KING OF THE BLUES
The Rise and Reign of B.B. King

Daniel de Visé

Grove Press UK

First published in the United States of America in 2021 by Grove Atlantic

First published in Great Britain in 2021 by Grove Press UK,
an imprint of Grove Atlantic

1 3 5 7 9 8 6 4 2

A CIP record for this book is available from the British Library.

Grove Press UK
Ormond House
26–27 Boswell Street
London
WC1N 3JZ

www.groveatlantic.com

Hardback ISBN 978 1 61185 654 5
Ebook ISBN 978 1 61185 880 8

Printed in Great Britain by Bell & Bain Ltd, Glasgow

KING OF
THE BLUES

Also by Daniel de Visé

*The Comeback: Greg LeMond, the True King of American
Cycling, and a Legendary Tour de France*

*Andy & Don: The Making of a Friendship
and a Classic American TV Show*

I Forgot to Remember: A Memoir of Amnesia (with Su Meck)

To Mom

CONTENTS

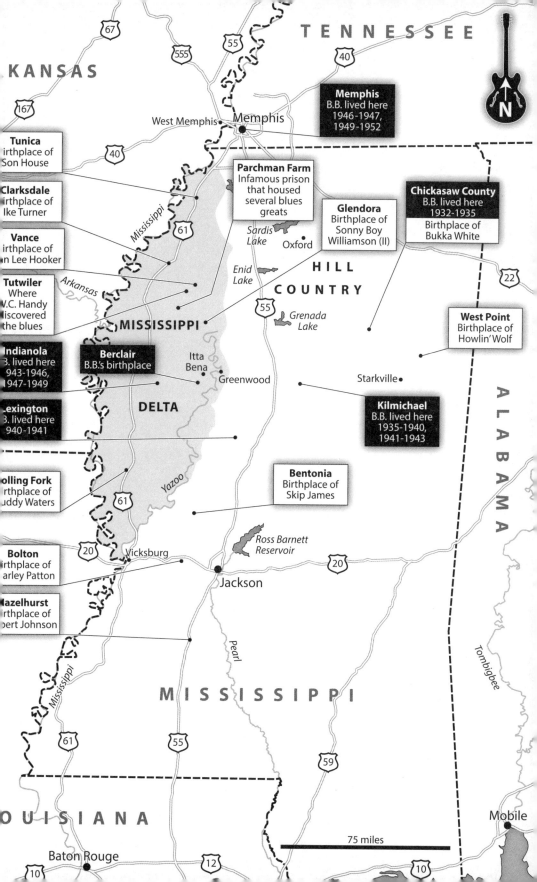

TENNESSEE

ARKANSAS

KANSAS

67

555

55

40

167

40

West Memphis

Memphis

Memphis
B.B. lived here
1946-1947,
1949-1952

N

Tunica
irthplace of
Son House

Clarksdale
irthplace of
Ike Turner

Vance
irthplace of
n Lee Hooker

Tutwiler
Where
V.C. Handy
iscovered
the blues

Parchman Farm
Infamous prison
that housed
several blues
greats

Chickasaw County
B.B. lived here
1932-1935
Birthplace of
Bukka White

Glendora
Birthplace of
Sonny Boy
Williamson (II)

Mississippi

61

Sardis Lake

Oxford

Enid Lake

HILL COUNTRY

Arkansas

MISSISSIPPI

55

Grenada Lake

22

West Point
Birthplace of
Howlin' Wolf

Indianola
B. lived here
943-1946,
1947-1949

Berclair
B.B.'s birthplace

Itta
Bena

Greenwood

Starkville

DELTA

Kilmichael
B.B. lived here
1935-1940,
1941-1943

ALABAMA

exington
B. lived here
940-1941

Yazoo

Bentonia
Birthplace of
Skip James

olling Fork
irthplace of
uddy Waters

61

Ross Barnett Reservoir

Bolton
irthplace of
arley Patton

20

Vicksburg

20

Jackson

azelhurst
irthplace of
bert Johnson

Pearl

M I S S I S S I P P I

Mississippi

61

55

59

Tombigbee

OUISIANA

Baton Rouge

10

12

75 miles

Mobile

10

KING OF
THE BLUES

INTRODUCTION

BACK INSIDE A JAIL WAS ONE PLACE B.B. King thought he would never go. He had spent only a single night in a cell, after a white cop flagged him down on a Mississippi highway for doing eighty in a sixty-mile-per-hour zone. That was in 1950. B.B. was then a struggling musician and underpaid radio performer in his twenties, still picking cotton to make ends meet, racing to a gig in a borrowed car. The fine was ninety dollars. B.B. didn't have it, and the imperious cop knew it.

Two decades later, on September 10, 1970, B.B. stood on the cusp of his forty-fifth birthday. In those forty-five years, Riley B. King had risen from penniless sharecropper to sidewalk busker to Memphis deejay to chart-topping singer to King of the Blues. Guitar heroics defined popular music in 1970, and B.B. King was the first guitar hero.

B.B.'s story was the story of the Great Migration, the northward journey that delivered millions of African Americans from southern plantations into the urban North. B.B. had hitchhiked out of Mississippi, found fame in Memphis, and then set out across the nation in a bus called Big Red. After two decades on the fabled Black chitlin' circuit, B.B. had crossed over, capping his symbolic breakthrough with a triumphant performance for a throng of white hippies at San Francisco's pot-scented Fillmore Auditorium in 1967. After that, B.B.'s audience had changed color. He played mostly for whites now.

But this gig was different: a show inside Chicago's infamous Cook County Jail, conceived by an African American warden to entertain 2,400 inmates, most of them African Americans. B.B. rejoiced at performing for Black people again.

B.B. and his band entered the jail around eleven that morning. Stony-faced guards patted them down and escorted them through heavy steel doors, which closed with a sickening clang. The group proceeded down endless, windowless tunnels, past offices and cells and the jail's electric chair, to a mess hall, followed everywhere by eyes "empty of everything except deep, numbing pain," one musician recalled. B.B. chatted with the inmates, trying to push down the primal terror of being locked inside a prison, a place that felt "final and scary and rock-hard." A beefy guard shadowed the bluesman, his eyes searching for the flashing blade of a shank. Most of the men were young enough to be B.B.'s children. One by one, they shared stories of languishing inside cells for months without end, awaiting trial, unable to post bail, powerless to leave.

After a tasteless meal, guards led the band outside to a bleak and gusty courtyard. The entourage headed toward a small stage, a raised platform where condemned men had once been hanged. A stubborn wind tore sheet music from the musicians' stands and whisked it over the forbidding thirty-foot stone walls. But a warm autumn sun shone on the yard, and the air was a perfect seventy degrees. The weather had held, and that was good, for organizers had committed to a concert on this day. B.B. was playing for free, but his label had spent $10,000 on transportation, salaries, and equipment to record the performance for eventual release as a live album.

The musicians warmed up, played a sound check, and jammed with men from the jailhouse band as the audience filed out to the yard. Two hundred female inmates sat in folding chairs at stage left. More than two thousand men sprawled out in roped-off sections of grass. The men on death row remained locked in their cells, listening through opened windows.

The concert began at 1 p.m. "Hello out there," a female jail official announced. She introduced the white sheriff and a prominent white judge to the jump-suited crowd, setting off a chorus of violent boos that echoed across the yard. Fifty guards with thick batons and .50-caliber semiautomatic rifles roamed the perimeter and perched atop towers. Concerts didn't get much more real. Sensing tension in the air, the announcer hurried things along, beckoning, "Would you please come forth, Mr. King?" And then B.B. climbed atop the old gallows, clad in an olive-green plaid suit. A gunshot blast from Sonny Freeman's snare drum announced the first song: "Every Day I Have the Blues." The six-piece band raced forward, shuffling in matching powder-blue suits, propelled by Freeman's galloping swing beat. B.B. spun the volume knob to awaken Lucille, his sinuous, symmetrical Gibson guitar. He played his first notes, climbing up to a "blue" third, bending the string with his powerful fingers to rise from D flat to D natural, then dancing back down and ending the solo phrase on a sustained note. B.B. flailed his left wrist up and down to create the shimmering vibrato that was his trademark. B.B. felt that he and Lucille spoke with the same voice, one picking up where the other left off. A few bars later, it was B.B.'s turn. "Ev'ry day, ev'ry day I have the blues," he sang, a rich, booming baritone that formed way back in his clenched throat. Two minutes later, the song was over, and the yard erupted in applause and cheers. This audience, surely, could relate to the blues.

Now the band slid into B.B.'s signature song, "How Blue Can You Get." Lucille unleashed an aural fireworks display that recounted the history of urban blues, much of it written by B.B. on his guitar: soaring bends, rapid-fire staccato bursts, and sustained, tremulous tones. And then B.B. sang: "I've been downhearted, baby, ever since the day we met," he growled, reminding his audience that he was not just the world's greatest blues guitarist but also an archetypal rhythm-and-blues singer. B.B. sang, and Lucille cried, and the crowd talked and cried and shouted back. As B.B. slowed into a campy, feminine reading of the song's climactic bridge, the audience clamor threatened to overwhelm the band, a release of pure, electric energy that B.B. breathed in like oxygen.

Much as B.B.'s new white fans adored him, they did not know how to engage, how to participate in a B.B. King show, any more than they would have known what to do in an African American church. But here at the jail, as the band proceeded into an obscure 1950s single titled "Worry, Worry, Worry," B.B. called out to the audience and the audience responded, singly and collectively. "Throw your arms around him," he cried, and the crowd shouted back, "Yeah!"

"Hold him close to you!"

"Yeah!"

"Look him straight in the eye!"

"Yeah!"

The song ended. Now, B.B. reached back almost twenty years to sing and play his first big hits, "3 O'Clock Blues" and "You Know I Love You," songs he mostly saved for Black audiences. He knew that many in this crowd had heard them the first time around. This was B.B. King, blues crooner.

"Don't forget 'Sweet Sixteen,'" someone cried. "All right, baby," B.B. cooed. He played that one next. Some of the loudest cheers came from scattered male inmates wearing dresses and wigs. At first, the band mistook them for women.

The concert climaxed with a slow-burning take on "The Thrill Is Gone," the song that had secured B.B. a future in the pop-music pantheon of white America. "I'm free, free, free now, baby," B.B. roared. The men in the grass and the women in the chairs, not free, roared back.

Looking out across the sea of Black faces "made me sad and glad," B.B. recalled. "Sad that so many brothers were behind bars, glad that I was reaching out to my own people." Such moments reminded B.B. of the miles he had traveled and of the sun-bleached sharecropper cabin where his journey had begun.

CHAPTER 1

SHARECROPPER

B.B. KING'S FATHER, ALBERT KING, was born on February 28, 1907. The King family crisscrossed Mississippi in a perennial search for farm work. Albert probably entered the world in Glaston, a pinprick of a place in southern Mississippi, one hundred miles north of the Gulf of Mexico.

Events tore Albert's family asunder. His mother left his father and promptly died. A sister perished, as well. Infant Albert and his father migrated two hundred miles north to join their kin in Monroe County, part of the larger expanse of Hill Country, a rugged slab of northeastern Mississippi bordering Tennessee on the north and Alabama on the east. Sometime after 1910, Albert's father exited his life, leaving Albert in the care of an older brother named Riley, who in turn deposited Albert with a sharecropper family named Love and vanished into the mists. Albert joined the Love family as an adoptive nephew. They lived in Sunflower County, part of the fabled Mississippi Delta. Flat and fertile, the Delta lay west of Hill Country along the Arkansas border, the cradle of Mississippi's cotton industry. The Loves would carry Albert out to the fields in a tub, draped with a cotton sack to keep the mosquitoes at bay.

Nora Ella Pulley, B.B.'s mother, was probably born in 1908 in Chickasaw County, a Hill Country province named for the Indian tribe that had long dwelt there. Nora Ella was the daughter of Elnora and Jasper Pulley. Elnora's parents, Pompey ("Pomp") and Jane Davidson, had been born slaves.

By 1920, Nora Ella's father was gone. She and her mother had joined the expansive household of Elnora's new husband, another Chickasaw sharecropper, named Romeo Farr. A few years later, Elnora left Farr and took Nora Ella west to the Delta. There, probably in 1924, Nora Ella met Albert King. They were teenagers of sixteen or seventeen. When Albert called on Nora Ella, he observed the old rules of courtship, arriving at her house in shirt and tie and departing at the stroke of 9 p.m. Soon, they became a couple. By the close of 1924, Nora Ella was pregnant.

Today, the official marker for B.B. King's birthplace sits at a remote crossroads, a mile or two south of a settlement called Berclair along gravel roads, where Leflore County Routes 305 and 513 intersect. For the birthplace of a legendary bluesman, it is a satisfying spot. Blue Lake—in truth, more stale creek than lake—sits east of the crossroads, a ribbon of stagnant water choked with logs and dotted with turtles basking in the warm Delta sun. Forest lies to the south, field to the west.

The plaque does not reveal the actual location of the King cabin, and perhaps that is just as well, for no trace of the dwelling remains. To reach that patch of earth, the blues pilgrim must follow the creek a bit farther south and east along Route 305 to Route 281, turn left, and cross the creek. The cabin stood there, in a lonely field. Decades later, archivists led B.B. back to the site by playing a tape recording that preserved the guttural Delta growl of Albert King, his father, recounting a series of twists and turns along those ancient roads.

B.B. would sometimes claim Berclair as his hometown, though it is barely a town, a few shacks scattered haphazardly along the railroad tracks that lead east to Greenwood and west to Indianola. At other times, he would name his birthplace as Itta Bena (pronounced "*bean*-a"), a real town, albeit a small one. In fact, the land where B.B. was born belonged not to a town but to a man. B.B. recalled that his parents lived and worked on the plantation of a white farmer named Jim O'Reilly.

Wednesday, September 16, 1925, dawned hot and bright, suffusing the O'Reilly plantation in a ninety-degree Delta swelter that belied autumn's approach. Nora Ella King awoke that morning to pangs that announced her baby's impending arrival. She alerted Albert, who set out to find his landlord. "When Mama went into labor and Daddy went looking for a midwife," B.B. recalled, "O'Reilly helped him find the right woman." O'Reilly attended the delivery. Albert gave the baby his landlord's name, which also belonged to his lost brother. The birth certificate rendered it as "Rileigh," perhaps reflecting the limited literacy of his parents. Albert trimmed the "O" because, he later joked, his son "didn't look Irish." The middle initial "B," so consequential in Riley's later life, didn't stand for anything.

The King family lived in the Berclair cabin for four more years. The town sat on some of the highest ground in the Delta. When the Great Mississippi Flood swamped twenty-seven thousand square miles of farmland in 1927, Berclair and the Kings were spared. Neighboring towns Moorhead and Indianola and Inverness vanished beneath the muck just a few miles away.

Albert could not read or write. Nonetheless, he ascended to tractor driver, a job atop the food chain for African Americans working on Delta farms, paying fifty cents a day. Tractors plowed and tilled the land with the power of five or six of the mules they replaced. Farmers ran their tractors around the clock. Albert sometimes worked consecutive double shifts, forty-eight hours, earning two dollars for a bone-rattling two-day marathon of driving.

In 1928, Nora Ella bore a second child, a son named Curce. A year or so later, Curce died, apparently after eating glass. His death, and the sorrow that followed, was very nearly the only concrete memory Riley retained from those blurry years with his mother and father. "My mother told me that I took it pretty bad, pretty hard," Riley later recalled, hinting ominously that he might have carelessly left shards of glass within his infant brother's reach.

"I wish he were here," Riley later wrote of the departed brother, recalling his thoughts at the time. "Wish I had someone to play with. I don't understand death. Death is a cold chill, frightening beyond reason."

Shortly after Curce's death, in 1929 or 1930, Nora Ella packed her surviving son into the back of an old pickup truck and left Albert King. Riley recalled his father as a receding figure on the horizon, waving goodbye, "growing more and more distant until he finally disappears. It's a gray day and the roads are bumpy and I'm not sure what's going on, except I've never been on a trip like this." As they began their journey,

Nora Ella told Riley, "It's hard for you to understand, but your daddy and I, well, we're not living together no more."

Nora Ella left Albert for another man. The shock of losing a child might have factored in her departure, or perhaps Albert's drinking drove her away. By the spring of 1930, according to the census, mother and son were living in the home of George Herd, a farmer, like Albert, who worked the same cotton fields around Berclair. Once Nora Ella was gone, Albert knew better than to confront the man into whose arms she had fled. "When a woman decides she don't want a man," he later explained, "you let her go."

THE BREAKUP of Riley's family came as the nation sank into the Great Depression. The stock market had lost nearly half its value between September and November 1929. In 1930 and 1931, thousands of banks failed, and unemployment reached double digits. By 1932 and 1933, the low ebb, the Dow Jones Industrial Index had lost nine-tenths of its value, unemployment peaked at 25 percent, and two million Americans lacked homes.

No one, perhaps, suffered more in the Depression than the people of Mississippi. Two-thirds of Mississippians were sharecroppers or tenant farmers whose livelihood depended on the price of cotton, which plummeted from twenty cents a pound in 1929 to less than five cents in 1932. Overall farm income collapsed from $191 million to $41 million in that span.

"I didn't know about no stock market crash or Depression," Riley recalled. "Our world was small." He and his mother lived in a remote farming village, one whose citizens were barely scraping by when the downturn hit. Riley and his neighbors didn't generally own bank accounts, let alone stocks. They had little to lose.

Nora Ella remained with George Herd for a year or two, providing Riley some semblance of a stable family life. The Herd cabin sat within the village of Berclair, along the railroad tracks. Riley would remember the sound of the train whistle and the sight of the conductor waving as the trains rumbled past. Riley might have taken his first classes at the

Leflore County Training School, the designated "colored" campus for African Americans in Itta Bena and environs.

One day in 1931, an illustrious visitor stopped by George Herd's cabin. His name was Booker T. Washington "Bukka" White. He was a Delta-blues master, and he was Riley's cousin.

Bukka White was born around 1904 in Chickasaw County, the cradle of Riley's grandparents. Bukka's mother, Lula, was a sister of Elnora, Riley's grandmother. By 1910, Bukka was living with Elnora's kin in Hill Country. He learned the guitar from his father, who was an amateur performer. Bukka also learned the "slide," a cylinder of metal or pop-bottle glass that Delta bluesmen used to animate their guitars. Around age thirteen, Bukka was jumping on and off a freight train with some friends when it suddenly accelerated, carrying him clear to St. Louis. Bukka found work there in a roadhouse, sweeping floors and playing blues. He married at sixteen. Three years later, his wife died of a burst appendix.

Bukka traveled to the provincial music capital of Memphis in 1930, around age twenty-five, and recorded fourteen tracks for the Victor imprint, whose producers were exploiting a national blues craze. But the deepening Depression dampened the label's enthusiasm, and only four sides saw official release. Still, by the time he met Riley in 1931, Bukka was an accomplished bluesman.

Bukka arrived in town for a gig at neighboring Itta Bena. He recalled Berclair as "a little, one-store town at the end of a road": "My Auntie Nora was living there, and Riley was about six. So I was sitting talking to my auntie, and I looked over in the corner and seen that boy looking at my guitar, and he looked so pitiful to me, just sitting there so quiet." Riley gazed at Bukka's red Stella acoustic. A voice in Bukka's head told him, "Get that boy a guitar." He handed the Stella to Riley. The boy replied with a barely audible "Thank you." Then he sat and gazed at the instrument.

At least three people would later claim to have given Riley his first guitar. If Bukka's story is true, then Riley had his own guitar by age six. But Riley recalled no such gift. Perhaps Bukka only allowed his young cousin to pluck a few strings on the instrument before taking it back. In any case, Riley would not make a serious study of the guitar for a few more years.

After that, Bukka visited Riley a couple of times a year, "looking like a million bucks," Riley recalled. "Razor-sharp. Big hat, clean shirt, pressed pants, shiny shoes. He smelled of the big city and glamorous times." Bukka had a round face framing warm eyes and wide-spaced teeth, revealed when his face cleaved into a brilliant smile. A born storyteller, Bukka reeled off tales of Arkansas roadhouses and Chicago skyscrapers. He would serenade Riley, coaxing sweet sounds from his guitar with his slide. "His vibrato gave me goose bumps," Riley recalled.

Not all of Riley's kin brought joy into his life. He shuddered at the memory of visiting the "old folk" of his grandmother's clan, who spun tales of headless bodies in open coffins as Riley lay in bed, shivering with fear in the next room. "The dark became a tomb," he recalled. For the rest of his life, Riley slept with a light on.

Some of the elders might have been Riley's neighbors. Sharecropper clans often traveled en masse from one settlement to the next as word spread of fresh opportunities to eke out a living. One distant relative recalled Riley living with members of Nora Ella's extended family in Berclair around 1931, during her time with George Herd. Riley might have passed back and forth between his mother and her kin. That pattern would shape the next decade of his life.

Riley had a playmate in Berclair. Her name was Peaches, she was seven, and she taught six-year-old Riley the rudiments of lovemaking.

"We climb into my mom's bed," Riley recalled, "take off our clothes, and Peaches shows me what she learned by watching her folks."

Once, Nora Ella caught Riley and Peaches in the act. She pulled him off her, hurled him across the room, and beat him. She didn't touch Peaches. Riley asked her why. "'Cause you know better than to do a thing like that," she replied.

IN 1931 OR 1932, Nora Ella left George Herd. Her declining health might have driven them apart. Riley's mother probably suffered from untreated diabetes. Though still in her early twenties, Nora Ella was losing her eyesight. Perhaps Herd decided his new wife was no longer pulling her weight, a harsh but necessary consideration in the cruel economy of sharecropping. So Nora Ella and her son journeyed one hundred miles east, leaving the Delta to join Nora's mother, Elnora, in Hill Country.

By 1932, Elnora Farr was back in Chickasaw County, her Mississippi birthplace, living alone and working as a sharecropper on farmland near the tiny county seat of Houston. Elnora was entering her forties. The men in her life, Jasper Pulley and Romeo Farr, were long gone. She would not remarry.

Elnora had three children, all in their early twenties, migrating back and forth between Hill Country and the Delta in search of an elusive living wage. In the early 1930s, all three were living in Chickasaw County: William Pulley, Nora Ella's older brother, stern patriarch of the Pulley clan; Nora Ella herself; and Jack Bennett and his wife, Nevada, Nora Ella's younger sister.

Riley seems never to have told anyone he lived in Chickasaw County. Perhaps those memories merged with subsequent memories from other places into a blurry Mississippi Hill Country montage. But census data and relatives' accounts put Riley in Chickasaw for roughly three years, from about 1932 until 1935, along with his mother and grandmother and much of their extended family.

"When Albert and Nora separated, she took her baby and went to Houston, Mississippi, to stay with her mama," recalled Lessie Fair, a distant relative who would enter Riley's life a few years later. "Her mama and her and all of the rest of them was in Houston."

Riley's exact address during his Chickasaw years, from about age seven to ten, is hard to pinpoint. Charles Sawyer, his first biographer, believed Riley spent those years with his grandmother Elnora. Others remembered him living with his Uncle William. Uncle Jack would claim Riley as a dependent on the census. Riley himself recalled living with his mother.

Nora Ella was a loving mother, however fleeting her presence in Riley's life. He adored her. "She has a radiant face, luminous brown skin, and a shapely body," Riley recalled, later in life. "It's raining, and her hair is glistening wet. She hands me a towel and asks me to dry her off."

The scenes of Riley and his mother that would later populate Riley's memoir read like soft-focus flashbacks from a movie. In one vignette, Nora Ella sat Riley down in their cabin and taught him to braid her hair, which fell to her shoulders. He wanted to do it just right, so that when she walked out to work the soil, "everyone will see she's the prettiest woman in the world." In another, Riley recalled sitting in church, alternately stealing glances at the comely girls behind him and "listening to Mama singing with the choir with a voice so sweet," it made him want to cry.

Riley's mother also figures in the more harrowing memories of his childhood. In one story, Riley recounted a night of "jagged lightning," a fierce summer squall that "felt like the end of the world." Riley and his mother huddled together "in the corner of that little shotgun shack," her arm around him, as a funnel cloud roared near. Wind ripped the roof from their shack. And then, just as suddenly, the tempest was gone. The next day, Riley and his mother walked outside into crisp sunshine and found fish wriggling in the fields. Riley could not believe the storm's wrath hadn't touched them: "It was just me and Mama, standing alone in that corner, thanking Jesus for the miracle."

In another episode, Nora Ella dressed Riley in a sailor suit for a trip to view a dead body in a sharecropper cabin. She instructed him not to stare, nor to eat all the food. Spooked by the cadaver, Riley impulsively grabbed a piece of sweet potato pie from the serving table. Then he spotted his mother, who shot him a stern look. He slipped the slice into his pants pocket. He sat down, and the piping-hot pie burned through the skin of his leg. Riley began to cry. Nora Ella led him outside and asked what was wrong. "I'm sorry, Mama," he explained, "I know you d-d-d-d-d-didn't want me to eat no m-m-m-m-more, so I snuck this pie." Nora Ella was horrified: "Oh, baby," she told him, "you took my look the wrong way." Mother and son wept together.

From Riley's earliest memories, he spoke with a pronounced stutter. Perhaps it formed within the cyclone of emotion spawned by his parents' separation. Stutters are said to stem from emotional trauma. Riley's great-grandfather Pomp Davidson, born a slave, also stuttered.

Riley learned his place in Mississippi society, directly or indirectly, from his great-grandparents Pomp and Jane Davidson, Elnora's parents. Riley recalled Pomp as a fearless swashbuckler who "talked with his shotgun and liked to ride his mule while swigging moonshine whiskey out of a jug. . . . No one got in Pomp's way." Grandma Jane exuded her own quiet authority. "She'd put me on her lap and, up close, I'd notice wrinkles around her mouth and over her lips. Her eyes would twinkle and her voice was steady."

Riley's great-grandparents were born into slavery around 1860. They raised a large family in Chickasaw County. Riley met Grandma Jane when he arrived in Chickasaw in the early 1930s. Riley remembered Pomp, too, but the Davidson patriarch died in 1923, before Riley was born. Riley's memories of his great-grandfather probably came from Grandma Jane's vivid stories.

Jane Davidson taught Riley about the blues. Riley had already heard them: Albert, his father, and Jack, his uncle, were consummate field shouters whose deep, husky voices could fill the plantation. The field holler was an African American work song, typically bellowed by a lone worker in a rhythm and cadence to complement the day's toil, at a volume audible across the field. Other workers would answer and echo the call, passing the song across the plantation like a signal fire. The holler sounded very much like unaccompanied blues. Folklorists theorize that plantation work songs more or less inspired the blues.

Riley's great-grandmother explained what it all meant. Singing the blues helped the day go by. "But the blues hollerers shouted about more than being sad," Riley recalled. "They were also delivering messages in musical code. If the master was coming, you might sing a hidden warning to the other field hands. Maybe you'd want to get out of his way or hide. That was important for the women, because the master could have anything he wanted." Riley could see that the blues were about survival.

Great-grandma Jane told an old Chickasaw story about a Black boy who fell in love with the white master's daughter. "When the moon was slim and the night was dark," Riley recounted, "they'd meet undercover and steal a kiss." In time, someone caught them and told the master. He tied the boy to a tree and covered him in boiling tar and feathers. He meant to burn the boy alive. Then his daughter appeared, hysterical and pleading. "He didn't rape me," she told her father. "I let him take me. I love him." The father asked what she wanted him to do. "Don't let him suffer," she replied. "It'd be kinder to shoot him."

AROUND THE START of 1935, Elnora Farr left Chickasaw County and traveled more than fifty miles southwest to a community of interlocking farms that would be her home for the next five years. Much of her clan joined her, including Nora Ella and Riley. Their destination was Kilmichael, a tiny hamlet, population five hundred. Kilmichael lay in north-central Mississippi, near the southern border of Hill Country. When Riley and his family arrived there, he recalled, "we got out of the truck and into a rickety old wagon pulled by a horse that went deeper into the hills, deep into the country," across the Big Black River toward an expanse of farmland and forest tucked between two creeks.

Elnora and her family settled on the farm of George and Mary Booth, a childless couple in middle age. Their stay was probably brief. The Booth family, like Chickasaw County, barely figures in the King legend.

"All of them moved from Houston down on the George Booth's place," recalled Lessie Fair, one of Riley's Kilmichael kin. Nora Ella, in declining health, sent Riley to live with his Uncle William, her brother, who had a new wife and an infant daughter. Riley helped with the baby.

After a short stay on the Booth property, Elnora and her kin decamped to a neighboring dairy farm owned by Edwayne and Bertha Henderson. The Henderson property sat on a few hundred acres, six miles south of Kilmichael along Highway 413. The farm comprised perhaps one hundred milking cows, along with corn, hay, and, of course, King Cotton.

Most of the actual farming on the Henderson land fell to a colony of sharecroppers. Under the sharecropping system, the landowner would provide each tenant family a parcel of five or ten acres to farm. Sharecroppers lived in unpainted wooden shacks without plumbing or electricity or telephones, fitted with windows that lacked panes, lit with kerosene lamps, and heated by wood-burning stoves. (The farm owner did not necessarily live much better, typically occupying a painted house of three or four rooms without running water or electricity.) The owner would supply farm implements, fertilizer, and seed. Sharecroppers grew much of their own food. The landlord would also provide a monthly "furnish," an allowance that covered costs of daily life, including clothing and medicine. At harvest, owner and sharecropper would split the profits from selling the yearly crop—but only after the landlord recovered the furnish, plus interest, and deducted half the cost of seed, fertilizer, and sundry other expenses. In a good year, a sharecropper might earn a tiny surplus. More often, sharecropping fed an endless cycle of debt. The economic successor to slavery left African Americans free but living in perpetual bondage to the landlord and the land.

The sharecroppers who occupied the Henderson farm and neighboring tracts in 1935 included most of the characters who would populate Riley's life for the next several years: Riley's Uncle William and new Aunt Lucille; his Uncle Jack and Aunt Nevada; Myony "Mima" Stell, a sister to Riley's grandmother, whose windup Victrola would change his life; the Hemphill family, whose five lovely girls would forever distract Riley from his studies; Archie Fair, brother of Aunt Lucille, the preacher whose guitar young Riley would covet; Denzel Tidwell, the white youth who would sell Riley his red Stella guitar; and Luther Henson, the schoolteacher who would show Riley a world beyond the cotton fields.

Riley now inhabited an insular realm defined by four points: the Henderson farm, along Crape Creek east of the state highway; the Elkhorn School, a one-room wooden structure and adjoining church set atop a hill overlooking a pond, west of the farm; Austin Chapel, a boisterous Sanctified Church that sat northwest of Elkhorn School; and the church and cemetery at Pinkney Grove, two miles to the south.

Elkhorn School was the domain of Luther Henson. "Professor" Henson would become the father figure Riley craved, perhaps the most enduring among several male role models who would guide him into a prosperous adulthood.

Luther's father, Syrus Henson, was born a slave in 1835 on the Henson plantation in North Carolina. When the Henson family journeyed southwest to Mississippi in the 1850s, Syrus drove the ox cart. Some years after their arrival, Syrus was freed. He purchased more than one hundred acres near Kilmichael. He founded the Elkhorn Primitive Baptist Church and the adjoining school. He taught his children to read and write, perhaps in the hope that they would one day lead the Elkhorn School. That job eventually fell to the twentieth of Syrus Henson's twenty-one children, Luther.

Five dozen students, from prekindergarten through high school, huddled within a single classroom at Elkhorn School. A cast-iron stove sat at the center, rows of wooden benches arrayed around it to capture the radiating heat. Kilmichael sharecropper children attended school for about four months of every year, from the end of the annual crop cycle in winter until the start of the next one in spring. Every morning, students assembled outside the school door and lined up by gender and height. The bell rang, and students marched into the chilly classroom. Mr. Henson led them in the Lord's Prayer and a cheery wake-up song: "Good morning to you. Good morning to you. We're all in our places with sunshiny faces."

Luther Henson, a man of about thirty-five, projected quiet dignity. He spoke slowly and deliberately, punctuating every sentence with a warm smile. He ran his school with almost military precision, the only way to maintain order in a space filled with children of a dozen grades. Henson would call each grade in turn, youngest to oldest, summoning children of like age from their benches, a few at a time, to line up at the chalkboard for brief lessons.

"We had about five or six books," recalled Jessie Hemphill, one of Riley's classmates. "Reading, writing, arithmetic, geography, spelling. We also had one called *Healthy Living*."

Henson's pedagogy went well beyond academics. He taught his students the skills to someday escape the prison of toil and debt into which they had been born. (Henson himself would never earn more than thirty dollars a month.) He taught them about nutrition, encouraging their families to raise chickens and hogs for protein and grow trees for fruit. "Everything we ate, we knew what part of the body it was for," recalled Fannie Henson Draine, Luther's daughter.

Professor Henson urged his students to manage their assets, however meager, and to strive for financial independence. He taught the class little songs whose words reminded them to brush their teeth and wash their hands and that dipping snuff would "snuff your little life away." He instructed them how to live in wedlock. "He taught the boys, when they were grown, how to treat their wives," Jessie Hemphill recalled. "He said, 'Don't give your wives wood and water. Wood on the back, water come out of the eyes.'"

Riley had seen white-owned newspapers, such as the *Greenville Democrat-Times* and the *Memphis Commercial Appeal*, that seemed to write of African Americans only when they stood accused of crimes. Henson showed his class African American newspapers such as the *Pittsburgh Courier* and the *Oklahoma City Black Dispatch* that ran articles about successful Blacks, such men as musician Louis Armstrong and boxer Joe Louis. He taught the class about educator Booker T. Washington, abolitionist Frederick Douglass, and activist Mary McLeod Bethune. He implored his students to complete their education: "It's the one thing, if you get it, white people can't take it away from you."

Mississippi in the 1930s was a dystopian society for African Americans, governed by the framework of codified racism known as Jim Crow, after a racist minstrel character. The U.S. Supreme Court had ruled in 1896 that separation of the races was constitutional, so long as Black and white accommodations were "equal." Luther Henson helped Riley decode the separate-but-equal fiction. African Americans tipped their hats as they passed whites on the streets, but whites did not return the courtesy. African Americans called whites "sir" or "ma'am," while whites called Blacks by their first names. White pedestrians on sidewalks enjoyed a perpetual right-of-way. Blacks stepped aside.

Henson helped Riley imagine a life beyond Jim Crow, a repressive system of which his own segregated school was an expression. Mississippi in 1930 spent $31 on a white student, $6 on a Black one. Riley and his classmates walked to their schoolhouse. The white children of Kilmichael were driven to theirs in a flatbed truck, an inequity that would haunt Riley all his life.

"Y'all hear about lynchings, where our people are punished for something they didn't do," Henson told his students. "Remember, not all the whites are behind this. If the whites wanted to, they could kill every one of us. But there are good men among the whites, just like there are bad men. Crazy people come in all colors. And one day soon, the good people will win over the crazy people." More than anything, Riley recalled, "Mr. Henson gave me hope."

Henson counseled Riley on his stutter. "Riley," he said, "just slow down and let your mouth catch up to your mind." Riley pleaded, "W-w-w-what if I can't g-g-g-get the w-w-w-word out and everyone's w-w-w-waiting for me?" Henson smiled: "Well, they'll just have to wait, won't they?"

Riley recalled schoolwork as a daily struggle and claimed he performed near the bottom of his small class. Classmates remembered otherwise. "He was an A-1 student," recalled Ted Hemphill, brother of Jessie. Jessie herself said of Riley, "He was eager to learn, he was obedient to his teacher, and he would absorb everything he heard."

However voracious Riley's appetite to learn, he was, by his own account, "more drawn to the girls than the books"—especially the Hemphills, one of whom sat on the bench in front of him. When he saw a chance, Riley would reach around Leona Hemphill's body and attempt a surreptitious embrace. She would respond by biting his hand. Henson sometimes caught him groping a breast or attempting to peer beneath a dress. Then, Henson would stride outside, break a switch from an elm tree, and administer a whipping, punctuating the blows with the admonition, "YOU . . . WILL . . . RESPECT . . . WOMEN."

Riley was not a large boy, but he was strong, especially in his hands. Jessie Hemphill recalled a playground game called Let Buddy Out, heartbreakingly symbolic, in which children took turns trying to break free from a circle of students with clasped hands. "I would always make it my business to hold B.B.'s hand," Jessie recalled, "because he could hold your hand tight."

From Riley's earliest days, he found his thoughts consumed by girls. Around age seven, it dawned on him that he could find them all at church, lined up on pews, wearing their prettiest outfits. From that day, Riley never missed church.

Sometimes Riley would attend the solemn Elkhorn Primitive Baptist Church on the hilltop across from his school, and at some point, he was baptized into the Baptist faith. But he preferred the Austin Chapel. This was the Church of God in Christ, a livelier congregation than the Baptists, led by the Reverend Archie Fair and his guitar.

Sundays at church belonged to Reverend Fair, a sanctified preacher, his sermons "part séance and part conjuring act." From his pulpit, Fair invoked the Pentecost, the moment when the Holy Spirit descended on Jesus and his followers to possess their bodies and speak in tongues. The congregation shook, rattled, and rolled on the church floor while the reverend filled the room with the low thunder of his voice and the sweet twang of his guitar.

In Riley's insular world, the reverend was a rock star. "Archie Fair is the nearest thing I know to God on earth," he recalled. "He talks like his words have already been written out in a book. . . . His sermon is like music, and his music—both the song from his mouth and the sound of his guitar—thrills me until I wanna get up and dance. He says one thing and the congregation says it back, back and forth, back and forth, until we're rocking together in a rhythm that won't stop. His voice is low and rough and his guitar is high and sweet; they seem to sing to each other, conversing in some heavenly language I need to learn."

One Sunday, Riley averted his eyes from the girls in the pews long enough to regard the reverend's guitar, whose shapely curves he suddenly found even more alluring.

After church, the reverend would visit his sister Lucille, Riley's aunt. The adults dined first, the children second, devouring whatever scraps their parents had left. The routine left Riley time, one evening, to sneak into the bedroom and find the reverend's guitar reclining on the bed.

"While they're not looking, I reach over and, oh-so-carefully, touch the wood of the guitar," Riley recalled. "Touch her strings to see how they feel against my fingers. Feels good. Feels like magic. I wonder: *How do you get her to make those sounds? How do you get her to sing?*"

A voice interrupted his reverie: "Go ahead and pick it up," Archie Fair beckoned. Nora Ella objected, mad that Riley had touched something that didn't belong to him, Riley recalled, "but Reverend calms her down. Reverend understands."

The reverend told Riley his guitar was a Silvertone, a line of inexpensive acoustics sold by Sears, Roebuck and Company through its catalog.

"You can touch it, boy," Fair told Riley. "Ain't gonna bite you." Riley recalled the moment in sensuous tones: "He shows me how to hold her, how to take her in my arms. She's bigger than me, but I still put her on my lap. She feels good against my body."

The reverend guided Riley's fingers to various combinations of strings and frets, showing him how to form three chords. They were the I, IV, and V chords, fundamental to every blues song Riley would ever learn.

RILEY'S OWN FIRST GUITAR was probably a diddley bow, a single-stringed concoction that a penniless sharecropper could fashion from household flotsam. (If cousin Bukka had really given Riley a guitar back in Berclair, the instrument did not follow him to Kilmichael.) A diddley bow was a length of wire stretched tight between two nails hammered into a board. The wire might come from the head of a broom. Folklorist Alan Lomax believed the diddley bow was descended from the ancient African mouth bow, an impromptu instrument created by placing a hunter's bow in front of an opened mouth and plucking the bowstring. The oral cavity served as a resonator, amplifying the plucked string. The mouth bow evolved into a one-stringed zither, a vibrating sliver of palm frond tethered to a bridge and placed atop a hollow gourd. Lomax believed the diddley bow, or something like it, traveled with slaves to the United States and served as "a crucial step in the birth of the blues."

Riley appeared one day at the door of the Henderson home. "Ms. Bertha," he asked the lady of the house, "do you have an old broom?"

"Yes," she replied, "but what do you want with it?"

Bertha Henderson watched as Riley unwound the wire that held the straws to her old broom. He used the handle as the bridge. "When I tightened or clamped down on the string," he recalled, "the sounds would change and I'd think I was making music."

Before long, Riley was dreaming of growing into a guitar-slinging country preacher like Archie Fair, if he could only tame his stutter and master his studies. Riley was developing an ear for music. Already familiar with the cotton-field shouters and the heavenly harmonies of the choir, Riley found new sounds inside the cabin of his great-aunt Mima.

Myony "Mima" Stell was the younger sister of Riley's grandmother. Born in 1891, Mima was in her forties when Riley arrived in Kilmichael. Mima was the settlement's resident hipster, the "most modern" of all Riley's relatives, he recalled. She dipped snuff, and she smothered Riley with snuff-scented kisses whenever he visited. Riley endured her embraces to gain entrée to her windup Victrola. Mima owned the first record collection Riley had ever seen. Her Victrola spun hard plastic or wax cylinders, candle-shaped rolls that were the first media to be termed "records." Later, Mima upgraded to a turntable and collected flat, fragile 78-rpm discs made of shellac. They looked to Riley like little flying saucers. She taught him to place a disc on the platter and cue the needle. "A second passed," he recalled, "and then— *pow!*—those beautiful, scratchy sounds flew in my face, cutting right through me, electrifying my soul."

Within those grooves, Riley discovered a whole new world of recorded sound. In Mima's cabin, Riley encountered Blind Lemon Jefferson, a Texan whose muscular, moaning melodies and intricate, mercurial guitar lines reminded Riley of the field hollers of his Mississippi kin. Riley reveled in the rich, ribald blues of Bessie Smith, the orchestral big-band jazz of Duke Ellington, and even the seminal Mississippi country-blues yodels of Jimmie Rodgers.

But nothing moved Riley like the satiny guitar strains of Lonnie Johnson. Born in New Orleans, Alonzo "Lonnie" Johnson mastered the violin before he embraced the guitar. He immediately viewed the guitar as a solo instrument, and he codified an entire vocabulary of single-note virtuosity that would influence every guitarist to follow. Lonnie Johnson was probably the first guitarist "to base his style on cleanly articulated single-string lines rather than heavily strummed chords—the first guitarist to phrase like a horn, in other words," writes blues historian Francis Davis. Johnson roamed freely between blues and jazz, which had not yet been walled off into separate silos. He played diminished and augmented chords, constructs beyond the imagining of most bluesmen. He bent and relaxed the strings to push notes higher or lower. He played lightning-fast riffs. Sometimes he lingered on a single note, like Louis Armstrong, fluttering his hand across the neck and wobbling the string to create an unmistakable vibrato. Violinists had cultivated vibrato for centuries, but, before Lonnie Johnson, no guitarist of consequence seems to have fluttered a string.

Johnson might have emerged as the first superstar of jazz guitar, but fate intervened when he won a talent contest in 1925 in St. Louis, playing the blues. That led to a recording contract, and Johnson rose to the forefront of popular blues. He recorded roughly 130 sides for the Okeh label between 1925 and 1932, making him one of the most successful and prolific artists of his day. Riley couldn't hear enough of him.

BY THE LATTER MONTHS of 1935, Nora Ella was living in the French Camp settlement, nearly a dozen miles from her mother and young son. She had a new man, Elger (or Elder) Baskin, who was not particularly interested in her Kilmichael kin or in raising a child. "He seed Riley one time, to my knowing," Lessie Fair recalled.

Nora Ella was not much past twenty-five, but her health was spent. Riley dared not ask his grandmother any questions about his mother: "I was afraid of the answers." One day, probably in the closing weeks of 1935, Nora Ella sent word that the end was near. Elnora awakened Riley, who knew what was coming from the look in her eyes. "Are we going to see Mama?" he asked. His grandmother nodded. They climbed into a horse-drawn wagon for the journey to Nora Ella's deathbed.

"It's winter and nothing is growing and the fields are empty and I wonder how many people have died between this winter and last,"

Riley recalled. "I don't say anything, and neither does Grandma. The sound of the horse's hoofs striking the ground strikes my heart like a clock that won't stop ticking. My throat is dry and my nose is runny and freezing cold. . . . I wonder if I'll ever be warm again."

At last, the wagon stopped at an old shack.

"Mama's eyes are half-closed," Riley recalled, and "covered by a film that gives her a hazy, faraway look." He noted with horror that blood trickled from Nora Ella's eyes. "When I stand above her, her gaze does not meet mine. That's when I realize she's gone blind." He fantasized of leading her to the wagon and taking her back home, but he knew he could not. "Her arms are thin as toothpicks, her body so frail it looks as though she'll break in half. She breathes heavily, and when she speaks it's with tremendous effort."

Nora Ella feebly grasped Riley's hand and began to speak. Her lips moved, but she lacked the strength to push words out. Riley lowered his head to her chest and placed his ear to her mouth to hear her hoarse whisper. "Kindness . . ." He waited for more, but her voice cracked. She gathered strength and continued: "People will love you if you show love to them. . . . Just remember that, son. I love you, Riley."

"I don't want you to go away," he pleaded. "I don't want you to leave."

"I'll never leave," she replied. "I'll always be with you. I'll always be your mother."

And then, Elnora told Riley it was time to depart: "It's going to be dark soon."

Nora Ella died that night. She was twenty-six or perhaps twenty-seven. Her lone surviving child was ten. Nora Ella's body was embalmed, returned to the shack, and placed on a cooling board, a perforated platform with ice layered beneath. The next day, her remains were loaded in a coffin and transported to Pinkney Grove for burial at the African American cemetery there. Years later, Riley could not recall the service.

Hindsight sheds little light on the brief life of Nora Ella King. There seems to be no official record of her death, no photograph to document her very existence. Her body lies in an unmarked grave at Pinkney Grove, a humble cemetery in a clearing across from the church, a spot at the very center of Riley's universe. A few dozen worn stones populate the cemetery today, scattered among fallen leaves and patches of moss in a glade threatened by encroaching pine forest. None bears Nora Ella's name. Riley rejected repeated entreaties to erect a tombstone in her honor. Close friends guessed at the reason: to erect a marker at his mother's grave was to concede that she was gone, and that was something Riley was never quite prepared to do.*

---

*Some prior accounts suggest Riley did not know the exact location of his mother's grave. But Lora Walker and Alan Hammons, both longtime friends, recalled him pointing out the gravesite with precision. Charles Sawyer, the biographer, notes another possible reason for Riley's reluctance to erect a headstone: he was frightened of graveyards.

CHAPTER 2

ON THE RUN

FOR MANY YEARS, Riley King would tell interviewers that he lived with his mother until the day she died and that he lived alone after her death. In his account, Riley declined invitations to move in with kin and opted instead to remain in the cabin where he and his mother had dwelt. That narrative would endure as a central tenet of the B.B. King legend. "Staying in the cabin was like staying with Mama," he recalled. "Her smells and her memories were in the walls and the floors, in the washtub and the wood-burning stove. Leaving the cabin would be leaving Mama."

But the evidence suggests Riley had not seen much of Nora Ella in her final years. Since his arrival in Hill Country, around 1932, Riley had probably passed back and forth between the households of his grandmother and his Uncle William, head of the Pulley clan. With his mother's passing, that temporary arrangement became more or less permanent.

Later in life, Riley rarely acknowledged the starring roles his uncle and grandmother had played in raising him. What little he said of Uncle William hinted that he didn't much like the man. Nora Ella's older brother "could be a little mean," Riley recalled, "a right-to-the-point kinda guy. Uncle William's thing was: 'If you don't do like I say, boy, you got trouble.' So I did what he said. He was the main man in the family. I loved him but was afraid of him."

The few times Riley breathed his grandmother's name sound almost like slips of the tongue. "Everybody cared about me," he told one interviewer. "But how much? The house where we lived—my room, my grandmother and I—I wanted to stay there. I felt that it was nobody but me. I just felt it was me against the world." Even here, Elnora is all but invisible, as if Riley were looking right through her.

After Nora Ella's death in late 1935, Elnora remained as a sharecropper on the Henderson farm. She also cooked and cleaned in the home of another farmer, Marshall Flake Cartledge. The Hendersons and Cartledges were neighbors, their farms sprawled across adjoining properties off Highway 413, south of Kilmichael. By 1936, Flake and Zelma Cartledge had a four-year-old son, Wayne. Ten-year-old Riley entertained the younger boy while his grandmother cleaned. "He would play with me and show me things," Wayne recalled.

On Sundays, Riley and his remaining family attended church in rotation: Elkhorn Primitive Baptist Church one weekend, followed in successive weeks by the Missionary Baptist Church at Pinkney Grove and then the Church of God in Christ at Austin Chapel, where Archie Fair serenaded worshipers with his guitar.

Riley begged the reverend to teach him how to play. But he needed a real guitar: Riley wasn't going to learn much on a one-stringed diddley bow. Word of his obsession reached the Henderson patriarch, Edwayne Henderson. One day, probably in 1936, Edwayne presented Uncle William with an old guitar for ten-year-old Riley to play. The instrument was probably another Stella, a simple acoustic model, ubiquitous in the Deep South, sold by the Oscar Schmidt Company in dry-goods stores. Well-crafted and modestly priced, Stellas were a cheap alternative to the costlier, metal-bodied National guitars of that era. And they were loud: an unamplified Stella produced enough volume to match the most boisterous blues shouter. Blind Lemon Jefferson played one.

Now, whenever John and Lessie Fair visited Riley's Uncle William, Riley "would go and drag out the old guitar for John to tune it," Lessie recalled. "John would take it and tune it and play some for him."

On one visit, Uncle William chastised Riley for pestering his elders. "Boy," William said, "John don't feel like foolin' with you with that thing."

"William," Lessie snapped back, "don't dog at him like that. You don't know what that boy's gonna come to. Someday he may be a sho' nuff musician."

RILEY WOULD SPEND the years after his mother's death surrounded by family but feeling very much alone. He passed endless hours in Aunt Mima's cabin, sitting on the floor, ear pressed to her Victrola, losing himself in the music until Mima feared he wasn't quite right in the head. Perhaps he wasn't. Riley recalled wandering into the thicket near his cabin and communing with woodland creatures, feeding breadcrumbs to field mice and talking to squirrels. "Sometimes a bird would settle on my shoulder or a bunny would hop right up to my nose," he recalled, raising eyebrows among incredulous loved ones in later life. "I felt too wounded from Mama's death to get close to other kids." Riley found it easier to befriend animals, because they didn't talk back.

Rural Mississippi's paternalistic structure insulated Riley from many horrors. He lived within a vast buffer of farmland overseen by two families, Henderson and Cartledge. Whatever their faults, those families were far from the cold-blooded racists Riley would encounter outside their farms.

In 1904, well before Riley's birth, a Black man named Luther Holbert was accused of killing a white landowner, the most grievous affront imaginable against Mississippi's established order. Luther and a female companion were captured and taken to Doddsville, sixty-five miles west of Kilmichael. The victims were tied to a tree and forced to extend their hands. Volunteers from a white mob stepped forward to chop off their fingers, one at a time, and distributed them as souvenirs. The mob severed their ears. They beat Luther, fracturing his skull and gouging one eye from its socket. Torturers used a corkscrew to bore holes into the victims' bodies and remove chunks of flesh. Finally, they threw Luther and his companion into a fire. All this unfolded in a picnic atmosphere, watched by white families sipping lemonade and eating deviled eggs.

Riley recalled just one instance of violence that touched him in Kilmichael, probably after his mother's death. He ran with a group of five or six boys. In a summer ritual, they would pick watermelons from a white farmer's patch and run down to the creek to build a bonfire and eat the melons. After one such incursion, the farmer sent word that he would shoot the next trespasser who purloined a melon. Undaunted, the boys returned to the patch—and the farmer opened fire. "I remember hearing the shots," Riley recalled. "Two, three shots rang out." The boys sprinted away. When they reached the creek, Riley felt wetness inside one of his boots. He removed it and saw a pool of blood. Riley had been shot.

After that, Riley chose safer pursuits. On Wednesday evenings, he would catch a ride into town and sit in the street with the other African American field hands to watch a movie on an outdoor screen. (Unlike the Henderson farm, downtown Kilmichael seems to have been wired for electricity.) If he spotted a girl sitting away from her parents, Riley would sidle over and smile, hoping she might allow him to hold her hand. These were white-people movies, films about Tarzan and Dick Tracy and the evil Dr. Fu Manchu. Riley particularly loved Gene Autry, the singing cowboy. "Cowboy music might have been white and coming from a world far from my own," he recalled, "but I could feel its soul." More important, Riley saw the effect Autry's singing had on women, on-screen and off: "When the girl sitting beside me would sigh and maybe rub up against me, I silently thanked Gene and made a mental note associating sensuous music with sensuous women."

One day on the Henderson farm, probably around age twelve, Riley idled in the barnyard, passing some time by bouncing a ball repeatedly off the head of a ram, a vaguely sadistic exercise spawned by sheer boredom. The ram endured the abuse with stoicism—until Riley missed a throw, forcing him to approach the ram and collect the ball. When the boy bent over, the ram saw his moment and charged, catching Riley squarely in the backside with his horns. A horn smashed into Riley's testicles. No doctor could be found, and the mangled organs were left to mend on their own. "And for the longest time, they thought that he would never heal," said Lora Walker, Riley's close friend and confidante in later years. The wounds eventually closed, but the episode would have dire consequences for Riley's fertility.

Riley's first sexual experiences had come with his childhood friend Peaches. Around 1938, Riley had an encounter with a full-grown woman, one whose companionship exacted a price.

"The guys had been tellin' me about her," he recalled, "so I'd worked hard for about two months trying to save me five dollars to go to bed with this lady. Well, I went to town that day, and I had to go 'cross the track, as we called it, to see this lady. She was kind of a heavy lady. So she was setting on a couch eating peanuts." Riley, by contrast, was rail thin. "I stood at the door, man, and she's sittin' with one of those kind of dresses lie between the thighs. And she had big thighs, looked real good. She's still eating peanuts, and she says, 'Whatchou want?' And when she said that, all the heart went out, in other words, my little feelings and everything about sex vanished. Yeah. But she started to talk to me, and she said, 'Did you come to see me?' and I said, 'Yes'm'. She said, 'Well, you got the money?' and I said, 'Yes'm', and she said, 'Ya don't have to say 'Yes'm', and I said, 'Yes, ma'am', and she said, 'You don't have to say *that.*' Then she started to take her clothes off, right there on the couch. I ain't never seen this before, you know? So I went over there, boy, and I guess the very moment I touched her, I was over."

The episode left Riley "so ashamed," he recalled, that he "never did it again."

RILEY'S FAMILY REMAINED in Kilmichael, including Aunt Nevada Bennett, her husband, Jack—Riley's field-shouting uncle—and their children, one of them a son named Flim who was a year younger than Riley.

Cousin Flim may be the unnamed antagonist in a story Riley told that illustrates how he learned to play the cruel hand fate had dealt him. Walking home from school one day, Riley and his cousin stopped at the cousin's house. The cousin asked his mother for something to eat. Both boys were famished. "Your food's in the safe," the mother replied, referring to a sealed compartment where families kept food safe from pests. The cousin reached into the safe, retrieved his meal, and sat down to eat. Riley waited hopefully. The cousin regarded him and asked cruelly, "Where's your dinner?" He knew Riley had none.

"It was his way of reminding me that I was stone alone, and too bad," Riley recalled. "I could have killed him. I could have cried. . . . But me being me, I did nothing. Didn't say a word to my cousin or my aunt. Didn't give either of 'em the slightest notion that I felt like the most useless, worthless thing on Earth. I watched him eat and left. I kept the hurt inside for the rest of my life." Riley had learned from his mother not to hurt other people the way his cousin had wounded him.

No one who worked on Edwayne Henderson's farm lived particularly well. Aunt Mima would end 1939 owing her landlord $8.31, a sum equal to two months' living expenses. Uncle William finished the year owing Henderson more than $100. The Hendersons themselves fared better. According to the 1940 census, Bertha Henderson earned $180 in 1939 working at the local library. The farm itself netted $1,000.

Toward the end of the 1930s, Riley passed into the sole custody of his grandmother. Uncle William now had three children of his own. Riley was probably glad to be rid of him. Riley toiled on with his grandmother, raising cotton on the acres the Hendersons had provided her. Farm records for 1939 show Elnora and Riley borrowed a monthly furnish, amassing a debt of $30 by August. Fertilizer costs padded the sum to $34.61. The pair earned $25.27 that fall by selling their crop and reaped another $10 working for the Hendersons, leaving them a profit of 66¢. Elnora borrowed $8 more in November and December.

Over the winter of 1939, Elnora began coughing up blood. She had probably contracted tuberculosis. Edwayne charged her 10¢ for pills and 20¢ for black draught, a dubious tonic. Finally, a doctor was summoned, and $8 further were charged to Elnora's account.

On January 10, 1940, someone transported Elnora to the Winona Infirmary, twenty miles away. Riley probably never saw his grandmother again. Elnora died on January 15, 1940, a chilly Monday. She was fifty-four. The Hendersons paid $5 for her burial and charged it to her estate. A farm subsidy check for $18.12 arrived some months later: government subsidies helped Mississippi farmers break even. But it was not enough to cover Elnora's debts. Riley's grandmother died owing the Hendersons $3.63. Mourners buried Elnora beside her daughter in the unmarked plot at Pinkney Grove. Riley, now fourteen, was both impoverished and alone.

Riley recalled that he remained in his grandmother's sharecropper shack after her death. But here, again, the evidence suggests otherwise. Jack and Nevada Bennett listed Riley in their household on the 1940 census, along with their own children. Aunt Nevada was Nora Ella's younger sister and faintly reminded Riley of his departed mother. One survivor of that era, Jessie Hemphill, likewise recalled Riley living with "Big Jack" after his grandmother passed. Even among sharecroppers, fourteen-year-old boys did not generally live alone.

Now, Riley himself entered the descending spiral of sharecropper debt. In the spring and summer of 1940, he borrowed a furnish of $12.50 from Edwayne Henderson. He purchased a pair of pants for $1 and a wrench for 50¢, and he spent another 40¢ on sacks to hold the cotton he picked. Henderson fronted the money and charged Riley interest on the debt, which swelled to $16.72. Over the summer, Riley earned $5 for work. At harvest, he earned another $4.18 by selling his cotton. At season's end, Riley owed Henderson $7.54.

Riley reviled the unending cycle of debt, but he felt a kinship to the soil. "I knew it was the system left over from slavery," he recalled. "I knew the system was cheating me and my people. But the work itself . . . well, I actually liked it. Liked being close to the land. Liked seeing that white world of freshly bloomed cotton sprouting out every summer. A new crop was like a new life."

AROUND THIS TIME, probably at age fourteen, Riley formed his first musical group. He had been singing in choir at the Elkhorn church, and adolescence had blessed him with a strong, resonant tenor. (Years later, it would settle into a rich baritone.) He organized a vocal group with two classmates and a cousin, Birkett Davis. They called themselves the Elkhorn Jubilee Singers.

At the start of the 1940s, African American teenage boys across the South were launching gospel groups inspired by the Golden Gate

Quartet, which had formed in 1934 in Norfolk, Virginia. In 1938, the group appeared at a historic Carnegie Hall concert organized by folklorist John Hammond, titled "From Spirituals to Swing." The quartet signed with the Okeh label in 1940, launched a nationwide radio program, and played at Franklin Delano Roosevelt's 1941 inauguration. The ensemble wedded the tight harmonies of barbershop quartets to the syncopated rhythms of jazz and blues. Voices would bounce in and out of the mix, adeptly mimicking the sounds of train whistles and muted horns, bouncing bass and skittering drums, all as a means to reinvent classic spirituals as pop songs.

Riley was equally smitten with the Ink Spots, a secular pop quartet that had developed a trademark "top and bottom" attack: tenor Bill Kenny would croon a verse or two in the style of a syrupy white balladeer, enunciating every round syllable, then Hoppy Jones would sweep in with his "talking bass," speaking, rather than singing, the next verse in a voice that was unmistakably Black. One voice established the group's crossover appeal, and the other affirmed its roots. Their 1939 breakthrough, "If I Didn't Care," sold nearly twenty million copies.

Consciously or not, the Elkhorn Jubilee Singers drew their name from an even earlier source: the Fisk Jubilee Singers, an ensemble formed in 1871 to raise funds for the historically Black Fisk University in Nashville. The Fisk Jubilee Singers had performed at the White House for President Ulysses S. Grant. They popularized the a cappella gospel style and would be credited with introducing the music of African American slaves to American whites.

More than pop or blues or anything else, Riley yearned to sing gospel. Raised within a community of fervent faith, he idolized Archie Fair and wanted nothing more than to follow his path. "I could see God's hand in the creation of the natural world," Riley recalled. "That made me wanna sing about him. Thank him for my life. Thank him for the rain that brought out the blossoms. Thank him for giving me the get-up-and-go to find a guitar and start plucking."

Riley sang tenor for the Elkhorn Jubilee Singers, taking the lead on "When the Saints Go Marching In" and on the group's unofficial theme song, "When the Roll Is Called Up Yonder."

Riley's group "tried to sound like the great Golden Gate Quartet, but didn't," he recalled. "We also wanted to sound like the Ink Spots, but couldn't." Yet, within the narrow walls of the Elkhorn church, the Jubilee Singers were a hit.

The gospel group afforded Riley a new status. He emerged from the shadows of anonymity. Girls noticed him. He certainly noticed them. Adolescence raged within him, and Riley became relentless in pursuit of sex. His weekly quest would begin at Sunday service, where he would take a lusty visual inventory of the pretty girls. He would try to pry one away from her mama for a walk home. If the walk went well, Riley would bid for a secret meeting in the woods. "Once in a great while," he recalled, "you might even convince her to give you a little—maybe a little feel, maybe a little more." Rarely, Riley would coax a girl into intercourse. None would allow him to climax inside her, a source of endless frustration, Riley recalled, for it was the part he "liked best." Otherwise, most of Riley's sexual encounters involved other boys, who would gather in a circle and masturbate. Riley usually finished last.

ONE FALL AFTERNOON in 1940, around Riley's fifteenth birthday, a pickup truck rolled up to the Elkhorn School. A man met Luther Henson at the door. They spoke. Henson walked over to Riley. "Get your books," Henson instructed. "Your daddy's here."

After splitting with Nora Ella, Albert King had settled down with the former Ada Lee Bingman. Ada bore a striking resemblance to the lovely Nora Ella. She and Albert had married in 1931 and settled in Lexington, a bustling trade center and the seat of Holmes County, Mississippi, forty miles southeast of Riley's birthplace. Albert and Ada started a new family. By 1940, they had three daughters. Albert was now a tractor mechanic earning $14 a week in farming season, enough to support his own family along with Ada's mother and brother in a seven-person household. Albert had earned $312 in 1939.

Though Albert was only thirty-three, he had borne the responsibilities of adulthood for nearly twenty years. He spoke in a gruff Delta

patois and drank "rivers of whiskey with no apparent effect." Riley had
inherited his father's broad nose and expressive eyes. Albert's adult
personality combined "qualities of pluck, roguishness, and good humor
with a touch of arrogance," biographer Charles Sawyer writes. He was
a hard man.

William Pulley, Riley's severe uncle, might well have summoned
Albert from Lexington after Elnora's death. As Elnora's eldest child,
William ruled Riley's fate. "After [Elnora] passed," one relative recalled,
"William decided to send him to Lexington, Mississippi, where his
daddy was."

On this autumn afternoon in 1940, Luther Henson brought Riley
out from the one-room Elkhorn schoolhouse to see his father. Albert
asked, "You all right, Jack?" Albert called Riley "Jack" to show warmth.
That was the closest he would ever stray to an outright expression of love.

"I'm okay," Riley replied.

"You're gonna come live with me now," Albert announced.

Riley hadn't seen his father since the day he and his mother left
Itta Bena, a decade earlier. "I guess she really tried to keep me away
from where he was," Riley recalled. Riley found himself both anxious
and excited at the prospect of leaving the only permanent home he had
really known. But he never seriously considered saying no: "Daddy
wasn't the kind of man you challenged." So Riley gathered his things
and left the Elkhorn School.

"I looked out the window," Riley's classmate Jessie Hemphill
recalled, "and he was going down the road with his daddy."

Riley said goodbye to almost no one. Albert stopped only at the
home of Edwayne Henderson, who assured Riley he would tell his
family where he had gone.

The trip southwest to Lexington covered about fifty miles. As
Albert drove, he told Riley a new family awaited him in Lexington,
a thought that, like the journey itself, elicited both exhilaration and
fear. Unlike Riley's mother, Albert was neither affectionate nor sweet.
"With Daddy there was strong silence, the road ahead, no stopping, no
questioning, no touching," Riley recalled. "We both stared down the
afternoon sun and listened as the tires crunched over the dirt road."

The first meeting between Riley and his new family was tense. Ada King was about twenty-three, eight years older than Riley. Her resemblance to Riley's mother was startling. Riley thought to himself, "Daddy found himself another Nora Ella." But Ada did not gaze on, speak to, or touch Riley with any of Nora Ella's warmth. "I didn't come out of her body," Riley recalled. "I came on a borrowed truck."

Riley regarded Albert's Lexington home with wonder. His father had electricity: not even the white farm owners outside Kilmichael had power. Albert owned a radio. His family had an indoor bathroom, fitted with a toilet that Riley did not know how to flush. (And he was too ashamed to ask.) Albert's new children owned toothbrushes. Riley had cleaned his teeth with twigs.

Nearly everything about Riley's new life put him ill at ease. His new stepmother, who worked as a laundress, ran her household with a seemingly endless slate of rules dictating where to place one's shoes and where not to set one's behind. Riley had three new stepsisters and a step-uncle. All of them would one day grow close to Riley. But at their first meeting, he felt like an ugly duckling and an outsider. It didn't help that Riley's father, the genetic link to his new family, was seldom home. He drove his tractor on a plantation near the town of Tchula, fifteen miles away, returning only on weekends. When he was home, Albert spent much of his time out drinking with friends.

The racial tension between Blacks and whites coiled even tighter in Mississippi's towns than on its plantations and farms. White plantation owners enjoyed absolute dominion over their lands, and benevolent owners could protect the African American sharecroppers living on their property. In towns and cities, by contrast, racial perils seemed to lurk around every corner. Albert took his son to a service station and drew his attention to three doors, one each for white men, white ladies, and "colored." Riley could no longer simply avoid white people, as he had so easily done on the expansive Henderson farm. Now, he would have to interact with whites every day. Riley's father instructed him to choose his fights. "I was never taught to hate," Riley recalled. "I was taught to try not to make trouble. I was taught to try to get along in the world."

Albert was a Black man of some means, and Riley apparently spent some of his time in Lexington attending private school. Saints Industrial and Literary School, founded in 1918, offered middle-class African Americans an alternative to public education on a picturesque campus run by the Church of God in Christ. Riley seems to have mentioned the school only once, in an early interview, perhaps because his brief tenure there ran so counter to the rest of his hardscrabble narrative. A short time later, for reasons unknown, Riley left the Christian school and enrolled at Ambrose Vocational High School, a sprawling, segregated public campus serving hundreds of African American students. At the tax-funded school, Riley saw the separate-but-equal fiction play out on a large stage. Black students roamed an overcrowded and dilapidated building and read tattered books handed down from white students when they got new ones. Ambrose boys wore clean shirts and neat trousers and spoke with erudition. Riley owned a single pair of overalls, and he spoke in a country twang. The well-spoken city boys belittled him. And Riley soon fell into trouble with the principal, Professor Seal, who answered every disciplinary lapse with a whipping. "Professor Seal would talk nice while he whacked the hell out of you," Riley recalled.

One sunny Saturday afternoon, Riley passed through Lexington's busy downtown, carrying a basket filled with clothes his stepmother had washed and ironed for a customer. When Riley reached the town square, he noticed a commotion around the courthouse. People were gathering there, most of them white. His instinct told him to stay away, so he stood at a distance and watched. Across the square, he saw several white men carrying the body of a Black man to the courthouse steps. There, they hoisted the body up with a rope hanging from a makeshift platform.

"Someone cheers," Riley recalled. "The dead man is young, nineteen or twenty, and his mouth and his eyes are open, his face contorted. It's horrible to look, but I look anyway. . . . I hear someone say something about the dead man touching a white woman and how he got what he deserves.

"My anger," Riley recalled, "is a secret that stays away from the light of day because the square is bright with the smiles of white people passing by as they view the dead man on display. I feel disgust and disgrace and rage and every emotion that makes me cry without tears and scream without a sound."

Mississippi would document 654 lynchings between 1877 and 1950, more than any other state. The archives of Lexington's weekly *Advertiser* newspaper for 1940 and 1941 record no lynching during Riley's time there. But white newspapers seldom covered lynchings.

Riley had seen enough. Taunted at school, ostracized at home, terrorized by what he had glimpsed at the courthouse, he wanted out of Lexington. Riley sought jobs outside town, climbing into trucks that transported Black workers to the fields to pick cotton and pull corn at harvest time. He squirreled away money to fund a trip back to Kilmichael.

Riley had lived barely a year in Lexington, from the autumn of 1940 till the autumn of 1941, when he climbed onto a bicycle purchased with his field-hand earnings and pedaled away. He was sixteen.

"The pressures of Lexington had been building," he recalled: living in a home where he felt unwelcome, attending a school "that seemed big as a factory and just as cold," and walking the streets among people who could transform into soulless monsters at any moment. "The more I thought," he recalled, "the harder I pumped the pedals." Riley would see little of his father, and nothing of his stepfamily, for the next six years.

Riley's journey back to Kilmichael spanned fifty miles over two days. At nightfall on the first day, he followed some cows into a barn and slept on hay. He awoke the next morning aching with hunger but had enough money only for a few crackers and a bottle of Barq's grape soda, and his bicycle needed grease. He spent his cracker money on grease. His stomach growled and his heart pounded as he struggled up the hills toward Kilmichael. Just when he thought he might collapse, he spotted an elderly African American lady in a rocking chair on a porch. He dismounted, wobbled toward her, and stuttered, "Excuse me, ma'am, but I was w-w-w-wondering . . . well, if you have s-s-s-something to eat."

The woman regarded Riley. Then she arose and disappeared into her house. She returned with a platter of buttered biscuits and a quart of buttermilk. Riley devoured it all. His energy restored, he thanked the lady profusely, climbed back onto the bicycle, and completed the journey. He wondered later if he had met an angel.

Jessie Hemphill was walking back from school when she spotted Riley in her path. "He was sitting on the road on his bicycle, waiting on us," she recalled. Riley greeted his classmates warmly and explained where he had been. "He told us his daddy'd married again," Jessie recalled, "and he said they all treated him bad."

Riley pedaled off to look for his kin. He hoped to rejoin the household of Aunt Nevada, his mother's sister, whose face reminded him of Nora Ella. He arrived at the cabin and found no trace of her family. He pressed on to the home of John and Lessie Fair, the brother and sister-in-law of the Reverend Archie Fair.

Lessie and John watched the shambling cyclist approach their porch. "Who is that?" Lessie asked. "I don't know," John replied. When the rider drew near, Lessie squinted in recognition. "Oh, that's Riley," she said.

Riley was a pitiful sight, his clothing torn and smeared with bicycle grease.

"What become of all my people?" Riley asked.

"They moved to the Delta," John replied.

"Lord have mercy," Riley said. "What am I gonna do?"

"Listen, boy," John replied. "Don't worry and carry on that way. As long as I have a roof over my head, you'll have one over yours. You hungry?"

"Yes, sir."

Lessie hurried into the shack and prepared a plate of biscuits. Riley devoured them. The boy "could eat like a log mule," one friend recalled.

Riley pedaled off to visit his old friends, the ones with whom he had sung gospel in church and purloined watermelons from fields.

"When you ready to go to bed," John Fair instructed, "come back here to the house."

Riley found his friends. He returned to the Fair cabin after nightfall, exhausted, for sleep.

The next morning, John Fair took Riley to see Flake Cartledge.

Marshall "Flake" Cartledge, born in 1897, was a cousin of Edwayne Henderson, Riley's former employer and landlord. Flake's mother was Mary Henderson. When Mary wed John Cartledge in 1892, her father deeded them forty acres of Henderson land. That became the Cartledge farm.

Flake married Zelma Landrum in 1928. A son, Wayne, arrived in 1932. They settled on the family farm. Flake "raised cotton and corn and vegetable crops and had cattle and mules and horses and stuff like that," Wayne recalled. Riley's grandmother Elnora had helped Zelma with the household chores. Riley had babysat young Wayne. By the time Riley returned to Kilmichael, Wayne was nine and Flake had a second job, grading dirt roads for the state highway administration.

Riley wanted to find his own family. But first, he told Flake Cartledge, he wanted to earn some money. John Fair suggested Flake house Riley in an old corn crib on the Cartledge farm, a twelve-by-twelve shack that had once housed John and Lessie. Riley embraced the new arrangement without hesitation. He knew the Cartledge family. Flake, the patriarch, "looked like a combination of John Kennedy and John Dillinger," Riley recalled. His voice was high-pitched and nasal, with a Mississippi twang "too thick for adequate metaphor," by one account. Riley recalled Flake as "a fair-minded and liberal man." Flake never uttered the N-word, and he seemed uncomfortable when other men did. He referred to Riley not as "boy" but as "son" or by his given name.

Flake crossed the Big Black River into Kilmichael. He bought Riley shirts and overalls, paper and pencils. He returned to the farm and fixed up Riley's new home, furnishing it with a bed and an oil-drum stove. Flake accepted Riley as a lodger on two conditions: that the boy resume his studies at Elkhorn School and that he help the Cartledge family with household chores, as his grandmother had once done.

Over the next year, Riley King would find a joy he hadn't known since the passing of his mother, six years earlier. He lived with the Cartledge family, working in their home, splashing in the creek with Wayne, and dining at the family table.

"B.B. was my babysitter," Wayne recalled. "We had a good time. He learned me how to ride a bicycle. And anything I wanted to do," he smiled, "I got away with it when I was in his care."

The Cartledge family had no electricity, telephone, or indoor plumbing. Water came from the well or from Crape Creek, where Zelma Cartledge washed clothes. Much of the family's diet came from the land: sausage and ham from slaughtered hogs, fried and boiled chicken, dried peas, butterbeans, canned peaches and blackberries, milk and butter from the cows. Riley and Wayne toiled on the farm every day. When spring arrived, they cleared a half acre outside Riley's shack and planted a turnip patch.

The Cartledge home comprised two bedrooms, a dining room, and a kitchen. The status Riley enjoyed in the household fell somewhere between houseboy, sitter, and son. Riley's presence at the family table marked a shocking affront to segregationist tradition. "It's a little hard for people to get their heads around," said Allan Hammons, Riley's longtime friend and archivist, "because it's unheard-of." Riley wasn't quite a Cartledge, but he was no longer a sharecropper. Flake paid Riley $7.50 a month for his work. Riley had no debt and no real expenses.

Riley spent most of his waking hours with Zelma and Wayne, his constant companions on the Cartledge farm. Like Riley's father, Flake was seldom home. When they weren't working or studying, Riley and Wayne would play.

One morning, nine-year-old Wayne was chopping down a tree when the axe glanced off the wood and sliced into his foot. Riley ran over, scooped him up, and carried him into the family house. While Zelma tended the wound, Riley sprinted off to find Flake's elderly mother, whose car carried Wayne into town to the doctor. Wayne's foot healed.

Wayne approached his father one day, probably in 1942, and asked if he could have a guitar. Denzel Tidwell, a white boy around Riley's age, was selling his fire-red Stella. The guitar cost fifteen dollars. Flake didn't want to spend that kind of money on his young son. He said no. Somehow, perhaps from Wayne's lips, Riley learned of the guitar. Riley asked Flake if he could purchase the guitar for himself. It was probably the boldest thing he had ever done.

Flake agreed: Riley was now sixteen, and he earned money of his own. Flake paid the fifteen dollars to Denzel Tidwell. He recovered the funds from Riley's next two paychecks.

This was probably Riley's second guitar, but the first he could call his own. "I was in love," he recalled. "Never have been so excited. Couldn't keep my hands off her. If I was feeling lonely, I'd pick up the guitar; feel like talking, pick up the guitar; if something's bugging me, just grab the guitar and play out the anger; happy, horny, mad, or sad, the guitar was right there, a righteous pacifier and comforting companion. It was an incredible luxury to have this instrument to stroke whenever the passion overcame me, and, believe me, the passion overcame me night and day."

Riley scrounged up another dollar to order Nick Manoloff's *Complete Chord and Harmony Manual for Guitar* from the Sears catalog. Riley was looking for blues. What he found in the Manoloff book was a generous helping of folk and cowboy songs. Undaunted, he set about learning notes and chords, teaching himself to play "You Are My Sunshine" and "Oh My Darling, Clementine." The guitar gave him "new life," he recalled. "It helped me cope. And gave me a little discipline."

Riley put his ears to work. He "had a battery-operated radio," Wayne Henderson recalled. In the shack, Riley caught every weekly broadcast of *Grand Ole Opry*, the radio "barn dance" from Nashville. The Opry revealed a world of white, working-class music, from the western swing of Bob Wills and his Texas Playboys to the Tennessee fiddle of Roy Acuff and his Smoky Mountain Boys. Riley procured a harmonica and ordered a neck-brace holder from the Sears catalog. After that, Wayne recalled, "he could play the harmonica, play the guitar, play anything he wanted to." One day, Riley serenaded Wayne with a harmonica-and-guitar rendition of "Walking the Floor over You," the breakthrough hit of Ernest Tubb, the Texas Troubadour.

One of the Hemphill boys went to spend the night with Riley in his corn crib, to see his red Stella. He and Riley slept in a single bed.

The boy returned home the next day covered in bedbug bites. He told his sisters Riley had spent the evening playing him songs on the guitar.

Riley took to his guitar in a way that he had not taken to his schoolbooks. He was a natural musician. Soon, he could play the guitar well enough to accompany the Austin Chapel congregation on a hymn, just like Archie Fair. Luther Henson sat Riley down at school one day and told him, "God has given everybody a talent. And your talent is playing that guitar."

RILEY WAS CONTENT on the Cartledge farm, but he would remain there for less than two years. After the 1942 harvest, he resolved to leave Hill Country. Most of Riley's kin had already decamped to the more fertile land of the Delta. Riley yearned to join them. His opportunity arrived in the form of Birkett Davis, his cousin and erstwhile bandmate.

Birkett was technically Riley's cousin once removed. His mother, Beulah Davis, was a sister of Riley's departed grandmother. Despite the generational difference, Birkett was Riley's age. Birkett was a strapping young man, an inch or two taller than Riley, with a narrow face and rakish good looks. Around 1941, Birkett and his family left Kilmichael for Indianola, the seat of Sunflower County, sixty-five miles due west at the heart of the Delta. In 1942, Birkett returned to visit Riley and told him the cotton paid better in Indianola. Later that year, Riley sent word to Birkett that he was ready to move. Birkett arrived in the spring of 1943 with a borrowed car. Riley and the Cartledge family parted warmly, and seventeen-year-old Riley King left Kilmichael for the last time.

CHAPTER 3

INDIANOLA MISSISSIPPI SEEDS

T HE DELTA SITS LIKE A VAST, muddy leaf across the map of northwestern Mississippi. It is not the actual delta, or terminus, of the mighty Mississippi River: that spot lies hundreds of miles south, beyond New Orleans. This Delta—*the* Delta, the only one anyone would name with a single word—is a narrow swath of Mississippi plain, bounded by the meandering paths of two rivers, the Mississippi on the west and the Yazoo on the east. The Delta's northern border lies below Memphis, where the Yazoo forks off from the Mississippi. The plain widens as it stretches south through towns of blues legend, past Clarksdale and Rosedale, Tunica and Greenwood, finally narrowing to a point where the rivers rejoin at Vicksburg. The Delta region spans 220 miles from north to south and, at its widest point, 87 miles east to west. It holds more than four million acres of alluvial floodplain: land covered in loose soil and sediment deposited over millennia by persistent floods. The mix of silt, clay, sand, and gravel bonds with rainwater on damp days to form Delta mud, a substance so dense and adhesive, Riley recalled, "it'll suck the soles off your shoes." It is some of the richest soil on Earth.

Farmers reclaimed large swaths of the Delta from pine forest and swamp before the Civil War, building an empire of cotton on the backbreaking labor of slaves and their descendants. Then came the Great Flood of 1927, submerging entire towns in muddy water, drowning hundreds of people—most of them Black and lacking the means of escape—and hundreds of thousands of animals. Charley Patton, the great Delta bluesman, recounted the deluge in a 1929 recording titled "High Water Everywhere": "So high the water a-risin', I been sinkin' down. . . . It were fifty men and children, come to sink and drown."

The Flood Control Act of 1928 yielded the world's longest system of levees, draining and drying much of the untamed Delta land. The introduction of International Harvester's Farmall row-crop tractor in the 1920s and the mechanical cotton picker in the 1930s transformed the cotton industry, which had relied on human pickers and mules. Riley King would return to the Delta amid this reorganization.

Riley arrived at Indianola and moved in with the family of Beulah Davis, his great-aunt. They lived on the thousand-acre farm of Johnson Barrett, a planter with a property so expansive that "you could start walking in the morning, walk all afternoon, and still be walking while the sun set," Riley recalled. The farm sat a few miles southwest of Indianola, along the Sunflower River.

Barrett owned roughly 350 acres near Indianola and rented perhaps 650 more. Fifty sharecropping families worked the land with tractors and mules. Barrett was Jewish, unusual for a Mississippi planter, and he held progressive ideas about race. When a nephew mismanaged the general store on his plantation, Barrett fired him and gave the job to his top field hand, Booker Baggett, who was African American. When Baggett set things right at the store, Barrett promoted him to plantation manager, a job that paid $2.50 a day plus food, shelter, and an automobile, a position of authority "unheard of for a black man at the time." Baggett kept the books, hired and fired, withdrew funds from the bank, and purchased equipment and supplies from the white merchants in town. Or he tried to: white shopkeepers sometimes refused to serve Baggett until Barrett assured them that a Black man controlled his purse strings.

Barrett sometimes forgave the debts of his sharecroppers when they finished the year in the red. He seems to have recovered those lost funds by short-changing his tenants in good years.*

---

* Riley's kin ultimately left the Barrett plantation in 1947 in a dispute over pay, according to Delcia Davis, the widow of Riley's cousin Birkett: "The last time we had a crop, they took a lot of our money," she recalled in an interview with the author.

However, Barrett was a far more benevolent landlord than the heartless racists Riley saw all over Indianola. A family photograph of Barrett pictures a weather-beaten man in a fedora, elbows bent, fists balled at the hips, Delta mud caked to his boots, staring off defiantly into the horizon. "He wore khaki pants, all starched and ironed, like he was on his way to church," Riley recalled. "He wasn't the kind to yell or scold or abuse his workers, but if you did something wrong he'd eye you until you felt shame." Barrett exuded quiet power.

Riley settled in with cousin Birkett and his family in a sharecropper house on Barrett's land, boasting three bedrooms and a kitchen. "They let me into their life," he recalled, "at a time when I was yearning for something stable."

Aunt Beulah dressed her own family in new clothing but attired Riley in hand-me-downs, sometimes leaving him without a clean shirt to wear to church. "We used to say some of Riley's clothes had every kind of patch on them but an okra patch," one Indianola friend recalled. Yet the same aunt purchased a new guitar for Riley to replace his beloved Stella, which he had lost to theft shortly before departing Kilmichael.

At seventeen, Riley was growing into a strapping young man, entering his prime earning years as a sharecropper, assuming he was fortunate enough to avoid injury and illness. Riley briefly attended the segregated Bay Lake School, near the Barrett farm. He never got past the tenth grade. In later years, Riley's unfinished education would linger as perhaps his greatest regret.

Riley set to work driving one of Barrett's mules, pacing behind the flatulent beast twelve hours a day, six days a week. Riley and his mule became a well-trained team, plowing the land, turning the soil, communicating with simple commands. "Git up" meant go; "Gee," turn right; "Ha-hee," left; "Whoa," stop. Riley enjoyed watching the soil go pliant behind the mule, ready to receive its seeds "like a woman receiving a man."

Riley thought a lot about women: they softened life's rough edges. Not long after his arrival in Indianola, he and cousin Birkett called on Delcia Davis, a beautiful, freckle-faced girl who had come to the

Delta to visit her sister. The boys quarreled affably over who would get to invite her to the movies. Riley asked Delcia to choose. She chose Birkett.

Undaunted, Riley pursued other farm girls. Sometime in 1943, he fell in love with one. He called her Angel. "She was a dark-skinned beauty with big, laughing eyes, a smile that lit up my day, and a body that fired my blood," he recalled. Riley was seventeen or eighteen, Angel perhaps a year or two younger. Like many girls Riley met at church, Angel would not consent to sex before marriage. So the couple kissed and hugged and walked hand in hand, following the time-honored rituals of courtship. They spoke of eventual nuptials. "She said she wanted to have my babies," Riley recalled, "and I said I'd love her right or die trying." Her parents admired Riley's industry. Angel's mother reminded him of his own.

One Sunday, Angel and her family failed to appear at church. Riley prayed they'd arrive by the end of the service, but they did not. He sensed something wrong, something other parishioners weren't telling him. "Finally, after the benediction," he recalled, "someone broke the news." Angel and her family had been passengers in the back of a truck when it struck a car and overturned. The entire family was crushed. Their bodies were returned for burial in closed caskets.

"When I started crying over Angel, I couldn't stop," Riley recalled. "I'm back living in a world where you could lose anyone anytime, just like that. Like my little brother. Or Mama. Or Grandma."

Robbed of love, Riley poured his energy into cotton. Farms around Indianola still employed human pickers. They paid better than Kilmichael farms, and the cotton was heavier. Riley could now pick as many as 480 pounds in a day. Birkett, his stronger cousin, could surpass 500 pounds. Each could earn $1.75 a day, a dollar more than the minimum rate. The two became so skilled at picking that they could sleep in, heading out to pick at eight in the morning instead of the customary six. (Sharecroppers were generally said to work from "cain" to "cain't": that is, from the first shaft of sunlight to the final shadows of sundown.) Riley also worked corn and soybean fields and maneuvered logs into a sawmill. He particularly disliked baling hay, painful and bloody work performed by hand.

RILEY AND BIRKETT REAPED some unexpected help with the fall harvest in 1943. In early October, according to an account in the daily *Indianola Enterprise*, one thousand prisoners of war, probably Germans captured in North Africa, arrived at a new internment camp outside of town. Army guards hauled the prisoners around Sunflower County in trucks, dispatching them to the cotton fields as pickers. Farmers evidently compensated the government at a rate of two dollars per hundred pounds picked, several times what Riley and Birkett earned for the same work.

The conflict had remained far away until Japan's attack on Pearl Harbor in December 1941. After that, Riley recalled, "the war got close." By the autumn of 1943, one-quarter of the crops Riley harvested in Mississippi went to feed and clothe the army and navy. One by one, Riley's friends on the Barrett plantation marched off to war.

African Americans had fought bravely in every military conflict since the Revolution. Yet, at the outbreak of World War II, only a few thousand African Americans served in the army, segregated into units commanded by white officers. Black civil rights leaders like labor unionist A. Philip Randolph prevailed on Congress to add language to the 1940 Selective Service Act that forbade draft boards to discriminate by race. The number of Black servicemen rose dramatically. But President Franklin D. Roosevelt, placating southern lawmakers, proceeded to reaffirm the age-old policy of racial segregation in the military. Black soldiers lived and trained away from white soldiers, often sleeping in older barracks and shopping at a second-rate post exchange (PX).

African Americans likewise remained largely shut out of the economic bonanza of war production. When Randolph threatened a mass protest in Washington, DC, in the summer of 1941, Roosevelt agreed to sign an order that banned employment discrimination in the defense industry, but the military remained segregated.

Black America never wavered in its patriotism, nor in its quest for equality. On February 7, 1942, two months after Pearl Harbor, the *Pittsburgh Courier* announced the Double V (for Victory) Campaign, calling on all African Americans to unite behind the war effort abroad while also lobbying for equal rights at home. The *Courier* was then the largest African American newspaper in the nation. The federal lobbying effort and Double V Campaign foreshadowed the modern civil rights movement. But the armed forces would not desegregate until 1948, three years after the war's end. Until then, Black servicemen would endure the same separate and unequal treatment as most Black civilians.

By the end of 1943, "quite a number" of Black Indianolans had enlisted or answered the draft, according to an account in the white-owned *Indianola Enterprise*: "There are many privates and sergeants, also one second lieutenant, who is a pilot, and two captains in the Medical Corps." One African American father claimed three sons in military service, one of them the aforementioned pilot, with a fourth "soon to be called." Black Indianolans eagerly commanded the local Civilian Defense effort, protecting the home front in the city's African American neighborhoods. Black citizens contributed generously to the city's war-bond drive, part of an urgent national campaign to finance the fight. Black leaders "got people to turn into bonds their savings of nickels and dimes," the *Enterprise* reported. The article concluded, with some apparent surprise, that "Indianola has a number of negroes who are well educated and are leaders among their race, and they usually cooperate freely with the white people."

MONEY, MUSIC, and lust inspired Riley in equal measure. He had seen the potent spell his gospel quartet cast on the girls at church. He and some friends organized a new group, aspirationally named the Famous St. John Gospel Singers. The ensemble began as a humble street-corner trio, Riley playing guitar and singing sacred songs in three-part harmony with cousin Birkett and a friend named John Matthews. They soon expanded to a quintet.

This group drew inspiration from the Golden Gate Quartet and also from the Soul Stirrers, a Texas ensemble. The traditional gospel quartet employed two tenors, one singing the "lead," or melody, the other a high harmony, joined by a baritone and bass on progressively lower harmonies. To this mix the Soul Stirrers added a fifth man, a second lead, who traded melodic duties with the first, backed by a four-part harmony. The "swing lead" added emotional tension and vocal depth. Radio exposure and relentless touring made the Soul Stirrers a national sensation by the time Riley arrived in the Delta.

Yet the Soul Stirrers, revolutionary as they were, didn't play guitars. Gospel groups of that era generally performed a cappella. Riley learned to accompany the Famous St. John Gospel Singers on guitar when the group performed at churches around Indianola. The act bordered on heresy: to church folk, the guitar symbolized the blues, and the blues symbolized sin.

Blues was a uniquely American music form that had probably taken shape around the turn of the century. It was African American music, seemingly rooted in African musical traditions brought to America by slaves. As writer Peter Guralnick famously observed, blues "came out of Mississippi, sniffed around in Memphis and then settled in Chicago," where it had arrived by the time of Riley's childhood, following the steady northward march of American Blacks.

Classic blues employed three chords, just like country music, its counterpart in the working-class white communities of the South. Blues was far simpler than jazz, a form that had emerged in New Orleans, arguably as an African American response to European classical music. But blues was more than music.

"The blues, to all or most of us Blacks, is a feeling," said Charles Evers, brother of civil rights leader Medgar Evers. "It comes out of suffering, being denied, refused, abused, misused. That's what the blues is."

Blues was the province of Delta roadhouses and taverns. Country bluesmen strummed guitars and sang about sex in thinly veiled lyrical slang. Some blues performers sang of dark dealings with the devil. Most God-fearing Mississippians, including Riley's Aunt Beulah, forbade the blues within their homes.

The rule against guitars was not inviolable. Riley's boyhood preacher, the Reverend Archie Fair, had strummed one in his Kilmichael church. But many congregations around Indianola had never seen such a thing. "If they found out we had a guitar," Riley recalled, "some churches would cancel our show."

The Famous St. John Gospel Singers also played secular gigs. Riley noticed a difference: At church, "we would sing, and they would pass the basket or the hat. People would say, 'Bless you.' But if we'd sing at a juke joint someplace and play, they'd have some guy standing at the door: 'You can't come in here unless you pay.' I liked that pretty well."

Whenever Riley heard the Soul Stirrers or Golden Gate Quartet on the radio, broadcast from some station in West Memphis or Helena, Arkansas, he would ask himself, "Why not us?" He saw the Famous St. John Gospel Singers as a way to combine his "love of the Lord, . . . music, and . . . money." He lobbied the other singers: the group could be their ticket out of the Delta. "I succeeded in convincing only me," he recalled.

Riley increasingly turned his attention to downtown Indianola. On weekends, he could glimpse the musical world beyond its borders. At the movie theaters, upstairs in the "colored" section, he sat transfixed through film shorts that featured Louis Armstrong. The New Orleans trumpeter had transformed jazz into a showcase for solo performers. His predecessors had favored a rapid, staccato attack. Armstrong played his horn like a human voice, slowing the melody, stretching the notes, and shaking his hand atop the valves to create the rich, vocal vibrato that was his trademark. Riley became equally mesmerized by another star of the shorts, Cabell "Cab" Calloway, a New York jazz singer who improvised wordless melodies. (Calloway had learned "scat" singing from Armstrong.) In their performances, horn and voice seemed to flow together into a single melodic stream. It was hard to tell where one left off and the other began.

Riley absorbed other musical influences on the smaller screen of the Mutoscope, a coin-operated moving-picture machine that played short films for single viewers. A ten-cent Mutoscope film introduced Riley to bandleader Benny Goodman, the King of Swing, who hastened the integration of American popular music by employing a succession of African American musicians. Riley found himself transfixed by one of those sidemen, a guitarist named Charlie Christian. He was the first great electric-guitar soloist in jazz.

Charles Henry Christian was born in 1916 in northeastern Texas but raised in Oklahoma: Like most of Riley's boyhood idols, Christian was conspicuously not from Mississippi. Christian came from a musical family. He took up the guitar in adolescence and became a star on the regional jazz scene, jamming with the big names when they passed through Oklahoma City. In 1939, he auditioned for the legendary producer John Hammond. The producer recommended Christian to Benny Goodman, who hired him, ignoring the color line that still divided much of the music world. The resulting exposure, along with Christian's gift for melody and improvisation, would thrust the guitar to the front rank of jazz, the genre that dominated American popular music. Christian played his amplified guitar like a horn, executing extended solos on a single string and manipulating the strings to produce a sound that could carry a melody, bending notes with his fingers and sometimes coaxing a subtle vibrato from the string. Lonnie Johnson had done the same things a decade earlier, without an amplifier. Amplification allowed Christian to compete with the other instruments in a big band, a revolutionary advance.

Surviving photographs picture Christian in a suit and tie, gazing at his guitar in rapt concentration, forever young. By the time Riley had discovered this brilliant young Black man playing in a white man's band, Charlie Christian was already dead. Tuberculosis had claimed him in 1942, at twenty-five. All the same, Riley's heart pounded in his chest as he watched Christian play. To Riley, Christian was "a miracle man, doing things to a guitar" that he "never imagined possible."

Riley found his way to Jones' Night Spot, an Indianola club operated by an African American entrepreneur. Still a teen and too young to gain entry, Riley pressed his face up against gaps in the wall. Inside, he beheld a throng of "women in tight dresses of red and yellow and baby blue dancing with men all decked out in big suits and ties and wide-brimmed hats." From that perch, through that crowd, Riley glimpsed the stars of the chitlin' circuit, the network of African American clubs that brought the nation's greatest rhythm and blues and jazz acts to their public. He saw Count Basie and his orchestra, dressed in matching green suits and playing music "as bluesy as anything I'd heard in the Delta"; and Jay McShann, another great bandleader whose sidemen briefly included a fiery young alto-sax player named Charlie Parker; and Alex Ford, a bona fide Mississippi bluesman who had found national fame playing harmonica on the *King Biscuit Time* radio show in Arkansas under the borrowed stage name Sonny Boy Williamson. Sonny Boy played with Robert Lockwood Jr., one of the finest slide guitarists working the Delta. Lockwood played solo and rhythm patterns beyond Riley's grasp. He and Charlie Christian seemed to come from another musical universe, one populated with chords Riley could not find in Nick Manoloff's *Complete Chord and Harmony Manual for Guitar.* Riley had learned only the bare rudiments of guitar craft. But he dutifully memorized all that he heard. "I believe I listened harder," he recalled, "than anyone in the history of listening." Music rang in Riley's ears as he trudged back to Johnson Barrett's farm.

AMONG RILEY'S MANY DREAMS, the first to come true was the most mundane. About a year after his arrival in Indianola, in 1944, Riley earned a promotion to tractor driver. Riley's father was a tractor driver. There was no bigger job for an African American farmer working a white man's land. (Booker Baggett, the Black foreman of the Barrett plantation, was the rare exception.) Barrett's nine tractors could do the work of several dozen mules. Riley's pay rose from $1 a day to $2.50, more than his father had earned in Lexington.

"I'd climb up on the tractor and, as far as the eye could see, look over acres and acres of hard soil," he recalled. "I liked the smells of the cold morning air and the hot engine's fumes; I liked looking at the uncovered dirt, the fat worms and the crawling bugs, the hungry birds flying overhead, the clouds in the sky, the changing light of day, the sound of the hardworking motor, the sense of accomplishment sweeping over me."

Johnson Barrett also promoted Riley's cousin Birkett to tractor driver. This was their first taste of prosperity. Now, Riley and Birkett could actually make a living, could even raise a family.

"Working the fields all the time, you couldn't do anything but eat, hardly," recalled Delcia Davis, who was now, to all intents, Birkett's wife. "But when you got to be a tractor driver, you could buy things for your home and food and clothes and go where you want to go when Sunday comes. You might even get to go out on Saturday evening."

The money was good. But now Riley and Birkett had two jobs: they still toiled as sharecroppers, planting and picking cotton between tractor shifts. Sometimes they drove through the night, taking after Riley's workaholic father. One morning, Delcia Davis recalled, Riley and Birkett slept in after driving their tractors all night. Johnson Barrett appeared at their cabin and demanded, "How come you ain't in the field?" Birkett replied, "I drove the tractor last night and I had to get some sleep before I go to the field." Unmoved, Barrett went to Birkett's parents and commanded, "You go in there and talk to those boys, 'cause they're supposed to be in the field, and they're not in the field."

Riley's success on the plantation only fed his nonagrarian ambitions. Having met one of his goals, Riley realized the others might not lie so far out of reach. His dreams alighted on the Famous St. John Gospel Singers. The quintet played a widening circuit of churches and halls around Indianola, sometimes opening for more established ensembles, groups as famous as the Soul Stirrers, so popular that they made a living on music. By contrast, the Famous St. John Gospel Singers barely scraped by. Church gigs didn't pay, apart from a collection that was shared with the church and then split five ways. Riley approached his bandmates and proposed, "Maybe we could take off after the crop's been picked and start traveling." His bandmates demurred. Most of them earned less than Riley, toiling from one paycheck to the next. "All the guys had families," Riley recalled, "and some just couldn't see traveling as I could see it." Riley felt trapped.

Though Riley could not persuade his group to leave Indianola, he did convince them to make a brief pilgrimage to Greenwood, thirty miles east, at the edge of the Delta. Greenwood sprawled three times larger than Indianola. There, inside a narrow brick building, Riley and his friends went on the air.

The same tradition of segregation that barred African Americans from white theaters and clubs kept most Black musicians off the radio. Throughout the 1920s, the segregationist American Federation of Musicians had blocked African American musicians from joining the first generation of radio dance bands. Black bandleaders broke through only on scattered provincial broadcasts that fell outside the union's control. Jazz pianist Earl "Fatha" Hines performed on KDKA in Pittsburgh in 1921, blues singer Bessie Smith on WSB in Atlanta in 1923. Duke Ellington orchestrated the New York airwaves between 1927 and 1930. Riley probably heard Deford Bailey, a diminutive blues harmonicist who performed regularly on the *Grand Ole Opry* out of Nashville. Segregation endured through the 1930s, but after the outbreak of World War II, the Armed Forces Radio Service produced a series of national shows that prominently featured titans of African American music, from Louis Armstrong and Count Basie to the Ink Spots and Golden Gate Quartet. By the 1940s, Black performers had also gained a foothold on southern radio. Local businesses with African American customers sponsored live shows to target their customers. The most famous was *King Biscuit Time*, launched in 1941 on KFFA in Arkansas to sell flour and featuring Sonny Boy Williamson, the harmonica master. *King Biscuit* provided a template for blues and gospel broadcasts that other stations would follow.

WGRM went on the air in Greenwood in 1938. The station mostly presented the usual white radio fare, a mix of popular music, comedy, drama, and variety shows. On Sunday afternoons, however, WGRM aired live performances by gospel groups, some of them Black. The success of the Golden Gate Quartet and its ilk had created a market for Black gospel music on white radio. Riley's group proved a popular addition to the Sunday broadcasts. Soon, the Famous St. John Gospel Singers added a banner to their flyers that announced, "Stars of Radio Station WGRM."

In the summer of 1944, with a well-paying job and a radio gig, Riley trained his full attention on a young woman named Martha Lee Denton. Martha was the youngest of eight, born in 1929. Most of her family lived in Eupora, a small city not far from Kilmichael. In 1944, Martha traveled to Indianola to join her brother John, who was working on the Barrett plantation. She and Riley met at church. She was fourteen. He was eighteen.

Martha "was a light-skinned beauty," Riley recalled, "beautifully built, with big legs, a small waist, and heavy hips," and the prettiest smile he had ever seen. "I longed for her."

But Riley would have to wait. Martha meant to remain a virgin until marriage. So they courted. Martha would nod to Riley as he drove past on his tractor. He would nod back and smile. Her face would linger in his mind all day. In the evening, he'd appear at John Denton's house and invite Martha for a walk.

"At first," he recalled, "I didn't even dare to hold her hand. That would have been too bold. She was a shy girl, and I worried that my aggressiveness would scare her away." They talked about her brother, about Eupora, and about the Famous St. John Gospel Singers. Riley told Martha how he yearned to leave Mississippi. He bemoaned his bandmates' reluctance to join him. He invited Martha on a tractor ride into town on a coming Saturday. After an agonizing pause, she assented.

Saturday arrived. Riley rode the tractor hard all morning. Then, he cleaned up for the drive into Indianola. There was no question of privacy for Riley and his date: A farmhand steering a motorized vehicle into town was duty bound to transport other farmhands, who would clamber into the wagon Riley towed behind him. Riley saved the passenger seat in the cab for Martha. When he saw her walking toward him, he recalled, "Her smile warmed me from the inside out." The two sat quietly as the tractor lumbered forward, each occasionally catching the other in a secret glance: "We tried looking straight ahead, but our eyes kept going back to each other."

Riley parked the tractor and escorted Martha around town. Martha spotted a bolt of yellow fabric through a store window and popped inside to ask its cost. She returned disconsolate: the price was too steep. Riley had an idea. He asked Martha if she wanted to listen while he played his guitar, which he had conveniently brought. "I guess I wanted to show off," he recalled. He boldly launched into a song, and passersby gathered, listening appreciatively and dropping coins into Riley's hat. After half an hour, he had enough change to fill his pocket. Riley steered Martha back to the store. He ducked inside.

"What are you doing?" Martha asked.

"Wait here," he replied, "and you'll see."

Minutes later, Riley returned with the bolt of yellow fabric.

"You shouldn't have," she beamed.

"I wanted to," he replied. Her smile was thanks enough.

Riley and Martha returned to town on subsequent Saturdays, sipping lemonade and dining on chicken and greens. One evening, Riley took Martha to Jones' Night Spot and showed her the holes in the rickety walls. Together they watched Louis Jordan and His Tympany Five, a red-hot rhythm-and-blues ensemble that could do more with five musicians than most big bands could achieve with a dozen. The couple marveled at the bug-eyed bandleader and his golden alto sax as he led the combo through his number 1 hit, "What's the Use of Getting Sober (When You're Gonna Get Drunk Again)." When the moment felt right, Riley turned to Martha and planted a kiss on her lips.

On the ride back to the plantation, Riley and Martha couldn't keep their hands off each other. When they reached her brother's house, Riley spoke: "Martha, you know how I feel, baby. You know I love you."

"Well, Riley," she replied, "I love you too."

That was his cue. "Will you marry me?" he asked.

This time, his wait was brief. "Yes!" she replied.

RILEY AND MARTHA'S ENGAGEMENT would play out against a backdrop of war.

Riley had turned eighteen in September 1943. By the summer of 1944, he was several months tardy in registering for the draft. He reported on June 22, 1944, nine months after his birthday, around the time he and Martha met. Perhaps to escape punishment from the Indianola draft board, Riley made himself younger, giving his birth date as April 15, 1926.

Riley passed his preinduction physical and was ordered to report for duty a few months later, toward the end of 1944. He was summoned to Camp Shelby in Hattiesburg, two hundred miles south of Indianola, farther than he had ever traveled before.

Johnson Barrett was already short of hands, and he did not want to lose another good driver. He told Riley he would ask the draft board for an occupational deferment: crops such as cotton and soybeans were essential to the war effort, and men who harvested them could serve their country simply by staying at work. More than one and a half million men, disproportionately Black and from the South, would be deferred as essential farm workers by the war's end. This fit a larger federal strategy that largely excluded African Americans from actual combat in World War II: the vast majority of enlisted Black men populated support units and replacement depots, working menial jobs rather than firing guns or flying planes. "Once the fighting actually began," a historian notes, "neither white political leaders nor military commanders were interested in sociological experiments of equality for African Americans in the military."

Barrett told Riley getting married could improve his chances for deferment. And so, on Sunday, November 26, 1944, Riley and Martha wed. He was nineteen, she a month shy of fifteen. "Just me, Martha, and a witness," Riley recalled. "No party, no honeymoon. That's how it was done in those days." Cousin Birkett, also seeking deferment, married Delcia on the same day.

Riley probably could not read or write well enough to file deferment papers, so Barrett completed the forms on his behalf. While they awaited a reply, Riley reported for basic training, eager, even excited, to serve his country. "For years I'd been hungering to see the world, and this was a righteous reason to take off," he recalled. "We'd also been taught that the black soldier enjoyed greater freedom than the black civilian. The uniform was supposed to give you respect. Naïve or not, we truly believed that."

One morning in the winter of 1944, Riley boarded a bus filled with Black conscripts. He waved back to Martha as she receded into the distance. Not long into the journey, the bus passed a small group of young white women. One of the conscripts yelled, "How y'all doing?" For a Black man to greet a white woman that way in Mississippi was unthinkable, but these men were heading off to war. The women smiled politely, and the bus rolled on, disaster apparently averted. Some time later, the Greyhound stopped for lunch in Jackson. Before the conscripts could disembark, a white man with a rifle climbed aboard, eyes ablaze. He demanded, "Which one of you n——s was yelling at my daughter?"

Riley and the other conscripts stared straight ahead, no one making a sound.

"I ought to shoot all of you," the man snarled. The white military officers on board sat silent as the man with the rifle proceeded down the aisle, jabbing the barrel into each conscript's neck. "When he got to me," Riley recalled, "I felt the cold metal of the gun barrel against my Adam's apple. I didn't blink. Didn't swallow. I was sweating bullets inside, but I didn't want to give him the satisfaction of seeing my fear." After a long moment, the man withdrew his rifle and went on to the next passenger. "No one budged," Riley recalled. "There was an unspoken unity among us." The bus driver finally intervened, explaining to the rifleman that these passengers were serving their country. His fury eased, and he exited the bus. The conscripts collectively exhaled.

The bus arrived at Camp Shelby. A sergeant marched the conscripts to the barracks at a breathless trot. Then he announced that the white PX, with its subsidized cigarettes and alcohol, was off-limits to Blacks. Half of the company ignored his orders and entered the military store anyway, prompting the sergeant to punish the entire group with a shift spent cleaning toilets with toothbrushes.

Riley's experience as a tractor driver served him well at Camp Shelby: officers put him to work hauling supplies in army trucks, an assignment that gave him time to breathe between the more rigorous chores of basic training. When he wasn't in a truck, he recalled, "they ran me ragged and exercised me so hard until all my bones ached at night." Riley endured this routine for nearly three months before he learned his deferral had been granted.

In the end, Riley felt the army had made him a better man. He was surely pleased to return to Martha and the meager comforts of home. But deferral compelled him to remain on Barrett's farm until hostilities ended, for that was the term of his release. And Riley would never reap

KING OF THE BLUES

the bonanza of veteran benefits, including a college education. To be eligible for veteran's benefits, a soldier had to serve ninety days. Riley was sent home just shy of that threshold. In later years, Riley recast the entire episode as a conspiracy, plantation owners (including Riley's boss, Johnson Barrett) colluding with draft boards to bind sharecroppers in agrarian servitude.

Cousin Birkett met a similar fate. His wife, Delcia, recalled that Birkett "went to Camp Shelby and passed and everything, but Mr. Johnson Barrett told him he needed him to drive a tractor," just like Riley. "And he kept him out every six months until the war ended. He kept both of them out."

The army offered up one final indignity. On the train ride home, Riley and the other African Americans rode in separate, dilapidated cars. German prisoners of war rode in modern cars, with the whites.

Venereal disease proliferated around military bases. Syphilis, gonorrhea, and related ailments disqualified roughly 4 percent of drafted men in World War II and sidelined roughly six hundred active servicemen per day. And it was around this time, possibly upon Riley's return from military service, that he appeared at the door of a country doctor. He had contracted a sexually transmitted disease, probably gonorrhea. His scrotum had swelled to the size of a melon. The doctor led Riley to the backyard and rested his genitals atop an old tree stump. Then, to drain the wound, he lifted a heavy book high over his head and brought it down, hard, on Riley's testicles. That was how country doctors treated swollen scrotums in that day.

"He said it was the most painful thing that ever happened to him in his life," recalled Dr. Darin Brimhall, a physician in whom Riley later confided.

This was probably the third assault on Riley's fertility. A childhood bout of the mumps had brought an attendant swelling of his testicles, a condition known as orchitis. In adolescence, he had been gored by a ram. He never shared the ram story with Dr. Brimhall, and he apparently never told the country-doctor story to anyone else. In any case, Riley King entered adulthood with little chance to father biological children.

Riley returned to his tractor to wait out the war, resuming a life that left him increasingly restless. Martha had moved in with Riley, Birkett, and Delcia, all of them joining Birkett's extended family in the three-room cabin on the Barrett plantation. In the spring of 1945, Barrett moved Aunt Beulah's family out of the crowded dwelling, leaving the two young couples to live there alone. They still lived without electricity, cooling food with a block of ice wrapped in a burlap sack. They split the costs of a cow, which Riley and Birkett took turns milking. Martha and Delcia traded shifts at the butter churn. They raised a crop together, working the fields in tandem. When they took breaks, Riley and Burkett would sing, blending their voices in an a cappella rendering of "Precious Lord, Take My Hand" or "I Know the Lord Will Make a Way." On Sunday mornings, the gospel quintet would head off to WGRM in Greenwood or WJPR, twenty-five miles west of Indianola in Greenville, a station run by a diminutive, balding young radio man named Bert Ferguson. Delcia and Martha would sit at home by a battery-powered radio and wait for the boys to come on.

The Famous St. John Gospel Singers now performed regularly at Black churches a hundred miles away, driving on "maypops," tires so worn from years of rationing and retreads that a puncture was inevitable. "About every weekend, they'd go somewhere to sing," Delcia Davis recalled. "They would go to Arkansas and sing, Kilmichael and sing, Cleveland, Mississippi, and sing. It was a packed house. Everybody would stand. They would pat their hands." Once in a while, an overwrought female parishioner "would go up there and grab them." Worshipers would bob in their seats, crying out, "Amen!" and "God bless you!" and shout out requests for the quintet's showstopper, "Moses Smote the Water."

The taste of success left Riley hungry for more. One Sunday at a church gig, as one of the group's dignified gospel songs faded, Riley ignored his bandmates and launched into a defiant solo guitar-and-voice performance of an Andrews Sisters boogie-woogie standard, "Shoo-Shoo Baby." All in an instant, the congregation exploded into dance as Riley's bandmates fumed. When the song was over, the quintet segued into another gospel number, the kinetic episode forgotten.

After the show, a friend asked Riley, "Why you do that?" He replied, "Oh, they was dancing, so I just gave them some dancing music."

Emboldened, perhaps, by that rebellious act, Riley summoned the courage to plant himself in downtown Indianola on Saturdays to play his guitar alone, reprising his brave sidewalk display for Martha in the prior summer. He chose a spot at the intersection of Second Street and Church Avenue, across from the county courthouse. Second Street traversed Indianola's downtown, while Church Avenue led into the city's Black community. Here, Riley could ply pedestrians with familiar gospel tunes, "The Old Rugged Cross" and "I'm Working on a Building." Some stopped to listen, and a few offered praise or a pat on the shoulder, but no tips.

And so, Riley changed his tune.

To that point in his life, Riley had never dared to sing or play the blues, at least not in public. It was the devil's music. His Aunt Beulah had forbidden it within her home, just as she had forbidden Riley to perform any genre of music on a street corner. But Riley no longer lived beneath her roof. One Saturday, on a Church Avenue sidewalk, Riley performed a blues number he'd heard Sonny Boy Williamson play at Jones' Night Spot a week earlier. He remembered half the words and made up the rest. As he played, a pedestrian appeared. The man had stopped by earlier and praised Riley's gospel songs. "It's later in the afternoon," Riley recalled, "but I'm the same and he's the same; the only difference is that 'my Lord' has turned into 'my baby.'" The man smiled like before, encouraging Riley with a cry of, "Sing those blues, son!" But this time, when the song was over, the man reached into his pocket, pulled out a dime, and dropped it into Riley's hat. The blues had loosened his purse.

Riley had dreamed of living his life as a gospel singer or perhaps as a gospel-singing preacher, like his beloved Reverend Fair. But "blues meant money," he recalled. "And money meant a better life." Powerful, warring impulses of faith, ambition, and lust churned within Riley's soul. And then came an epiphany: *God has the blues.*

"Look at the story of Jesus," he would later reason. "I'll be damned if that ain't a blues story. And I'll be damned if Jesus wasn't a bluesman.

Wandering around. No home. No money. Yet all that time talking about love. But not everyone's loving on him. . . . Sitting in that garden, he knows the world's about to do him in. That's the blues, son. The sure-enough blues."

Soon, Riley had a new weekend routine, playing the blues. "After I got off work, I'd take my bath, get my guitar and hitchhike to other little towns like Itta Bena or Moorhead or Greenville," he recalled. "Most times I was lucky. I'd make more money that evening than I'd make all week driving tractors." Riley's pockets jingled with coins as he walked home to the Barrett farm. On Sunday afternoons, after church, he would sit on the porch of the plantation commissary and play for the sharecropper children. "Everyone on the place would come to listen," recalled Lillian Barrett, Johnson's wife. "And the children would dance and stir up so much dust."

Riley spent ever-longer hours at home, listening to records on cousin Birkett's windup Victrola, practicing chords and scales on his guitar, to the detriment of his marriage and day job. "He'd play that guitar all night," Delcia Davis groused. "My husband would say, 'Riley, why don't you go to bed?' Riley would say, 'Birkett, I got one more tune I got to play.'"

Sidewalk busking was not socially acceptable for a churchgoing Indianolan. Bandmates pressured him to stop, warning, "You can't sing in the St. John Gospel Singers and sing blues on a Saturday night." But Riley could make a lot more money playing blues on the sidewalk than his band would ever earn at a church. Riley wanted to leave town for good, to hit the road with his guitar and make a living as a musician. His bandmates wanted to stay in Indianola and raise families. But Riley also had a good job and no good reason to leave it. And Martha was trying to start a family.

Riley would later claim that his wife miscarried repeatedly during their marriage. In truth, Martha was probably never pregnant. At the time, the couple's failure to conceive surely mystified both partners. Later on, the fiction of miscarriage protected Riley's image as a virile Delta bluesman.

"We were stuck," Riley recalled. Or at least, he was stuck.

A year or two into their marriage, Martha was learning to endure life as a bluesman's wife, though her husband was not yet quite a bluesman. Riley wasn't home much, and the tractor-driver job gave him celebrity status among the other young women of Indianola.

"Hey, you could steal the girls," Riley laughed in a latter-day interview about his Indianola days. "I've always been crazy about the girls."

AROUND THIS TIME, Riley heard a musician who would influence his career more than any other.

Aaron Thibeaux "T-Bone" Walker was born in 1910 in Linden, Texas. His mother was a musician who would lull him to sleep with her guitar. When T-Bone was two, his mother left his father, moved to Dallas, and married a new man, who was also a musician. The Walker household hosted endless jam sessions: visitors included Blind Lemon Jefferson. By age eight, T-Bone was following Jefferson around town. By twelve, he was playing the banjo for change. By sixteen, he was proficient on guitar, banjo, mandolin, violin, and piano, and he could read, write, and arrange music. He had the same depth of musical training as Lonnie Johnson, an artist he saw in person around that time. By his early twenties, Walker was performing with Charlie Christian.

Around 1935, Walker moved to Los Angeles. Crowds filed in to watch this novel performer, who wore double-breasted suits and spellbound audiences with acrobatic stage moves. Walker was a skilled dancer and singer. He worked the crowd to a frenzy, playing the guitar behind his head and then dropping into a split, all within the confines of a crisp white suit. With his pencil mustache, close-cropped pompadour, and big, wolfish smile, Walker "separated women from their undergarments using only his guitar." The cheers grew so loud that Walker invested in a Gibson ES-250 electric guitar and plugged into an amplifier. He might have been the first prominent blues performer to go electric.

T-Bone Walker established the electric guitar as a solo instrument in rhythm and blues, just as Charlie Christian had done in jazz. Walker joined Les Hite's Cotton Club Orchestra. His virtuosity proved so distracting that Hite relegated him to vocal and rhythm duties.

In 1942, Walker recorded some sides that featured his guitar. Those songs, "Mean Old World" and "I Got a Break, Baby," were among the first pressings to feature electric guitar as a lead instrument. But then, the American Federation of Musicians went on strike over unpaid royalties, hobbling the recording industry for two years and preventing the release of Walker's sides. Walker recorded many more singles between 1945 and 1947, songs such as "T-Bone Boogie," featuring his guitar and voice in equal measure. Riley heard them, and they blew his mind.

"His sound cut me like a sword," Riley recalled. "His sound was different than anything I'd heard before. Musically, he was everything I wanted to be, a modern bluesman whose blues were as blue as the bluest country blues with attitude as slick as those big cities I yearned to see."

An army buddy returned from the war with a stack of 78s by another guitarist whom Riley might otherwise have missed. Like T-Bone, Django Reinhardt came from well outside the Delta—from another continent, in fact.

Born into a family of Belgian gypsies, Reinhardt learned the guitar after first mastering the violin, like Lonnie Johnson. He coaxed a gentle vibrato from the strings. He reeled off single-string melodies and diminished jazz chords with equal fluidity. When a fire left him badly burned, Reinhardt learned to play with the three good fingers on his left hand. Improbably, he grew into one of the most technically gifted guitarists in jazz, cutting a series of classic sides with violinist Stéphane Grappelli in the late 1930s.

The guitar remained a back-bench rhythm instrument in the popular music of the 1930s and 1940s, rarely seen and seldom heard, a rule to which Reinhardt and Walker were exceptions. In their hands, the guitar could hold its own as a solo instrument with the saxophone or the trumpet or the human voice. Riley saw its promise. But he found that he could not begin to approach either man's masterful technique. He made a pledge to himself: "I had to keep working until, by accident or default, I developed a sound that became me."

Riley's thoughts increasingly turned to Memphis, 130 miles to the north, provincial capital of the blues. Again he begged his Famous St. John Gospel Singers to leave Indianola. Again they refused. Riley decided to go alone. He bragged of his plans to the other tractor drivers. Booker Baggett, the Black foreman, slapped him down: "You'll never do any of those things, Riley, so long as the Earth stands."

"Mister Booker," Riley replied, "someday I'm going to drive up in a brand-new car and give you a dollar. Then you'll know I wasn't jivin' when I said I'd do those things."*

Those were big words, but Riley had no real plan. And then, one disastrous day in the spring of 1946, a plan revealed itself. Riley had been driving the tractor all day. It was payday, and he was in a hurry to collect his earnings. In some versions of the story, he was rushing to make a gig with the gospel quintet or a date with a woman who was not Martha.

Johnson Barrett's barns stood on pilings that kept their contents dry during floods. The dirt-floored space beneath, only six feet high, was the "shed" where Barrett's men stowed their tractors. Drivers parked tractors in gear so they would not roll loose. After being turned off, the tractor engines could backfire, sometimes so powerfully that the machine lurched forward. To prevent that, Riley usually stayed in the driver's seat, foot on the brake, until the danger of backfire was past. On this afternoon, Riley steered his tractor into the shed, a maneuver he'd performed many times before. He killed the engine and leapt from the cab. He had walked a few paces, his back to the tractor, when he heard a loud "POP!" His heart stopped.

Riley turned and watched the tractor jolt forward to collide with the barn wall, snapping off the exhaust pipe that ran straight up from the engine. Riley knew in an instant that his negligence would cost hundreds of dollars in repairs. He panicked, fearing Johnson Barrett's reaction. He couldn't possibly hide such a colossal misdeed from the boss. And he'd have to labor for years, even at his lofty salary, to pay Barrett back.

"I didn't know what to do," he recalled. "I didn't know what to tell him. I didn't know anything. So I just started to walking."

---

*Several years later, as promised, Riley rolled into town in a shiny new Chevrolet, tracked down Booker Baggett, and handed him a crisp bill.

Riley recalled the rest of the day as a blur. In some retellings, he dashed home and instructed Martha to rejoin her own family in Eupora. In others, Martha wasn't home, and Riley didn't take the time to track her down. He did pause to scoop up $2.50 in dollars and change lying around the house and to sling his guitar over his back. Perhaps he scrawled a note. Then, Riley left his marital home and headed east to Highway 49, the road to Memphis.

CHAPTER 4

THE BLUES

HISTORY HAS FORGOTTEN how long the blues endured as an American music form before it reached listeners with access to recording equipment or music paper—with the means, that is, to transcribe the new sounds for posterity.

Perhaps the blues traveled to America with African slaves. Robert Palmer, the longtime *New York Times* pop music critic, devoted nearly a chapter of his classic history *Deep Blues* to that theory. Palmer's case is compelling but, absent recorded evidence, hard to prove. What can be proved is that elements of the blues arrived on American shores with African slaves.

In the 1806 book *Notes on the West Indies*, English abolitionist George Pinckard described an encounter with slaves on a ship bound for Savannah, Georgia, singing and dancing on deck. "Their song was a wild and savage yell, devoid of all softness and harmony, and loudly chanted in harsh monotony," Pinckard wrote. Perhaps Pinckard's ears recoiled from the "monotony" of standard blues verse and the savagery of bent third and seventh notes in a musical scale he hadn't previously heard.

Half a century later, at a campfire in South Carolina in the 1850s, journalist (and future architect) Frederick Law Olmsted observed an African American work crew in a midnight ritual of "merry repast." Suddenly, Olmsted wrote, one of the workers "raised such a sound as I never heard before, a long, loud, musical shout, rising and falling, and breaking into falsetto, his voice ringing through the woods in the clear, frosty night air, like a bugle-call. As he finished, the melody was caught up by another, and then another, and then by several in chorus." Olmsted's description sounds uncannily like the field holler, the tradition of shared work song that would reach Riley King's ears on the plantations of central Mississippi eighty years later.

Many blues histories begin with a Harvard archeologist named Charles Peabody. In the spring of 1901, Peabody led a crew to Mississippi's Coahoma County, near the Arkansas border, home to the mythic town of Clarksdale and a historic stretch of Highway 61. Peabody had come to excavate ancient burial mounds left by Choctaw Indians. The expedition yielded a bonanza of bones. But Peabody was equally struck by the songs he heard the African American workmen sing as they dug. His report appeared in 1903 in the *Journal of American Folk-Lore*.

"Our ears were beset with an abundance of ethnological material in song," Peabody wrote, "songs sung by our men when at work digging or wheeling on the mound," sometimes backed with strummed guitar. The archeologist struggled poignantly to describe what he had heard: he said it sounded like "a bagpipe played pianissimo, or a Jew's harp played legato . . . monotonous but weird."

Peabody had heard the blues. He recounted "syncopated melodies," a rhythmic emphasis on the spaces between the beats that set blues music apart. He recalled lyrics that told "hard luck tales" and a curious tendency in the singers to bend their notes. "So frequent was this," he wrote, "that it seemed intentional or unavoidable, not merely a mistake in pitch." The professor helpfully jotted down some of the world's first published blues lyrics, including these:

The reason I loves my baby so
'Cause when she gets five dollars she gives me fo'.

In 1902, a year after Peabody's expedition, a young African American singer named Gertrude Pridgett encountered the blues in Missouri, a discovery she later recounted to folklorist John Work. Pridgett, destined for fame under the stage name "Ma" Rainey, was traveling with a tent show. One day, a local girl came to the tent and sang a moaning dirge about "the 'man' who left her. The song was so strange and poignant that it attracted much attention," ultimately winning the singer a spot in the lineup. "Many times she was asked what kind of song it was, and one day she replied, in a moment of inspiration, 'It's the blues.'"

A year or so after that, the African American bandleader William Christopher "W. C." Handy was in Tutwiler, a Delta town south of Clarksdale, waiting for a train. Handy led a dignified African American orchestra, based in Clarksdale, that played the same operatic overtures and popular songs favored by white ensembles of the day. Handy was from Alabama, and he had formal music training. A photograph pictures Handy bald-headed in a crisp tuxedo and black bow tie, holding his trumpet, an expression of calm gravitas on his mustachioed face, looking more like an orchestral section leader than a forebear of hardscrabble Delta bluesmen.

As Handy awaited the train in Tutwiler, one night in 1903, he noticed that "a lean, loose-jointed Negro had commenced plunking a guitar" beside him while he slept. "His clothes were rags," Handy recounted. "His feet peeped out of his shoes. His face had on it some of the sadness of the ages. As he played, he pressed a knife on the strings of a guitar in a manner popularized by Hawaiian guitarists who used steel bars. The effect was unforgettable. His song, too, struck me instantly: *Goin' where the Southern cross' the Dog.* The singer repeated the line three times, accompanying himself on the guitar with the weirdest music I had ever heard."

Around the same time, Handy was leading his orchestra at a gig in Cleveland, Mississippi, when someone in the African American audience sent up a request for "native" music. Handy's musicians could not play the blues: all of them, Handy recalled, "bowed strictly to the authority of printed notes." The orchestra responded with a stiff southern medley. Another note came forward: Would the band mind if a local group took the stage and played a few songs? Handy yielded the stage, and the local combo stepped forward.

"They were led by a long-legged chocolate boy, and their band consisted of just three pieces," Handy recalled, "a battered guitar, a mandolin and a worn-out bass."

The band struck up a song, "one of those over-and-over strains that seem to have no very clear beginning and certainly no ending at all," Handy wrote. "The strumming attained a disturbing monotony, but on and on it went, a kind of stuff that has long been associated with cane rows and levee camps."

Handy wondered whether anyone could possibly endure this music. "The answer was not long in coming. A rain of silver dollars began to fall around the outlandish, stomping feet. The dancers went wild. Dollars, quarters, halves—the shower grew heavier and continued so long, I strained my neck to get a better look. There before the boys lay more money than my nine musicians were being paid for the entire engagement. Then I saw the beauty of primitive music."

Handy realized then, as Riley King would learn four decades later, that people would pay to hear the blues. Within a day or two, Handy had written up arrangements of several local blues songs and featured them in performance. He found them popular with audiences both Black and white. A few years later, he brought the blues to Beale Street in Memphis, a bustling hub of African American art, entertainment, and commerce. In 1909, Memphis mayoral candidate Edward Crump hired Handy to write a campaign song. The resulting "Mr. Crump" might have evolved into "The Memphis Blues," Handy's breakthrough, published on sheet music in 1912. "The Memphis Blues" was arguably the first hit blues song—or at least the first hit song with "blues" in its title.

The basic blues song follows a few rules. Each verse comprises twelve measures, or bars, hence the term "twelve-bar blues." The first four bars are played in the root chord, which corresponds to the key in which the song is written, such as G. The fifth and sixth measures move to the IV chord, derived from the fourth note in the scale. (If the song is in G, the IV chord is C.) The song returns to the root chord in measures seven and eight. The ninth and tenth bars ascend to the V chord. (In a G blues, that is D.) In its simplest form, the song then "resolves" back to the root chord in bars eleven and twelve. A traditional blues song never strays from those three chords.

A classic blues lyric follows a similarly predictable pattern. The first line is sung over the four opening bars of music. The second line, sung over measures five through eight, echoes the first or repeats it verbatim. The third line, in measures nine through twelve, is distinct from the first two and might offer a lyrical punch line.

Portions of W. C. Handy's "The Memphis Blues" follow the twelve-bar form. But the song begins on the V chord, rather than the customary I, and at times it strays completely outside the blues lexicon. Many other early blues hits would follow a similar formula, meandering into pop or jazz, "almost as if the undiluted blues were too raw, too overpowering to be consumed on its own."

Searching for a worthy successor to "The Memphis Blues," Handy came up with "St. Louis Blues," perhaps the most famous of the early blues songs, published as sheet music in 1914. "St. Louis Blues" alternates between classic blues and tango, a style quite unlike anything Blind Lemon Jefferson would ever play. No matter: "St. Louis Blues" was a smash.

Handy moved himself and his publishing business to New York in 1917, the same year that the Original Dixieland Jass Band produced the first jazz recording. Handy's move triggered an explosion of urban blues. In 1920, a vaudeville singer named Mamie Smith recorded perhaps the first blues sides by an African American singer, over threats of record-company boycotts by white segregationists. (The first recordings of W. C. Handy's songs were instrumentals.) One single, "Crazy Blues," was said to have sold a million copies, chiefly to Black buyers, a hitherto untapped market. Like "St. Louis Blues" and "The Memphis Blues," "Crazy Blues" might be termed "titular" blues: a work that blends elements of blues and other forms, leveraging a bluesy title and sound in the service of popular song. "Crazy Blues" sounds more Dixieland than Delta.

A few months later, *Metronome* magazine reported, "One of the phonograph companies made over four million dollars on the blues. Now every phonograph company has a colored girl recording. Blues are here to stay."

Through most of the Roaring Twenties, women ruled the blues. Promoters dubbed Mamie Smith "Queen of the Blues," though she continued to blend blues, jazz, and pop. In any case, she was not the first African American blues singer to find fame. Ma Rainey, born in Georgia in 1886, had added blues to her repertoire well before 1923, when Paramount signed her, capitalizing on the success of Mamie Smith. The label dubbed her "Mother of the Blues." Rainey cut several dozen recordings, the best known being "See See Rider Blues," later a curtain raiser for Elvis Presley. Rainey, too, recorded sides filled with chirping ragtime flourishes: her sidemen included Louis Armstrong. Mamie Smith was a striking woman, with round, luminous eyes and a dreamy smile. She dressed in beads and furs. Ma Rainey, by contrast, was "a short and stubby woman," with ample proportions "and broad features that didn't quite match." She was edgy, bawdy, and blunt. She might have been bisexual. In the now-legendary single "Prove It on Me Blues," Rainey sang of wearing a collar and tie and talking "to the gals just like any old man." Historian Jonathan Ned Katz termed the song "unique in pre-Stonewall American history" as a declaration of queer pride.

Ma Rainey's recording career coincided neatly with that of her archrival, Bessie Smith. Bessie was considerably younger, born in 1894 in Tennessee, and she might have been discovered by Ma or someone in her entourage. The two women began recording in the same year. Bessie became the bigger star.

Beautiful, tall, and curvaceous, Bessie Smith projected both power and vulnerability. Her voice, one of the richest ever put on disc, quivered with carnal tension. Musicians adored her. One recalled her as "all the femaleness the world ever saw, in one sweet package." Bessie cherry-picked the best of her competitors' songs and recorded them herself, outselling the originals: blues historian Francis Davis calls her the first great cover artist. Bessie's 1923 recording of Alberta Hunter's "Down Hearted Blues" sold 780,000 copies in six months. By 1925, the year of Riley King's birth, Bessie was the nation's highest-paid Black performer. Seeing that the honorifics "mother" and "queen" were taken, Bessie's promoters called her "Empress of the Blues." Like her peers, Bessie blurred the lines, not yet clearly drawn, between blues and jazz.

Bessie had a distinct advantage over Rainey: her singles didn't sound as if they had been recorded underwater. Bessie sang for Columbia, a label whose recording equipment apparently far surpassed the technology at Paramount. Thus, Bessie Smith is probably the earliest superstar of blues whose talent is properly preserved on tape. To fully appreciate the recorded oeuvre of Ma Rainey (and some blues greats who followed) requires both attentive ears and imagination.

The great blueswomen of the 1920s and early 1930s sang playfully and euphemistically about prostitution, drugs, homosexuality, and sodomy. Much of this content arrived in record stores uncensored: white studio executives and other arbiters of decency didn't know what they were hearing.

On a 1929 Columbia single titled "It's Tight like That," Clara Smith sang about a man who "put the key in the hole, but he couldn't get in." In a 1935 recording, Lucille Bogan celebrated the bull dyke: "Comin' a time, B.D. women ain't gonna need no men." In another side, titled "Shave 'Em Dry," Bogan sang about "something between my legs that'll make a dead man come." This was apparently too much even for the "race" market, and the 1930s recording did not see official release for thirty years. The song might have been recorded for underground distribution as a "party record." It hints at the bawdy heights Bogan and her compatriots could reach in unfettered late-night live performance. The Rolling Stones, boundary pushers themselves, seemed to pay homage to Bogan when they sneaked the "dead man" line into the fade of their own hit single "Start Me Up," five decades later.

The Great Crash of 1929 sank the blues market. At Columbia Records, the standard first pressing of new releases declined from eleven thousand copies in 1927 to a few hundred copies by 1932. Ma Rainey cut her last side in 1928. Bessie Smith had her final hit the next year, aptly titled "Nobody Knows You When You're Down and Out."

Oddly enough, Bessie Smith and her peers might have exerted more direct influence on Riley King than most of the Delta bluesmen who followed them, though they shared neither his gender nor his birthplace. Unlike Robert Johnson and most of his Delta brethren, Bessie Smith, Mamie Smith, and Ma Rainey enjoyed massive popularity in their day. Riley's Aunt Mima owned copies of Mamie's "Crazy Blues," Bessie's "Empty Bed Blues," and Rainey's "See See Rider Blues." When Riley heard those songs, he recalled, they "tore off the top of my head."

* * *

THE FIRST of the great bluesmen captured on disc, Blind Lemon Jefferson, made his debut recordings in 1926, when Bessie Smith was at her peak. Born blind (or nearly so) at Couchman, now an East Texas ghost town, Jefferson traveled the Lone Star State as a street musician for years before someone escorted him to Chicago to record his first sides. A lone surviving photograph reveals a thickly built, stern-faced man in suit and tie with close-cropped hair and eyes narrowed to slits behind spectacles. The eyeglasses, and accounts of a wrestling career, suggest that Jefferson was not entirely blind. "He darn sure could *feel* his way around," blues singer Victoria Spivey once quipped.

Ragtime instrumental jazz ruled the mid-'20s marketplace: few artists had recorded tracks featuring solo voice and guitar, and none of those had yielded a hit. Jefferson would record nearly one hundred scratchy sides for Paramount between 1926 and 1929, and many sold well, establishing him as a star on par with Bessie and Rainey.

Though Blind Lemon Jefferson was hardly the first bluesman to pluck a guitar, he was the first guitar-playing bluesman to attain national fame. He would be credited with popularizing many conventions of acoustic blues. One was the three-line verse, with the first line repeated twice and the third echoing the first two in rhyme. Another was the single-string guitar riff, a pattern of notes that answered and repeated the melody Jefferson had just sung. Jefferson used his guitar as both rhythm section and solo vessel, strumming chords on three or four strings interspersed with descending, two-note arpeggios. He introduced a whole repertoire of blues standards, songs such as "Black Snake Moan," "Matchbox Blues," and "See That My Grave Is Kept Clean," that would influence every blues artist who followed. But Jefferson's heyday was tragically brief. Two months after the market crash, in December 1929, he froze to death on a Chicago street. He was thirty-six.

Charley Patton emerged a few years after Blind Lemon Jefferson. He took the blues deep into the Mississippi swamp, singing with a powerful, hoarse baritone that was said to be audible a quarter mile away. Patton effectively founded the school of Delta blues.

The Delta region has yielded no president or vice president, no secretary of state or Supreme Court chief justice. Yet, both Charles Peabody and W. C. Handy first identified the blues in the Delta. And in the half century that followed, an absurdly disproportionate share of master bluesmen would emerge from the Delta, a royal lineage that runs from Charley Patton through Son House and Skip James to Robert Johnson and thence to Muddy Waters and Willie Dixon, John Lee Hooker and B.B. King. "The influence of the Delta on the sound of our musical lives is so pervasive today that it is almost impossible to take full measure of its impact," historian Ted Gioia writes. Patton and his descendants mapped out a new musical landscape around the flatted third and seventh notes of the blues scale. Delta singers and guitarists might or might not have invented the three-chord, twelve-bar structure of classic blues, but they explored it and exploited it and perfected it, writing and rewriting foundational songs that would steer the course of popular music for generations.

Charley Patton does not command the name recognition of Robert Johnson or Muddy Waters. But music historian Robert Palmer was not alone in rating Patton "among the most important musicians twentieth century America has produced." Patton was small and slender and walked with a limp. Wavy hair framed his narrow face. He was probably of African, European, and Native American ancestry, but Delta society regarded him as Black. Patton wore a bow tie and suit and an enormous chip on his shoulder. Blues historian Samuel Charters described him as "a small, intense, fretful man who blustered his way out of fights," surviving "as best he could in a violent countryside." Patton spent most of his life near Indianola in Sunflower County. He learned the musical trade on the Dockery Plantation, a vast cotton farm and country-blues incubator.

Prideful and restless, Patton scripted his escape from the plantation. In 1929, he penned a letter to H. C. Speir, a white Mississippian who sold blues records out of a mercantile and music store in the state capital of Jackson. Speir served a mostly African American clientele and operated a modest recording studio. Around 1926, Speir began scouting

Black blues talent wherever he went, recording promising artists in his store and sending the best of them up north to the major labels. Over the next decade, nearly every Delta-blues artist of consequence would seek out H. C. Speir, if he didn't find them first. Charley Patton was his first great find.

Patton's sides aren't an easy listen. Mostly they are Paramount recordings—scratchy, hissy tapes that somehow sound both muffled and shrill. Yet, with those recordings, Charley Patton defined the vocabulary of Delta blues. His raspy delivery was the first recorded iteration of the Delta growl. He would lay down a rhythm by tapping bass notes on his guitar and answer it with strummed notes on the higher strings. Atop that he would erect a second, contrasting rhythm with his voice and solo guitar, using a slide to alternately accompany or answer his sung lyrics. At times, as on the remarkable "A Spoonful Blues," Patton would stop singing and let his guitar complete a lyrical phrase or lapse into spoken word to comment on what he had just sung. He was truly a one-man band.

In a series of seminal recordings Patton made between 1929 and 1934, powered by his booming baritone and stinging slide, he introduced songs and themes that would be passed down, copied, and interpreted for decades, including "Spoonful," "Pony Blues," and the Great Flood epic "High Water Everywhere." Patton played plantations and taverns across the South. He ranged north to Chicago and east to New York. His showmanship was legendary. "All the strutting and flaunting we associate with rock stars since Jimi Hendrix were already part of Patton's repertoire in the 1920s," Gioia writes. "He worked up the crowd with the shrewdness of a medicine show barker, taunting and teasing, and mouthing off with an endless stream of lively banter."

Improbably, Patton recorded many more songs after the 1929 collapse than before. His final sides were cut a few months before his untimely death, in 1934, possibly of complications from an earlier bout of rheumatic fever or bronchitis. He was in his early forties.

Eddie James "Son" House Jr. was born in 1902 near the mythic blues hub of Clarksdale, subsequent home to Muddy Waters. His family was both musical and spiritual, and his love for the church and the blues raged in perpetual conflict. He first heard a slide guitar at age twenty-five and promptly learned the style, entranced by its lyricism. "I could make [the guitar] say what I say," he recalled, voicing an impulse that would later inspire Riley King. House wielded the slide as counterpoint to his resonant voice, "the most penetrating and haunting the Delta has ever produced."

House was tall and gangly, with a thin and handsome face and deep-set, penetrating eyes. He spoke softly and favored polite string ties. But when a man opened fire one night at a juke joint where he was playing, around 1928, House produced his own gun and shot the man dead. Despite his protestations of self-defense—House himself was wounded in the leg—the bluesman was sentenced to fifteen years at Parchman Farm, a state penitentiary that would become a holding tank for several blues masters. Details of his incarceration are hazy: House evidently served only two years, and he was back in circulation by 1930. Charley Patton took House under his wing. House accompanied Patton to the headquarters of Paramount Records in Grafton, Wisconsin, in 1930. House recorded nine sides, half of them two-part epics, all now the stuff of legend, including the love ode "My Black Mama" and the irreverent "Preachin' the Blues." Paramount released eight scratchy recordings. They went nowhere, and Son House soon faded into obscurity.

Nehemiah Curtis "Skip" James was born in 1902 in Bentonia, well south of most other Mississippi blues towns. He studied piano and organ, completed high school, and never picked cotton, all measures of his family's relative prosperity. He learned the guitar, eschewing the slide in favor of a deft, three-fingered picking style all his own, a powerful influence on latter-day pickers from Chet Atkins to John Fahey. James found his way to Jackson, Mississippi's capital, where, in 1931, he auditioned for H. C. Speir. By this time, Speir had already steered both Charley Patton and Son House to Paramount Records. Speir sent Skip James to Wisconsin. He recorded around twenty Paramount sides, including the haunting "Devil Got My Woman" and the oft-covered "Hard Time Killing Floor Blues." James sang in a delicate, almost supernatural moan, and he knew enough music theory to turn the blues form on its ear. "Devil Got My Woman" opens on the minor

V rather than the conventional root chord, hanging there in mounting tension as James moans about his mind "ramblin' like a wild geese" above a fingerpicked guitar figure that anticipates the modern "riff," before settling back to the I. With this song, James wasn't merely populating a conventional blues with melody and verse: he was composing.

But the 1931 singles failed to sell. The next year, Skip James abandoned the blues to enter the ministry.

None of the early Delta bluesmen left much of an impression on young Riley King. Charley Patton was a big name in 1930s Mississippi: Aunt Mima played some of his records. Son House and Skip James, by contrast, barely registered with the listening public. Patton and his disciples took the genre one way: Riley's ears went another. From the primordial power of Blind Lemon Jefferson, Riley proceeded directly to Lonnie Johnson, a contemporary of Patton's who dressed up the blues in a jacket and tie. Riley's tastes tracked the evolution of popular music, which largely abandoned the country bluesmen after Patton in favor of full ensembles populated with rhythm sections and horns and guitarists who played through amplifiers. In effect, Riley skipped over the entire generation of classic Delta country bluesmen, the one that started with Patton and ended with Robert Johnson.

Johnson is the quintessential Delta bluesman. Scholars and fans have spun a vast mythology around the sparse facts of his life. Never, perhaps, has so little been known about so great a modern musical artist. Historians may quibble about the year of Charley Patton's birth, but for a very long time, blues historians weren't entirely sure Johnson was a real person. This is partly a matter of slapdash recordkeeping in rural Mississippi and partly down to how little Johnson impacted the music industry in his lifetime. And it is partly his own doing. Johnson labored tirelessly, for example, to propagate the tale that he had sold his soul to the Devil. In a sense, all of the subsequent myth-mongering across seven decades of pop music—from the "Paul is dead" rumors to Mick Jagger's satanic flirtations to the exploding drummers of Spinal Tap—begins with Robert Johnson. As an influence on modern blues and rock music, Robert Johnson looms larger than anyone, save perhaps the great Muddy Waters and B.B. King himself.

Robert Leroy Johnson was born in Hazlehurst, near the southwest corner of Mississippi, possibly in 1911. His father was a fleeting presence. Johnson spent his early years with his mother "in Delta labor camps and on various plantations," according to historian Robert Palmer. By the late 1920s, the teenage Johnson was living in Robinsonville, a town along Highway 61 south of Memphis. He learned the harmonica and then the guitar, and he took up a dogged pursuit of any established bluesman who came to town. He trailed Charley Patton. He shadowed Son House. The older men considered Johnson a pest.

In 1929, Johnson married a sixteen-year-old girl. She died in childbirth the next year. Johnson abruptly left Robinsonville, destination unknown. He returned perhaps a year later as a changed man, "singing and playing with the dazzling technique and almost supernatural electricity" eventually captured in his recordings. It was during this mysterious absence that the bluesman purportedly sold his soul at a lonely crossroads.

The crossroads myth probably originated with Tommy Johnson, an older bluesman (no relation), gifted with an unearthly falsetto, whose "Canned Heat Blues" would inspire the name of a Woodstock-era white blues band. In 1930, Tommy Johnson was living near Hazlehurst. Robert Johnson probably met him there. Assuming he did, then Robert Johnson also heard the local legend that Tommy Johnson had sold his soul to Satan in trade for fame. Robert Johnson made that legend his own.

As for Robert Johnson's uncanny improvement during that span, scholars theorize that he perfected his technique the traditional way, through hours of practice, perhaps with help from a Hazlehurst guitarist named Isaiah Zimmerman, who claimed to have acquired his own skills by visiting graveyards at midnight.

In 1936, Robert Johnson traveled to Jackson and sought out H. C. Speir. The talent scout sent him to the American Record Corporation, and Johnson recorded sixteen songs at a hotel in San Antonio. The recordings, released on the Vocalion label, represent the apex of Delta blues. Johnson had mastered Charley Patton's polyrhythms, thumping thick bass notes with his thumb to set the beat and filling in the spaces with a dizzying array of notes and chords, played in triplets, sixteenth notes, and even denser, rapid-fire bursts. His guitar work is an ongoing rhythmic commentary, revealing the endless permutations of syncopation and subdivision possible in a twelve-bar blues. Johnson had mastered both the pervasive slide-guitar style and the novel fingerpicking of Skip James, as well as Lonnie Johnson's single-string attack, and he had learned to play aggressive solo runs. He did it all with a single guitar, topped off with his plaintive, potent tenor. Hearing his songs today, listeners might assume Johnson is backed by a second guitarist. Johnson neither required nor desired an accompanist: he didn't want anyone stealing his style.

A detailed analysis of Robert Johnson's style is possible because the recordings sound remarkably rich and clear, especially by contrast to the noisy Paramount sides recorded by Charley Patton and Blind Lemon Jefferson. (The master copies of those inferior Paramount recordings are lost, leaving even worse secondhand copies as the only aural evidence of Patton's and Jefferson's genius.) Perhaps that is why Johnson is now a household name and Patton and Jefferson are not. To some extent, blues history is written by the well recorded.

The titles Robert Johnson cut in 1936 include the first iteration of "I Believe I'll Dust My Broom," an archetypal anthem of the bluesman's itinerant restlessness, and "Cross Road Blues," a self-referential tale of his rendezvous with the Devil. Johnson traveled to Dallas in 1937 and recorded thirteen more songs. Many of these were darker in tone. "Love in Vain Blues" posited a departing train as a metaphor for unrequited love. With "Hell Hound on My Trail" and "Me and the Devil Blues," Johnson again traded on his own Faustian legend. Some of this was familiar macho posturing. But other bluesmen "never recorded anything as chilling and apparently dead serious" as Johnson's tormented verse about hellhounds and sinister spirits and Satan.

Muddy Waters, born a few years after Johnson, saw him once and recalled him as a "dangerous man." Much like frail Charley Patton, the mature Robert Johnson menaced not with his body but with his very presence. He was "slender, small-boned, brown-skinned, and handsome enough, with his delicate features and wavy hair, to attract legions of female admirers, but he started more fights than he finished." Johnson frightened other men with his manic intensity, his diabolical bluster, and his paranoiac conviction that the hounds of Hell pursued him.

With barely enough recordings to fill two long-playing records (fewer than thirty compositions in all), Robert Johnson would exert as much influence on pop performers of the 1960s and beyond as all of his Delta-blues forebears combined. Johnson seemed to understand the concept of a pop song better than his antecedents had. He consciously crafted blues songs that fit on 78-rpm records. He wrote lyrics that seemed more linear, and less disjointed, than those of his predecessors. His songs had definite beginnings and ends. Yet, in his lifetime, Johnson had just one tiny, regional hit, "Terraplane Blues," an exercise in sexual innuendo that sold around five thousand copies.

In the end, Johnson might have accomplished more as a performer and interpreter than as a composer of original music or verse. Many of his best-known recordings borrowed melodies and lyrical schemes from earlier works. "Sweet Home Chicago" recalls an earlier song by Kokomo Arnold that celebrates Arnold's namesake town. Johnson's "32-20 Blues" makes obvious reference to Skip James's "22-20 Blues." Johnson's "Preachin' Blues" recalls Son House's "Preachin' the Blues." And so on. Then again, most of Johnson's musical ancestors and descendants did the same, for that is the blues tradition.

Robert Johnson died in August 1938, at age twenty-seven. He might have been poisoned with tainted whiskey after flirting with someone's wife. He is said to have perished in agony, a sign to the superstitious that the Devil had taken his due.

The quintessential Delta bluesman was also "the last *great* performer" in the lineage that began with Charley Patton. The Depression was ending, tastes were changing, and the greatest of all Delta-blues stylists died virtually penniless and alone. Had Johnson lived just a few months longer, his fortunes might have turned: John Hammond, a prominent New York record producer, had hoped to feature Johnson at a blockbuster concert in December 1938 at Carnegie Hall, the aforementioned "From Spirituals to Swing."

Riley King was twelve years old when Robert Johnson died. He was too young to have seen Johnson perform. Riley was clearly aware of

Johnson's music, but it never moved him—not even when a subsequent generation of white musicologists embraced Robert Johnson as the great lost master of Delta blues.

"Because his music was made so close to my home—and exactly during the age of my growing up—you'd think I'd be under his spell," Riley recalled. "But I wasn't. He didn't speak to me with the power of Lonnie Johnson or Blind Lemon. I listened to Robert Johnson and I liked him, but that was all."

To understand why Robert Johnson and the other Delta-blues masters exerted so little influence on Riley, consider the record charts. Country-blues performers enjoyed a brief and tenuous hold over the record-buying public in the late 1920s. From about 1930 until Muddy Waters's arrival on the charts in 1948, Delta blues retreated from the public consciousness. Record buyers and radio listeners, Riley included, gravitated toward slick jazz-blues ensembles with horns that played sophisticated dance music and smooth ballads.

A typical number 1 R&B hit of 1943, the year Riley arrived in Indianola, was "That Ain't Right," by the silken-voiced singer and pianist Nat "King" Cole. Riley would recall Cole as "the epitome of taste, musicianship, and serious swing." Benny Goodman, the storied white bandleader, hit number 1 in 1944 with "Solo Flight," a posthumous showcase for the brilliant Charlie Christian, whom Riley worshiped. In 1945, Louis Jordan and His Tympany Five topped the charts with "Caldonia." All of those songs rang in Riley's ears in the spring of 1946, as he set out for Memphis.

CHAPTER 5

MEMPHIS

THE CITY OF MEMPHIS was formed in 1819 and named for a city in ancient Egypt that abutted the Nile River. Memphis in Tennessee straddles bluffs above the Mississippi River at a spot where three states meet: Tennessee to the north and east, Arkansas to the west, Mississippi to the south. Memphis grew into a major trading post for slaves and the cotton they picked. The city seceded along with its state in 1861 but fell to Union troops a year later, whereupon it became a destination for escaped slaves, who formed camps and opened schools. In 1866, white citizens rioted against the city's newly empowered African American population, killing forty-six Blacks. The brutal murders spurred passage of the Fourteenth Amendment, establishing equal rights, at least on paper, for African Americans. Yellow fever epidemics in the 1870s nearly wiped out the city. But Memphis rebounded on the strength of the cotton and lumber trades. The nation's first supermarket chain, Piggly Wiggly, debuted there in 1916, and the elegant Peabody Hotel became a center of southern society. In 1935, Mississippi author David Cohn wrote, "The Mississippi Delta begins in the lobby of the Peabody. . . . If you stand near its fountain in the middle of the lobby, where ducks waddle and turtles drowse, ultimately you will see everybody who is anybody in the Delta."

Everybody, that is, who wasn't Black. African Americans could not stay at the Peabody.

The Memphis population tripled to three hundred thousand between 1900 and 1940. The city fell under the sway of a Chicago-style machine led by E. H. "Boss" Crump, a white Democrat who manipulated elections, empowered cronies, and thwarted rivals in collaboration with a network of agricultural barons known as Cotton Row. Crump dispensed a modicum of power to the city's growing Black minority, extending patronage jobs and leadership posts to select African Americans at the fringes of his empire. Jim Crow–era Memphis became one of the largest southern cities where Blacks could vote. Yet, in daily life, segregation reigned.

Beale Street, a two-mile span that runs east from the banks of the Mississippi, took shape in 1841 as Beale Avenue. At its west end, in the heart of downtown, Beale housed merchants who traded with the vessels that navigated the river. In the 1860s, with the arrival of freed slaves, the thoroughfare became a destination for Black musicians. One of the first musical groups to call Beale Street home was the Young Men's Brass Band, formed in 1867. After the yellow fever epidemic, a Black entrepreneur named Robert Church bought up much of the land around western Beale. That shrewd investment would make him perhaps the South's first Black millionaire. At the close of the nineteenth century, Church paid the city to build a park and auditorium at Beale and Fourth Street. Church Park became a mecca for musicians, while the auditorium would host speakers as disparate as Woodrow Wilson and Booker T. Washington. By the early 1900s, Beale bustled with restaurants, nightclubs, and shops, many of them owned by African Americans. Ida B. Wells, cofounder of the NAACP, campaigned against lynchings in the antisegregationist paper *Free Speech* from an office on Beale.

W. C. Handy moved to Memphis in 1909 and made Beale his base. When he relocated to New York eight years later, he left "Beale Street Blues" as a parting gift. Over the decades to follow, a parade of performers would pass through Beale Street. Lizzie Douglas, better known as Memphis Minnie, worked as a blues guitarist, singer, and prostitute on Beale in the 1920s before a Columbia Records talent scout discovered her. Walter "Furry" Lewis rose to prominence as a Beale Street bluesman in the 1920s while working days as a street sweeper. The Memphis Jug Band formed in 1926 and became a favorite of "Boss" Crump. Country-blues icon "Sleepy" John Estes recorded his first sides for Victor in Memphis in 1929. Harmonica virtuoso Walter "Shakey" Horton first recorded there in 1939.

Beale Street cannot claim the same birthright to blues as New Orleans does to jazz. As Peter Guralnick observed, all roads on the great blues trail lead back to Mississippi, to the Delta, if not to any town or plantation in particular. But Beale and Memphis would come to be viewed as the capital of blues, a title it eventually, grudgingly ceded to Chicago. (The succession was complete by 1936, when Robert Johnson recorded "Sweet Home Chicago.") This northward journey of blues capitals tracked the Great Migration of African Americans from Delta plantations to better-paying jobs up north.

The Beale Street mystique spread "by word-of-Negro-mouth." That talk drew Handy to Memphis. By 1919, white actress Gilda Gray was singing "Beale Street Blues" on Broadway, with lyrics "glorifying chitlin' cafes, pickpockets, and ladies of the night," announcing Beale to the broader world. In 1931, the greatest stars of country and jazz, Jimmie Rodgers and Louis Armstrong, brazenly crossed racial lines to collaborate on a historic recording titled "Blue Yodel No. 9," set in Memphis, at the corner of Beale and Main. Beale Street had arrived.

RILEY BEGAN his 135-mile journey to Memphis one evening in May 1946. On the way out of Indianola, he happened on a friend and somehow persuaded him to come along. Riley had his guitar and his $2.50 in change. His companion had half a sausage, which the travelers shared. They spotted a Lewis Grocery Company truck heading north. In exchange for free passage, the boys helped the trucker unload his flour. They arrived after three in the morning. Riley knew he had kin in town, but he didn't know where. Unsure of his destination, he asked the driver to drop him at the bus station. The driver didn't know the address, so he steered Riley and his friend to the train station. They slept there till sunrise, and then they went their separate ways.

Riley had probably never set foot in a city larger than Greenville, population twenty-five thousand. The sheer scale of Memphis left him breathless. "I'd never seen anything like it," he recalled. "Never seen factories and plants and stores selling flashy jewelry and smelly fish and silk suits and, best of all, records and musical instruments. Music was in the air. Ladies were everywhere. I arrived in summer and the women, compared to those on the plantation, seemed half-undressed in their frilly dresses and revealing blouses. I didn't know about parks, where you could just sit and relax and enjoy. And then there was the river running along the banks of the city, the wide and mighty Mississippi, with its barges and boats carrying great loads of cotton to the merchant buildings where high finance was conducted by men in starched white shirts."

Once the awe had subsided, Riley set out to locate cousin Bukka White, his only relative who qualified as a professional bluesman. Riley hadn't seen Bukka in at least seven years and wasn't even sure he lived in Memphis. But if Bukka was in town, Riley figured he'd find him on Beale Street. Riley walked along the storied street, past the One Minute Café, where twenty-five cents could fill your belly with chili and crackers and Barq's orange soda, and Mitchell's Hotel, run by local Black entrepreneur Andrew "Sunbeam" Mitchell. Riley passed movie palaces, variety stores, and pawnshops. He had never seen white people and Black people shopping on the same street.

Riley heard music. He made his way to Handy Park, across from Sunbeam Mitchell's hotel, and discovered an impromptu gathering of musicians, men playing guitars and harmonicas, clarinets, trombones, and even the odd violin.

"The sounds got me so excited, I started to run," he recalled. When he arrived in the middle of the green space, he stood transfixed. "I wasn't about to play; all I could do was listen and learn. I listened for hours and, even though my guitar was under my arm, I never struck a note. All my confidence from all those Saturdays playing all those little Delta towns vanished—just like that. Before Beale Street, I thought I was pretty hot stuff. After Beale Street, I knew I stunk."

Riley noticed three men shooting dice behind a hedge. He had never seen men gamble out in the open. He stood mesmerized until someone shouted, "Number One!" That was code: A white police officer approached. The men leapt to their feet and scattered.

It took Riley three days to track down his cousin, whom he could not locate on Beale. He slept one night in a boxcar, another in an all-night gambling hall. His search eventually led to an address on

Spottswood Avenue, southeast of downtown. He knocked on the door, but no one answered. He fell asleep on the curb with his arm cradling his guitar. He awoke, some hours later, to the words, "Riley? That you?"

Bukka White invited Riley inside. He listened sympathetically to his young cousin's story and counseled him on his debt to his employer: "Mr. Johnson is surely mad as a motherfucker," he said, "but in time he'll cool off. Meanwhile, we better get word to Martha that you're all right." The two men talked late into the night. Bukka had just returned from a house party and was still high on the adrenaline of performance. He regaled his cousin with the Steinbeck-worthy saga of his life.

Bukka was a contemporary of Son House and Skip James. He had grown up admiring Charley Patton and had become a fine slide-guitar player with a profound sense of rhythm and a deep Delta growl. Some of his early recordings might be termed hobo blues: Both "The New 'Frisco Train" and "The Panama Limited" evoke the cadence and clatter of train travel. Bukka had ridden the rails, collecting stories of Depression-era America.

Bukka himself would become one of those stories. His records didn't sell, and Bukka couldn't make a living playing music in Memphis. He returned to farming in the Delta, marrying again in 1934. But Bukka was restless, and he spent the next few years wandering the eastern United States. He claimed to have pitched for a baseball team in the Negro Leagues. He boxed in Chicago. He also continued to perform. In 1937, between gigs in Mississippi, Bukka got into a scuffle with some men, possibly over a woman. He shot one in the thigh. A judge sentenced Bukka to two years at Parchman Farm.

Bukka was under contract to record more sides for the Vocalion label in Chicago. Legend has it Bukka skipped bond and fled north for the session. In some accounts, the Mississippi sheriff caught him in the studio. More likely the jailers allowed him to fulfill the contract before his incarceration.

Bukka recorded two songs for Vocalion. One, "Shake 'Em On Down," became a hit while he served his time. Inmates and guards pooled their funds to buy him a guitar and formed a prison band for him to lead. His songs drew the attention of Alan Lomax, the Library of Congress folklorist, who visited Parchman periodically to harvest country-blues recordings. Lomax recorded Bukka there in 1939. Another visitor was Riley, who made the eighty-mile journey from Kilmichael with relatives sometime during Bukka's confinement. "After that visit," Riley recalled, "I knew I wanted to stay far away from that place."

Bukka emerged from prison in 1939 "with a head full of some of the finest classic blues songs ever written," according to biographers F. Jack Hurley and David Evans. He returned to Chicago and recorded twelve more sides, including "Parchman Farm Blues" and "Fixin' to Die Blues." Some or all were issued in the summer of 1940, "the last of the classic Delta recordings to be released on a commercial market," according to historian Samuel Charters. Bukka's songs stood out for their lyrical depth: while most Delta blues traded on lewd sexual euphemism, Bukka sang about freedom and sorrow and injustice and death. No one else recording blues sides in 1940 would release a song quite like Bukka's "District Attorney Blues," with socially conscious lyrics about a system that "will take a woman's man and leave her cold in hand."

Bukka spent the next two years traveling between Chicago and the Delta, where his second marriage was unraveling. In 1942, he settled down, renting an apartment in the Orange Mound section of Memphis, which is where Riley found him.

The morning after their reunion, Bukka awakened Riley with the instruction, "We'd better start thinking about getting to work." Riley thought Bukka meant gigs. In fact, he referred to the Newberry Equipment factory, where Bukka built underground gasoline tanks for service stations. Bukka got Riley a job there that very day, and Riley learned to weld. The job paid sixty dollars a week, the most money Riley had ever seen. Bukka charged Riley three dollars a week for room and board.

When Riley wasn't working, he would follow Bukka around from party to party, watching him play and studying his style and his presence as a performer. Consciously or not, Riley apprenticed himself to his cousin, in much the same way that Robert Johnson had followed Son House around Robinsonville, Mississippi, and that T-Bone Walker had trailed Blind Lemon Jefferson in Dallas.

"His blues was the book of his life," Riley recalled. "He sang about his rough times and fast times and loving times and angry times. He'd entertain at a party for two hundred people with the same enthusiasm as a party for twenty." Riley could see that Bukka was born to play the blues. He wondered if he was, too.

In hindsight, those months of apprenticeship feel like a pivotal moment in the development of B.B. King, musician. It's hard to imagine that Riley, with his burning ambition and attentive ears, didn't memorize every nuance of his cousin's slide-guitar attack. Bukka was a Delta-blues master, and Riley spent many nights in his company. The cousins often played together but never in public. Riley was too insecure of his own abilities to join Bukka onstage. Perhaps to seed confidence, Bukka took Riley to the Houck music store and helped him pick out a new guitar. It was probably a Gibson L-30, a budget-priced instrument that looked more like a cello than a bluesman's guitar.

ORVILLE GIBSON had patented a design for a mandolin in 1898 and opened a factory in Kalamazoo, Michigan, to build them. In 1922, the Gibson factory introduced the L-5 guitar, a striking departure from the classic acoustic-guitar design of the prior century. It lacked a round sound hole and relied for amplification on twin "f holes," vaguely f-shaped designs cut from either side of the strings, in the style of a violin. The instrument produced less natural volume than a round-holed guitar but proved better suited to amplification, an innovation that became possible by adding a "pickup," a metal rectangle that functioned as a microphone for the strings, picking up the vibrations and transmitting them to an amplifier. The L-5 came to dominate both big-band jazz and western swing in the 1930s and 1940s.

The first true electric guitar emerged in 1932 from the Electro-Patent-Instrument Company of Los Angeles, shortly renamed Rickenbacker. Gibson released an electric instrument by 1936. T-Bone Walker first recorded with an electric guitar in 1939. Amplification transformed the guitar and the guitarist. At first, electric and acoustic guitars followed similar designs, and most performers played more or less as they always had. But manufacturers soon learned they could design electric guitars with strings that were thinner and set closer to the instrument's wooden neck. The volume of an acoustic guitar depended on both the breadth of the strings and their distance from the neck, qualities that enhanced their vibrations over the sound hole when they were strummed. None of that mattered with an electric guitar, whose volume was controlled at the amplifier. Electric guitars became suddenly and dramatically easier to play. Now, guitarists could dash off lightning-fast solo "runs," and, thanks to the amplifier, the audience could hear them. In time, some guitarists would dispense with chords altogether and subsist entirely on single-string solos.

Gibson's L-30, introduced in 1935, was a budget instrument, designed for amplification but lacking a pickup. Bukka told Riley he could economize by purchasing the items separately. Riley selected a DeArmond pickup, a brand introduced in 1939. They returned to the Houck store a short time later so Riley could buy a small Gibson amplifier. Riley began to think of himself as an electric guitarist.

On Saturday nights, Bukka would take Riley downtown to the Palace Theatre, a Beale Street institution. Opened in 1920, the Palace was reputedly the largest theater in the South to serve African Americans. Since 1935, the Palace had hosted weekly amateur nights as a showcase for local talent. The emcee was Nat D. Williams, a diminutive high-school history teacher who seemed to host every African American event in Memphis. His sidekick was Rufus Thomas, a tap-dancing comedian. Williams would halt struggling acts by firing a blank from a revolver. Bukka and Riley became regulars at amateur night, where everyone who performed earned a dollar and the weekly winner reaped a five-spot.

"B.B. used to come with holes in his shoes, his guitar all patched up, just to get that dollar," Thomas recalled.

Bukka was a proud mentor, happy to shepherd Riley along in his music career. Bukka's kin were excited for Riley, as well. The lone dissenting voice came from Riley's father.

Though not entirely estranged, Albert King and his son were not close. "Once in a great while," Riley recalled, Albert had paid brief visits to his son in Indianola. "We'd see each other for a quick minute," Riley recalled. Desperate for affirmation, Riley would tell his father how hard he was working. Albert would call him "Jack," and that told Riley he still cared. But the brevity of the visits must have stung: the stolid King patriarch drove sixty miles on country roads to see Riley, only to spend a "quick minute" with his son before moving on.

Albert and Bukka had stayed in touch. Now, when Bukka apprised Albert of Riley's budding passion for the blues, Albert told Bukka he was a "damned fool" to encourage Riley's pursuits. Bukka replied that he could see the good in it, even if Albert could not.

BY EARLY 1947, Riley had resolved to return to Johnson Barrett's plantation in Indianola. He hadn't seen Martha for nearly a year and "missed her something fierce," he recalled, notwithstanding the strains in their relationship. He also owed a debt to his former employer. He hoped the passage of time had softened Barrett's mood. Riley finally telephoned his old employer to apologize, and one can imagine his relief when Barrett responded with laughter and a gentle appeal: "Come on home."

Riley had left a mess back in Indianola. He hadn't told anyone where he was going. Martha fled to Eupora to rejoin her mother. Their departure drove a wedge between Johnson Barrett and Birkett Davis, Riley's cousin, prompting his family to leave the plantation. Barrett held Birkett and Delcia responsible for Riley's ignominious exit. "You see, when you run off from a plantation, you owe that man," Delcia explained, years later. Abandoning their crops drained the Davis family's earnings. Birkett and Delcia and their two young children barely survived the year.

The bus ride back to Indianola felt to Riley like retreat. His reunion with Martha was tense: each suspected the other of infidelity. Riley surely had broken his marital vows during his time in Memphis. Perhaps Martha had, as well. "I don't think she lived so true to him," one Indianola friend recalled. The lingering bitterness over their separation left a rift that would not heal.

Riley found it easier to make amends with Johnson Barrett.

"Riley, where you been?" Barrett said when he opened his front door. But the warmth in his voice told Riley he was happy to see him again.

"I'm sorry," Riley offered.

"You know, Riley, all you had to do was tell me what happened," Barrett said. "We could have talked about it. Everyone screws up at least once."

In a few minutes, the two men had worked out a plan for Riley to repay the $500 Barrett had spent to repair the tractor. And then, with surprising ease, Riley reclaimed the life he had fled. He returned to his tractor. He resumed performing with the Famous St. John Gospel Singers. More than ever, the gospel group was ripe for fame, but Riley remained the only one willing to chase it.

Riley passed two unremarkable years driving tractors and raising crops on the plantation, practicing his guitar for hours a day and amassing funds to repay Johnson Barrett. He and Martha moved into a new home on Lincoln Avenue in the Black section of Indianola. In 1947, the house was wired for electricity. This was another epochal event in Riley's life. Now, he could purchase an electric radio and play the guitar through his new amplifier.

Radio adorned Riley's life with a soundtrack of postwar rhythm and blues, especially the riotous Louis Jordan and His Tympany Five, who owned the R&B charts in 1947. But Riley's big ears took in more than Black music. He also became smitten with Arthur Godfrey, the folksy white broadcaster with a crooked smile and bulbous nose, whose delivery gave listeners the impression he was speaking directly to them. Godfrey transformed talk radio by rejecting the stiff, newsreel cadence of his era for a direct and neighborly style that held Riley transfixed.

In the spring of 1948, another new sound burst forth from Riley's radio. It was a song called "I Can't Be Satisfied," a breakout recording by a hot new blues talent in Chicago. Muddy Waters was born McKinley Morganfield around 1913, a decade before Riley, probably in a forgotten Delta community called Jug's Corner. Muddy's sad narrative faintly echoed Riley's. His parents split while he was a baby. His mother died in 1918, and McKinley was dispatched to a grandmother, who took him a hundred miles north to the Stovall Plantation, outside Clarksdale. He acquired the nickname "Muddy" for playing in the mud. By age three, Muddy was banging on bucket lids and tin cans. He progressed to an accordion, a Jew's harp, and then a harmonica. At seventeen, he learned the guitar and formed a band. In early adulthood, Muddy encountered Son House at a Mississippi roadhouse. He sat mesmerized for weeks on end, soaking up the master's voice from a back corner of the club. Muddy's other obvious influence was Robert Johnson, though the two blues giants never met. Muddy's "thick, heavy tone, the dark coloration of his voice and his firm, almost stolid manner were all clearly derived from House," Peter Guralnick writes, "but the embellishments which he added, the imaginative slide technique and more agile rhythms, were closer to Johnson."

In the summer of 1941, the Library of Congress folklorist Alan Lomax found Muddy and recorded him. He was now an accomplished local performer well into his twenties, albeit one who lived in a shack. The recordings emboldened Muddy. He moved to Chicago to become a full-time bluesman. Chicago rivaled Memphis as a destination for African Americans migrating north out of dead-end sharecropping jobs. At the moment of Muddy's arrival, the reigning stars of Chicago blues included Big Bill Broonzy, a country-blues guitarist from Arkansas who had filled in for the deceased Robert Johnson at John Hammond's legendary 1938 Carnegie Hall concert, and John Lee Curtis "Sonny Boy" Williamson, an accomplished harmonica player who had scored a career-defining hit in 1937 with the leering "Good Morning, School Girl." (Confusingly, this Sonny Boy and the Mississippi harmonica virtuoso performed under the same name.)

In Chicago, Muddy took immediate command. He was regal and inscrutable, with "high Indian cheekbones, striking, almost oriental features, and an impassive expression" that left observers unsure what he was thinking. He strode onstage "with all the dignity of a king."

An uncle gave Muddy his first electric guitar around 1945. Muddy found Chicago audiences too boisterous for an unamplified acoustic. Thus, noisy Chicagoans deserve some credit for spawning electric blues. Amplifiers changed Muddy's sound. His band evolved into a prototype for a thousand pop acts to follow: a lean, muscular, and aggressive ensemble, with Muddy on vocals and electric slide guitar, "Little" Walter Jacobs sharing lead duties on harmonica, and Otis Spann on piano, along with a second guitar and drums. Both Muddy and Walter learned to push amplifiers into overdrive, harnessing waves of distortion to create thick, angry sounds Chicagoans had never heard.

Muddy recorded a few sides for Columbia in 1946 without his backing band. They went nowhere. The next year, he recorded more songs for the new Aristocrat label. These were better, but barrelhouse piano dominated the sides, overshadowing Muddy's guitar and sapping much of the molten energy his band could harness onstage. At that time, across popular music, the guitar was an afterthought.

Aristocrat Records passed into the hands of a Jewish immigrant from Poland named Leonard Chess. By the time of Muddy's next session, Chess was sufficiently intrigued to unleash the undiluted Muddy on the record-buying public, backed only by an upright bass. The crown jewel of that session, "I Can't Be Satisfied," might be the most important blues recording of the postwar years. Chess cranked up the volume, distorting Muddy's electric slide lines and his round baritone on purpose in a song built around a stinging, three-note riff played on a single guitar string. It was an act of aural assault. The *Billboard* magazine reviewer missed the point, opining, "Poor recording distorts vocal and steel guitar backing." But the first pressing of "I Can't Be Satisfied" sold out in twelve hours. The record reached number 11 on the R&B charts, perhaps the genre's first national hit powered by a single-string riff on an electric guitar.

Riley didn't know Muddy, but he knew of the bluesman and his pilgrimage to Chicago. Riley considered following him there but balked at the city's legendary winter chill. "I'd already been to blues heaven," he recalled, "and it wasn't called Chicago."

Riley remained restless. He and Martha remained childless. Martha wanted Riley to play the role of conventional husband, earning good money on his tractor, coming home every night for dinner, and staying there. Riley wanted to play his guitar, and that was evening work.

"For some reason," he recalled, "my mind was not settled at being a husband like a husband should be. Now I wanted to play an instrument.

Now I'm thinking that there's something out there for me. I don't know what to do, but I'm seeking. I'm looking for it. She'd fight me on it."

Martha was stubborn and jealous, just like her husband. If he wanted to play his guitar at some rowdy house party, she wanted to come along. Riley took to sneaking out alone. One night, Martha burst into a party to find a woman sitting on her husband's lap. "I didn't know the lady," Riley recalled. But the trust was gone. In subsequent romantic contretemps, he said, "she never believed I was telling the truth."

The agrarian calendar governed life in the Delta. Riley chose the fallow months between the 1948 and 1949 growing seasons to make his second trip to Memphis. He probably departed in March 1949. This time, Riley left no loose ends, bidding a proper farewell to his boss and his wife. "I'll send for you, soon as I get settled," he told Martha. She accepted his terms and packed to move back in with her parents in Eupora, perhaps sensing Riley would go to Memphis with or without her blessing.

Riley left Indianola at dawn. He hitched a ride in another Lewis Grocery truck, helping the driver make his deliveries in exchange for free passage. This time, Riley didn't stop in Memphis: he traveled on, across the Mississippi River, past the Arkansas border into the city of West Memphis.

By the time of Riley's arrival, a prolonged attack on gambling and prostitution on Beale Street had driven the vice trade across the river to West Memphis, transforming its downtown into Beale Street West. "Wild West" might have been a better descriptor. By 1949, more than thirty all-night clubs dotted the downtown strip on Broadway, pulsing with gambling and prostitution, drawing much of the blues scene away from Beale.

Riley's destination was 231 East Broadway, the studios of KWEM. The West Memphis radio station had launched in 1947 on a pay-to-play system. Local performers could pony up fifteen or twenty dollars of their own money to go on the air, or they could find a sponsor. One of the station's first stars was Chester Burnett, a giant of a man from Mississippi Hill Country who performed as Howlin' Wolf and assembled a backing band in West Memphis that rivaled the Muddy Waters ensemble in Chicago for power and bite. Wolf would prowl the stage, alternately rolling on the floor, climbing the curtains, or thrusting a broom handle suggestively between his legs. Wolf's voice, a bone-rattling bass-baritone growl, froze listeners to their seats. Never had the Delta delivered such a potent set of lungs.

The station's other star was Sonny Boy Williamson. Born around 1912 on a Mississippi plantation and first known as Alex Ford, he mastered the harmonica, and by the 1930s, he was traveling around Mississippi and Arkansas and performing with many singers and guitarists of subsequent renown, including Robert Johnson. In 1941, Ford landed the role of a lifetime as a deejay on radio station KFFA in Helena, Arkansas, to play music and tout baking flour on *King Biscuit Time*. Sponsors supposedly rechristened him Sonny Boy Williamson to exploit the brand of the Chicago musician who was already recording under that name. For chronological reasons, the Arkansas musician is now generally known as Sonny Boy II. In 1948, Sonny Boy moved to West Memphis and KWEM.

Sonny Boy arrived at KWEM shortly after Wolf. They were friends: Sonny Boy had taught Wolf the harmonica. Sonny Boy's new show touted a sponsor called Hadacol, a patent medicine marketed as a vitamin supplement for the whole family. But the "Wonderful Hadacol Feeling" was actually inebriation: Hadacol was 12 percent alcohol.

Riley had been listening to Sonny Boy on the *King Biscuit* show for so long, he recalled, "I felt like I knew him." He and the other hands would come in from the fields at lunchtime and relax with the broadcast. Still, Riley could not explain how he summoned the nerve to walk into the KWEM studio that Wednesday morning—the exact date might have been May 23, 1949—clutching his guitar, and ask for Sonny Boy. He found the harpist with his band, Robert Lockwood Jr. on guitar and Willie Love on piano. Sonny Boy "was huge, tall as a basketball player and brawny as a boxer," Riley recalled. "He looked like he was ready to brawl at the drop of a hat."

Riley had caught Sonny Boy finishing a song. When Sonny Boy saw Riley, he took the harmonica out of his mouth and regarded him with a resentful look. Riley took a deep breath and tried to remember all the warm memories of Sonny Boy on the radio.

"What do you want?" Sonny Boy asked, curtly.

"I-I-I-I wanna sing a song on your program."

"You do, huh?"

"Yes, sir."

"Go ahead. Lemme hear you."

Sonny Boy and his band remembered Riley as the stuttering boy who had prodded them with questions at Jones' Night Spot in Indianola, a few years earlier. Perhaps that flash of memory had earned Riley an audition.

Riley swung his guitar around to play. He had prepared "Blues at Sunrise," a top-ten R&B hit by singer-pianist Ivory Joe Hunter. "I sang with all the soul I could muster," he recalled. "I surprised myself, 'cause I didn't falter. My guitar hit the right notes and I sang in tune." Riley awaited Sonny Boy's verdict.

"What do you call yourself, son?" Sonny Boy asked, his voice finally betraying just a flicker of warmth.

"Riley B. King."

"All right, Riley B. King," Sonny Boy replied. "You can sing your song at the end of my program. Just be sure you sing as good as you did just now."

Near the close of Sonny Boy's lunchtime show, Riley pulled up to the microphone and sang his song on the air. He played and sang as well as he ever had. When he was through, Sonny Boy reclaimed the mic.

"The boy ain't bad," he said, "but you tell me what you think. Call in if you like him."

Sonny Boy wrapped up his show. Riley sat and waited. A short while later, a white man entered the studio and announced that many listeners had called in with praise for Riley's performance. Then he leaned in and whispered something in Sonny Boy's ear.

"Shit," Sonny Boy said. "I done messed up." He turned to Riley, who became gripped with panic. He thought he had messed up.

"Lookee here, Riley B.," Sonny Boy said. "Seems like I double-booked myself. I'm working down 'round Clarksdale tonight, but I also got me another date at the Sixteenth Street Grill here in West Memphis. You wanna play the Grill for me?"

"Yes, sir," Riley replied in an instant.

Riley was "thrilled beyond reason," he recalled, "giddy and silly and screaming hallelujah inside." In the space of an hour, he had debuted as a radio bluesman and earned his first paying solo gig.

Sonny Boy picked up the telephone and placed a call. "Did you hear the boy who just sang?" A pause. "How did you like him?" Another pause. "Well, I'm gonna let him work for you tonight." He hung up.

"I want you to go down and play for Miss Annie at the Sixteenth Street Grill. And you better *play*," Sonny Boy said, now with menace in his voice.

"Yes, sir," Riley replied.

The club on South Sixteenth Street, a block off Broadway in West Memphis, was variously known as the Square Deal Café, the Sixteenth Street Grill, or Miss Annie's Place, after its owner, Annie Jordan. Miss Annie showed Riley around. "The joint was just a couple of rooms," he recalled, "one up front for music and sandwiches, one in the back for gambling." Annie told Riley, "I got me a jukebox in here, but I turn it off 'cause the ladies like to dance to a live man."

A live man. The words danced in his head. And sure enough, as the hour of Riley's gig approached, a procession of ladies filed into the café, some with escorts, some without. The men retreated to the gambling parlor, leaving their dates up front to dine and dance.

Riley took the stage in his old army jacket. He had no better clothes. The ladies didn't seem to mind. "For the first time," he recalled, "I played for dancers, played for these ladies who moved so loose and limber that I played better than I'd ever played before. Might have messed up my musical measures or screwed up a lyric or two, but, baby, the beat was there."

Riley filled Miss Annie's Place with the blues, playing through his Gibson guitar into his diminutive amplifier and singing through a tinny sound system, unaccompanied. He held down the beat, and the dance floor filled with hot, heaving bodies.

When Riley's set was over, Miss Annie told him, "I want to hire you. But you can't help me get business unless you're on the radio, like Sonny Boy is. If you can get on the radio, I'll pay you twelve dollars a night and give you room and board."

"Yes, ma'am," Riley replied. "I *will* get on the radio." Exactly how was a matter for later.

Miss Annie offered Riley a room above her club. "That night," he recalled, "I couldn't sleep for the pictures running through my head": women in various states of undress, "bending over and stretching, grinding and grinning and showing me stuff I ain't ever seen before."

The next morning, Riley grabbed his guitar and boarded a bus to downtown Memphis. This time, his destination was another radio station, with the call letters WDIA.

CHAPTER 6

THE BLUES BOY

WDIA COMMENCED OPERATIONS in the summer of 1947 on Union Avenue in Memphis, founded by a pair of white broadcasters looking for a niche to fill. John Pepper was the businessman, scion of an affluent Memphis family. Bert Ferguson was the radio man, short on money but long on experience. Eight years earlier, Pepper had brought Ferguson in to run WJPR in Greenville. They regrouped at the new Memphis operation, named for John Pepper's daughter, Diane.

The station started with a country-western format. When that failed to ensnare an audience, the owners tried pop and even classical music. Nothing worked. Five other Memphis stations with celebrity deejays from national networks controlled the market. Christine "Chris" Cooper, Ferguson's young programming director, searched in vain for the right format.

Cooper was a striking woman of twenty-three, taciturn and serious, with soulful brown eyes and a sharp mind. She had skipped two grades in school. Ferguson had lured her away from an ad agency to become one of the first women in Memphis radio.

By the spring of 1948, Cooper wondered if she had made the right choice. WDIA hovered near bankruptcy, and its owners seemed desperate. One night, to save on hotel bills, four station employees drove back to Memphis from an industry convention in Nashville, a journey of two hundred miles past moonlit farmhouses along winding two-lane roads. Bert Ferguson held the wheel. Midway through the trip, Ferguson leaned in to Cooper in the passenger seat and whispered, for her ears only, "What do you think of programming for Negro people?" Cooper considered. The other Memphis stations had divvied up the white audience. Black listeners represented an audience nearly as large as the entire white market—"tens of thousands of people with names and faces who had served me at restaurants and ridden on the same bus," she recalled. Black Memphians had their own clubs, their own festivals, and even a newspaper but no radio station. She told her boss she loved the idea. Ferguson pressed: "Would you object to working alongside Negro people at the station?" No, Cooper replied, she would not.

After that furtive exchange, Ferguson avoided the topic for weeks. Cooper feared he had lost his nerve. But then, one day in October 1948, Ferguson greeted her at the WDIA studios and announced that he had decided to "go ahead with it." She knew instantly what "it" was.

THE STORY of African American radio had really begun two decades earlier, with a visionary African American named Jack Cooper. Born in Memphis in 1888, Cooper made his name as a journalist in Chicago before launching a variety show on radio station WCAP in Washington, DC, in 1925. On the air, Cooper performed comedy skits in a variety of dialects: he would later joke that he had been "the first four Negroes on radio." In 1929, Cooper launched *The All-Negro Hour* on radio station WSBC in Chicago, hosting a broadcast patterned on African American vaudeville.

Radio of that era favored live performance, so broadcasters could skirt the hefty fees charged by the American Society of Composers, Authors, and Publishers to play recorded music on the air. The modern disc-jockey format did not exist—until 1932, when Jack Cooper invented it. A musician walked out of a scheduled broadcast in a dispute over pay. To fill the dead air, by one account, Cooper "got a barrel and set some little record player on it and held a mike to it." Cooper thus became the first deejay.

By the time of WDIA's debut, fifteen years later, African American radio performers were popping up all over the South. Bert Ferguson himself had put Riley's gospel quartet on the air in Greenville. But Black deejays remained largely taboo, and no U.S. radio station had adopted an all-Black format. That became Ferguson's goal.

His first choice for deejay was Nat D. Williams, perhaps the most visible African American in Memphis. When Williams wasn't teaching his high-school history class, he was writing a column for the Black *Memphis World* or hosting the Palace Theatre's weekly amateur night, broadcast on another Memphis station. His short, stocky frame and Coke-bottle glasses were familiar to all of Black Memphis.

Williams agreed. Now came the ticklish subject of naming his broadcast. The terms "Black" and "African American" were unknown in polite white society of the day. "Negro" was acceptable but too blunt, apparently, for the weekly radio listings in the *Memphis Commercial Appeal*. So Ferguson and Chris Cooper were left to choose among several other descriptive euphemisms. They rejected "Sepia" and "Brown" and ultimately settled on "Tan," which sounded like a day at the beach. Williams would host *Tan Town Jamboree*.

The new deejay appeared at the studio just before the scheduled start of his first broadcast at 4 p.m. on Monday, October 25, 1948. He was breathless after racing across town from his classroom at Booker T. Washington High School. He took his position at the microphone. At the top of the hour, the white announcer pointed to Williams and gave him a cue. Williams sat there in silence: in the gravitas of the moment, his mind had gone blank. Seconds ticked by. Finally, Williams realized the absurdity of his predicament and erupted into a long peal of laughter. Soon, everyone in the studio was howling. That big, cathartic laugh would become Nat's trademark, an ice-breaker to open every broadcast.

Not everyone was laughing. The backlash to *Tan Town Jamboree* came swift and fierce. "For the first three weeks, we were just plagued with calls—'Get that n—— off the air,'" Chris Cooper recalled. "My boss got death threats." Station hands politely reminded callers that if they didn't like what they heard, they were free to turn the dial.

Protests from white listeners died down, and WDIA's Black listening audience exploded. African American communities in Tennessee, Arkansas, and Mississippi had never fully experienced the unifying power of radio. Now, the most famous Black man in Memphis was on the air daily. *Tan Town Jamboree* became a virtual town hall for every Black settlement within sixty miles.

MISS ANNIE had told Riley about the new radio station that was hiring African American talent. Riley already knew Nat Williams from amateur nights at the Palace with his cousin Bukka. The famed Memphian reminded Riley of Luther Henson, his old schoolmaster.

Riley set out for WDIA, securing a cotton-sack strap tightly around his army-fatigue jacket to ward off the chill. The quarter in his pocket took him only to the downtown Memphis bus station. The radio station lay three miles away. Riley walked. The morning was cold and wet. As rain fell harder, Riley clutched his guitar to his chest so that his precious instrument, still without a case, would not fill with water. He lifted his pace to a trot. He came to a stop in front of the studio, a brick box that vaguely resembled a giant radio, with the station's name bolted to the front wall in art-deco metal letters.

By Riley's account, he peered into a large plate-glass window and saw "a black man with super-short hair and super-thick glasses": Nat Williams. The red studio light was on. Riley knew that meant Williams was on the air. He waited till it turned green. He tapped on the window. Williams looked out through the pane and saw, in his words, "a brown-skin fellow standing there with water dripping off his battered old hat, water oozing out of the soles of his shoes. Drenched all over with a worn and really battered old guitar under his arm. He stood there looking wistfully at me through that glass partition."

A less evocative retelling comes from Chris Cooper. She said Riley simply appeared at the WDIA front desk. "He went to the receptionist with his dripping-wet umbrella and his guitar held tight to his chest," Cooper recalled. "She called the manager, Bert Ferguson, and he came down from his office, and she said, 'Somebody's here who wants to record.'"

Riley recalled Ferguson as "a short Jewish man, not much hair, with a serious air about him." Ferguson regarded the sodden visitor. A short, ragged pompadour topped Riley's smoothly symmetrical, clean-shaven face, with wide-set eyebrows above mournfully expressive eyes. Full lips and flared nostrils overpowered a subtle chin. His body was slender and wiry, his powerful hands rough from farm work.

"We don't make records," Ferguson told Riley, but "we might be able to use you. If I put you on the radio, would you be too nervous to talk?"

"I might do a little s-s-s-stuttering," Riley stuttered, "but no more so than the average person. I think the average person will take to me."

Ferguson asked Riley about his background. Riley answered honestly. He sensed Ferguson was a fair man, and he did not embellish. He told Ferguson about singing blues on the Indianola street corner and singing gospel on the radio. Now Ferguson remembered Riley as the guitarist for the Famous St. John Gospel Singers, the ensemble Ferguson had broadcast in Greenville. Riley told Ferguson about singing for Sonny Boy on KWEM and about his new gig at the Sixteenth Street Grill.

Don Kern, the production manager, entered the room. Riley performed a song for the two men. After years of busking for tips on street corners in Black neighborhoods, this might have been the first time Riley played the blues for an attentive white audience. White people knew little or nothing of real blues. Riley probably weighed his options and decided that the leering sexuality of the typical blues lyric would leave his listeners slack-jawed. So he selected lighter fare, performing Louis Jordan's "Caldonia," an ode to a woman with "great big feet."

"You're all right," Kern said when Riley had finished. Both men smiled. "And mentioning Sonny Boy gives me an idea," Ferguson said. "Sonny Boy's made quite a splash advertising Hadacol. Well, we have a sponsor called Pep-ti-kon. It's a tonic like Hadacol. Good for whatever ails you. And we're looking for someone who can sell it. I'm thinking that one way to sell it is through a song. You ever written a jingle?"

"No, sir," Riley replied.

"Willing to try?"

In West Memphis, Sonny Boy Williamson was driving a brisk business in Hadacol from his platform at KWEM. Ferguson wanted to enter that market with Pep-ti-kon, a competing product with similar ingredients and similarly dubious benefits. He and his WDIA business partner had already formed a company to market the tonic. Ferguson had approached Cooper to write a series of Pep-ti-kon ads, but the principled program director refused. Now, the assignment fell to Riley. He sat with his guitar for a few moments, humming a tentative melody over simple blues chords. Then he burst out in song:

> *Pep-ti-kon sure is good*
> *And you can get it anywhere in your neighborhood*

Ferguson beamed. He went off and returned with his program director. Cooper saw a guitar leaning against a wall, still dripping, and a slender man standing with his head bowed, also dripping, looking like some Delta apparition. Ferguson instructed the visitor to sing something. When the reticent young man reached the microphone, he seemed to transform. "He just straightened up," Cooper recalled, "and he hit his guitar like he knew what he was doing."

She thought the visitor might play "Old Black Joe" or "Swanee River," old Stephen Foster chestnuts written in the previous century by a white man about African Americans: they were the only "Black" songs she knew. Decades later, she could not remember much about the song Riley did play except her reaction: "It just tore me apart."

Chris Cooper had never heard Delta blues. The song Riley played was raw and sexual and coarse. His voice burned with menace and lust, and his sodden guitar buzzed with an angry twang.

Riley recalled the song as "Somebody Done Changed the Lock on My Door," another Louis Jordan hit. Even this comparatively mild fare, nearly as playful as "Caldonia," featured a lyric whose meaning, beneath the paper-thin veneer of double entendre, was shockingly carnal stuff about a "key" that "won't fit that lock no more." The music and the words made the young programming director want to rip open the studio door and run out into the street. She felt shaken, upset, unnerved. And then she thought that maybe this rough, sexual music was exactly what the new WDIA listeners wanted to hear. When Riley had finished playing, Cooper gasped, "Let's put him on the air."

Riley sat down with the staff of WDIA to plan a daily, fifteen-minute performing segment for the bluesman and his guitar. He would be only the second African American hired by the new Memphis station. (Or possibly the third: accounts vary on the exact date of Riley's arrival.) "Hired" may not be the right word: Riley would receive no pay for his on-air performances. He could, however, use the airtime to promote his gigs and spread his name around the tristate African American community. Riley would open and close every set with his Pep-ti-kon jingle, whose simpering melody quickly wore thin on the WDIA staff. "Man, it was horrible," fellow broadcaster Rufus Thomas recalled.

The half-hour meeting concluded with Ferguson making a spontaneous decision. Turning to Riley, he announced, "I'm going to rename you *BB King*." According to Cooper, Ferguson chose Riley's on-air name by pure impulse. "No periods," he instructed. "Just *BB*." Like Riley's middle initial, the two letters stood for nothing.

This unromantic account pales beside the legend that has arisen around those enigmatic initials. Years later, Riley would tell interviewers he made his radio debut as Riley King. Only later, he said, did announcers begin calling him the "Beale Street Blues Boy." Over time, fans shortened the moniker to "Blues Boy" and then to "B.B." Friends called him "B."*

Confusion likewise swirls around the details of Riley's first appearance on WDIA. Riley recalled that the station manager put him on the air at 3:30 that very afternoon. Cooper said she and Ferguson assigned Riley a fifteen-minute slot on weekday mornings, around 9:30, starting the next day. ("He was on every morning," she said. "I remember, because I got the calls.") Other accounts have Riley debuting as a guest of Nat Williams.

Any of those scenarios is possible. This much is certain: the name "Bee Bee King" first appeared in the radio listings of the *Memphis*

---

* Prior biographers have suggested yet another account: an early profile, published in 1952 by the African American *Tri-State Defender*, reported that the listening public christened Riley the "singing black boy" and that those words—rather than "Beale" or "Blues"—supplied the requisite *B*s.

Commercial Appeal on Saturday, March 26, 1949, in the 5 p.m. slot, an eponymous, fifteen-minute program tucked between news and *Songbirds of the South.* (The listing seems to confirm Cooper's account that her boss, rather than radio listeners, coined the famous initials.) The next Monday, March 28, he played another fifteen-minute slot at 3:30 p.m., ahead of Nat's four o'clock show. A week later, his show moved to 5:30 p.m., after Nat's *Tan Town Jamboree.* Riley would remain in that slot for several months.

Riley's arrival on the airwaves proved Bert Ferguson's enduring commitment to creating the first Black radio station. Yet, white announcers introduced Nat and Riley, and white producers supported them. And neither performer was allowed to touch the controls or spin records. "That was ridiculous and frustrating and made me mad," Riley recalled.

Aside from that injustice, Riley found a kind of utopia at WDIA. "The radio station reminded me of Beale Street in this respect," he recalled. "It was a world apart. In the middle of a strictly segregated South, WDIA was a place where blacks and whites worked together." All station employees, white and Black, addressed one another as "Mr.," "Mrs.," or "Miss," a courtesy few white southerners extended to African Americans.

Riley sent for Martha to join him in Memphis. They rented two rooms in a boarding house north of downtown. Martha took a job as a housecleaner. Riley's job with Miss Annie paid several times his tractor-driver salary.

The marriage remained tense, riven by both infidelity and infertility. After five years together, Riley and Martha had not yet conceived a child. By now, surely both partners suspected Riley's damaged testicles were to blame. Imagine Riley's reaction, then, when a woman tracked him down in Memphis and told him he was a father. She and Riley had carried on a secret relationship in Indianola. Now she had a son, Willie. She pressed her case to a man who earned as much money as any African American in Indianola.*

---

*Riley did not identify the child when he recounted the episode in his memoir. But when he listed his adoptive children in a 1970 interview, only one, Willie, was a son born before 1950.

"I didn't tell Martha," Riley recalled, "but I did tell the woman I'd care for the son." Riley diverted some of his newfound wealth to the woman in Indianola.

By mid-April, WDIA had three African American employees. Maurice "Hot Rod" Hulbert, hired around the same time as Riley, was a Memphis entrepreneur and showman with an on-air talent for wordplay. "Hot Rod" cut a more dashing figure than either Riley or Nat D. Williams, with his checkered suits, megawatt smile, and goatee. He began his daily broadcast by ticking off names of Black Memphis neighborhoods—"Orange Mound! New Chicago! Hollywood!"—to the sound of a rocket blast. Hulbert hosted *Sepia Swing Club* at three on weekday afternoons, before Nat's *Tan Town Jamboree*.

Throughout WDIA's first year of African American programming, the station retained a split personality, still offering *Cracker Barrel* and *Hillbilly Party* for white listeners in the mornings before turning to its new Black stars in the afternoons. As Black listeners drove ratings skyward, Ferguson and Cooper eased out the hillbilly fare, and Ferguson filled the station roster with new Black deejays, including Dwight "Gatemouth" Moore, an established blues singer, and A. C. "Moohah" Williams, a high-school biology teacher who led a vocal group called the Teen-Town Singers and penned a column in the African American *Memphis World*. By summer's end in 1949, WDIA had shed its last vestiges of white programming.

A FEW MONTHS into Riley's Memphis journey, he must have felt he was living someone else's life. He was spending his days at the city's ascendant Black radio station. He was playing nearly every night at Miss Annie's over in West Memphis. On weekends, he rode around the city's Black neighborhoods in a flatbed truck. Sponsors would place Riley atop the cab to play the guitar and sing the blues while merchants hawked bottles of Pep-ti-kon out of the flatbed. If the Pep-ti-kon boys hit their sales quota, they would reward Riley with a bonus, sometimes fifty dollars, sometimes a hundred, dizzying sums to the former sharecropper. Riley would tout his nightly gigs and the ubiquitous tonic on his radio show. He promoted his radio show at his gigs and on the weekend truck tours. His face, his name, and his music were rapidly suffusing the city's Black community.

Riley's next goal was to make a record. He pestered Bert Ferguson until, in the summer of 1949, Ferguson arranged for his Pep-ti-kon star to cut four sides in the station's studio. Riley didn't have a band, so the station heads went down to Beale Street and found one.

Richard "Tuff" Green was an established Memphis bassist and bandleader. His Rocketeers were one of the hottest acts on Beale. Phineas Newborn Sr. joined the session on drums, son Phineas Newborn Jr. on piano, and brothers Ben and Thomas Branch on horns, along with Sammie Jett, a female trombonist. Riley knew them all. Don Kern packed the musicians into a tiny recording room off the main WDIA studio and supervised the session.

Riley had never heard himself on tape. When Kern played back the songs Riley recorded that summer day, he did not recognize his own voice. "Who's that?" he asked. "That's you, fool," someone replied.

The standout was "Miss Martha King," an ode to Riley's long-suffering wife. It opened with Riley playing a descending riff that sounded more like an exercise than a hook. Then Riley started to sing, and his guitar was barely heard again. Ben Branch played the first solo on the saxophone, and Sammie Jett took the second on the trombone. The song featured not Riley's guitar but his confident, slightly clenched, back-of-the-throat tenor. The sparse and colorless guitar work suggested that Riley had not yet developed any of the aural techniques for which he would eventually be known. The other featured single, "Got the Blues," featured even less of Riley's guitar. But the real shocker on this recording was the plain fact that Riley had not mastered the twelve-bar blues form. Despite a valiant effort by bandleader Tuff Green, whose elementary bass line all but cried out "one-two-three-four" behind him, Riley sang right over the chord changes, his lyric falling progressively further behind the beat until, by the end, his seasoned backing band churned in rhythmic disarray. At moments in "Got the Blues," everyone seemed to be playing a different chord.

The session revealed not just Riley's musical naïveté but also how little experience he had playing with other musicians. The star of these WDIA sides was the weakest link in the ensemble that recorded them.

Nonetheless, Riley was an artist of growing stature in Black Memphis. Surely the records would sell. Kern dispatched the tapes to the independent Bullet imprint in Nashville, the nearest label, two hundred miles away. They emerged on 78-rpm shellac discs as Bullet singles 309 and 315, under the name "B. B. King." Riley would remain "Bee Bee" in the Memphis radio listings for another year or two, but "B. B."—with a space at first, later without—was the name that stuck.

In July, B.B. King earned his first published review. *Billboard* awarded "Miss Martha King" fifty-three of a possible one hundred points. "A low-down, heavy beat keeps this blues-shouting ballad from dying," the reviewer opined. Three months later, the dreadful "Got the Blues" earned forty-four points. The records made no mark on the national charts but sold well in Memphis, whetting the appetites of B.B. and his radio-station handlers to explore further recordings.

With fame came offers for B.B. to play larger gigs in Memphis and the tristate region around it. He needed an agent and soon had two.

Robert Henry was the top concert promoter on Beale. He "stood no taller than a pool cue," Preston Lauterbach writes, "light-skinned and fleshy, with a broad nose, pointy little eyes, and round shoulders. He wore his hair and mustache scraggly and his shirttail out."

Henry had come to Memphis in 1909 and started out as a ticket taker. By the 1940s, he was bringing Duke Ellington and Count Basie to the Palace Theatre and running a record store and pool hall on top of his booking business. He kept tabs on every talented African American performer in town. "For a roadhouse booking, he could assemble an orchestra from spare parts in Handy Park and the saloons, usually in under an hour."

Accounts differ on precisely when Robert Henry entered B.B. King's life. In B.B.'s memoir, he recalled approaching the Beale Street kingpin only after he had attained national fame. Henry, by contrast, would later take credit for virtually every step in B.B.'s ascent: he even claimed to have persuaded Nat Williams to give B.B. his job at WDIA.

Whatever the case, Henry was probably working with B.B. by the time he played his first gigs outside Memphis.

But Robert Henry mostly booked expansive theaters and auditoriums, and B.B. was not yet that famous. He needed someone who could place him in roadhouses and juke joints, places like the Jones' Night Spot back in Indianola. For those engagements, B.B. had to see Sunbeam Mitchell.

Andrew "Sunbeam" Mitchell had grown up along Beale Street, toiling on his father's horse-drawn vegetable cart. In 1944, Mitchell leased space above the Pantaze Drug Store and opened a rooming house. By 1945, he was operating both the Mitchell Hotel and the Domino Lounge. He ran liquor across the state line into Mississippi, a dry state. He was "a casual, heavyset fellow with a high hairline," according to Lauterbach. "His hands shook. He stammered in a high, nasal voice. He dressed like a barkeep," with sagging jowls and protruding belly. Between the hotel, the club, and the liquor business, Sunbeam almost single-handedly built "an interstate vice distribution system that worked like an old-time medicine show, albeit with sex, gambling, bottled-in-bond booze, and entertainment by the rising stars of black music."

Those credentials may explain why the name Sunbeam Mitchell does not appear in most accounts of B.B.'s rise. In B.B.'s memoir, he hails Sunbeam as the "patron saint of Memphis musicians" but assigns him no role in nurturing his own career. In fact, Sunbeam handled many of B.B.'s early bookings into clubs "as far out as the WDIA signal traveled," down Highway 61 into Mississippi and across the river in Arkansas. The only condition was that B.B. return to Memphis in time for the next day's radio show.

Henry and Mitchell reaped a cut of B.B.'s earnings, probably 5 or 10 percent, on gigs they booked. B.B.'s employers at WDIA also got in on the action, leveraging bookings to raise the station's profile. B.B. had always performed the blues alone. He played solo for a few months after his arrival in Memphis, much like his Delta-blues forebears, except that B.B. played Louis Jordan songs through an amplifier on an electric guitar. His first real blues collaborator was evidently Walter "Shakey" Horton, the Memphis harp legend, who blew with kinetic abandon.

"He and I had a duo along the lines of Brownie McGhee and Sonny Terry," the folk-blues duo, B.B. recalled. "We'd play little places that held maybe twenty-five people, and we'd make ten or fifteen dollars apiece."

To satisfy his growing schedule of club dates, B.B. would need a proper backing band. Over the summer of 1949, he recruited musicians from a loose fraternity of talented Beale performers who took turns serving each other as sidemen and some of whom would later be remembered as the Beale Streeters (at least by historians and fans: the Beale Streeters apparently never uttered the name themselves). They included John Alexander Jr., a talented but unstable pianist who would later rocket to national fame under the stage name Johnny Ace; Earl Forest, a drummer and singer who would likewise ascend to headliner; Richard Sanders and Herman Green, a pair of well-traveled saxophonists; Bobby "Blue" Bland, an illiterate Memphis teen with a silken voice but no particular instrumental prowess; and Robert Lockwood Jr., the virtuosic guitarist who had played with Sonny Boy Williamson.

B.B.'s first band was probably a humble trio. Personnel varied from gig to gig, but a typical lineup might find B.B. on guitar, Sanders or Green on sax, and Forest on drums: the bass would come later. Bobby Bland served mostly as tagalong, always welcome because he owned a car. By day, the band would head into the WDIA studio to join B.B. on his show, racing through three or four songs, the Pep-ti-kon jingle, and a breathless pitch for that night's gig. Gradually, tip jars gave way to booking fees, and the ensemble turned a profit.

"We were traveling up to the state line between Arkansas and Missouri, and to Covington, Tennessee and Birdsong, Arkansas," Earl Forest recalled, describing the movements of B.B.'s first real blues ensemble. "In the other direction, we traveled in Mississippi all the way to Louisiana. We had solid engagements where we played every week. . . . Since B.B. was on the air, he could advertise where we were going to be. He would do his radio show, get the band together, travel, do the show, and then get back to Memphis to do his radio show the next day."

Some of the sidemen were veteran musicians. B.B., the front man, was only a few months removed from busking on sidewalks. Much like the unschooled country bluesmen before him, B.B. thought nothing of adding a measure here or there or lingering on a note for a few extra beats when the feeling took him. Such quirks drove the sidemen crazy. Some were ashamed to accompany him. Privately, they marveled at how this Indianola hick had grown so popular. One of them finally sat B.B. down and taught him how to keep time.

Robert Lockwood Jr. was an extraordinary talent. Born in Turkey Scratch, Arkansas, in 1915, Lockwood grew up in a middle-class home and studied piano and organ, instruments out of reach to poor Delta sharecroppers, before he learned the guitar. Lockwood was the only guitarist known to have learned directly from Robert Johnson, who had lived on and off with Lockwood's mother as her boyfriend. Lockwood learned many styles, even mastering Johnson's own approach so completely that listeners reputedly could close their eyes and not tell them apart. In 1941, Lockwood began his longtime radio association with Sonny Boy on *King Biscuit Time*. Together they formed the first prominent electric-blues band in the Delta. By the time he met B.B., Lockwood was a soft-spoken journeyman in his midthirties with close-cropped, thinning hair and large, piercing eyes, supremely confident in his abundant talent and impatient with lesser musicians. He could play chords with names B.B. had never heard in time signatures he had never learned.

However flawless Lockwood's technique, he still needed to make money, and that was something B.B. knew how to do. Lockwood first encountered B.B. at a club in Arkansas in 1949. "I went out there with the intention of sitting in with him, but he was sounding so bad, I left my stuff in my car," Lockwood recalled, only partly in jest. "And he begged me to help him play, so I went out and got it." The decision would cost Lockwood a year of his life.

That night, Lockwood agreed to help B.B. with his guitar playing. The two men returned to the rooming house where B.B. and Martha lived. Lockwood lay down in the extra room, ate some barbecue in bed, and fell asleep. Some time later, B.B. awakened him. It was the middle of the night. The young bluesman wanted Lockwood to teach him. Lockwood sleepily protested, "Can't it wait till tomorrow?" "Naw," B.B.

replied: he feared that his teacher would flee before B.B. had learned anything of value.

Though Lockwood was B.B.'s employee, B.B. was also Lockwood's student—at least indirectly. "He'd never just sit me down and show me things," B.B. recalled. Instead, Lockwood would chide B.B. each time he played something wrong—which, in the beginning, seemed to be all the time. "I taught him because I was working with him, and I knew, and he didn't," Lockwood recalled. "I couldn't play with him without teaching him." Lockwood taught B.B. how to follow a time signature and how to play with other musicians in the recording studio. He taught him to listen to the bass, because the bass notes revealed what chord the rest of the band was playing. He schooled B.B.'s handlers, as well, telling them to bury the singer within a large ensemble until he had learned how to play. "He can't work with no trio," Lockwood warned, "because he don't know what he's doing. Put him with eight pieces and he'll have to listen. He will *have to listen*."

LESS THAN A YEAR after B.B. had arrived in Memphis, he felt his career taking off. And then, it seemed to come crashing down. B.B. fell gravely ill. He had survived the mumps, venereal disease, and sundry other ailments, most of them mild. Now, for the first time in his life, B.B. feared he was going to die. The mystery affliction sapped his strength, leaving him too weak to work, too frail to rise from his bed. Fever and nausea wracked him. His whole body ached. Blood streaked his bowel movements. He couldn't swallow, focus his mind, or even lift his arms. Doctors finally diagnosed hepatitis. He summoned his wife to his side—and his father.

B.B. and Albert King had not been close in the eight years since B.B.'s abrupt departure from Lexington. Albert had paid a few brief visits to his son in Indianola, but that, it seems, was the extent of their contact. Albert had left Lexington in 1948 and taken a job at the Memphis Firestone plant, grinding up old tires and melting the rubber into new ones. B.B.'s decision to reconnect with Albert now, as he hovered near death, changed the course of their relationship. Albert would play a recurring role in B.B.'s life for the next four decades.

Perhaps B.B.'s newfound success emboldened him to seek out Albert, the patriarch whose approval he craved. He wanted his father by his side as he lived out his final hours on Earth. This was B.B.'s first taste of mortality. As he lay in bed, B.B. recalled, "I could only visualize the death of my mother and grandmother, imagining that I was going through the same thing. I prayed to God to take me. Wanted to stop suffering. Wanted to just stop." He prepared to rejoin Elnora and Nora Ella.

Gradually, though, that thought gave way to another: "Maybe it's not my time." It occurred to B.B. that he didn't know God's plan and that perhaps he was wrong to wish for death. A friend brought ice cream, and B.B. ate it and kept it down. A doctor, a real one, prescribed medications. Bit by bit, B.B.'s health returned.

B.B.'s brush with death might have inspired one of Albert's most fatherly acts toward his son: he found B.B. a guardian angel. Norman Matthews, born in 1929, was a Beale Street hustler. He claimed to have crisscrossed the country as a child with the chitlin' circuit comedy duo Butterbeans and Susie. By his teens, Matthews worked as a driver for the Memphis mayor (possibly James J. Pleasants Jr., one in a long line of "Boss" Crump cronies). He also ran shipments of whiskey two hundred miles from Memphis to Jackson, Mississippi. His perpetual search for retread tires led him to B.B.'s father, who could get them at the Firestone plant. The two men arranged a barter system, tires for whiskey. Albert deemed Matthews a gangster, which wasn't far from true. One day, probably in late 1949, Albert instructed the streetwise teenager, "Take care of my son." Though only five foot six, Matthews was tough. His face seemed locked in a perpetual glare. His eyes pointed in disarmingly divergent directions. He kept one eye on B.B. while working ill-defined jobs for a procession of Memphis musicians, including Johnny Ace. No one in B.B.'s entourage was more loyal. "He take care of me," Matthews once observed, "and I take care of him." In the prosperous years to come, Norman Matthews would help B.B. remember who he was and where he came from.

Illness did not bring B.B. closer to his estranged wife. He and Martha would remain together for three more years, but the thrill was gone. An event in late 1949 would further complicate the marriage. Another woman, this one from rural Arkansas, informed B.B. that she had given birth and that the child was his. B.B. had met Mary Jackson in a kitchen at a juke joint where she worked as a cook. Jackson lived in Gilmore, Arkansas, roughly thirty miles from West Memphis. Her daughter, Shirley Ann, was born on October 26. The timing alone would seem to exclude B.B. as the father: he had probably arrived in Memphis only seven months earlier. But B.B. again accepted the paternity claim without question, adding a second child to his family. Shirley remained in Arkansas with her mother, who eventually married another man. B.B. dropped by for the occasional visit and sent some of his earnings to Shirley's mother.

"It was a pattern he would follow for his entire life," Shirley recalled. "He promised any woman that he was involved with that he would stay in her life forever."

Newly invigorated, his health restored, B.B. took stock of his success and raised his ambitions anew. He took yet another job, rising at dawn and traveling across the Mississippi River to Arkansas to spend mornings picking cotton. Arkansas planters paid up to a dollar for a hundred pounds of cotton, three times what B.B. had earned in Mississippi. He would race back to WDIA for a new fifteen-minute lunchtime segment, created in the final months of 1949 when the days grew too short for B.B.'s rush-hour slot. (WDIA was a "daytimer," an AM station that broadcast only during daylight hours and went dark at night, when its signal might interfere with other broadcasts.) The dawn-to-dusk schedule meant that WDIA signed off around 5 p.m. in winter.

After B.B.'s lunchtime gig, he would hang around the station through the afternoon. He was being groomed as a deejay, a big step up from playing guitar and pitching Pep-ti-kon. Full-time deejays at WDIA made forty or fifty dollars a week, while B.B. still earned nothing for his daily on-air performances. If he was around the studio at two o'clock, he might be asked to sit in for Hot Rod Hulbert and anchor the *Sepia Swing Club*. If not, he might return to the cotton fields. That exhausting schedule became his routine. "It was rough," he recalled, "but it paid." Between gigs, deejay shifts, and cotton hauls, B.B. now earned the princely sum of roughly eighty-five dollars a week.

But B.B. was not a frugal man, and he was developing a gambling habit. West Memphis teemed with gambling houses. The big game was craps, bets placed on dice rolls. Card players favored a game called Georgia skin: each player got one card and placed a bet. The dealer flipped the remaining cards until one matched a player's card. Memphis musicians played a variation on gin rummy called kotch. B.B.'s addiction commenced within months of his arrival in town. "I liked betting, and naturally I liked winning," he recalled, "but I was mostly losing." B.B.'s increasingly spendthrift lifestyle left him perpetually short of cash. Fortunately, B.B. was still young enough to get away with hitting up Nat Williams for a few dollars whenever their paths crossed.

B.B.'s deejay work opened up a whole new world. The typical Delta bluesman synthesized the styles of the men he heard at the local juke joint into one of his own, with direct and obvious antecedents in the work of his predecessors. B.B., by contrast, drew inspiration from music he heard on records and film reels and radio. His greatest influences were men he had never seen, at least not in person: Blind Lemon Jefferson, Charlie Christian, and T-Bone Walker from Texas; Lonnie Johnson from New Orleans; and Django Reinhardt from Belgium. Never, perhaps, had a blues guitarist drawn from such diverse influences. And now, with an entire radio station at his disposal, B.B.'s ears were about to explode.

"Before Memphis," he recalled, "I never even owned a record player. Now I was sitting in a room with a thousand records and the ability to play them whenever I wanted."

The WDIA station heads let B.B. select whatever songs he liked, though only white producers could play them. He chose plenty of rhythm-and-blues sides, like Charles Brown's slow-burning "Trouble Blues" and Dinah Washington's brassy "Baby Get Lost." But he also played pop hits like Nat Cole's "Nature Boy" and Frank Sinatra's "Five Minutes More" and even Bing Crosby's "Too-Ra-Loo-Ra-Loo-Ral." He sought out songs that "had the most feeling" to him "as a blues musician," even if they weren't blues songs and even if they weren't performed by

African Americans. B.B. was a natural deejay. He had learned the art of studied sincerity from Arthur Godfrey. In his first disc-jockey shifts at WDIA, B.B. aimed to forge the same intimate connection with African American listeners. "I spoke what I believed," he recalled, "and I would say it as I really felt it."

AMONG ALL OF B.B.'S early gigs, the most storied was an engagement in the tiny hamlet of Twist, Arkansas, in December 1949. The booking sent the bluesman forty miles northwest of Memphis to a nightclub that "isn't really a nightclub," B.B. recalled. "Just a big room in a chilly old house where the owner has set a tall garbage pail in the middle of the floor and half-filled it with kerosene for heat."

"Well, I get to playing and the room gets to rocking," he recalled, "couples get to jitterbugging, snake-hipping, and trucking, and that kerosene is burning hot. I'm up there stoking their fire—the better my beat, the bigger my tips—singing some barn-burning Pee Wee Crayton blues and having a ball. I hear some scuffling, but don't pay no mind, figuring it's only a couple of extra-happy dancers. When the voices get loud, though, I know something's wrong."

Two men at the center of the dance floor were locked in an argument that was escalating into fists. The combatants threw punches and hurled each other to the floor. Soon enough, one of them crashed into the garbage pail, knocking it over and filling the dance floor with a river of fire. Then came "screams and panic and running and everyone, including B.B. King, heading for the only door," B.B. recalled. "Bodies crushed and elbows in faces and folks falling down until everyone finally escapes into the freezing night air."

B.B. was standing within the shivering throng, gasping for breath and grateful to be alive, when he realized he had left his guitar inside. He appraised the burning structure. It would be foolish to run back in, he thought, but just as foolish to allow his guitar to burn. B.B. did not have the funds to buy another Gibson L-30.

"I look at that fire and figure I've got about one second to decide," he recalled. "I go for it. . . . Fire all around me. Heat unbearable. Burning like hell. Flames licking my feet, scorching my arms. I find the guitar, just as a beam crashes down in front of me. But I got the guitar. Grab it by the neck. Jump back over the beam just as a wall collapses, missing my ass and my guitar by a couple of inches. Can barely see the door for the all-roaring fire. Put my head down, cradling the guitar in my arms, and make a mad dash for the exit. The black night is a welcome sight. I'm burned on my legs, but the guitar is fine."

As B.B. caught his breath, he heard one patron tell another, "Damn, you wouldn't think two guys would near kill each other over a gal like Lucille." He decided, then and there, to name his guitar after the woman who had inspired the fight.

B.B. recalled that two men had died in the blaze. No news account seems to survive, but history left an eyewitness: John Francis Twist Jr., a young farmer and landowner for whose family the town was named. On a scratchy audiotape, he recalled driving home from Memphis with his wife one night to discover "a large fire" burning in the direction of their home. Twist remembered the date as "the early '50s," rather than 1949. (A subsequent historical marker would put the fire even later, in the mid-1950s.) The couple tore around hairpin turns on gravel roads toward their home, where their two babies lay in a sitter's care. Only after rounding the final turn did they see that the fire raged two miles beyond their house, at the African American boarding-house-cum-juke-joint. "A large crowd, mostly partygoers, were watching the blaze," John Twist recalled. "The house was gone."

CHAPTER 7

LUCILLE

I N A WAY, THAT NIGHT IN Twist marked the fiery dawn of the guitar era in American popular music. Up to that moment, the guitar had seldom played a starring role in any musical genre. B.B.'s heroes—jazzmen Django Reinhardt and Charlie Christian and bluesmen Lonnie Johnson and T-Bone Walker—were exceptions to the rule that relegated the guitar to the back lines of recording and performing. Singers sang, horns wailed, guitars accompanied.

On the night B.B. anthropomorphized his Gibson L-30 guitar into Lucille, he nudged popular music into the future. Where other guitarists had heard scales and chords and arpeggios, B.B. heard a voice. "I wanted to sustain a note like a singer," he recalled. "I wanted to connect my guitar to human emotions." He wanted his guitar to sound like Lonnie Johnson's. He also wanted it to sound like the full-throated tenor of Roy Brown and the silky baritone of Nat Cole.

By the time B.B. named Lucille, he had given up trying to copy other guitarists. He abandoned that quest "out of frustration, not conviction," he recalled. B.B. lacked the "chops," the basic manual dexterity, to play like Lonnie Johnson or Charlie Christian, the men who had pioneered the single-string solo. He had likewise failed to master the slide, the cylinder of metal or glass that Delta bluesmen used to animate their acoustic guitars with an angry-wasp buzz. But it is too simple to say B.B. gave up trying to play like his guitar heroes because he couldn't do it. In truth, none of them had the sound B.B. wanted, because none invested his guitar with the spirit of a human voice. At the close of the 1940s, B.B. found the final ingredient for his own guitar sound. As with so many of his musical influences, this one came from far beyond the Delta.

The six-string acoustic guitar had undergone a peculiar transformation on the islands of Hawaii, where it arrived from Europe in the nineteenth century. Hawaiian musicians, working in isolation and following an impulse for simplicity, developed a new tuning sequence for their guitars based on the notes in the A Major chord: E-A-E-A-C#-E. (A traditional guitar tuning, E-A-D-G-B-E, does not correspond to any musical chord.) Hawaiian guitarists could now produce a chord simply by strumming the open strings, and they could change chords by sliding a length of pipe over the fret board, much like their counterparts in the Delta, who also experimented with unorthodox tunings. As a final concession to ease, the Hawaiians laid the guitar across their laps. The "lap" steel worked in much the same way as the bottleneck slide of the Delta bluesman, but it yielded a sweeter, more mellifluous sound. In contrast to the rough, piercing wail of the Delta bottleneck slide, the Hawaiian lap steel produced an ethereal, flowing melody and a natural, warbling tremolo, almost as if the guitar were crying. "That cry," B.B. recalled, "sounded human to me."

Hawaiian musicians brought the lap steel to the United States, igniting a brief Hawaiian craze. The first electric stringed instrument, released in 1932 by the Electro-Patent-Instrument Company, was the A22 Frying Pan: an electrified lap steel guitar. In 1933, the Noelani Hawaiian Orchestra entered a New York studio and recorded arguably the first sides to feature an electric guitar. The lap steel swiftly colonized America's country-western genre. In 1936, Bob Wills and his Texas Playboys released "Steel Guitar Rag," a single that featured Leon McAuliffe, the band's star guitarist, on lap steel. "Kick it off, Leon," Wills cried, and McAuliffe embarked on a guitar solo for the ages, anchored by a sliding riff built around the notes of a major chord and answered by Wills's piercing yodel. The song popularized the lap steel as a showcase in country-western music.

B.B. once saw a man playing a lap steel guitar in Beale Park, and he surely heard "Steel Guitar Rag." He embraced the graceful slide work of McAuliffe and the Hawaiians. B.B. would never master the lap steel. But with his strong, thick, cotton-picking fingers, he found that he could bend and trill the strings of his own Gibson guitar to similar effect, and he could do it without a slide. He called his new technique the "Butterfly."

"I swivel my wrist from the elbow," he recalled, "back and forth, and this stretches the string, raising and lowering the pitch of the note rhythmically. With my other fingers stretched out, my whole hand makes a fluttering gesture, a bit like a butterfly flapping its wings." This was a more aggressive vibrato than the subtle, violin-styled quaver of Lonnie Johnson and Django Reinhardt, more muscular than the elegant tremolo of T-Bone Walker. Those men had taught their guitars to sing. B.B. taught Lucille to cry.

B.B. practiced his new style in earnest. He played as he spoke: slowly and deliberately, always pushing down the old stutter. "I play lazy," B.B. once explained. He experimented with the volume knobs on his guitar and amplifier to create a warm blanket of buzz called "feedback," a loop of sound between the amplifier speaker, the guitar strings, and the instrument's pickup microphone that compels the strings to vibrate on their own. Feedback allowed B.B. to sustain Lucille's cries.

B.B.'s idols had shown him how the guitar could break out of rhythmic anonymity as a solo instrument. B.B. took their experiment a step further, breathing human life into the instrument. He sang to Lucille, and Lucille sang right back to him. Music and sex had always dueled for supremacy in B.B.'s mind. In his love of the guitar, sex and song found a sort of union, an impulse that had gripped B.B. from the moment he first glimpsed Archie Fair's guitar lying on the bed in a Mississippi sharecropper cabin. His face pinched and stretched in ecstasy and pain with every note he coaxed from Lucille, visual testimony to the depth of his concentration as he labored to telegraph the sounds in his head. B.B.'s exertions inspired Martha to call her husband "Ol' Lemon Face."

"I liked seeing my guitar as a lady. I liked seeing her as someone worth fighting or even dying for. I liked giving her a name and attitude all her own," he recalled. "I sit down with Lucille. I put her on my lap and wait until some happy combination of notes falls from her mouth and makes me feel all warm inside. With the possible exception of real-life sex with a real-life woman, no one gives me peace of mind like Lucille."

From the winter of 1949 through the summer of 1950, B.B. toured all over the tristate region that encircled Memphis. By the end of that span, he had introduced his Butterfly vibrato technique in public performance.* Some credit for B.B.'s innovation must go to Robert Lockwood Jr., whose very presence in the B.B. King band allowed B.B. to focus on playing solos. Most R&B bands of that era had no guitarist at all, and surely no other Memphis band featured two. The King-Lockwood collaboration, barely noted in its day, feels in hindsight like a pop-music milestone, a prototype for the two-guitar attack that would come to define rock 'n' roll.

B.B. ceased to think of his guitar as his accompanist. He found he could no longer play a solo and sing a lyrical melody at the same time. "Both sounds—guitar and voice—were coming out of me," he recalled, "but they issued from different parts of my soul." That B.B. could not sing and play at once would become part of his legend. This was really two deficiencies, both reflecting B.B.'s deep-seated insecurity as a musician. B.B.'s inability to play solos as he sang is a universal dilemma: it is difficult, if not quite impossible, for a guitarist to improvise a solo and sing a melody at the same time. B.B.'s second problem was more reluctance than incapacity: once he started playing with bands, B.B. came to mistrust his skills as a rhythm guitarist. B.B. could play chords as he sang, but he lacked confidence as a timekeeper. So he stuck to solos. "He just didn't think he was a good background musician," recalled Ford Nelson, an early bandmate.

---

*This timing is informed by pianist Ford Nelson, who accompanied B.B. in that era and distinctly recalled B.B. playing "just straight notes" in their first months together in an interview with the author. The aural evidence of B.B.'s "Mistreated Woman" single suggests he had developed his signature vibrato by the time he entered the Sam Phillips studio in the summer of 1950.

B.B. was now a Memphis celebrity and reasonably prosperous. But profligate spending left him perpetually short of cash. Thus, he sputtered from gig to gig in a 1935 Ford coupe, a two-seater with a rumble seat and a leaky fuel tank, which compelled B.B. to store fuel in a five-gallon drum tethered to the running board. Circumstances sometimes grew so dire, he recalled, that the band dug up earthworms and caught fish for sustenance. In one story from this time, possibly apocryphal, a man appeared at the apartment where B.B. and Martha lived to repossess the draperies from their windows while Martha hectored her husband to find a real job. "Martha's disgusted, man," B.B. confided to Phineas Newborn Sr., one of his musical cohort, as he recounted the episode. He was ready to quit the music business. Newborn urged him on: "[There's] money in it," he said, "if you can ever get to it."

One night, on the road to Clarksdale, the old Ford stalled in the rain. B.B. and his bandmates grabbed their gear and ran the rest of the way. They arrived at the roadhouse and were greeted by a local boy named Izear "Ike" Turner. Just eighteen, Turner already worked at a local radio station and led his own band. Turner's long, narrow face topped a strikingly slender body, angular and edgy. Turner could not read music but possessed such a strong ear that he could learn piano and guitar parts from records and play them verbatim from memory.

"Y'all are a mess," Turner observed when B.B. and his dripping sidemen limped in. "Is this your whole band?"

"This is it," B.B. replied.

Turner sized up the ensemble and said, "I better sit in with you."

The precocious teen played with B.B.'s band that night and made them "sound a whole lot better," B.B. recalled. After the gig, Turner invited B.B. to stay for a few nights at his family's comfortable Clarksdale home. When they parted, the two young bandleaders must have known they would meet again.

BY 1950, EVERY AMBITIOUS blues musician in Memphis was vying for a chance to play on the radio with B.B. King, whose daily show placed him atop the pecking order of Memphis musicians. One was pianist Alfordson "Ford" Nelson, a Memphian who alternated with Johnny Ace in B.B.'s touring band. B.B. and his Blues Boys, as he christened the group, now ranged hundreds of miles from Memphis to play midnight gigs at remote chitlin' circuit outposts before racing back to the city for B.B.'s midday radio broadcast. "We would go out sometimes five, six, or seven nights a week, playing Tennessee, Arkansas, Missouri, Mississippi," Nelson recalled. The ensemble would meet at a Beale Street restaurant called Hamburger Heaven, devour stacks of hamburgers, and then climb into a car, sometimes with teenaged Bobby Bland at the wheel.

This was an exciting band, with the two-guitar attack of B.B. and Robert Lockwood Jr. backed by a revolving cast of sidemen: Nelson or Johnny Ace on keyboards, Herman Green or Richard Sanders on sax, and Solomon Hardy or Earl Forest on drums. (No one, oddly, played bass.) Some gigs grew so crowded that bandmates couldn't see B.B. ten feet away. "They would be dancing and responding to him," Ford Nelson recalled. "They kept knocking the guitar out of his hand." Robert Lockwood's virtuosic rhythm freed B.B. to take ever longer and more intricate solos. B.B. might collect twenty-five dollars on a good night, while the backing band could expect ten or even twenty dollars apiece. The Blues Boys once played gigs on 105 consecutive nights. It was good money but exhausting work, and the musicians had day jobs. B.B. himself briefly worked shifts driving trucks for the Memphis Furniture company.

B.B. never tired of that schedule, but Martha did. She periodically returned home to Eupora, Mississippi, and on one of those visits, she fell ill. B.B. drove down to see her. Then he raced back to Memphis for a gig. Along the way, a small-town patrolman stopped him for speeding. "By the way he spoke and looked down at me," B.B. recalled, "I could see he was a stone racist." A judge fined B.B. ninety dollars, money he didn't have. He telephoned his father. Albert listened patiently as B.B. explained his predicament. When he was finished, Albert asked, "You all right?" "Yes, sir," B.B. replied. "Then I'll see you tomorrow." He hung up. B.B. spent the night in jail. Albert arrived the next morning with the money. From then on, B.B. took great care with speed limits and police officers, especially in the South. "I thought about that [jail] every time I started to get in trouble," he recalled. "I didn't like that place."

B.B. recalled just one other spell in a cell, probably in early 1950. He was determined to make a gig in Osceola, Arkansas, an hour's drive north of Memphis, against long odds. He lacked both a car and a guitar, having just lost the original Lucille (the one he'd rescued from the fire) to, ironically, another fire, this one inside his own home. B.B.'s father reluctantly loaned him his beloved eight-cylinder Buick with the admonition, "Be careful with the car."

Herman Green, B.B.'s dignified saxophonist, knew where he could get a guitar. "B.," he said, "my father's a preacher, and he's got a guitar sitting in his church we could borrow. But we'll just have to climb through the window and take it." The two men broke into the church, snatched the guitar, and made the gig. After the group collected their pay, they climbed back into Albert King's Buick and headed for the church, hoping to break in and return the guitar. On the way, B.B.'s driver veered off the roadway to avoid another car and slammed into a bridge support. The impact left Albert's cherished eight-cylinder engine in B.B.'s lap, as he recalled. The band survived the wreck mostly unscathed, but police jailed them all. B.B. had no choice but to call his father.

B.B. explained what had happened. "You wrecked my car?" Albert asked. "Yes, sir," B.B. replied. "Anybody hurt?" "No, sir." In the silence that followed, B.B. heard his father curse under his breath. "That meant things was bad," he recalled, "worse than I thought." B.B. summoned the courage to instruct his father, "You've got to come get us." Albert showed up a short time later, retrieved his car, and helped B.B. and Herman return the borrowed guitar to the church, along with a ten-dollar bill as an offering. Albert's car was not beyond repair, a revelation that surely eased the strain in his relationship with his son.

HOWEVER LITTLE B.B.'S feeble recordings of 1949 had impressed the *Billboard* reviewers, the artist held such commercial potential in Memphis that he seemed destined to record again. As a professional courtesy,

Don Kern of WDIA sent B.B.'s debut recordings to the Bihari brothers of Los Angeles, owners of a new independent rhythm-and-blues label. By the summer of 1950, the Biharis were ready to invest in B.B. King.

Edward and Esther Bihari were Hungarian Jews who had wed in Philadelphia. Edward, a grain and seed man, suffered a fatal heart attack in 1930 while hoisting a hundred-pound sack of flour. He left Esther to raise eight children alone. She moved the family to Los Angeles and dispatched the younger children to a Jewish orphans home in New Orleans. A maintenance man at the Jewish home introduced Joe Bihari, the youngest son, to the music of Blind Lemon Jefferson. A few years later, Joe and his older brother Jules Bihari reunited in Los Angeles to work for a jukebox outfit, searching for R&B recordings to stock taverns in South-Central Los Angeles. Both were passionate R&B fans, and they noticed a scarcity of "race" recordings from the major labels. They resolved to make some of their own.

In 1945, the brothers took a chance and cut a record for Hadda Brooks, a boogie-woogie pianist they had heard at a dance studio. Joe loaded pressings of "Swingin' the Boogie" into his car and sold them at record stores to finance further pressings. They parlayed that song's success into Modern Music, one of the nation's first independent record labels, operating outside the music-industry mainstream and featuring mostly African American artists. The Biharis scored a number 1 R&B hit in 1949 with "Boogie Chillen'," from an emerging Delta-born Detroit bluesman named John Lee Hooker.

In May and June 1950, the Biharis made a series of trips to Memphis, a city as important as any in America to the kind of music they wanted to record. On one of those visits, they met B.B. King. He took an immediate liking to the Bihari family and especially to Jules, the de facto chief executive of Modern Records. Jules, thirty-six, was the brains of the Bihari outfit, a shrewd businessman who played tough but also seemed to play fair. Jules reminded B.B. of Flake Cartledge, the farmer back in Kilmichael. "He was more a buddy than a boss," B.B. recalled. "Jules didn't show the prejudice or reserve of many white men of that era. He hated segregation and paid it no mind, crossing the color line like it wasn't there. We'd go to Beale Street, hanging in clubs, listening to music, eating chili, chewing the fat. Jules gave me confidence." Jules told B.B. he was an artist with a future. No one in the music business had told him that before.

The Biharis were businessmen. Whatever future they saw in B.B. probably lay more in his rising currency as a Memphis radio celebrity than in the quality of those Bullet singles, which B.B. himself would later joke had put the label out of business.

Jules returned to Memphis in July with his brother Saul to make a record with the bluesman. Saul Bihari, younger and handsomer than Jules, was the smooth-talking salesman of Modern Records. Instead of recording again at WDIA, Jules and Saul negotiated a deal with a Memphian who had just opened a new studio.

Sam Phillips had come to Memphis from Alabama in 1945 and worked as a radio announcer and soundman. In January 1950, Phillips opened the Memphis Recording Service on Union Avenue. He was twenty-seven but looked younger, with angular, bushy eyebrows framing manic eyes. A frozen wave of red hair that no pomade could tame swept up from the left side of his freckled face. The young producer's plan was to record the amateur talent buzzing around Memphis and sell the recordings to record labels, but most of his initial profits came from recording weddings and funerals. He met the Biharis on one of their Memphis visits and agreed to let them record B.B. in his studio in exchange for a cut of the royalties when the records came out.

The first B.B. King session was set for late July 1950. B.B. arrived at the Sam Phillips studio with Tuff Green's combo: child prodigy Phineas Newborn Jr. on piano, Phineas Sr. on drums, and Tuff on bass. Phillips himself served as engineer. In the twelve months since B.B.'s last recordings, he had played hundreds of gigs, practiced for countless hours in his home, and synthesized the sounds of his idols into a sound of his own. The hard work showed: on the first singles he recorded with Phillips, B.B. sounded transformed. He could now march in time with the bass and drums, no longer leading his sidemen off a musical cliff.

The real revelation here was Lucille. She opened "B.B. Boogie" with a stabbing riff, then descended into a jazz-swing solo that glided up and down the blues scale, dazzling the ears with a sprinkling of grace notes—swift, polyrhythmic melodic flourishes wedged between the beats, a tradition passed down from Bach to Louis Armstrong to Charlie Christian to B.B.* More marvels unfolded: Lucille paused on the second note of the scale, and then B.B. bent her string to raise the pitch to a flatted third and held it there for a breathless moment. Several bars later, B.B. hit two of Lucille's strings together, ringing a dissonant dyad—and then he bent the higher string a half step upward, resolving the jarring harmony into a perfect jazz interval. Throughout the remainder of the song, B.B. slashed away at two- and three-note chords, some of them simple blues triads, others complex jazz derivatives. This was not the same guitarist who had stumbled through "Miss Martha King" a year earlier.

B.B.'s playing on "B.B. Boogie" was a revelation, but the flip side may be the more historic track. On "Mistreated Woman," B.B. introduced his signature vibrato to the record-buying public. Midway through the nearly three-minute song, B.B. unleashed a soaring, remarkably loud and lyrical solo on Lucille. At the end of each two-bar melodic passage, he settled back to the root note of the blues scale. He held that note for two or three bars, whipping his wrist up and down to create Lucille's distinctive, stinging tremolo. His sound was the angry snarl of an electric guitar in overdrive. Several of B.B.'s idols had employed vibrato, but it had never sounded quite like this.

Decades later, amid lingering confusion over the primacy of B.B.'s approach, an interviewer from *Guitar Player* magazine asked the guitarist, bluntly and directly, whether he had indeed invented it. "Let's put it this way," B.B. replied. "I won't say I invented it, but they weren't doing it before I started." Then he laughed.

But Sam Phillips was torn on B.B.'s merits as a recording artist. By one account, the young engineer thought B.B.'s blues "too conventional,

---

*The guitar work on this performance is so accomplished that some archivists have questioned whether it is B.B.'s. Some believe the guitar on "B.B. Boogie" was played by Calvin Newborn, of the musical Newborns. B.B. denied it. If Newborn played lead, then we must accept that B.B. played no guitar at all on these sides, because only one guitar can be heard. And if you take the guitar out of his hands here, when do you give it back?

too *predictable*, too much along the lines of what every other popular blues shouter of the day was inclined to do." The irony here, of course, is that B.B. and his guitar were about to change the direction of popular music. Phillips seems to have missed that point entirely: he regarded B.B. primarily as a singer. But Phillips was not blind to B.B.'s promise. Beneath the bluesman's deep-seated shyness and enduring stammer, Phillips sensed "a burning ambition, a need to have not just Memphis and Mississippi but the world know of him." Not for nothing did Phillips later term B.B. "a black Elvis."

Jules Bihari flew back to Los Angeles within hours of completing B.B.'s new recordings, telling Phillips he would waste no time in putting out a single. Smooth Saul Bihari stayed in Memphis. He told Phillips he and B.B. would return to the Union Avenue studio the next day to sign a deal. B.B. would remain under contract to the Biharis, but Phillips would claim a share of the royalties and some stake in the artist's future.

Yet, when Saul arrived at the studio the next day, he was alone. He told Phillips that he had already signed B.B. to a contract and that Jules, the boss, would be in touch. Phillips "protested vehemently," but Saul politely demurred, saying the decision was not his. Some days later, Jules telephoned from Los Angeles and told Phillips icily that the deal was off. The Biharis would pay Phillips for his studio time, but B.B. King would remain under the sole artistic and financial control of the Biharis. Phillips exploded in anger, but there was little he could do: he had nothing in writing.

B.B.'s first single with the Biharis, "Mistreated Woman" backed with "B.B. Boogie," emerged in September on a new Modern Records subsidiary called RPM Records. The 45-rpm format had just appeared, and the acronym loomed large in the public consciousness. The label billed B.B. as "singing star of station WDIA Memphis." *Billboard* awarded the songs seventy-one and sixty-six points, respectively, in a pair of capsule reviews that ignored the guitar work on both songs. "High-pitched warbler does okay," the reviewer wrote. Many years would pass before B.B. King was recognized, let alone celebrated, for his guitar.

One reason for B.B.'s vast improvement as a guitarist on the 1950s singles was his year-old apprenticeship to Robert Lockwood Jr., the virtuoso guitarist and mentor. B.B. had learned to keep time, hear jazz chords, and play along with other musicians, all thanks to Lockwood. "He taught me how to be a musician," B.B. recalled. "Not a blues musician, not a jazz musician, just a musician." Sometime in 1950, that partnership ended. Lockwood traveled north to Chicago, where he would become a valued session musician and sideman.

Another possible factor in B.B.'s technical leap was his new guitar. B.B. had purchased a Fender Esquire, the first mass-marketed electric guitar with a solid body. Leo Fender's design completed the guitar's evolution away from its acoustic origins. The Esquire was tailored explicitly for an emerging breed of "lead" guitarist: slender, lightweight, and durable, easier to hold and to play than its hollow-bodied predecessors. Up to that point, most guitars had been crafted with large, symmetrical tops to boost their natural amplification. In the amplifier age, there was no need for such bulk. Fender carved out a slice of the guitar's body—a modification now termed a "cutaway"—so that players could reach ever higher up the fret board while playing single-string solos.

Blues-guitar aficionados will recoil at the image of B.B. King playing anything other than the lovely, hollow-bodied Gibson guitars with which he is inextricably linked. But in the early years of his fame, B.B. had not yet settled on a single make or model of guitar. And all of B.B.'s early instruments were eventually stolen or lost, leading him to regard guitars as interchangeable. "In those days, it was hard to keep a good guitar," he recalled, "so I played anything I could get. . . . I had a Fender, a Gretsch, a Silvertone and a Gibson." Given a choice, though, the B.B. King of this era favored the Fender Esquire.

ONE NIGHT in February or March 1951, Ike Turner was driving back to Clarksdale from a gig with his band when he came upon a mass of cars parked outside a roadhouse and a sign announcing that night's performer as B.B. King. Turner walked into the club and found B.B. At their last meeting, Turner had sat in with B.B.'s band as a favor. Now, Turner asked B.B. if his band could play a song. B.B. agreed, and, by Turner's account, the Kings of Rhythm "tore the house down." At night's end,

B.B. told Turner, "Y'all got a good group. Have you ever made any recordings?" Turner, still a teenager, confessed to B.B. that he didn't know how. B.B. replied, "I think I can set up a recording for you in Memphis with Sam Phillips." He told Turner to show up at Sam's studio around 10 a.m. on the next Wednesday.

B.B. turned up at the Memphis Recording Service studio shortly after Turner and his band. He pulled Phillips aside to tell the producer what he had heard at the club. At this session, Phillips was about to hear something else altogether. On the way to the studio, someone in Turner's band had dropped a guitar amp. When the guitarist plugged in, the amp produced a horrible rasp. Everyone was deflated—except Phillips. He told the band the guitar would sound "different," in a good way. He ran out to find brown wrapping paper to wad up inside the cabinet as a mute. Turner didn't know quite what to make of the frenetic young producer, and he didn't really care. "All I could picture was B.B.'s picture being tacked up on the posters," Turner recalled. "That's the next thing I was gonna be."

The session yielded "Rocket 88," a song later claimed by Phillips as the first true rock 'n' roll single. Its distinctive quality lay in the sonic interplay between the saxophone and the oddly distorted guitar, which doubled the bass part through most of the song before briefly harmonizing with the horns at the end. Just as Phillips had predicted, it sounded like nothing that had been recorded before. The song rocketed to the top of the rhythm-and-blues chart, establishing Phillips as a major producer.

IN APRIL 1951, WDIA lost one of its stars. "Hot Rod" Hulbert decamped to radio station WITH in Baltimore. His exit left an opening for host of his three o'clock daily show, *Sepia Swing Club*. Bert Ferguson awarded it to B.B., who, after two years at WDIA, finally became a regular deejay with a weekly salary. The distinction is more important than it sounds. With his fifteen-minute slots singing the blues and hawking Pep-ti-kon, B.B. had enjoyed growing fame in juke joints around Memphis. But he had not been recognized, let alone embraced, by the city's larger African

American community, the rarified world of black-tie charity balls and award dinners. By the spring of 1951, B.B. ruled the roadhouses, but he had not been mentioned in any news article or column in the African American press in Memphis or anyplace else. He had not attained the civic currency of fellow deejays Nat and A. C. "Moohah" Williams, both established Memphis celebrities with newspaper columns of their own. All of that was about to change.

B.B.'s first singles on Modern Records sold well around Memphis but failed to chart nationally. The Bihari brothers, still trolling for a hit, sent B.B. back to the Memphis Recording Service several times between the fall of 1950 and spring of 1951. The rift with Sam Phillips over B.B.'s contract quietly faded: Phillips needed their business. Affable Joe Bihari, at twenty-five the youngest of the Bihari boys, supervised a session in May 1951. B.B.'s backing band included the full Newborn family: Phineas Sr. on drums, Phineas Jr. on piano, and younger brother Calvin a new presence on second guitar, with other musicians supplying bass and horns.

The single Joe Bihari culled from this date was a cover of a rollicking boogie-woogie number by the Chicago blues guitarist Tampa Red, titled "She's Dynamite" and chosen for its commercial promise. B.B.'s recording, like Tampa Red's original, was prototypical rock 'n' roll, anchored by a galloping boogie-woogie bass line, doubled on piano, and adorned with stabbing, two-string guitar bursts and tinkling piano triplets. The production hummed with overdrive. B.B. sang with abandon, capturing the sensuality of Tampa Red's lyric. No one could fail to divine the meaning of the raucous refrain, celebrating a lover who "knows what to do" and "knows what it's all about." Sam Phillips harbored high hopes and dispatched the single to several deejays. But the *Billboard* reviewer dismissed "She's Dynamite" as "ordinary." The song appeared on a few local charts, but it made no mark on the national stage.

B.B.'s Modern Records singles weren't selling well, but his career as a disc jockey stood in full flower. In October 1951, "Gatemouth" Moore departed WDIA for a new African American radio station in Birmingham. Once again, the beneficiary was B.B., who took Moore's prized 1 p.m. slot with a new show titled *Bee Bee's Jeebies*. Lucky Strike cigarettes bought time on B.B.'s shows, making him WDIA's first African American personality with a national sponsor. B.B. made a credible Lucky Strike pitchman, being a smoker himself, even if the product he now touted was far worse for one's health than Pep-ti-kon. In November, the radio station put B.B.'s face atop a display ad in the *Tri-State Defender*, a new weekly newspaper for the African American population of Memphis and environs, for its annual Goodwill Revue, a Christmastime fundraiser for the city's Black community. B.B.'s currency was rising.

"You know, I've watched that boy go up the ladder, from just a 5-minute [*sic*] segment on Nat's *Jamboree* to where he now has a series of programs all his own, and every one a hit," wrote A. C. "Moohah" Williams, B.B.'s fellow deejay, in his column for the *Tri-State Defender*. "I've tried to figure what makes him click . . . and I've come to the conclusion. . . . The reason B.B. is banging at the top of nearly every Hooper Rating is his all-fired SINCERITY." Hooper Ratings measured a radio program's listening audience, and the latest numbers revealed B.B. as a bona fide Memphis radio star. His close study of Arthur Godfrey had paid off.

B.B. had now cut several strong singles with Sam Phillips and the Bihari brothers. Had their collaboration continued, who knows what direction B.B.'s career might have taken. But in 1951, Sam and the Biharis fell out for good. This time, Phillips betrayed the Biharis. The brothers had the right of first refusal on everything Phillips recorded. That spring, Phillips sold the master of "Rocket 88" to a rival record maker from Chicago, Leonard Chess. The Biharis felt double-crossed.

The Chess brothers already controlled Chicago's greatest bluesman, Muddy Waters. Now they sought to corner the market on Chicago blues, most of which was really Mississippi blues, by way of Memphis. Phillips gave the Chess brothers both "Rocket 88" and Howlin' Wolf, who migrated north after making his name as a West Memphis deejay. Wolf's Chess debut, "How Many More Years," emerged in August 1951 and further redefined the Chicago sound.

Sam Phillips had no contractual power over B.B., so the rising star of Memphis blues remained in Memphis, out of the clutches of Chess. The Biharis set about finding new studio space for B.B.'s next session. They settled on the "colored" YMCA—conveniently, a block away from the rooming house where B.B. and Martha now lived. Joe Bihari rented a room at the Y for the September 1951 recording date and drove over with a Magnecord reel-to-reel tape machine in his car. He hung blankets over the windows to mask the sounds of passing cars.

Many men have claimed to have played at the Memphis Y that day: success, it is said, has many fathers. Hank Crawford, a teenager destined for jazz stardom, might or might not have played sax on B.B.'s session, possibly joined by Fred "Sweet Daddy Goodlow" Ford or Evelyn "Mama Nuts" Young or Ben Branch or Richard Sanders or Adolph "Billy" Duncan—but surely not by all of them. Bandleader Tuff Green might have handled the crucial bass part, or perhaps it was James "Shinny" Walker. Willie Mitchell, bound for fame as Al Green's producer, might have played trumpet. Either Earl Forest, Phineas Newborn Sr., or Ted Curry manned the drums. Calvin Newborn might have provided a second guitar. If memories seem fuzzy, that is partly because Joe Bihari was recording several artists that day: the corridors of the Y hummed like a Memphis blues convention.

The song chosen for B.B.'s session was "3 O'Clock Blues," a 1948 hit for Lowell Fulson, a West Coast blues guitarist. B.B. had the single on heavy rotation on *Sepia Swing Club*. Fulson rewarded the deejay by allowing him to record it. B.B. set out to put his own stamp of sincere intensity on Fulson's song, whose lyrics "start out as an insomniac's lament, but end up with a weepy farewell more suited to a suicide note." It seemed perfect for B.B.'s emerging vocal style, fervent, intimate, and intense. But after the first take of "3 O'Clock Blues," Joe Bihari recalled, "nothing was happening. It was just not working." Joe called a fifteen-minute break. Part of the problem was the pianist, whom Joe recalled as young Phineas Newborn. Joe found his playing too jazzy: this song needed a blues beat. During the break, Joe heard someone playing the very piano part he imagined. He ran back into the recording room, shouting, "That's what I want!" and found Ike Turner sitting at the piano. Joe hired Turner on the spot and sent Phineas Newborn home.

Joe tried a second take, and the song came together. "3 O'Clock Blues" was the first recording to showcase B.B. and Lucille in equal measure. It was also the first to feature both his voice and guitar high above the rest of the mix, if "mix" is the right word for a recording made on a monaural reel-to-reel tape recorder. Sam Phillips and his engineers had given plenty of space to B.B.'s voice but less to Lucille's. No one in B.B.'s entourage had given him much credit as a guitarist. Now, at last, B.B. and Lucille stood front and center in a recording, commanding the listener's attention. Lucille opened the song with a long, confident run of emotive notes. The horns fell into place as B.B. began to sing, marching along like a funeral procession. "Three o'clock in the morning," he lamented, "can't even close my eyes." Lucille wailed a wordless reply. Ike Turner's barroom piano tinkled in the background, combining with the dirge-like horns to weave a chilly veil of suspense.

"3 O'Clock Blues" was a triumph both for Lucille and for B.B., whose warmth and humanity finally prevailed over his native reticence on disc. Perhaps his newfound success as a deejay had loosened him up. As B.B. concluded the second verse, vowing to go down to the boilin' ground if he couldn't find his baby, he retreated into his speaking voice, just like Charley Patton of old, to comment on what he had just sung: "That's where the mens hang out at." His commentary rolled on as Lucille proceeded into an emphatic solo. He punctuated her forceful licks with cries of "Yeah!" and "Come out, baby!" The solo was simple and tasteful and masterful. Some of Lucille's velvety phrases ended in long, sustained tones, drenched in vibrato. Others just stopped, as if B.B.'s guitar were catching her breath. B.B. erred only on the song's final chord, which he played a half step too high. Tape was expensive, so Joe Bihari didn't bother with another take. The rest of the performance was breathtaking. For all of Sam Phillips's genius, the youngest Bihari brother had finally coaxed greatness from B.B. King.

"When I got back to California," Joe recalled, "I listened to it, and I knew we had a hit record then."

CHAPTER 8

ON THE ROAD

3 O'CLOCK BLUES" entered the *Billboard* charts in the penultimate week of 1951, at number 6. Someone seized the momentum to book B.B. into a January 14 showcase at the city auditorium in Atlanta, as far from Memphis as B.B. had traveled. An ad in the African American *Atlanta Daily World* touted B.B. as "No. 1 Blues Singer" on a bill topped by doo-wop group the Clovers, whose "Fool, Fool, Fool" had just scaled the charts. "3 O'Clock Blues" faded to number 8 in early January, suggesting that it had already peaked. But then it rebounded to number 5, and then to number 2, just behind "Weepin' & Cryin'," a maudlin ballad by Tommy Brown and the Griffin Brothers that featured actual recorded sobs. Finally, in the week of January 25, 1952, "3 O'Clock Blues" reached number 1.

Guitarists had topped the *Billboard* R&B chart only rarely since its 1942 inception. Lonnie Johnson, B.B.'s hero, had held the number 1 spot for seven weeks in 1948 with a strummed acoustic ballad titled "Tomorrow Night." Later that year, Pee Wee Crayton, B.B.'s stablemate at Modern Records, topped the chart with "Blues After Hours." John Lee Hooker, another Modern artist, hit number 1 with "Boogie Chillen'" in 1949 and again with "I'm in the Mood" in 1951. Lowell Fulson, author of "3 O'Clock Blues," scored with "Blue Shadows" in 1950. A rare female guitarist, Sister Rosetta Tharpe, just missed the top in 1945 with her crossover hit "Strange Things Happening Every Day."

B.B. and his guitar had the attention of the music industry. "For the first time in many months," *Billboard* noted in February 1952, "the down-home, Southern-style blues appears to have taken a solid hold in the current rhythm and blues record market." The writer named B.B. King among Delta artists with recent hits, including Howlin' Wolf, Muddy Waters, and John Lee Hooker. "Even the sophisticated big towns, like New York and Chicago, have felt the Southern blues influence in wax tastes."

B.B.'s hit slipped from the top of the charts in March, after six consecutive weeks at number 1, but he was now a big name. Offers poured in from booking agents up north. The likes of Sunbeam Mitchell and Bert Ferguson would be no help in mapping and managing a cross-country tour. B.B. approached Robert Henry, the Beale Street gangster-entrepreneur who had booked some of his local gigs, and asked for his help.

In March 1952, Robert Henry became B.B.'s first manager, marshaling the ascendant bluesman's career in exchange for a larger share, perhaps 15 percent, of B.B.'s future earnings. Henry touted the partnership in the March 29 edition of the *Tri-State Defender*. The article brimmed with hyperbole and blather, apprising Black Memphians that B.B. had been orphaned at age three and raised by a "God-fearing uncle." Henry painted himself as a benevolent Svengali: "Acting on a tip, Riley searched out the veteran Memphis showman, Robert Henry. He found the friend of struggling artists one wet and dreary afternoon in Memphis, and soaking wet with drenched guitar, Riley sought his help."

Henry arranged for B.B. to sign a six-month contract with Universal Attractions, a New York booking agency. The firm packaged B.B. into a showcase, a touring company of artists who would take the stage and sing three or four songs each, backed by a single band. The company featured two headliners, saxophonist Tab Smith and the great, clownish bandleader Myron Carlton "Tiny" Bradshaw. B.B. sat well down the bill, pigeonholed into a two-way "battle of the blues" against another ascendant singer, Robert Percell "H-Bomb" Ferguson. Joining the tour meant B.B. had to drop his own touring band. He left the Blues Boys in the care of his piano player, Johnny Ace.

B.B. took leave of his deejay job at WDIA for the duration of the tour, a span dictated by the shelf life of his hit. Bert Ferguson found creative ways to keep him on the air in his absence. B.B.'s *Sepia Swing*

Club passed to Rufus Thomas, the tap-dancing comedian. *Bee Bee's Jeebies* gave way to *Wheelin' on Beale*, hosted by A. C. "Moohah" Williams. But B.B. did not relinquish the fifteen-minute music spots for which he was best known. Instead, station hands stockpiled dozens of new segments and played them back, "live," at the appointed hour, hoping listeners would never know.

In March 1952, B.B. boarded his first airplane, bound for Washington, DC. He somehow fell asleep en route and awoke as the plane was banking low across the Potomac River. B.B. feared the aircraft was going down. He curbed an impulse to run to the cockpit and warn the pilot. His destination was the Howard Theatre, an icon of the chitlin' circuit, a stage previously graced by Duke Ellington.

FIVE GRAND PALACES RULED the chitlin' circuit: the Howard in Washington, the Regal in Chicago, the Royal in Baltimore, the Uptown in Philadelphia, and the Apollo in New York. The circuit took shape along the route of the Great Migration, a northward and westward march of six million African Americans that reshaped both Black and urban America. In 1910, nine African Americans in ten lived in the South. The exodus commenced around 1915, when droves of African American families left tobacco farms and cotton plantations for better-paying industrial jobs in Chicago and Detroit, New York and Philadelphia, repelled from the South by decades of Jim Crow inequity. "At one point," journalist Isabel Wilkerson writes, "ten thousand were arriving every month in Chicago," the address adopted by Mississippians Muddy Waters and Howlin' Wolf. Between 1910 and 1950, the share of African Americans remaining in southern states plummeted from 89 percent to 68 percent. Weary of whites-only signs and "colored" schools, Klan rallies and lynchings, the migrants voted with their feet. "It was the first big step the nation's servant class ever took without asking."

B.B. did not follow Wolf and Muddy to Chicago: his was not a linear path. Instead of settling for one northern city, B.B. would visit them all, over and over again, for the rest of his life.

* * *

BEFORE THE WASHINGTON TRIP, Robert Henry had taken B.B. to a Beale Street tailor for a new wardrobe. They had picked out two custom suits in lavender-blue and red, two pairs of matching leather shoes, and a red and black shirt festooned with flowers. B.B. previewed the colorful outfits for Jesse "Tiny" Kennedy, an enormous, ironically nicknamed singer in Tiny Bradshaw's touring band who had been appointed to chaperone B.B. (The nickname better fit the slender Bradshaw.)

"Goddamn," Kennedy said, shaking his head in dismay. "You can't wear this shit." Kennedy took B.B. to another tailor and helped him pick out a classy black-and-white ensemble with dinner jacket and bow tie.

Next, Kennedy asked B.B. about arrangements. A musical arranger writes sheet-music "charts" for a song, assigning melody, harmonies, and rhythmic flourishes to each piece in an ensemble. The parts fit together like a puzzle. Adding or subtracting musicians seeds chaos. Kennedy played for an eighteen-piece swing band. B.B. showed Kennedy his chart for "3 O'Clock Blues," written for six pieces. "Won't work," Kennedy said. "This is a big band. You need a big-band chart."

"Where do I get one?" B.B. asked.

"At the liquor store," Kennedy replied. He explained that B.B. would have to approach the musicians in Tiny Bradshaw's band who wrote arrangements. The negotiation would go better if B.B. plied them with Scotch. B.B. procured the Scotch and presented it to Kennedy's bandmates, who delivered a fine arrangement. The showcase opened at the Howard on a wintry Friday, March 7, 1952. B.B. triumphed, with the band at his back. He had learned a lesson lost on his costar, H-Bomb Ferguson, a cocky young performer who failed to curry favor with the band. In retribution, B.B. recalled, the musicians "played in keys that gave him fits." H-Bomb bombed.

One night during the stand at the Howard, B.B. met a young woman who invited him back to her home. Before the couple disrobed for bed, the woman produced a cache of heroin paraphernalia and announced that she was going to shoot up. B.B. couldn't watch: he hated needles. She persuaded B.B., against his better judgment, to join her: "It'll make you feel good." Within seconds after the drug entered B.B.'s bloodstream, he fell violently ill. He showed up for his nightly gig with his fly unzipped and no socks on his feet. B.B.'s chaperone realized immediately what had happened.

"That shit will kill you," Kennedy admonished. "And if it don't kill you, it'll turn you into a raggedy-ass junkie like her. You better check whether you got outta there with your rings and watch." B.B. discovered his watch was gone. He never did hard drugs again.

The showcase proceeded to Baltimore for a stand at the Royal Theatre, another fixture on the chitlin' circuit. In April, B.B. and H-Bomb Ferguson split off to headline their own smaller revue, joined by sundry comedians and tap-dancers. They played one-nighters at the 81 Theatre in Atlanta and the Lyric in Lexington, Kentucky. An item in the African American *Atlanta Daily World* of April 12 pictured B.B. with his Fender Jaguar and billed him as "the nation's newest singing sensation," making no mention of the guitar.

BARRELS OF INK would later be spilled about the roots of B.B.'s guitar sound. Less would be written on his voice, which was the wellspring of his initial fame. B.B. recalled drawing vocal inspiration from Nat Cole, the jazz balladeer who sang in big, round notes that appealed to listeners Black and white; from the prototypical rock 'n' roll stylings of Wynonie Harris; and from Louis Jordan, the campy jump-blues bandleader who sang with the syncopated snap of a saxophone. (Jump blues was an up-tempo style delivered by small, horn-heavy acts.) But B.B.'s overarching vocal influence was a former choirboy and welterweight boxer named Roy Brown. Had B.B.'s career ended after "3 O'Clock Blues," he might have been remembered as one in a succession of promising Roy Brown imitators.

All but forgotten today, Roy Brown scored thirteen top-ten R&B hits between 1947 and 1951, and he wrote the jump-blues classic "Good Rocking Tonight." Born in Louisiana, Brown found his calling when he won a song contest by singing an old Bing Crosby standard. He was six feet tall, with a slender build and a rounded face topped by a crown of processed hair. His sweet, insistent tenor retained traces of both the choirboy and the boxer. Brown brought gospel's swooping, melismatic style to the blues idiom. He would slide up to the first note of each vocal line. At the end of the phrase, he would slide up even higher in a piercing cry, an electrifying flourish that kept his audience in hysterics. He sang with the syncopated punch of Black rhythm and blues but with the round vowels and crisp enunciation of white pop, always with a plaintive clench in his voice. "He had a big-throated, full-throttle way of singing, and a vibrato that went right through me," B.B. recalled. "As a singer, he had balls."

One irresistible Roy Brown single from 1951 opened with his glorious, unaccompanied tenor: "I met a fine beautician," he proclaimed, "in a very fine condition." The band cried "Yeah!" at the end of each line. B.B. loved this sort of genteel ribaldry. He would cover "Beautician Blues" a decade later. Brown's song clearly informed B.B.'s own up-tempo blues sides. But Brown's work also sounds in hindsight like early rock 'n' roll. His melodies provided a template for the white rock 'n' roll classics "Rock Around the Clock" and "Blue Suede Shoes," and his churning piano rhythms would influence "Tutti Frutti" and "Great Balls of Fire."

B.B.'S FIRST UNIVERSAL ATTRACTIONS tour paid a stratospheric $2,500 a week. After that, his regular weekly pay ranged from $1,000 to $2,000. He frittered most of it away. "I bought some jewelry, got a ring with B.B. set in diamonds, made money, lost money on gambling, pawned jewelry, stopped gambling, got the jewelry out of hock, and started all over again," he recalled. "Bought me a white Cadillac and always put up a good front."

B.B. bought a new home for Albert, his father, a three-bedroom dwelling on Hubert Avenue in Memphis. He spent freely on wine, women, and gambling. He thought nothing of extending a hundred-dollar loan to an old friend from the Newberry Equipment factory. (The unnamed "friend" might have been cousin Bukka.) B.B. was in no hurry to collect on the loan and grew perplexed when the borrower avoided him. He finally approached Robert Henry, one of his few well-heeled associates, and asked his advice. Henry explained that a hundred dollars was twice what B.B.'s friend earned in a week. "That kind of loan puts him in another place," he told B.B. "If you really like the person, just give him the money." B.B. followed that advice for the rest of his life.

For all his newfound wealth, B.B. still found himself frequently falling into debt. Once, during a front-porch chat with his father, B.B. remarked, "For all this work I'm doing, seems like I'm just living day to day."

"Heard you been gambling," Albert replied flatly. "That true?"

"Yes, sir."

"You make money gambling?" Albert asked his son.

"No, sir."

"You make money with your music?"

"Yes, sir."

B.B. waited for his father to continue, but he had already made his point. That was how Albert communicated with his son, in occasional, terse, enigmatic observations that stopped short of rendering actual advice or declaratory judgment.

At first, B.B. didn't lose much when he gambled, because he didn't earn much. By 1952, B.B. was a high roller. The gambling habit became the costliest of his many vices. Until he found a way to kick it, B.B. would live from paycheck to paycheck, no matter how large the checks.

Desperate to impress his father, B.B. worked harder than ever. At one point during his six-month tenure with Universal Attractions, B.B. recalled playing sixty gigs on consecutive nights in different cities. On a rare breather, he took his father to the ball field at Russwood Park to watch the Memphis Chicks, his hometown minor-league baseball team. Between bites of a hot dog, B.B. mused, "I'm wondering if I'm working too much."

"Work too much?" his father replied. "I don't know what that means. How can a man work too much?" For the rest of the game, apart from cursing the umpire, Albert said nothing.

B.B. was back on the road in mid-1952 when word reached him that Martha had left Memphis and planned to file for divorce. B.B.'s lengthy absences had laid the final straw. Both partners had tormented themselves with thoughts of infidelity. Martha had a waitress job and was learning to get along without her husband. B.B. appealed for help to Delcia Davis, wife of his cousin Birkett, who loved Martha like a sister. "She says I'm liking too many women," he pleaded to Delcia. "I ain't liking so many women."

Delcia urged Martha to reconsider. "Girl, why you leaving?" she asked.

"'Cause he won't stay home," Martha replied. "He's playing, going everywhere."

"B.B. can't help all those women liking him," Delcia countered. "His playing is good. Girl, you crazy. You should stay with your husband."

Martha did not.

"Maybe it would have been different if we had had children," B.B. mused in his memoir, "or maybe it would have ended just the same. There was more disappointment than bitterness. I still loved her and cherished her ways. But I couldn't stay home and, as our disagreements increased, I couldn't stay faithful."

Martha would remarry one of B.B.'s distant relatives and bear seven children, bolstering the case that B.B. was solely responsible for their failure to conceive.

Nonetheless, bad love made good blues. B.B. chronicled the death of his marriage in a succession of RPM singles released in the spring and summer of 1952. B.B. rejected his lover in "She Don't Move Me No More," issued in April as a follow-up to "3 O'Clock Blues" and similar in dirge-like cadence. He descended into a muddle of regret, anger, and self-blame in "My Own Fault, Darlin'," issued in May. This sloppy, passionate performance, based on a Muddy Waters single of the previous year, pointed squarely to the future of the electric guitar in popular music. B.B. turned his guitar and amplifier all the way up, yielding perhaps the loudest, angriest snarl yet committed to acetate. Lucille dominated the song from her opening two-string riff, punctuating each melodic phrase with a ringing vibrato that channeled all the anger and pain of broken love. B.B. sounded close to tears, and possibly drunk, as he careened up and down his vocal register, his aching falsetto climbing toward the heavens as he sang of romantic resignation. B.B. became so absorbed in the song that he forgot his backing band, pushing the musicians into a round of jazz-like improvisation behind him. Lucille's solo brimmed with violence and menace: B.B. slashed the strings with such force that he occasionally struck two at once.

B.B.'s next major single, "You Know I Love You," moved from rage and recrimination to wistful acceptance. He had sobered up, settled down, and collected himself in a mournful blues shuffle about a lover who's "gone and left me for someone else." Released in August, "You Know I Love You" stalled at the number 2 spot in the *Billboard* R&B chart for several weeks—held off by "My Song," the debut of Johnny Ace, B.B.'s old piano player, backed by the Beale Streeters, his former band. Finally, in November, "You Know I Love You" reached number 1.

B.B.'s second number 1 hit proved the first had been no fluke. His New York agents happily extended his contract beyond the probationary six months. By the late summer of 1952, however, B.B. himself was souring on the arrangement. The traveling showcase had sent B.B. all over the Midwest and South, west to Oklahoma and north to Cleveland. He had shared a bill with Ray Charles, the brilliant, blind young singer. He had met Antoine "Fats" Domino, a boogie-woogie pianist whose 1949 single "The Fat Man" would be cited among the first million-selling rock 'n' roll records. But the showcase lineups were erratic, and so were the backing bands. As the novelty of B.B.'s first hit wore off, he sensed diminishing returns.

He approached Bill Harvey, a sax man who led the house band at Sunbeam Mitchell's Beale Street hotel. Harvey was "the George Washington of Memphis musicians," B.B. recalled: a gifted tenor saxophonist, bandleader, musical arranger, and talent scout. After weekend gigs, B.B. would sometimes unwind with Harvey's band at the Mitchell Hotel. Harvey had big, expressive eyes, a ready smile, and a fondness for drink, which would be his undoing. B.B. was now an artist of sufficient stature to tap Harvey as his bandleader. Harvey agreed, and at summer's end, B.B. hired Harvey's swing orchestra as his road band.

B.B. and Harvey raided the jazz band at Manassas High School, an illustrious African American institution in Memphis whose student ensembles recorded professionally under the tutelage of the program's founder, Jimmie Lunceford. One of the first Manassas students to play with B.B. was George Coleman, a teenaged saxophone prodigy. Charles Lloyd, three years younger than Coleman, joined up a year or two later. Both men went on to long careers as jazz recording artists. Their very presence in B.B.'s band set him further apart from Muddy and Wolf and the other electrified country bluesmen.

B.B. now hired his first employee who was not a musician. One night, out on the road, B.B. lost control of the station wagon he was driving. The wagon veered off the road and flipped over. B.B. escaped without serious injury but decided it was time to enlist a full-time driver.

B.B. had often prevailed on others to do his driving, particularly Bobby Bland, the younger Memphis singer who idolized B.B. and yearned to replicate his fame. But Bland had a nascent recording career of his own. So B.B. approached Cato Walker Jr., a railroad porter with a knack for vehicular repair. Cato quit his railroad job and joined B.B. on the road.

Late in 1952, an executive of Lucky Strike cigarettes stopped by the WDIA offices in Memphis for an unannounced visit to check up on the program his company was sponsoring. B.B.'s show blared over the studio speakers, but B.B. was nowhere in sight: the studio sat empty. Lucky Strike was paying for live broadcasts, not taped reruns. The company pulled its support, and the station arranged an amicable parting with its biggest star. B.B. thus bade a reluctant farewell to WDIA, the radio station that had seeded his stardom.

"It was hard for us Kings to quit *any* paying gig," B.B. recalled, alluding to his father. But Riley King's pilgrimage to WDIA on that rainy morning in March 1949 had paid off handsomely. B.B. King had literally made his name at the upstart radio station. The station had also launched B.B.'s recording career, and the recordings had made him a national star.

HOUSTON, TEXAS, a bustling regional capital of blues and jazz, became a sort of second home to B.B. in the 1950s. One night in early November 1952, B.B. crossed paths there with Dizzy Gillespie and Charlie "Bird" Parker, men he knew by reputation as the greatest jazz artists of the celebrated "bop" movement. The pair were in town with a traveling jazz show that also featured Nat Cole, bandleader Stan Kenton, and singer Sarah Vaughan, a tour justly billed as "The Biggest Show of '52." For B.B. to happen upon them all was no great coincidence: everyone stayed in the same segregated hotel. Gillespie told B.B. he liked "3 O'Clock Blues," B.B. recalled, "and that made me feel like a million bucks." They shared stories of farm life. Gillespie confided that he was worried about getting the mercurial Bird to the auditorium. B.B. was honored to offer a ride.

"Charlie Parker was a handsome man who spoke like a professor and smiled like a saint," B.B. recalled. "I'd heard the stories about drugs. But I didn't see any drugs, not that day. Bird was clear-eyed and well-mannered and treated me with so much respect, I felt humble." B.B. told Parker of watching him play through a peephole at Jones' Night Spot in Indianola, a decade earlier. Bird smiled. "I'm a blues player, B.," he told B.B. "We're all blues players. It's just that we hear blues in different ways. The day we get away from blues is the day we'll stop making sense." Later on, as Bird's legend swelled, B.B. came to view the meeting as communion with the messiah.

The press had written little or nothing about B.B.'s guitar playing by Thanksgiving of 1952, when B.B. returned to Houston for another gig. The event is thus historic, if only for its focus: a "battle of guitars," pitting B.B. against Clarence "Gatemouth" Brown, a rival African American blues guitarist and virtuoso fiddler born in Louisiana and raised in Texas (and not to be confused with WDIA deejay Dwight "Gatemouth" Moore). Someone, it seems, had finally noticed Lucille.

Battles of the bands in that era were generally settled by measuring applause. Costumery helped, so B.B. outfitted his band in matching engineer overalls for the Thanksgiving showdown with Gatemouth. B.B.'s set reaped a warm ovation. He retreated backstage and waited, only to be stunned, a short while later, when the audience exploded in rapture for Gatemouth. The iconoclastic Texan had taken the stage alone with his fiddle, clad in cherry-red long johns, shiny boots, and a cowboy hat.

Around this time, Joe Bihari joined B.B. in Houston for a recording session with a band. By now, B.B. would simply tell the Bihari brothers

when he was ready to record, and they would fit sessions into his schedule. When the appointed day arrived, B.B. tested Joe's largesse with
the unsolicited comment, "Gee, I'd really like to have a new guitar."
Joe escorted B.B. into a music store. B.B. vowed, "You buy a guitar, I'll
make you a hit record." Joe bought two.

It was probably on the same Houston trip that Bill Harvey introduced B.B. to the Buffalo Booking Agency. Founder and owner Don
Robey, an African American restaurateur and concert promoter, had
built a musical empire beyond the wildest imaginings of Robert Henry or
Sunbeam Mitchell. Robey was half Black and half Jewish. With his hair
parted in the middle and slicked back, he could pass for white or Black.
Like Sunbeam, Robey plied the vice trades. He seldom traveled without
a shotgun or revolver at his side. Robey's Bronze Peacock club, opened in
1945 in Houston's Fifth Ward, became "a laboratory of early rock & roll."
Robey rejected the big-band craze and embraced a new breed of small,
electrified ensembles that often replaced four or five horns with a single
electric guitar. Buffalo Booking became one of the nation's first Black-
owned talent firms. In 1949, Robey established Peacock Records, with
Gatemouth Brown as his first recording artist. In 1952, Robey acquired
the Duke label, a Memphis imprint founded by a WDIA producer (a
would-be partner Robey later chased off with his revolver), and inherited
a wealth of Memphis talent, including Bobby Bland and Johnny Ace.

Most of B.B.'s old Memphis cronies seemed to work for Robey, and
Robey dearly wished to add B.B. King to his stable. B.B. met Robey's
partners: Morris Merritt, a fellow gambler-entrepreneur, and Evelyn
Johnson, a college-educated Black woman who ran the Buffalo agency
and was widely regarded as the brains of the outfit. Robey himself "didn't
know a record from a hubcap," Johnson later quipped.

"Let Evelyn book you, and let me manage you," Merritt told B.B.,
"and I'll advance you some money to cover transportation. That way
you can tour exclusively with Bill Harvey's band." Merritt offered to
lay out more than $2,000 to cover down payments on a new Cadillac
for B.B. and a pair of station wagons for the band. That kind of largesse
impressed B.B.: Robert Henry hadn't spent a dime on him since the red
and blue-lavender suits for his first tour.

Henry, the Beale Street pool-hall entrepreneur, had served as B.B.'s de facto manager since "3 O'Clock Blues," if not before. Their working relationship had peaked with B.B.'s first national tour. After the first blush of fame, the novelty faded, and B.B. found his drawing power diminished. By the close of 1952, promoters were offering B.B. $350 or $400 a gig, half of what he'd earned a few months earlier: B.B. was no longer the hot new star. Henry turned those gigs down, leaving B.B. no money at all.

"Robert was a nice guy," B.B. recalled, "and long as I was hot, everything was great, but when my records got cold, he still wanted to charge the same amount of money I'd been getting, and it just wasn't gonna happen. He didn't care. He had his poolroom. I was starving."

Naturally, Robert Henry opposed the management change. He told B.B. the market for his talent would rebound. B.B. faced a choice.

"If you'd placed Henry and Robey side to side," Preston Lauterbach mused in his definitive chitlin' circuit history, "and asked an ambitious black musician to choose his manager on appearances alone, it wouldn't have been a contest. Henry, plump and slouchy, looked his sixty-four years. His wiry gray hair poked out from under his blown-out cap, and the chalky Beale Street dust clung to his brogans. Robey, with his dark hair slicked down, appeared younger than his fifty-one years, peering alertly from behind black horn rims. His suits fairly shimmered, and a prosperity-minded fellow would not have missed his diamond tiepin and gold ring."

B.B. went with Robey, choosing money over loyalty. The new Cadillac spoke volumes. When Robey approached Henry the following spring to purchase thirty B.B. King dates, effectively buying out the rival manager, Henry acceded. But hard feelings lingered on both sides. "Forget him," Henry recalled, years later. "I went a long ways to try to help him. When he got to the place he could make some money, he broke his contract."

When B.B. played on Beale Street in the summer of 1953, Henry had his car impounded and his wages garnished through legal writ. B.B. responded by largely expunging Robert Henry from his life story.

* * *

IN EARLY 1953, B.B.'S contract with Modern Records came up for renewal. B.B. felt that a new three-year contract was worth a $5,000 advance. He wanted to buy a house. The Biharis balked at the sum. Much as the brothers indulged B.B. with attention, praise, artistic respect, and the occasional flashy gift, they remained notoriously stingy with cash. They were known to sleep on studio couches rather than pay for hotel rooms when they left Los Angeles on recording expeditions. B.B. detested conflict, so he raised no protest. Instead, he compelled the brothers into negotiation with another suitor: Don Robey, who effectively served as B.B.'s manager and agent and dearly wished to produce him. "If you give me $5,000," B.B. told Robey, "you got B.B. King." Robey agreed without hesitation, cut B.B. a check for the full sum, and set out to arrange recording sessions before the Biharis could intervene. Now, B.B. had the brothers' attention. They pleaded for more time. B.B. told them it was too late. The Biharis swiftly counteroffered: they would buy back B.B.'s contract and pay him an additional $2,000, or $7,000 in all. B.B. said that would be just fine. The Peacock recording sessions were quietly scuttled, no doubt to Robey's chagrin.

B.B. hit the road with Bill Harvey and a seven-piece ensemble, touring as B.B. King and the Bill Harvey Orchestra. Morris Merritt delivered B.B.'s new Cadillac in May 1953, announcing the gift, the new artistic collaboration, and a "Socko Tour" in the African American press. Later that month in Atlanta, an unnamed correspondent of the African American *Daily World* reported that a "blues shouting tornado" had entertained a sellout crowd that "applauded his titanic drive, floor-pounding rhythm and blissful beat." B.B. had his first concert review.

Sometime during that busy spring of 1953, B.B. met a man who would become his closest confidant outside of Norman Matthews, his best friend and guardian angel. B.B. met Willis "Bebop" Edwards Jr. when he climbed into a cab Bebop was driving outside a Houston hotel. "3 O'Clock Blues" was playing on the car radio. Bebop carried B.B. to a series of business meetings, and they chatted along the way. B.B. mentioned that he needed a valet. (Matthews played that role on and off and drew sporadic pay, but he was too close to B.B. to be termed an employee.) By the time they reached the airport, B.B. had persuaded Bebop to abandon his cab in the terminal parking lot and join him on the road. Born in 1923, Bebop was a navy veteran and a natty dresser, fond of alligator shoes and tailored suits. Now, B.B. had two wingmen. Bebop Edwards and Norman Matthews would devote most of their adult lives to B.B.

With a pair of 1953 singles, B.B. exorcised some of the hurt over his parting with Martha while simultaneously delivering Joe Bihari the pair of hits he had promised in Houston in exchange for the new guitars. The narrator of "Woke Up This Morning" and "Please Love Me" had worked through the sorrow of romantic dissolution and resolved to move on. In "Woke Up This Morning," the first single, the singer leveraged his heartbreak to entice a new partner into bed: "I'm in misery . . . Oh baby, come on stay with me." In "Please Love Me," B.B. embraced the new love with a worship that bordered on obsession. Like many of the best early B.B. King songs, this one struck a balance between B.B. and Lucille. The solo was a triumph of fierce melodicism, all stinging vibrato and snarling bends.

"Woke Up This Morning" peaked at number 3. A few months later, "Please Love Me" reached number 2 on the *Billboard* National Best Sellers chart. Its further ascent was blocked by a mournful ballad titled "The Clock," yet another hit for Johnny Ace, B.B.'s former piano player. But "Please Love Me" scraped number 1 on an alternate chart of records Most Played in Juke Boxes. A song that topped either chart counted as a number 1 hit, and now B.B. had three. Together with "3 O'Clock Blues" and a handful of less-celebrated cuts, "Please Love Me" would provide a model for chart-topping, guitar-driven songs from Chuck Berry, Bo Diddley, and many others.

The fine print on the RPM single credited "Please Love Me" to two songwriters: B.B. himself and a cowriter named Jules Taub. A survey of B.B.'s other singles from that era finds many such collaborations. Labels listed B.B. as sole author of the chart toppers "3 O'Clock Blues" and "You Know I Love You." The mysterious Taub was credited as cowriter of "Woke Up This Morning," as well as "B.B. Boogie," "My Baby's Gone," and "Story from My Heart and Soul." Later on, B.B. would collaborate with songwriters named Sam Ling and Joe Josea—at least on paper. All three were pseudonyms for the Biharis, who appended their names to dozens of singles recorded by B.B. and other Modern Records artists.

Songwriting credit was a nebulous business in the blues, a musical genre built on imitation, appropriation, and theft. Modern Records listed B.B. as writer of "3 O'Clock Blues," a Lowell Fulson composition, and "She's Dynamite," a Tampa Red song. A 1952 single called "Shake It Up and Go," also ostensibly penned by B.B., was in fact a well-traveled boogie, previously recorded by Memphis jug-band singer Charlie Burse as "Oil It Up and Go," by Piedmont blues guitarist Blind Boy Fuller as "Step It Up and Go," and by Delta bluesman Tommy McClennan as "Bottle It Up and Go." Many other songs, including the hits "Woke Up This Morning" and "Please Love Me," were evidently genuine B.B. King originals.

When a record company released a single, the imprint generally paid two royalties, one to the performing artist, the other split between the song's composer and publisher. Independent labels of the 1950s typically paid artists and composers only a penny or two per record sold, after steep deductions for sidemen and studio time: practically speaking, no royalty at all, beyond whatever cash the label had paid out as an advance.

A top-ten B.B. King single might sell fifty thousand copies. Precise sales figures were elusive, because independent "race" labels flew below the radar of recording-industry tabulators. B.B. collected the artist royalties. The Biharis pocketed publishing royalties. On songs B.B. wrote alone, he claimed the composer royalty. On songs cowritten by B.B. and "Taub," he and the Biharis split the composer royalty, the pseudonymous credits allowing the Biharis to collect an extra (and arguably unearned) share. The Biharis helped B.B. and themselves by claiming composer credit for songs none of them had written, reaping royalties that should have gone to the true authors. (Such pilferage pervaded the R&B industry and endured into the rock 'n' roll era, with blues-rockers Led Zeppelin among the most notorious scofflaws.)

B.B. saw few royalty checks. The bulk of his recording income arrived in four-figure advance payments he collected whenever he signed a new contract with Jules Bihari. The brothers also gave B.B. cash when he needed it, helping him meet his own payroll with musicians and aides, bailing him out when his bus broke down, and charging the funds against his account.

Early on, B.B. knew little of songwriting credits or royalties. The Biharis spelled out their business practices in carefully worded contracts B.B. signed for Jules Bihari, documents B.B. did not generally read. Independent record makers routinely cut themselves in on publishing and songwriting royalties for other people's songs. Don Robey, proprietor of the Duke and Peacock labels, claimed composer credit for songs he didn't write for Bobby "Blue" Bland and Johnny Ace. The Biharis defended their methods unblinkingly. "We worked with artists in recording sessions," Joe Bihari recalled. "We rehearsed with them and changed things."

Had those methods been entirely defensible, then presumably the brothers would have listed their own names on the labels and not the pseudonyms, derived from various maiden names and nicknames in the Bihari clan. The ruse would haunt B.B. in years to come. "I'd never met 'Taub' or 'Josea,'" he later quipped. "How could they write with me?"

B.B. SPENT THE REST of 1953 and all of 1954 crisscrossing the chitlin' circuit with the Bill Harvey orchestra. The Black press chronicled their travels. An ad from June 1953 promoted a gig for B.B. and Harvey at Club Morocco in Little Rock, Arkansas. A clipping from August 1953 put them at the Atlanta city auditorium on a bill with fellow Buffalo Booking clients Gatemouth Brown, Johnny Ace, and Willie Mae "Big Mama" Thornton, riding high on her "Hound Dog" single. B.B. toured Ohio, Wisconsin, and Michigan in the fall before returning to Memphis in December for WDIA's annual Goodwill Revue fundraiser, sharing a bill with the Soul Stirrers and their hot new lead singer, Sam Cooke. An account in the *Chicago Defender* of January 30, 1954, put B.B. in Texas, bound for California, Nevada, and Oregon, his first real West Coast tour. An Easter gig at the City Auditorium in Houston drew ten thousand fans: two thousand more were turned away. "The B.B. King orchestra, one of the top blues aggregations, is popular the nation over," the *Defender* reported. "The crew touring the state of Texas on one-nighters set all kinds of records and broke many of its own marks in other cities."

It was a punishing schedule, even compared with the pace B.B. had endured in previous years. "We took our little review wherever Evelyn Johnson could book us," he recalled. "There were tiny clubs and big barns, nice black theaters and nasty roadhouses." Johnson set the itinerary without particular regard to geography: a gig she described as "just up the road" could lie several hundred miles away. "We might get up on a Monday in L.A. and drive straight through to New York City, alternating drivers, not stopping for nothing except bodily functions, watch the sunset, watch the sunrise, keep on keeping on till we found ourselves driving down 125th Street in Harlem."

Blacks could not patronize hotels or motels through much of the South, so B.B.'s entourage stayed in private residences, which might be "pleasant or uncomfortable, depending on the hosts," he recalled. Often, the entire band slept in their cars.

In April 1954, B.B. made the cover of *Cashbox* magazine, chief competitor to *Billboard*. B.B. beamed as he shook hands with a Los Angeles deejay and accepted a trophy "commemorating the artist's last seven releases on RPM, all of which have attained top popularity." Joe Bihari, clean-cut and handsome, smiled indulgently at B.B.'s side. B.B. had reached the *Billboard* top ten with five consecutive singles, starting with "You Know I Love You" in the fall of 1952 and ending with "Please Hurry Home," a rock 'n' roll romp released in September 1953.

A few years earlier, B.B. had been the weak link in his own band. Now, B.B. was an electric-blues master, breaking new ground and finding new sounds with each successive release. He was outgrowing Bill Harvey's big band. A typical single from the spring of 1954, "The Woman I Love," revealed a growing contrast between B.B.'s electrifying guitar attack and Harvey's increasingly anachronistic arrangements. The song featured a breathtaking solo, a savage assault on the blues scale. Lucille sat high in the mix, her angry tone drenched in "reverb," an electronic innovation that re-created the natural echo of a cathedral or cavern. To modern ears, the overall effect is something like a Hendrix-era guitarist fronting an Ellington-era band.

On May 28, 1954, a warm and pleasant Friday, B.B. debuted at the Apollo in Harlem, the most storied theater on the chitlin' circuit. To mark the occasion, B.B.'s managers at Buffalo Booking presented him with thirty tailored suits. Dizzy Gillespie, now a besotted fan, hyped B.B.'s arrival around the city's jazz community. The show drew B.B. his first coverage in the Hollywood trade journal *Variety*, whose review illustrates the frenetic pace of the showcase era. B.B. and his troupe played for just forty-three minutes. B.B. himself sang just four songs. The reviewer noted, almost as an aside, that "the young colored performer twangs a guitar to accompany his modest vocalizing." This was very nearly the first published acknowledgment that B.B. King played the guitar.

B.B.'s romantic life, like his professional life, must have seemed a blur. He could now expect adoring female fans backstage after every performance, and he was never one to turn a willing woman away. He mostly dated African American women: B.B. had spent his life working around racial confrontation, and nothing invited trouble like interracial romance. So, when a lovely white woman chatted him up backstage one night in Little Rock, Arkansas, B.B. carefully skirted sexual talk. But when he mentioned he was heading to New York, she said she was heading there, too. Dating a white woman in New York was an entirely different matter. B.B. invited her to dinner and then back to his hotel room in Harlem, where they "indulged in pleasures that went on and on." They became lovers, and eventually B.B. found himself escorting her to Black-owned hotels in Little Rock, despite—or perhaps because of—the danger implicit in the liaison.

AROUND THIS TIME, Albert King welcomed a new child into his Memphis household: Shirley King, B.B.'s daughter, whose mother had befriended the bluesman at an Arkansas juke joint.

When Shirley reached school age, her mother persuaded B.B. to allow the girl to live with B.B.'s father and stepfamily in Memphis during school months. B.B. had acknowledged no more than two or three children by 1954, although several claims would surface later from children born earlier. Shirley grew up unaware she had any siblings. She would be the first of B.B.'s adoptive children to live with his biological family.

Shirley spent long stretches of childhood in Albert King's home. She loved to play with Albert's grandchildren, and she cherished her time with B.B. when he visited. She also recalled enduring regular beatings from Albert, who lost his temper when he drank. She never mentioned the abuse to B.B., she said, for fear of upsetting him. "He lived his whole life trying to make his daddy proud of him," she recalled. If Shirley complained, she feared she might be sent back home to her mother.

B.B. LANGUISHED THROUGH MUCH of 1954 without a chart hit, but his studio prospects were about to change. Early that year, the Bihari brothers hired a new arranger and producer named Maxwell Davis. Born and raised in Kansas, Davis first made a living as a virtuoso tenor saxophonist, then settled into a lucrative role as freelance musician and arranger in the booming West Coast rhythm-and-blues scene until the Biharis hired him full-time. Davis proceeded to arrange and produce a series of singles that B.B. would later recall as his finest recorded work.

"He looked like Nat Cole and dressed just as sharp," B.B. recalled. "The man could think, write, and adapt." Davis reminded B.B. of Luther Henson, the loving teacher of his childhood. B.B. embraced him as a mentor. "I'd bring in the songs," he recalled, "and sometimes I'd run them down for him beforehand; sometimes he'd write the arrangements right there in the studio. He was that good." Bill Harvey had done a fine job arranging B.B.'s music for his orchestra, but Harvey was no record producer. B.B. knew how he wanted to sound. The Biharis knew Maxwell Davis could interpret B.B.'s aural instructions and commit them faithfully to tape. Davis proved to be "the only arranger," B.B. recalled, "who could put on record 95 percent of everything I was hearing in my head." Perhaps most important, Davis "always left room for Lucille."

The timing suggests Maxwell Davis produced "Everything I Do Is Wrong," a standout single from May 1954 that showed further evolution in Lucille's sound. B.B. was manipulating the rudimentary tone controls on his guitar and amplifier to favor treble over bass, because he heard the high sounds better. His trebly attack positioned Lucille perfectly atop the mix here, occupying a range of frequencies that set her apart from B.B.'s voice and his backing musicians. Lucille's tone boasted a new richness, a quality as piercing and urgent as an air-raid siren yet somehow warm and melodic. Jimmy Page, of future Led Zeppelin fame, would attain a similar sound with an arsenal of Woodstock-era technology. B.B. had little more at his disposal than a tweed amplifier, a guitar, and a few switches and knobs.

On "When My Heart Beats like a Hammer," released in July 1954, B.B.'s new producer finally struck a balance between Lucille and the backing band. Seemingly for the first time, the wall of horns and punchy rhythm section truly accompanied B.B.'s guitar. Neither faction dominated, and the backing musicians no longer sounded quite so antiquated. B.B.'s solo included a lengthy phrase composed primarily of dyads, B.B. plucking two strings at once. He was playing licks well beyond the ken of most of his peers.

The next single, "You Upset Me Baby," delivered B.B.'s fourth number 1 hit. A spirited blues shuffle, it boasted neither his greatest lyrics nor his most accomplished guitar work. Yet, as a finished song, it was somehow more memorable than anything B.B. had recorded before. The reason was B.B.'s vocal: in hindsight, this recording seems to mark the emergence of his unique voice as a blues stylist. B.B. was no longer channeling Roy Brown. His relaxed delivery, his conversational singing style, his tendency to lag behind the beat, the warm rasp that engulfed his voice at the end of each melodic phrase—from first to last, the vocal on "You Upset Me Baby" was unmistakably B.B. King. It was also unapologetically ribald: B.B. opened the song by tabulating his lover's measurements and celebrating her "real crazy legs," earning him a mild rebuke from *Variety* and a ban on some stations. "Still sold over a million of 'em," B.B. laughed, a few years later.

B.B. had been a fine singer from the outset. In the four years between his Modern Records debut and "You Upset Me Baby," he had evolved as a vocal stylist alongside his vast improvements on the guitar. Now, all the elements of his singular style fell into place. This was B.B. King, Blues Traveler, man of a thousand gigs, who had crisscrossed the chitlin' circuit, had bedded women in a hundred towns, had loved and lost and loved again. "Like being hit by a falling tree," he sang, "woman, what you do to me." World-weary and wise, laid-back and lustful, "You Upset Me Baby" introduced the mature B.B. King.

"You Upset Me Baby" entered the charts at number 9 in October 1954. In December, it reached number 1.

THANKSGIVING WEEK FOUND B.B. in Hollywood, celebrating his fifth anniversary as a recording artist, joined by the Biharis and his Buffalo Booking agents. Evelyn Johnson told the press B.B. had performed for more than one and a half million people in that span: nearly a thousand patrons a night, surely an exaggeration.

Notably absent from the festivities, according to the *Billboard* account, was the Bill Harvey orchestra. Harvey had long struggled with drink. In the first year of his partnership with B.B., Harvey had held his demons at bay. By 1954, his alcoholism had resurfaced, and his band had descended into bacchanalia, "partying every night, all night, all day, drinking," in the words of sideman Calvin Owens. As Harvey's grip on sobriety loosened, the ensemble behind him grew increasingly sloppy, its performances erratic. "Gigs dwindled and money faded," B.B. recalled. "I fell into another rut. I felt myself moving horizontally, while I wanted to go up."

Around the close of 1954, B.B. parted ways with Bill Harvey. In B.B.'s memoir, he blames Harvey's alcoholism for the split. Another reason was money. B.B. had been dividing his tour income with Harvey and Morris Merritt, his manager, with Merritt apparently claiming the lion's share. B.B. remedied the imbalance by firing both men.

B.B. held on to Evelyn Johnson and Buffalo Booking, his most dependable source of income. But he seeded rumors of an indefinite hiatus, staging a series of West Coast dates that looked like a victory lap: a sellout show on Christmas night in Oakland opposite the riotous Louis Jordan, one of his idols, followed by a mysterious "farewell dance" at the stately Elks ballroom in Los Angeles on December 27 featuring Roy Brown, another hero. As to why a chart-topping blues artist would throw a farewell dance, press accounts offered no clue.

CHAPTER 9

BIG RED

DUKE ELLINGTON AND HIS ORCHESTRA rolled around
the country in a bus with the words "Duke Ellington, Mr. Hi-Fi
of 1955" emblazoned on the side. A bus signaled status for a Black performer in that era, and B.B. wanted one. At the start of 1955, he plotted
to rejoin the road under his own name, with an ensemble even larger
than the seven or eight musicians who traveled with Bill Harvey. His
plan defied the trend in the rhythm-and-blues industry, which favored
smaller, nimbler ensembles like Louis Jordan and His Tympany Five.

B.B. initially kept the plan to himself. He finally confided in Evelyn Johnson, his trusted booking agent. Then, B.B. quietly set about
assembling an entourage of musicians, drivers, mechanics, ruffians, and
rogues, some of whom would remain with him for decades.

Cato Walker Jr. had been B.B.'s first real employee, working as his
driver since 1952. When B.B. first laid eyes on the lovely Polly Walker,
he commenced a lusty flirtation, unaware she and Cato were married.
Polly politely retreated, and Cato announced, "Well, Boss, you met my
wife." B.B. offered Polly a job as his personal secretary. From then on,
B.B. treated Polly with the utmost respect, always addressing her as
"Mrs. Walker." They shared a relationship intense but familial, "more
like brother and sister," recalled Lora Walker, daughter of Polly and Cato.
"If you wanted to tell him something he didn't want to hear, you told
Polly." Given B.B.'s peculiar hours, Polly performed most of her secre-
tarial duties on evenings and weekends, all while holding down another
full-time secretarial job at a Memphis school. James "Shinny" Walker,
Cato's brother, joined B.B.'s crew as road manager and sometime bassist.

The B.B. King Orchestra convened in the spring of 1955. Cato found a used Trailways bus for $5,000 and spent another $3,000 making it roadworthy. B.B. called it "Big Red."

Among the seventeen musicians and roadies who populated Big Red, only one was an artist of sufficient stature to merit separate mention in newspaper ads. She was Evelyn Young, "Mama Nuts." Born in 1928, Young had backed B.B. in the Bill Harvey orchestra until she left Harvey to join B.B. Her fame probably stemmed both from her considerable talent on the alto sax and from her gender: she was B.B.'s only female instrumentalist. "Evelyn was fierce," B.B. recalled, bold enough to jump onstage with Dizzy Gillespie and Charlie Parker for an impromptu jam at the Birdland jazz club in New York. Only insiders knew the derivation of her nickname, "Mama Nuts": Young liked both men and women. She had dated Bill Harvey. When she joined B.B., Young swiftly became embroiled in a relationship with Bonita Cole, B.B.'s backup vocalist. Young sometimes invited fellow musicians to hide under the bed while she and Cole carried on: "to prove to us how tough she was with the girls," one bandmate recalled. One of the rules posted inside B.B.'s tour bus read, "Don't mess with Mama Nuts."

B.B.'s other backing vocalist, Harold Conner, was bisexual or gay and fond of strutting around naked in front of Calvin Owens, a trumpet virtuoso from Houston with whom Conner was smitten. Owens, who was straight, would protest in vain.

Some musicians recruited for B.B.'s first big band had worked with him before, including Owens and drummer Earl Forest. Others were new. Kenny Sands provided a second trumpet. Lawrence Burdine and Floyd Newman fortified the sax section.

Pianist Millard Lee, another Bill Harvey alumnus, was "old enough to be everybody's father," Owens recalled. He assumed Harvey's old role of bandleader. The others took to calling him "Mother." Mother called B.B. "Black Bitch." That was a term of endearment for B.B., who, for all the dues he had paid, was still in his late twenties. Older bandmates viewed him as a spoiled diva. B.B. told Mother things he couldn't confide in his own father. Mother would snap back, "You know better than that,

Black Bitch." Lee would serve B.B. as a mentor and father figure, like Robert Lockwood Jr. and Luther Henson before him.

But B.B. was the boss. He covered all of his musicians' expenses except food. He tolerated romantic companions, provided they found an empty seat on the bus and carried the carfare to get home. One thing B.B. stressed above all to the passengers on Big Red: "You must learn to get along with each other."

B.B. did not demand perfection from his musicians or fine them for playing wrong notes: he was not James Brown. But B.B. prized promptness. A musician who missed the "call time" for Big Red's departure to the next gig was left behind. (In later years, B.B. would fine sidemen who missed airplane flights, a costlier lapse.) Whenever B.B. felt the backing band was growing complacent, he might call a rehearsal at the end of a gig, starting at three or four in the morning and playing through daybreak, an exercise that generally yielded a tighter show the next night. B.B. was quick to dismiss any band member who fought, used drugs, or showed up to work drunk or stoned—although he could hardly object to the copious drinking that went on outside of work. B.B. was himself a heavy drinker. He later recalled his Memphis years as "drinking days": "maybe my heaviest." But B.B.'s drinking never became a problem. He was addicted to gambling and sex and life on the road but not to alcohol.

B.B. had, by his own account, sworn off hard drugs after the lone, disastrous experiment with heroin. Bandmates claimed never to have seen him take so much as a single drag from a joint. That is not to say B.B. took no drugs at all. He later admitted to the cannabis chronicle *High Times* that he "would just as soon smoke a stick of good grass than some Kools or Prince Alberts." B.B. smoked Kools in public. He smoked pot in private, and he counseled his musicians to do the same. His scrupulous attention to public decorum would bear fruit years later, when presidents and ambassadors screened him for White House visits and diplomatic tours.

Cousin Bukka had taught B.B., on his first trip to Memphis, to dress like he was "going to the bank to borrow some money." Onstage, B.B. and his band wore suits and ties. B.B. sometimes wore Bermuda shorts beneath his jacket and tie in a bid for *Esquire*-style hipness. He grew a slender, Louis Jordan–style mustache. Onstage, he cut a sharp contrast to the classic Delta bluesman, slouching on a stool in smelly overalls, drinking from a hip flask. B.B. detested that stereotype: he thought it gave the blues a bad name. He took his stylistic cue instead from men such as Jordan and Nat Cole and T-Bone Walker, who dressed like they were going out on the town, rather than out to butcher a pig.

B.B. HIT THE ROAD in 1955 with renewed confidence. But his first year as bandleader proved comparatively lean for record sales: only two singles scraped the top ten, one at the start of the year, the other at the end. The first was "Every Day I Have the Blues," a reboot of an old Memphis Slim single. Maxwell Davis wrote a big-band chart for B.B.'s version, a vigorous shuffle that reached number 8 on the *Billboard* charts in February. The arrangement perfectly suited B.B.'s new ensemble. "Every Day" would become a sort of B.B. King theme song, an opener to nearly every show. The second hit was "Ten Long Years," which peaked at number 9 in September. Inspired by Eddie Boyd's 1952 hit "Five Long Years," B.B.'s "Ten Long Years" sounded like a lament for his failed marriage ("for ten long years / she was my pride and joy"), even if the years didn't quite add up.

The road remained a blur of gigs, gas stations, and indignities. Music palaces like the Regal and the Apollo proved the exception. Mostly, B.B. recalled, the band played beer halls and juke joints: "places so hot the moisture in the air condensed on our instruments, so cold we'd have to thaw out our hands with matches before we could play, places with no bathroom, no dressing room: we'd have to change clothes in the manager's office, or in the car." Only the largest chitlin' circuit cities had hotels that served African Americans. The B.B. King Orchestra spent many nights on Big Red.

"We were playing one-nighters," recalled Floyd Newman, B.B.'s affable baritone saxophonist. "We'd go to work at 9 and play till 2. Then we'd get on the bus and go to the next place. The only place you'd get to wash up was at the club. It was rough out there, sleeping on the bus.

You had to wash your shirts in the restroom and hang them in the bus to dry." B.B. and his entourage "really lived off the bus," recalled tenor saxophonist George Coleman. "Everybody had a box with crackers, sardines, and beans. You didn't have time to stop at a restaurant because you was jumping from one part of the country to the other at all times. A lot of times, when you got off stage you had to jump right on the bus to get to the next town."

The actual gigs were relatively consistent. B.B.'s band would take the stage and play an instrumental warm-up, often a jazz workout penned by Onzie Horne, a former Memphis music teacher whom B.B. brought in to replace Bill Harvey as musical arranger on the road. B.B.'s backing singers would lead the band in a ballad or two, followed by more warm-up music. Finally, amid rising protestations from the crowd, B.B. would take the stage and plow through the hits they had come to hear: "Every Day I Have the Blues," "You Upset Me Baby," "3 O'Clock Blues." If B.B. was opening a multiact showcase, he might play a single forty-minute set. On a full night at a roadhouse, the music might go till two or three in the morning. Once the encores were over, B.B. would return to the stage to sign autographs until every last patron had gone home. "When you rode with B.B. King, you never knew what time you were going to leave," recalled Lora Walker, B.B.'s lifelong friend. "He would shut the place down."

Between gigs, Big Red staged strategic stops at service stations with restaurants attached, leveraging the 150-gallon gas tank as an economic incentive to secure food at white-owned establishments. "We need gas *and* food," Shinny Walker would announce to the attendant. Even then, the group usually settled for sandwiches handed out through a back door and eaten on the bus. Once, when Bebop Edwards dared to drain a cup of coffee inside a segregated diner, the waitress smashed the empty cup to pieces on the floor. The Big Red odyssey "was a lesson in segregation," Floyd Newman recalled.

B.B. and Norman Matthews later recalled that, more than once, the band beheld African American bodies hanging from trees as they journeyed through the Deep South. At such moments, they recalled, the musicians would fall into a sickened silence. Someone would finally break it by asking, "I wonder what they say he did." Someone else might add, "And you know that at the next gas station, you mess up and it'll be you."

ON MAY 17, 1954, the U.S. Supreme Court struck down the legal fiction of "separate but equal," at least in public schools. "Separate educational facilities are inherently unequal," the court reasoned.

Rather than integrate, most of the Deep South girded for battle. Southern governors and senators roared segregationist rhetoric to leverage white votes. Mayors and police chiefs allied with a reenergized Ku Klux Klan. A new column of resistance formed under the banner of Citizens' Councils, a sort of white-collar Klan. Founded by a plantation man from B.B.'s own Indianola, the councils fought desegregation in the courts and chambers of commerce. "Somebody has to be the spokesman for the majority of the white people," an unnamed Citizens' Councilman told the Greenville, Mississippi, *Delta Democrat-Times*, "and it is a lot better to have that somebody be on the side of reason and the law."

One evening in August 1955, a Chicago boy of fourteen named Emmett Till stopped at Bryant's Grocery and Meat Market in the tiny community of Money, Mississippi, forty miles northeast of Indianola. Till was a visitor, staying with relatives and unaccustomed to Mississippi's segregationist traditions. Till entered the store to buy some candy. The white, female shopkeeper later claimed that Till flirted and grabbed her hand on the way out. Till and his companions drove away. A few days later, on August 28, two white men appeared at the cabin where Till was staying to seize the "boy that done the talkin'." An elderly relative pleaded for mercy, but the men dragged Till off. His body surfaced three days later in the Tallahatchie River, tethered by the neck to a cotton-gin fan. Investigators found a bullet in his skull. One of his eyes had been gouged out, and his forehead was crushed. Till's mother insisted on an open casket, so the world would see what had become of her child. *Jet* magazine, the African American weekly based in Chicago, published a photograph of the mutilated body. A parade of African American witnesses testified against the two white defendants at trial, in shocking defiance of Jim Crow rules. But an all-white, all-male jury found them not guilty. Decades later, the shopkeeper admitted that much of her story was false.

LATE ONE NIGHT on the road, somewhere in the Deep South, Big Red stopped beside an overturned car. B.B.'s crew rushed out to find a family trapped beneath the wreck—a white family. The men carefully flipped the car back over and freed everyone but the wife, whose body could not be extracted from the twisted metal. Then, another car pulled up, and two white men got out. They asked, "What are you doing to these people?" B.B. attempted an explanation, but the white men did not want to hear it. The white motorists took charge and summoned paramedics. A growing crowd of white rescuers stood and glared at the African American rescuers who had preceded them: "looking at us like we're perverts or thieves," B.B. recalled. "No one can believe we're just people helping other people."

By the late 1950s, B.B. had joined the Prince Hall Masons, the African American branch of freemasonry. B.B. seems never to have discussed freemasonry with any interviewer or biographer, perhaps to honor the masonic tradition of secrecy, but it's easy to guess why he joined. The masons were segregated, but membership in the world's largest fraternity of African American men gave B.B. invaluable net-working opportunities on the road. Freemasonry had opened doors for a great many African American musicians, including Duke Ellington, Nat Cole, Count Basie, and W. C. Handy. Several others in B.B.'s entourage joined him in the masons, including brothers Cato and Shinny Walker, trumpeter Calvin Owens, and faithful friend Norman Matthews.

The masonic brotherhood occasionally reached across racial lines. Once, when Big Red suffered a flat tire on the road, a white patrolman pulled up to the scene, climbed out of his car, and announced, "You n——s are going to jail." When B.B. approached the officer, he spotted a masonic symbol on his uniform or car. "Officer," B.B. pleaded, "we're really sorry. We're gonna get this bus off the road as soon as possible." Then he telegraphed to the officer that he was a mason, perhaps via a secret handshake. The white officer gave a start, and then he seemed to reconsider. "All right," he huffed. "But when I come back, you n——s better be gone." B.B. escaped incarceration.

The informal network of segregated lodgings presented its own perils. Once, B.B. and Norman Matthews were packing to leave a guest house in Macon, Georgia, when they heard shots. After the shooting had stopped, they ran out of their room to find the African American proprietor slumped against the wall, covered in blood. They would later learn the owner had doubled back from work to find his wife in bed with another man, who had opened fire. Before B.B. and Matthews could react, the dead man's brother arrived, seeking revenge. He produced a gun and fired on the murderous lover. And then the cops arrived, "shooting at anyone who's moving," B.B. recalled. "We ain't moving." When the body was removed and arrests made, B.B. and Matthews dusted themselves off and set out for the next gig.

Groupies could be a blessing or a curse. B.B. had his pick. His bandmates shared the wealth. They did not necessarily share B.B.'s impulse for discretion. Saxophonist George Coleman recalled a young woman once "taking care of all the cats" as they stood in line, awaiting their turns at some chitlin' circuit lodging. That bacchanal ended without incident, but on another occasion, Coleman and a second musician landed in jail over an underage girl who had been "giving it up" at the band's Houston hotel. The mother had called the police. Only exculpatory testimony from the girl spared them from prosecution.

After a show in Austin, Texas, B.B. sat on a stool and signed autographs for fans. One autograph seeker flirted with B.B., and he flirted back. At the end of their exchange, B.B. rose to hand her the paper he had signed. When he sat back down, the stool was gone, and B.B. collapsed to the floor. A jealous boyfriend had intentionally moved it. B.B. arose and exchanged tense words with the boyfriend, now surrounded by his friends. B.B.'s entourage gathered around him. Millard "Mother" Lee somehow produced a Winchester rifle and leveled it at the man who had moved the stool. All in a moment, guns were pointing in every direction. B.B., who had no gun, stood his ground with leaderly calm and waited patiently until the weapons were lowered and his band allowed to leave. As Big Red pulled away, shots rang out. B.B.'s band returned fire. B.B. left Austin in a hail of bullets. After that, B.B. enacted a no-guns policy on Big Red.

Sometimes the threat of violence emanated from club owners. B.B. and his band often played for a percentage of ticket sales, rather than a set fee. That system invited corruption on all sides: owners could keep any ticket revenues they concealed from the performer. Agents and managers sometimes struck secret side deals with promoters. B.B. mostly trusted his agents at Buffalo Booking. He would post a man at the club door with a click counter to track sales. Someone else would prowl the perimeter looking for a secret entrance.

B.B. periodically dispatched Shinny Walker, his road manager, to mete out a beat-down to an uncooperative club owner. Sometimes, an owner gained the upper hand. One night in Milwaukee, B.B.'s men counted the crowd at just shy of 1,000 heads. The promoter's count came to 750. "That's what you're getting paid on," he said. After some heated words, the promoter summoned the local sheriff, who asked B.B., "You want to take the count or go to jail?" B.B. took the count.

Gatemouth Brown, the flamboyant, cowboy-hatted Texas guitarist, recounted another standoff with a crooked Mississippi promoter, a scene more violent than anything B.B. himself ever shared: "We had about 3,500 people in the house, and this guy didn't want to pay off nobody. Had a big .45 sittin' on the table, and he didn't know I had a pistol in my pocket. So I pulled my pistol and I laid it right up above his head. I told B.B. to count his money out and count mine, too. And he did, and I backed out the door with my gun, just like the Wild West days. I hollered at my driver, I said, 'Get this Pontiac rollin'!' He had the motor runnin'. I got in that car and we burned rubber from there back to Texas."

B.B. almost never canceled a show. Once, Big Red broke down amid torrential rain en route to a gig on the Mississippi-Alabama border. B.B. telephoned the promoter, said he was running late, and gave him the option to pull the plug. The promoter replied, "We got a house full of people who ain't leaving till you get here." B.B. got the bus repaired and raced to the show, arriving less than an hour late. Rather than reward his efforts, the promoter tried to wriggle out of B.B.'s $4,000 fee. B.B.'s solution was elegant. He proceeded with the show and played his heart out. Once he had whipped the crowd into a frenzy, he called for quiet. "Folks," he announced, "I'm playing the dance for free. Get your money back." Fans stormed the ticket booth, and the promoter frantically issued refunds to avert a riot. B.B. left town feeling justice had been served.

JOHNNY ACE, B.B.'S erstwhile pianist and perennial nemesis on the charts, was now his stablemate in Don Robey's Buffalo Booking operation in Houston. Still in his early twenties, Johnny was a shy young man with boyish good looks who hadn't really sought the spotlight and never seemed quite at ease once he had it. Johnny wasn't much of a singer, either, but something in his smooth, sincere baritone ensnared listeners. Johnny's consecutive number 1 hits in 1952 and 1953 made him Robey's first breakout artist. By the spring of 1953, Robey had a second star: Willie Mae "Big Mama" Thornton, the gay blues growler from Alabama whose defiance of feminine stereotypes made her a spiritual descendant of Lucille Bogan and her "B.D. Woman's Blues." Thornton exploded out of radio speakers in 1953 with "Hound Dog," a Leiber-Stoller song that she transformed into primordial rock 'n' roll. Robey sent Thornton and Johnny Ace out on tour, playing the Apollo eight times in two years. Yet, by 1954, Johnny had fallen into a rut. His singles in the spring and summer of 1954 reached only number 6 and number 9 on the charts, respectively. And so it was with diminished hopes that Robey rolled out Johnny's final 1954 release, "Pledging My Love," at Christmas.

On Christmas night, Johnny played a gig with Thornton at the Houston City Auditorium. They closed out their first set just after 11 p.m. and retreated to a dressing room for intermission.

Johnny was a wild man. His idea of fun was "driving his Oldsmobile 90 miles per hour, his pistol in hand, shooting out the zeroes on roadside speed-limit signs." Johnny delighted in terrifying his retinue of girlfriends, coperformers, and hangers-on with a disturbing good-luck ritual: he would spin the empty cylinder of his revolver, as if playing Russian roulette, snap it back into place, lift the barrel to his temple or point it at someone else's, and pull the trigger.

That Christmas night in the Houston dressing room, Johnny sucked down vodka and toyed restlessly with his revolver. He pointed it at a couple sitting nearby. Thornton told him to stop. She asked to see the gun. When she examined the cylinder, a bullet fell out. Johnny told her to put it back. (Or that, at least, would be Thornton's account.) She did, and she returned the firearm. Johnny then proceeded to press the barrel against the head of his girlfriend and pull the trigger, producing an empty click. Johnny cackled. "Stop that, Johnny," Thornton barked. "You're gonna get somebody killed."

"There's nothing to worry about," Johnny replied. "Look, I'll show you." He raised the barrel to his right temple and again pulled the trigger. The gun discharged the bullet into his brain. His body went limp and crashed to the floor. Johnny Ace was, in a sense, the first real casualty of the rock 'n' roll era. He was twenty-five.

Questions swirled for months after Johnny's death. The coroner called it Russian roulette, which it was. B.B., who had watched his former sideman grow increasingly erratic with his rising fame, wistfully observed, "I think the pressure was beginning to get to Johnny."

Why had Johnny added a bullet to his good-luck ritual? If he sought suicide, if he knew the gun was loaded, then why had he pointed it at his girlfriend's head and pulled the trigger? Conspiracy theorists wondered if Don Robey, no stranger to firearms, had somehow persuaded Thornton to load the bullet into the gun in a bid to boost record sales.

If that was Robey's plan, it worked. Death rekindled Johnny Ace's career. Robey organized a star-studded funeral in Memphis on January 2, with B.B. and band as honorary pallbearers. "Pledging My Love" rose to the top of the R&B charts and remained there for ten weeks, becoming the best-selling "race" single of 1955. It even reached number 17 on the pop charts, the white charts, which was somewhere B.B. and most of his label-mates had never been.

The big names on the rhythm-and-blues charts of the early 1950s— Roy Brown and Ruth Brown, Fats Domino, Big Joe Turner, and Ray

Charles among them—made little impression on the *Billboard* pop charts. Then, in January 1955, a doo-wop vocal group called the Penguins cracked the top ten on the *Billboard* Hot 100 with "Earth Angel." The next summer, Fats Domino reached number 10 on the pop chart with "Ain't That a Shame," a fast-paced blues shuffle with all the trappings of early rock 'n' roll: amped-up guitar, pounding piano triplets, boogie-woogie bass, and Earl Palmer's insistent snare drum hammering away on the second and fourth beats. Some weeks later, Chuck Berry hit number 5 with "Maybellene," a song oft cited as the starting point for rock 'n' roll guitar. *Billboard* noted the trend in a November article beneath the headline "1955: The Year R.&B. Took Over Pop Field."

B.B. remained captive to the chitlin' circuit, performing for, and selling records to, an audience composed almost entirely of fellow African Americans. Few whites knew his name, and fewer attended his shows. The white press hadn't yet covered him, save for the occasional squib. Nonetheless, B.B. was now an established rhythm-and-blues journeyman, filling houses in Black theaters and reaping plenty of coverage in the African American press. A piece in the December 8, 1955, *Los Angeles Sentinel*, a few months after B.B.'s thirtieth birthday, termed him a "guitar magician," recognizing B.B. as a guitarist, rather than a singer. The writer floated a new honorific: "King of the Blues."

A reader poll conducted by the African American *Pittsburgh Courier* in the spring of 1956 hinted at the full reach of B.B.'s fame after four years of relentless national touring. Readers voted B.B. the top male rhythm-and-blues artist, over veterans Big Joe Turner and T-Bone Walker and relative newcomers Fats Domino and Ray Charles. A subsequent feature in the same paper, one of the first real profiles of B.B. and his band, neatly encapsulated the bluesman's life in the middle 1950s. Headlined "R-B Star B.B. King's Group Lives in Style," the spread pictured B.B. behind the wheel of his latest ride, a pink-and-cream Cadillac El Dorado fitted with blue-and-white tires and a battery-powered television set. (This at a time when nearly one-third of American families lacked television sets.) The B.B. King bus boasted two more televisions, a record player, and an electric piano. B.B.'s Cadillac probably had air conditioning, which would become standard on the El Dorado by 1957, but B.B. didn't use it. Years of Delta heat had conditioned him to a life of near-perpetual swelter. Air conditioners hurt his throat and strangled his voice. He couldn't sleep in an air-cooled space. When B.B. entered a room or a car on a warm day, an aide switched off the air conditioner and threw open the windows.

Paradoxically, the same *Courier* profile that enumerated B.B.'s automotive riches also found his road company reduced from seventeen pieces to thirteen. After touring for a year with a full, Ellington-style big band, B.B. had lightened his load, surely to save money. Saxophone wild-woman Evelyn "Mama Nuts" Young was gone, along with star trumpeter Calvin Owens, saxophonist George Coleman, and one or two others.

B.B. earned a lot and spent a lot. He paid his musicians top dollar, and B.B. himself lived as luxuriously as was possible in a life on the road. But he didn't save much, and he seldom set aside money to cover his federal taxes. He and his band lived from paycheck to paycheck. Every so often, a cash crunch would compel him to cut back. That economic cycle would play out several times in the years to come.

BY 1956, the segregated charts were breaking down. "The Great Pretender," a late-1955 release from African American doo-wop combo the Platters, became the first song of the new crossover era to reach number 1 on both the white and Black charts, peaking after the new year. Then came Little Richard, whose "Long Tall Sally" reached number 6 in the spring. Richard Penniman's pompadour hairdo, pencil mustache, pancake makeup, and primal squeals ushered androgyny into pop music. His voice was a revelation: a wild banshee howl, an octave higher than Howlin' Wolf's graveyard rasp but no less powerful. Surely this was the loudest, lustiest sound ever to invade the pop charts. Earl Palmer, Fats Domino's powerful drummer, framed Richard's songs with a thundering backbeat on the snare. More than any other songs, Little Richard's "Tutti Frutti" and "Long Tall Sally" fired the first shrill volleys in the rock 'n' roll revolution.

Momentum drew B.B. into this battle for the hearts and souls of American teens. On July 27, 1956, promoters billed a dance at Robinson

Auditorium in Little Rock, Arkansas, as an absurd "Blues Battle" between Richard and B.B.

Happily, B.B. had a hit of his own that summer, one that almost rivaled Richard's for ribaldry. "Sweet Little Angel" was a remake of "Black Angel Blues," a 1931 single from Lucille Bogan, the bawdy blues-woman of "Shave 'Em Dry" fame. The lyrics traded on imagery of angels suggestively spreading their wings. Perhaps B.B. and the Biharis chose the song in conscious response to the hormonal delirium whipped up by Little Richard at his shows. B.B. himself was now an established sex symbol on the chitlin' circuit, drawing screaming female fans to every gig. But B.B. had never seen anything like the shrieking, sobbing throngs that greeted Richard on the Little Rock stage. B.B. immediately grasped that he could not compete with Richard's leg kicks or with his sheer youthful energy. Richard "was lighthearted and funny and filled with the fire of youth," B.B. recalled. "My audiences were always my age or older. And I was thirty-one years old." B.B. had no pompadour, no duck walk, and, frankly, nothing in his repertoire as irresistibly catchy as Chuck Berry's "Maybellene" or Little Richard's "Tutti Frutti." But B.B. did have a few moves. One was to strike a note on his guitar and then spin his pick hand around and around over his head while the note rang, as if he were magically coaxing the vibrato from the instrument. Another was to plant his hand on his hip and sing in falsetto while gyrating in an effeminate wiggle. Either could bring the house down.

History does not record who won the Blues Battle. But B.B.'s new single served up a master class on electric blues. B.B. had perfected his muscular technique for bending notes, and he bent to breathtaking effect on "Sweet Little Angel." When he finished a particularly dramatic vocal line in the second verse, Lucille replied with a ringing tone that B.B. bent with abandon, a moment of tonal anarchy as revolutionary as Little Richard's shrieks. "Angel" also revealed B.B.'s newfound ability to play outside the rhythmic structure of a song—on purpose, this time. Whereas once he had dictated Lucille's solos in neat eighth notes and triplets, now he dared to break out of the song's 6/8 time signature (six eighth notes to a bar), sometimes dragging subtly behind the beat, other times pushing edgily ahead. When he stopped to bend a note or settled into a burst of vibrato, B.B. ignored the rhythm completely, holding a note until he felt like releasing it. Lucille kept her own pace, sometimes pausing and lingering on a sorrowful tone before lurching forward and crashing to a halt in a jumble of notes. This was musical expressionism, B.B. and his guitar voicing feelings so powerful that the rhythmic structure could not contain them. "Sweet Little Angel" reached number 3 on the *Billboard* R&B charts.

Astute listeners might have noticed a subtle change in lyrical theme among B.B.'s RPM singles of this era, from the cautionary "Ten Long Years" and "Crying Won't Help You" in 1955 to the lustful "Sweet Little Angel" and the amorous "On My Word of Honor" in 1956.

B.B. had played the role of eligible bachelor since his split with Martha, meeting, dating, and bedding women with nearly the same tireless ambition that drove his musical career. He had surely been spotted with many paramours. An item in *Cash Box* in early 1956 prophesied an impending marriage to a Miami dancer named Dorothy Anderson. That was not to be. But a few short months later, B.B. was in love. On a visit to Indianola early in 1956, he became smitten with a girl of fifteen named Sue Carol Hall. She was a "bright-eyed, light-skinned beauty," B.B. recalled, with a white, Jewish father and an African American mother. With her olive skin and lustrous brown hair, Sue didn't visually register as either white or Black, an ambiguity that promised trouble for her relationship with B.B.

Sue's mother owned Club Ebony, a chitlin' circuit fixture. "I worked in the club," Sue recalled. "And musicians [my mother] would book, she would introduce me to all of them: 'This is my daughter; if you need anything, let her know.' There were no child labor laws then, not in Mississippi."

Sue met B.B. on his tour bus, parked outside the club. "Come out," her mother instructed. "I want you to meet him." Sue obliged. "And it was just an introduction, and that was it," she recalled. "He stayed on the bus and got dressed and went to work. And I was there working." B.B. "had a façade that he could put up," Sue recalled. He revealed none of his feelings in that first meeting. But Sue had made an impression.

"When I'd play the Ebony," B.B. recalled, "Sue would show up, telling me how she liked my music and how she planned to go to college and improve her lot in life. I liked that talk. I liked her mom and I liked coming home to play for folks and family from my earliest memories. When I went away from Indianola, Sue stayed on my mind."

Sue and B.B. kept in touch. She turned sixteen in March 1956. Two months later, she completed high school, finishing early because she had skipped two grades. B.B. sent her a graduation present: a set of luggage for her trip to Howard University, where she would enroll in the fall. Their correspondence continued. "It was kind of at arm's length, really," Sue recalled. "My mom was a terror, and she had a reputation, and he was afraid of her." B.B. knew he would have to seek the blessing of Sue's mother if he wished to marry her before she turned eighteen. That was not a conversation he wanted to have, so B.B. bided his time.

IN AUGUST 1956, B.B. extended his contract with the Bihari brothers for two more years. Little Richard and Fats Domino had scored multiple hits on the white charts with songs the deejays called "rock 'n' roll." B.B. and his Modern Records label made a few halfhearted efforts to adapt. As a follow-up to "Sweet Little Angel," they released "On My Word of Honor," a maudlin ballad. B.B. crooned like Nat Cole, backed by a choir-of-angels chorus. It sounded nothing like B.B. King, but the song reached number 3 on the R&B charts—though it failed to dent the white pop charts, which was the real goal. The flip side, "Bim Bam," was an abomination, B.B. singing "toodly-do, I sure love you," over an arrangement that sounded like Little Richard's band on helium. B.B. would later say it was the only one of his songs that he hated.

There was no need for desperate measures. A 1956 poll of five hundred stores by the Harlem record dealers association named B.B. the nation's most popular blues performer, his records outselling those of his nearest rivals two to one. This news spawned a raft of "King of the Blues" headlines. A piece in the African American *New York Age* mused that B.B. had conquered the idiom by singing "with the proper feeling and interpretation."

Back home in Memphis, B.B. put some of his earnings to work. In August, he broke ground on a fifty-unit motel as an investment property. (It's hard to know what came of that project, which seems never to have been mentioned in print again.) In December, he announced the formation of a new record company called Blues Boys Kingdom, installing $20,000 worth of recording equipment in an office at 164 Beale Street. The imprint was not for B.B. to record himself—he remained happily under contract to the Biharis—but rather to cultivate neglected talent in the Black community. "Unless someone takes time out to aid kids," B.B. explained, "then the world may never hear a future Sammy Davis, Jr., Pearl Bailey or Fats Domino." Blues Boys Kingdom sounded like a potential competitor to Modern Records, but the Biharis indulged B.B.'s pet project, probably reasoning that he would never find the time to properly pursue it. B.B.'s label released a handful of singles over two years before quietly shutting down.

A short time later, probably in 1957, B.B. spent $5,000 to purchase a twenty-acre farm outside Memphis in Bartlett, Tennessee, not for himself but for his father, Albert, and his extended family. Albert kept his job at the Firestone plant and put his family to work tending the farm.

"We had cotton, corn, sorghum, and we had livestock as well. Pigs, turkeys, geese, we had all of that," recalled Walter Riley King, B.B.'s nephew. Born in 1951, Walter was the son of Barnell King, the eldest daughter of Albert and Ada, but raised by his grandparents. Albert and his wife ran a tight ship. Walter recalled grandmother Ada as "a matriarch, a disciplinarian, as well as making everybody go where they're supposed to go." Albert, he said, was "very simple": "You just didn't cross him."

Albert never told Walter he loved him, just as he never professed love to B.B. He betrayed his affections in other, subtler ways. "He worked the midnight shift," Walter recalled. "He'd get off at eleven, and it would be cold, because sometimes the fire goes out. And he would throw his overcoat over his kids to keep them warm. And that was one of the things that let you know that he cared."

When B.B. bought the property, he recalled, "I suppose I was dreaming how one day we might live on the farm." But B.B. was seldom home. When he and his father reunited, all of B.B.'s recording-star gravitas would melt away. "There were no distractions from who was Dad and who was Son," Walter recalled.

ON DECEMBER 1, 1955, Rosa Parks boarded a city bus in Montgomery, Alabama. She aimed to challenge one of her state's separate-but-equal policies. City rules required that Black bus passengers exit the front door after paying their fare and then reenter the vehicle through a rear door. Whites sat in front, Blacks in back, behind an invisible color line that shifted when more white people boarded. No Black person could sit while a white passenger stood.

Parks found a seat that Thursday evening. But then the bus filled, and its driver asked Parks to yield her seat to a white man. She refused. Police arrested her. Organizers printed up thirty-five thousand handbills instructing the city's Black community to honor a citywide boycott of public buses on December 5, the date of Rosa Parks's trial. Most of the Black community opted in, and city buses sat largely empty on the day a court found Parks guilty of violating segregation laws. For leadership, boycott organizers tapped a twenty-six-year-old church minister named Martin Luther King Jr. That night, King gave his first big speech to an audience of nearly five thousand protesters at the Holt Street Baptist Church. "My friends," he said, "there comes a time when people get tired of being trampled over by the iron feet of oppression. There comes a time, my friends, when people get tired of being thrown across the abyss of humiliation, where they experience the bleakness of nagging despair. There comes a time when people get tired of being pushed out of the glittering sunlight of life's July, and left standing amidst the piercing chill of an Alpine November." Deafening cheers finally drowned him out.

The Montgomery bus boycott dragged on for months. Membership soared in the local white Citizens' Council. On January 30, 1956, segregationists bombed King's Montgomery home. He and his family escaped injury. Local prosecutors indicted King and other Black leaders for conspiring in the boycott. King was convicted and fined $500. In November 1956, a U.S. Supreme Court ruling effectively outlawed segregated buses. On December 21, Blacks returned to Montgomery buses. White segregationists fought on, firing guns at the buses and bombing African American churches and pastors' homes. A grand jury later indicted four white men in the bombings. Two confessed to their crimes, but a sympathetic jury acquitted them. Prosecutors dropped charges against the others.

Throughout the nascent civil rights struggle, white segregationists had variously portrayed the Black activists as radicals, outside agitators, or communists. Much of their ire focused on the National Association for the Advancement of Colored People, a group formed in 1909 to combat lynchings and racial disenfranchisement. The NAACP's agenda was hardly radical and certainly not communist, and Dr. King himself was a Montgomery resident. To counter the segregationist propaganda, local organizers formed a new group called the Southern Christian Leadership Conference, with King at its head and the church at its back.

THE PLATTERS HAD LIFTED BLACK rhythm-and-blues to the top of the white pop charts in February 1956 with "The Great Pretender." Seven months later, on September 5, a white recording artist appeared atop the R&B charts, and the crossover was complete.

Sam Phillips had proceeded from his work with B.B. and Howlin' Wolf to record a succession of other Memphis rhythm-and-blues talents, releasing many sides but failing to score a breakthrough hit. It was perhaps his commercial failure with Black artists that drove Phillips to focus increasingly on white artists. Phillips had discovered, and B.B. was fast learning, that the R&B charts could take an artist only so far. "If I could find a white man who had the Negro sound and the Negro feel," Phillips said, "I could make a billion dollars."

The producer's hopes alighted on Elvis Presley, a white, working-class teenager from northeastern Mississippi, one of many young singers prowling around downtown Memphis looking for work. Something about Elvis—an odd blend of deep humility, painful insecurity, and iron resolve—reminded Phillips of B.B. King. The producer indulged Elvis and tried out one song after another until something clicked: an old Arthur Crudup blues titled "That's All Right," which Elvis and his little combo sang almost as a goof, jumping around the studio, hamming it up. Phillips finally had the sound he wanted. When the recording hit the radio in the summer of 1954, listeners couldn't tell if Elvis was white or Black. The single sold to patrons of both races.

Elvis moved to RCA Victor before scoring his first number 1 pop hit, "Heartbreak Hotel," in 1956. Elvis remained every bit the ham, singing with exaggerated vibrato, gasps, and yelps, sounding as intimate and unguarded as someone caught crooning in the shower. His vocal delivery was as over-the-top as Little Richard's, and African American listeners loved it. "Heartbreak Hotel" hit number 3 on the Black charts, a rarity in the prior history of the *Billboard* "race" market. Elvis then topped both the Black and white charts with a searing cover of Big Mama Thornton's "Hound Dog," perhaps the most powerful song he would ever cut, released in tandem with a masterpiece of restrained lust titled "Don't Be Cruel."

Years later, B.B. recalled meeting Elvis in the Sam Phillips studios, where B.B. had cut sides in 1950 and 1951. "When I'd go over there, several times Elvis was there," B.B. told an interviewer. But Elvis first entered Sun Studios in 1953, two years after B.B.'s last session there. Thus, B.B. probably met Elvis on a return visit to the studios, as a celebrity guest. He met the rest of the vaunted Million Dollar Quartet: Jerry Lee Lewis, Carl Perkins, and Johnny Cash. "I saw all of them, but they didn't have much to say. It wasn't anything personal, but I might feel a little chill between them and me," B.B. recalled, never elaborating on whether their silence signaled rivalry, racism, or something else.

"But Elvis was different. He was friendly. I remember Elvis distinctly," B.B. recalled, "because he was handsome and quiet and polite to a fault"—not unlike B.B. himself. "Spoke with this thick molasses Southern accent and always called me 'sir.' I liked that. In the early days, I heard him strictly as a country singer," which is how most people regarded Elvis in the early years. Elvis made his first television appearance on a program titled *Louisiana Hayride*. "I liked his voice, though I had no idea he was getting ready to conquer the world."

On December 7, 1956, B.B. returned to Memphis for the Goodwill Revue, WDIA's annual benefit concert to help the city's poor Black children. B.B. was a headliner that Friday night, along with Ray Charles, whose career and B.B.'s were rising apace. Organizers wondered if they could get Elvis, now a bigger star than either B.B. or Uncle Ray, to make a guest appearance. It was a big ask: the Goodwill Revue was an all-Black show, and Elvis would be very nearly the only white person in the Ellis Auditorium if he turned up. Elvis gave his enthusiastic assent, though he could not perform: his contract with RCA forbade it. So Elvis stood quietly in the wings and watched his heroes. Near the end of the show, Rufus Thomas led Elvis to the stage. Elvis greeted the throngs with one of the leg gyrations the television networks would not show. The audience screamed and rushed the stage. Police whisked Elvis off.

Elvis found B.B. backstage. They posed for pictures, Elvis in a striped jacket and tie, B.B. in a white tuxedo, both men wearing easy, crooked smiles. B.B. had watched Presley's rise with a mix of fascination and envy. "The new stuff was R&B sung by a good-looking white boy," he recalled, with a measure of irony. Still, B.B. couldn't help but like Elvis, and his presence at the Revue spoke volumes: "I believe he was showing his roots. And he seemed proud of those roots."

The iconic image of Elvis and B.B., arm in arm at the peak of each man's youthful fame, would become the stuff of legend, particularly among Elvis fans seeking proof that the King had honored his rhythm-and-blues forebears. It was no act. Elvis treated B.B. "like royalty" that night, the bluesman recalled, recounting how B.B. had inspired his career.

Black teens remained smitten with Elvis, buoying "All Shook Up," "Teddy Bear," and "Jailhouse Rock" in turn to the top of the R&B charts at a time when B.B. was scrapping for hits. That stoked resentment. Nat Williams mused in his syndicated column, "How come cullud girls would take on so over a Memphis white boy . . . when they hardly let out a squeak over B.B. King, a Memphis cullud boy?"

B.B. spoke diplomatically of the rock 'n' roll revolution as it unfolded. Decades later, in a moment of candor, he would dismiss the genre as "just more white people doing blues that used different progressions": "Elvis was doing Big Boy Crudup's tunes, and they were calling that rock and roll. And I thought it was a way of saying, 'He's not black.'"

At the close of 1956, Evelyn Johnson and her Buffalo Booking Agency honored B.B. for playing 342 gigs that year, nearly one a day. His earnings for the year topped $100,000. He now owned one hundred suits. At Christmas, generous to a fault, B.B. presented a Cadillac to every member of his seven-piece band. He rewarded himself by taking off the entire month of February, the first real vacation of his working life.

Yet, B.B. was not entirely pleased. "Can't knock the money, but it's a tough way to live," he told an interviewer in 1957. "The hours are terrible and the traveling is worse." B.B. was king of the chitlin' circuit but virtually unknown to white America. "Records are funny," he observed. "You aim them for the colored market, then suddenly the white folks like them and, Wham!, you've got both markets, plus whites at your dances. That's what happened to Fats Domino."

Fats had released his first long-playing album, *Rock and Rollin' with Fats Domino*, in the spring of 1956 on the independent Imperial label. The LP format, introduced by Columbia Records in 1948, marked a gradual shift from brittle shellac 78s to slower-turning records pressed from more durable vinyl. By the late 1950s, LPs accounted for roughly one-quarter of all records sold and more than half of the money spent. Ray Charles, Little Richard, and Chuck Berry all issued their first long-players in 1957.

B.B.'s bold foray into the LP market appeared in the spring of 1957 as *Singin' the Blues*, at a rock-bottom price of $1.49. Even discount records of that era generally fetched twice that sum. Like many early LPs, *Singin' the Blues* merely repackaged B.B.'s greatest hits. Each of the dozen tracks had been a single, and most were obvious choices: the number 1 hits "3 O'Clock Blues," "Please Love Me," "You Upset Me Baby," and "You Know I Love You," along with top-ten entries "Every Day I Have the Blues," "Woke Up This Morning," "Ten Long Years," "Sweet Little Angel," and "Bad Luck." The Biharis rounded out the collection with "Crying Won't Help You," a lower-charting song, and two numbers that hadn't charted at all: "Blind Love" and "Did You

Ever Love a Woman." The back-cover liner notes, evidently compiled without B.B.'s participation, described him as a former dockworker who had started out "plunking his father's battered old guitar."

Singin' the Blues emerged on Crown Records, a new Bihari imprint. While most of the music industry moved in one direction, the Bihari brothers lumbered off in another. Major labels seized on the profit potential in high-quality long-playing records, packaging albums in dust jackets tucked within thick cardboard sleeves adorned with lavish cover art, liner notes, production credits, and dire warnings about stylus wear, even as they hiked the retail price by a full dollar to $4.98. The Biharis, by contrast, priced Crown releases at $1.98 or less and dispatched them to budget bins in general stores and service stations, to be sold alongside discount fare from the Pickwick and Camden labels. As a rule, the Crown factory pressed records on vinyl of such inferior quality that they sounded scratchy on the first play and packaged them without dust covers inside sleeves that lacked production credits. Customers who purchased *Singin' the Blues* might even find an entirely different record inside.

As an African American and a bluesman, B.B. already felt consigned to the music industry's bargain basement, an inferiority he would later liken to being Black twice. The discount-bin stigma haunted him. "I thought I was being undervalued and undersold," he recalled.

But B.B. continued to release fine singles at a steady pace. He opened "I Want to Get Married," a minor hit from the spring of 1957, with a pair of jazz chords in descending chromatic sequence, a gentle reminder that B.B. played three-chord blues by choice, not because he knew no other chords. When B.B. sang that he had known true love "three times" in his life, perhaps he alluded to Angel, his childhood love; Martha, his first wife; and Sue, the girl he intended to wed—although subsequent references to one paramour as a "juicehead" and a second as "another man's wife" frustrate such analysis.

Sue surprised B.B. in his New Orleans hotel room one day in May 1957, walking in unannounced. She faced a grim task: to tell him that she had just given birth to a son named Timothy and that he was not the father. Sue had continued to date other men. She sat on the bed, broke the news, and braced for B.B.'s wrath. Instead, his face cleaved into a smile. He took her hands. "Now you're an adult," he beamed. "Now we can get married." Sue was a mother, which meant she was a woman, even if she was not yet eighteen. "Do you want to get married?" B.B. asked, uncertainly. "Yes!" Sue replied, terror melting to joy. B.B. had no ring to offer his new fiancée, but he promised they would wed after her next birthday.

B.B. soon had another cause for celebration. His next single, "Be Careful with a Fool," became his first hit on *Billboard*'s Top 100 Sides chart, later renamed the Hot 100, which ranked the best-performing singles across all musical genres. It peaked at number 95. Nearly all of B.B.'s singles now featured guitar solos. On this one, he squeezed a flatted "blue" third until the underlying tone was gone and only the harmonic overtone remained—a technique, later named "pinch harmonics," that legions of rock guitarists would exploit in decades to come.

AT THREE THIRTY in the afternoon of October 14, 1957, B.B.'s band motored toward a gig in Dallas. Big Red rolled along Highway 80, east of the city, on a cool and blustery Monday, with Millard "Mother" Lee at the wheel and seven other men inside. (B.B., traveling separately, was miles away.) As the bus approached a narrow bridge, Mother suddenly found himself running out of road. A speeding car had pulled up alongside Big Red—or, by a conflicting account, Big Red had pulled up alongside the car. Both vehicles were moving too fast, and a butane truck barreled toward them from the opposite direction. Neither vehicle had time to pass the other. The three rigs converged on a bridge with space for only two. Mother lurched to the right to avoid the car. Big Red bounced off the bridge wall and careened into the approaching truck. The truck burst into flame. Fire engulfed the truck, the car, and the front end of Big Red. B.B.'s crew managed to crawl out of the back of the bus, escaping serious harm. But the truck driver perished in his cab. The woman in the passing car somehow emerged unscathed, although her car did not.

B.B. heard of the accident by telephone, and apparently some time passed before he learned the full magnitude of his predicament. Big

Red was not insured. As B.B. recalled, regulators had just suspended the insurer, along with his policy. He was personally liable. The truck driver's widow sued B.B. for $375,000. By one account, possibly apocryphal, the court papers reached B.B. onstage in Galveston, Texas, and he promptly fainted.

The case would crawl through the courts for years, finally reaching the Texas Supreme Court. A jury found Mother—and, by extension, B.B.—partly to blame and awarded the dead trucker's family $368,000, a sum later reduced to $210,000 and split between B.B. and the driver of the ill-fated car. B.B. emptied his $10,000 savings account toward the $27,000 purchase of a new Starliner bus, and he worked out a payment plan with the grieving family that would leave him in debt for a dozen years.

CHAPTER 10

FALLOW

S UDDENLY, IMPROBABLY, B.B. KING WAS BROKE. He was also behind on his taxes, and after the Big Red wreck, he had even less motivation to pay them. B.B.'s first priority was his musicians: he would pay them in full even if it meant shortchanging the taxing authorities. IRS agents appeared at his gigs and garnished the nightly kitty. The feds ultimately limited him to a weekly personal allowance of seventy-five dollars. B.B. was accustomed to blowing through that much and more in a single night.

B.B. had gradually thinned the ranks of his band to rein in costs. But his downsizing proved self-defeating. A smaller ensemble limited him to smaller clubs: "We couldn't work nice enough places to make any money." So he hired more musicians and aimed for larger and classier venues. Fronting an Ellington-style big band also allowed B.B. to transcend the label of "blues," which, in the new rock 'n' roll era, was becoming a liability.

Sam Phillips, B.B.'s onetime producer, remained a prime mover in the rock 'n' roll genre. Phillips had moved on from Elvis. His biggest new star, boogie-woogie wild-man Jerry Lee Lewis, scored consecutive crossover smashes in 1957 with "Whole Lot of Shakin' Going On" and "Great Balls of Fire." The Killer's reign would endure until May 1958, when a British reporter discovered Lewis had married his thirteen-year-old cousin. His pop career never recovered.

B.B.'s betrothed, Sue Carol Hall, remained months away from legal adulthood. She had a new blue-and-white Chevy station wagon, a high-school graduation gift from her mother. In the winter of 1957, she climbed into the car, alone, and drove from Indianola to Greenwood. Baby Timothy remained with Sue's mother. Sue intended to dine with B.B., who was passing through Mississippi en route to Florida, and return to Indianola. But when Sue readied to leave, B.B. persuaded her instead to join him on the road. Sue had brought no clothing and wore winter attire. She melted in the Florida heat until the band reached Tampa and B.B. bought her some new clothes. She and B.B. traveled together for two months, crisscrossing Florida, Alabama, and Georgia and logging tens of thousands of miles on the new station wagon before Sue returned home. Her mother was not pleased. "I caused her a lot of grief," Sue recalled. After the wedding, Sue would try to make it up to her.

IN THE SPRING of 1958, B.B.'s contract with Modern Records again came up for renewal. B.B. was desperate for cash, so he opened an earnest round of negotiations with the Bihari brothers. B.B. asked for a $5,000 advance. The miserly Biharis balked.

The Biharis were drifting away from the music-industry mainstream. In 1958, they announced they would eliminate both their Modern and RPM labels, the very heart of their brand, in favor of two budget imprints: Crown for LPs and Kent for singles. Crown evoked "King," the surname of their famous artist. A cigarette brand inspired "Kent." Together, the moves took the Biharis "out of the record business, really," Joe Bihari later conceded, and into the ticky-tacky realm of drug stores and five-and-dimes.

The impasse in contract talks sent B.B. into the arms of the Chess brothers, archrivals of the Biharis: once again, the conflict-averse bluesman averted conflict by courting another suitor. The Chess men promised $5,000 up front and paid for a session in Miami, where B.B. recorded at least four sides. Only then did the Biharis capitulate, matching the Chess dollars and buying back the Chess tapes.

"I would have stayed with Chess, 'cause I liked Chess," B.B. recalled, "but I thought maybe it was better to be a big hog in a small pond than to be a little pig in the ocean." Chess had several artists as big as B.B. King.

That drama unfolded as the Biharis rolled out B.B.'s second long-playing record, titled simply *The Blues* and released in June 1958. It was another collection of singles, inevitably weaker than its predecessor, its contents cherry-picked from across B.B.'s career. The track list included just two top-ten R&B singles, "When My Heart Beats like a Hammer" from 1954 and "I Want to Get Married" from 1957. The latter title proved prescient.

In March 1958, Sue Carol Hall turned eighteen. There was no further need for B.B. to ask the permission of her formidable mother. Still, B.B. and Sue waited another three months to wed. He timed the ceremony for a June visit to Detroit, home to the Reverend Clarence LaVaughn Franklin. C. L. Franklin was a massive celebrity in the African American community, a radio preacher with a national following and a fiery oratorical growl. When his sermons reached a moment of liturgical climax, his voice would crack with passion and pain, a technique that Bobby Bland parlayed into the finest blues voice of his generation. In the decade to come, Franklin would see his daughter Aretha emerge as perhaps the greatest voice of the entire rock and soul era.

Franklin had started his career in Memphis. Now, both he and B.B. were famous, and the two were close. When the time came for nuptials, B.B. "really was adamant that he wanted [Franklin] to do the ceremony," Sue recalled.

The June 4 service unfolded in Room 609 of the Hotel Gotham in Detroit, with the celebrated reverend orating to an audience of four: B.B., Sue, and two witnesses. One of the witnesses was Reece "Goose" Tatum, a Harlem Globetrotter basketball star who happened to be staying down the hall. The other was "Cups" Wilson, a friend and employee of B.B.'s who sold souvenirs at his shows. Neither bride nor groom had any family in Detroit. After the service, the couple "left immediately to go to Cleveland, to work," Sue recalled: "no fanfare." And no honeymoon.

Sue left Howard University and joined B.B. on tour. B.B. objected. "The road, after all, was my private territory, where I'd always done what I'd wanted," he recalled, a freedom that surely extended beyond thermostat settings and bedtimes. To his argument, Sue replied, "But if you're living on the road and I'm waiting at home, it'll never work. I want to be your wife and be with you wherever you are." In the end, B.B. was too smitten to refuse. He drew the line, though, at touring with baby Timothy. "B. did not believe in having children on the road," Sue recalled. "Tim stayed with my mom."

Sue challenged B.B.'s sensibilities about the role of a woman in marriage. B.B. was earning mountains of cash but spending too much of it on his band and his vices, falling ever further in arrears with the tax collectors. She scolded him: "B., your musicians love you because you pay them well and treat them good. But until you treat the IRS just as good, you'll stay in trouble."

Sue tolerated her husband's gambling. Her mother had run a gambling house at Club Ebony. She watched B.B. play poker for money with the musicians on the bus for hours every night. She spoke up about it only once, repeating an axiom her mother had taught her: "The house always wins."

But B.B. never warmed to the IRS or, by all accounts, to Sue's wifely advice. "No woman had ever been so blunt with me," he recalled. Sue's ambition, her financial savvy, her persistent invitations to help—part of him found it sexy. And part of him felt threatened. B.B. ultimately rejected her appeals. He didn't want her advice. He didn't want her to work for him. He didn't want her to work for anybody. She knew better than to persist. Sue's only job would be that of B.B.'s driver, sleeping on the tour bus during his gigs and taking the wheel of his Cadillac Fleetwood when they were over.

B.B. and Sue had fun together on tour. One sunny day, he took her fishing with Arthur Prysock, the jazz singer, in New York's Sheepshead Bay. But Sue eventually tired of the road, and unlike B.B., she felt no compulsion to remain there. She lived for a time in the household of Albert King, her new father-in-law, on his farm outside Memphis. Sometimes B.B. joined her, the closest he would come to a permanent address in an era when he spent six days of every seven on the road. Sue resumed her studies at the segregated Henderson Business College. But she wasn't particularly happy in Memphis. She broached the topic of a move. B.B. told Sue to pick a place. "He worked everywhere," Sue recalled, "and he didn't care where he lived. He wanted me to be happy."

Sue chose Los Angeles. In March 1959, the couple purchased a home in South Pasadena, an arboreal suburb with a small-town feel. The Biharis advanced the money for a down payment. B.B. liked the thought of living close to them. He also liked warm weather, and he thought a Los Angeles address might boost his career. Now he could hold court at the famed 5-4 Ballroom in South-Central Los Angeles, a western outpost on the chitlin' circuit, playing to capacity crowds of female fans unleashing "screams of awe reminiscent of the old Frank Sinatra era," as one account put it, as his young wife sat at home with her child.

IN THE AUTUMN of 1957, Arkansas governor Orval Faubus went on television to announce that "blood will run in the streets" if nine African American students attempted to enter Central High School in Little Rock, the state capital, that fall. A campaign to integrate one Little Rock school had galvanized segregationist sentiments among whites, emboldening the governor to defy both the federal government and the civil rights community. On the morning of September 4, the first Black student, Elizabeth Eckford, arrived at Central High to find that Governor Faubus had activated the National Guard to bar her way. A cordon of guardsmen surrounded the school, brandishing bayonets, as a white mob cried, "Lynch her!" The Little Rock Nine finally gained entry on September 23, but a riotous mob compelled police to remove them. The next day, President Eisenhower dispatched federal troops. He spoke on national television, framing Little Rock not as a righteous cause but as a dispassionate case study that "mob rule cannot be allowed to override the decisions of our courts." On September 25, a convoy of paratroopers escorted the nine students to their classes. Over the 1957–58 school year, white students kicked and tripped them in the halls and threatened them with more serious harm. But in May 1958, sixteen-year-old Ernest Green became the first Black student to graduate from Central High. The white governor redoubled his segregationist rhetoric, his popularity among white voters buoyed to an all-time high.

The next spring, somewhere in the endless expanse of Texas, B.B. and Sue King stopped at a diner for food. They were heading to Los Angeles on their cross-country move. Diner employees asked them to wait in their car while the kitchen staff prepared a meal. Some minutes later, a patrol car arrived, summoned by the diner staff, who didn't like the looks of this dark-skinned man traveling with a light-skinned woman and blond-haired baby. The patrolman walked to B.B.'s car at a glacial pace, positioned himself at the driver's window, and stood there, peering at the young family. Eventually, B.B. broke the silence: "Something wrong, officer?" he asked, through clenched teeth.

"Been a kidnapping 'round here," the officer replied. "We're stopping suspicious cars."

"This is my wife and my son," B.B. offered.

"What's your name, girl?" the officer asked, ignoring B.B.

"Sue."

"You okay with this guy?"

"He's my husband."

By this time, B.B. was "mad enough to chew glass." But he tamped down his temper, as he always did at such times. Cold silence hung between the men. Finally, the officer dismissed B.B. in the most demeaning terms imaginable: "You drive on, boy. Just be careful."

B.B.'s second marriage was problematic, and not just because of the age difference. Sue was so light-skinned that many observers assumed she was white. After a gig in Ocala, in central Florida, B.B. learned that police had detained Sue on the pretext that a white woman had no business in a Black club. B.B. restrained his fury while he negotiated her release. After that, Sue mostly avoided her husband's gigs.

"If we got into town a little early, he and I would just slip off and go to a movie or something and hide in the movie house until it was time for him to go to work," she recalled. "He would go to work, and I would stay on the bus."

The appearance of interracial marriage would fuel several more disturbances over the years. "I just didn't pay attention to half of it,"

Sue recalled, and B.B. "probably interceded a number of times that I just didn't know."

A CONFLUENCE of events in 1958 and 1959 sent the nascent rock 'n' roll movement into full retreat. Rock 'n' roll was Black music, raw and sexual. Elvis and his pelvis sparked backlash among the nation's cultural guardians. Mainstream labels churned out milquetoast covers of Black rock 'n' roll hits by white artists such as Pat Boone, whose versions of "Ain't That a Shame" and "Tutti Frutti" out-charted the originals. Little Richard abruptly left music for the ministry in 1957. Elvis entered the army in March 1958. Scandal brought down Jerry Lee Lewis. Buddy Holly, the rockabilly icon from Texas, died in a plane crash in February 1959. Later that year, police arrested Chuck Berry on suspicion of sexual relations with a girl of fourteen. Of the early rock 'n' roll titans, only Fats Domino remained.

Into the breach swept a new breed of manufactured white teen idols, Frankie Avalon, Bobby Darin, Paul Anka, and Ricky Nelson—talented artists all, but groomed, coiffed, and sanitized. They battled for supremacy of the pop charts against the remaining rock 'n' rollers, including a post-army Elvis, the Everly Brothers, and crossover African American vocal stars the Platters.

Into that fray, in the fall of 1958, B.B. released a Platters-style doo-wop single titled "Please Accept My Love." He sang in big, round, crooning vowels, backed by a choral group called the Vocal Chords. The Biharis buried Lucille in the mix. B.B. even abandoned the 1-4-5 blues style, an early foray into pop. The song marked a musical dead end, but it supplied B.B. his only top-ten R&B hit of that year or the next.

Another long-player, *B.B. King Wails*, appeared in June 1959. Largely forgotten today, *B.B. King Wails* feels in hindsight like a watershed moment for B.B. and the Biharis. It was the first B.B. King record to feature a collection of songs recorded (at least in part) as an album, rather than an assemblage of unrelated singles. The record revealed an emerging quality in B.B.'s voice, rich, muscular, and rough-hewn, perhaps inspired by a certain full-throated Detroit cleric. The opening track, "Sweet Thing," was one of the finest things B.B. had ever done, clearly in loving homage to his new bride: "When I first met you," he sang, "you were almost out of school." Another standout, "The Woman I Love," featured a breathtaking machine-gun volley from Lucille and an overpowering vocal from B.B. Tucked in among the filler was another doo-wop experiment, "I Love You So," written and arranged by an erudite Miamian named Hampton Reese. Reese would loom large in B.B.'s later life.

The cover image of *B.B. King Wails* depicted B.B. in classic game face, eyes squinting, brow knitted in concentration, mouth half open as he wordlessly "wailed" the notes pouring forth from his guitar. More interesting, perhaps, to guitar aficionados was B.B.'s choice of instrument: the Gibson ES-175, a lovely, hollow-bodied jazz guitar.

Around this time, B.B. settled not necessarily on a guitar of choice but at least on a manufacturer. For a full decade, the name "Lucille" had passed from Gibson to Fender to Gretsch as B.B. dithered among competing brands. By 1958, B.B. had recognized the branding power of the electric guitar, the elegant visual appeal of a shapely Gibson set against the crisp lines of a freshly pressed suit. Soon after, he embraced a single line of Gibson guitars: the ES-335, released in 1958 and marketed as the first "semi-acoustic" guitar, neither entirely solid nor fully hollow. A solid block of maple ran through its center, flanked by hollow "wings" on either side fitted with f-holes. (To minimize the feedback generated by the open space, B.B. stuffed towels into the holes.) B.B. would eventually trade up to the ES-355, the 335's wealthier cousin, costing twenty dollars more. Most photographs of B.B. from 1960 on show him cradling some variant of the 355.

B.B. was the unrivaled king of blues guitar. No one sounded quite like him, and precious few performed his lyrical style of solo guitar—at least, not on the radio. But a new generation of guitarists awaited his every single with tingling pick fingers. As archivist Colin Escott notes, a lesser album track from *B.B. King Wails*, titled "I've Got Papers on You Baby," spawned cover versions by two ascendant African American Chicago blues guitarists: "Magic" Sam Maghett and Henry Lee "Shot" Williams. Other axe-slingers loomed in the wings.

One night in late 1959, B.B. stood at a urinal in the men's room at Birdland, the New York jazz club, between sets of the Miles Davis Sextet. He was there to see Miles, and the mournful melody of "'Round Midnight" played in his head. A raspy voice broke up his reverie: "Motherfucking, blues-singing B.B. King. Yeah, that's one cat who plays his ass off. Nigger can blow some nasty blues." A shiver ran up B.B.'s spine. Miles was also in the men's room, talking about B.B. That night, the bluesman met the jazzman. Thereafter, whenever they played the same town, B.B. and Miles religiously attended each other's shows.

Davis was a dentist's son, raised on a midwestern estate and trained at Juilliard. He never knew poverty. He bowed to no one, Black or white: you bowed to him. But neither wealth nor fame could fully insulate him against racial horrors. One night during the celebrated Birdland stand, a white policeman confronted Davis outside the club. Davis had just walked a young woman to a cab. The patrolman barked at him to move on. "Move on, for what?" Davis asked. "I'm working downstairs. That's my name up there, Miles Davis," he said, pointing at the marquee. "I don't care where you work," the officer replied. "I said move on." Davis stared him down. The officer closed in to arrest him. A scuffle ensued, drawing more police. One of them clubbed Davis over the head. Photographs of the great jazzman, defiant in his bloodied khaki suit, circled the globe. The bogus charges were dropped, but Davis took that night to heart. "I was surrounded by white folks," he recalled, "and I have learned that when this happens, if you're black, there is no justice. None."

TOWARD THE END of 1959, B.B. released another album, *B.B. King Sings Spirituals*. This was his fourth long-player and probably the first composed entirely of new material, all of it gospel. The record revisited B.B.'s roots with the Famous St. John Gospel Singers. It provided a fascinating glimpse at how the bluesman's career might have played out, had he followed his first musical calling. B.B. recorded *Spirituals* as a peace offering to his Mississippi kin who had forbidden the blues within their homes. Even now, B.B.'s elders greeted his fame with disdain. His Aunt Beulah chided, "What you're doing is all right, I guess, to make a living with. But you ought to make something for God." Beulah was ill. B.B. made the record for her. His lone gospel album showcased the new, throaty richness in his singing voice. Lucille, by contrast, was nowhere to be heard.

B.B. and his young wife were working hard at starting their own family. Though B.B. and Martha remained childless, B.B. either failed to connect the dots or proceeded in willful denial. In 1959, after a year of marriage, B.B. asked Sue if she was "doing something to keep from having children," she recalled. Sue was not, so B.B. submitted to a fertility test at a Detroit clinic. A doctor reviewed the results and told him, "You don't have enough sperm to have impregnated anybody." B.B. then confessed: "When I was young, I had an STD, and I guess I never recuperated from that." He proceeded to recount his previous bouts of hepatitis and gonorrhea, skirting the gruesome details of the country doctor's cure. It was news to his doctor and to his wife, who believed that Shirley King was B.B.'s biological daughter. Suddenly, her husband's failure to conceive a child in his first marriage made sense. B.B. took his infertility harder than Sue did: she already had a child.

In later years, B.B. would weave an elaborate fiction of fatherhood, acknowledging his low sperm count even as he claimed to have sired several children and falsely asserting that both of his wives had miscarried. The truth—that B.B. probably never stood a chance to father children—remained a closely guarded secret to the end.

"At the time," Sue recalled, "I cared more about how he felt about it than about my not having any [more children]." Later on, Sue would learn from a mutual friend that Martha, like her, had successfully borne children with another man. "So I knew," she said. "It was the one thing that he was denied. And he carried it with him to his grave."

Sue contented herself with her small family, touring sporadically with B.B. and spending the rest of her time with Timothy at their South Pasadena home. She reprised her business studies at Los Angeles State College. If she wished to catch more than a fleeting glimpse of her husband, Sue recalled, "I'd have to go out on the road. And sometimes I'd be out there for a year. Sometimes I'd be out there two or three months. Very haphazard. And he'd only be home when he worked there." B.B. always returned to Southern California in the coldest months of winter.

B.B. OPENED the 1960s on a promising note, releasing a single titled "Sweet Sixteen." It was probably the most important side he had cut in half a decade. "Sweet Sixteen" was, at heart, a fairly ordinary blues song, adapted from a Big Joe Turner hit of eight years earlier. The melody was neither memorable nor hummable. The decision to credit B.B. and the Bihari pseudonym "Josea" as the song's authors on the label triggered a letter from an attorney for Atlantic Records, whose cofounder, Ahmet Ertegun, had actually written it. Even then, years would pass before Ertegun received proper credit as songwriter. "Sweet Sixteen" was big, bold, and long—clocking in at more than six minutes, twice the duration of the typical 45. The Bihari brothers split the song in two, placing half on each side of the single. B.B. delivered a commanding vocal, set against a thick, floor-shaking bass that anticipated recording techniques of a later era. Suspense mounted as the minutes ticked by, and "Sweet Sixteen" built to an explosive climax (with the band shouting "Yeah!") in the final verse. The song reached number 2 on the R&B charts. It would endure in B.B.'s set list for decades to come.

The B.B. King orchestra of 1960 little resembled the group that had first boarded Big Red five years earlier. Bandleader Millard "Mother" Lee remained on piano, Kenny Sands on trumpet, and Lawrence Burdine on alto sax. Most of the rest were gone. The newcomers included drummer V. S. "Sonny" Freeman, hired away from Bobby Bland. Freeman was five foot five, and a childhood accident had left his snare-drum hand permanently curled. He remained steadfastly faithful to his wife, a rare trait among B.B.'s musicians.

B.B. had trimmed his entourage from eleven or twelve musicians and singers in 1956 to seven or eight in 1960. His earnings, too, were diminished. B.B.'s bookings dropped apace with his chart performance, from 281 gigs in 1957 to 230 in 1959, with a corresponding dip in gross income from $159,000 to $143,000. "Sweet Sixteen" marked a legitimate comeback, but it would arrive in the next year.

B.B. recorded, and the Biharis released, a torrent of music in 1960 and 1961. Some of the impetus came from B.B.'s revival on the charts, but surely the bigger reason was the collective sense that B.B.'s days with Modern Records were numbered. B.B.'s peers were decamping to major labels. Sam Cooke moved from the independent Keen Records to RCA in 1960 and promptly scored a pop smash with "Chain Gang." Ray Charles moved from Atlantic to ABC-Paramount at the end of 1959 and negotiated an annual advance of $50,000. B.B. visited Louis Jordan at his home in Phoenix and shared his frustrations with the Biharis and their $5,000 advances. Jordan produced one of his own royalty checks. The sum was $160,000. "The big companies are more accountable than the small ones," Jordan explained, in fatherly fashion. "Remember, B., it's a business. Ain't nothing but a business."

B.B. stayed with the Biharis out of loyalty, especially to Jules, who had swept into Memphis a decade earlier and crossed the color line like it wasn't there. "Jules was my man," B.B. recalled.

Well-timed gifts of guitars and cash kept the Biharis in B.B.'s good graces. But B.B. King albums remained cut-rate affairs. After a pair of forgettable LPs that scraped the vaults, the Biharis released *King of the Blues*, which at least brought B.B. back to the present. *King of the Blues* emerged in late 1960 or early 1961 and featured a pair of top-ten R&B hits, "Partin' Time" and "Got a Right to Love My Baby." Throughout these ten sides, B.B. demonstrated a remarkably versatile vocal instrument and a full arsenal of guitar tools—sweeping note bends; effortless subdivisions of quarter notes into eighth- and sixteenth-note runs; crisp, staccato arpeggios; and a velvet-whip sting of vibrato—that white blues-rock guitarists would spend the rest of the decade trying to decode.

B.B.'s next LP was even better. Crown Records hustled out *My Kind of Blues* shortly after *King of the Blues*, with nearly identical cover art. Hard facts on the release are few, and that is remarkable, considering that *My Kind of Blues* is an essential album by a major artist. British blues archivists later theorized it was cut in a single day in March 1960, amid a jumble of other recordings for various slipshod Crown LPs. Little or nothing about it appeared in any newspaper. The session was led by Lloyd Glenn, an accomplished blues pianist based in Los Angeles, the

Biharis' backyard. The full ensemble was just four pieces, probably the smallest group B.B. had fronted at any recording session and a stark retreat from the big-band sounds of his past. "Wanted just drums, bass, and piano behind me and Lucille," B.B. recalled. "Wanted to stay with the basics."

Lucille opened the album with thirty seconds of unhurried, unaccompanied solo before B.B. wailed, "Oh, baby, you done lost your good thing now." The full band didn't kick in until the second minute, and it entered at a loping pace, lagging gently behind the beat, giving the recording the feel of last call at a late-night club. This was the sort of expansive, exploratory music that the long-player era allowed. B.B.'s solo ebbed and flowed between loud, assertive passages and quieter, hushed runs, as if Lucille were stopping to breathe. The record closed with "Please Set the Date," an elegant symphony of interplay between B.B.'s guitar and Lloyd Glenn's effervescent piano. B.B. would later cite *My Kind of Blues* as his favorite among his albums, with the attendant lament, "I don't think anybody bought it much but me." The album didn't sell, and B.B. struggled through a string of moribund singles. He finally scored again in the summer of 1961 with "Peace of Mind." He crooned like Sinatra, another departure from straight blues (with diminished chords, no less) that peaked at number 7 on the R&B charts. It would be B.B.'s last top ten on any chart for five years.

For every high-gloss appearance at the Regal or the Apollo, B.B. and his orchestra endured a night at the Moon-Glo Roller Rink in Kent, Ohio, or someplace like it. B.B.'s agents managed to book him into the Alan Freed Spectacular, hosted by the star-maker deejay at the Hollywood Bowl in June 1961. But newspaper ads relegated the King of Blues to fine print, behind the likes of Brenda Lee and Bobby Vee.

"I could see I wasn't getting anywhere," B.B. recalled. When his contract with the Biharis came up again at the close of 1961, B.B. launched a concerted search for another label. He took a hard look at Chess Records, now perhaps the premier independent imprint in rhythm and blues, home to Muddy Waters, Howlin' Wolf, and Chuck Berry. The Chess brothers also had Willie Dixon, a bassist, producer, and prodigious songwriter who was probably the most important bluesman in Chicago outside of Muddy Waters. Dixon had written "Hoochie Coochie Man" and "I Just Want to Make Love to You" for Muddy, "Spoonful" and "Back Door Man" for Wolf. The Chess brothers surely promised B.B. that if he came over to Chess, Dixon could start writing blues classics for him. B.B. and the Chess men were "just about to get together," Dixon recalled, until Dixon himself talked B.B. out of it. "Look," Dixon said, "you'd be doing the wrong thing if you worked for Chess." Dixon explained that the Chess and Bihari brothers were alike in their stingy ways.

The other suitor was ABC-Paramount. Formed in 1955 as a unit of the American Broadcasting Company, ABC Records had scored big hits with Paul Anka's "Diana" and the doo-wop classic "At the Hop." Those were white songs, but ABC had since crossed over into the R&B marketplace, launching a million-seller for Black vocalist Lloyd Price with "Stagger Lee" in 1958. Ray Charles had signed to ABC the next year and promptly charted the smash "Georgia on My Mind." Other artists weighed a move to ABC, renamed ABC-Paramount at the close of 1961. One was Fats Domino. He and B.B. were close.

Fats counseled B.B., "You need a good company with good distribution." Fats told him to keep his standards high, in business as in love. Fats was about to jump to ABC. He lectured B.B. on record sales and certification. "Not everyone could talk to me like this," B.B. recalled, "but coming from Fats, I took it to heart."

The Biharis told B.B. he "had never sold less than fifty thousand of anything" and said his releases routinely topped one hundred thousand in sales. But none of them were tabulated by the Recording Industry Association of America, because Modern Records was an independent label. The Biharis tried to assuage B.B. for his lack of industry recognition by making up dummy gold records and presenting them to him with great fanfare. But they weren't real.

B.B. was ready to bolt. In mid-1961, he met with the suits at ABC-Paramount headquarters in New York. The office was stiff and formal compared to the warm, familial Bihari operation. But then, label president Samuel Clark offered B.B. a $25,000 advance.

B.B. told Joe Bihari about the fat offer. He added, "I'd like to stay with you." It was a fond sentiment, but surely B.B. knew the Biharis would never counter.

"B.," Joe replied, "let me talk to Jules."

Joe wanted to keep B.B., no matter the cost. Jules disagreed. Voices rose. Hands flailed. "I'm not going to give anybody $25,000 to sign a contract," Jules seethed. And that settled it.

Joe called B.B. back in. "Go with ABC," he said. "They'll do a lot better than we'll do for you."

CHAPTER 11

REGAL

A T SOME IMPERCEPTIBLE MOMENT, around the start of the 1960s, the musical genre known as rhythm and blues split in two. R&B had itself been a catchall term for the segregated pop music of Black America, formerly known as "race" music. Now, a new species of rhythm and blues emerged under the proud heading of "soul." A succession of songs conspired to consolidate the soul movement: "Shop Around," in the autumn of 1960, the first number 1 hit from Smokey Robinson's Miracles; "Stand by Me," in the spring of 1961, from Ben E. King, former lead singer of doo-wop group the Drifters; and "Hit the Road Jack," in the summer of 1961, from Ray Charles. Then came the Marvelettes, Motown's first great girl group, with "Please Mr. Postman." Sam Cooke followed with "Twistin' the Night Away" in early 1962.

The new songs weren't blues, but they weren't very far from blues (four chords rather than three, and eight bars to a verse instead of twelve). They blended compositional elements of Black blues and white pop with a rock 'n' roll backbeat and swooping vocal flourishes of gospel. Soul music marked a distinctly African American response to rock 'n' roll, a genre that had become dominated by white artists following the declines of Little Richard and Chuck Berry. But soul music quickly crossed over to white America, reaching the same listeners who had propelled Richard and Berry to pop fame.

Berry Gordy Jr., the man behind the Miracles and Marvelettes, marketed his Motown labels as "The Sound of Young America," as opposed to Black America. Gordy initially resisted picturing his artists on record sleeves. He carefully curated the Motown Sound, adorning singles with orchestral strings and tapped tambourines and toning down their overt "Blackness." Motown singers covered show tunes and standards and sang lyrics cleansed of sexual double entendre: Gordy probably wouldn't have touched a song like "Poison Ivy," a number 1 R&B hit for the Coasters in 1959 with a lyrical theme of venereal disease. No one in the Motown stable sang with the feral lust of a James Brown, the Pentecostal passion of a Sam Cooke, or the winking hedonism of a Ray Charles. Motown transformed the pop charts, but only the combined efforts of many African American artists and labels would fully integrate the nation's white and Black musical traditions.

By the time B.B. signed with the ABC label, on January 14, 1962, he felt like the last bluesman standing. No other practitioner of pure blues was playing the circuit of theaters and civic centers where B.B. dwelt. (One possible exception was Bobby "Blue" Bland, B.B.'s old Memphis friend. But Bland was hardly a pure blues singer, notwithstanding his nickname, which alluded to the blue undertone of his skin.) Muddy Waters hadn't logged a hit since 1958. John Lee Hooker cracked the charts in 1962 with the rousing "Boom Boom," but his act and B.B.'s lay worlds apart.

The decade since B.B.'s ascent had yielded a bumper crop of young blues guitarists. But none could yet approach him in drawing power or record sales. Otis Rush, born in 1934 in the central Mississippi town of Philadelphia, made the customary journey to Chicago and scored a top-ten hit in 1956 with "I Can't Quit You Baby," playing a B.B. King–style lead over a slow-burning, Muddy Waters–style band. Freddie King, a Texan, found his way to Chicago and channeled B.B. in his 1960 classic "Have You Ever Loved a Woman." But both men would knock around in relative obscurity through most of the 1960s.

Elmore James, "King of the Slide Guitar," started recording two years after B.B. and first scraped the charts in 1952 with his defining song, "Dust My Broom." But James was no B.B. King disciple. If anything, he was an antecedent. Born in 1918 in central Mississippi, James played with Sonny Boy Williamson and learned slide-guitar licks from Robert Johnson. After a stint in the navy, James emerged as the greatest electric slide guitarist since Muddy Waters. He and B.B. carved out parallel paths in the blues.

When it came to B.B. King pretenders, no one could top Albert King. Born Albert Nelson (and not to be confused with B.B.'s father), Albert adopted his hero's surname and hometown and claimed to be his half brother to anyone who would listen. He scored a modest hit in 1961 with "Don't Throw Your Love on Me So Strong," featuring B.B. King–inspired guitar work set against Albert's warm, husky voice. Then he, too, retreated into comparative anonymity. There were others, including Albert Collins in Houston and Buddy Guy in Chicago. For all their talent, none of them had B.B.'s versatility or his drive, the qualities that had kept him on the road and in the charts for so long.

B.B. knew of his younger, African American followers. Never, though, had he seen or heard a white person play the blues as he did. B.B. had no white acolytes because there were no white blues stars. In the United States of 1960, the blues remained an African American endeavor. The rigid segregation of Black blues clubs all but ensured that no white guitarists would even see B.B. play, unless they took great pains (and considerable risks) to seek him out. Perhaps that is why B.B.'s singular, lyrical style of solo guitar barely registers as an influence on the nation's great white guitarists of the late 1950s and early 1960s, men such as virtuoso fingerpicker Chet Atkins, distortion maestro Link Wray, Elvis Presley sideman Scotty Moore, and Ricky Nelson sideman James Burton.

But a few white savants were hip to the blues. One night in 1961, a shockingly white teenager walked into an all-Black Texas club where B.B. was playing, joined by some white friends. B.B. took them for tax men. The pale youth approached the stage, holding a guitar. Closer inspection revealed him to B.B. as an albino. He asked B.B. if he could sit in. B.B. normally spurned such requests. But he admired the boy's chutzpah and didn't want to make a scene, so he agreed. The albino boy proceeded to "set the people on fire," B.B. recalled. And he played like B.B., whose technique he had clearly studied. When the song was over, the milk-white boy reaped a standing ovation. His name was Johnny Winter. At decade's end, he would emerge as one of the great white bluesmen.

* * *

WHEN B.B. SIGNED with ABC-Paramount Records, he parted with Evelyn Johnson and Buffalo Booking, his theatrical agent for nearly a decade. He hired Shaw Artists of New York, the agency that represented Ray Charles. Milt Shaw could book B.B. as a supporting act on hotselling soul revues, with B.B.'s band backing every performer.

"I played bills with Marvin Gaye and Jackie Wilson and just about everyone else you can name, dozens of bills all over the country," B.B. recalled. "But I was the outsider, the bluesman, just like I'd been the outside bluesman in the rock 'n' roll shows of the fifties. I still felt like a sheep among cows."

Once the Biharis knew of B.B.'s impending departure to ABC, they persuaded him to record a series of sessions in the final months of 1961, leaving Modern Records a vast backlog of unreleased songs upon his exit. The next few years would see a glut of B.B. King, with old Crown and Kent recordings competing for rack space against new ABC pressings. By a conservative count, eight LPs and two dozen singles would issue from three different labels under B.B.'s name between 1961 and 1964. The first and best of the Crown albums, aptly titled *More B.B. King*, appeared in late 1961, brimming with spectacular guitar work and novel vocals. On "Bad Case of Love," B.B. experimented with a storytelling style of talk-singing that would become a signature in later years. "You're Breaking My Heart" showcased the gruff power of B.B.'s thirty-something lungs.

The torrent of competing releases should have provoked a reaction from B.B.'s new bosses at ABC-Paramount. But they "never said a word about it," Joe Bihari recalled. The silence left the brothers feeling as if their little label didn't exist.

On March 1, 1962, B.B. recorded his first session for ABC-Paramount at the label's Los Angeles studios. Producers allowed Maxwell Davis to remain B.B.'s main arranger, which put him at ease, and hired top session players such as pianist Lloyd Glenn. For the first time, B.B. worked with a professional lyricist, Ferdinand "Fats" Washington, a talented songwriter whose "Pledging My Love" had delivered Johnny Ace his posthumous number 1 hit. Studio hands taught B.B. to "punch in" his vocals and solos, recording them separately from the instrumental backing track, the easier to fix mistakes. He still recorded most songs in a few takes.

By 1962, American folk singers both white and Black were performing songs about the civil rights movement. But the protest song was not yet an established genre in the new soul idiom, let alone in the broader canon of rhythm and blues. B.B. still hewed to the classic themes of blues: love, lust and longing, heartbreak, betrayal, and loss. And nothing changed with his first ABC single, notwithstanding its title, "I'm Gonna Sit In till You Give In." B.B. strained at the upper end of his register, his voice actually cracking around the halfway point of a lyric that invoked language of the civil rights movement in a whimsical bid for sex. The brisk soul arrangement owed little allegiance to blues and none to Lucille, who sat silent. On his major-label debut, B.B. King played no guitar.

B.B.'s second ABC single, "My Baby's Comin' Home," proceeded at the same frenetic pace. But at least it was a blues song, and Lucille was allowed a solo. B.B.'s guitar vanished again on the next release, "Sneakin' Around," but resurfaced on the flip side, "Chains of Love." And so it went. Some of these songs weren't bad, but the singles still issuing forth from Modern Records were better.

The April 1962 edition of *Ebony* magazine included a B.B. King profile, one of the most in-depth features yet published on the busy bluesman. The photo spread pictured him in suit and tie on his tour bus, a book in his lap and young wife, Sue, cradling him lovingly from behind. A close-up showed B.B. chatting with two other young women while signing autographs backstage. But wider-framed images from gigs in Chicago and Michigan told a different story: B.B. King's audience was aging. B.B. was now thirty-six. Most of the fans at his shows were his age or older. And younger fans who flocked to Milt Shaw's soul revues were not coming to hear B.B. King. Middle-class Black America recoiled from the blues. Soul music represented a fresh start: hip, urbane music that could compete with white rock 'n' roll. Soul meant progress. Blues, to young African Americans, invoked segregation and slavery, juke joints and Jim Crow. When B.B. opened for Sam Cooke or Curtis Mayfield, he sometimes heard boos.

"It hurts me to my heart to hear young audiences heckle me, because they don't understand what I am singing," B.B. told *Ebony*. "They think all blues singers drink gin and smoke pot and beat their wives every Saturday. They don't realize we can be gentlemen, too, and have families and want respect. But I intend to prove they are wrong."

B.B. now grossed $250,000 a year, a large sum, the attainment of which kept him on the road more than three hundred days a year. Salaries, travel expenses, and IRS penalties left him nearly broke at year's end. And, major label or not, B.B. still played dingy Elk lodges and smoky union halls.

Around this time, B.B. was riding shotgun in a Ford van heading from a show in New Orleans to another in Dallas. The night was rainy, and B.B. warned his driver about slick roads. Around Shreveport, B.B. fell asleep. The next thing he felt was "a thump and a bump and a crash, and excruciating pain." The van had veered off the road and hit a tree. "The tree wound up in my seat," B.B. recalled. Fortunately, B.B. was no longer there: he hadn't worn a seatbelt, and the impact had thrown him from the van. He had instinctively raised his right arm, which smashed through the windshield. When B.B. collected himself and took stock, he saw a large flap of flesh dangling from his arm where it had met the windshield. B.B. beheld the white of his own bone.

A surgeon dug the glass from B.B.'s partially severed triceps, sewed up the arm with 163 stitches, and apprised him that he owed his life to the good fortune that the windshield glass had missed major arteries. B.B. flirted with the nurses. That night, he made the gig in Dallas. His right hand was useless, so B.B. coaxed sounds from Lucille by hammering the strings against the fret board with his left. His amplifier did the rest.

B.B.'s second recording session for ABC-Paramount convened in September 1962. Rather than consolidate B.B.'s growing reputation as a blues guitarist, the ABC producers marched hard the other way, placing him before an eighteen-piece orchestra as a Sinatra-style crooner. The first single was a sappy take on a lovely song, "Tomorrow Night," that had been immortalized by B.B.'s hero, Lonnie Johnson, fourteen years earlier. Surely B.B. knew his new major-label bosses were distancing him from his strengths. He can't have enjoyed butchering Lonnie

Johnson's song. "He never liked any recording, during that time, that was not blues," his wife, Sue, recalled.

In concert, B.B. played the blues harder than ever. One night, he decided he was tired of the boos that greeted his customary opener, "Every Day I Have the Blues." B.B. reworked his set to open with "Sweet Sixteen." He sang it with "real-life pain," he recalled. "When I got to the part that says, *Treat me mean, but I'll keep on loving you just the same . . . one of these days, baby, you'll give a lot of money to hear someone call my name*, I couldn't stop the tears from running down my face. And when I stopped singing, the tears kept coming, but instead of boos, I heard cheers."

But B.B.'s audience was shrinking, and his major-label contract wasn't helping. By the time ABC released its first B.B. King album, *Mr. Blues*, in the summer of 1963, most of the dozen songs had already been issued as singles. They hadn't sold, and neither did the album, probably B.B.'s least bluesy collection yet, its title notwithstanding. The best cuts were those, such as "Blues at Midnight," that featured more Lucille and less orchestra. The other keeper was "A Mother's Love," a dreamy, Nat Cole–style ballad penned by the prolific African American songwriter Clyde Otis. B.B. would later call it an all-time favorite.

A fine new B.B. King record did appear in 1963—from the Bihari brothers. Remarkably, almost all of the ten tracks on *Blues in My Heart* were new, recorded shortly before B.B.'s departure to the major label. The musicians assembled in an uncluttered studio: guitar, vocals, bass, and drums, with pulsing Hammond organ and the occasional saxophone or piano. Lucille answered B.B.'s impassioned growls with sensitivity and restraint. The standout song was "Down Hearted." Written by jazz critic Leonard Feather and his wife, Jane, "Down Hearted" was originally titled "How Blue Can You Get" (and probably renamed by the Biharis to muddle the question of songwriter credit). Johnny Moore and his Three Blazers recorded it in 1949, interpreting the song as cocktail jazz. Louis Jordan picked it up a couple of years later, delivering it with customary panache. The big payoff came in the bridge, one of the finest lyrical buildups in the jazz-blues idiom. The singer buys his girl a brand-new Ford, but she wants a Cadillac. He buys her a ten-dollar dinner. She says thanks for the snack. He lets her live in his penthouse. She says it's just a shack. He gives her seven children, and now she wants to give them back. In the months and years to come, "Down Hearted" would work its way to the center of the B.B. King repertoire.

One more B.B. King album would emerge from the Bihari vaults in 1963, under the eponymous title *B.B. King*. All but forgotten today, *B.B. King* offered the most powerful set of songs B.B. had ever recorded for a studio LP. Most of the ten tracks were new and sounded like the product of a single session at the end of B.B.'s Modern Records tenure, although one song, "Please Remember Me," was a full decade old. Producers set the volume on B.B.'s microphone so high that it crackled with distortion from the opening notes of the first song, "Going Home." From there, B.B. delivered one raw, riveting performance after another, raging over Maxwell Davis's crisp, intricate horns. The backing band sounded barely contained. The brothers culled "The Letter" and "You Never Know" as a single, both sides buoyed by B.B.'s impassioned baritone and impeccable guitar. B.B.'s powerful lungs burst from the speakers on "Sundown" and "You Shouldn't Have Left," demanding the listener's attention. The energy didn't let up until the final notes of the closer, "Shake Yours." At this point in his career, B.B. King could have sung his grocery list and brought his fans to their feet.

THE CIVIL RIGHTS movement hummed all around B.B. and his band as they logged one-nighters across the Deep South in the early 1960s. B.B. had yet to address the movement publicly, apart from the regrettable "Sit In" song. His apolitical tendencies would eventually stir ire among younger African Americans.

In February 1960, four African American freshmen at the all-Black North Carolina Agricultural and Technical College walked into an F. W. Woolworth store in Greensboro, North Carolina. They made small purchases and settled into seats at the all-white lunch counter for coffee. Denied service, they remained seated in peaceful protest until the store closed for the day. Their action sparked a sit-in movement at five-and-dimes across the South. White hooligans set upon many protesters, dousing them with condiments or dragging them from their stools and beating them. Racists dynamited the home of an African American Nashville councilman who had represented protesters in court. The bombing inspired a silent march on Nashville's city hall by twenty-five hundred students and supporters, the first such demonstration in the modern civil rights movement. In May, Nashville's lunch counters began to integrate.

At year's end, a Supreme Court ruling effectively desegregated bus stations that served interstate travelers. Activists challenged the government to enforce the ruling in a series of Freedom Rides. A group of thirteen Black and white passengers left Washington, DC, on May 4, 1961, on a slow procession to New Orleans. On May 14, a mob fire-bombed the riders outside Anniston, Alabama. A second mob beat the protesters at the bus station in Birmingham. Photographs of bloodied Freedom Riders filled newspaper front pages the next day. Alabama governor John Patterson refused to protect the riders, calling them "a group of renegades who are here for the avowed purpose of stirring up trouble." The violence stalled the journey until May 20, when a group of Nashville students boarded a bus to resume the Freedom Ride. This time, Alabama leaders promised police protection, but the escort evaporated when the bus reached Montgomery. Again, thugs beat the riders, even knocking a presidential aide unconscious. The Kennedy administration dispatched federal troops to help the riders safely leave Montgomery, only to see them arrested in Jackson, Mississippi. A segregationist judge sent the Freedom Riders to Parchman Farm. Three hundred more Freedom Riders followed over the summer of 1961.

NO STATE POSED a steeper challenge to civil rights organizers than Mississippi. In 1950, the state had a larger share of Black citizens than any other, around 45 percent. Mississippi also led the nation in racially motivated beatings and lynchings. Only 5 percent of the state's African Americans were registered to vote, the lowest share in the nation, thanks to a coordinated effort at voter suppression. More than three hundred thousand African Americans left the state between 1950 and 1960, along with three-quarters of Mississippi-born college graduates of any race. In a 1959 survey, the National Association for the Advancement of Colored People found only five Black lawyers in the state.

In September 1962, a federal court ordered the desegregation of the University of Mississippi, where a lone African American student named James Meredith had sought admission. Rather than obey the court order, white Mississippi governor Ross Barnett termed it "our greatest crisis since the War Between the States." Barnett fanned the conflict, encouraged by the surging popularity of local leaders who fought integration in other Deep South states. "There is no case in history where the Caucasian race has survived social integration," he said in a televised speech. "We must either submit to the unlawful dictates of the federal government or stand up like men and tell them, Never." On September 30, 1962, federal agents secreted Meredith onto the Ole Miss campus. Racists rioted outside. Rather than calm the mob, the governor went on the radio and vowed, "We will never surrender." By dawn the next day, two men lay dead. Meredith quietly registered for classes.

B.B. steered himself and his band clear of civil rights protests, just as he had avoided confrontations with white racists for his entire life. "We didn't hang in those places where we thought we gonna be in trouble," recalled Norman Matthews, B.B.'s closest friend. "We didn't go lookin' for that. They said they gonna have a march, we try to be marchin' out 'steada marchin' in."

But marching away from trouble wasn't always an option.

In May 1963, B.B. was staying at the Gaston Motel in Birmingham. Martin Luther King Jr. was also there, using the Black-owned motel as a staging ground for his campaign to pressure city leaders toward desegregation. A series of spring protests had filled Birmingham's jails. In May, organizers raised the stakes by recruiting children for non-violent demonstrations. Birmingham police took the bait, arresting nearly one thousand children on May 2 and herding them into cells. The next day, Birmingham police chief "Bull" Connor loosed police dogs and fire hoses on a fresh wave of child protesters. By May 6, more than two thousand demonstrators of all ages sat in jail, some in a temporary encampment at the state fairgrounds. Business leaders, horrified by national news coverage of white police attacking Black children, brokered a truce with King. On May 10, King's group announced the Birmingham Truce Agreement, a tenuous desegregation commitment from civic and business leaders to begin lifting color bans on restrooms, water fountains, lunch counters, and fitting rooms, among other modest concessions. King declared victory and left Birmingham the next day. B.B. remained at the Gaston Motel. That night, a group of white supremacists, some of them policemen, hurled a bomb at the motel. The device detonated beneath room 30, the dwelling Reverend King had just left. The blast shook B.B.'s room. "We were two doors apart," B.B. recalled. "We knew it was for him."

B.B. wasn't a hero of the movement, like singer-activists Harry Belafonte and Mahalia Jackson. He didn't perform at historic rallies. He was, by his own admission, "just a blues singer, working the chitlin' circuit." B.B.'s friendship with Dr. King played out behind the scenes, in telephone conversations and chance meetings at segregated motels. "He would talk to [Dr. King], he would donate, he would do what he needed to do," recalled Lora Walker, B.B.'s lifelong friend. "When he'd play certain shows, whatever he was paid, he would give it to the civil rights movement."

B.B. was also friends with Medgar Evers, the fellow Mississippian who had been named the first field secretary of the National Association for the Advancement of Colored People in B.B.'s home state. Evers staged boycotts and protests, working tirelessly to integrate schools, buses, and parks. He led voter-registration campaigns, and he crisscrossed plantations to recruit sharecroppers to join the NAACP. An incurable optimist, Evers would engage the racists who telephoned his home with death threats, hoping to change their minds.

"Medgar Evers showed me more courage than a thousand pistol-wielding militants," B.B. recalled. "I knew those plantations. And I knew how plantation owners lorded over their land like absolute dictators. They could do anything on their land they wanted to; they could get away with murder. So to come on a plantation, to walk right into the lion's den and openly say, 'Here I am. I'm an organizer. I'm here to change the way things have been done for hundreds of years,' man, that took guts."

On June 12, 1963, hours after John F. Kennedy's historic Civil Rights Address, a bullet struck Evers as he emerged from his car at his home. His family rushed him to the nearest hospital, operated by the University of Mississippi, where workers denied him entry because of his race. Once his identity was known, the hospital staff dared not turn him away. And so, Medgar Evers became the first African American admitted to a white hospital in Mississippi, fifty minutes before he died. The shooter, a white segregationist named Byron de la Beckwith, was acquitted after two trials ended in hung (and all-white) juries.

Medgar Evers had lived and died for the Black people of Mississippi. B.B. was one of them. Evers's death hit him hard, B.B. recalled: "because this man gave his life, and he was from Mississippi, and I am from Mississippi, and people think nothing good comes from Mississippi."

By 1963, civil rights leaders feared the movement had stalled. A hundred years after the Emancipation Proclamation, African American families earned fifty-four cents for every dollar earned by whites. The unemployment rate for Blacks was twice that for whites. A. Philip Randolph, now an elder statesman, met with other leaders to plan a March on Washington for Jobs and Freedom at summer's end. Two decades earlier, Randolph had threatened a mass gathering at the nation's capital to leverage desegregation in the defense industry. This time, his goal was to pressure Kennedy and Congress to pass the Civil Rights Act, a measure proposed by Kennedy in his June speech to outlaw segregation in public spaces and halt employment discrimination.

On August 28, 1963, a warm and pleasant Wednesday, 250,000 demonstrators joined the March on Washington. Many arrived on specially charted "freedom buses" and "freedom trains." Folksingers Bob Dylan, Joan Baez, Odetta, and Peter, Paul and Mary and gospel legend Mahalia Jackson entertained the throngs. Martin Luther King Jr. delivered his "I Have a Dream" speech. It was, at the time, the largest human-rights demonstration in the nation's history.

Eighteen days later, on September 15, segregationists bombed a Black church in Birmingham during a Bible-school class. Four African American girls were killed.

* * *

B.B. HAD FAILED to chart a hit in 1963 with ABC-Paramount. In the spring and summer of 1964, the label scraped the bottom of the Hot 100 chart with a pair of singles that, though still mired in orchestral morass, at least signaled momentum in B.B.'s career. The first was "How Blue Can You Get," an updating of his "Down Hearted" single that acknowledged its place in the B.B. King songbook. The second was "Help the Poor," an irresistible Brazilian-style bossa nova penned by Charles Singleton, author of "Strangers in the Night." Lyrically, the song suggested social consciousness, a theme B.B. still had not tapped in song. This time, though, the joke was warmhearted and genuinely funny. "Help the poor," B.B. pleaded. "Won't you help poor me?"

In the spring of 1964, B.B.'s old label released a single titled "Rock Me Baby," perhaps the most important song among many the Biharis had held back upon B.B.'s departure. Though based on an old Bill Broonzy song titled "Rockin' Chair Blues," B.B.'s "Rock Me Baby" was a more disciplined affair, setting a strong and memorable melody against a simple, repeated guitar riff, doubled on piano. The riff was really just two notes, descending from C to a bluesy B flat. It would become one of the most famous hooks in blues. The song reached number 34 on the *Billboard* pop chart, the first time B.B. had cracked the elite Top 40.

"Rock Me Baby" entered the repertoire of James Marshall Hendrix, a young rhythm-and-blues guitarist from Seattle who met B.B. on the road in 1964. Hendrix was playing guitar for "Gorgeous" George Odell, a flamboyant singer, on a tour that included B.B., Bobby Bland, and Sam Cooke. Hendrix was twenty-one and unknown. He sought an audience with B.B., who told him "about entirely new approaches to the guitar, and the powerful effect the Hawaiian and country and western pedal-steel guitars had had on him," and how he had "achieved a cry that sounded human, that had emotion, that sang," David Henderson writes in his Hendrix biography. B.B. pointed to his fat hands, and he explained how Jimi could use his long, supple fingers to make his guitar sound "like a woman singer's vibrato," like Lucille. That little chat "put enough in Jimmy's ears to keep him occupied for months, years."

Blind Lemon Jefferson, the first great bluesman captured on disc, appeared not in the Mississippi Delta but in East Texas. His scratchy Paramount recordings delivered early inspiration to Riley "B.B." King.
WIKIMEDIA COMMONS.

No one influenced young Riley King more than Lonnie Johnson, a virtuoso jazz and blues guitarist from New Orleans, pioneer of the single-string solo.
LIBRARY OF CONGRESS, PRINTS AND PHOTOGRAPHS DIVISION.

Charley Patton, the first great Delta bluesman, appeared on disc in 1929, a few years after Blind Lemon and Lonnie Johnson. Oddly, neither he nor his successors, including the legendary Robert Johnson, made much of an impression on Riley King.
DOCKERY FARMS FOUNDATION.

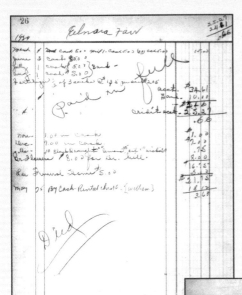

This yellowed page from Edwayne Henderson's farm ledger records the 1940 death of Elnora Farr, grandmother of Riley King. She died owing the landowner $3.63.

COURTESY OF CHARLES SAWYER.

Johnson Barrett (standing), the Indianola plantation boss who promoted Riley King to tractor driver. Barrett was Jewish and racially progressive. Riley admired him.

COURTESY OF CHARLES SAWYER.

Teenaged Riley King posed for this picture postcard and sent it to a girl he was courting.

COURTESY OF CHARLES SAWYER.

Riley (back right) with the Famous St. John Gospel Singers, a quintet that formed in Indianola around 1943. At far left is Birkett Davis, Riley's cousin.
COURTESY OF CHARLES SAWYER.

Riley with Martha Denton, whom he wed in 1944. He was 19; she was 14.
© ERNEST C. WITHERS.

T-Bone Walker, a smart-dressed, acrobatic Texas guitarist, established the electric guitar as a solo instrument in postwar rhythm and blues. More than anyone else, Walker laid the groundwork for the B.B. King sound.
INDIANA UNIVERSITY ARCHIVES OF AFRICAN AMERICAN MUSIC AND CULTURE, JACK GIBSON COLLECTION.

T-BONE WALKER

Direction
SHAW ARTISTS CORPORATION
565 Fifth Avenue
New York 17, New York

B.B. King (at center, with guitar) with the deejays of WDIA in Memphis, the first all-Black radio station, around 1950. At far right is Nat D. Williams, the station's first star.

PICTORIAL PRESS LTD / ALAMY STOCK PHOTO.

B.B. in his WDIA days.

PICTORIAL PRESS LTD / ALAMY STOCK PHOTO.

B.B. in Bermuda shorts, around 1954. At right is Bill Harvey, the saxophonist-bandleader. At left is Evelyn "Mama Nuts" Young, B.B.'s only female instrumentalist.

PICTORIAL PRESS LTD / ALAMY STOCK PHOTO.

B.B. hits the road in 1955 with Big Red, his first tour bus, leading his own big band.

© ERNEST C. WITHERS.

B.B., sans guitar, with the B.B. King Orchestra, around 1955. Several more years would pass before he was regarded primarily as a guitarist.

© ERNEST C. WITHERS.

B.B. with Shirley King, one of his fifteen adoptive children, and nephew Walter Riley King, who was a blood relation, around 1955. Walter would later join B.B.'s band.
© ERNEST C. WITHERS.

B.B. and the King, 1956.
© ERNEST C. WITHERS.

B.B.'s first long-playing record, *Singin' the Blues*, released in 1957.
COURTESY OF ACE RECORDS.

B.B. with his second wife, Sue King, around 1960.
COURTESY OF SUE KING EVANS.

Bukka White, B.B.'s cousin. Bukka was a Delta slide-guitar master and one of B.B.'s greatest inspirations, though B.B. seemed loathe to admit it.
COURTESY OF WAYNE T. HELFRICH.

This 1968 jam at the Generation club in Greenwich Village signaled the meeting of the Black and white blues traditions. From left, B.B., Eric Clapton of Cream, and Elvin Bishop of the Butterfield Blues Band.
MICHAEL OCHS ARCHIVES, GETTY IMAGES.

B.B. tinkers on the piano at the aptly named Hit Factory, New York, 1969.
These sessions would yield "The Thrill Is Gone," his biggest hit.

B.B. chats with Mick Jagger and Keith Richards during the 1969 Rolling Stones tour.
As opening act, B.B. reaped a vast new audience of white rock fans.

B.B. in concert in Boston, 1970. In the space of two or three years, his audience had shifted from mostly Black to mostly white.

PHOTO BY CHARLES SAWYER.

B.B. with his father, Albert King, around 1970. Whenever they reunited, one observer recalled, "there were no distractions from who was Dad and who was Son."

© BOB ADELMAN.

Publicity photo, early 1970s. "If you ever watch his mouth while he's playing," one listener observed, "the words are coming out of those strings."
AUTHOR'S COLLECTION.

B.B. King becomes Yale University's first doctor of blues, 1977. Willis "Bebop" Edwards, B.B.'s lifelong friend and sometime valet, stands behind him.
PHOTOGRAPH BY WILLIAM FERRIS, WILLIAM R. FERRIS COLLECTION, SOUTHERN FOLKLIFE COLLECTION, THE WILSON LIBRARY, UNIVERSITY OF NORTH CAROLINA AT CHAPEL HILL.

B. B. KING   **SONNY FREEMAN & The UNUSUALS**

Paiste Cymbals

Fibes Drums

B. B. KING PRODUCTION
Management: Leroy Myers
1414 Ave. of Americas
New York, N. Y. 10019
212 - 421 - 2021

B.B. King with his backing band, early 1970s. Standing: Eddie Rowe, Bobby Forte, Ron Levy, Li'l Joe Burton, Louis Hubert, Sonny Freeman, unknown fan, B.B., Milton Hopkins. Seated: Driver Cato Walker, Jr., bassist Wilbert Freeman, valet Bertrand English, arranger Hampton Reese.
COURTESY OF RON LEVY.

The friendship between B.B. and singer Bobby "Blue" Bland (left) dated to Memphis
circa 1950, when Bobby sometimes drove B.B. around in his car.
They cut two records together in the 1970s.
AUTHOR'S COLLECTION.

B.B. performs in Leningrad, 1979.
The Soviet fans sat in silence with hands folded in laps.
PHOTOGRAPH BY VALENTIN GOLDIN, AUTHOR'S COLLECTION.

By 1978, B.B. seldom played to African American crowds unless he revisited old chitlin' circuit spots, such as Chicago's Burning Spear.
PHOTO BY CHARLES SAWYER.

B.B. entertains an adoring fan backstage in Chicago, 1978.
PHOTO BY CHARLES SAWYER.

B.B. greets inmates at Mississippi's infamous Parchman Farm prison in 1981.
PHOTOGRAPH BY WILLIAM FERRIS, WILLIAM R. FERRIS COLLECTION, SOUTHERN FOLKLIFE COLLECTION, THE WILSON LIBRARY, UNIVERSITY OF NORTH CAROLINA AT CHAPEL HILL.

B.B. presents Lucille to Pope John Paul II at the Vatican in 1997.
He later joked that the pontiff seemed to know his way around a guitar.
COURTESY OF SPECIAL COLLECTIONS, UNIVERSITY OF MISSISSIPPI LIBRARIES.

B.B. with Eric Clapton, 1987. Their *Riding with the King* collaboration,
thirteen years later, would become B.B.'s biggest seller.
AUTHOR'S COLLECTION.

B.B. with Bono, frontman of U2, 1990. Bono's song, "When Love Comes to Town,"
would rejuvenate B.B.'s career.
COURTESY OF SPECIAL COLLECTIONS, UNIVERSITY OF MISSISSIPPI LIBRARIES.

B.B. and longtime manager Sid Seidenberg at the Great Wall of China, 1994. B.B. credited Sid with propelling him to global fame.
COURTESY OF LARRY SEIDENBERG.

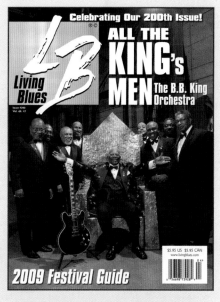

President George W. Bush pins the Medal of Freedom on B.B. in a 2006 White House ceremony.
UPI / ALAMY STOCK PHOTO.

The King's Men, 2009. By this time, B.B.'s revolving-door backing band had evolved into a relatively fixed unit. From left: Charlie "Tuna" Dennis, Ernest Vantrease, Stanley Abernathy, Melvin Jackson, Calep Emphrey, Reggie Richards, James "Boogaloo" Bolden, Walter Riley King.
COURTESY OF SPECIAL COLLECTIONS, UNIVERSITY OF MISSISSIPPI LIBRARIES.

B.B. with Norman Matthews, his best friend and near-constant companion, on the tour bus in Connecticut, 2009. Norman's death, a few years later, was a blow from which B.B. would not recover.

B.B. watches President Barack Obama sing a verse of "Sweet Home Chicago" at a 2012 White House performance. An observer said the octogenarian bluesman appeared "lost beneath two layers of fog."

B.B.'s employers at ABC-Paramount hadn't paid much heed to the flood of competing Bihari releases or to their own new blues artist, whose recording career seemed to be winding down. The former star of Modern Records was just another artist on a corporate label. B.B. felt invisible—until "Rock Me Baby," which proved that he could still sell records, given the right material. Now, ABC executives faced mounting pressure to exploit that shred of hope. They turned to Johnny Pate. A fine jazz bassist turned producer, Pate had teamed up with Curtis Mayfield and his Impressions on a string of soul hits, including "It's All Right" in 1963 and "Keep On Pushing" in 1964. The latter became an anthem of the civil rights movement.

Pate conferred with B.B. on how best to capitalize on his Modern Records hit. "We figured that the quickest way to do this would be to do a live performance, instead of trying to sit down and try to figure out a studio concept," Pate recalled. Thus, sheer convenience inspired the most famous live album in recorded blues.

B.B. seemed to play Chicago's Regal Theater every few months in the middle 1960s. The Regal had opened in 1928, a gem in the necklace of chitlin' circuit palaces. Its auditorium held three thousand patrons on leather seats beneath a ceiling hung like an enormous canopy, with a hole at the center revealing a painted vista of deep-blue sky on a starry night. An arch of maroon, blue, and gold framed the stage, giving it the look of an ancient and vaguely Asiatic temple. Gilded columns lined the walls. Little Stevie Wonder, child star of Motown, scored his first number 1 hit with "Fingertips," a vocal and harmonica workout recorded live at the Regal in the summer of 1962 and featuring the audience as much as the singer. Soul shouter James Brown brought New York's Apollo to its knees a few months later in a show recorded by his King Records label. *Live at the Apollo* would spend sixty-six weeks on the *Billboard* pop chart, establishing Brown as a crossover star on par with Ray Charles. The *Apollo* album documented the riotous energy of a James Brown show for legions of Black and white fans. Pate saw similar potential in B.B.'s stagecraft.

The temperature dipped below fifteen degrees on a frigid Saturday as patrons filed in to the Regal on November 21, 1964. They didn't know B.B.'s sets would be recorded. Neither did the band.

Drummer Sonny Freeman and trumpeter Kenny Sands were probably the lone holdouts from B.B.'s lineup of three or four years earlier. Pianist and bandleader Millard "Mother" Lee had retired. B.B. had hired multi-instrumentalist "Duke" Jethro Pollard to replace him. Bassist Leo Lauchie served as bandleader. Promoters padded out B.B.'s seven-piece combo with another full ensemble, the Regal house band. The last-minute addition of those unrehearsed musicians seemed an odd choice, at a gig to be recorded for posterity.

A sound crew set up beneath the stage, the only space available. The recording apparatus was "probably the best in the world," engineer Ron Steele recalled: legendary conductor Fritz Reiner had used the same gear to record his Chicago Symphony Orchestra. Steele assembled the band at nine that morning for a sound check that "was more like a party," he recalled. Between sets, B.B. and his musicians played poker. The sets would be recorded on three audio tracks. Steele hung two microphones high above the seats to capture the crucial interplay between B.B. and his audience.

Duke Jethro, B.B.'s new keyboardist, was a Black Sephardic Jew from Meridian, Mississippi, east of the Delta. Duke held a commercial pilot's license. Though he was ten years younger than B.B., Duke brought dignity and ladies-man *suavité* to the band. B.B. immediately embraced him as a friend and confidant.

On the day of the Regal gig, Duke's Hammond B3 organ was out for repairs. No one had bothered to return it in time for the curtain call. Duke waited for the right moment to inform B.B. Shortly before the first set, B.B. gathered the band and announced, "Oh, by the way, they're gonna record us tonight." Duke replied gravely, "The organ is not here." B.B. considered. "Well," he said, "you're gonna have to play piano." Duke said, "I can't play piano." B.B. said, "Well, just sit there and pretend you're playing. That's what you do most of the time anyway." The musicians burst into laughter.

The Regal touted continuous shows starting at 1:30 p.m. and running past midnight. B.B. and his band probably played four sets that November day as the headliner on a bill that included Mary Wells, of "My Guy" fame, among other acts. The sound crew recorded at least two of B.B.'s sets, probably the rowdier evening performances.

Johnny Pate lined up deejays from Chicago's premier Black radio station, WVON, to introduce B.B.'s sets. Their participation encouraged airplay for B.B.'s music. In the first recorded set, preserved on side one of the resulting record, the announcer was Pervis Spann, a Mississippian from B.B.'s own hometown of Itta Bena.

"Ladies and gentlemen," he cried, "how about a nice warm round of applause to welcome the world's greatest blues singer, the King of the Blues, B.B. King!"

Sonny Freeman struck a thunderous upbeat on the snare, the band launched into a frenetic reading of "Every Day I Have the Blues," and "the audience just went wild," recalled Arthur Gathings, a boy of fifteen who attended the show. Twelve bars in, Lucille made her entrance with a mellow and understated solo. Then B.B. sang, his calm delivery counterbalancing the band's harried pace.

Barely two minutes later, the song was over. "Thank you very much," B.B. intoned, as the band listened intently. By this stage in his career, B.B. always opened his shows with "Every Day I Have the Blues." After that, Duke Jethro recalled, "every night was different. We never knew what the next song would be. You'd just watch and keep your ears open. He would hit a little note on the guitar, and you'd know what key it was in. And then he'd start playing, and you'd know whether it was fast or slow. And then it was up to Sonny Freeman."

B.B. held court. "And now, ladies and gentlemen," he offered, "we would like to go back and sort of reminisce just a little bit and pick up some of the real old blues. If we should happen to play one that you remember, let us know it by making some noise." B.B. launched into the next song, playing a rising riff in the odd key of D flat that his bandmates instantly identified as "Sweet Little Angel." Goodness knows how the Regal house band caught on.

The crowd was warming up. One young woman cried, "Come on, B.B.," amid scattered screams. Lucille led out the song for nearly a full minute before B.B. opened his mouth. Then he sang the opening line, his voice rising to a sensual growl as he lingered on the words "I love the way-ay-ay she spreads her wings," and the scattered screams became a chorus. Some fans swayed in full delirium. On the second and third verses, the band gradually swelled in volume and urgency, prompting still more desperate cries. Sonny Freeman's powerful bass-drum kicks and snare-drum blasts propelled the song forward with metronomic precision, even as he dazzled the crowd with breathtaking fills. (Mick Fleetwood, drummer and cofounder of Fleetwood Mac, later confessed having listened to Freeman's drum work on *Live at the Regal* until his "eardrums fell out.") In purely musical terms, the performance was a three-way conversation among Sonny, B.B., and Lucille.

B.B. unfurled a solo on "Sweet Little Angel" as complex and rewarding as anything he had recorded. At one point, he peeled off a riff on two strings at once, an impressive feat of improvisation. A few bars later, he hit a sour note, proving that, yes, this was a live recording.

The song eased, and B.B. launched into another little story about "a guy that loses his girl": "Oh, it happens, believe me," he said. B.B. spoke with a preacher's cadence, and his flock responded in kind. "I know it," a man cried from the audience, prompting a chuckle from B.B. as he slid into the next number, "It's My Own Fault," to another round of screams.

Side one of *Live at the Regal* reached its dramatic peak on the fourth cut, "How Blue Can You Get." B.B. beseeched the crowd to heed the lyrics, and they fell to a polite hush in the opening stanzas. B.B. could command an audience the way Fritz Reiner had led the Chicago Symphony. Their communion provided the dramatic arc to this recording. B.B. approached the climactic section of "How Blue Can You Get" with the band and its listeners reaching simultaneous crescendo. When B.B. roared the payoff couplet, "I gave you seven children / And now you wanna give 'em back," the room exploded in a single, cathartic cry.

Much of the Regal set transported the audience back to the 1950s: of the ten songs featured, only "How Blue Can You Get" and "Help the Poor" were relatively new. B.B.'s audience was aging, but it was loyal. Only a room filled with veterans of five or ten B.B. King shows could have erupted in joyous cries at the opening lines of "Worry Worry," an overlooked single that had endured in B.B.'s concert repertoire.

More than anything, perhaps, *Live at the Regal* showcased the broad emotional palette of B.B.'s blues, from the brisk shuffle of "You Upset Me Baby" to the jazz-club smolder of "Worry Worry," from the breakneck rhythm assault of "Woke Up This Morning" to the *Bolero*-style buildup of "You Done Lost Your Good Thing Now." Fittingly, the set closed with "Help the Poor"—"and we need it," B.B. laughed.

When the show was over, the crowd poured out onto Forty-Seventh Street into the frigid Chicago night, many voices hoarse from "yellin' and screaming and singing along. There were very few people who left there that could actually speak the next day," Arthur Gathings recalled. "The Regal was Woodstock without the drugs. . . . That's how much excitement was in the theater that night."

CHAPTER 12

REVIVAL

BRITAIN, RATHER THAN THE UNITED STATES, produced many of the first white artists to learn and play the music of the Black blues greats. Britons had grown up with the blues. In World War II, the BBC broadcast sides by folk-bluesmen Lead Belly and Josh White to soothe shattered nerves during bombing raids. In the years to follow, British clubs and radio stations had no qualms about featuring Black performers.

A small community of white, English bluesmen took shape in the postwar decade. The prime mover was Chris Barber, a trombonist and bandleader from Hertfordshire, just north of London. Barber became swept up in a movement known as "trad" jazz, a revival of American Dixieland inspired by the raft of old jazz and blues recordings that had arrived at British ports with American GIs. (The same wartime exchange of recorded music put Belgian guitarist Django Reinhardt in B.B.'s hands.) British jazzmen arranged for several prominent African American bluesmen to visit English clubs. The first, in 1951, was Big Bill Broonzy, the blues guitarist who had replaced the deceased Robert Johnson in John Hammond's landmark 1938 Carnegie Hall gig. Broonzy touted himself as "the last American bluesman," a myth that endured until the arrival of Lonnie Johnson, very much alive, at Royal Festival Hall in the following year. Subsequent visitors included Josh White himself and harmonica-guitar duo Sonny Terry and Brownie McGhee.

By the 1950s, many country bluesmen had followed Muddy Waters's lead and gone electric. But on these British pilgrimages, the musicians found white audiences lagging a decade or two behind: they expected acoustic guitars and overalls. The Americans happily obliged, playing acoustic instruments and even donning country garb.

Chris Barber hired a guitarist named Tony Donegan. After seeing Lonnie Johnson in London, Donegan adopted the stage name "Lonnie." Barber and Donegan led a uniquely British revival of an American country blues form called "skiffle," a movement that elevated the pompadoured Donegan into an Elvis-style icon of cool. Their recording of the Lead Belly standard "Rock Island Line" launched a short-lived skiffle craze in Britain, inspiring the formation of numerous ragtag bands, whose members would go on to populate the Beatles, Rolling Stones, and Who.

When Donegan briefly exited Barber's band for military service, his replacement was Alexis Korner, a Paris-born pianist and guitarist with a powerful affinity for blues. Korner eventually left Barber along with another enthusiast, Cyril Davies. Together they opened the London Blues and Barrelhouse Club in 1957, repurposing an old skiffle joint. They had tired of skiffle.

In 1958, Barber arranged for Muddy Waters to tour Britain. Korner and Davies saw Muddy perform. Few Brits had heard Muddy or anyone else play amplified Chicago blues, and no one had forewarned Muddy about the acoustic sensibilities of his audience. His music both shocked and inspired.

In early 1962, Korner and Davies formed their own electric-blues combo, which they named Blues Incorporated. Around this time, childhood pals Michael "Mick" Jagger and Keith Richards started a band called Little Boy Blue and the Blue Boys, a name evidently inspired by "Blues Boy" King. When the Blue Boys learned of the more polished Blues Incorporated, they contacted Korner and talked their way into his band. Jagger and Richards quickly defected from Blues Incorporated to form another band, eventually poaching both Korner's former drummer, Charlie Watts, and mercurial slide guitarist, Brian Jones. They dropped the "Blue Boys" moniker for a more enigmatic name lifted from a Muddy Waters song. The Rollin' Stones, as they were first known, debuted in the summer of 1962.

That fall, promoters imported a full armada of African American blues legends to Britain under the banner of the American Negro Blues Festival. Performers included T-Bone Walker, John Lee Hooker, and Chess Records polymath Willie Dixon. The Rolling Stones sat, mesmerized, in the audience.

In 1963, three more members of Blues Incorporated defected to form the Graham Bond Organisation. The important names were Bond's sidemen, Scottish bassist Jack Bruce and temperamental drummer Ginger Baker, later two-thirds of the vaunted power trio Cream. Another seminal group, the Metropolitan Blues Quartet, formed in the London suburbs in 1962. By late 1963, they had hired a hot young guitarist named Eric Clapton and renamed themselves the Yardbirds. They would later evolve, sans Clapton, into Led Zeppelin.

October 1963 brought the epochal return of the American Negro Blues Festival, with Muddy Waters headlining. Five years earlier, Muddy had caught flak for playing through an amplifier. This time, he played acoustic, drawing fresh criticism from fans who now expected an electric set. The bill also featured harmonica legend Sonny Boy Williamson (Sonny Boy II, who had put B.B. on the radio) and Lonnie Johnson, now aged sixty-four. The Yardbirds served as occasional backup band.

The British ensembles had come together for love of the blues. But the music industry rewarded them with hits mostly when they strayed into rock and pop. None could escape the gravitational pull of the Beatles, who single-handedly codified the British guitar-rock sound with a string of singles in 1962 and 1963, including the back-to-back smashes "She Loves You" and "I Want to Hold Your Hand." The Beatles drew inspiration not from the blues per se but from the best of American pop and rhythm-and-blues music in that decade and the preceding one: pioneering rock 'n' rollers Chuck Berry and Little Richard; rockabilly icons Elvis, Buddy Holly, and Carl Perkins; soul shouters the Isley Brothers and Larry Williams; and even the new wave of African American girl groups. "We didn't know any blues," bassist Paul McCartney recalled. "It was all rock and roll, really." The Beatles themselves proved such gifted songwriters that, by the time they had any real competition on the charts, they were writing hits of their own.

Nearly every record label in London had rejected the Beatles. A man at Decca supposedly told them groups of guitars were going out of fashion. In truth, groups of guitars had never really been in. Almost none of the artists who topped the UK pop charts at the start of the 1960s were proper groups. They were individuals *with* groups: Emile Ford and the Checkmates, Cliff Richard and the Shadows, Johnny Kidd and the Pirates.

The Beatles presented themselves as a more or less democratic collective. After they hit number 1, with "From Me to You" in May 1963, nearly every rock 'n' roll band in Britain followed suit. Anachronisms like the Dave Clark Five and Gerry and the Pacemakers gradually gave way to the Animals, Rolling Stones, and Kinks, who hit number 1 in swift succession in the summer and fall of 1964. This democratization of British bands helped set the stage for the guitar hero: a musician, such as Keith Richards or Eric Clapton or Jimmy Page, who could claim a stature equal to or greater than that of a lead singer.

The Beatles' guitar-guitar-bass-drums format defined the rock 'n' roll band for the balance of the twentieth century. Their decision to play guitars, as opposed to saxophones, keyboards, or kazoos, can be traced to the skiffle craze that forged the band. British skiffle ensembles of the 1950s were essentially groups of guitars, augmented with banjos and washboards, overturned trash cans, and other ephemera. Skiffle groups employed neither pianists nor horns: thus, the Beatles learned to play guitars.

Skiffle led a generation of young British musicians to the work of African American blues guitarists. The American rock 'n' roll explosion and the first stirrings of soul delivered further inspiration. The first long-playing album from the Kinks, a North London band formed in the Beatles mold, covered material from prototypical Black rock 'n' roll guitarists Chuck Berry and Bo Diddley and bluesmen Slim Harpo and Lazy Lester. The first Who album covered Bo Diddley and James Brown. The first Rolling Stones LP paid homage to Muddy Waters, Berry, and Diddley. These were (relatively) democratic recordings from democratic bands, showcasing voice and guitar in equal measure.

The Rolling Stones achieved their first international hit in 1964 with a Buddy Holly song, "Not Fade Away." The Yardbirds released a pair of blues singles to little notice before scoring with "For Your Love," a pop song so removed from blues that it drove away the group's star guitarist, Clapton. Their first choice for a replacement, ace session man Jimmy Page, turned them down. They hired the man he recommended, Jeff Beck. A year later, Page joined the Yardbirds, briefly placing two of Britain's greatest blues-rock guitarists in the same group.

The modern guitar hero had not yet taken shape in 1964 and 1965, the peak years of Beatlemania. The Beatles themselves emphasized vocal melody and harmony over guitar virtuosity. Their lead guitar-ist, George Harrison, played short, economical solos that recalled the rockabilly guitarists of the 1950s: Eddie Cochran, Carl Perkins, and Scotty Moore. Those men played guitar like a bank of horns, pealing off simple, rhythmic riffs on two or three strings at a time, emulating two or three horn parts on one guitar.

"With an amplified electric guitar, you could play two harmony notes and you could basically save money on two saxophones and a trum-pet," Keith Richards recalled, summing up the lead-guitar philosophy of that era. The Rolling Stones' lead guitarist played like Chuck Berry, who developed a rhythm-as-lead style of solo guitar that replicated the sound and feel of absent horns. Pete Townshend, guitarist for the Who, played in a singular, slashing style that suggested no one else in the guitar pantheon, at least no one sane.

Eric Clapton's arrival rewrote the rules. Clapton didn't figure in the first wave of the British Invasion, led by the Beatles and Rolling Stones. Those bands had forged their guitar sounds before Clapton's career took off and well before "Clapton is God" graffiti appeared on London walls.

Clapton moved on from the Yardbirds to the Bluesbreakers, a decid-edly unfashionable ensemble led by John Mayall, an older bluesman with a knack for selecting sidemen. The resulting LP, *Blues Breakers with Eric Clapton*, sold briskly in Britain in 1966 and introduced the broader public to a cross-section of the African American bluesmen who had inspired Clapton and his peers. The record opened with Clapton's string-shredding cover of the great Otis Rush single "All Your Love." The band burned through Freddie King's "Hideaway" and Robert Johnson's

"Ramblin' on My Mind," along with choice cuts from Little Walter and Ray Charles. Mayall, the nominal bandleader, claimed top billing. But the real star was Clapton's guitar, a Gibson Les Paul turned all the way up, drenched in distortion, fed through a Marshall JTM-45 amplifier, and recorded at ear-splitting volume, at Clapton's insistence and much to the consternation of the engineers. Clapton had learned what B.B. already knew: if you turned the volume down, you lost that magical sound. *Blues Breakers* marked the full flowering of blues in Britain.

Clapton's guitar-as-voice approach had obvious touchstones in African American electric blues: he had synthesized the sounds of B.B. and his greatest disciples.

"At first I played exactly like Chuck Berry for six or seven months," Clapton recalled. "Then I got into older bluesmen." He progressed from Bill Broonzy to Skip James to Robert Johnson as if flipping through a stack of albums, which he probably was. Then, in an epiphany, he "turned on to B.B. King, and it's been that way ever since." Decades later, Clapton would write that B.B. "is without a doubt the most important artist the blues has ever produced."

Clapton came late to B.B. because the bluesman arrived late in Britain. The first B.B. King single released in England was "Tomorrow Night," in 1962. B.B.'s sappy Lonnie Johnson cover wasn't particularly bluesy, and it didn't sell. The breakthrough came two years later with "Rock Me Baby," the powerful single that had sparked a comeback in the States. Released on the British Ember Records imprint, "Rock Me Baby" arrived just as Clapton and his peers were discovering urban blues. The Animals covered it, among many others. But B.B. himself would not visit Britain for another five years. His guitar style reached London via his recordings and his acolytes: Buddy Guy toured Britain in 1965, Otis Rush in 1966.

After the *Blues Breakers* record, seemingly every guitarist in Britain wanted to sound like B.B. King. Nearly all the prominent lead guitarists of the latter 1960s, from Peter Green of Fleetwood Mac to David Gilmour of Pink Floyd, would bring B.B.'s lyrical style of single-string solo guitar to their bands.

* * *

THE "REVIVAL" of American blues on American shores began within a scrum of record collectors and more specifically with a particular record collector named Harry Everett Smith. He was an abstract painter and experimental filmmaker with vast holdings of blues and country records. In 1947, Smith met with Moses Asch, founder of the new Folkways label. They agreed to issue a mammoth six-album compilation of songs culled from Smith's collection on the emerging LP format. The resulting *Anthology of American Folk Music*, released in 1952, actually spanned the genres of folk, blues, and country and artists both Black and white, covering the era from the advent of modern recording in 1926 to the Depression-era collapse of the music industry in the early 1930s. The *Anthology* launched both the folk and blues revivals of the 1960s in white America. "That set became our bible," recalled Dave Van Ronk, a founder of the Greenwich Village scene that spawned Bob Dylan.

Harry Smith had big ears, and he made wise choices in selecting country-blues sides for his collection. He included classic cuts from several nearly forgotten bluesmen, including Charley Patton's "Mississippi Boweavil Blues," Blind Lemon Jefferson's "See That My Grave Is Kept Clean," Furry Lewis's "Kassie Jones," and the Memphis Jug Band's "Bob Lee Junior Blues," alongside truly mysterious cuts from an entirely forgotten bluesman, "Mississippi" John Hurt.

The term "folk revival" is a bit misleading: "revivals" is more apt. The first took shape in the 1940s around Woody Guthrie, Josh White, Burl Ives, Lead Belly, and especially Pete Seeger and the Weavers, the singing group Seeger formed in 1948. The Weavers scored a huge hit in 1950 with Lead Belly's "Goodnight, Irene." But the group's politics—Seeger first performed his song "If I Had a Hammer" to benefit the U.S. Communist Party—led to its ostracism, along with Guthrie and White, amid the Red Scare of the early 1950s. The American folk genre would require a second revival.

A new generation of white folk guitarists took shape around Harry Smith's *Anthology*. The first neofolk artist to top the *Billboard* album charts, in 1958, was the Kingston Trio, a clean-scrubbed ensemble that studiously avoided the left-wing politics that had hobbled the Weavers. The second, in 1962, was Peter, Paul and Mary, a combo no less commercial than the Kingstons but more political. Changing times allowed the latter trio to reinvigorate both the social consciousness of folk music and the musical careers of Seeger and the Weavers. Following Joe McCarthy's downfall, the Weavers recorded a celebratory comeback concert at Carnegie Hall in 1955. The recording saw release in 1957 and finally became a hit in 1961.

In the summer of 1959, Pete Seeger and the Kingston Trio played the inaugural Newport Folk Festival, a landmark gathering of folk revivalists in Rhode Island that would spawn an annual tradition. A second compilation of lost blues treasures, *The Country Blues*, emerged that year on the Folkways label. This one was assembled by Samuel Charters, a voracious record collector. The disc accompanied a book of the same name, now regarded as the first modern history of blues. The Charters LP added to the canon of "revived" country blues such titles as Bukka White's "Fixin' to Die," Big Bill Broonzy's "Key to the Highway," Blind Lemon Jefferson's "Matchbox Blues," and Blind Willie McTell's "Statesboro Blues." All of those songs would find their way onto white rock and folk records by the next decade's end. Another compilation, Columbia's 1961 Robert Johnson retrospective, catapulted the late Mississippian from near anonymity to the front rank of blues legend.

In 1962, a mellifluous, politicized, Mexican American folksinger named Joan Baez made the cover of *Time*. But the signal moment of the second folk revival was arguably the recorded debut, that same year, of Bob Dylan. He had a voice "like sand and glue," to quote David Bowie, and his first Columbia LP charted only in Britain. He had come to New York from Minnesota a year earlier as a Woody Guthrie disciple on a pilgrimage. Dylan had also heard Harry Smith's *Anthology*, and in Greenwich Village he absorbed the repertoires of established folkies Dave Van Ronk and Eric Von Schmidt, white men who unabashedly performed Black country blues. John Hammond, the famed Columbia producer, provided Dylan the forthcoming Robert Johnson LP upon signing him to the label.

The Weavers and Kingstons had traded largely on folk, rather than blues, traditions. Both ensembles had a way of reshaping every song, no matter its source, into an earnest campfire sing-along. Dylan, on his eponymous first LP, headed straight down Highway 61 to the Delta. Alone with guitar and harmonica, Dylan recorded Bukka White's "Fixin' to Die," which he had surely heard on the *Country Blues* anthology; "See That My Grave Is Kept Clean," the Blind Lemon Jefferson song immortalized by Harry Everett Smith; "Baby Let Me Follow You Down," an old Blind Boy Fuller song that reached Dylan via Von Schmidt; and "House of the Risin' Sun," a Lead Belly song whose arrangement Dylan purloined from Van Ronk. Had an African American recorded and released those songs in 1962, then perhaps *Bob Dylan* would have been termed a blues album. All this, of course, preceded Dylan's emergence as the greatest songwriter of his milieu.

Many Dylan listeners assumed the other blues legends were as dead as Robert Johnson. Eventually, the possibility dawned on the nation's record collectors that a few of their heroes were alive and well and living in obscurity, unaware of their new currency. Tracking them down— the bluesmen themselves or proof of their death—became an obsessive quest to a knot of aficionados with flexible calendars.

One of the first to be targeted was Mississippi John Hurt, a bluesman more enigmatic even than Robert Johnson, his very existence affirmed only by a few old, scratchy 78s. Dick Spottswood, a record collector and musicologist from the DC suburbs, set out to find him in early 1963, armed with an encouraging lyric from one of the 78s that instructed, "Avalon, my hometown." Spottswood located Avalon, Mississippi, a tiny speck in an ancient atlas, midway between Memphis and the state capital in Jackson. Another DC hipster named Tom Hoskins was planning a trip to Mardi Gras. Spottswood asked him to stop at Avalon along the way. Hoskins arrived at the Avalon general store one day and asked the shopkeeper whether John Hurt still lived. Not only was Hurt alive, but he had left the store with two sacks of groceries that very morning. Hoskins proceeded to Hurt's cabin. Hurt saw him and assumed he was a lawman. The visitor ultimately persuaded Hurt to travel to Washington and reprise the musical career he had abandoned thirty years earlier to work as a common laborer.

Hurt thus commenced an autumnal comeback whose basic pattern would play out for several other forgotten blues greats in his wake. He recorded a new album, performed at coffeehouses to mostly white audiences, and staged a triumphal performance at the 1963 Newport Folk Festival. The Rhode Island festival had already hosted John Lee Hooker, Sonny Terry, and Brownie McGhee, but those men had never gone missing. Mississippi John Hurt was a revelation: to hardcore folkies, it seemed almost as if Robert Johnson had returned to life.

For the purpose of rekindling a lost bluesman's career, the festival stage functioned much like the resonator on an old National guitar. Records like Harry Smith's *Anthology* revealed forgotten talents such as Hurt to a small knot of musicians and collectors. Outside that insular world, "the number of people who had heard of John [Hurt] or Son [House] or Bukka [White] was really very small," recalled Dick Waterman, a folk-blues revivalist who eventually served as booking agent for all three men. "And that's why you needed a Newport Folk Festival or a Philadelphia Folk Festival or a new record to bring them to a new audience." On the Newport stage, Waterman recalled, "you came on pretty much unknown. And if you really, really played really well, the word of mouth would sweep over the festival."

After Hurt, the hunt was on. Sometime in 1963, a record buff named John Fahey posted a card to "Booker White, Old Blues Singer, c/o General Delivery, Aberdeen, Mississippi." Fahey took a clue from "Aberdeen Mississippi Blues," wherein Bukka sang, "Aberdeen is my home." Bukka was a missing person, as far as the folk movement was concerned, although B.B. could have easily told Fahey where he was. Happily, someone at the Aberdeen post office knew Bukka and forwarded the postcard to Memphis, where he still worked at the old tank factory. Fahey traveled there with E. D. Denson, his musical coconspirator. Bukka proved more than happy to revive his moribund career. When the rediscovered bluesman told the young visitors B.B. King was his cousin, they took it for another of his tall tales.

Fahey was more than a record collector: he was one of the finest finger-style guitarists of his era, incorporating old country blues,

Episcopal hymns, and a classical sensibility into a unique and eccentric style. He and Denson founded Takoma Records, a label named for the DC suburb of Takoma Park, the leftist bedroom community where Fahey had grown up. In 1964, Takoma Records released the first new Bukka White recording in more than twenty years.

Bukka's comeback tour led to the University of California at Berkeley, where he performed for a group of enthralled (and mostly white) students in a succession of folklore classes. During Bukka's Berkeley residency, B.B.'s own itinerary brought him to nearby Oakland, where he performed to a mostly Black audience at Sweet's Ballroom. Bukka turned up at the gig and took a seat near the stage. B.B. spotted him and offered a "moving tribute," by one account, which sadly included no further details.

The great blues search marched on. The leading candidates for rediscovery were now Skip James and Son House, the finest Delta bluesmen who were neither demonstrably alive nor provably dead.

Fahey took up the hunt for James in 1964, joined by two blues-loving pals. They tracked him to central Mississippi, where an aunt referred them to a place called Dunbar. The men could not locate such a town, so they searched maps for soundalikes and found Dundee. There, they encountered James's wife, who directed them to a bed at Tunica County Hospital, where doctors were treating the bluesman for a genital tumor. Skip James proved a more cantankerous quarry than either John Hurt or Bukka White. When the blues pilgrims showed him a discography of his recordings that someone had painstakingly assembled, James scornfully replied, "Now, isn't that nice." But he eventually agreed to travel to Washington and reprise his career. A month later, in July 1964, Skip James took the stage at the Newport Folk Festival, to rapturous applause.

Another group climbed into a red Volkswagen Beetle in New York in June 1964 and set out for Memphis in search of Son House. A series of tips led them to a telephone, through which they finally reached House in Rochester, New York. House, like James, had stopped playing music and knew nothing of his new celebrity. He also had a drinking problem. The entourage escorted him to Boston, where House entered into a sort of reverse apprenticeship with another young, white record collector, named Alan Wilson. Like Fahey, Wilson was an accomplished musician, soon to found the band Canned Heat. In his Boston apartment, Wilson reminded House how to play his own songs.

"He sat and played with Son, knee to knee," recalled Dick Waterman, one of the blues pilgrims, who watched the lessons. "Al would say, 'In 1930, you did this as "My Black Mama,"' and then he would play it. 'And when [Alan] Lomax came, eleven years later, you called it "My Black Woman,"' and then he would play it. And Son would play with him. And Son would say, 'I'm getting my recollection back!'" Another comeback was under way.

In Chicago, the Chess brothers scrambled to remind young fans that their artists, too, had once worn overalls and played folk blues. They released *Muddy Waters, Folk Singer* in 1964, followed by a series of *Real Folk Blues* LPs featuring Muddy, Howlin' Wolf, and other Chess greats.

To that point, the blues revival had dwelt mostly in yesteryear. On May 26, 1965, many white Americans heard their first strains of contemporary urban blues. The Rolling Stones appeared on *Shindig!*, the ABC musical variety show, on the condition that producers also invite Howlin' Wolf. Wolf performed "How Many More Years" with a full band. The Stones sat reverentially at his feet.

One small faction of young, white Chicagoans had already jammed with Muddy and Wolf. Paul Butterfield was a lawyer's son from Hyde Park who had trained in classical flute. But he looked like a dockworker, and Butterfield found his calling in blues. Mike Bloomfield was a wealthy businessman's son with probing eyes, a slicked-back Jew-fro, and a rebellious streak: his boisterous guitar playing had gotten him expelled from a fancy suburban high school. Elvin Bishop grew up on an Iowa farm but landed at the University of Chicago as a National Merit Scholar to study physics. He retained the rough-hewn features of a farm boy, with an untamed mop of brown hair and wild, Harpo Marx eyes.

At the close of the 1950s, Butterfield started turning up at Black Chicago blues clubs to see Muddy, Wolf, and Little Walter. He met Bishop around 1960. Bishop was a fine blues guitarist, so Butterfield switched to harmonica. They procured a gig at a white North Side folk club and, in 1963, cheekily prevailed on two men from Wolf's touring band to join them. Bloomfield, who was playing the same venue, added a second guitar. By 1965, the Butterfield Blues Band was playing East Coast clubs and drawing notice as a rare integrated band playing electric blues.

Bloomfield and Bishop played like none of the guitarists in American pop music. When journalists or other guitarists asked how they had learned to play that way, they would answer, "By copying B.B. King's licks," to which the questioner would invariably reply, "B.B. who?"

American rock guitarists got a late start. The British Invasion mobilized the first wave of American rock bands, centered in Los Angeles and San Francisco. The new groups recruited mostly from the coffeehouse scene, a community of young men and women still caught up in the folk revival and strumming acoustic guitars. Britain's electric-blues movement, the one that spawned Clapton and Richards and Page, had no real counterpart in the States. "The Black blues culture just had not spread to the mass of white people," Elvin Bishop recalled.

The Butterfields were the exception. Albert Grossman, Dylan's hard-charging manager (and cofounder of the Newport festival), saw the band's promise and prepared to sign them. In June 1965, Dylan recruited Bloomfield, alone, to participate in one of the most storied recording sessions of the decade, yielding Dylan's "Like a Rolling Stone" and *Highway 61 Revisited*. Dylan's sole instruction to Bloomfield was, "I don't want any of that B.B. King shit, man." Bloomfield played on *Highway 61* with uncharacteristic restraint.

The next month, the Butterfield band was a last-minute addition to the 1965 Newport Folk Festival, which had emerged as a sort of national convention for fans of both folk and blues. Organizers slotted the band into a down-ticket "workshop" on July 23, a cool and breezy Friday. The Butterfields would perform last on a bill that featured several great country bluesmen. Emcee duties fell to Alan Lomax, the aging Smithsonian archivist, who introduced the young Chicagoans as if he were auditioning them. "Us white cats always moved in, a little bit late, but tried to catch up," he told the audience, scornfully. "I understand that this present combination has not only caught up but passed the rest. That's what I hear. I'm anxious to find out whether it's true or not."

Albert Grossman, planning to sign the Butterfield band, confronted Lomax backstage. Grossman growled, "What the fuck kind of a way is that to introduce a bunch of musicians?" Lomax reportedly replied, "Do you want a punch in the mouth?" Grossman then opined, "I don't have to take that from a faggot like you." Lomax shoved Grossman. Grossman shoved Lomax. All in an instant, the two men were rolling in the dust.

The crowd ignored Lomax's misgivings and cheered the Butterfield band's revelatory electric-blues attack. Many in the audience had never heard amplified blues. Nor had most of them heard long, lyrical, B.B. King–style guitar solos, which Bloomfield now delivered "with the gyrations and grimaces of a man possessed," by one account. Bloomfield exited the stage as the first in a new breed of white, American guitar heroes.

"Like a Rolling Stone" was just days old when Newport convened, lending palpable excitement to Dylan's approaching appearance as the Sunday-night headliner. Surely many in attendance expected him to play electric: both "Rolling Stone" and his previous single, "Subterranean Homesick Blues," had featured full bands. But Dylan apparently arrived at Newport that Friday expecting to play a solo acoustic set. The notion of a backing band struck him only on Saturday, by which time the Butterfields were the talk of the festival. Dylan asked Bloomfield to assemble a band. Bloomfield enlisted Butterfield's African American rhythm section and found an organist. Rehearsals began Saturday evening and stretched into Sunday morning. The band mastered three songs. On Sunday night, as pop history dutifully records, Dylan went electric. When he was done, according to one attendee, the folk movement's poet laureate had "electrified one half of his audience and electrocuted the other." Folk purists booed him.

Dylan's famous Newport set endures as a landmark in rock music history. Almost forgotten, by contrast, was the rabble of Chicago bluesmen who had inspired him to plug in. "To me, the Butterfield Blues Band was the most important thing to happen at Newport in 1965," said Geoff Muldaur, a prominent folkie who attended. After the festival had passed, "in the blink of an eye, there would be two hundred thousand blues bands in the world based on that model."

After several abortive attempts, the folk-oriented Elektra Records label released the Butterfield band's first full-length LP in the fall of 1965. The eponymous record barely charted, but white Americans purchased it in large numbers, probably a first for an electric-blues album. The Butterfields and their blues carved a deep impression on the landscape of post-Beatles American rock 'n' roll. The very notion of white and Black musicians playing in the same band upended generations of tradition. But the real revelation was Mike Bloomfield. Most white record buyers and musicians had never heard anyone like him.*

---

*A few other guitarists would emerge in the early 1960s with the chops to play like B.B. King. Among them were Lonnie "Mack" McIntosh, a white Indianan whose 1963 debut LP attained cult stature among aficionados; Danny Kalb, a New Yorker whose virtuosity was revealed on the first Blues Project record in 1966; and Jaime "Robbie" Robertson, who joined Dylan's touring band after the legendary Newport gig. (The author thanks Elvin Bishop and Al Kooper for their help in compiling this list.)

CHAPTER 13

FILLMORE

M ANY YEARS AFTER *Live at the Regal*, B.B. King would recall the album as a turning point, if not quite *the* turning point, in his career. "The critics went a little wild," he recalled. "Called it my best ever."

The reality was more nuanced. *Live at the Regal* reached number 6 on the new *Billboard* Hot R&B LPs chart in May 1965, the first of B.B.'s albums to chart at all. But in the broader world of white pop music, *Regal* barely registered. Major newspapers and periodicals failed even to identify the album, let alone review it, just as they had mostly ignored every prior B.B. King release. What little attention B.B. reaped for his milestone recording came in the African American press. "Baby, you talk about something so funky and beautiful and basic that no one with an ounce of soul can resist it," the *Pittsburgh Courier* opined. "Well, B.B. is this thing."

Live at the Regal was required listening for anyone with a serious interest in either the blues or the electric guitar. Eric Clapton later said the record was "where it really started for me as a young player." Carlos Santana termed it the "DNA" of rock guitar. *Rolling Stone* would one day rank it 141st on a list of the 500 greatest albums ever pressed.

Clapton and Santana might have heard *Live at the Regal* when it came out. Most white people did not. The *Billboard* Hot R&B LPs chart did not track white tastes. B.B.'s record would not enter the pop charts for another six years.

B.B. himself never cared for *Live at the Regal*. He once lamented to his bandmate Duke Jethro, "Duke, they treat it like that was the only time that we played well. And if you remember, that wasn't one of our best gigs." B.B. and his musicians remembered the Regal date as an awkward musical mashup. "It sounded like shit to me," Duke recalled.

But it was a hit. The Bihari brothers, suddenly outflanked, rushed out a competing release that spring titled *Live! B.B. King on Stage*. Upon closer aural inspection, that record revealed itself as a rehash of old singles stitched together with random, unrelated crowd noises, surely the nadir of the storied relationship between the Biharis and B.B. King.

Neither album did much to change B.B.'s fortunes. He continued to play package tours as the token bluesman, a supporting act to younger and less experienced performers. A typical ad of that era, from an Atlanta show in April 1965, put B.B. fourth on a concert bill, behind soul crooners Jackie Wilson, Solomon Burke, and Ben E. King. His biggest press clipping of the year was an ill-advised tirade against his shrinking audience, published in the *Baltimore Afro-American*: "For a blues singer, going on stage before an audience of teenagers is like going before a firing squad," B.B. bemoaned. "They don't give you a chance. You don't always expect them to be quiet, but you expect them not to say things to you, not to heckle." He went on to castigate the nation's Black deejays, the other constituency to which he owed his livelihood, as "ashamed to play the blues."

B.B. still played upward of three hundred shows a year, often at "clubs where you could see the moon shining through the ceiling," Duke Jethro recalled. On the road, the overt racism of the 1950s marched right on into the 1960s, oblivious to the federal government's ongoing campaign to enforce civil rights in a recalcitrant South. White-owned service stations still denied food to B.B.'s band unless threatened with the loss of a twenty-dollar gas purchase. On rare occasions, a promoter would cordon off a section of seats for white patrons in a Black venue. Most of the chitlin' circuit remained off-limits to whites. Duke recalled an episode in Shreveport, Louisiana, around this time, wherein a gaggle of white, teenage boys burst through the doors of a segregated Black club where B.B. was playing, trailed by police who sought to deny them entry. The scene unfolded like some dystopian mockery of Beatlemania. "They wanted to get in to hear B.B.," Duke recalled, "and they were running around through the audience, running across the stage, and the police were chasing them." Duke claimed that Elvis himself was turned away from a B.B. King show in Meridian, Mississippi.

IN THE FREEDOM SUMMER of 1964, civil rights volunteers poured into Mississippi to register African Americans to vote, a right that segregationists had categorically and violently denied. On June 21, the campaign's second day, three civil rights workers vanished. Michael Schwerner, James Chaney, and Andrew Goodman had traveled to central Mississippi to investigate a fire in a Black church. Police jailed them on a purported speeding charge. After that, the three men simply disappeared. An exhaustive search turned up other bodies, victims of hate crimes long past. Those chilling discoveries raised no outcry, even as a nation anguished over two missing whites. (Of the three abductees, only Chaney was Black.) In August, searchers recovered the workers' buried remains on a farm outside Philadelphia, Mississippi. One unrepentant local congressman noted ominously, "When people leave any section of the country and go into another section looking for trouble, they usually find it."

The Freedom Summer movement nudged the proportion of Mississippi's registered Black voters from roughly 5 to 7 percent of the adult population. After that, the voting-rights drive moved to Alabama. Martin Luther King Jr. launched that effort in January 1965 in Selma, where only 1 percent of eligible Blacks had registered to vote. Local leaders blocked them by threatening their lives or livelihoods and by limiting registration hours to two days a month. Those few African Americans who actually turned up at the registrar's office might face a twenty-page qualification test that asked applicants, among other things, to enumerate constitutional limitations on the size of the District of Columbia. Local sheriff Jim Clark told reporters Blacks did not vote "largely because of their mental I.Q."

On February 1, 1965, police arrested 250 protesters, including Dr. King, on a march to the Selma courthouse. When Black children marched to protest King's arrest, police jailed five hundred of them. Two days later, three hundred more children marched off to mass arrest.

Police forced prisoners to relieve themselves in buckets. Malcolm X, the Black Muslim leader and national symbol of rising African American rage, spoke at a Selma church. Malcolm apprised the city that "white people should thank Dr. King for holding people in check."

Nonviolent protests continued. Police beat marchers in Selma on February 16 and in nearby Marion, Alabama, on February 18. Protesters defied them, organizing a fifty-mile march from Selma to the Alabama capital of Montgomery. Six hundred marchers set out from Selma on March 7. As they crossed the Edmund Pettus Bridge, they met an army of state troopers armed with gas masks and billy clubs. The troopers charged, beating the unarmed marchers and choking them with tear-gas. Television networks interrupted programming to run live footage of mounted police running down children and elderly women. (Their horses, by contrast, showed humanity, carefully stepping around fallen protesters.) A week later, moved by that appalling display, President Lyndon Johnson announced federal voting-rights legislation in a speech to Congress. "We *shall* overcome," Johnson intoned, pointedly invoking a slogan of the movement. At month's end, Dr. King led twenty-five thousand marchers into Montgomery in triumph.

A gunman killed Malcolm X in a Manhattan ballroom a few weeks after his Selma speech, a slaying linked to the Nation of Islam, with sinister hints of FBI complicity. In August, race riots erupted in the Los Angeles enclave of Watts. Modern Records, B.B. King's old label, owned a pressing plant in Watts. Employees managed to save it by forming a picket line and hoisting a large sign that read, "B.B. King's Record Company." In autumn, B.B. spent $15,000 to bulletproof his bus and took out $50,000 life-insurance policies on each of his musicians.

Musically, 1966 was the revolutionary year of *Revolver*, *Blonde on Blonde*, and *Pet Sounds*, arguably the apex of the entire rock 'n' roll move-ment. Motown scored number 1 hits that year from pop-soul vocal com-bos the Supremes and Four Tops. In Memphis, the independent Stax label scaled the charts with harder stuff from soul growlers Sam & Dave and Otis Redding. Thanks to the blues revival, many of B.B.'s peers enjoyed a lucrative new currency among young, white record buyers. But B.B. was, once again, left out. For him, the year started with *Confessin' the*

Blues, an ABC album that beat an ignoble retreat from the vérité of *Live at the Regal* to the big-band schmaltz of his earlier ABC releases.

The far greater sin was ABC's decision to hire a second guitarist to play some or all of the solos on *Confessin' the Blues*. B.B. later recalled his producer "using another guitarist to play the instrumental breaks" on one of his *Regal*-era albums. He never identified the producer, the guitarist, or the album, being conflict averse, but the record was probably *Confessin' the Blues*: a second, unidentified guitarist is clearly audible on the finished recording. "Man, that ticked me off," B.B. recalled. "I still have bad feelings about that session and promised myself it'd never happen again." In hindsight, the notion that anyone would hire a session guitarist to play the solos on a B.B. King album defies comprehension. Yet, even by 1966, most of the music industry still regarded B.B. primarily as a singer. The guitar hero was a new and untested commodity, and B.B.'s producers somehow failed to grasp that they had the premier guitar hero in their employ.

Meanwhile, new B.B. King singles continued to appear at regular intervals from the Modern Records vaults, like old girlfriends. Odder still, B.B. returned to the Modern studios for a one-off session in December 1965, almost as if he were cheating on his new label. Around the time of B.B.'s resurgent "Rock Me Baby" single, the Biharis alerted ABC that B.B. had remained under contract to Modern Records when he signed with the major label in January 1962. ABC agreed to the bonus session as compensation.

Apart from *Live at the Regal*, nearly every B.B. King release from ABC-Paramount suffered by comparison to whatever the Biharis had out at the same time. The first single released from that 1965 Bihari session, a cover of Sonny Boy Williamson's "Eyesight to the Blind," delivered the sort of effortless, authentic B.B. King blues that ABC seemed unable or unwilling to match. It reached #31 on the R&B charts in March 1966, B.B.'s first successful single in several months.

But B.B. felt like a falling star. And things were about to get much, much worse.

The IRS had haunted B.B. like "a noose around [his] neck" since the Big Red crash, almost a decade earlier, he recalled. B.B. was paying his musicians partly with money withheld from his booking fees that was meant to cover his taxes. "It was a bad business decision," Sue King recalled. "But he wanted a big band, and he kept hoping that things would change. So he kept getting in deeper and deeper."

Now, the taxing agency placed a $78,000 lien against his income. If B.B. had any doubts that the auditors were serious, they were dispelled a short time later, when the IRS placed another lien on a safe-deposit box that he had just filled with $50,000 in gambling winnings.

In June 1966, shortly after the IRS clampdown, B.B. formally disbanded the B.B. King Orchestra. Truth be known, it was hardly an orchestra anymore. The ensemble of the *Live at the Regal* era never numbered more than a dozen men, including road crew and hangers-on. Personnel came and went, but B.B. typically employed a drummer and bassist, organist, and three horns (trumpet and alto and tenor sax), along with a road manager, driver Cato Walker, and wingmen Bebop Edwards and Norman Matthews. When he played a chitlin' circuit palace, B.B. might hire an extra horn or two. Thus, the Great Purge of 1966 left only a few men jobless, including Leo Lauchie, B.B.'s bandleader and bassist, and loyal sax man Lawrence Burdine. B.B. so abhorred discord that he fired the entire band: that way, no one would feel singled out. He quietly rehired the men he wished to keep. In later years, he would delegate such dirty work to road managers and other aides. The dismissals left B.B. with a four-piece backing band, his smallest touring company since the big break in 1952. Kenny Sands, now the band's nominal senior member, stayed on trumpet, Sonny Freeman on drums, Bobby Forte on tenor sax. Duke Jethro, B.B.'s closest friend on the bandstand, played both organ and bass. B.B. put his remaining musicians on salary: up to then, he had paid them after every gig, in cash. "It was a matter of money," Duke recalled. "He couldn't support a big band any more."

B.B.'s marriage, too, was falling apart. Sue, B.B.'s lonely wife, had spent eight years trying to reconcile her life to his. She had entered the marriage without illusions: "I knew he was going to be on the road. He didn't have to tell me." With a young son and professional aspirations of her own, Sue finally gave up trying to follow her husband around the country. "I think it was just a point where I realized that I couldn't keep going out and being on the road and being a mother," she recalled. "And he didn't want kids on the road. So you get torn, and you have to make a decision." Sue lobbied instead to play a larger role in managing her husband's career, or at least his finances, which stood in dire need of management. B.B. rebuffed her. "My temperament told me marriage and business should stay separate," he recalled. "My temperament probably told me wrong, but my temperament was strong."

In late 1965, Sue threatened divorce. B.B. agreed to a radical reordering of priorities. He pledged to perform only around weekends, leaving him free to join his wife and child at home in Los Angeles for half of every week.

"That was the plan," B.B. recalled. But deep down, Sue knew he would never carry it out. By March 1966, he was back to playing a weeklong engagement at the Apollo in New York and performing in St. Louis on Easter, a day any family man would have spent at home.

B.B. told Sue he had to resume working three hundred nights a year to pay the IRS. (Sue remembered differently. In her account, taxes weren't the problem: B.B. simply could not resist rejoining the road, which was his real home.) Sue resolved to leave.

No other woman figured in Sue's decision. That is not to say there were no other women. B.B. routinely booked rooms, sometimes blocks of rooms, to lodge female companions in the hotels where he stayed—nice hotels, not the Holiday Inns where the band bedded down—and to keep them in easy reach. It fell to a procession of long-suffering valets "to babysit the women (yes, plural) who weren't in B.'s bed at whatever particular moment for later on," one bandmate recalled. Wilson Ester, a valet from this era, once rented nine rooms for nine women at the same hotel in the same city. B.B. visited each in turn on a single night. Bandmates called him Doc Sausage.

B.B. and Sue had reached an agreement early in their partnership. Sue would hide any extramarital affairs from B.B., and he would never be seen in public with another woman. B.B. conducted his romantic affairs with utmost discretion, never traveling with anyone but Sue and almost never—apart from one or two squibs in the African American press—being sighted with a paramour.

"He told me that he would always respect our relationship," Sue recalled. And he did. "On TV or at the White House or an awards ceremony or anything, he'd never have a woman there," she said. "And that was because of our marriage."

July 1966 was a turbulent month. African Americans rioted in Chicago and Cleveland and Omaha. Bob Dylan crashed his motorcycle in Woodstock. Protesters boycotted Beatles records over John Lennon's vainglorious quip about Jesus. The U.S. military stepped up bombing raids on North Vietnamese troops along the Ho Chi Minh Trail.

The month also marked perhaps the low ebb of B.B. King's professional career and arguably the deepest trough of his life, for his life and his career were intertwined. Sue filed for divorce in July, citing mental cruelty. After nearly a decade of marriage, she was all of twenty-six, and he was forty. Timothy, her son, was eight. B.B. surrendered the couple's $38,000 South Pasadena house, his '66 Mustang, a Volkswagen camper, and $35,000 in cash.

"I hope she changes her mind," B.B. told an interviewer. She did not. Yet, in years to come, Sue would remain as close to his heart as anyone, offering friendship, support, and counsel. B.B. would never be publicly linked with another woman.

"It's tough," Sue recalled. "Usually divorce comes because of cheating, or you fall out of love, or you have money problems. And we've had all of those things, and we've survived them. The love always stayed."

B.B. was now twice divorced, with no children from either marriage. Feature articles of that time credited B.B. with one child, Timothy, who wasn't technically his. Sue knew about Shirley, B.B.'s daughter. Shirley grew up unaware she had any siblings.

Behind the scenes, B.B.'s family was growing. A second daughter, Gloria, arrived at Albert King's farm around 1958, "basically dropped on Mr. Albert's and Mrs. Ada's doorstep" by a woman who had dated B.B. in Florida, Lora Walker recalled. Lora's mother, Polly, served as intermediary between B.B. and the children. A short time later, B.B. introduced Polly to a third daughter, Barbara, born and raised in Memphis. Willie King, B.B.'s son, surfaced in Chicago around the same time.

By the end of the 1960s, still more children would appear, much to the surprise of B.B.'s friends and former wives.

AFTER FOURTEEN YEARS of national touring, perhaps five thousand performances, and more than one hundred recordings, B.B. seemed to command a smaller audience in the summer of 1966 than when he had first hit national fame, in the spring of 1952. Young African Americans booed him. Most white people had never heard of him.

No one knew those sad facts better than Charles Keil, a young, idealistic, white New Englander. Keil had graduated from Yale in 1961. Two years later, he was at the University of Chicago, preparing a master's thesis in anthropology. Keil played stand-up bass, and he knew the musicians in Paul Butterfield's band. He sometimes joined Elvin Bishop in jam sessions in the apartment building where both men lived.

For his thesis, Keil set out to study the Black, urban musical culture that surrounded him on Chicago's South Side. He drew inspiration to write from the same scene that had moved the Butterfields to play. Keil quickly found, in Chicago and across U.S. society, a blues endeavor hopelessly riven by race.

White people embraced the unamplified blues of antiquity. White record collectors and folkies treasured the music of prewar, Delta-blues fingerpickers. They only grudgingly admired the more recent work of Muddy Waters and Howlin' Wolf and their ilk, who had taken that music to Chicago and electrified it.

"We were looking for the people who played old-time, acoustic country blues," recalled E. D. Denson, the Takoma Records cofounder and Bukka White benefactor. "You had to have recorded in the '20s and '30s, or you just weren't cutting it."

Revivalists rejected the entire school of modern blues, the genre that had taken shape around B.B. and T-Bone Walker and their postwar peers. That genre, which Keil termed "urban blues," featured songs written, arranged, and performed in the pop-music tradition. Urban bluesmen employed full bands that featured the same electric guitars and amplifiers, musical charts, and horns that populated hundreds of other ensembles vying for position on the *Billboard* charts. Urban blues guitarists favored the flat pick of rhythm-and-blues and jazz, a rounded triangle of plastic held between the thumb and forefinger, over the thumb pick of country blues and bluegrass, which amounted to a plastic extension of the thumbnail. For revivalists, flat picks and horn charts were deal-breakers. "They didn't like B.B. King. They didn't like T-Bone Walker," recalled Dick Spottswood, the music buff who had helped rekindle the career of Mississippi John Hurt.

Urban blues, B.B.'s world, was the exclusive province of African Americans. "I doubt that more than a few thousand white Americans outside the Deep South have ever heard B.B. King's music," Keil wrote in his thesis. Urban blues populated the Black rhythm-and-blues charts in the 1960s. Within the Black community, Son House and Skip James, Mississippi John Hurt and Bukka White, and other champions of the blues revival were forgotten commodities.

If the urban blues movement had a leader, Keil reasoned, it had to be B.B. King. For all his recent struggles, B.B. was a survivor. He was the only identifiable practitioner of contemporary blues who had built and retained a national following across two decades, consistently cracking the charts. Keil organized his thesis around B.B., featuring him along with one other artist of similar stature: Bobby Bland, B.B.'s old Memphis crony.

Keil interviewed B.B. backstage in Chicago on August 28, 1963, the day Martin Luther King Jr. delivered his "I Have a Dream" speech in Washington. The meeting provided a snapshot of B.B.'s life on the road in those lean years. B.B. told Keil he had slept just twelve hours over six preceding days, performing three shows a day and holding court with Chicago admirers. "Whenever there isn't something happening, I drop off for a few minutes or a few hours, whatever I can get," B.B. told the anthropologist. He shared his frustration at being pigeonholed as a blues singer and his fascination at the growing number of young African American guitarists who fancied themselves the next B.B. King. He voiced poignant hope that he might open a small nightclub when his touring days were over, a time that now seemed close at hand.

Keil typed up the interview verbatim from memory. He spent many nights at Chicago blues clubs, where, he recalled, "I would scan the audience and not find another white face." He wrote his thesis in the summer of 1964. He was working on final edits when *Live at the Regal* came out. Keil's advisers persuaded the University of Chicago Press to publish the thesis as a book. Someone decided to put B.B. on the cover. The book wasn't really about him, but his spirit suffused it. One emphatic passage leapt out: "B.B. King is the only straight blues singer in America with a large, adult, nationwide, almost entirely Negro audience. If the adjectives 'unique,' 'pure,' and 'authentic' apply to any blues singer alive today, they certainly apply to B.B. King."

By the time the book was published, in the summer of 1966, Keil was living with the Tiv people in Nigeria, the subject of his doctoral research. He was, to put it mildly, out of the loop. Only upon his return to the States, a year later, would he discover the impact of *Urban Blues*.

The critics gave Keil a rough ride. His book had, after all, started out as a thesis, one whose first sentence announced, "I am primarily concerned with an expressive male role within urban lower-class Negro culture." But the *New York Times*, *Washington Post*, and *Guardian* all reviewed it, signaling a major work. For the first time, B.B. was the subject of serious journalism in the nation's leading newspapers. The *New York Times* termed B.B. "possibly the best of the big name blues singers," quoting Keil directly. The *Post* mocked Keil's egghead prose but reprinted the author's assertion that B.B. was the nation's most important modern blues performer. Leonard Feather, America's preeminent jazz critic, more or less panned *Urban Blues* in the *Los Angeles Times*. But the review trained Feather's full attention on B.B. King, an artist who clearly had not been on his radar before. Keil could not have given his subject better press.

IN MID-1966, the Bihari brothers exhumed another classic B.B. King single from their vaults, a smoldering take on the standard "Ain't Nobody's Business." This time, B.B.'s new label had a worthy response. "Don't Answer the Door," released in the fall, sounded unlike anything else B.B. had recorded for ABC. It opened like a church dirge, with shimmering organ and a long, reverb-drenched solo from Lucille, who purred with understatement and subtlety. B.B. displayed his mastery for silence, never striking a second note until the first one was finished, to paraphrase archivist Colin Escott. Lyrically, the song was an ode to romantic paranoia, a theme of B.B.'s failed marriage. "Don't Answer the Door" was a triumph of mood and an enduring showcase for Lucille: the aural information embedded in those five minutes could document B.B.'s cumulative influence on the guitar craft, were it his lone surviving recording. "Don't Answer the Door" reached number 2 on the R&B charts and, more important, number 72 on the pop charts, evidence that white America was beginning to take notice.

After the divorce from Sue, B.B. decamped from the South Pasadena home that was no longer his. He would spend the next four years living in a procession of hotel rooms, seldom remaining in one city for more than a week. By this stage, B.B. didn't check into a hotel so much as he moved in. He traveled with a veritable flotilla of luggage, a dozen bags and boxes filled with changes of clothing, snacks, tape recorders and record players, and volumes of the Schillinger System of Musical Composition, an obscure method of music notation that he studied daily. B.B.'s valet patiently packed, transported, unpacked, and guarded the parcels. B.B. seldom kept a valet for long.

One bag, known as "the Grip," held the cash. Half of the money B.B. earned on the road went to New York, to be parceled out in commissions to his manager, accountant, and booking agents. The other half went into the Grip. B.B. traveled with thousands of dollars in cash, which he paid out in musician salaries and dispensed to various hoteliers, restaurateurs, and service-station attendants on the road. Among all the items in B.B.'s traveling horde, perhaps only Lucille rivaled the Grip for gravitas. When Norman Matthews traveled with B.B., his most sacred duty was guarding the Grip.

Albert King, B.B.'s father, still lived with his family on the farm outside Memphis. B.B. surprised him one day with a brand-new Ford tractor, top of the line. But B.B. never lingered at his daddy's farm. "No matter how old you get," he told a reporter, "they," meaning Albert, "still think of you as a little boy." Nor did B.B. ever live at the apartment building he purchased in Memphis around this time as an investment. The building sat in a white section of town. The landlord could not live among his tenants.

B.B. gradually shifted his base from Los Angeles to New York, home to his record label and historical center of the music industry. But the music business was changing. The Beach Boys and the Byrds, arguably the most important American rock bands of the era, were Los Angeles ensembles. By 1966, new bands were springing up along the Sunset Strip, and a rival scene was taking shape in San Francisco, centered on the Haight-Ashbury neighborhood and a band called Jefferson Airplane.

In March 1966, promoter Bill Graham had invited the Butterfield Blues Band to San Francisco for a series of epochal shows at Graham's Fillmore Auditorium and Winterland Arena. The performances exposed young folkies to the B.B. King style of electric-blues guitar via B.B.'s fervent disciples, Bloomfield and Bishop. More than a concert promoter, Bill Graham was helping to shape the San Francisco sound with the ever-broadening palette of bands he brought to town. "He was pulling the whole thing together and making the whole thing make sense," Elvin Bishop recalled. One night, Graham asked Bloomfield and Bishop to name a Black blues performer he might approach to book a show. They replied, probably in unison, "Well, the number-one guy you've gotta get is B.B. King."

Graham scheduled B.B. to perform at the Fillmore several months later, in February 1967. B.B. had played at the Fillmore before: the venue had been a stop on the chitlin' circuit. B.B. did not know Graham had transformed it into a hippie palace.

Bit by bit, Charles Keil's *Urban Blues*, the *Regal* album, and the promotional efforts of Bloomfield and Bishop moved the needle on B.B.'s stalled career. On October 29, 1966, during a swing through Ohio, B.B. visited the studios of WEWS-TV in Cleveland for his first television appearance. The program was *Upbeat*, one in a seemingly endless number of productions—*Shindig!*, *Shivaree!*, *Shebang!*—that packed fashionable teens into a studio to gyrate to a pop beat. *Upbeat* aired in more than one hundred cities via syndication. Its producers were remarkably colorblind, for their era. By the time of B.B.'s appearance, the show had already hosted James Brown, Bobby Bland, and the Miracles. B.B.'s band was one of at least ten to perform on his appointed date. He probably played "Don't Answer the Door," his current hit. *Upbeat* performers usually played along in pantomime to prerecorded songs, as was the fashion. But producers apparently permitted B.B. to perform live, a concession to the impossibility of pantomiming an extended guitar solo.

B.B.'s producers seemed finally aware of him. In November 1966, B.B. signed a new contract with ABC Records (the "Paramount" had been quietly dropped). B.B.'s side of the deal was negotiated by a Chicago musician named Lou Zito, who was his new manager. Neither side disclosed the terms.

In the years since B.B.'s departure from Memphis, he had relied mostly on Polly Walker, wife of driver Cato, to oversee his business affairs, a job she still performed on evenings and weekends from her home. His booking agency, Milt Shaw in New York, handled the gigs. Polly remained in Memphis, where she saw to hotel reservations, worked with agents and reporters, kept the books, and marked out B.B.'s itinerary on an enormous wall map. In 1966, B.B. moved Polly into an actual office on Beale Street, a block or two from the dilapidated remains of the city's faded entertainment district, framed by slums. Polly quit her day job.

"At that time," Polly recalled, "I got to decide where he wanted to work and where he didn't want to work. I got to haggle with the booking agents. I got to listen to him fuss when I didn't take the gigs that he thought I should have."

B.B. himself kept an office there, "a large, wood-paneled room with a blue-green carpet, a long black leather couch, a table-topped desk," and a bookcase filled with reference titles ranging from foreign-language courses and *High School Subjects Self-Taught* to *The Key to Winning at Dice* and *Female Sexual Anatomy*, by one account. B.B. sometimes slept on the couch. Visitors arrived to find the suite littered with record players, tape recorders, and stacks of old 78s, part of a record collection that was vast and still growing. While B.B. himself seldom opened up to visitors, he made so little effort to conceal his hobbies and habits that his lifestyle was, quite literally, an open book.

"There was a bottle of Johnny Walker Scotch (red label) open on the desk," a journalist noted upon his arrival for a midday interview. "B.B. poured us both a drink in Coca-Cola paper cups. In a moment his secretary, Mrs. Polly Walker, a large, good-humored lady, came in, saw the Scotch, and said, 'Sure makes a good breakfast, don't it?' She was carrying a newspaper-wrapped plate with B.B.'s lunch, which consisted of corn bread, pig's knuckles, collard greens with a thick onion slice, sweet potatoes, and black-eyed peas with fat bacon. 'Soul food,' B.B. said."

Lou Zito, a former big-band drummer, appeared in B.B.'s life around the time he disbanded his orchestra. B.B. makes almost no mention of the manager in his memoir, an omission suggesting either that the collaboration was brief—which it was—or that B.B. found Zito ultimately unworthy, or perhaps both.

After the aural disaster of *Confessin' the Blues*, B.B.'s handlers at ABC wisely plotted a sequel to *Live at the Regal*. The label again enlisted producer Johnny Pate, who selected another Chicago venue, this one smaller and more intimate than the Regal. Formerly Club DeLisa, the space on South State Street was now known simply as The Club. Pate recorded two of B.B.'s shows there, on November 5 and November 17, 1966. The band was the same lean ensemble B.B. had employed since the purge of the previous summer, with Duke Jethro handling the bass notes on his Hammond organ as a cost-saving measure. Producers later overdubbed an actual bassist, Louis Satterfield, onto a few tracks in the studio, the only trickery in an otherwise honest recording.

Literally and figuratively, the new *Blues Is King* LP was everything *Live at the Regal* was not. *Regal* presented B.B. backed by a big band in a large theater, playing his greatest hits. *Blues Is King* put him in a small club with a tight quintet, playing just one hit, "Don't Answer the Door," and nine lesser-known but incendiary tracks, one of which, "Night Life," had been penned by country-music songwriter Willie Nelson. Whereas *Live at the Regal* celebrated love, *Blues Is King* stewed in anger and despair. *Blues Is King* was a breakup album. It was almost a concept album. On the opening track, "Waitin' on You," a man sits alone in his home at four o'clock in the morning, awaiting a woman who has stayed out too late. With the second song, "Gambler's Blues," his lady is gone. The third track, "Tired of Your Jive," finds our narrator angry and bitter. On the fourth song, "Night Life," his anger softens to introspection. By the fifth track, "Buzz Me," he is begging his woman to come home. Without her, he moans, "I'm like the ship that's lost at sea."

B.B. "was playing what he felt," Duke Jethro recalled. The divorce "was tough on him, and it really affected his playing. Sonny [Freeman] and I, I remember us talking about it: 'What can we do to get him out of this?' . . . I noticed in the dressing room he would take a few shots, which normally he wouldn't do. He was playing sadder songs."

Blues Is King was a powerful recording. It didn't chart, but the young acolytes who sought it out were rewarded with another clinic on the B.B. King style of electric guitar. B.B. explored his "magic switch," the Varitone dial on his Gibson ES-355, whose various positions "pinched" the guitar's sound by selectively muting frequencies in the middle range between treble and bass. The effect was to compress and sharpen Lucille's tone, much like the effect of turning up the treble and bass knobs on a receiver. B.B. played on *Blues Is King* with as much distortion as he had ever unleashed on an audience. He produced the overdrive naturally, using the volume knobs on his amplifier and his guitar. Some tracks drenched Lucille in reverberation echo. Elsewhere, her tone was immediate and clean. B.B. claimed not to know what all the switches and knobs were for, but he knew how to get the sounds his ears wanted to hear.

Blues Is King emerged in early 1967 as a flagship release for a new ABC subsidiary called BluesWay. The label recognized the rising currency of the blues generally and B.B. King in particular. ABC executives marketed BluesWay releases to the connoisseur, presenting B.B. and his peers in a context of reverent liner notes and studious production credits (and dust jackets). In this, BluesWay was the antithesis of Modern Records.

Blues Is King was hot off the press when B.B. arrived in Los Angeles in February 1967 for a series of shows on the fabled Sunset Strip. Louis Zito and Polly Walker had probably inserted the L.A. dates into B.B.'s schedule as a warm-up for the February 26 show in San Francisco at the Fillmore. The original plan was for B.B. to play the Crescendo, a Sunset Boulevard landmark that hosted mostly biracial jazz acts and was thus friendly territory to B.B. But the Crescendo had closed, leaving B.B. without a venue. His band was a last-minute addition to the calendar at Gazzarri's, a room at Doheny and Sunset that hosted teen pop acts such as the Doors. And that, it seems, is how B.B. King secured his first high-profile booking at a white club.

Years later, B.B. recalled that he had performed for white audiences only twice before. Both gigs were "complete fiascos," according to biographer Charles Sawyer. At one date, the club owner had insisted that B.B.'s backing band perform behind a stage curtain.

The L.A. press hailed B.B.'s six-day residency at Gazzarri's. The bluesman was visibly nervous on the first night, according to a *Los Angeles Times* reviewer, repeating himself absentmindedly and groping for words as he introduced songs, quite the contrast to his cool command on the chitlin' circuit. He broke two guitar strings in the first set. But B.B. settled in, a *Variety* critic wrote, delivering "an indescribably soulful guitar solo" on "How Blue Can You Get?" and utterly enthralling the crowd with a smoldering "Sweet Little Angel."

Around this time, *Jazz* magazine printed an extended interview with B.B., the first white periodical to do so, penned by British critic Stanley Dance. B.B. dwelt in a shared space between blues and jazz. He played with jazz-trained sidemen, and his singular style honored the tradition of Charlie Christian and Django Reinhardt. Blues revivalists rebuffed B.B., but Stanley Dance embraced him.

"He bears down on the beat, intensifying the feeling in his voice as the long guitar notes wail in pain and release," Dance wrote. "Now he is playing on the people's emotions as surely as on the guitar strings. The response is vibrant and, sensing it, he is himself uplifted, for it is when he is moving people who understand the blues that he is truly inspired."

After the triumphal week in Los Angeles, B.B. and his band proceeded toward San Francisco.

February 26 dawned fair and cool in California's emergent hippie capital. The Fillmore had long served as an African American venue.

But when B.B.'s tour bus arrived at the band entrance for the Sunday performance, he realized something was very different. He saw "long-haired kids in tie-dyed outfits," sitting, cheek to jowl, all the way up the stairway leading to the door, none of them African Americans. "Wasn't nothin' there but white," Norman Matthews recalled.

B.B. said, "We're in the wrong place." He summoned an aide, probably Cato Walker, and told him, "I think they made a mistake this time." B.B. instructed Cato to press through the corridor of bodies and find Bill Graham, a man he had never met. Cato disappeared into the throng. A few minutes later, he returned with Graham, a man fifteen years older than most of the hippies, with thick, shoulder-length hair and an expressive, olive-complected face. Graham waded through the sea of hippies and walked up to B.B. "Yeah, B.," he said. "You're in the right place. C'mon in."

The band entered the auditorium. To reach the dressing room, B.B. had to plot a course across the length of the hall, a solid hippie mass. This wasn't the Fillmore he remembered, was not, in fact, like any club he had ever seen. There were no chairs. "All of the kids were sitting on the floor," B.B. recalled, "body to body, body to body." A cloud of sweet-scented smoke hung in the air. B.B. tiptoed tentatively through the flock, squinting to find a bare patch of floor whenever he took a step. The kids watched him in silence, their glassy eyes betraying curiosity but no flicker of recognition. B.B. thought to himself, "They don't know who I am." With each step, his anxiety swelled. After what seemed an interminable march, the group finally reached B.B.'s dressing room. The walls were covered in psychedelic posters advertising bands B.B. had never heard of. The most prominent piece of furniture was a couch whose upholstery had been slashed with a knife.

B.B. looked Graham straight in the eyes. "Bill," he said, "I got to have a drink."

"We don't sell liquor here," Graham replied, "but we can send someone out and get you a bottle." He did. When the bottle arrived, B.B. took two swift belts. They didn't help.

The opening acts were Moby Grape, a psychedelic combo with a ferocious, three-guitar attack, and the Steve Miller Blues Band, a new ensemble that provided a sort of trippy, West Coast answer to Chicago's Butterfield band. (Steve Miller, the front man, had grown up around rhythm and blues in Dallas and completed a musical residency in the Chicago blues scene.) B.B. was a spiritual godfather to both groups.

A night at Bill Graham's hippie cathedral was something more than a concert. Ralph J. Gleason, the illustrious San Francisco jazz critic, had taken notes on an evening spent within those walls: "Inside, a most remarkable assemblage of humanity was leaping, jumping, dancing, frigging, fragging and frugging on the dance floor to the music of the half dozen rock bands. . . . The costumes were freeform Goodwill-cum-Sherwood-Forest. Slim young ladies with their faces painted a la *Harper's Bazaar* in cats-and-dogs lines, granny dresses topped with huge feathers, white Levis with decals of mystic design; bell bottoms split up the side."

Fillmore shows were not discrete events. B.B. arrived amid a non-stop, three-day blues party. Friday's and Saturday's gigs had featured Otis Rush, the resurgent Chicago bluesman. Rush shared a bill with the Grateful Dead, purveyors of acid blues, and Canned Heat, whose leader, Alan Wilson, had helped Son House relearn his own songs. Those bands probably played two sets each on Friday and Saturday and another two on Sunday, starting at 2 p.m. and ending shortly before B.B.'s show began. B.B. and his supporting acts would play two shows, scheduled for 8 p.m. and 2 a.m. Many young revelers stayed in and around the Fillmore for the entire weekend.

"There wasn't a real dividing line between the band and the audience in those shows," recalled Peter Lewis, of Moby Grape. "Everybody's going through this experience to try to become free of . . ."—he paused briefly—". . . the tyranny of themselves."

The Steve Miller Blues Band opened the first show around nine o'clock, fashionably late, with Moby Grape following an hour later. As eleven o'clock drew near, Bill Graham appeared at B.B.'s dressing room to summon him to the stage. B.B. took another swig from his bottle. It still wasn't helping. Graham led B.B. back across the auditorium floor, through the herd of colorful bodies and the sweet cloud of cannabis.

This time, B.B. carried Lucille. He thought to himself, "They still don't recognize me." They reached the stage. Graham approached the microphone. "Ladies and gentlemen," he said, and suddenly the hall fell as silent as church. "I give you the chairman of the board, B.B. King."

At those words, the vast crowd rose as one and erupted into the loudest cheer B.B. had ever heard. Tears welled in his eyes.

CHAPTER 14

MYTHOLOGY

B.B. HAD RECEIVED STANDING OVATIONS before in his forty-one years, but always at the end of a performance, never the beginning. Now he stood on the Fillmore stage, tears streaming down his cheeks, facing a kaleidoscope army of hippies whose cheers rang louder than any of the music that would fill the hall that Sunday.

Carlos Santana, the guitarist from Tijuana, stood in the audience and beheld his hero through the smoky glare. "The light was hitting him in such a way that all I could see were big tears coming out of his eyes, shining on his black skin," Santana recalled. "He raised his hand to wipe his eyes, and I saw he was wearing a big ring on his finger that spelled out his name in diamonds. That's what I remember most—diamonds and tears, sparkling together."

B.B. had feared this audience would give him nothing. Instead, the fans were giving him everything. He wondered how he could possibly answer such an outpouring. He led the band into "Every Day I Have the Blues." The answer would come in his music.

"I played that night like I've never played before," B.B. recalled. He fed on the energy of his audience, an interaction not unlike the feedback loop between guitar and amplifier that provided Lucille her signature sound. B.B. had been allotted forty-five minutes but played for nearly an hour and a half. All the while, the audience remained on its feet, dancing and leaping, screaming and clapping, frigging, fragging, and frugging. The cheering never really stopped.

"It was hard for me to believe that this was happening," B.B. recalled, "that this communication between me and the flower children was so tight and right."

Peter Lewis, the Moby Grape guitarist, watched from the wings. "The kids were tripping out under these strobe lights," he recalled. "And he's playing blues like he's in a smoky bar. He fit. That's what I remember about that night. He fit. He was perfect."

B.B.'s jaded sidemen never paused to appraise the moment. To them, the Fillmore was one more stop on an unending tour, much like that chilly night at the Regal back in 1964. "I guess for most of us in the band, it was just another gig," recalled Duke Jethro, the organist. "Except that the audience was different. I remember psychedelic lights and all that. I wasn't paying attention to a lot, except girls."

Nonetheless, when the pot smoke had cleared, B.B. King stood revealed as the greatest blues musician of his time. Perhaps the hippies hadn't recognized him as he stumbled through the crowd, searching for the refuge of a dressing room and a bottle of scotch. But they recognized his sound, for it was the sound of Eric Clapton and Mike Bloomfield, their rock-guitar idols. And they recognized his name, a name B.B.'s white acolytes had been chanting in San Francisco and Los Angeles and London. That Sunday night, B.B. bade farewell to the chitlin' circuit, vacating the fringe genre of blues to join the mostly white and male fraternity of rock music.

In the movie version of B.B.'s life, a camera would now pan across the gyrating Fillmore audience to settle on the face of a graying man with a walrus mustache and pipe. With a column penned two days after the Fillmore show and published around the country, Ralph Gleason became the next white journalist to celebrate B.B. King. Gleason was a jazz head, familiar with B.B.'s many touchstones in rhythm and blues.

"They call him B.B. King, King of the Blues," Gleason opened, "and he is exactly that. And if you ever want to know what the blues is all about, how it should sound and how much it can mean, you go hear B.B. King. He'll show you."

Gleason proceeded with the breathless enthusiasm of a critic revealing a new talent, which B.B. was to most of Gleason's readers. "He can reach down deep inside you with his voice like all the great singers in the blues tradition have been able to do," he wrote. "He is also one of the greatest guitarists of his time." A B.B. King concert is "a guitar-players convention," Gleason wrote. "They all come to hear him do it and he stands up there and lets the guitar hang those notes out there, sustained and vibrating through the hall."

All through the spring and summer of 1967, writers, musicians, and fans celebrated B.B. King with the same euphoric thrill of discovery. Here was a towering figure in American music, the preeminent exponent of modern blues, a living legend—but also unknown, at least outside the African American community, where he had lain in hiding for nearly twenty years.

In May, Chicago's stuffy *Tribune* dispatched a reporter to a South Side club to review a B.B. King show. "Tho most white Americans have never heard his name," the reviewer instructed, "King is important as perhaps the most authentic, 'pure,' blues singer today, and as such is being discovered by collegians and young adults hungry for real feelings and beauty amidst an increasingly steel-souled world." Later that month, the white-owned *Memphis Press-Scimitar* published a full profile of B.B., "the boy from Beale Street." The writer portrayed B.B. as a Memphis icon even as he recited the basic facts of his life to readers who had never heard them.

In June, Miles Davis turned up at a B.B. King show at the 20 Grand in Detroit. Miles and B.B. had been friends and mutual admirers for more than a decade. Between songs, B.B. announced, "Ladies and gentlemen, I'd like to acknowledge one of the greatest jazz musicians in the world, Mr. Miles Davis." Davis was a notorious grump. Now, amid polite applause, Davis rose and loosed a torrent of hoarse invective. "Motherfucker," he growled, "I didn't come by to be introduced. I just wanna listen to your ass."

"Then sit your ass down," B.B. shot back, "and enjoy the compliment, 'cause this is my show, and you're my man, and I'll damn well introduce you if I wanna."

Stunned at the rebuke, Davis cracked a rare, sheepish smile. The 20 Grand crowd erupted in a rapturous cheer.

That summer, Modern Records released an album titled *The Jungle* to capitalize on B.B.'s newfound fame. B.B. had recorded the namesake single in 1962, at the end of his formal association with Modern Records.

The Biharis unearthed it five years later, added a thick slab of Stax Records–style horns and bass, and released it as a single, which proceeded to crack the *Billboard* Hot 100. The clumsy overdubs left the song's drum track badly out of synch. Even so, "The Jungle" was a great song, perhaps the most passionate blues ever written about a federal agency. B.B.'s lyric was a lament about income tax: "a little for the state, a little more for Uncle Sam." The balance of the *Jungle* LP collected a string of superb Kent singles the Biharis had released over three prior years. Five of them, "Beautician Blues," "Blue Shadows," "Eyesight to the Blind," "I Stay in the Mood," and "It's a Mean World," had cracked the charts. The latter song paid loving tribute to T-Bone Walker, down to the elegant, chromatic jazz riff that opened it.

July brought B.B. his first extensive coverage in *Down Beat*, America's premier jazz magazine. B.B. told the interviewer his audience was changing. "I noticed in the last year or so that I've had a lot of the white kids, more of the white kids, come to me than ever before," he said. "They often come up and tell me the tunes, a lot of the tunes that I've forgotten about. And they remember them."

B.B. didn't miss segregation or the chitlin' circuit, but he missed his African American fans and the exchange of Pentecostal energy that had breathed life into *Live at the Regal*. "I can remember standing in the wings, looking out and trying to find a Black face," Duke Jethro recalled. "[B.B.] was really sad about it."

Now, when B.B. arrived at a concert hall, one of Norman Matthews's official duties was to peek through the curtain and gauge the racial mix of the audience, to help his boss refine his set list and onstage style. During the show, B.B. kept the house lights bright enough for him to see how the crowd responded to his music.

If the Sunset Strip in Los Angeles had a counterpart in 1960s New York, it was Greenwich Village, within whose smoky clubs Dylan had gotten his start. On September 15, 1967, B.B. played his Village debut at the Café Au Go Go. The jaded New Yorkers greeted B.B. with a standing ovation.

More important than that Friday-night gig was the afterhours jam that followed. Eric Clapton was in town with his blues-rock band

Cream. Clapton was perhaps B.B.'s most talented follower among British guitarists, on a par with Mike Bloomfield in America. Bloomfield was not there, but his bandmate Elvin Bishop was.

The guitarists had met once before, on August 22, at the Fillmore in San Francisco, a gig that featured Cream and the Butterfields. The two acolytes had joined B.B. in conversation around a table in the dressing room, "just thrilled to be in his presence and to get a chance to meet him," Bishop recalled. By the time of their next meeting in the Village, the ice was broken. That September night, three guitarists gathered onstage for a reverential exchange of licks. A photographer captured the moment, B.B. in a dark suit and tie and shiny black boots, Clapton and Bishop in jeans and billowy shirts, both sporting Dylan-styled perms. In one shot, the three are talking, Clapton looking earnest, B.B. droopy-eyed after a long night. In another frame, the men sit and play together, heads bowed almost as if in prayer. "I had to play the hardest I have ever played in my life," Clapton recalled.

The very next day, three thousand miles away, B.B. played his first festival: not the Newport Folk Festival, where so many of his friends and forebears had performed, but the Monterey Jazz Festival, an event of similar renown staged on the opposite coast. Perhaps it was a better fit.

Three months earlier, Monterey had hosted an International Pop Music Festival, kicking off the fabled Summer of Love. Monterey Pop more or less introduced the American public to Jimi Hendrix, the R&B guitarist from Seattle who had deconstructed the B.B. King guitar sound and reimagined it through a prism of lysergic acid and war. A few years after meeting B.B. on the chitlin' circuit, Hendrix now emerged as the first rock-guitar superstar. "Because of Jimi, millions of kids wanted to play guitar," B.B. recalled. "And when the guitar is the center of musical attention, that's good for my business." Still, B.B. didn't much like the way Hendrix played "Rock Me Baby," and he hated seeing anyone light a guitar on fire.

B.B. was now an artist of sufficient stature to serve as a Saturday-afternoon headliner at the jazz festival, presented in tandem with his idol, T-Bone Walker, and an all-star band. To cap the evening, T-Bone sang "Happy Birthday" to B.B., who had just turned forty-two.

In December, B.B. and his band assembled in the KQED studio in San Francisco for another television taping. This was *Jazz Casual*, Ralph Gleason's show, launched in 1960 as a showcase for his favorite acts. Gleason had recorded Dizzy Gillespie, Louis Armstrong, and John Coltrane in turn. One can only imagine B.B.'s delight when Gleason invited him on. The broadcast put B.B. on public television stations across the nation, exposing millions of new listeners to his music. Gleason captured a powerful set. The program commenced with a blistering reading of "Whole Lotta Love": not the Led Zeppelin song but B.B.'s hit single of the same name from 1954. B.B. sported a pencil-thin mustache and hair processed into a side part, and he wore a trim dark suit and broad tie, slightly askance, his shirt unbuttoned at the top. The four-piece backing band featured new organist James Toney, a man whose family would one day loom as large as Cato Walker's in B.B.'s life. Toney replaced Duke Jethro, who had finally tired of the road.

From "Whole Lotta Love," B.B. proceeded into a mesmerizing, gospel-inspired dirge titled "All Over Again." The song played to B.B.'s strengths. He sang a lyric both sorrowful and darkly mirthful—"I've got a good mind to give up living, and go shopping instead"—atop a bank of horns playing Chopin's funeral march. The lento pace, about sixty beats a minute, opened up a world of space for B.B.'s swooping vocal delivery, which alternated between ominous growls and a sweet croon. Lucille responded with a mournful solo as the camera captured every twitch of B.B.'s brow, every purse of his lips. B.B.'s face alternately smiled and grimaced and frowned in unconscious communion with Lucille. That was why Martha, his first wife, had called him Ol' Lemon Face.

After three more songs, the band broke, and Gleason interviewed B.B., whose speaking voice proved surprisingly gentle, almost childlike. B.B. rambled nervously, interrupting himself in midsentence, wandering off topic, and frequently stopping to correct himself, almost as if he were under oath. His halting progress betrayed a faint echo of the ancient stutter.

Gleason asked his guest to review his influences, including T-Bone Walker and Bukka White, Charlie Christian and Django Reinhardt. B.B. seemed to understand that Gleason and his viewers were mostly concerned with his instrumental influences, and he barely touched on his vocal touchstones. Henceforth, B.B. King would be known primarily as a blues guitarist, rather than a singer.

"That feeling on the guitar, that singing string, what was the phrase you used for it before?" Gleason asked.

"Twinging," B.B. laughed.

"Twinging. This is your own," Gleason continued. "This is your contribution," he said, more an assertion than a question.

B.B. answered slowly, taming the stutter. "I think so. I think it is. Because I've heard so many guys since I started playing sound that way, and I don't remember ever hearing anybody before that. Not before that." He smiled.

Gleason asked if B.B. thought of his voice and guitar as interchangeable.

"I can hear myself singing when I play," B.B. replied. "That may sound weird, but I can hear—the words that I'm saying, a lot of times, don't mean as much to me as the way I say it, and I think this is the same thing I've tried to do on the guitar. There's been a sound that I've heard for years, but I haven't quite got it as I want it."

That exchange spun a new narrative thread about the B.B. King guitar sound. Over the next forty-eight years, countless interviewers would ask B.B. how he came to play his guitar with the tremulous lyricism of a human voice. B.B. always offered more or less the same reply. When he played Lucille, when he winced and grimaced and wrung notes from her neck, B.B. was struggling to re-create the sound he heard in his head. The voice wasn't B.B.'s own voice, exactly, but a counterpoint to that voice, an answer to the call of his hoarse baritone, higher pitched and angular, feminine and defiant. B.B. would always insist he had never quite captured that inner voice the way he heard it. There lay his essential modesty.

Gleason's transcribed interview ran in *Rolling Stone*, the nation's new periodical of record for "rock" music, cofounded in late 1967 by Ralph Gleason and his young protégé Jann Wenner. The journal's very name, borrowed from Muddy Waters by way of Britain's greatest blues-rock band and Bob Dylan's most famous single, underscored how thoroughly B.B. and Muddy and "urban blues" had transformed white rock 'n' roll. Dropping the "roll" freed *Rolling Stone* writers to craft a whole new vocabulary of compound nouns: country rock, folk rock, psychedelic rock, progressive rock, blues rock. Blues bands that strayed from their roots, such as the Rolling Stones and Yardbirds, were now generally termed "blues rock," although even that label would ultimately prove too confining. Those that clung obstinately to the blues, including John Mayall and Canned Heat, were still termed "blues" artists, like B.B. himself.

On December 7, 1967, B.B. returned to Bill Graham's Fillmore Auditorium, followed by two nights at another Graham venue, a converted ice rink called Winterland. Ralph Gleason devoted a full column to the Fillmore show. "He calls his guitar 'Lucille,'" Gleason wrote, "and as he plays it, he listens to its sounds, his head cocked to one side and a slight smile on his lips."*

B.B.'s bandmates and wives had known of Lucille for years. In the latter months of 1967, B.B. introduced her to the public, and Gleason's syndicated column gave her a national audience. This, for B.B., was a conscious act of mythologization. Lucille became part of the B.B. King legend.

All told, 1967 was probably B.B.'s biggest year since 1952, when "3 O'Clock Blues" had topped the charts. But B.B.'s record label seemed oddly oblivious. ABC had released B.B. King recordings at a positively glacial rate, four long-players in six years, this at a time when many pop acts put out two albums a year. B.B.'s label was squandering his new fame. As 1967 drew to a close, someone at the label must have noticed. ABC would issue five B.B. King records over the next two years.

The first, titled *Blues On Top of Blues*, was assembled from sessions recorded in July and September of 1967 and released the following February. This would be the last album of that era to feature B.B. with a big band, an anachronistic format that ultimately distracted from

---

*Over the years, some accounts have mistakenly cited this engagement, or B.B.'s well-publicized Fillmore gig in the summer of 1968, as the moment of his crossover breakthrough.

B.B.'s guitar. One single, "Paying the Cost to Be the Boss," managed to transcend those constraints, propelled by Sonny Freeman's insistent backbeat and a fat, modern-sounding bass line. The song reached number 39 on the Hot 100 chart, one of B.B.'s best showings to date.

The sessions that would yield B.B.'s next album, *Lucille*, took place in December 1967 under the guidance of Bob Thiele, the man who had produced *A Love Supreme* for John Coltrane, possibly the finest jazz LP ever pressed. Thiele disbanded the anachronistic orchestra. Half of this album was recorded with a ten-piece band—still large but passably modern. The other half was cut with a seven-piece ensemble, more like the group that now accompanied B.B. on the road.

B.B. must have had Lucille on his mind. During a break in taping, B.B. chatted with Thiele while noodling on his guitar. He began to recount Lucille's origin story, which he had told Ralph Gleason a week or two earlier. In a moment of inspiration, Thiele mobilized the rhythm section and signaled the engineer to record. B.B. then unfurled the ten-minute story-song "Lucille," reportedly in a single take. The track captured one of those intimate, extended monologues B.B. could roll out, deep in a set, to give his band a breather. "Lucille" sounded like nothing else B.B. had recorded. It was exactly the sort of performance that could bring him up to date with his peers in the blues and rock pantheon, many of whom were experimenting with longer and looser song forms.

"If I have a girlfriend and she misuses me and I go home at night, maybe I'm lonely—well, not maybe, I am lonely"—B.B. lamented, "I pick up Lucille, and then ping out those funny sounds that sound good to me."

"Lucille" wasn't even released as a single, but it probably did more than any other song to seed the B.B. King legend. Neil Young would have his Old Black, Willie Nelson his Trigger. Yet, among named guitars, Lucille was queen.

Lucille, released in the spring of 1968, became the first B.B. King studio album to crack the *Billboard* 200 chart, reaching number 192. Five decades later, a YouTube recording of the song had garnered twenty-five million views.

*   *   *

SOMETIME AFTER 3 a.m. on July 23, 1967, Detroit police crashed into an unlicensed afterhours club in an African American neighborhood. Inside, they found more than eighty partiers celebrating the safe return of two men from the escalating conflict in Vietnam. Officers arrested them all. As they rounded up the revelers, a crowd assembled. Someone hurled a bottle at a cop. A riot commenced. Dawn revealed a neighborhood in anarchy, looters breaking windows and emptying stores. Fire and mayhem spread across the city, fed by looters and rock hurlers of both races. By Monday, nearly five hundred fires raged. On Tuesday, President Lyndon Johnson sent in federal troops. A veritable army of police, National Guardsmen, and soldiers managed to quell the violence. Police arrested more than seven thousand accused rioters, nearly all of them African American. Forty-three people died. "We stand amidst the ashes of our hopes," said Jerome Cavanagh, Detroit's white mayor. The city never fully recovered.

The desolation of Detroit punctuated the Long, Hot Summer, a wave of urban upheaval that touched more than one hundred African American communities in 1967. The civil rights movement had won a major victory with passage of the Civil Rights Act of 1964. But African Americans now found themselves trapped within sprawling urban ghettos, communities hobbled by inferior schools and rampant unemployment and patrolled by racist police, while white families fled to cookie-cutter suburbs. The average African American household still earned barely half the income of a typical white household.

By the end of 1967, B.B. had not allied himself publicly with the burgeoning Black Power movement, nor had he released a single suitable as an anthem of either civil rights or Black pride. He preferred to serve the movement behind the scenes, as when he performed at benefits for the NAACP. Thus, his embrace of a "natural" hairstyle in 1968 turned heads. B.B.'s processed, parted hair was now sculpted into a close-cropped Afro.

"I had a process for years, partly because it was the fashion, and 'cause I thought it looked good," B.B. explained to some young, African American fans. "But I always knew it wasn't quite right; it was a mask I wore to hide something. Now I don't feel I need it anymore."

* * *

IN JANUARY 1968, a decade later than some of his peers, B.B. and his band finally performed overseas. The band made its European debut on January 10 in Strasbourg, the provincial capital of eastern France. The band swept through central Europe, playing in Berlin, Hamburg, and Frankfurt, Paris and Bordeaux, Geneva, Stockholm, and Amsterdam, fifteen concerts in all.

Nothing in the prior experience of B.B. and his sidemen quite prepared them for their reception in Europe. They had been all but invisible to white America for most of two decades, only to watch B.B. climb the ladder of pop currency over the prior year. B.B.'s sidemen, however, remained invisible—until they hit Europe, where they became instant celebrities. "They would stop you in the street and ask for your autograph," recalled Charles Boles, a Detroit pianist who joined B.B.'s band before the European tour. "And I'd say, 'But I'm not a star.' And they'd say, 'But you're in the band.'"

B.B. himself later recalled of his European debut, "I have never had so many standing ovations in my life, and I have never had to go back on stage so many times in my life." He and his band arrived as conquering heroes wherever they went. On the final night of the tour (in either Switzerland or Sweden, according to Boles), the band's European hosts threw a farewell party. "There was six of us in the band," Boles recalled. Just as things were heating up, a door opened at the far end of the room, and six lovely blondes walked in, one for each musician. B.B. and his sidemen fell silent. "And then," Boles recalled, "you were on your own, brother."

WHY HAD B.B. waited so long to tour Europe? Nearly every top-drawer act in the blues genre, from Muddy Waters and Howlin' Wolf to young upstarts Buddy Guy and Otis Rush, had preceded him across the Atlantic. And why, on this first tour, did B.B.'s handlers fail to book a single gig in England, home to some of his most ardent acolytes?

This was, in the end, a failure of management. Shortly after the European tour, B.B. made a change. He had grown increasingly frustrated with his manager, Lou Zito, the former jazz drummer. To be fair, Zito had done about as well as any of B.B.'s prior managers. Their greatest collective accomplishment was to keep B.B. on the road, plodding from one gig to the next. "It was all about survival," B.B. recalled. Now, B.B.'s career was taking off, and Zito seemed to have no broader ambition for his client. A lot of money was coming in, and B.B. suspected Zito of mishandling it. The dispute came to a head when B.B. learned one of Zito's nephews was using a business credit card, allegedly without his approval. B.B. confronted Zito. The two agreed to enter into an informal arbitration. The adjudicator would be Sid Seidenberg, a New York accountant who worked for Zito and, by extension, for B.B.

When Seidenberg completed his audit, he informed the two men that B.B. actually owed Zito several thousand dollars. But B.B. had seen enough of Zito. He hired a new manager, a man Seidenberg recommended. This was probably Pervis Spann, the Chicago deejay who had introduced B.B.'s legendary set at the Regal. A few months later, around May 1968, B.B. checked in with Seidenberg, who was still his accountant.

"How are we doin'?" B.B. asked.

"You're doing lousy," Seidenberg replied.

"Oh, my God," B.B. said, and he sulked out of the office. A short while later, he returned. He had fired his new manager. He asked if Seidenberg would step in and do the job himself.

Sidney Alexander Seidenberg was born in 1925, the same year as B.B., in the vowel-deprived Polish town of Szczuczyn. He emigrated with his family in 1930, settling in the New Jersey community of West New York, across the Hudson River. Sid's father worked as a wallpaper hanger, packing his wife and four children into a two-room apartment. Sid worked multiple jobs in high school and learned typing and stenography. After graduation, he took a civilian desk job with the military in Washington, DC. The draft sent him to Camp Shelby around the same time as B.B., although the tenets of segregation ensured they would never meet. He attended New York University on the GI Bill, graduating in 1949 with an accounting degree. He worked for a time at the law firm of Lee Eastman, the show-business attorney whose daughter, Linda, later married Paul McCartney. The showbiz bug had bitten him. Sid went out on his own as a celebrity accountant, keeping the books for such talents as Brill Building songwriter Neil Diamond and Welsh soul shouter Tom Jones.

Seidenberg was six foot one, three inches taller than B.B., with mutton-chop sideburns and an unruly mop of curly brown hair, long enough to brush the broad wingspan of his Technicolor lapels. His black-rimmed accountant's glasses framed large, probing eyes. He was energetic, articulate, and trustworthy. And he was all business: when Seidenberg wasn't sleeping, he was working. He shared that trait with B.B. From their first meeting, B.B. recalled, "I felt like I'd known Sid all my life."

The history of pop music is filled with larger-than-life managers, men who inspired respect, fear, and revulsion in equal measure. Peter Grant, the mercurial hulk who managed Led Zeppelin, single-handedly changed the calculus of concert tours by securing his band a full 90 percent of ticket proceeds. Allen Klein negotiated and renegotiated contracts between the Rolling Stones and Decca Records until his band reputedly earned more than the Beatles. Another manager of legend, Don Arden, is best remembered for dangling rival Robert Stigwood out a window. Bad manager stories vastly outnumber good ones.

"I knew what a manager is, and I don't like this business," Seidenberg recalled. "I didn't like what they did to people, most of the managers. An accountant sees the inside of the business, and I was not crazy about what their ethics were."

Seidenberg was an unlikely candidate for rock 'n' roll manager. "He didn't smoke, he didn't drink, he didn't gamble," recalled Larry Seidenberg, his son. "He had no hobbies. He was just twenty-four-hours-a-day business. He was as straight as you could get."

Seidenberg was reluctant at first to manage B.B., but misgivings soon gave way to a voracious ambition. "For every million you make, I'll get a hundred grand," Seidenberg crowed to his new client, emphasizing the *million*. (His actual cut was probably nearer two hundred grand.) Seidenberg was no *Spinal Tap* caricature. He evolved into a consummate pop-music manager, training all of his considerable financial acumen on a tireless quest to enrich B.B. beyond his wildest dreams.

Every aspect of B.B.'s career to that point had been undervalued. The world's greatest blues performer had toiled for years at a label that sold his records in discount bins at dime stores. He had played perhaps six thousand concerts over twenty years, but he had no appreciable savings. His booking fee was pennies on the dollar paid to the white rock bands that copied his songs and his style. His current label, ABC, still thought him a second-rate artist.

Sid Seidenberg's impact on B.B. King's career defies overstatement. For all of B.B.'s immense talent and singular accomplishments in his first two decades, it is easy to imagine his career ultimately fading into oblivion without the intervention of Seidenberg or someone like him. At the moment Seidenberg stepped in, B.B. was a respected bluesman with rising currency on the transatlantic pop-music scene—but hardly a household name. Perhaps global fame would have found him without a tireless, forward-thinking manager—or perhaps not.

For B.B. to cede control of his professional fortunes to anyone took humility, not a strong suit for most pop stars. "Had he not been humble, he probably wouldn't have let Seidenberg take over his career," recalled David Ritz, a biographer who would collaborate with B.B. on his memoir in later years. "And B.B. knew what he couldn't do, which was market himself in a world that was getting increasingly complex. Other artists shoot themselves in the foot because they can't give up control. B.B. was not controlling."

Seidenberg sat down with B.B. and wrote a five-year plan. His overarching goal: to elevate B.B. from American blues legend to global ambassador for American music and culture. Seidenberg was thinking of Duke Ellington and Dizzy Gillespie and Louis Armstrong.

Seidenberg admired Joe Glaser, the manager and superagent who had helped Louis Armstrong climb to the top of the music business, even as he rubbed shoulders with Al Capone. Seidenberg sacked B.B.'s agent, Milt Shaw, the party largely responsible for keeping him on the road three hundred nights a year, playing places like the Corpus Christi Carousel Lounge and the Hobson City Recreation Center. B.B. signed with Joe Glaser.

"Do you know Louis Armstrong?" Glaser growled, when B.B. sat down in his New York office for the first time, his eyes casting across stacks of five- and six-figure royalty checks that Glaser had helpfully arrayed across his desk.

"Yes, I do," B.B. replied.

"And Fats Domino?"

"Know him, too."

"Well," Glaser said, "if you can get your career going like them, you'll be all right."

Glaser died a year later, after a stroke. But his Associated Booking agency would elevate B.B.'s itinerary, paring the remaining juke joints, community centers, and VFW halls from his calendar and dramatically raising his minimum fee, which had languished at $750 to $1,000 a night. Seidenberg told B.B. his days as opening act were over.

Money poured in. Seidenberg took steps to ensure B.B.'s new riches wouldn't evaporate like rain in the Delta sun. He set things right with the IRS, brokering a reasonable plan for B.B. to repay the million dollars he now owed. The taxmen had haunted B.B. like an apparition for a decade: now, they faded away. Seidenberg set new rules for B.B.'s ceaseless gambling binges. "B.," he instructed, "when you want gambling money, always write yourself a check." That way, B.B. would see the true cost of his addiction. Seidenberg helped B.B. trim the fat from his bloated payroll. B.B. had a hard time saying no. Seidenberg patiently counseled him, "You don't need two bus drivers. You don't need two valets."

Seidenberg persuaded B.B. to embrace the convenience of air travel. Serendipitously, B.B.'s $27,000 Starliner bus vanished from an Atlanta street around this time in a mysterious theft. Cato Walker, his faithful driver, would spend the rest of his days watching the roads for the lost rig, Charles Sawyer writes, "like Ahab scanning the sea for Moby Dick." B.B. and his band now flew more often than they drove.

Out on tour, Seidenberg blasted through the last remnants of chitlin'-circuit-era segregation. Once in a while, when B.B.'s entourage entered a venue, the owner would try to separate Seidenberg from the band, sending B.B. and his African American musicians around to a service entrance while allowing the white manager to pass through the front door. That would light Seidenberg's fuse. He would snap back, "If you want to work with me, I go with them." The owner would relent, or the band would leave.

Seidenberg's next target was ABC Records. He called a meeting with label executives and demanded to renegotiate their contract with B.B. "You've got a major artist in your midst," he barked, "and you'd better start treating him like one." No one revealed the particulars of the new, seven-year deal, announced in the trade press in June 1968, but every subsequent B.B. King record would roll out with considerably more fanfare. Seidenberg "didn't think in terms of tens of thousands of dollars," B.B. recalled. "He thought in terms of hundreds of thousands. I finally had someone fighting for me."

AT TWILIGHT on April 4, 1968, Dr. Martin Luther King stepped out onto the balcony of the Lorraine Motel, a haven for African American travelers in downtown Memphis. His eyes drifted down to the parking lot and found Ben Branch, a saxophonist who had recorded with B.B. in Memphis almost two decades earlier. Branch was to appear alongside Dr. King at a rally that night. "I want you to play 'Precious Lord' for me," King shouted to Branch. "Play it real pretty." Moments later, a bullet knocked King to the ground. The man at the center of the civil rights movement died an hour later, aged thirty-nine.

Riots soon ignited African American communities across the nation. Fire and mayhem raged for four days, the nation's largest episode of social unrest since the Civil War. The final toll, more than forty deaths and twenty-five hundred injuries nationwide, could have been much worse. An unlikely cast of civic leaders—Mayor John Lindsay in New York, singer James Brown in Boston, and Black street gangs in Chicago—stepped forward with heroic appeals that spared entire neighborhoods from ruin.

Dr. King's death hit B.B. as hard as the assassination of Medgar Evers, five years earlier. More than ever, B.B. embraced their philosophy of protest through peace and love. "I felt I was doing all I could by bringing people together through music," he recalled. "I had a clear picture of courage, and it had nothing to do with style or muscle or hip political slogans. You didn't have to be a genius to realize brute force wouldn't work. Mama always talked about kindness and self-respect. Daddy was about work, about feeding his family. In my mind, the two go together. Respect requires work. Medgar Evers and Martin Luther King worked fearlessly so our people could realize respect. That's why they died. And why they live on."

On April 7, a national day of mourning, B.B. played the Generation club in Greenwich Village on a bill with Janis Joplin. The gig evolved into a star-studded wake, with Joni Mitchell, Buddy Guy, Jimi Hendrix, B.B., the Butterfield Blues Band, and Richie Havens performing in turn. Buddy and his guitar raged and sobbed through T-Bone Walker's "Stormy Monday." Havens strummed Bob Dylan's apocalyptic "All Along the Watchtower." A week later, on April 15, B.B. jammed till dawn with Hendrix and the Butterfields, a meeting memorialized on bootlegs as "The Kings' Jam." Hendrix evidently had not crossed guitars with the bluesman before and would not again.

Shortly after midnight on June 5, Palestinian American militant Sirhan Sirhan shot Robert F. Kennedy in a hallway at the Ambassador Hotel in Los Angeles. JFK's younger brother, a hero of the civil rights movement, had launched his own campaign for president on a platform of peace and reconciliation. He died the next day.

That night, B.B. returned to Bill Graham's Fillmore. He arrived with Stanley Booth, a music journalist from Memphis who was preparing a profile for *Eye* magazine, a short-lived knockoff of *Rolling Stone*. Just twenty-six, with shoulder-length hair and a penchant for bandanas, Booth could easily be mistaken for a roadie. His narrative recounted an epic duel between B.B. and another bluesman who was becoming a rival.

"When B.B. comes downstairs and starts toward the stage (the crowd parting before him, murmuring gentle respect), his smile seems a bit tight around the corners," Booth wrote. "The Fillmore's manager has announced that Albert King, whom the audience knows as another strong old Guitar Man, is on hand. Albert has flown up from L.A. for this one night, to play with B.B. and, as everyone including B.B. is aware, to try to cut him."

After an early blush of fame, Albert King had knocked around for years before gaining traction in 1967 with a collection on the Stax label called *Born under a Bad Sign*. The new songs were positively volcanic. Albert was backed by the M.G.'s, the Stax house band, yielding a powerful marriage of B.B. King–style blues guitar to muscular Memphis soul. The record sounded better, frankly, than anything B.B. had recorded in a studio since his departure from Modern Records. White rock guitarists lapped it up.

Albert was a six-foot-four mountain of a man. His Gibson Flying V guitar, named for its distinctive shape, looked like a child's toy in his massive hands. Sweat poured from his body as he carved up notes beneath the stage lights. His star was rising. To B.B., Albert looked like the standout among the 1960s class of Black blues guitarists, the one man who might even best him in a cutting session. B.B. once confided in Duke Jethro, "Albert King bears watching." B.B. never talked that way about other guitarists. "He didn't fear no other guitar player, no other musician," Duke recalled.

Albert King's very existence threatened B.B.'s singular identity as King of the Blues. Albert was going around the country telling people he was B.B.'s half brother, a depth of homage that seemed almost creepy. The two Kings would later become dear friends. But on this night at the Fillmore, B.B. was seething.

With Albert towering in the wings, B.B. walked onstage and began his set. He led his band through "How Blue Can You Get" and two more songs. Then he paused for the inevitable confrontation, gamely bidding his audience to welcome "one of the great ones." Albert lumbered forward and plugged in, and the battle commenced.

"Albert's style, though based on B.B.'s, is much simpler and harsher; it is powerful, however, and a great crowd-pleaser," Booth wrote. "B.B.'s more relaxed and melodic lines are soon overpowered by Albert's longer, and louder, bent notes, which provoke steadily increasing howls from the audience." The aural exchange came to resemble a prize fight, and Albert was winning. B.B. finally retreated to the side of the stage and stood idle "while Albert puts down riff after driving riff," Booth reported.

On the ropes, B.B. punched back. He struck Lucille's strings, "as hard as he can, one note at a time, playing a blues chorus so strong and high and wild that the audience, shocked, becomes silent; then he pauses, takes two steps forward to the mike, and sings. *'My brother's in Korea, baby, my sister's down in New Orleans.'* The last part of the line is drowned out by the screams of the audience, who had forgotten, in the heat of the guitar duel, that B.B. is not only the master of the modern blues guitar, he is also the founder of entire schools of blues singers. Albert must have forgotten this, too; and now the pain of miscalculation is as plain on his face as it had been on Sonny Liston's that night in Miami Beach when he miscalculated his chances against Cassius Clay. As he stands flat-footed, stunned, B.B. turns and, between phrases, finishes him off: 'Where the fiddle, boy?' he asks, and Albert meekly starts to play accompaniment."

The song ended, and the crowd exploded in cheers. B.B. retreated back to the side of the stage, again yielding the spotlight to Albert. "He is a generous man," Booth wrote, "and his point has been made."

When B.B. performed his 1958 single "Please Accept My Love" at the Fillmore that night, he dedicated it to the ghost of Bobby Kennedy.

BEFORE SUMMER was over, under Sid Seidenberg's influence, B.B.'s career soared in full flight. B.B. appeared in June on *The Steve Allen Show*, a popular spin-off of Allen's iconic *Tonight Show*, serenading perhaps the bluesman's largest broadcast audience to date. July brought *For Love of Ivy*, a Sidney Poitier film whose soundtrack featured two B.B. King vocals on songs composed by two future giants of the arts, Quincy Jones and Maya Angelou. At month's end, B.B. made an overdue debut at the Newport Folk Festival, the granddaddy of music gatherings, before seventeen thousand fans.

Sometime in the fall of 1968, the blues-rock movement B.B. had largely inspired reached its raucous peak. Big Brother and the Holding Company, Janis Joplin's psychedelic blues group, topped the *Billboard* album chart in October before yielding the number 1 spot to Jimi Hendrix. Eric Clapton's Cream had three albums on the chart. Blues purists

Mike Bloomfield, the Butterfield Blues Band, John Mayall, and Canned Heat all stalked the *Billboard* 200 list, along with Yardbirds alumnus Jeff Beck and a host of other acts on the blues-rock spectrum, including Ten Years After, the Electric Flag, Blue Cheer, the Steve Miller Band, and Eric Burdon's Animals. B.B. himself scaled the chart that autumn with his *Lucille* album, vying with his old friend Muddy Waters and his new nemesis, Albert King.

Among front-rank U.S. newspapers, only the *New York Times* had failed to publish an article about B.B. In the autumn of 1968, the *Times* finally assigned a feature on the bluesman to Michael Lydon, twenty-six, a San Francisco freelancer and founding editor of *Rolling Stone*.

One September night, Lydon counted himself the only white patron inside Club Streamline, a cinder-block dump in Port Allen, Louisiana. B.B. was an hour late. The crowd was edgy. These were B.B.'s regulars, a gathering of "field workers in collarless shirts, city dudes from Baton Rouge, orange-haired beauticians, oil refinery workers with their wives," Lydon wrote. The space was hot and ripe. "We want B.B.," shouted a woman with several gold teeth, over the pulsing beat of Sonny Freeman and the Unusuals, B.B.'s backing band and warm-up act, punching through a jazzy, wordless chorus of the Beatles' "Eleanor Rigby."

The crowd stirred as an aide appeared from the wings, carrying Lucille. He plugged her into an amplifier and laid her unceremoniously atop a chair, gleaming fire red in the pale light. Lee Gatling, B.B.'s tenor-sax man, lowered his horn and stepped to the microphone: "Ladies and gentlemen," he announced, "it's show time, and we're *happy* to present the *star* of the show, the King of the *Blues*, Mr. B. . . . B. . . . *King*."

B.B. took the stage, clad in a shiny ox-blood suit. He strapped on Lucille. The band hit "Every Day I Have the Blues." B.B. shut his eyes, lowered his head in concentration, and struck his first note.

"From that instant," Lydon wrote, "the very molecules of the air seemed alive; King and his guitar were a magic source of energy, from which came fine glistening notes in leaping curves, drawing the whole club into their tremulous, hesitant intensity. 'Put the hurt on me,' a man yelled. Women stood twisting their hips, heads bowed, hands held high in witness. *Evra day, evra day I have the blues,* B.B. sang, rocking back and forth, both fists clenched beside his head, and the shouting went on."

The band departed Port Allen at 3 a.m. B.B. rode in his green Cadillac Fleetwood with his valet and road manager and the *Times* reporter. The band traveled in a Ford Econoline van. They planned to drive 200 miles to Mobile, Alabama, sleep till afternoon, then log another 170 miles to Montgomery for the next gig.

On a gas stop in Baton Rouge, three men from B.B.'s entourage walked over to an adjoining restaurant for sandwiches. Lydon tagged along. B.B. warned them to be careful: this was still the South. Some of his men wore dashikis, colorful West African tunics that African Americans had embraced as a symbol of Black pride.

The attendant at Neyland's Fine Food and Gift Shop turned the men away, refusing to serve them at the counter or wrap the food to go. "We're Wallaces," sneered a man at the counter, one of several white ruffians seated there, referring to Alabama's segregationist former governor.

"Great, man," replied Wilson Ester, B.B.'s valet.

"Whah, you n——," cried one of the men at the counter. He lunged and knocked Ester to the ground. Another man cried, "Git 'em!" The white patrons tumbled outside to confront the three African Americans. One of the white men produced a chain. B.B.'s retinue fought back. The man with the chain struck Pat Williams, B.B.'s trumpeter, on the forehead. Someone else stabbed Lee Gatling in the shoulder. Big Frank Brown, B.B.'s driver, charged in and wrested the chain away, and the attackers scattered. The two musicians were bleeding.

Police arrived, asked a few listless questions, announced that they could not find any suspects, and then lingered beneath the gas-station lights, glaring coldly at the wounded men. The white attackers had left the scene in a freight truck. A witness, presumably white, told officers he had watched B.B.'s musicians unearth the incriminating chain from the trunk of their own vehicle and plant it on the ground after the fight.

B.B., freshening up in the men's room, had missed the whole thing. Now he swept in and took charge, summoning an ambulance and calming both his own men and the police. At such moments, the great bluesman possessed a gravitas that even racist cops could not ignore.

"Wanted something to eat," B.B. told Lydon, when the skirmish was over. "Just something to eat."

B.B. still traveled with a bare-bones band, but with Sid Seidenberg in charge, he would not play many more cinder-block dives like the Club Streamline. No longer would he play anywhere for a paltry $400, the sum B.B. had grudgingly accepted that night when the club manager said he didn't have the promised $650.

"Maybe soon I'll just work weekends, maybe even have a club of my own," B.B. told the *Times*. "I got four kids by various women; they're all grown and have children. Maybe I'll enjoy my grandchildren like I never had a chance to with my own."

Since B.B.'s divorce from Sue, more women had come forward with paternity claims. B.B. never pressed a mother for proof a child was his, a tenet of Mississippi chivalry he had learned from his father. "When a lady says the baby is yours," Albert would say, "the only question you ask is, 'Was you in there?' If the answer is yes, then it's yours." By 1970, B.B.'s family had swelled to six: Barbara, twenty-two; Shirley and Willie, both twenty; Gloria, nineteen; Riletta, eighteen; and Riley Jr., thirteen. B.B. paid for their college educations, and some of his progeny would later work for him.

B.B. had lost his infant brother and then his mother and then his grandmother. He had no siblings. His father had another family. Now, at last, he had a family to call his own. B.B.'s prolific paternity became a part of his virile-bluesman legend, something to brag about in hundreds of interviews to come, even if it wasn't provably true.

CHAPTER 15

LIVE AND WELL

AROUND THE END OF 1968, B.B. King finally quit the chitlin'
circuit. He performed at Yale University and drew a standing ovation, seeding a new future for B.B. on the college circuit. At year's end,
he fulfilled a weeklong residency at New York's Village Gate, where the
jazz masters Thelonious Monk and Sonny Rollins had cut albums. On
February 6, 1969, the B.B. King band appeared on *The Tonight Show*,
the nation's leading late-night talk show. The booking was probably the
handiwork of Flip Wilson, the African American comic, whose status
as perennial substitute for Johnny Carson was itself a triumph of pop-
cultural desegregation.

"All of a sudden, it seem like people remember that I'm still alive,"
B.B. told an interviewer in March. "And I'm grateful."

A few years earlier, B.B. had traveled in circles so remote from
America's white population that even sage music writer Leonard Feather
did not know his work. Now, B.B. King was one of the most recognized brands in popular music, his renown threatening to transcend
the insular genre of blues. "King has had the kind of impact on the
young guitar players that Ray Charles has had on the singers, which is
to say, the kind of impact Allen Ginsberg has had on the poets," Ralph
Gleason wrote in his column.

In March, work began on the first in a string of B.B. King albums
that would bring his sound up-to-date. B.B. had a new producer, Bill
Szymczyk. He was white and twenty-six, with a mop of dark-brown
hair set atop a rugged face and dimpled chin. Szymczyk (pronounced
sim-zik) had grown up in Muskegon, Michigan, listening to R&B music
on a Nashville station with a homemade radio. After working sonar

systems in the navy, he enrolled in New York University and took a job as a floor sweep at a music studio. By 1969, Szymczyk had worked his way up to producer at ABC, drawing inspiration from such studio wizards as Glyn Johns, the man who had engineered the triumphal *Beggars Banquet* for the Rolling Stones. Szymczyk was a blues freak, and he begged the studio heads to let him produce B.B. King. He thought the label was squandering the bluesman's immense currency among white blues-rock fans. "At the time," he recalled, "the Stones were breaking, and all the English bands were breaking, and they're just feeding American blues back to us that we fed to them in the '40s and '50s." Szymczyk wanted to reverse that polarity. He wanted to see what B.B. could do with a group of modern rock and blues musicians in a loose, unscripted, contemporary studio session. At first, the label bosses told Szymczyk he was "too young and too white." He wore them down. He had not yet produced a major album, but the ABC suits still allowed him to produce B.B. King. "They did not know what they had," Szymczyk recalled.

Szymczyk told B.B. he wanted to "liven up the energy" around him. He proposed a studio session with musicians drawn from the cream of the New York R&B and rock communities. B.B. was only half convinced. At his request, one side of the record would be recorded in March 1969 at the Village Gate, capturing the electricity of a live B.B. King show performed by his regular road band. To engineer that session, Szymczyk chose Phil Ramone, another producer of subsequent renown. Side two took shape in the studio, where Szymczyk would show what B.B. could do in a modern aural setting.

From the opening notes of "Don't Answer the Door," side one of *Live & Well* registered as the highest-quality live B.B. King recording yet captured on tape. One or two songs in, it became equally clear that *Live & Well* would never equal either of B.B.'s prior live releases. The problem lay with the audience, which sounded barely awake. B.B. had gained much in his ascent to the front rank of popular music, but he had also lost something. The audience captured at the Regal in 1964 had been full participants in the recording, as important as B.B. or his band. Now, with B.B. playing to a mostly white audience at an elegant jazz club, much of that rousing, shouting, stomping, Pentecostal energy was gone. The applause that opened and closed each song was just that—polite applause, not wild cheers, not full-throated exhortations to "Play it for me, B.B.!" By the album's second track, "Just a Little Love," B.B. was sufficiently perturbed by the dearth of audience response to engage the crowd in a tepid sing-along.

Side two of *Live & Well*, recorded over two nights at New York's famed Hit Factory, sounded unlike any prior B.B. King record. In the past, B.B. had generally walked into a studio and performed with a band that played scripted notes from printed arrangements. On *Live & Well*, B.B. entered the studio with lyrics printed on a legal pad, sat down, and simply started to play. "I'd watch his foot to get the time," recalled Jerry "Fingers" Jemmott, the bass player. "He would sing, we would listen, we would get a groove, and then we would record it." The multiracial backing band included a second guitarist, versatile white session man Hugh McCracken, a concession to the two-guitar attack that was now the norm in pop music. The band's deft polyrhythms reworked B.B.'s customary blues shuffles into sleek, subdivided funk. Before *Live & Well*, most B.B. King songs had followed the blues shuffle rhythm, which is the essence of swing. The rhythm is based on the triplet, a musical note split into three. The "swing" comes from an accent on the first and third notes, a cadence familiar to anyone who has heard "The Pink Panther Theme." On *Live & Well*, the session band reshaped B.B.'s triplets into "straight" eighth notes, the rhythm of funk. B.B.'s studio work had fallen behind the times. *Live & Well* sounded modern, and that was what B.B. wanted.

The best track by far was the album's closer, "Why I Sing the Blues," an eight-minute explosion of anger and hurt, a performance so propulsive and powerful that it left the listener wondering why the band had been holding back. "Why I Sing the Blues" was B.B.'s first overtly political statement. It appeared as a single several months after James Brown's landmark "Say It Loud—I'm Black and I'm Proud." B.B.'s message was both longer and angrier. "When I first got the blues, they brought me over on a ship," he sang. "Men were standing over me, and a lot more with a whip." B.B. had not addressed race in a song before, let alone slavery. Now, he raged about urban blight and slum housing, the chitlin' circuit and the welfare state. The Dylan-length lyric, apparently cowritten with African American R&B songsmith Dave Clark, unfolded as an extended sociological observation on Black America, a theme Marvin Gaye would explore at album's length two years later with *What's Going On*.

B.B. had reaped more press in 1967 and 1968 than in the entirety of his prior career. The marketplace was ripe for a good B.B. King record, and now it had two: *Live & Well* and *The Electric B.B. King*, a rush-job collection of ABC singles and scraps. Seven songs from those albums charted as singles. "Paying the Cost to Be the Boss" reached number 39 on the pop chart in 1968. "Why I Sing the Blues" reached number 61 in 1969. Both would endure as blues classics. *Down Beat* declared *Live & Well* "the most important blues recording in many years," arguably the first mainstream blues album produced like a modern rock record.

On April 22, 1969, a cloudy Tuesday, B.B. and his band at last debuted in Britain. His visit was long overdue. The center of the rock universe lay in London, not in San Francisco or New York. England had spawned most of the greatest electric guitarists in pop. The list included Jimi Hendrix, the greatest pop guitarist of them all. After several years as an R&B sideman in the United States, Hendrix had journeyed to England to launch his own career. His psychedelic blues rock was too "white" for Black radio stations back home, but Hendrix was too Black for white radio. In England, none of that mattered.

B.B.'s band arrived in London to a scene from a Beatles newsreel. Two thousand Britons greeted them at the airport, waving American flags. "And as we walked through customs, everybody started hollering, 'B.B.! B.B.!'" he recalled. "By God, I was frightened." Throngs of fans did not camp out at airports back home for B.B. King.

B.B.'s British hosts booked his first performance at Royal Albert Hall, the grand arts palace. He headlined a bill that included the old folk-blues duo of Brownie McGhee and Sonny Terry and Peter Green's Fleetwood Mac. The Mac were a blues band fronted by a Jewish Brit who played B.B. King–style guitar as well as anyone. The concert felt like a tender homecoming. "This is the moment for all blues men," one observer reported. B.B. fed off the adoring crowd: "working away in his own public agony, his face feeling every note, sweat hidden but seeping, we know, across pale blue cotton ruffled shirt, neat, dark worsted suit, still crisp from the steam iron, shoes laced up and well shone," the reviewer observed. "Suddenly he hollers a piece of high camp earthy blues, sashaying his thighs to the retort lines; and we break up in the moment's relief. The audience is hysterical with gratification." At the end of the set, B.B. and his audience wept together in reciprocal gratitude.

LIVE & WELL EMERGED in May and entered the pop album charts, peaking at number 56, B.B.'s best showing to date. His label quickly booked more studio time. Bill Szymczyk now sought to replicate the studio setting from *Live & Well* across a full album, fittingly titled *Completely Well*. He summoned his studio men.

The studio recordings on *Live & Well*, for all their strengths, sounded like the work of a major artist backed by session men. B.B. hadn't played with the ensemble before, and it showed. When the same musicians regrouped for *Completely Well* in June 1969, they met as friends. "It's not so much instruments coming together as people coming together," recalled Jerry Jemmott, the bassist. Herb Lovelle, the drummer and bandleader, outfitted the studio with copious quantities of wine, weed, and women. Spirits ran high by the time the music began.

The *Completely Well* sessions yielded a series of long, loose jams. "We had gotten the taste of playing long songs from 'Why I Sing the Blues,'" Jemmott recalled. The performance chosen as the opening track, penned by Jemmott and titled "So Excited," ranked among B.B.'s most distinctive works. It began, deceptively, with a straight-ahead rock beat before opening up into a funky, syncopated polyrhythm, anchored by an ear-candy riff from the organ and a confident vocal from B.B., who had seldom sounded so fresh. B.B. fed off the band just as he drew energy from an audience in concert.

Side two offered a raucous reprise of B.B.'s 1955 single "Crying Won't Help You." The performance stretched into a six-minute jam and segued into "You're Mean," which combusted for another ten minutes, B.B. and Hugh McCracken locked in musical duel. McCracken played musical chameleon, sounding like Jimi Hendrix in one phrase, Jimmy Page in the next, all the while pushing B.B. to deliver some of the best licks he had ever played. B.B. thrived on competition, friendly or not. Midway through the second song, after a blistering exchange, the two guitarists paused, and spontaneous applause erupted in the studio. B.B. broke up in laughter. "That's good," he gasped, as he dove back into the fray. When the performance ended, B.B. deadpanned, "Whatchall tryin' to do, kill me?" No backing band had pushed him so hard.

But that jam and the rest of *Completely Well* would be overshadowed by the song chosen to close the album, perhaps the most important single performance of B.B.'s career.

"The Thrill Is Gone" was another old R&B hit that B.B. had filed away in his disc-jockey brain. It was a top-ten single in 1951 for Roy Hawkins, a rhythm-and-blues singer and noted sad sack who once penned a side titled "Gloom and Misery All Around." Hawkins had been B.B.'s label-mate at Modern Records. He performed "The Thrill Is Gone" as a mournful shuffle. B.B. carried the song around in his head for years, reimagining it in various arrangements and even trying to record it once or twice. One night during the sessions for *Completely Well*, B.B. arrived at the studio with a new version that he liked. He had raised the key, lifted the tempo, and shifted the rhythm to Otis Redding–style soul. Whereas the original ballad hewed to the twelve-bar, three-chord formula of minor blues, B.B. had introduced a note of compositional complexity: a fourth chord, in the third line of each verse, a baby step into the province of pop.

Szymczyk "set up the sound nice and mellow," B.B. recalled. And then, "without tellin' them what I was gonna do, I slipped into this tune. And everybody fell right in, and it seemed to be the sweetest sound ever to me." The recorded performance opened with a single, ringing, vibrating note from Lucille, held for three full beats before B.B. proceeded into his introductory solo, soaring over a pulsing bass and watery splashes of organ. And then he sang: "The thrill is gone, the thrill is gone away."

B.B. had rewritten Roy Hawkins's melody, taming it into a simple, hummable, descending line. Jemmott found the perfect bass pattern to complement B.B.'s melody, built around a little riff on the first and third beats that tiptoed up to each note. Lovelle, the drummer, anchored the bass to a spare, slightly lagging 4/4 rock tempo. Together, bass, drums, and melody conspired to render the song unique and memorable.

Yet, according to Szymczyk and Jemmott, no one went home that night thinking they had recorded a hit. B.B. would later claim that he, and maybe he alone, had heard its promise: "I was thrilled."

In the hours after the session ended, Szymczyk replayed the tapes from that night, looking for keepers. When he reached "The Thrill Is Gone," he began to hum along, imagining a bank of strings suspended above the mix. Excitement seized him. Around two in the morning, he telephoned B.B. in his hotel room. "B.," he said. "'The Thrill Is Gone.' I like it." A groggy B.B. replied, "I told you so." The producer continued, "I want to put some strings on it." Ten seconds passed in silence. "Go ahead and do it," B.B. replied. "I'm not sure if I'm gonna like it." Violins on a B.B. King song seemed as unlikely as acoustic guitar on an Otis Redding song. But "(Sittin' On) The Dock of the Bay" had delivered Redding a posthumous number 1 hit.

B.B. was in the studio when the string section recorded the overdub. Szymczyk wondered how the bluesman would react. When the recording reached the second verse and the bank of strings swelled to life, the producer saw a wide grin break across B.B.'s face. Strings perfected "The Thrill Is Gone," imbuing the brooding ballad with cinematic suspense, not unlike the effect of the dirge-like horns on B.B.'s very first hit, "3 O'Clock Blues," eighteen years earlier.

Decades later, at an event in Indianola, a man from National Public Radio approached Sue King, B.B.'s ex-wife, and inquired coyly, "Are you the thrill?" The question caught her off guard. Sue had never asked her former husband if she inspired his most famous recording, and he hadn't told her. "I don't know," she confessed. "You need to ask him." Hours later, the reporter found Sue. He had spoken to B.B. "It was you," he told her. Deep down, Sue already knew.

For B.B., the *Completely Well* sessions unfolded during a month-long residency at the Village Gate, two shows a night, perhaps the longest B.B.'s band had ever played the same room. No doubt he enjoyed

waking up every morning in the same city. The calculus of live performance was shifting to his favor. He played fewer concerts in 1969 than
in previous years, but each gig seemed to bring a progressively larger
audience. In the summer, he entertained twelve thousand fans at the
Newport Jazz Festival, five thousand at the Ann Arbor Blues Festival,
another twenty thousand at Tanglewood in Massachusetts, nearly fifty
thousand at the Atlantic City Pop Festival, and one hundred thousand
at the Texas International Pop Festival outside Dallas, along with an
appearance in New York's Central Park bandshell on a bill with Jimmy
Page and his red-hot Led Zeppelin. That fall, B.B. launched a marathon
college tour, stopping at the universities of Illinois and Wisconsin,
Colorado State and Cornell. By the end of 1969, Sid Seidenberg would
claim that B.B. had played to more people in that year than in all prior
years combined.

In October, news leaked that B.B. King would join the Rolling
Stones on most of their month-long U.S. tour. The 1969 Rolling Stones
tour was the event of the year in rock music, the Stones being the second
most important rock 'n' roll band in the world behind the Beatles, who
were breaking up. *Village Voice* critic Robert Christgau later termed it
"history's first mythic rock and roll tour."

The Stones had admired B.B. since the beginning, had even made
a pilgrimage to the famous 20 Grand club in Detroit to catch a B.B.
King show during their first U.S. tour, in 1964. Now, B.B. was the most
celebrated performer in blues. Perhaps the Stones thought it fitting that
he share a bill with the greatest rock 'n' roll band in the world, as they
touted themselves on this tour. Several dates would reunite B.B. with
his old Mississippi friend Ike Turner, whose wife, Tina, possessed one
of the most powerful contraltos in popular music. Ike & Tina were the
hottest act in soul, and Mick Jagger had made a careful study of Tina's
lioness-in-heat stage act. B.B. and Tina would be hard acts to follow. It
was another of those awkward situations, and B.B. had endured many,
that cast him as warm-up act for younger artists who had built careers
more or less on his back.

Drummer Sonny Freeman still anchored B.B.'s band. The newcomers included Ron Levy, B.B.'s first white sideman. An alumnus of

the Albert King band, Levy was a Jewish kid from Cambridge, Massachusetts, slender and tall, with a shoulder-length mop of hair and an easy smile. Just a few years earlier, he would have had trouble gaining entry to the clubs B.B. played. B.B. treated him like a son.

However much the vainglorious Stones loved B.B., they didn't show it on opening night at the Forum in Los Angeles. B.B. played cards at a folding table with his band as he waited in vain for his hosts to stop by his dressing room, a repurposed locker room, and pay respects. Ike Turner finally escorted B.B. into the Stones' opulent camp and made introductions. Only once, later in the tour, did the Stones find the time to be photographed with B.B. According to *Rolling Stone*, "no sooner had the shutter clicked than they were gone."

B.B. recalled of Jagger and Richards, "They told me how they named themselves after a Muddy Waters tune, and they showed me respect." But he approached the gig with unease. "I wasn't used to being around rock 'n' roll stars. I wasn't comfortable. It was another new situation that had me worried about fitting in. I felt like I was being forced on the fans," nearly all of them white, "like I was going to someone's house without being invited."

An army of rock critics descended on the Forum on November 8, a cool and breezy Saturday, for the tour opener. Thirty-six thousand tickets for two shows had sold out in eight hours. The scribes included Stanley Booth, now twenty-seven and armed with a book deal to write about the Stones.

As B.B. took the stage and wrestled with a dead microphone at the start of his set, someone from B.B.'s entourage invited Booth into the dressing room and revealed a stash of heroin, which the two men proceeded to snort. That was a flagrant violation of B.B.'s road rules, which, within the twenty-four-hour bacchanal of a Rolling Stones tour, would prove difficult to enforce.

The dead microphone revived, B.B. started his set. It included some new banter tailored to an audience of white hippies, who might misconstrue his old chitlin' circuit soliloquies on spousal abuse and infidelity. Booth transcribed some of B.B.'s Delta patois: "'Laze and gennlemen, if we just had more love, we wouldn't have no . . . wars.'

[Applause.] 'Than kyou. And if we had more love, we wouldn't have no . . . jails.' [Applause.] ''An kyou.'"

"Then B.B. stopped talking," Booth recounted, "was quiet for a moment, played eight searing bars of blues, and sang, 'When I read your letter this morning, that was in your place in bed.' The crowd, white city people, hooted and hollered, and for the moment even the cops seemed to stop harassing bystanders. Rising on his toes, B.B. lifted the guitar neck on the ascending notes. With his blue suit shining in the blue spotlight, so intent on what he was doing, B.B. was, for all his eight children by six different women, a saint of the blues."*

One of the children, Gloria, visited with B.B. backstage after his first set, joining B.B.'s father and stepsisters in his locker room. B.B. now routinely paid for members of his burgeoning family to travel to his concerts and handed them fifty-dollar bills when they arrived.

Ike & Tina followed B.B. and laid down another electrifying performance. Then the Stones shambled onstage and somehow held their own as headliners. "The kids stood up on their seats and danced," a *Variety* reviewer wrote, "long hair flapping like rags in the wind, eyes glazed, totally stoned by the beat and the presence." And so it went, from one city to the next. Ike & Tina and B.B. whipped crowds into a rhythmic frenzy that threatened to upstage the band they had been hired to support. And then the Stones arrived to command the sweaty throng, proving themselves, after all, the greatest rock 'n' roll band in the world. The nightly challenge forced the Stones to raise their game.

The Stones held court backstage after the first Forum show, joined by B.B.'s cousin Bukka. Keith Richards, Bukka's besotted admirer, produced an old National steel guitar and launched into some country blues. Mick Jagger fell in on vocals.

"That's good," Bukka said, when they had finished. "These boys is good. Has you ever made any records?"

Bukka seemed not to recognize the Rolling Stones. Richards regarded him with puzzlement and then replied that, yes, they had

---

*B.B.'s adopted offspring actually numbered six on the night of the show. Two more would arrive by the time Booth completed his book.

made records. "I knew good and well that you had," Bukka said, nodding in smug satisfaction.

B.B. knew the stakes of this tour for his own career. When he played a subpar set in Philadelphia, he went off by himself and got drunk. "It's good that he still gets so upset," Keith Richards said, when someone told him the story. "You got to be able to do it every night, and it ain't easy."

B.B. and the Rolling Stones parted ways after a gig in Boston on November 29, 1969, a week before the Stones' infamous free concert at the Altamont Speedway in California. The month B.B. spent on tour with the Stones would boost his currency in white America like no other episode in his career. "It's one of the great ironies in music today," Lillian Roxon observed in her *Rock Encyclopedia*, "that American kids had to learn about one of their own big blues men from a bunch of English kids."

THE YEAR, and the decade, ended in a flurry of activity for Sidney A. Seidenberg, Inc., the new firm formed in December by B.B.'s busy manager. Seidenberg announced that B.B. would appear in a series of television and radio commercials, his first since the WDIA days, singing the praises of Pepsi Cola, American Telephone & Telegraph, and Axion laundry soap. More important, perhaps, was his deal with the Gibson guitar company, a relationship that would make the name Lucille more or less synonymous with Gibson's line of shapely, hollow-bodied blues guitars. A B.B. King book appeared, a compendium of sheet music and clippings titled *B.B. King—The Personal Instructor.* Big-shot music writer Albert Goldman profiled B.B. in *Life,* weekly circulation eight million.

Completely Well, surely B.B.'s best recording since his crossover ascent, emerged in the final weeks of 1969 and spent half of the next year on the *Billboard* album chart, peaking at number 38, his best placement to date. "The Thrill Is Gone" entered the Hot 100 chart in December and reached number 15, the highest B.B. would ever go on the pop singles chart. That statistic, though, doesn't quite capture the magnitude of

B.B.'s achievement. The song was "being played on Top 40 radio stations that never before played a B.B. King disc," or any other Black blues single, Ralph Gleason reported. "The Thrill Is Gone" would endure on the radio for decades, would become known as *the* B.B. King song, the one any casual music fan could identify after a few bars. In 2004, *Rolling Stone* would include the single on its list of the 500 greatest pop songs. At number 183, "Thrill" was the highest-placed pure blues song on the list.

Taken together, the Stones tour and "The Thrill Is Gone" completed B.B.'s metamorphosis into Major Artist, exposing his music to a vast new audience of young, white Americans, many of whom wanted nothing more than to play guitar like B.B. King. As aide Norman Matthews recalled, "We didn't have to eat no more grits."

B.B.'s big hit opened big doors. In April 1970, he debuted on the Las Vegas Strip. B.B. had played the Black clubs at the edge of Vegas since the 1950s but never one of the grand gambling palaces. He now secured a two-week stand at Nero's Nook, the second stage at Caesar's Palace, home base to Frank Sinatra. When Sid Seidenberg had sought Sinatra's blessing, the entertainer had telegraphed, "Hell, yes." The band arrived at the elegant casino with a new member, trombonist "Li'l" Joe Burton, a veteran rhythm-and-blues sideman, though he was not yet twenty.

"We stood out there," Burton recalled, "looking at that marquis all night long, with B.B.'s name up there."

B.B. was hardly the first Black entertainer to do Vegas: a decade earlier, Sammy Davis Jr. had played the Strip without a dressing room, unable to sleep in the hotel where he sang. But B.B. was evidently the first modern blues artist to perform along the famed entertainment corridor. The music press ascribed symbolic gravitas to his tenure at the Nook, a 250-seat lounge with a reflecting pool, where he broke attendance records. Sammy Davis himself showed up on opening weekend. "The King is in the palace," Leonard Feather proclaimed in the *Los Angeles Times*. "A new regime has begun."

B.B. eventually gained an audience with Sinatra himself. "It was 3 a.m., and we'd finished our last set," B.B. recalled. "I rode the elevator up to the penthouse. Big double doors, big entryway. Inside, lots of gorgeous girls milling around an enormous suite overlooking the

Strip, a billion watts of neon aglow below." An aide announced that Sinatra had just arrived from Palm Springs on his private jet. He would be out in a moment. And then the man appeared, flanked by henchmen. "Hi, B.," he said. "I'm happy to see you."

"Happy to see you, too, Frank."

"Hear you're packing 'em in downstairs."

"Things seem to be going well, Frank."

"Look, B. I'm dead tired. I need to go to bed. But I got some booze and I got some broads. Help yourself."

And he was gone.

Las Vegas was big-band territory. B.B. would need a professional arranger, someone to write charts for a full orchestra. B.B. hadn't much use for an arranger in the lean years or during his ascent of the pop charts. Now, in Vegas, the need arose anew. B.B. turned to Hampton Reese.

Reese had entered B.B.'s life in the late 1950s and contributed a song to the *B.B. King Wails* LP. Over the next decade, Reese became a friend and occasional arranger. With B.B.'s Vegas debut, Reese took on a larger role and became his frequent traveling companion. Born in Alabama, Reese studied trombone at the New England Conservatory and emerged with a faux British accent. "He wore horned-rim glasses, a goatee, usually a shirt with an almost matching ascot, tweed jacket and smoked Benson & Hedges 100mm cigarettes from a long holder, all giving his modest height a very professorial countenance," recalled pianist Ron Levy. Upon departing a gig, Reese might announce, "Yonder vehicle contains my worldly goods and chattel." Bandmates thought him an insufferable ass.

Reese and his wife were New York swingers with an open marriage. Levy once walked in on him performing oral sex on a young woman while snapping photos with a camera mounted on a tripod. But B.B. took to Reese like Eliza Doolittle to Henry Higgins in *Pygmalion*, embracing him as tutor, mentor, and symbol of upward intellectual mobility, a man in the spirit of schoolteacher Luther Henson. "His thing was books, books, books," B.B. recalled. "If you don't know something, go to a book."

Reese had taught B.B. to read music, via the Schillinger instruction books. He had taught B.B. and Sue to play chess to fill the long hours on the road. And Reese seeded in B.B. a fascination with the printed word that would endure until his death. When B.B. briefly flirted with recreational flying, Reese escorted him to a used-book store to purchase a stack of aviation texts.

B.B. had emerged into adulthood functionally illiterate, according to biographer David Ritz. "He taught himself how to read as an adult," Ritz recalled. B.B. could read and write by the time he met Sue, in the middle 1950s. But Sue never knew if her husband read well enough to digest the contracts Sid Seidenberg presented him to sign. Such a failing was not something B.B. would have confided, even to his wife. "He was too proud," Sue recalled.

ON MAY 2, 1970, B.B. made another auspicious debut, at New York's Carnegie Hall, headlining a program titled "B.B. King and His Friends." The friends assembled on this pleasant Saturday night ranged from 1950s jump-blues shouters Big Joe Turner and Eddie "Cleanhead" Vinson to Peacock Records alumna Big Mama Thornton and electric-blues icon T-Bone Walker. For B.B., such an assemblage of influences and peers must have felt a bit like an episode of *This Is Your Life*. His set that night "was, essentially, the same one he has been doing at concerts and festivals for more than a year," the *New York Times* reported. "But he projected everything he did with such a ringing sense of conviction that it might have been the first time. That's showmanship."

All the breakthroughs and firsts betrayed the influence of Sid Seidenberg, who seemed to be finding a new artistic watershed for his client to cross with every passing month. Even as he secured a future for B.B., Seidenberg reached into the past, setting out to correct historical wrongs across B.B.'s two-decade career. In the spring of 1970, Seidenberg helped B.B. file a $2 million federal lawsuit against the Bihari brothers and their Modern Records empire, alleging the company had infringed B.B.'s copyright on more than one hundred songs by falsely claiming songwriter credit under the "Taub" and "Josea" pseudonyms. The parties settled out of court, and the bluesman's credits were quietly restored.

Another raft of press and plaudits arrived in June. B.B. returned to *The Tonight Show*, this time as a guest of Johnny Carson himself. Carson had been cool on the idea until Doc Severinsen, his trusted bandleader, saw B.B. in concert and changed Carson's mind. A week or so later, B.B. drew his first coverage in the *New Yorker*. The *Billboard* album chart of June 13 featured a new number 1 album, the Beatles swan song *Let It Be*. Within that choppy collection, on a free-association jam titled "Dig It," John Lennon cited B.B. by name. The rock pantheon could offer no higher praise.

Of all the gigs B.B. played on the Woodstock-era festival circuit, one performance lingered in his memory: the Atlanta International Pop Festival, staged over three days in July 1970 on a Georgia raceway. All but forgotten today, the Atlanta festival was the southern Woodstock. Hundreds of thousands of people—no one really knows how many— gathered among the pecan trees for one of the largest explorations of hippie music and hirsute culture. Headliners included B.B. and Jimi Hendrix, two months before the latter's fatal barbiturate overdose in a London apartment. Hell's Angels escorted B.B. on motorcycles to his trailer, where his bandmates awaited. They were giggling, and they wouldn't say why. B.B. entered the trailer and sat down to practice. Then came a knock on the door. "Come on in," he said, without looking up. When he finally did, he beheld a young, naked white woman. "I'm your escort for the festival," she smiled. B.B. had heard about such rituals at the hippie festivals. She wasn't there for sex, more as living artwork. B.B. found himself gripped by nerves. This was still the Deep South. Old fears returned. "I really don't know how to act," he recalled. "Don't wanna be rude; don't wanna insult the lady; but I sure do wanna stare." He summoned the nerve to speak, inviting the visitor to sit down while he retreated to the bathroom to change his own clothes for the show.

B.B. CUT TWO of his most successful albums in quick succession in 1970, both comparatively lavish productions from a record company that now found itself controlling the world's most marketable blues artist.

The first was a studio album, *Indianola Mississippi Seeds*. Conceived by producer Bill Szymczyk, the record completed the journey of musical modernization that B.B. had begun two albums earlier, with *Live & Well*. The sessions put B.B. in a Los Angeles studio with a coterie of cutting-edge pop artists. One was Carole King, a Brill Building songsmith. Another was Leon Russell, a wild-eyed musical shaman. A third was Joe Walsh, a formidable guitarist from Kansas who was B.B.'s label-mate at ABC.

The album began with a charming little snippet of B.B. noodling at an out-of-tune piano, an instrument he could barely play, setting things off on a suitably mellow note. The first proper song, "You're Still My Woman," revealed further evolution in B.B.'s blues, set here against a sturdy 4/4 rock beat. Carole King's prominent piano sounded overcaffeinated, but B.B. and the rhythm section kept a calm groove. Leon Russell provided a more bluesy touch on "Ask Me No Questions." After that, *Indianola Mississippi Seeds* veered into derivative terrain. A meandering jam failed to recapture the magic of the *Completely Well* sessions. "Chains and Things," a slow and stately minor blues laced with gentle strings, suffered by comparison to "The Thrill Is Gone," a song it was clearly meant to emulate. The enigmatic lyric—"just can't lose these chains and things"—might have been another meditation on race and oppression, or it might not. The album closed with Leon Russell's piano-driven "Hummingbird," a performance that strayed about as far from the blues idiom as B.B. had ever ventured. "Hummingbird" was a gamble, and it worked, bringing *Indianola Mississippi Seeds* to a dramatic finish with a swell of gospel-hued chorus, not unlike what the Rolling Stones had recently achieved with their woozy epic "You Can't Always Get What You Want."

Indianola Mississippi Seeds was an uneven album. But B.B.'s label packaged it beautifully, with cover art of a watermelon sliced in half and wired up like a guitar, a wry sendup of African American cliché. The album reached number 26 on the *Billboard* album chart. Three singles, "Hummingbird," "Ask Me No Questions," and "Chains and Things," cracked the top fifty. Indianola's weekly *Enterprise-Tocsin* featured the record on its front page. The blurb did not mention that B.B. hadn't actually set foot in Indianola since 1962, when he and his band could not find a hotel in town that would accept African American guests.

B.B.'s second album of 1970 took shape during a two-week stint at Mister Kelly's, the Chicago jazz club. He opened there on August 31, evidently as the venue's first blues performer. A man came up to B.B. and introduced himself as Winston Moore. He ran the Cook County Department of Corrections, including the notorious Cook County Jail, where he had been the nation's first African American warden. "B.," Moore said, "it's the first time for you at Mr. Kelly's, and it's the first time for me at the correctional center, so why don't we do another first?"

Moore, a big bear of a man, had swept into the jail in 1968 and broken up a ring of corruption, seizing weapons and drugs and disempowering prisoners who ran cell blocks. A psychologist by training, Moore thought it might lift morale if B.B. performed for the inmates, most of whom were African Americans. B.B. asked for time to think it over. He consulted Sid Seidenberg, who not only liked the idea but suggested B.B. cut an album in the jail. Johnny Cash had revived his flagging career in 1968 with an LP recorded live at California's Folsom Prison, an exercise that rebranded him as the banner man of "outlaw" country music. Cash connected deeply with the prison folk. Seidenberg had a hunch that B.B. would, too.

Released in 1971 in a faux-denim prison-blues sleeve, *Live in Cook County Jail* surpassed all of B.B.'s prior long-players on the charts, reaching number 25 on the pop album chart and number 1 on the R&B album chart, which he had never topped before. *Cook County Jail* was a recording for the ages.

B.B.'s journey from chitlin' circuit to global fame had commenced in 1967, on the stage of Bill Graham's Fillmore Auditorium. The final symbolic stop was *The Ed Sullivan Show*. A rite of cultural passage for the Beatles, Elvis, and the Stones, *Sullivan* was a fading national pastime in 1970, with a dwindling audience of several million households. B.B. and his band arrived at the New York studio in a haze of exhaustion on the morning of the October 18 broadcast, having played consecutive nights at Bill Graham's Fillmore East. The Fillmore gig ended a few hours before the 9 a.m. call for *Sullivan*. B.B. took the stage for the taped

broadcast in a tuxedo, set against a purple backdrop. His band was allotted six minutes. In a fog of fatigue, anxiety, and haste, B.B. attempted
to count off "one-two-three-four" to start the first song, "Just a Little
Love," a recent ABC single. B.B. never counted off songs, because he
was no good at it. He counted wrong, and the performance began with
B.B. and his drummer playing a beat apart. The band righted itself,
and the rest of the six minutes went well, B.B. finding time to cover
both "The Thrill Is Gone" and "How Blue Can You Get?" in medley
form. When B.B. had finished, Sullivan did not reward him with the
congratulatory handshake that he extended to favored acts.

Nonetheless, Ed Sullivan, Ralph Gleason, "The Thrill Is Gone,"
and the Rolling Stones each had introduced B.B. King to a new audience. He was a household name.

CHAPTER 16

BACK IN THE ALLEY

IN A 1971 INTERVIEW, *Rolling Stone* founder Jan Wenner asked former Beatle John Lennon how he rated himself as a guitarist. Lennon replied that he wished he could "do it like B.B. King."* Lennon was probably the most important person in pop music, and readers hung on his every acid word. B.B. emerged from the interview as one of the few musicians Lennon seemed to like.

B.B.'s currency stood at an all-time high. He had cleared half a million dollars in 1970. Sid Seidenberg, ever the accountant, calculated that the B.B. King band had performed for 2,980,716 people that year, a tally he termed "one of the greatest records in the history of American show business."

Toward the end of 1970, B.B. rented a luxury apartment on the twenty-ninth floor of Park Ten, a new, thirty-three-story tower on West Sixty-Sixth Street in Manhattan. This was B.B.'s bachelor pad, decorated in blue and cream, with picture windows overlooking Central Park. He filled it with musical instruments, stacks of records, and all of the flotsam his beleaguered valets had dragged from one hotel to the next.

B.B. closed out the year at Club Paradise in South Memphis. The venue belonged to Sunbeam Mitchell, B.B.'s first patron, who had withdrawn from blighted Beale Street. Now well into his sixties, Sunbeam "waddled around contentedly on his 200-pound-plus frame, like a chocolate Buddha, grinning a jagged-toothed grin between puffs on

---

* On the taped interview, Lennon swallowed the word "it," and the pronoun was omitted from the published piece. Lennon was thus widely misquoted as wishing he could "do like B.B. King."

a giant cigar," visibly delighted at the night's receipts, according to an account in *Look* magazine. B.B. played till 3 a.m.

Early in 1971, the B.B. King band traveled to Japan, their first journey farther than Europe. When they reached customs at the Tokyo airport, an agent dropped a ceramic jar he had pulled from Ron Levy's luggage. The jar shattered, and white powder exploded atop his desk. The customs hall fell silent. B.B. shook his head and muttered, "Oh, Slim, say it ain't so," using his sideman's nickname. Levy himself wasn't quite sure what had spilled. To everyone's relief, the powder was Old Spice. The customs man never found the actual drugs Slim had concealed on his slender person.

Drugs were as common as drumsticks in pop music of the day, and B.B. knew some of his musicians were using. He vowed vengeance on anyone who showed up loaded to work or who, God help him, got caught. Sonny Freeman, B.B.'s drummer and bandleader, prowled hotel hallways, sniffing for weed. Anyone he found smoking cannabis faced a fifty-dollar fine. That was B.B.'s way of policing his band's public image, a precious commodity as Sid Seidenberg assembled increasingly ambitious international itineraries for his star. "He didn't want anybody getting arrested," Levy recalled. "He didn't want any notoriety."

Legal disaster averted, the band proceeded with a two-week Japanese tour of public venues and U.S. military bases, even recording a pair of shows at Sankei Hall in Tokyo on March 4 and 7. The Japanese crowds sat through every song in impassive silence, hands folded in their laps as if they were attending a cello recital. They held that pose until a song reached its end, whereupon the entire audience would explode in rapture, screaming and rushing the stage, only to retreat like a spent wave and sit in silent vigil as the next number began.

Between gigs, B.B.'s sidemen explored Tokyo clubs and found themselves "treated as the international celebrities" they imagined themselves to be, Levy recalled. One musician broke a bathroom sink at an Osaka hotel while carousing with a woman in his suite at 3 a.m., flooding several floors. Such mishaps aside, the tour proved a conspicuous success, delivering packed houses and a double album of new B.B. King recordings— another first—titled *Live in Japan*. B.B.'s ABC label released it only in

Japan, no doubt deeming it redundant. The longer format allowed the band to stretch out on long, live jams, instrumental workouts that had not been captured on vinyl before. On the nine-minute "Japanese Boogie" and the six-minute "You're Still My Woman," B.B. reeled off chromatic, jazz-inflected solos that ventured as far outside the blues scale as he had ever dared to go. *Live in Japan* became a coveted collectible.

B.B. returned home in time for the March 16 Grammy Awards. He had been nominated for a Grammy just once before, for the 1969 album *Live & Well*. This time, B.B. was nominated in the category of Best R&B Vocal Performance, Male, for his new signature song, "The Thrill Is Gone." He won, and *Indianola Mississippi Seeds* snagged a trophy for its front-cover artwork.

In May, a B.B. King single titled "That Evil Child" peaked at number 97 on the *Billboard* pop chart. This would be B.B.'s last hit from Modern Records, a full decade after his departure from the label. The Biharis had never stopped repackaging old B.B. King product on singles and albums. Some of them, including the double-LP compilation *From the Beginning*, sold in large quantities, drew serious attention from reviewers, and schooled a new generation of fans in B.B.'s best work.

Two of B.B.'s greatest albums, the live sets at the Regal and Cook County Jail, had been inspired by James Brown and Johnny Cash, respectively. His next LP would follow the same pattern.

John Lee Hooker was scaling the *Billboard* charts in the spring of 1971 with *Hooker 'n Heat*, a record cut with the white blues band Canned Heat. Howlin' Wolf had completed a "super session" in London with Eric Clapton, British pop wunderkind Steve Winwood, and two Rolling Stones. Those sessions provided a template for Black blues masters to record with their white disciples, helping Hooker and Wolf reinvigorate their careers. B.B.'s career needed no revival. Still, producers reasoned that a transatlantic B.B. King album would underscore his influence on the fertile British pop scene, perchance to boost sales at home and abroad.

Bill Szymczyk, the producer who had shepherded B.B. into pop music's mainstream, was no longer available. The 6.5-magnitude Sylmar earthquake of February 1971 had driven Szymczyk from L.A. to Colorado, where he would guide a band of mellow country rockers called the

Eagles to rock stardom. Szymczyk didn't want B.B. to fall back into the hands of some studio hack, so he enlisted a trusted friend, Ed Michel, a seasoned jazz and blues producer who had cut records for avant-garde jazz artists Alice Coltrane and Pharaoh Sanders as well as John Lee Hooker.

Nearly every musician in Britain seemed to want to cut sides with B.B. King. Michel and his colleagues assembled a list of stars who might pair well with the bluesman. Calls were placed. The two biggest names, John Lennon and Eric Clapton, proved unavailable. (Michel's handwritten notes describe Lennon's response as "uptight.") But Michel was able to land Lennon's post-Beatles bassist, Klaus Voormann, and an actual Beatle, drummer Ringo Starr. The final lineup for *B.B. King in London* included Steve Winwood on organ, the other big catch, and guest artists including the New Orleans pianist Dr. John and Fleetwood Mac alumnus Peter Green.

B.B. landed in England amid pouring rain. Sessions commenced on June 9 at Command Studios in London. The proceedings were predictably decadent. B.B. recalled a typical scene: Bobby Keys and Jim Price, the Rolling Stones' horn section, were laying down a backing track. "They were behind sound baffles," B.B. recalled, "so all you could see was their heads poking above the top, and Jim Price was getting a blowjob from a chick while he was playing the trumpet. So he was getting his trumpet blown while he was blowing his trumpet."

The resulting album was neither a masterpiece nor a disaster. The opening track, Louis Jordan's jump blues "Caldonia," sounded like drunken Dixieland. From there, *B.B. King in London* played like a series of sonic experiments. The album closed with an ambitious foray into soul titled "Ain't Nobody Home." Peter Green, a brilliant but unstable guitarist, contributed several memorable solos to the LP, only to later demand that they be stricken from the mix. When it was all over, Michel had enough leftover material for a second album. Four decades later, the tapes remained in a file in his home.

"Ain't Nobody Home" reached a respectable number 46 on the *Billboard* singles chart. But *B.B. King in London* topped out at number 57 on the album chart, halting B.B.'s upward march over four previous albums. The missing ingredient was Szymczyk, the canny producer, whose absence somehow outweighed the combined efforts of two dozen pop stars, backup singers, and session men.

Szymczyk seeded a tradition of artistic interplay between B.B. and other accomplished guitarists: Hugh McCracken on *Live & Well* and *Completely Well*, Joe Walsh on *Indianola Mississippi Seeds*, Peter Green in London. But B.B. hadn't toured with a second guitarist since Robert Lockwood Jr., twenty years earlier. In the spring of 1971, at long last, B.B. hired Lockwood's replacement.

Milton Hopkins was a veteran axe-man from Houston. A cousin of country-blues guitarist Lightnin' Hopkins and an acolyte of fellow Texan Gatemouth Brown, Milton Hopkins spent his early years in Don Robey's entourage, touring with Little Richard and recording with Johnny Ace. He and B.B. were casually acquainted. One night in 1971, B.B. spotted Hopkins in the audience at a show near San Francisco. He dispatched an aide to invite Hopkins backstage. B.B. hired the guitarist that night. B.B. wanted to resume the musical conversation he had started with Robert Lockwood two decades earlier. B.B. gave Hopkins just one instruction: stay out of my way.

THE SUMMER of 1971 brought an unprecedented honor to B.B. from his spiritual hometown. Memphis leaders designated August 27, 1971, as Day of the Blues. Festivities opened with a motorcade from the airport to City Hall, B.B. and his band waving to the crowds from Lincoln convertibles. Mayor Henry Loeb presented B.B. a key to the city. Two hundred people gathered at W. C. Handy Park, around the statue of the self-professed Father of the Blues. B.B. placed a wreath of red roses at its feet. This postage stamp of a park was the city's only standing tribute to any bluesman. Beale Street was a dump.

"I want to apologize to Mr. King for the City of Memphis," said the Reverend James M. Lawson Jr., a prominent African American pastor, speaking at the Handy Park ceremony. "It has been stingy in dedicating only this small park to men like W. C. Handy and B.B. King, who have influenced music all over the world." Few in the crowd could hear Lawson's apology, because he spoke without a platform or microphone.

The day closed at Sunbeam's Club Paradise with a beauty contest to empanel a Miss Blues-zette, followed by B.B. and his band. When the party ended, a few men from B.B.'s entourage went to hear Memphis soul impresario Isaac Hayes perform at another venue. Around dawn, keyboard man Ron Levy returned to the Holiday Inn. As Levy passed through the lobby, he heard a woman yelling, "This is MY man . . . I am HIS woman, and ain't no bitch gonna steal him away from me this time." Levy approached the woman, whose red wig hung at an odd angle. B.B. sat beside her in a drunken stupor, head listing, eyes rolling vacantly, body teetering dangerously close to a platter of food. The woman recognized Levy and beckoned, "Come sit here, baby, and join us for breakfast." Levy accepted her invitation but excused himself to wash his hands. He raced to the lobby phone and summoned two of B.B.'s aides-de-camp. The men appeared in the lobby and carried B.B. up to his room. One of them slipped some bills to B.B.'s companion, silencing her protests and sending her home.

B.B.'s father, Albert, remained on the farm outside Memphis. B.B. brought the band around to visit him. Albert strutted around with a flask of whiskey sloshing in his back pocket. When Joe Burton, the trombonist, said something B.B.'s father didn't like, Albert produced a bullwhip and cracked him in the behind. "I could've killed that man," Burton recalled. "It hurt like hell."

A year later, in 1972, Albert retired from his job at the Firestone plant and moved to a new home purchased by his son in the Los Angeles suburb of Gardena. Albert sold the Memphis farm, which B.B. had put in his father's name. When B.B. found out, he was crushed. "He loved that farm," Sue King recalled. The hard-drinking, whip-cracking King patriarch would spend the rest of his days in Gardena, tending his rose garden.

IN THE YEAR SINCE B.B.'s breakthrough performance at Cook County Jail, he had emerged as the figurehead of a concerts-in-prisons campaign and the larger prisoners' rights movement. In September 1971, inmates at Attica Correctional Facility in upstate New York rose up, took hostages, and demanded reforms. The standoff ended with thirty-three inmates slain, along with ten guards and civilians. Undeterred by the ongoing threat of violence, Sid Seidenberg booked B.B. into fifteen prisons in 1971, always at B.B.'s expense. On November 2, two months after Attica, the B.B. King band performed at the Massachusetts Correctional Institution in Walpole, a maximum-security prison.

The Massachusetts show sparked a long-term collaboration between B.B. and F. Lee Bailey, the celebrity Boston attorney. In early 1972, B.B. and Bailey formed the Foundation for the Advancement of Inmate Rehabilitation and Recreation, or FAIRR. The nonprofit pledged to help inmates acquire musical instruments and sound systems and ultimately stage prison concerts of their own. "If you want to reform a man, give him something he can do while he's behind the wall," B.B. told the *Chicago Tribune*.

B.B. spent the rest of 1972 settling into the role of superstar. In April, he headlined the New Orleans Jazz and Heritage Festival. In Mississippi, new governor Bill Waller, an antisegregationist, declared June 15 B.B. King Day. This was B.B.'s first real recognition in his home state, twenty years after his first national hit. In July, B.B. played Yankee Stadium as a headliner at the Newport Jazz Festival, which had relocated to Gotham. He proceeded to the Astrodome in Houston and Riverfront Stadium in Cincinnati as part of a Lollapalooza-style touring festival organized by Newport founder George Wein. In September and October, B.B. toured Japan, Europe, and, for the first time, Israel. While climbing a slippery stone staircase at the River Jordan, B.B. slipped. The fall injured his right wrist and drove his teeth through his lip. He played the remainder of the tour one-handed, producing sound from his guitar by hammering the strings on the fret board, just as he had done after the car crash a decade earlier.

"We buckled up in a military transport plane and flew to a remote military base to entertain the Israeli Defense Force troops," recalled Ron Levy, B.B.'s bedazzled pianist, who had kin in Israel. "The cats stared in disbelief at the cute Israeli girl soldiers carrying Uzis in full military garb along with the boys, all young, tanned and strong."

In 1973, B.B. ascended to Las Vegas headliner. On February 24, he commenced a three-week run at the Las Vegas Hilton, working the main room, not a second-tier venue like Nero's Nook. B.B. fronted his own band and a thirty-one-piece orchestra on a bill with Ann-Margret, the female Elvis. B.B. took to calling his costar "Miz Ann," in the deferential manner he had learned in Depression-era Mississippi, mortifying his younger, hipper sidemen.

Elvis had headlined at the Hilton. Sid Seidenberg saw the booking as a step forward in B.B.'s career. B.B. would play many more stands in Vegas, earning enormous sums of money, some of which remained in his pockets after the inevitable gambling binge. B.B. now wagered mostly on keno, a lottery-style game whose players bet on a series of numbers drawn at random. "He would bet thousands of dollars a night, usually at one time, and go to his room to sleep," recalled Sue King, his ex-wife. "He would wake up to find out if he had won." He usually lost.

B.B. and his band jammed with Glen Campbell and Kenny Rogers. Elvis himself sometimes stopped by B.B.'s dressing room to chat with his old Memphis friend. "He used to invite us to his suite for parties," Li'l Joe Burton recalled. "He would have Hefner up in there," he said, referring to the *Playboy* founder. But B.B.'s new Vegas identity subtly rebranded him as a certain type of act, more entertainer than artist. And it chipped away, bit by bit, at the aura of authenticity that was his Mississippi birthright. Muddy and Wolf did not perform with thirty-one-piece orchestras or party with Elvis.

In the recording studio, too, B.B. seemed to be losing his edge. *L.A. Midnight*, released in February 1972, was his first truly aimless recording in half a decade. A tuba, of all things, drowned out some interesting interplay between B.B. and guest guitarist Joe Walsh on the opening track, "I Got Some Help I Don't Need." On two promising jams, the producers buried B.B.'s solos beneath a jarring layer of overdubbed horns. *Guess Who*, released later that year, strayed far from the three-chord vocabulary B.B. had spoken with such fluency in the past. The cover pictured B.B. sprawled on a beach, canary-yellow shirt riding up to reveal a middle-age paunch: success had gone to his waistline. The title track took an honored place in B.B.'s repertoire. The next year brought *To Know You Is to Love You*, cut in Philadelphia and scripted to sound like the latest releases from red-hot soul acts the Spinners and O'Jays.

B.B. sounded tired, as if he were struggling to keep pace with his young session men. No less than Stevie Wonder contributed the title song, cowritten with his former wife Syreeta Wright and buoyed by Wonder's unmistakable synthesizer runs. A pair of singles, "I Like to Live the Love" and the title cut, reached number 28 and 38, respectively, on the *Billboard* pop singles chart, B.B.'s best showings since "The Thrill Is Gone." But the album itself reached only number 71, continuing a downward slide.

An archivist surveying B.B.'s recorded output through 1973 might partition it into three chapters. The first, and best, was the decade he'd spent at Modern Records, cutting more than one hundred sides and marching at the vanguard of electric blues. The second, and probably the worst, comprised B.B.'s first half-dozen years at ABC Records, a time of mostly misguided sessions led by men who mistook him for a big-band singer. The third chapter opened with Bill Szymczyk, the ace producer, leading B.B. into a prosperous reconciliation with the guitar-rock genre he had inspired. But now that chapter was drawing to a close, with steadily dwindling returns.

In the pop-music landscape of the 1970s, a greatest-hits package often signaled the end of a good thing. In 1973, B.B.'s label released two. One, titled *Back in the Alley*, collected B.B.'s best work from his years as a lost soul on the ABC roster. The other, misleadingly titled *The Best of B.B. King*, took up where the first left off, capturing the high points of B.B.'s work with (and since) his collaboration with Szymczyk. Neither collection covered any of B.B.'s magnificent work from the 1950s.

"B.B. King has, in his belated flush of success, become almost as frustrating for the aficionado of the Real Shit as Ray Charles," *Rolling Stone* reported, in a review penned by the inimitable Lester Bangs. "B.B. plays Vegas now, no fault there, and hits both the colleges and TV talk shows. So he's finally out of the scuffle, at late long last. Unfortunately, his music has also gotten less interesting with each successive album. Vintage King wasn't just something for punks to prove they could tell a good blues guitar solo from a bad one; it was stark, evil stuff. Troubled and troubling."

B.B.'s best recording of the early 1970s, *Cook County Jail*, marked a subtle but certain shift in artistic direction. Throughout the 1950s and

1960s, B.B. had shaped popular culture with his music. In the 1970s, as his music lost focus, B.B. would make a deeper impact with his social agenda.

One inspiration was B.B.'s friendship with Charles Evers, the older brother of slain civil rights leader Medgar. A loquacious former dee-jay, Charles Evers had dabbled in prostitution and organized crime in Chicago before his brother's death drew him back to Mississippi. He had his younger brother's fierce gaze and perpetually knotted brow but none of his legendary patience. "I wasn't the kind of guy Medgar was," Charles once told a *Rolling Stone* reporter. "I came here to Mississippi and wanted to kill every white person I saw." The rage endured until Charles buried his brother. He decided then, "There must be a better way of getting even with them." Charles reinvented himself as a righteous if volatile politician. By 1973, he was mayor of tiny Fayette, Mississippi, the state's first African American mayor in generations.

B.B. had been close to Medgar and closer to Charles, who had traveled in the same circles where B.B. performed on Chicago's South Side. As the tenth anniversary of Medgar's death drew near, B.B. met with Charles and proposed an annual gathering to celebrate his brother's life. "I'll come every year," B.B. told Charles, "and bring who I can bring, if you'll run it for me and set it up. All you've got to do is manage it for me and make sure it comes off."

B.B. and Charles assembled an impressive cast for the inaugural Mississippi Homecoming, including actor James Earl Jones, comedian Dick Gregory, and gospel's Staple Singers. Governor Bill Waller declared June 12 a statewide Medgar Evers Memorial Festival Day.

The day began with a memorial service in the sweltering gymnasium of Jefferson County Senior High School. From there, a motorcade coursed through Fayette along Highway 61, Charles Evers leading the procession in a car driven by one of Mississippi's three Black highway patrolmen. The entourage traveled ninety miles to the state capital in Jackson for a marathon concert at the Mississippi Coliseum. B.B.'s father attended, along with an endless procession of more distant family. "It seemed like everybody there was related to B.B.," recalled Joe Burton, B.B.'s trombonist. In years to come, B.B.'s kin and not-quite-kin arrived at these festivals by the busload, to B.B.'s delight—and on his tab.

* * *

THE SLOW ROT AFFLICTING B.B.'s recordings did not hinder his steady rise as a performer. In June, B.B. hosted a three-hour celebration of blues at the prestigious Philharmonic Hall in New York, handing the microphone to Muddy Waters, Big Mama Thornton, and Arthur "Big Boy" Crudup in turn. In the latter months of 1973, B.B. performed on national television for variety shows hosted by Helen Reddy and Flip Wilson and comedian George Carlin, and he played on the live-act showcase *Midnight Special*. In a September ceremony, Tougaloo College in Mississippi conferred an honorary doctorate on B.B., who hadn't even finished high school, making him the world's first doctor of blues. B.B. melted into a puddle of humility on such occasions. Yet, a quarter century into his musical career, B.B. now roamed the same cultural airspace as Ellington and Sinatra and the late Louis Armstrong, artists whose impact and import transcended genre. And he was about to enter an arena where only they had trod.

By 1973, B.B. had appeared on the radar of the U.S. Information Agency, an organization of Cold War–era propagandists who had sent Ellington and Armstrong on international tours under the banner of "Jazz Ambassadors." Launched in the 1950s, the Jazz Ambassadors program countered Soviet propaganda with aural images of Americana.

The blues was no less American than jazz. A March 15 telegram to Washington from the U.S. embassy in Dakar, the capital of Senegal in West Africa, announced, "Post would welcome opportunity present B.B. King as major cultural event fall season."

B.B.'s careful attention to professionalism and public image continued to pay dividends. The State Department considered and rejected at least one other potential candidate for government backing that year, a prominent San Francisco pop band. "Although Jefferson Airplane artistically qualified, other negative considerations would preclude embassy sponsorship," a cable from Washington advised. The Airplane sang about revolution and acid trips.

Both B.B. and Duke Ellington signed on for government tours of Africa in the fall of 1973. B.B.'s band spent the second half of November performing in Ghana, Senegal, and Nigeria. B.B. thus became the first blues artist to represent his country on a diplomatic tour and the first to perform in Africa. The trip drew almost no press coverage back home. But a jubilant embassy cable from Nigeria on November 28 announced, "B.B. King's appearances in Lagos were an unequivocal success, due in large part to his winning personality. King was modest, unassuming, down to earth, but straightforward, which made him a true cultural ambassador. [He] came to Nigeria and established rapport with local colleagues in a way unrivaled by previous American performers. From the arrival press conference to the last of many interviews that he graciously permitted, [King] easily grasped local considerations and handled tricky questions with cool, diplomatic awareness."

B.B. always employed two or three "heavies," burly drivers and cranky road managers he could assign to threaten hoteliers or dismiss pesky paramours. By the time of the Africa trip, B.B.'s top lieutenant was LeRoy Myers, a former tap dancer from Philadelphia and charter member of Harlem's famed Copasetic tap club. In his autumn years, Myers carried more than two hundred pounds on his five-foot-five frame. He and B.B. flew first-class, leaving the rest of the band in coach. B.B. assigned men such as Myers the role of bad cop, and they played it with panache, freeing B.B. to glide through the daily tangle of reservations, timetables, and social functions in a life of nonstop touring.

B.B.'s diplomatic hosts had moved his band from one Lagos hotel to another, apparently in protest over exorbitant fees. B.B. happily acceded, but not Myers, who, according to one cable, "preferred raising his voice to diplomacy" and "unilaterally demanded" that the band return to the overpriced hotel they had left. B.B., alone, remained at the lesser hotel, a gesture that left the diplomats deeply moved. Upon his departure from Africa, B.B. announced, "I'll be back, so save my room." The band returned home to perform at a lavish State Department charity ball on November 30. B.B. shook hands with Richard Nixon, the first time B.B. or his band had met a president, albeit one ensnared in the Watergate scandal.

"And I gotta say, no matter what your politics are, when you meet someone that's president, there's a certain aura around them that's more than just another person," Ron Levy recalled.

Back in 1968, Sid Seidenberg had sat down with B.B. and plotted a five-year plan for his client to supplant Louis Armstrong as the global face of American music. At the close of 1973, Seidenberg had managed B.B. for five years. Right on schedule, B.B. was performing for the State Department and shaking hands with a president.

THOSE ACCOLADES NOTWITHSTANDING, a distressing torpor had settled over B.B.'s recording career. He needed a hit.

For sheer longevity as a nominal blues artist, B.B. had few peers. One was his old Memphis friend Bobby "Blue" Bland. Perhaps the finest male R&B singer of his generation, Bland had retained his currency on the charts across nearly two decades, from his first number 1 single, "Farther Up the Road," in 1957 through his soulful mid-'70s output, songs such as "Ain't No Love in the Heart of the City" and the irresistible "I Wouldn't Treat a Dog (The Way You Treated Me)." B.B. called Bland his favorite blues singer. "I liked hearing that," Bland recalled.

The mature Bland presented an enigmatic persona, onstage and off-: "helpless, naïve, childish" but also self-assured and very much in control, according to *Urban Blues* author Charles Keil, who termed Bland a "baby-boss." Around B.B., Bland acted more baby than boss, rather like a deferential kid brother, a relationship forged back when the younger singer drove the older one around in his car.

With the 1973 retirement of gangster-producer Don Robey in Houston, Bland and the rest of the Duke-Peacock stable passed into the hands of ABC Records. Steve Barri, a fine pop producer who worked with Bland, ran into B.B. in the ABC offices one day and suggested a collaboration. B.B. loved the idea.

Barri proposed to present the two artists on the same stage with their respective bands inside a Sunset Boulevard studio to perform a live set before an audience of friends and VIPs. If it all worked out, the resulting recording would pop with all the spontaneous energy of a live show but with the meticulous preparation and production gloss of a studio album. B.B. and Bland had performed many times in the same venues on the same tours but never on the same stage. Barri set about scheduling rehearsals and assembling song lists.

Almost immediately, the partnership broke down. "B.B. was always ready to rehearse," Barri recalled, "to do anything we wanted. But Bobby, for some reason, I dunno . . . he was just never available." When the date of the August 1974 session arrived, B.B. and Bland had completed no full rehearsals. No one had even written a set list. "Other than the sound check," Barri recalled, "they just winged it."

A writer from the rock magazine *Crawdaddy!* caught the show. "Both bands were massed on opposite sides of the stage," he reported, "and somewhere in the middle, at a proposed meeting ground, were Bland and King, poised to make history. But nothing had been planned, neither band knew what songs they were supposed to play. Bland and King didn't know either. After the first couple of songs (decided on the spot) it was obvious that something was wrong. With both bands playing at the same time, confusion was rampant."

Over the years, Bland's idolatry of B.B. had hardened into prideful resentment. "Whenever they would get together, they would always be sniping at each other," Barri recalled. The bad vibes came mostly from Bland, who quarreled with B.B. like a sibling with a short fuse. "B.B. King was a big star," Barri said, "and Bobby was looking for that same kind of success." Bland had no crossover hit like "The Thrill Is Gone."

On this night, B.B. acted outwardly gracious and humble, as he always did. Bland responded with thinly veiled contempt. At one point, Bland shrugged B.B.'s hand from his shoulder and barked, "Don't tell me what to do." When the two unmatched bands collided in cacophony at the conclusion of Bland's "Driftin' Blues," B.B. observed, "Kind of a bad ending there," in case anyone had missed it. The hostilities bewildered the musicians in the assembled bands, who were friends. "There was some weird shit going on," Ron Levy recalled. A couple of songs later, B.B. muttered about throat problems. He sounded hoarse, and his extraordinary voice was no match for Bland's on a good night. B.B. took great care of his vocal instrument, avoiding air conditioners, drinking tea with honey and tall glasses of water before taking the stage. He knew other tricks, such as lowering the keys of his songs when his voice was weak. But three hundred gigs a year had taken a toll. On bad nights, nothing helped.

The resulting set, released in late 1974 as *B.B. King & Bobby Bland: Together for the First Time . . . Live*, delivered exactly what the title advertised. Across the double LP, B.B. and Bland sounded like men who had never performed together before. But the recording sold well among fans who had grown up with B.B. and Bland, reaching number 2 on the R&B charts and earning B.B. the first gold-record award of his career. B.B. would later claim, "I loved it better than practically any album I'd ever made." Bad reviews bruised B.B., prompting him to shower superlatives on his worst records. Perhaps he did love *Together for the First Time*, at least in monetary terms. Bland did not. "We're both pros," he told an interviewer, "and they don't think pros make mistakes."

B.B.'s stature as ambassador of the blues was better served by his role in Zaire '74, a three-day music festival in sub-Saharan Africa. The event took shape around the storied "Rumble in the Jungle" boxing match between Muhammad Ali and George Foreman in Kinshasa, the Zairian capital. Zaire '74 was the brainchild of Stewart Levine, a tough-talking, wild-haired music producer from the Bronx who had explored South African music in collaboration with South African trumpeter Hugh Masekela. "I was reading about the announcement of the fight," he recalled, "and I just came up with the idea of 'three days of music and fighting.' It was kind of like a piss-take on Woodstock."

The prospect of African American stars performing for Black Africans attracted the biggest names in pop. But Aretha Franklin and Stevie Wonder dropped out for fear of political tumult in a host country ruled by Mobutu Sese Seko, a vainglorious dictator. Those defections left James Brown as a formidable headliner, with B.B. claiming second billing ahead of the Spinners and several other acts. Levine offered $15,000 to every artist except Brown, who would not play for less than $100,000. Mobutu pledged $14 million for the fight but would not finance the attendant festival, so Levine struck a side deal for funding from the nation of Liberia, where trumpeter Masekela was living in exile. Disaster loomed when Foreman injured his eye in training. The bout was postponed, forcing organizers to wedge six empty weeks between the fight and festival, which was set for a September weekend and could not be rescheduled. Levine withheld the news of Foreman's injury from the musicians until they were safely aboard the charter plane.

The flight itself barely cleared the runway, its engines straining against the forty thousand pounds of extra equipment James Brown had insisted be loaded into the hold, mostly speakers and amplifiers. (Brown also demanded eight airplane seats for his personal use, which, given the extra weight, was probably a blessing.) After the jet had landed, one passenger recalled, "all three hundred people on board kissed the ground."

Ron Levy, B.B.'s keyboard man, recalled Zaire as "a non-stop, no-holds-barred party" that stretched for ten days. Festival producers told the musicians to charge everything on the hotel tab, which swelled to $280,000. "We had an open bar and free food," Levy recalled. "Hugh Masekela delivered a garbage bag full of African ganja for us to smoke. . . . Clothing was deemed optional, hedonism ruled, Caligula was an amateur. Life was grand." B.B. did not partake. He was ensconced at another hotel, a better one. In any case, B.B.'s intolerance of drugs did not extend to cannabis, provided his musicians exercised discretion, which was not an option here. The bacchanal paused only once or twice for bursts of rocket fire across the river from the hotel. The party resumed when the group's security escort, military police with machine guns, assured the celebrants that all was well.

The revelry ceased on September 21, when the festival commenced: the Kinshasa stadium sat nearly empty. Promoters had charged up to twenty-four dollars a ticket, expecting busloads of international tourists for the prize fight, which had been postponed. The top ticket price approached half of a Zairian's monthly pay. A parade of performers played to sparse applause. But James Brown rallied the crowd with a triumphant closing set, dancing and sweating and reaching down from the stage into a sea of outstretched hands.

B.B. was scheduled to headline the second night. Mobutu sent army trucks to roust citizens from their homes, and organizers admitted them for free, filling the Kinshasa seats. Levine padded B.B.'s backing band with members of the Crusaders, a tight jazz-pop-fusion ensemble from Los Angeles that had worked with the producer. The concert lagged behind schedule, and B.B. didn't take the stage until 3 a.m., late even for him. He warned Levine, "I'm running out of steam, Stew." But those who heard B.B. that night remembered it as one of his finest performances. "The heavier the competition, the deeper he went," Levy recalled. On the Kinshasa stage, B.B. played Ali to James Brown's Foreman, an aging champion facing off against a younger, fresher foe. He powered through a set of his greatest hits, ensnaring and entrancing an audience of "80,000-plus crazed, hot, sweaty, dancing and bouncing heads," Levy recalled. "We all realized this was not just another gig. It was history, good history." B.B. had nothing in his repertoire like James Brown's Black Power anthem "Say It Loud—I'm Black and I'm Proud." But when he hit the final verse of "The Thrill Is Gone," B.B. lingered on the words "I'm free," balling his hands into fists and contorting his face into a grimace of exertion and pain that compressed all the energy and emotion of Brown's anthem into a few words.

CHAPTER 17

MOSCOW ON THE
MISSISSIPPI

IN FEBRUARY 1975, B.B. King announced a new company under the inscrutable name Promotions Consolidated, Inc. The firm would handle all of his "personal business transactions," he said in a press release. B.B. would serve as president. Notably absent from the release was the name Sidney Seidenberg.

B.B. had dominated Seidenberg's life and work for seven years. But sometime in 1974, the balance of power had shifted. Another Seidenberg client, Gladys Knight & the Pips, broke out in the autumn of 1973, reaching number 1 on both the pop and R&B charts with the song that would become their signature, "Midnight Train to Georgia." The single put the band's career in high gear, spawning three more top-ten pop hits and a short-lived variety television show. Knight's career waxed as B.B.'s waned, and B.B. found that he no longer commanded Seidenberg's full attention. The doting manager had always dealt with B.B. directly. Now, he communicated through underlings. That, for B.B., was the final straw.

Seidenberg accepted his ouster with magnanimity. "If he doesn't want to have a manager, it's his prerogative," he told an industry journal. "In other words, he's a free agent."

Perhaps the rift went deeper than the Pips. According to producer Stewart Levine, who knew both men, Seidenberg despaired over B.B.'s spiraling gambling addiction. Seidenberg had helped B.B. earn millions of dollars, and then he had watched B.B. gamble most of it away. Sometimes B.B. played keno twenty-four hours straight. Bandmates would spot him pacing the casino floor, head downcast, searching for tokens hidden within the swirling carpet patterns when he had run out.

"The first time [B.B.] played keno in Vegas, he put down a dollar and won $23,000," Levine recalled. By B.B.'s own admission, that brief taste of victory "probably cost him $40 million over the years. And Sid couldn't stand to watch him doing that."

At first, not much changed for B.B. or his band in the new, Sid-less universe. The year began with a month-long stand at the Las Vegas Hilton and another tour of Japan. B.B.'s business office remained in Memphis, where the indulgent Polly Walker now served as executive secretary and de facto manager, overseeing a staff of five. A prominent Memphis banker named Jesse Turner took over as B.B.'s accountant.

Soon enough, though, B.B.'s bandmates found their A-list lifestyle slipping away. To save money on airfare, B.B. purchased an old Greyhound bus. This was an act of defiance: one of Seidenberg's first moves as B.B.'s manager had been to put the band on planes. The Greyhound promptly broke down.

LeRoy Myers, B.B.'s tap-dancing road manager, had goaded him for months to drop Seidenberg, boasting, "I could do better than that." Now, Myers happily inherited managerial duties, including the crucial role of scheduling gigs. But LeRoy Myers had none of Seidenberg's clout. After years of stadiums, television appearances, and international tours, B.B. and his band suddenly found themselves playing dank New Jersey casinos, threadbare urban nightclubs, and unsung civic auditoriums.

"When Sid was there, we were going first-class," Li'l Joe Burton recalled, "playing all the hot spots and playing all the TV shows. And when Sid left, it dried up, dried up like desert—back to the chitlin' circuit."

Once more, B.B. felt abandoned. That B.B. walked out on Seidenberg didn't lessen the hurt. His temper turned mercurial. B.B. fired half of his band, including Sonny Freeman and brother Wilbert. Sonny had been with B.B. for fifteen years.*

"Sonny was a blues drummer," recalled trumpeter Eddie Rowe. "Sonny had a hell of a left-hand shuffle." But by this time, B.B. had forsaken swing for the modern polyrhythms of funk. To replace Sonny, B.B. enlisted John "Jabo" Starks, a funk titan, who had backed James Brown on the seminal singles "Super Bad" and "Soul Power." Sonny Freeman, for all his talent, "could never play with James Brown," Rowe recalled.

B.B. rechristened his backing band the King's Men. Eddie Rowe took over as bandleader and arranger. Journeyman Bobby Forte had returned on tenor sax, James Toney on organ, relegating Ron Levy to piano. They were fine musicians all, but, as Levy recalled, "the old camaraderie and family familiarity was gone for good." B.B. even dropped "Every Day I Have the Blues" as his opening number, after two decades. Now, he opened shows with "Let the Good Times Roll." Perhaps it was wishful thinking.

Around the same time, Cato Walker Jr., B.B.'s very first employee, found his own role diminished by advancing diabetes that cost him a leg, amputated below the knee. B.B. could not employ a one-legged driver. He found a new one, and Cato quietly retired. His son, Cato Walker III, carried on the family name as saxophonist in B.B.'s band.

B.B.'s next decision marked a final act of spite against the departed Sid. If there was one place B.B.'s former manager and accountant did not want him to live, it was Las Vegas. In the fall of 1975, B.B. moved there. He chose a $200,000 ranch house in a neighborhood of large homes framed by shade trees and ample lawns. B.B. was the first African American on the block. "Later I heard the people who sold me the house caught hell," he recalled, "but no one said a word to me. I'm sure that's because I'm an entertainer. If I was an unknown black man, they might have burned a cross on my lawn."

---

* By this time, B.B. didn't do his own hiring and firing. "The word would come down from B.B., and then he might have somebody else to do the dirty work," typically the road manager or loyal wingman Bebop Edwards, Eddie Rowe recalled in an interview with the author.

Biographer Charles Sawyer visited B.B. at the ten-room home on Alta Drive a few years later. He described it as "dark, spacious, thickly carpeted, and furnished with deep, soft chairs that envelop the sitter. The walls are crammed with memorabilia—citations, plaques, photographs—from the many stages of his career. The house spreads out in many directions from a central room which opens onto the terrace and pool at the rear. There are four guest rooms, an office, a very large living room with a dining area, a large kitchen, a master bedroom at the extreme end, and the central room connecting the others." The L-shaped pool and adjoining tennis court lay unused and fell into disrepair.

James Toney's statuesque girlfriend, LaVerne, soon became a fixture in the Las Vegas home. LaVerne had lovely features, a mocha complexion, and a sprinkling of freckles around her eyes. She held a psychology degree from Iowa State University and had worked as a juvenile probation officer in Michigan, where she met B.B.'s keyboard man. James and LaVerne would marry in 1977. LaVerne worked as B.B.'s personal assistant, paying the bills, answering fan mail, and fielding calls from his expansive family. In her dealings with B.B.'s children, LaVerne embraced the role of gatekeeper like a supercilious stepmother.

"They would call and try to get to him," she recalled, typically with dire pleas for cash. "He wouldn't answer the phone, because he didn't want to be bothered." When it rang, B.B. would cry out, "I don't wanna talk to anybody. I'm not in." LaVerne would answer the call and make something up. "I had to tell a lot of lies," she said.

With her regal bearing, LaVerne left many visitors to B.B.'s home thinking she was his third wife, which in a sense she was, except in the bedroom. She resisted her employer's overtures. "He asked me plenty of times along the way," she recalled, "but I never did. I said, 'I'd rather be your friend.' I knew him too well."

B.B. entrusted LaVerne with The Book. After more than two decades on the road, B.B. had women in every town. "He used to have this big loose-leaf book, like you had when you were in school," recalled Stewart Levine, his producer and friend. B.B. called it "The Book." "And it was his phone book. And he had about six of them. And it was listed by cities. So he'd have, like, Akron. And then he'd have Athens. Not Georgia.

Then he'd have Baltimore. Then he'd have Berlin. And when he got to the city, he'd open it up, and it was who he knew there. And 90 percent of it was women. And he had descriptions: 'Lowell Fulson's ex. Big ass.'"*

Early in B.B.'s relationship with LaVerne, he presented her his directory of romantic partners, asking her to copy its pages by hand like a medieval monk. "Whatever you see," he instructed her, "you don't see."

One or two of B.B.'s adoptive children sometimes occupied the King household, having talked their way into his employ, but LaVerne never allowed them to take up permanent residence. B.B. himself was seldom home. When he was, he would turn up for dinner three hours late, infuriating his cook. Then he would retreat to the master suite, a space sealed off behind lock and key to protect the hoard within. B.B. filled closets with stacks of records from a collection that now surpassed twenty thousand items. That endeavor made sense: B.B.'s compulsion to stockpile videocassette recorders, reel-to-reel tape machines, and office supplies did not. "It is probably a compensation for his harsh childhood, fraught with deprivation," Charles Sawyer theorized. Every week, B.B. combed through *T.V. Guide* with a yellow highlighter and marked off an assortment of soap operas and old cowboy movies for LaVerne to tape. He filled thousands of videotapes and labeled none of them. Somehow, he always found what he wanted within the mountain of tapes.

Beneath the clutter, B.B.'s bedroom bore a striking resemblance to a Hilton hotel suite, "down to the cards that said what a long-distance call would cost you," recalled biographer David Ritz, who spent many hours in his quarters. After passing thousands of nights in the branded monotony of hotel rooms, B.B. found he could not fall asleep anyplace else.

Around the end of 1975, B.B. retreated to Las Vegas to recover from a grisly medical procedure that he had understandably postponed for decades. "I wasn't circumcised," he recalled, "and over the years my foreskin gave me problems. In cold weather, the skin would tighten and

---

* Trumpeter Eddie Rowe recalled in an interview with the author that the musicians had their own informal network of names and numbers passed back and forth between B.B.'s band and Bobby Bland's and Albert King's: "Hey, when you get to Mobile, you gonna run into Red Ruby."

sometimes break. Occasionally, bacteria would set in and swelling would occur. Urinating could be painful and sometimes sex was ruled out."

The last part, for B.B., was unacceptable. He finally went in for the procedure. Afterward, B.B. awoke feeling "like someone had dumped burning hot coals" on his "joint." He endured one of the most painful hours of his life, waiting for the pain pills to kick in. As B.B. convalesced, some impish friend sent him a gift subscription to *Playboy*.

SINCE B.B.'S CROSSOVER BREAKTHROUGH, reviewers and critics had given him a generous pass on the shortcomings of his recent recorded work, swept up as they were in his newfound fame. By the middle 1970s, the novelty had faded, and listeners gave B.B.'s music a harder listen. On his listless mid-'70s releases, there wasn't much to hear. "In recent years," one *Cincinnati Enquirer* critic wrote, "his playing has slipped into a self-parody." The last truly forgettable outing, released in the summer of 1976, reunited B.B. with Bobby Bland to cash in on the success of *Together for the First Time*. The second meeting repeated the errors of the first, the two artists assembling in Los Angeles without rehearsal or planning. The resulting album, *Together Again . . . Live*, was another mess, "with Bland and King sounding as if they were in different rooms (or cities)," the *San Francisco Examiner* wrote. But the record reached number 73 on the pop chart, delivering B.B. badly needed sales. The second hit validated the first: B.B. and Bland toured on and off for the rest of 1976. They would share hundreds of bills in years to come.

Notwithstanding that prosperous partnership, by 1977, B.B.'s own celebrated career seemed to have bottomed out. Ten years had passed since the triumphal performance at Bill Graham's Fillmore. That breakthrough had launched B.B. on a steep arc of global fame. Over the following years, with "The Thrill Is Gone" and *Indianola Mississippi Seeds*, B.B.'s celebrity had peaked. And then, across a span of lackluster recordings, inattentive management, and changing tastes, B.B. had slid back down to Earth. He now occupied a higher tier of the entertainment business than ten or twenty years earlier. But B.B. was in a rut and badly in need of a Szymczyk or Seidenberg or Johnny Pate to dig him out.

"Things were getting a little loose," B.B. recalled. "I felt myself losing control."

The next B.B. King record was a start. *King Size* was an album of more or less straight blues performed with a funky, conga-drum rhythm and backed with crisp horns. B.B.'s Philly-soul experiments were over. Veteran jazz producer Esmond Edwards placed Lucille front and center in the mix. B.B. summoned the necessary energy to match his band. A soul-pop excursion titled "I Wonder Why" sounded purposeful, rather than pandering. A half-dozen prior albums had presented B.B. as an old artist trying to sound new. On this one, he sounded mature, and that was progress.

King Size put B.B. back in the game. Shortly after its release, in March 1977, B.B. appeared on *Sanford and Son*, one in a string of vérité "urban" sitcoms, featuring chitlin' circuit journeyman Redd Foxx. B.B. played himself in an episode built around the fictional Fred Sanford's misplaced fears that he had stolen his wife from the bluesman. The broadcast reached fourteen million homes.

Amid this gentle upswing, B.B. received a welcome invitation. It came from Bill Ferris, a young, white Yale professor who had forged a friendship with B.B. over the prior decade. Born in 1942, Ferris grew up on a family farm outside Vicksburg, on the Mississippi River at the Louisiana border. He first heard B.B.'s music on a Nashville radio station as a child, and he entered adulthood with a voracious academic appetite for folklore and the South. After earning a doctorate in history at the University of Pennsylvania, Ferris returned home to teach at Jackson State University and cofounded the Center for Southern Folklore in Memphis. Then he moved to Yale, where he met B.B. on one of the bluesman's college tours. Barely thirty, with waves of long, tousled hair, swooping sideburns, and warm blue eyes, Ferris looked more like a grad student than a professor. B.B. became a regular visitor to Ferris's folklore classrooms. In 1977, Ferris told B.B. that Yale's senior class had selected him as a commencement speaker and that Yale president Kingman Brewster wanted to award him an honorary doctorate.

B.B.'s tenth-grade education had always embarrassed him. His propensity to travel with sack loads of instructional books on musical composition, elementary French, and reptiles of the world stemmed from educational insecurity. His vocabulary embarrassed him. Now he would be the first blues performer to collect an honorary doctorate from Yale and the second African American musician to do so, following Duke Ellington. B.B. would also be the very first speaker from outside the university to address graduates at the traditional Class Day ceremony, on the eve of graduation.

"Bill, I'm not a speaker," B.B. fretted to Ferris when he arrived on campus for the May festivities. "What am I going to tell them?"

"You share your life with them," Ferris replied.

B.B. told the Yale seniors of a life very different from theirs. He recounted walking five miles to school, picking four hundred pounds of cotton a day, and learning to sing the blues so he "could eat regular." Then, Lucille took over. B.B. performed "How Blue Can You Get" and "The Thrill Is Gone." The Yale seniors responded with a long standing ovation. B.B. dined with the other honorary-doctoral candidates, a group that included former president Gerald R. Ford, the second president he had met.

Perhaps this powerful affirmation, from an institution at the center of the white intellectual establishment, emboldened B.B. to return to his segregated Mississippi hometown for the first time in fifteen years.

In June 1977, B.B. journeyed to Indianola for a performance at Club Ebony, the chitlin' circuit nightclub where, two decades earlier, he had met his second wife. Word of the gig reached the editors of the weekly *Enterprise-Tocsin* newspaper. They found him inside an RV parked outside the club. After introductions, Jim Abbott, the newspaper's editor, told B.B., "I'm just wondering why you haven't been home until now."

B.B. took a deep breath. "Look," he said. "I've been around the world. And back in the sixties, I came with my band, and we could not stay in the motel here. We stayed at Top of the Mark in San Francisco. But my band could not stay in the hotel here, and we could not eat at the hamburger stand out on Route 82." B.B. told Abbott he had no wish to speak ill of Indianola: "But it just made me feel kind of bad. And I decided I don't wanna come back until things change."

Abbott told B.B., "Things have changed." A few days later, the *Enterprise-Tocsin* published a full-page feature on B.B. The article offered a primer on the bluesman's Indianola origins and recounted his many honors. This was for B.B.'s eyes and also for the many Indianolans who did not know the B.B. King legend. Abbott took care to note that B.B. "has a big place in his heart for Indianola." With that piece, the *Enterprise-Tocsin* launched a subtle public-relations campaign to popularize B.B. King among white Indianolans and to soften the bluesman's feelings toward his nominal hometown. Abbott would spend the next few years working to lure B.B. back.

AFTER THE CHART SUCCESS of *King Size*, executives at ABC Records approached producer Stewart Levine to gauge his interest in making a record with B.B. The two had become friends in Zaire. B.B. had even asked Levine to store his precious Lucille in the producer's hotel room. In 1977, Levine went to hear a B.B. King show at the Village Gate in New York. He found the blues king in a sorry state. "He was despondent," Levine recalled. "This was a different guy than I saw in 1974. It was hapless."

Little hints of B.B.'s mortality lay sprinkled among old news clippings. Chatting with rock journalist Michael Lydon backstage at the Fillmore in 1969, B.B. had confessed to seeing a doctor about his stomach, presumably for ulcers. The doctor had told him to foreswear fatty foods, liquor, and women—in other words, the entirety of his diet on the road. The doctor had given him pills, which had sapped his libido. "And then this morning," B.B. told Lydon, "I was with a sweet gal I been trying to make for fifteen years. She finally said the time was right, so there we was, [and] you know what? Wouldn't do a thing," he said, alluding to erectile dysfunction. "Not a blame thing. I played with it, *she* played with it, but it just lay there like a hound."

Five years later, at a March 1974 performance in Sydney, B.B. had collapsed onstage. He dismissed the episode as heat exhaustion. A few months after that, B.B. had abruptly quit smoking. "B. had a bad cold in Vegas," recalled pianist Ron Levy. "We were playing keno together, and after a coughing fit, he lit up a Kool. And I [asked] him, 'As a singer with a cold, doesn't smoking make it worse?' He gave me a look, and I never saw him smoke a cig again." Quitting smoking left him with a fierce craving for food. His weight ballooned to 250 pounds, 50 more than he had carried at the decade's start. By 1977, B.B. was in visibly poor health.

B.B.'s business was also ailing. With Sid Seidenberg out of the picture, B.B. was losing his grip. "Little by little," he recalled, "I was falling into the kind of money messes I'd fallen into before." On a visit to Mississippi, B.B. opened up to his old friend Charles Evers, who told B.B. he looked a little down. B.B. said, "I feel like the finances are getting away from me."

"You know what you need, don't you?" Evers replied. "Sid. You need Sid, and Sid needs you."

IN LATE 1977, Stewart Levine met with B.B. at Lake Tahoe to discuss making an album with the Crusaders. The group had started in Houston in the late 1950s as the Jazz Crusaders. They relocated to Los Angeles, and their sound drifted toward instrumental pop and funk over the 1960s and 1970s. The ensemble paid homage to the civil rights struggle with song titles such as "The Freedom Sound" and "Chain Reaction." The 1970 single "Way Back Home" became a sort of anthem to the radicalized Symbionese Liberation Army, kidnappers of Patty Hearst. The band's politics gradually softened, to the point that a late-'70s collaboration with B.B. King did not raise eyebrows.

Levine told B.B. he wanted to try something new: "To make another blues record wasn't gonna cut it." He proposed presenting B.B. a slate of songs penned by Crusaders keyboardist Joe Sample and lyricist Will Jennings for B.B. to record with the Crusaders as his backing band. B.B. agreed without hesitation. A recent Crusaders album, *Those Southern Knights*, had hit number 38 on the *Billboard* chart, higher than B.B. had reached in half a decade. B.B.'s only concern lay in learning new material. He preferred to work within the vast songbook of R&B standards that filled his encyclopedic musical mind. Levine told B.B. he would get the band to record crude demos, which B.B. could study before they hit the studio. B.B. gave just one instruction to his new producer: "Do not change me."

When sessions commenced, B.B. arrived without his guitar. Levine was aghast. B.B. had grown accustomed to adding guitar parts later, as overdubs, after laying down a vocal track with the band. That sterile method was how records were generally made in the late 1970s. But Levine wanted B.B. to "get a feeling," and that meant performing live in the studio with the band.

B.B. looked around. He spotted a Fender Stratocaster. "I'll play that," he said.

"B.B. King playing a fucking Strat?" Levine howled. "Are you kidding me?"

When work resumed the following day, B.B. brought Lucille. He asked Levine to start the daily sessions at 11 a.m., giving him time to fly back to Vegas every night for a round of keno. Still, he sounded fresh and energetic. After a week of recording, B.B. told Levine, "I feel something here."

The producer and the bluesman got to talking. B.B. sensed the new record could be a big one. He approached its completion with one regret. "I think I made a terrible mistake with Sid," B.B. told the producer. Levine and Seidenberg were old friends. "I really think I need Sid back on this one," B.B. said. "This is one that could work."

"What are you telling me?" Levine asked.

"I don't know. It'd just be great," B.B. wavered.

"Whaddaya want me to do, man? Do you want me to call Sid?"

B.B. exhaled a nervous chortle. "Oh, I don't think Sid wants any part of me."

B.B. did not know how wrong he was.

After losing B.B. as a client in 1975, Sid Seidenberg had gone all in with Gladys Knight and her Pips. After a couple of busy years, Knight had faded from the pop charts. By the summer of 1977, Knight had fired Seidenberg. She would accuse him of "general mismanagement" of her career and allege that their partnership had enriched him beyond her. Seidenberg had lost his biggest artist.

Levine telephoned Seidenberg.

"I think I have a record here," he said, meaning a good one. "And he asked me to get in touch with you," he said, meaning B.B.

"B. said he'd like to see me?" Seidenberg replied, incredulous.

"Listen, he's the one who asked me to make the phone call," Levine said. "So, you know, if I were you, I would come out and check it out, man. See what you think of the music."

Silence followed.

"B. really wants to see me?" Seidenberg repeated.

"Yeah."

"I'll be there tomorrow."

Seidenberg left New York that night, boarding a red-eye to Los Angeles, and arrived at the studio the next day. The bluesman and manager greeted each other awkwardly. Levine played them some of the songs he had recorded. "Then there were big smiles," Levine recalled. "And then they went off into a little room, and a few minutes later they came back in, and Seidenberg said, 'We're on.'" He was beaming. B.B. set one condition: "This time, I wanna deal directly with you, and no one else."

Midnight Believer emerged in the spring of 1978 as the strongest B.B. King album in years. Sample and Jennings had penned a stack of songs that elegantly wedded B.B.'s blues to the jazz-funk-pop formula that the Crusaders mined so successfully. The opening track, "When It All Comes Down (I'll Still Be Around)," offered a melody as memorable as anything on *Indianola Mississippi Seeds*, set atop a song that was pure late-'70s pop but rooted in blues. The superb backing band left plenty of room for Lucille, whose deft interplay with the sidemen reminded listeners why B.B. was so beloved among fellow musicians. B.B. and the Crusaders had found an immediate chemistry. The title track was funk verging on disco, but B.B. remained in control, no longer sounding like an old man trying to keep pace with the young. The album flirted with ragtime on "I Just Can't Leave Your Love Alone" and with Hall & Oates–style soul on "Hold On (I Feel Our Love Is Changing)," before cycling back to a propulsive, Marvin Gaye–inspired boogie-woogie blues on the remarkable "Never Make a Move Too Soon," one of the finest B.B. King songs of the 1970s.

Midnight Believer wasn't really a blues album, but it was a B.B. King album—and a good one. It outperformed B.B.'s three prior studio albums on the charts, and a raft of strong reviews gave B.B. a currency he hadn't enjoyed since the start of the decade. Critic Robert Christgau opined that the record would have marked a full-blown comeback, had it included even one more song as strong as "Never Make a Move Too Soon."

B.B.'s reunion with Sid Seidenberg paid immediate returns for the B.B. King band, which spent the first months of 1978 playing flagship state universities in Oregon, Montana, and Colorado and stately theaters in Milwaukee, Pittsburgh, and Buffalo. LeRoy Myers, the ambitious road manager who had encouraged B.B. to split with Seidenberg, made a quiet exit. The beneficiary was Bebop Edwards, B.B.'s old friend and sometime valet, who ascended to road manager with imperious glee.

Several new musicians had joined B.B.'s entourage in 1977. Two of them would remain with him for decades. One was Calep Emphrey Jr., a fine drummer from Mississippi. The other was Walter Riley King, B.B.'s nephew, born and raised in the household of B.B.'s father. Soft-spoken and temperate, Walter was the very antithesis of Albert. His broad, expressive visage faintly recalled a younger B.B. Walter learned the saxophone in high school and studied music theory in college. His career took him to Opryland USA, the Nashville amusement park, and thence to the legendary Muscle Shoals Horns. By his midtwenties, Walter had worked with the Spinners and O'Jays in soul, Hank Williams Jr. and Roy Clark in country. Oddly enough, he had never worked with his uncle. None of Walter's employers knew he was blues royalty. When a contractor from the musician's union telephoned to ask, "You ever heard of B.B. King?" Walter replied with a simple "Yeah."

B.B. sometimes padded his band with extra musicians for big gigs, putting the word out through sidemen or the union. When he needed a baritone sax for a charity performance in Nashville, the call reached Walter. B.B. didn't know he had hired his nephew until he beheld Walter onstage. "What are you doing here?" B.B. asked. "I'm on a job," Walter coolly replied. Walter would be B.B.'s first and only blood relative to play in his band. "I have to be harder on you than anybody," B.B. told

Walter gravely. Walter remained with B.B., on and off, for the rest of his uncle's career.

ANOTHER NEW FACE was Norman Matthews, B.B.'s best friend and sometime employee. Upon Bebop's promotion to road manager, Matthews supplanted him as B.B.'s personal aide. Matthews had been furloughed from B.B.'s entourage over a drinking problem, but he returned in good standing. This was a recurring pattern. Matthews "would do something, get fired, and he'd come back like a month later," Walter King recalled. One layoff found Matthews working in Jack Ruby's Dallas nightclub in November 1963. After President Kennedy's assassination, and Jack Ruby's fatal attack on the presumed assassin, Matthews telephoned B.B. with the plea, "Get me out of here." Years later, on a European tour, Matthews set out to find a glass of milk for his boss and disappeared, surfacing two weeks later at a rehab center in Phoenix. His comings and goings were so frequent that B.B.'s management paid him in cash, writing payroll checks only if he stayed around long enough to justify the effort.

"Norman held the record for most hired and most fired," recalled Stafford Davis, a security aide to B.B. for thirty years. Matthews would smile slyly to Davis and say, "You always want to keep that 'hired' number one more."

B.B.'s two closest friends cut an odd contrast. Bebop Edwards was haughty and flamboyant, so visibly infused with the powers B.B. had extended him that some observers mistook him for his boss. He wore a cowboy hat and sunglasses and dripped with gold jewelry to complement a prominent gold front tooth. Matthews, on the other hand, might be mistaken for a vagabond. He wore oversize suits, their lapels pierced with so many pins that they hung askew. His manner was gruff and belligerent. His rare smiles revealed missing teeth. The musicians called him "Black Devil."

Matthews would sit in the wings during shows and roll dice. At a gig's end, after the audience had filed out, he would take the stage and perform a shambling dance. If a particularly striking woman appeared backstage between sets, he would walk over to B.B. and murmur, "Got a live one," whereupon, with his employer's assent, Matthews would clear the dressing room and escort the guest inside. Matthews stuffed drawers on the tour bus with seemingly random flotsam. But at his boss's command, Matthews could produce an electric burner and conjure a meal, seemingly from thin air. Matthews and B.B. would bark and snap at each other in public, as only old friends could. Then they would retreat to B.B.'s hotel room to play cards while Matthews steamed B.B.'s suits in the shower. Matthews awakened before B.B. and retired only after his boss was asleep. B.B. spent endless hours teaching Matthews to read, just as Hampton Reese had taught him, using marking pens and sheets of cardboard from hotel laundries.

Matthews and Bebop functioned at various times as B.B.'s alter ego (or, perhaps, his id), shaking down club owners, corralling beautiful women, and ejecting troublesome backstage guests, all so that B.B. could play the consummate gentleman, delighting fans with autographs and dazzling bellhops with hundred-dollar tips. When B.B. was out of earshot, the aides quickly lost all pretense of civility. They would shoo away backstage visitors and hangers-on with outraged cries of "Get outta here!" and "You don't need no damn autograph!"

"Both of 'em was terrible, man," laughed Joe McClendon, B.B.'s valet of that era. But never in front of the boss.

IN FEBRUARY and March 1978, B.B. allowed a journalist to accompany him on the road, a level of access he had seldom granted before. The writer was Charles Sawyer, and he had waited ten years for his moment.

Born in New England in 1941, Sawyer spent most of the 1960s in academia, attending Yale, then teaching at a small New Hampshire college, all to the ultimate end of evading the draft. Sawyer studied physics and the history of science but, after abandoning a doctorate, wound up teaching photography and math. It was as photographer and journalist that Sawyer first encountered B.B. King, at a gig in 1968 at Lennie's on the Turnpike, outside Boston. B.B. was not yet much of a celebrity, so Sawyer sidled up with his camera and tape recorder and started posing questions. B.B. was booked at Lennie's for a full week, so Sawyer amassed a trove of pictures and notes. He hoped to submit an article to *Rolling Stone*; but he had no contacts there, and the plan fizzled.

The next year, Sawyer met blues historian Paul Oliver at the Ann Arbor Blues Festival. Oliver was organizing a series of blues monographs for a British publisher. He asked Sawyer to pitch a topic. Sawyer proposed a full biography of B.B. King. Oliver helped him broker a deal with a British publisher. Sawyer approached Sid Seidenberg, who gave his blessing. Sawyer conducted further interviews, finished his book, and submitted it to the publisher. Weeks turned to months, and Sawyer heard nothing. Finally, in 1971, Paul Oliver informed him the imprint had gone broke. Sawyer and his book spent years in publishing limbo. In 1977, he sold it to Macmillan. He commenced a fresh round of interviews to update the manuscript.

Sawyer joined B.B. one winter night in 1978 at the Burning Spear on Chicago's South Side, part of a network of urban, African American nightclubs along the former chitlin' circuit. Around 10 p.m., Bebop Edwards entered the dressing room, carrying Lucille in her case. "Hit at 11," he barked to the band, as he turned a key on a padlock to open B.B.'s separate dressing room. Shortly before eleven, Bebop mobilized the musicians: "Get your asses down on that stage. When you finish this here parade, you don't get no cotton candy, you get dollars." The King's Men marched out to play three instrumental numbers as a warm-up.

Backstage, Sawyer wrote, B.B. "peels off his camel's hair coat and opens a small valise from which he pulls a comb and a can of Afro Sheen. In the glaring light of a dozen bare bulbs, he sprays and combs his hair. As the band begins the second number downstairs, Bebop appears with a glass and a pitcher of ice water. B.B. pours a tall drink, drinks it at one go, and pours a second," hydration for the hours of perspiration to come. Lucille was already onstage, propped beside an amplifier, where Bebop had placed her.

Halfway through the third song, Bebop signaled Eddie Rowe, trumpeter and bandleader, to prepare for the introduction. A sudden shift in tempo told B.B. his time had come. He drained his second glass of water and strode toward the stage. "Every seat in the house is full,"

Sawyer wrote, "and the aisles are jammed with dancing, laughing, boozing patrons. The audience and the nightclub are almost timeless. This could be 1939 at Jones' Night Spot in Indianola, Mississippi, or 1950 at the Club Handy on Beale Street in Memphis, or the Apollo Theater in Harlem, around 1960."

The music swelled as Eddie Rowe announced, "Mister B. . . . B. . . . King!" B.B. took the stage and strapped on Lucille, as his band launched into a brisk rendition of "Let the Good Times Roll." When B.B. played his first notes, the crowd exploded in rapture.

Seventy-five minutes later, around 1 a.m., B.B. closed the set to thunderous applause. He returned to his dressing room, already filling with guests. The King's court, on this night, comprised a nephew of a distant cousin, a musician friend, and a bevy of women, one in knee-high vinyl boots, another in a snug snakeskin dress. The woman in the snakeskin dress asked if someone could turn on the air conditioner. B.B. politely refused: air conditioners gave him a sore throat. A waitress appeared with a tray of drinks and a forty-three-dollar tab. B.B. directed her to Bebop: "Take care of this, will you?" The party rolled on.

B.B. carefully parceled out attention to his guests, acknowledging all and allowing no one to monopolize his time. When a drunken man demanded to see B.B. in private, he demurred, telling him that such a sidebar might affront the other visitors. "But it's *business*," the drunk man slurred. "There's a time for business," B.B. replied firmly, "and it's not now." The man retreated.

Now and then, a house photographer appeared to fulfill a picture request from a fan, which B.B. dutifully honored. And so it went, for two full hours, until 3 a.m., when B.B. downed another glass of water and departed to begin his second set. "Gotta go to work, folks," he said. "You'll excuse me, please."

After three nights in Chicago, B.B. played one-nighters in bleak Elgin, Illinois, and chilly Milwaukee, Wisconsin, before boarding the tour bus for a ten-night stand in Detroit. An hour into the journey, half the band slept while the other half congregated around B.B., trading stories of sexual misadventure. B.B. dispatched someone to play an eight-track tape that he had filled with a selection of songs: Lonnie Johnson, Eddie "Cleanhead" Vinson, Ray Charles.

A job in the B.B. King band was a coveted thing. His musicians earned between $500 and $675 a week. B.B. still covered travel and accommodations: coach fares and midpriced lodgings for the band, first-class for B.B. and Bebop.

Sid Seidenberg flew in to Detroit to meet with B.B., one of their first face-to-face encounters in the renewed partnership. Seidenberg had already made his mark, elevating the gigs on B.B.'s itinerary and restoring order to his finances. B.B. now held a small portfolio of properties: his home in Las Vegas, his father's house in California, and the apartment building in Memphis. Yet, after nearly three decades on the road, B.B. felt far from rich.

"Out of every dollar I make," B.B. told Sawyer, "I pay ten cents to the booking agency and ten cents to my manager, off the top. I haven't done a damn thing, haven't put a drop of gas in my bus, and I've spent twenty cents already. By the time I pay overhead and my taxes, you know what I've got left over for myself? A dime. Maybe two." He spoke while devouring a meat casserole, cornbread, and fried rice in the company of a doting young woman on a hotel bed.

During his years away from Seidenberg, B.B. had fallen back into trouble with the IRS. He owed "something like a million dollars" in back taxes when the two reunited, according to Floyd Lieberman, a longtime Seidenberg aide who did B.B.'s accounting. One morning in 1978, an IRS agent telephoned the King residence in Las Vegas. LaVerne Toney took the call and innocently answered the man's questions. At noon, when B.B. awoke, LaVerne apprised him of the call and the questions. B.B. exploded, pacing the floor and hissing through clenched teeth that she "did not understand the magnitude of the situation." LaVerne would not make that mistake again.

Tax woes notwithstanding, B.B. rolled out of Detroit in a new, $12,000 Cadillac in eggplant purple, an emblem of newfound confidence. In June, Sawyer caught up with B.B. again in New York, where Seidenberg threw a $10,000 party at Studio 54 to promote *Midnight Believer*.

Sawyer delivered his manuscript to Macmillan that summer. Some weeks later, the publisher returned it, heavily rewritten. Aghast, Sawyer bought back the book. After a decade of work and two finished manuscripts, B.B. King's biographer had no one to publish his story.

B.B.'s currency had never been higher. In July, he headlined Festjazz '78, the first edition of an event that would become the Montreal Jazz Festival. In fall, a gushing, two-part feature in the jazz journal *Down Beat* declared that B.B. had "become the single most popular and successful of all blues performers," that, "in one way or another, every blues performer of the last quarter-century has been his heir, student or offspring," and that "there has been no major stylistic development in the music since his appearance that is in any way comparable to his."

B.B. had indeed transformed the blues. Before him, the genre had embraced acoustic slide guitarists and harmonica virtuosi, saxophonists and big-band singers. After B.B., those silos collapsed. By the late 1970s, the blues were played mostly by men with electric guitars, and all of them inevitably invited comparison to B.B.

In the autumn of 1978, B.B. initiated another musical purge. This one began with a confrontation between Bebop Edwards and Eddie Rowe on a sidewalk outside the Conrad Hilton hotel in Chicago. The bandleader and road manager had sparred for months. The encounter ended with Rowe pulling down his pants and instructing Bebop, "Either kiss my ass or kick it." Bebop fired Rowe. B.B. rehired Calvin Owens, the Texas trumpet talent whom he had fired two decades earlier in a prior purge. Owens was now forty-nine, four years younger than B.B. but older than most of his other sidemen. Since leaving the bluesman's employ in 1956, Owens had gone home to Houston and worked in the Maxwell House coffee factory before returning to music and recording with T-Bone Walker, among others. He now replaced Rowe as B.B.'s bandleader and supplanted both Rowe and haughty Hampton Reese as arranger. Owens fired everyone else in B.B.'s band except Calep Emphrey, the drummer. Not even Walter King was spared.

B.B. populated his new ensemble partly at the expense of Otis Clay, the great Chicago soul singer. B.B. had spent that summer and fall on a traveling blues festival, sharing a bill with Albert King and Bobby

Bland. The tour wrapped in Chicago on September 16, B.B.'s fifty-third birthday. An all-star jam session followed at the Burning Spear, anchored by Otis Clay's fiery young rhythm section. With B.B. at the mic, the musicians stunned him with a propulsive version of "Never Make a Move Too Soon" that put B.B.'s band to shame. B.B. promptly hired Clay's musicians.

Emboldened by success, B.B. rolled out one of the largest ensembles he'd led since the Big Red days of the 1950s: seven horns flanking a five-piece rhythm section. Owens, the bandleader, revealed himself as "a little dictator," recalled Russell Jackson, the new bassist. "He was deadly serious about the music, he knew B.B. really well, and you had to play things a certain way. Next to death, there were no excuses."

B.B. SPENT FEBRUARY AND March 1979 on perhaps the most consequential tour of his career: Sid Seidenberg, the patient architect of that career, persuaded the U.S. Information Agency to fly the B.B. King band to the Soviet Union. The Jazz Ambassadors program had been sending the likes of Benny Goodman and Duke Ellington to perform behind the Iron Curtain for two decades, but the Soviets resisted overtures from pop artists. An affable country-western troupe headed by singer "Tennessee" Ernie Ford finally toured Russia and environs in 1974, and country revivalists the Nitty Gritty Dirt Band visited in 1977. Some of the biggest rock acts tried to gain entry and failed, including Chicago and Fleetwood Mac. Rock's casual embrace of hard drugs and cutoff shorts were deal breakers.

Once again, B.B.'s manicured image played to his favor. A group from the Soviet cultural office attended a B.B. King performance at Harrah's in Lake Tahoe to ensure that his music posed no threat to the Soviet people. After three or four songs, they rose and filed out as one, having found his songs acceptable. The trip was on.

U.S. and Soviet officials bickered for weeks about logistics and pay, according to declassified diplomatic cables, finally settling on a per-concert fee of 1,150 rubles, or $2,875. The Soviets provided an extra airplane seat for Lucille. The Soviet concert bureau screened B.B.'s set list and rejected nothing. B.B. and Seidenberg bought Slavic-style rabbit-fur hats and coats for the trip.

The tour commenced in Baku, the capital of Azerbaijan, across the Soviet border from Iran. Backstage before the first show, B.B. confided to a Western reporter, "I feel like I did the day I joined the Army." He was profoundly nervous: "I don't know if these people can appreciate the blues." Soldiers lined the hall. Communist Party VIPs filled the front rows. The show began, and the crowd responded warmly, applauding at the start and end of each song and more or less continuously between numbers. The reception was intense but oddly ceremonial, much like B.B.'s experience in Japan. The restrained passion of this Azerbaijani audience poured forth only at the very end, when the crowd surged forward to the stage, patrons crying out for autographs and reaching up to touch B.B. "By Soviet standards," a reporter observed, "it was a raucous reaction."

The tour proceeded west to Armenia, where B.B. dined with farmers, and then north to the Georgian capital of Tbilisi. The band endured untold hardships. Soviet cities shut down at bedtime, leaving the musicians nowhere to go after gigs but back to the hotel. Temperatures dipped below freezing. Vodka was plentiful, but the band could procure no controlled substance, a deprivation that sent some sidemen into withdrawal. Black-suited Soviet escorts accompanied them everywhere. When one musician told another, within the privacy of their room, that he wished he had some coffee, someone appeared at the door with a steaming cup.

B.B.'s American chaperones proved equally unnerving. An Information Agency man sat next to B.B. on noisy Soviet airplanes, snapping surreptitious photographs with a tiny camera. "Every airport we passed over—*click, click, click*," B.B. recalled. "Every city or military base—*click, click, click*. If he wasn't a spy, I ain't a bluesman. 'Hey, man,' I said, 'put that camera away. They're gonna think I'm your partner.' But he kept on—*click, click, click*—and I kept praying no one would charge us both with espionage." No one did.

The Soviet itinerary demanded fifty-four performances in thirty days, a punishing schedule even by B.B.'s standards. Many shows were beyond sold out. "They had people sitting on the floors, in the aisles.

You couldn't step. You couldn't walk," recalled Russell Jackson, the bassist. Scalpers lined the streets outside the halls, fetching up to $150 per ticket. In Tbilisi, a reporter observed, "the impulsive Georgians nearly started a riot, shoving into the theatre until two people sat in every seat." Still, the gigs left B.B. unsatisfied. He fed off an exchange of emotion and energy with his audience. These crowds had passion, beyond a doubt, but B.B. wasn't bringing it out.

"When we finally made it to Moscow," B.B. recalled, "I was determined to get the audience going. I wanted some reaction." On March 22, a Thursday, B.B. and his band performed to three thousand Russians at the Hotel Rossiya, reputedly the world's largest lodging, a white-marble colossus that rose up from the Moscow River. He opened the set with "Every Day I Have the Blues," which had regained its rightful place atop the set list, and "played with all the fire" at his command. No response. He performed a rousing "Rock Me Baby." Still nothing: "'Sweet Sixteen' and 'How Blue Can You Get' didn't get 'em either. I did everything but buck dance, and still no response. After another half-dozen tunes, nervous desperation gave me an idea. I offered my guitar pick to a woman sitting in the front row," one of the party faithful. "She was shy at first, but I urged her on. She approached the foot of the stage and accepted my gift. She looked it over and then—miracle of miracles—she smiled at me before turning to the audience and smiling at them." B.B. had a pocketful of picks. He produced some more and started handing them out to the timid VIPs, who rose one by one from their seats. Taking their cue, the rank-and-file folk behind them arose from their seats and crept tentatively toward the stage. At last, the audience was alive. After the show, dozens of Russians mobbed B.B. backstage, some in military regalia, begging the bluesman for autographs and grabbing desperately at little blue-and-white B.B. King buttons. Outside, young Russians swarmed around B.B. when he emerged from the hall. "These kids, they wouldn't let us leave," recalled Joe McClendon, B.B.'s valet. "They lay down in front of the limousine. They wouldn't get off the ground. They wanted autographs." B.B. climbed out of the car and obliged them.

A *New Yorker* reporter caught up with B.B. at a performance in Leningrad and chronicled his uncanny breakthrough. "King teases his audiences, urging them to clap along, to whistle, to hoot their appreciation, like the congregations in the Southern churches in which he grew up," the correspondent wrote. "But to the Russians, such behavior suggests a lack of culture and an almost frightening disorder. Though obviously impressed, the audience at first kept a respectful silence during the numbers, as it might at a symphony. . . . Then, King played an irresistible riff, stopped, and leaned toward the audience with his hand cupped to his ear. The audience caught on and began to clap. King changed the beat, and waited for the audience to catch up. Then he changed it again. Soon the whole place was clapping along to 'Get Off My Back, Woman,' and there were even a few timid shouts and whistles. King, who has carried the blues to Europe, Africa, and the Far East, had broken the ice one more time." The reporter was stunned. "By the second half of the performance," she wrote, "the audience was looser than any other Soviet audience I've ever seen. People whistled, they hooted with delight, they clapped along, answering B.B. King's playful coaxing on the guitar. The guards standing against the auditorium walls looked uneasy."

Later, in the cloakroom line, a young woman told the journalist, "This is one of the greatest things that has ever happened to me in my life." An older man in a baggy suit observed, "He poured his whole heart and soul out there on the stage. Such feeling is very Russian. We believe in emotion, in the soul. I never thought that an American could feel that way."

Louis Armstrong had died in 1971, Duke Ellington in 1974. And now, on a Russian stage in 1979, B.B. King had proved himself their rightful heir. He was Mississippi's cultural ambassador to the world.

CHAPTER 18

HOMECOMING

ONE APRIL NIGHT IN 1979, B.B. King closed a set at the Great Southeast Music Hall in Atlanta with "I Got Some Help I Don't Need," a track from his forgotten 1972 album *L.A. Midnight*. Joining him onstage were Diana Ross, queen of Motown, and Eric Clapton, arguably the premier guitarist of rock. B.B. and Clapton jammed for half an hour, evidently their first publicized encounter since the now-legendary meeting in 1967. Backstage in Atlanta, Clapton told B.B., "I'd be honored to play with you anytime."

B.B. was King of the Blues. But Clapton had scored three number 1 albums, one each with the supergroups Cream and Blind Faith and a third as a solo artist. B.B., for all his fame, had never cracked the top twenty on the *Billboard* 200 pop album chart.

B.B. toured because he had to. By the late 1970s, A-list white rock acts Led Zeppelin, Pink Floyd, and the Who had proved that they could survive, even prosper, on a leisurely schedule, releasing an album and staging a tour every two or three years. Those bands earned enough money from albums and tours to sustain them in off years. B.B. did not.

"You don't see our names in the Top 100," B.B. told an interviewer, speaking of himself and his blues peers. "We've got to work to survive." The interviewer asked if B.B. alluded to a difference between blues and rock or something more fundamental. The writer mentioned Johnny Winter, the scrawny albino guitarist who had once asked to play with his idol in a segregated Texas club. At the close of the 1960s, a major label had signed Winter to a contract worth $600,000, more money at the time than B.B. had ever seen. Johnny and his brother Edgar Winter had since placed twenty albums on the *Billboard* 200, two of them in the vaunted top twenty.

"You don't even have to ask, man," B.B. replied. "You just said it. White."

Relentless touring kept B.B. from appearing in a landmark film that seemed scripted for him. *Saturday Night Live* comedian Dan Aykroyd wrote *The Blues Brothers* in homage to the giants of rhythm and blues whose careers had gone cold. A disco invasion colonized the charts in 1978 and 1979, compelling even rock superstars to record disco songs. James Brown, Aretha Franklin, and other R&B legends "were out of work," recalled John Landis, the film's director and cowriter. *The Blues Brothers* told a story of two white bluesmen reviving their band to save a church, but the film's real payoff came in powerful musical numbers that featured Brown and Franklin, Ray Charles, Cab Calloway, and John Lee Hooker, among others. *The Blues Brothers* would revive these artists' careers, a quest that Landis winkingly termed a "mission from God" in the script. The director invited B.B. to join the film, but Sid Seidenberg declined: B.B.'s tour schedule was too tight. "That guy never stopped working," Landis recalled. The director honored B.B. in the film by picturing him in a mural during the Ray Charles number.

ONCE, WHEN LAVERNE TONEY was making up B.B.'s bed, she encountered a hard lump beneath the sheets. It was a gun. When she asked B.B. about it, he laughed it off: "You never know what you might find in my bed." But she soon surmised the truth: B.B. had purchased the gun for protection. "He was, at times, quite fearful—of his children, some of them," she recalled.

Three decades after B.B. had embraced his first paternity claim, he was now the proud father of eight. His expansive family cost him thousands upon thousands of dollars a year in handouts, tuition, and gifts. Happily, given B.B.'s scrupulously clean public image, none of the children's lives had erupted in scandal. That changed in the summer of 1979 with the arrest of twenty-three-year-old Patty Elizabeth King.

Patty was the daughter of Essie Williams, owner of the Blue Note nightclub in the steamy Florida college town of Gainesville. B.B. and Essie had dated. Essie bore a child, and she named B.B. as the father.

By 1979, B.B.'s oldest children were entering their thirties. Two of them, Willie and Leonard, worked with him. Patty joined them for a time as a paid receptionist in B.B.'s Las Vegas home. After that, B.B. supported her with a $400 monthly allowance. By 1979, she was back in Gainesville and married to a man with a rap sheet. Florida police arrested them both on theft and burglary charges and recovered nearly $30,000 in stolen goods. Patty got off with probation, but the arrest of B.B. King's daughter made national headlines.*

In the autumn of 1979, Sid Seidenberg reframed the media's attention by staging a series of events to celebrate B.B.'s fifty-fourth birthday and thirtieth anniversary as a recording artist. In September, on *American Bandstand*, Dick Clark wheeled out a Lucille-shaped cake and led a round of "Happy Birthday," as B.B. laughed humbly. But B.B. refused to lip sync for Clark, compelling the program to air live music for one of the few times in its thirty-seven-year history.

While new momentum had infused B.B.'s recording career, his next record would bring it to a halt. This was B.B.'s fifth live set as headliner, recorded on the friendly turf of the University of Mississippi and released in the spring of 1980 by MCA Records, which had acquired rival ABC. Proceeds aided victims of the devastating Easter flood of 1979: a spring deluge had overwhelmed the Pearl River in southern Mississippi, forcing seventeen thousand souls from their homes. Despite noble intentions, the resulting double album fell far short of B.B.'s classic live recordings. The MCA executives seemed unable to agree on a title: three variations on *Live at Ole Miss* appear on the album's cover, credits page, and label. Producers sweetened the tapes in the studio with strings and sundry effects, one of which sounded uncannily like

---

* Patty King would make headlines again in 1992, when she filed into the front row of a B.B. King concert at the Gainesville Community Correctional Center, his first and only child to attend one of his signature prison shows as an inmate.

a lawn sprinkler. "B.B. didn't like it, and we didn't like it," recalled Russell Jackson, the bassist. The record stalled at number 162 on the *Billboard* 200, halting B.B.'s upward progress on the charts.

The year progressed with a recurring theme of homecoming. On June 5, 1980, B.B. returned to Indianola for B.B. King Day, a festival conceived by a local deejay and endorsed by the *Enterprise-Tocsin* newspaper. Jim Abbott, the paper's editor, had been seeking both formal and informal recognition for B.B. since their 1977 meeting. Now, on a hot and dry Delta day, B.B. pressed his hands in wet concrete at the corner of Church and Second Streets, where he had once played guitar for tips. He accepted the key to the city from the white mayor, who announced that a park would be named for him. The day concluded with an evening concert at the Indianola Industrial Park before a crowd of about three thousand, well short of the ten thousand that promoters had predicted. To judge from the photograph in the *Enterprise-Tocsin*, it was a mostly Black audience peppered with a few young, white faces.

In July 1980, the Gibson guitar company issued a B.B. King signature guitar titled, naturally, "Lucille." B.B. headlined a September concert at the Hollywood Bowl featuring Muddy Waters, Big Mama Thornton, Big Joe Turner, and Lloyd Glenn. *Variety* billed the event as "four legendary performers and one timeless giant," suggesting that B.B. had eclipsed even Muddy in renown. Muddy was enjoying his own artistic and commercial resurgence, with a series of albums produced by Johnny Winter, but his health was failing. At the Hollywood Bowl gig, everyone but B.B. performed sitting down. He was, quite literally, the last bluesman standing.

All B.B.'s résumé lacked was a proper biography.

Charles Sawyer had shopped his manuscript around and around, amassing fifty-three rejection letters. In 1980, his agent reached a deal with Doubleday. The new publisher wanted to market the book as an authorized biography, which meant Sawyer had to seek a signed release from his subject. Sawyer sent the book to B.B. and Sid Seidenberg for their review. The three men met in Germany that spring. Sawyer braced for B.B.'s reaction to his account, which, while reverential, flatly contradicted the bluesman on several points.

B.B. was pleased. He told Sawyer, "You did your part. You did your work, and you wrote this wonderful book." He held the signed release in his hand. He moved to offer the document to Sawyer. Seidenberg snatched it from the air. "Call me when you get back to the United States," he growled.

The next meeting unfolded in the office of a New York lawyer, who informed Sawyer that B.B. wanted half of the publishing royalties. (This was surely the lawyer's idea or Seidenberg's: B.B. would never have shaken down his old friend.) The three men argued back and forth. Someone asked Sawyer to name his price.

"You could not get a better treatment of your artist, more sympathetic, if you paid me ten times what the publisher is going to pay me," Sawyer said. He did some quick arithmetic in his head and promised B.B. half of any royalties beyond $20,000, a sum that would guarantee the writer a small profit.

The Arrival of B.B. King, published in late 1980, posited a richly detailed account of B.B.'s childhood, his journey to Memphis, and his artistic ascent where none had existed before. Sawyer set the record straight on dozens of facts that had decayed into fable and myth across the years.

By the time the biography went to press, Sawyer did not believe B.B. had fathered any children. He dutifully reported the fertility test that had proved B.B. was sterile. He also reported B.B.'s account of the eight children he claimed as his own. One or two reviewers noted the paradox. B.B. went right on telling interviewers he was a father.

Fatherhood "was a mark of manhood," Sawyer recalled. "And to say 'I have no biological children' would be to say, 'I was shooting blanks.'" And that was something B.B. would never say, not even to his biographer.

TAKEN TOGETHER, the biography, the Soviet Union tour, and two strong LPs with the Crusaders restored lost luster to B.B.'s career as the 1970s gave way to the 1980s. Now, B.B. needed another good album. He returned to Stewart Levine, who had produced the Crusaders collaborations. After two albums, *Midnight Believer* and the 1979 follow-up,

Take It Home, Levine felt that the jazz-pop conversation between B.B. and the Crusaders had run its course, so he sought fresh inspiration. He found it in a new artistic teaming.

B.B. had worked before with Mac Rebennack Jr., the New Orleans boogie-woogie pianist who performed as Dr. John, sometimes donning voodoo witch-doctor robes and feathered headdresses. By 1980, Dr. John was writing songs with another unlicensed physician of swing, Jerome Felder, aka Doc Pomus. Pomus had written or cowritten dozens of hits, including "A Teenager in Love" and "Save the Last Dance for Me." Levine asked the pair to write some songs for B.B. He wanted lyrics that evoked "the world that B.B. came from, not where he was at the moment." The B.B. King of 1955 or 1960 could have written those songs himself. The B.B. King of 1981 generally left the songwriting to others.

A month later, the writers sent Levine a cassette that contained an entire album. The six titles Levine chose for *There Must Be a Better World Somewhere* were strong compositions, suffused with Dr. John's barrelhouse piano and purring baritone but not straying too far from B.B.'s twelve-bar blues. The only problem lay with B.B., who, after hearing the demo tape, descended into a crisis of confidence. The demos sounded like a fully realized Dr. John album. Rebennack's masterful performances left B.B. intimidated and disheartened. "I don't know if I can do these," he told Levine. B.B.'s native humility and enduring insecurity were heartwarming, but they were also liabilities. Levine helped him overcome his self-doubt.

The sessions for the *Better World* album, released in early 1981, put B.B. back in New York at the Hit Factory, where he had worked with Bill Szymczyk a decade earlier. The band included keyboardist Dr. John, renowned saxophonists Hank Crawford and David "Fathead" Newman, celebrated drummer Bernard Purdie, and backup guitarist Hugh McCracken, who had memorably dueled with B.B. on the *Completely Well* album in 1969. If those dates had been debauched, these were deranged. Levine, the producer, recalled "drinking three, four, five bottles of white wine a night": "And I never even drank wine. It was delirious. Mac was on methadone and mixing it up with other stuff. Purdie was weird. The bass player was weird. Hank Crawford was fucked up, drunk, and stoned."

What emerged after two weeks of nocturnal bacchanalia was a sweet, smoky homage to the era of Woodstock and weed. B.B. reached a climax of gospel ardor on "More, More, More." On "The Victim," Drs. John and Pomus delivered a surprisingly accurate narrative of an embattled bluesman, fleeced by every woman he meets. B.B.'s melancholy musings on "Life Ain't Nothing but a Party" and the title track left listeners crying in their beer. Fittingly, B.B. won his second Grammy for the *Better World* album, in the category of "ethnic or traditional recording," at a ceremony in February 1982.

B.B. played 320 gigs in 1982, a year in which he turned fifty-seven. He was shedding weight, eating better, drinking less, and sleeping more. In September, he celebrated his birthday by completing the sessions for another strong album, *Blues 'n' Jazz*, with Sid Seidenberg producing. Calvin Owens, B.B.'s trumpeter and bandleader, provided Maxwell Davis–styled arrangements for a set of rhythm-and-blues chestnuts, including the old Louis Jordan tunes "Inflation Blues" and "Heed My Warning," the mid-'50s pop standard "Make Love to Me," and an old R&B instrumental called "Rainbow Riot," all for a 1940s-style jazz big band anchored by the inimitable pianist Lloyd Glenn. The session featured a handful of new B.B. King songs, the first such outpouring of original material from the once-prolific songwriter in nearly a decade. The album earned B.B. his third Grammy, in a new category that honored albums of traditional blues.

IN INDIANOLA, decades of white resistance to the B.B. King legend, and all it implied about race and class and local history, were finally melting away. B.B.'s Mississippi Homecomings had become an annual event. The celebration planned for June 1983 was the biggest yet, with festivities stretching across three days, capped with an official Friday ceremony to rename a two-lane street as B.B. King Road. But the real surprise came on Thursday, when, for the first time in living memory, leading citizens of Indianola's Black and white communities gathered for a garden party at the home of a prominent local banker to toast the most famous Indianolan.

Jim Abbott, editor of the *Enterprise-Tocsin*, had watched for years with mounting frustration as the same group of mostly African American celebrants turned out for the annual Homecomings. B.B. would graciously pose for a photo op with the white mayor and a few white business leaders. But when the time came to break bread and raise toasts, most of white Indianola vanished into the Delta mists. Abbott was himself a prominent Indianolan. At planning meetings for the 1983 Homecoming, he delicately broached the issue of race. B.B. "is such a gentleman, such a nice guy," he told fellow organizers. "Somehow, we've got to get these people to meet him," he said, meaning white people. Another organizer offered, "Why don't we have a party, and we'll invite these people, and that way, they'll meet him."

Abbott approached B.B. with the plan. "We'd like to have a party, a garden party, in your honor," he said. "And we're gonna invite half white and half Black." B.B. was "a bit stunned, kind of overwhelmed," Abbott recalled. He was also intrigued.

Party organizers asked a small but influential group of Indianolans to invite several dozen Black couples and an equal number of whites. Embossed invitations went out. Word leaked to the press, and soon dozens of news organizations wanted to cover the party. The planners called an emergency meeting. "These are whites and Blacks who have never socialized together, with drinks in their hands," one organizer fretted. With the news media hovering, she predicted, "they will go to opposite sides of the room." Organizers finally agreed to admit only Robert Palmer of the *New York Times* and only at the party's end. To judge from Palmer's account, he sneaked in early.

The party started at eight. Two hundred and fifty guests filed through a wrought-iron gate framed by crepe myrtles into an English garden filled with oaks and pecans. The garden backed into Indian Bayou, the stagnant waterway that bisected Indianola, its brown-black waters dotted with primeval cypress trees. Guests roamed the garden in a cool evening breeze, sipped drinks, nibbled hors d'oeuvres, and

watched videotapes of classic B.B. King performances on a giant outdoor screen. The event was scheduled to go until ten. But the attendees
were "having so much fun," Abbott recalled, that no one dared halt
the festivities. Around 11 p.m., Bebop Edwards approached Abbott
and announced, "The man wants to say something." B.B. took a flute
of champagne, climbed onto a low garden wall, and commenced to
speak. "For the first time in my life," B.B. said, "I don't feel like I'm the
prodigal son anymore. I feel like I'm home."

Palmer's account made the front page of the *New York Times*: the
great B.B. King had found a way to unite white and Black Mississippi,
at least for the span of a garden party. B.B. King Road was dedicated.
The Homecoming culminated Saturday night with a concert south of
town, in a wheat field not far from the old Johnson Barrett plantation
where Riley King had once toiled.

For all the party's success, Indianola had not been magically cured
of racism. A reporter from the *Jackson Clarion-Ledger* found a pocket of
opposition within a local pool hall, where a clutch of older white men
held court. "No, I don't think I'll make it out there to see ol' B.B.," one
regular chortled. "He'll have plenty of his people out there to keep him
company."

Later that summer, the University of Mississippi announced the
creation of the country's first blues archive. The opening underscored
the gravitas of the genre, the state's claim as its birthplace, and how much
had changed in the twenty years since white segregationists rioted over
the enrollment of a Black student at Ole Miss. The centerpiece of the
archive was a truckload of records, more than seven thousand, donated
from B.B.'s personal collection and valued at $178,000. The donation
included a single of Lonnie Johnson's "Rambler's Blues" from around
1942: B.B. called it his favorite blues recording. Mississippi governor
William Winter attended the dedication, which naturally segued into a
B.B. King concert. The Reverend Dwight "Gatemouth" Moore, B.B.'s
old colleague from radio station WDIA, served as master of ceremo-
nies. Someone asked B.B. how the blues came to be born in the Delta.
"That's like asking why life began where it did," he replied. "Who really
knows? The Delta was a good birthplace."

To thank B.B. for his gift, archive boosters found a tax attorney to negotiate a new settlement between the bluesman and the IRS. Federal taxing authorities stalked him like Robert Johnson's hellhounds after the chaotic years of self-management, despite Sid Seidenberg's best efforts to set things right. In the end, the feds emptied his vaults and compelled him to sell his sprawling Las Vegas home. B.B. downsized to a rented three-bedroom house nearby in a gated community called Spanish Oaks. Colonel Tom Parker lived across the street. It was a much smaller dwelling, but "he liked it better," LaVerne Toney recalled, "because it was a gated community, and the kids were getting to be more of a problem." Now, LaVerne could better control the children's comings and goings. B.B. would remain within the walled subdivision until the end.

B.B. HAD LOST TWO of his musical mentors in the 1970s. The first was T-Bone Walker, who died in 1975 in a California nursing home. The second was Booker T. Washington White, who died of cancer in a Memphis hospital in 1977. B.B.'s cousin was probably seventy-two, but the wire-service obituary aged him to eighty-nine, such being the vagaries of biography in Delta blues. B.B. evidently missed Bukka's funeral and later claimed not to have known where he had died. Though B.B. often distanced himself from his lesser-known cousin, Bukka had probably influenced his career more than any other musician, save T-Bone.

Two deaths in the early 1980s would further darken B.B.'s life. In April 1983, Muddy Waters passed away. Robert Palmer eulogized him in the *New York Times* as "the greatest contemporary exponent of the influential Mississippi Delta blues style." B.B. made it to Chicago for the wake. Inevitably, Muddy's death brightened the aura of legend around B.B., John Lee Hooker, and the few other Mississippi bluesmen of their generation who remained alive.

The following winter, Albert King, B.B.'s father, telephoned his son to say that he was dying. B.B. was out on tour. Albert promised B.B. he would try to hang on until his only son could get to Los Angeles. He wasn't sure he could. "One thing I want you to do for me, B.," Albert said, "I want you to take care of my family."

"Daddy," B.B. said, "I'll get home soon."

"Okay, son," Albert said, "I'll be waiting for you."

By the time B.B. arrived, on January 4, 1984, his father was dead. Albert King was seventy-seven. He left a wife, three children (aside from B.B.), and an estimated thirty-five grandchildren. Albert had outlived B.B.'s mother by forty-nine years. B.B. attended the funeral in Los Angeles and departed the next day for a gig in Alaska. His schedule left little time to grieve.

Albert had been born only eighteen years before his son. He had been mostly absent from B.B.'s life. There were many examples of Albert speaking derisively or dismissively of his son's fame and precious few of him offering admiration or even recognition. One of Albert's favorite put-downs was the preposterous claim that he played guitar better than his son. But B.B. loved his father, and he had spent his entire adult life trying to earn his unspoken esteem. Albert's voice would forever echo in B.B.'s ears, asking, "How can a man work too much?"

Shortly after Albert's death, B.B. played the Beverly Theater in Los Angeles on a bill with Bobby Bland. Among the backstage visitors was Michael Zanetis, a young, white session drummer. Zanetis had visited B.B. backstage before and knew Willie King, B.B.'s son and frequent companion. When Zanetis approached Willie before the Beverly gig, Willie warned him: Albert was dead. B.B. was "pretty down."

B.B. had friends like Michael Zanetis in every town. He always greeted them with genuine warmth, even if he couldn't possibly remember them all. Inside B.B.'s dressing room, Zanetis and his idol shook hands and struck up a conversation. Besotted visitors took these reverential exchanges to their graves. For B.B., they were about as memorable as a tooth brushing. All that changed when this visitor told B.B. he had nominated him for a star on the Hollywood Walk of Fame.

For all of B.B.'s laurels, no one had thought to ask the Hollywood Chamber of Commerce to award the bluesman a star on the famed Walk. Zanetis had taken it upon himself, a brainstorm that erupted one day when Zanetis discovered that Bugs Bunny had a star and B.B. did not.

"I thought it might raise your spirits," Zanetis said, after sharing his news. B.B. gazed upon the young visitor as if seeing him for the first time. His face melted from pain and grief into "a look of excitement and happiness, like he just got a lifetime pass to Disneyland," Zanetis recalled.

B.B. sleepwalked through his first set at the Beverly, looking "like he wasn't there," Zanetis recalled. Sometime during the second set, he came back to life. After the show, Zanetis returned backstage. He knelt before B.B. and told him that their backstage friendship, so ephemeral to B.B., had helped Zanetis bear the loss of his own father.

"Well, Michael," B.B. replied slowly, "I'm glad to hear I could help you, even when I didn't know I was helping you." B.B. thanked Zanetis for bringing him good news: it had helped him get through a rough night. Then he spoke of his own father. "We were not super close," B.B. said, "but I love my dad, and my dad loves me. My dad never told me he loved me, but I know he did."

IN THE WINTER of 1983–84, B.B. again reshaped his band. The key departure was Calvin Owens, B.B.'s longtime trumpeter and bandleader. Owens had been "fucking around with drugs and whiskey and wild women," by his own account, and he had carved out an increasingly prominent role within the band, including a bit where he walked through the audience, playing his horn and drawing attention away from his boss. Owens claimed he fired himself. B.B. didn't argue.

"I read once where Miles Davis said that it's not good to stay together too long," B.B. told an interviewer after the split, "because you might get stale and you could stop growing."

If B.B. had an equal in jazz, it was probably Davis. Each man had led his genre across three decades. They adored each other's work. A rare double bill in New York around this time brought forth a rare fire in B.B. "And the crowd picked up on it," a *Down Beat* reviewer observed, "applauding his falsetto leaps, vocal nuances, and passionate string bends. It was a great performance, totally redeeming the man from the dreadfully slick, overproduced albums he's released in recent years." After finishing his set, B.B. told the crowd, "It's really an honor to be on the same show with the maestro, because this guy has meant so much to the music and has done so much for it." B.B. paused, and someone in the cheap seats screamed out, "So have you!" And then the packed house at the Beacon Theater rose as one and applauded the blues master, shaking the room for two full minutes, reducing B.B. to tears.

The trumpeter's tirade at B.B. in the Detroit club, decades earlier, had set the tone for their friendship. Davis's hoarse invectives only endeared him to B.B. On a 1980s package tour of Europe, Davis arrived late to the chartered plane that carried B.B. and the other artists. No empty seat remained. Davis walked up to B.B. in first-class. He glared at Joe McClendon, B.B.'s valet, in the next seat. "Move over," he commanded.

"Man, you can't do that," McClendon protested. But Davis did. The valet shuffled off to sit in the cockpit with the pilot.

On another tour, McClendon was leaving B.B.'s hotel suite when Davis came stomping down the hallway. "Is this B.B.'s room?" he growled. "You with B.B.?" McClendon nodded. Davis shoved past. "Man, you can't go in there," McClendon cried. "I have to use the bathroom," Davis hissed. From inside the room, McClendon heard his boss's voice. "That's Mr. Miles," B.B. said. "That's all right."

PROFESSIONALLY, B.B. was descending into another trough, a span that saw him play smaller and less illustrious venues in the States, even as he remained an A-list talent overseas. B.B. had faded from the charts after a run of hit records produced by Stewart Levine. American tastes were shifting from blues-based guitar rock to synthesizers and drum machines. B.B.'s 1984 itinerary included the Executive Inn in Owensboro, Kentucky, the State Theatre in Kalamazoo, Michigan, and a jai alai fronton in Tampa, interspersed with performances in a dozen European countries and Japan. Critics increasingly worried of a creeping complacency, a slick predictability, in the nightly gigs. The B.B. King band of these years was a fine, dignified ensemble, swaying back and forth onstage in three-piece suits. But in an era of choreographed Michael Jackson videos, B.B.'s group looked increasingly anachronistic.

B.B. and Sid Seidenberg complained about being shut out of MTV. Launched in 1981, Music Television mirrored pop music's early-'80s embrace of big hair, spandex, and smoke machines. Success on the charts now required fashion-spread visuals. The new format opened a fresh chapter of music-industry discrimination: MTV mostly ignored Black artists, until former Motown child star Michael Jackson demolished the color barrier in 1983 with a video for his smash "Billie Jean."

In 1985, Seidenberg took a call from John Landis, the director who had made *The Blues Brothers* and, more recently, an epic video for Michael Jackson's "Thriller." Landis still wanted to work with B.B. He had a new film titled *Into the Night*, a comedy-thriller about international intrigue that starred Jeff Goldblum and Michelle Pfeiffer. He wanted B.B. to perform on the soundtrack.

When Landis and B.B. sat down together for the first time, B.B. asked, "Why wasn't I in *The Blues Brothers*?"

"Because you were booked," Landis replied. B.B. didn't know the filmmaker had called: Sid Seidenberg hadn't told him. B.B. had nursed a grudge for five years.

"But you put me on that mural," B.B. said, still puzzled.

"You're welcome," Landis smiled.

When the recording date arrived, the director "had B.B. sit with headphones and watch the movie," Landis recalled. "And he watched it like two or three times, twice one day and once again the next day. As he watched the movie, he just sort of played." Studio hands added orchestration to B.B.'s improvisations. They teamed him with a session band to perform a cover of Wilson Pickett's "In the Midnight Hour" and two new songs penned by Ira Newborn, a Hollywood soundtrack man. The titular "Into the Night" became B.B. King's first music video. Like many Reagan-era videos, this one was "very '80s," Landis recalled. B.B. and his big-haired backing band performed against a pastel backdrop, a scene interspersed with shots from the Landis film. The song was all stiff drum beats, gauzy synthesizer fills, and slap bass. Videos for "My Lucille" and "Midnight Hour" were more fun, featuring Pfeiffer and comedians Dan Aykroyd and Steve Martin in a mock horn section and Eddie Murphy on drums. Yet, after all that, MTV refused to air the videos. Landis offered them instead to the Black Entertainment Television cable network, where they went on heavy rotation.

Those songs set the tone for B.B.'s next album, *Six Silver Strings*, billed on the cover as his fiftieth long-player, though counting them all was a challenge. The record was a slick, '80s affair, and it's a wonder Michael Jackson didn't sue over the stark similarities between B.B.'s "Big Boss Man" and "Billie Jean." B.B. and Seidenberg were following the beacon of pop, rather than blues. B.B. did, however, win his fourth Grammy for "My Guitar Sings the Blues," one of the better tracks.

Two young bluesmen were breathing fresh vitality into the genre. One was Robert Cray, a reserved African American guitarist from the Pacific Northwest, whose *Bad Influence* LP was a modern blues-funk classic (featuring not a whiff of drum machines or shrill synthesizer). The other was Stevie Ray Vaughn, a white cowboy-bohemian from Dallas who was probably the most exciting revelation in blues guitar since the Hendrix era. Both artists were placing albums on the *Billboard* 200 chart, which B.B.'s *Six Silver Strings* failed to crack.

In time, B.B. would take both Cray and Vaughn under his wing. A well-traveled anecdote tells how one night onstage with B.B., in a gun-slinger guitar-dueling jam, Vaughan sought to impress his hero with a withering barrage of notes. B.B. answered with one long, pure, resonant tone. The master smiled as Vaughan doubled over in tears of laughter.

IN JULY 1985, B.B. delivered a celebrated set from Holland at Live Aid, a benefit show beamed around the world via satellite as a fundraiser to relieve an Ethiopian famine. In September, he celebrated his sixtieth birthday at Farm Aid, the iconic, agrarian fundraiser organized in part by Willie Nelson, whose "Always on My Mind" was one of B.B.'s favorite songs.

B.B. had some new employees. Walter King, B.B.'s nephew, returned as saxophonist and bandleader. Walter helped B.B. recruit a new bass player, Michael Doster, a tall, lanky, white Nashvillian known onstage as "Mighty Mike," although he looked more like a high-school math teacher. For a young jazz-blues bassist like Doster, a spot in the B.B. King band was a dream job. But his first impression did not encourage. "To tell you the truth, I thought it was unorganized and kind of chaotic," he recalled. "There appeared to be a lot of vitriol. Everybody was kind of grumpy. The band traveled on a regular Greyhound bus. They didn't have a sleeper coach. It was about a month before we had a rehearsal."

B.B. paid better than anyone else on the blues circuit. B.B. provided his sidemen medical and dental insurance, rare luxuries for working musicians. But a job in his band of this era was not particularly fun. An archaic, chitlin' circuit class system still ruled the B.B. King band. B.B., his road manager, and his valet occupied the top tier, flying first-class, staying in four-star hotels, and riding in an elegant coach equipped with beds. The musicians flew coach and stayed in Holiday Inns. Out on the road, B.B. slept comfortably while his musicians tossed and turned in Greyhound-style seats, a plight that left them perpetually tired and cranky. Bebop Edwards, the current road manager, cut a singularly caustic figure. When the band arrived at its nightly lodging, Doster and the others would languish in the bus until Bebop returned with a pile of room keys: "They didn't want to see a lobby full of Black people," Doster recalled. The chitlin' circuit was dead, but its legacy lived on.

IN LATE 1985, B.B.'S recurring throat problems caught up with him. Night after night, he delivered his signature line, "I gave you seven children / And now you wanna give 'em back," at a guttural roar. The effort pushed his voice into overdrive, unleashing a passionate growl that ravaged his vocal cords. His tour schedule left them no time to heal. When B.B. entered a studio to cut a song for the Paul Newman–Tom Cruise film *The Color of Money*, he could only summon a hoarse rasp, and someone on the production complained. B.B. went to a doctor, who inserted a probe down his throat and pronounced that one side of his larynx was badly inflamed. He prescribed rest. B.B. spent six weeks in convalescence at his new Las Vegas home over the winter of 1985–86, an unprecedented hiatus. B.B. was not yet an old man, but the years, and the miles, were adding up.

B.B. TOURED BRITAIN and Europe in the fall of 1986. As an October date in Dublin approached, word reached Sid Seidenberg that U2, one of the biggest bands in the world, planned to attend. "We're going to Ireland," Seidenberg told B.B., "and U2 is coming to the show. So why don't you ask Bono, the guy who sings lead, to write a song for you?"

Years earlier, on their way up, the Irish superstars had opened for B.B. in London. When B.B. played in Dublin, the young Irishmen would come to his shows and queue up for autographs. "Mr. King," they would tell him, "if we ever get big, we're gonna invite you to come on our show." B.B. would reply, "Keep it up. You're gonna be famous one day." Now, the tables were turned, and B.B. winced at the thought of leaning on Bono. B.B. preferred to be the one dispensing dollars and favors.

The Dublin date arrived. At concert's end, the members of U2 filed into B.B.'s dressing room, looking "like little kids in the candy store" as they approached their hero, recalled Tony Coleman, B.B.'s sometime drummer. Coleman recognized the illustrious visitors, but some of his older bandmates sat slack-jawed as they watched four young, white ragamuffins walk right up to the boss and start talking. "B.B. and them don't watch MTV," Coleman explained. B.B. and the Irish musicians "had a nice, relaxed chat": "They acted more like old friends than superstars," B.B. recalled. As his guests prepared to leave, B.B. summoned the courage to tell Bono, "I would love it if you guys would write me a song."

"Okay," Bono replied simply. "I will."*

---

*Tony Coleman's version of this encounter, recounted to the author, differs markedly and intriguingly from those of B.B. and U2. According to Coleman, Bono had a song ready when the band came backstage, and Bono boldly announced to B.B., "We wrote a song about you coming to Ireland."

CHAPTER 19

LOVETOWN

Y EARS ENDING IN SEVEN SEEMED to bring B.B. luck. In 1967, he had broken through the racial barrier of pop music at Bill Graham's Fillmore. In 1977, Stewart Levine and Sidney Seidenberg had conspired to revive his career. And now, in 1987, B.B. was on another roll.

One January night in New York City, the kings and queens of pop gathered at the Waldorf Astoria Hotel to induct twenty-three of their own into the sophomore class of the new Rock and Roll Hall of Fame, including B.B. King. Contemporary artists introduced each inductee. Bruce Springsteen gave a heartfelt tribute to Roy Orbison, and Beach Boy Brian Wilson honored the songwriting team of Leiber and Stoller. For B.B., the organizers could have chosen virtually anyone from the pantheon of rock guitar, including Billy Gibbons of ZZ Top, who was in attendance and who had more or less named his band after B.B. Inexplicably, the Hall chose Sting, founder of new wave superstars the Police, a band about as bluesy as Madonna.

No one had thought to invite Lucille. Event organizers somehow forgot to tell the most important guitarist in the house to bring his guitar. When the inductees gathered onstage for the customary post-awards jam, B.B. was reduced to shaking maracas. Someone finally handed him a Les Paul.

In August, B.B. hosted a delegation in Las Vegas from Indianola. The group included the Reverend Birkett Davis and his wife, Delcia, who had once shared a house in Indianola with B.B. and Martha King. Also along were James and Beatrice Fair, surviving kin of the Reverend Archie Fair, whose guitar Riley King had once coveted. Some of them had never traveled on airplanes before. B.B. covered airfare and hotels and provided each guest a jar of coins for the slot machines, a temptation from which Reverend Davis righteously abstained.

In October 1987, the Recording Academy awarded B.B. a Grammy for lifetime achievement, its most prestigious trophy. No other blues artist had one.

That fall, the cable-television service Cinemax broadcast an hour-long program titled "A Blues Session: B.B. King and Friends," a performance taped in April. The talent assembled on the studio stage was spellbinding, a testament to the man, his currency, and his legend. B.B.'s backup guitarists included Eric Clapton, Albert King, and Stevie Ray Vaughan, perhaps the three living axe-men who could give the King a run for his money. B.B. shared singing duties with some of the finest lungs in rhythm and blues: Gladys Knight, Etta James, Chaka Khan, and Billy Ocean. Dr. John tickled the ivories, and Phil Collins sat reverentially at drums. The performance captured electric-blues pioneer Paul Butterfield blowing a sublime harmonica in one of his final acts. Gladys Knight sang a captivating "Please Send Me Someone to Love." Etta James and Dr. John managed to top that with a steamy duet on "I'd Rather Go Blind." B.B. traded licks with a worshipful Clapton on an energetic "The Thrill Is Gone," finishing the performance mano a mano as an unaccompanied duo. Vaughan and Albert King answered them with a smoldering take on "The Sky Is Crying," handing the mic to Butterfield for a final turn in the spotlight and then enlisting B.B. for an incendiary cutting session. It was "that rare kind of music special," the *New York Times* opined, "that leaves you wanting more." Producers dedicated the program to Butterfield, who died of an overdose shortly after the taping.

In late 1987, B.B. returned to the radio for the first time since his departure from WDIA, thirty-five years earlier. A pair of Los Angeles producers conceived the *B.B. King Blues Hour* as a showcase for B.B. to share his favorite blues albums. B.B. would record shows three or four at a time, talking into a digital audio tape recorder in his tour bus or hotel room. A technician would stitch his words together with songs from the chosen record, usually an archival release from one of B.B.'s heroes. Launched in late 1987, the *Blues Hour* played on more than one hundred stations via syndication, mostly R&B outlets that reached urban Blacks. B.B. loved that.

"B.B. felt that urban contemporary radio kind of blew him off," recalled Gary Bird, who cofounded the show, "because they went to more contemporary R&B. The blues, like jazz, became like a subgenre. There were jazz stations in a lot of towns, but there weren't blues stations in a lot of towns. In fact, there were none."

The *Blues Hour* would remain on the air until 1990: by then, B.B. was too busy to host it.

One day in the autumn of 1987, Sid Seidenberg told B.B. that U2 wanted his band to open for them in Fort Worth, Texas. Bono had written a song for B.B. to sing. B.B. had forgotten all about Bono and his pledge.

B.B. arrived in Fort Worth ahead of the show to rehearse Bono's song. The concert film *Rattle and Hum* captured Bono, like a vulnerable child in a trilby hat, asking B.B. if he had liked it. "I loved the song," B.B. replied. "Real heavy lyrics. You're mighty young to write such heavy lyrics." Bono laughed nervously. A few minutes later, B.B. confessed to Bono that he was uncomfortable playing chords in performance, a humbling admission. Now both men looked nervous.

Bono had titled the song "When Love Comes to Town." He claimed to have written it "in about ten minutes" in a bathroom, with lyrics that celebrated the redemptive power of love, faith, and B.B. King. The band debuted it that night in November 1987 before fourteen thousand rapturous Fort Worth fans. Bono took the first verse. "I gave it my absolute, you know, everything I had in that howl at the start of the song," he recalled. "And then B.B. King opened up his mouth, and I felt like a girl."

Bono's song reached number 68 on the *Billboard* pop chart. The attendant video, shot travelogue style with imagery of B.B. and Bono, Sun Records and Elvis, Memphis and the Mississippi, went into heavy rotation on MTV, earning a coveted Video Music Award. Sung with real passion by Bono and with rare abandon by B.B., "When Love Comes to Town" was a highlight, maybe even the centerpiece, of the *Rattle and Hum* LP, which sold fourteen million copies.

For B.B., the collaboration paid immediate dividends in larger venues, younger crowds, and higher fees. In the summer of 1988, B.B. rolled into Indianola for the annual Homecoming in a new $400,000 Acron Magnum tour bus from Belgium, equipped with a full bar, closed-circuit television, and microwave oven. A few days later, B.B. closed out the Chicago Blues Festival before an audience of 225,000, possibly the largest group of American blues fans that ever saw him play.

U2 "gave B.B. a new crowd," recalled trumpeter James "Boogaloo" Bolden, a veteran of the Calvin Owens era. "Before Bono, it was a much older, much Blacker audience. I would say late forties to sixty. And once he met Bono, the audiences were much younger: teens and twenties and early thirties. And then you start to see the audience changing to whiter and whiter and whiter."

By the autumn of 1988, random people were recognizing B.B. at airports and on city streets. He'd been spotted by fans before but never like this. The bluesman now found it impossible to travel without a security detail. Like Elvis or Sinatra, B.B. could not get through a terminal or lobby or concert hall without a cordon of security, men whose principal job was to keep him moving past the endless parade of police, parking attendants, and doormen. "They, just like any other fans, would talk him to death," recalled Stafford Davis, B.B.'s longtime security aide.

This broadening and whitening of B.B.'s audience recalled his breakthrough of two decades earlier, when the Rolling Stones had invited B.B. on tour. B.B. responded then with *Completely Well*, one of the finest records of his career. Now, with U2 fanning the flames of his fame, B.B. and Sid Seidenberg rolled out *King of the Blues 1989*, enlisting an all-star cast of supporting talent to further burnish his brand. The album was dreadful. The combined talents of drummer Mick Fleetwood, guitarist Steve Cropper, singers Stevie Nicks and Bonnie Raitt, and the Muscle Shoals Horns were all wasted on a production of plastic Adult-Oriented Rock pap. Producers buried B.B. and Lucille beneath a sludge of synthesizers and drum machines. (And the drum machines buried Fleetwood, a fine drummer.) As for the actual music, biographer

David McGee called *King of the Blues 1989* "the least distinguished collection of songs B.B. had ever committed to a long-player."

Since the 1970s, B.B. had chased many pop-music trends: Philly soul and jazz-pop fusion in the 1970s, country and synth pop in the 1980s.* B.B.'s response was always the same: he was trying to stay fresh. That quality, his currency, set B.B. apart from the other great bluesmen of his generation. "I don't want to compare myself to President Bush," he told a skeptical interviewer from *Down Beat*, alluding to the forty-first president. "But in my own small way, doing what I do, I have to make some of the same kinds of decisions he does. He has so many different constituencies to please—so many more than I do, of course. But he has to walk a fine line about what they want. In my way, so do I." That rationale made sense when B.B. made good records, such as the jazz-pop collection *Midnight Believer*. When he made bad ones, fans and reviewers howled that he dishonored his own legend.

The tenure of President George H. W. Bush, elected in November 1988, raised B.B.'s profile in Washington. Bush's campaign manager, a white Georgian named Lee Atwater, revealed himself on inauguration night as a talented blues guitarist, performing for and even pretending to jam with the new commander in chief, who joined in on air guitar. Atwater idolized B.B. One night in February 1989, he turned up at a Washington club and jammed with his idol. The two men became fast friends.

The same Lee Atwater had helped President Ronald Reagan revive the racist "Southern strategy" of the 1960s with pointed references to states' rights, spending cuts, and the welfare state, framing an agenda that ensured "blacks get hurt worse than whites," in Atwater's words. In the 1988 campaign, Atwater infamously embraced a series of campaign ads that sensationalized the crimes of an African American felon named Willie Horton to cast the opposing Democratic Party as soft on crime. The ads stoked racist sentiments, but Atwater's love for B.B. looked genuine. "I don't let nobody tell me who I can speak to or who

---

*B.B.'s 1982 foray into country, the regrettable *Love Me Tender*, is reviewed in a separate discography.

I can be friends with," B.B. snapped at a *Rolling Stone* reporter who took a dim view of the friendship. Still, B.B.'s fans had a hard time processing Atwater's presence on a Mississippi stage at the annual Homecoming in the summer of 1989. Atwater's brief set drew both applause and boos.

After that, the two men fraternized mostly in private. But Atwater made good on his pledge to introduce B.B. to the president. In June 1989, shortly after the Homecoming, B.B. presented a replica of Lucille to Bush in the Oval Office. "He was just the nearest thing to God, for me," B.B. recalled. The following January, B.B. returned to Washington and serenaded the president at the Kennedy Center with a rendition of "Nobody Loves Me but My Mother" before a gathering of wealthy Republicans. Behind the scenes, Atwater wielded his influence to have B.B.'s ongoing tax audit reassigned from an adversarial Las Vegas field office to a friendlier agent in Northern Virginia. Barely a year later, in March 1991, at age forty, Atwater died of a brain tumor. In his final months, Atwater had publicly apologized for the "naked cruelty" of the '88 campaign.

IN LATE 1989, U2 invited B.B. on tour to support *Rattle and Hum* as an honored opening act. The band named the tour "Lovetown," after B.B.'s song. Half of the forty-seven shows were performed in Australia and New Zealand, with the remainder in Europe and the United Kingdom. The tour bypassed the United States, where some critics had savaged *Rattle and Hum* as an act of cultural plunder. The easy pace of U2's itinerary, three or four performances a week, left B.B. at loose ends. He was used to doing a show a day. He and his bandmates filled the empty hours with wagers on the most trivial of probabilities. "They would literally bet on which lift doors would open next," Bono recalled, using the British term for elevator. Bono asked B.B. if there was anything he wouldn't gamble on. "Yes," B.B. replied, "a bass player and a drummer."

B.B. turned sixty-four in Australia that September. U2 threw him a surprise birthday party. Thinking he was going on a fishing trip, B.B. arrived at Sydney Harbour to find a rented yacht filled with balloons and friends. A formation of Aussie fighter jets saluted the bluesman. A skywriter carved "HAPPY BIRTHDAY B.B." into the blue. After hours of jamming and singing, the entourage returned to the harbor at sunset for a fireworks display in B.B.'s honor. He wept in gratitude.

At year's end, B.B. invited Sue and her sister to see him perform with U2 in Dublin. When he met them in person at the airport, rather than send an aide, Sue knew how much the moment meant to him. "I remember how proud he was to go on the U2 tour," she recalled. "He wanted me to share that."

THE CLOSE of the 1980s marked a new era of unprecedented stability in the B.B. King band. Organist James Toney had played with B.B. on and off since 1968. B.B.'s drummer, Calep Emphrey Jr., and his saxophonist nephew, Walter King, had joined in 1977. Trumpeter James "Boogaloo" Bolden had arrived in 1980. Backup guitarist Leon Warren had joined around 1982, bassist Michael Doster in 1985. That ensemble would endure, almost unchanged, until the new millennium.

This stasis reflected B.B.'s preference for musicians he liked and trusted over those with more virtuosity but less humanity. He often said, "I look for someone who's 100 percent man. If he's only 50 percent musician, that's okay: We'll turn him into 75 percent musician after a while. But if he is not 100 percent man, there's nothing I can do."

B.B. had executed several brutal purges over the decades, casting out any number of likable, trustworthy men. However, the B.B. King of 1990 was a changed person. He had purged his bands to retain currency, to compete with younger, fresher artists for supremacy on the charts and top billing on festival stages. Now, as B.B. reached the traditional retirement age, his artistic restlessness was maturing into contentedness—or, perhaps, complacency. "I think he thought his creative years were behind him," recalled Stewart Levine, the producer.

B.B. went to greater lengths to protect this band than any before it. "We're a family," he told his musicians, "because we spend more time together than our own family." When Bolden became afflicted with gum disease, rendering him briefly unable to play the trumpet, B.B. stuck with him, paying his health insurance and permitting Boogaloo to earn his keep by playing the tambourine and working the crowd.

The B.B. King band of this era alternated between two drummers, faithful Calep Emphrey and brash soul journeyman Tony Coleman. B.B. called him Cole Man. Their mercurial relationship began in 1978. B.B. would hire Coleman periodically to replace Emphrey, who battled endlessly with alcoholism and addiction. "He was an enabler with Calep," Coleman recalled. "He'd get rid of Calep when he couldn't take it anymore, but then he'd take him back and give him another chance." Cole Man worked on and off for B.B. across four decades. B.B. loved Coleman's drumming—and, at times, hated his attitude. Coleman was thirty years younger. Like many much-younger African Americans, Coleman grew up in a post–Jim Crow world and lacked patience for B.B.'s tactful diplomacy toward bigots. "B.B. was afraid of white people," Coleman recalled. B.B.'s conciliatory manner drove Coleman crazy. He would periodically explode at his boss, "You don't have to kiss no one's ass. You're B.B. King." B.B. would reply, "Son, you don't have to tell me how to be B.B. King."

Coleman bragged that B.B. fired him five times. In truth, Coleman generally fired himself after backing into a rhetorical corner with B.B. during one of their many spats. Their relationship was like that of father and rebellious son. Cole Man could do a dead-on impression of his boss. His rhetorical flourishes could reduce the band to tears. Once, during one of B.B.'s annual pilgrimages to the Delta, Coleman sat in the tour bus outside a decrepit club, a place with grass growing through the floorboards and bugs consorting in the corners, pointing up the sheer absurdity that the great B.B. King should perform in such a place. The other musicians howled.

"And then we're getting ready," Coleman recalled. "And on my way out, B.B. says, 'Tony Cole Man, would you sit down please? I'd like to talk to you, son.'" Once the others had left, B.B. spoke. "You think it's funny that we're playing here. Well, you've been around the world with me. You've played for kings and queens and presidents. We've played at Carnegie Hall. Don't you think these folks deserve a good show, too, son? These people represent me. This is where I come from. And when you laugh at them, you're laughing at me."

For once, the drummer sat speechless.

* * *

B.B.'S HEALTH was no longer a trifling concern. On a February 1990 visit to Northwestern University, near Chicago, B.B. slipped on ice while stepping from a bus. Walter, his nephew, reached out and slowed his fall, but B.B. landed hard on his left knee. After a hospital trip, he appeared at the lecture on crutches.

Two months later, in April, B.B. closed out a set at Rockefeller's, a Houston club, feeling dangerously low on energy. "I hardly felt like picking myself up," he recalled. He pressed on to Louisiana, where he "couldn't make it out of bed" to play the New Orleans jazz festival, according to bassist Michael Doster. Paramedics stabilized B.B. and sent him home.

Back in Las Vegas, a few days later, B.B. set out on a road trip to California with his nephew Walter and returned with dozens of records and compact discs, as was his habit. "We got back to the house," Walter recalled, "and he didn't open one, not a single one, and he went to bed." B.B. complained of an unquenchable thirst. "And he drank this mix of orange juice and pineapple juice," Walter recalled. "He was really drinking a lot of that, to the point that he was drinking and peeing in the restroom at the same time." Walter told his uncle, "B., I think you have diabetes." Walter was diabetic.

Tests revealed B.B.'s blood sugar had spiked to six hundred milligrams per deciliter of blood, six times normal. "I've called the hospital and made a reservation for you," his doctor told him. "You should go now."

B.B. spent a week in May at the hospital and another week recuperating at home. The doctor told him that only a man of his strength could have soldiered on with such elevated blood sugar without slipping into a coma. Sid Seidenberg canceled half a month of gigs and a trip to London, where, according to Walter, B.B. had been invited to perform with former Beatles. (Walter didn't remember which ones.)

"In all of my forty-one years, I've never missed as many days as I canceled," B.B. told an interviewer. "But then you realize that your life is all you've got."

B.B. had more or less stopped drinking in the late 1980s. Faithful Norman Matthews, an admitted alcoholic, sobered up in solidarity and immediately became a more reliable companion.* B.B. knew diabetes ran in his family, but since he had never felt any obvious symptoms, he had gone right on eating what he wanted, a decadent southern diet interspersed with junky dressing-room fare and greasy Chinese takeout. Henceforth, he would have to take daily medication and get serious about diet and weight. Fans responded to the health scare with an avalanche of letters, cards, and flowers. B.B. wept as he read them.

That spring, a new prop appeared onstage at B.B. King shows: a chair. At sixty-five, with arthritis hobbling his legs, B.B. now performed the latter half of each show sitting down. He dismissed the poignancy of the prop with a quip: "I'll bet you thought you'd never live long enough to see B.B. King sit down." He worked the chair into his act, dismissing the horns and playing a series of softer, more intimate songs while seated, just as Led Zeppelin and the Eagles had done in the middle of their shows, and telling stories between songs.

B.B.'s lone LP of 1990, *Live at San Quentin*, reminded listeners how much energy the bluesman had commanded just a few years earlier. The performance had been recorded in May 1986 and inexplicably shelved. B.B. charged through his set, almost as if he were in a hurry to leave, which he was. B.B. had played dozens of benefit gigs at prisons. But when he arrived at this one, a prison official set the band on edge, warning the musicians that the prisoners might take them hostage and that if they did, "We do not negotiate. You're on your own." Inmates, rather than administrators, had invited B.B. to San Quentin. The chilly welcome inspired an electric performance. B.B. was in fine voice, he played Lucille with fire and flair, and he drew real energy from a crowd of hardened men, some young enough to be his grandchildren. The spooked sidemen galloped through "The Thrill Is Gone" at a disco pace.

"I remember big guys in the audience with arms that looked like tree stumps from working out, and they were wearing lipstick and makeup," recalled Mike Doster, the bassist. "They were whistling at

---

* Neither man gave up alcohol altogether. "They stopped drinking *heavily*," said Darin Brimhall, personal physician to both men, in an interview with the author. Years later, Matthews went on a bender in Italy and so infuriated B.B. that he left Matthews there.

me and making catcalls. Our road manager, Bebop, was egging them on and saying to me, 'Mike, they like you.'"

Around this time, Sid Seidenberg finally prevailed on B.B. to dismiss Bebop, his road manager of a dozen years and companion of four decades. "Sid wanted to ease out anyone he couldn't control," recalled Lora Walker, B.B.'s lifelong friend. After a tour stop in San Francisco, Bebop had left a rental car and hotel room in the care of an acquaintance, who had amassed a $25,000 tab, which B.B. eventually paid. B.B. and Bebop remained friends, and B.B. attended Bebop's lavish retirement party in Mobile, Alabama. But their professional association was over.

To replace Bebop, Seidenberg enlisted Sherman Darby, a veteran hand whom he deemed more professional. Calm and stern, taciturn and mysterious (he spent idle hours watching François Truffaut movies in French), Darby served B.B. as the next in a long line of surly aides. He barked at sidemen. He terrorized hotel receptionists. Like Bebop Edwards and LeRoy Myers before him, Darby embodied the antithesis of even-tempered B.B.

"We had gotten kicked out of a lot of hotels," Walter King recalled, "and we didn't know why. It wasn't so much the musicians destroying the rooms as it was the road managers making folks at the desk cry."

Nonetheless, Darby and Sid Seidenberg guided B.B. through 1990 with consummate skill, dispatching the band on its longest and, by Sid's account, most successful European tour to date, twenty-four shows in thirteen nations, including a gig in Prague at the invitation of Czech president Václav Havel.

In September, B.B. traveled to Hollywood to collect a star on the fabled Walk of Fame, between Milton Berle's and Vivien Leigh's. Michael Zanetis, B.B.'s friend and fan, had filed and refiled his application with the Hollywood Chamber of Commerce every year since the poignant meeting with B.B. in 1984. At last, in 1990, the chamber granted its approval. On September 5, three hundred spectators gathered in front of a leather boutique on Hollywood Boulevard for the lunchtime ceremony. At the 12:30 start time, only B.B. was missing. Johnny Grant, the radio personality and honorary Hollywood mayor, threaded through the crowd and found Zanetis. "They're gonna make us wrap this thing up," Grant hissed. "Is he OK? Do you know where he is?"

Zanetis reached B.B.'s driver by phone. He had lost his way in the Los Angeles maze. The limousine was five minutes away. B.B. hadn't time to stop at the hotel and change into his suit. He arrived, five minutes later, dressed in a blue plaid shirt, blue pants, and a clashing gray sport coat. He had not brought his guitar. B.B. apologized to Zanetis for his tardiness and his appearance. Zanetis pulled him close. "Everybody here loves you," he said into B.B.'s ear. "Nobody's even gonna notice what you're wearing."

B.B. told his assembled admirers, "I never thought I'd be worthy of being on this walk." He covered for his missing guitar by explaining that Lucille was "asleep. She'll be mad at me later for not bringing her today."

B.B.'S NEXT TOUR SPANNED five continents over three months in late 1990 with the Philip Morris "Superband," a Basie-style orchestra staffed with famed sidemen such as trumpeter Harry "Sweets" Edison, an actual Basie alumnus, and guitarist Kenny Burrell, a jazz star in his own right. B.B. coheadlined with Ray Charles, one of a few living musical artists with the gravitas to share a bill with him. The tour yielded an album, *Live at the Apollo*, that gives a fair hint of what the Superband delivered: a fast-paced, journeyman set that sounded about thirty years out of date. The format worked well on an R&B standard like "Ain't Nobody's Business," less so on the U2 anthem "When Love Comes to Town."

From the start of B.B.'s performing career, he had styled himself after Basie and Ellington, men for whom such distinctions as blues, jazz, and rhythm and blues held little meaning. For all his talk of "stupid fingers," B.B. could transpose a blues song into any musical key, crafting a beautiful solo on Lucille in C, G, or A flat with equal facility. He could "listen to a sixteen-piece orchestra on a record, and he could name every musician," recalled Stafford Davis, the security aide. B.B. heard each musician's tone as distinctly as a human voice.

"We'd be on these jazz festivals," recalled Russell Jackson, the bassist. "We'd be the only blues band out of twenty acts. We'd be on the plane with Miles Davis and Dizzy Gillespie. And then we'd come back and we'd be in the Kool Jazz Festival with Chaka Khan and Kool & the Gang and Earth, Wind & Fire. B.B. was the only guy who could do that."

The two live sets, *San Quentin* in 1990 and *Apollo* in 1991, snagged B.B. his fifth and sixth Grammy awards in the Traditional Blues category. The albums illustrated the good and bad about live B.B. King in the 1990s. Playing with his regular band at the prison, B.B. could approach the jaw-dropping artistry of his classic live recordings. But the San Quentin set also revealed a creeping malaise of carnival-act frivolity. The great bluesman now spent more time playing the ham. He handed longer solos to his sidemen and played fewer, shorter solos himself. He talked more. He sang less. Playing with the big band at the Apollo, by contrast, forced B.B. to reprise the no-nonsense, high-energy showmanship he had commanded three decades earlier. But B.B.'s weary voice on *Live at the Apollo* betrayed all of his sixty-five years. On such fast-tempo shuffles as "Paying the Cost to Be the Boss," the boss struggled to keep up.

As a concession to B.B.'s advancing age and ebbing energy, Sid Seidenberg gradually slackened the crazy pace of his concert itinerary. B.B. had averaged around 300 gigs a year through the 1980s. He would cut back dramatically in the early 1990s, playing 250 dates in some years, fewer than 200 in others. To hedge against the artist's dwindling strength, Seidenberg expanded B.B.'s commercial portfolio. B.B. played for Budweiser in Japan, for electronics giant JVC in Newport, and for Seagram's in New Orleans. He pitched personal computers for Commodore and the McChicken sandwich for McDonald's, "the one with that downhome taste." He played guitar with cartoon family the Simpsons.

Visitors to Seidenberg's office in Midtown Manhattan invariably left bearing bag loads of swag. Seidenberg "was, like, the original merchandiser," recalled Tina France, his longtime secretary. "We had pins. We had picks. We had necklaces, flashlights. It could be knives, it could be world maps," all emblazoned with logos for B.B. King and Sidney A. Seidenberg, Inc.

On May 3, 1991, B.B. returned to Beale Street in Memphis to open B.B. King's Blues Club, the first link in an eventual chain of home-cookin' eateries with live music. The day marked a new revenue stream for B.B. and the arrival of Beale Street as a legitimate destination on the Memphis tourist circuit.

After decades as a center of African American rhythm and blues, Beale had fallen into a deep, desolate slumber. The federal government had wishfully declared the district a National Historic Landmark in 1966, a local redevelopment effort commenced in 1973, and Congress named Beale the "Home of the Blues" in 1977. B.B. performed to six thousand people at the inaugural Memphis in May street festival that year, marking a sort of turning point. But Beale endured a belabored rebirth. When music writer Ed Ward visited the fabled strip in 1982, he observed, "It's only 11 at night, and as we stand staring down the short length of Beale Street, the loudest sound in the immediate area is a piece of paper, scraping against the pavement as the wind urges it along ahead of the thunderstorm that's brewing."

Many great Mississippi bluesmen had migrated north to Chicago, which, congressional proclamations notwithstanding, enjoyed a nearly unrivaled claim as home of the blues in the 1970s and 1980s. But Muddy and Wolf were dead. That left B.B. and Memphis.

The late Elvis and his Graceland mansion still ruled the Memphis tourist circuit. Elvis and Graceland and the old Sun Studios were great attractions, but they were largely white attractions, synonymous with rock 'n' roll. Now, with the city's embrace of B.B. King, Memphis forged a new identity, a majority-Black city reclaiming its mantle as a center of African American music. Memphis had Al Green, one of the greatest soul artists of the 1970s and pastor of his own Memphis church; and Stax Records, the defunct label of Otis Redding, Sam & Dave, and Isaac Hayes; and Beale Street.

The Memphis business community was slow to embrace a revital-ized Beale Street. "Nobody wanted to invest, because just about every-thing on Beale Street had failed," recalled Tommy Peters, a Memphis entrepreneur who stepped in to run B.B.'s namesake club. Yet, by the 1991 opening, a few dozen businesses had launched in the historic district, many drawn by B.B.'s name. The ribbon-cutting ceremony blossomed into a full-fledged civic event. City leaders presented B.B. a key to the city (his second). "I'm as happy now as I've ever been in my life," B.B. said at a mobbed press conference. "I hope this club will be the home of the blues all over the world."

The next month delivered B.B. a chilling reminder of what it meant to be Black in Mississippi. As the band prepared to perform its annual Homecoming concert at B.B. King Park in Indianola, a white woman strode up to Lora Walker in the parked van where she sat. "Are you Polly Walker?" the white woman asked, referring to Lora's mother.

"No, ma'am," Lora replied.

"Do you know Polly Walker?"

"Yes, ma'am."

"Do you know Sherman Darby?"

"Yes," Lora replied.

"Well, if Polly Walker don't want to see Sherman Darby lynched, she'd better get him."

B.B.'s gruff road manager "didn't have any tact," Lora recalled. Whatever Darby said to the white woman in the park had "probably cut her off at the kneecaps." The woman's response chilled Lora to the bone.

Two months later, on July 4, 1991, Memphians reconvened to dedicate a new National Civil Rights Museum on the hallowed grounds of the old, segregated Lorraine Motel, on whose balcony Martin Luther King Jr. had been fatally shot in 1968. The museum would one day rival both Beale and Graceland as the city's top tourist destination.

FOR B.B.'S FIRST STUDIO album after the abysmal *King of the Blues 1989*, Sid Seidenberg returned to Stewart Levine, B.B.'s finest producer since Bill Szymczyk. The resulting LP, *There Is Always One More Time*, revisited the strengths of the earlier King-Levine albums. Songwriters Joe Sample and Will Jennings contributed several fine compositions, including a spirited shuffle titled "I'm Moving On" and the slow-cooker "Back in L.A." B.B. played one for Johnny Carson, the other for David Letterman, looking elegant and sounding ageless. But the most moving track was the title cut. "There Is Always One More Time" was a song about mortality, with lyrics by B.B.'s friend Doc Pomus, cowriter of the *Better World* album, who was dying of lung cancer. B.B. sang the new song with startling conviction. Levine played the recording over the phone to Doc in his hospital bed. When the song ended, Doc was too choked up to tell B.B. how much he liked it. Doc Pomus died the next day. "It's almost like a fuckin' movie," Levine recalled. B.B. dedicated the album to Doc's memory.

B.B.'s own pace was slowing. By Sid Seidenberg's careful count, B.B. played 173 concerts in 1992 and 163 in 1993, possibly the first time his annual gig tally dipped below 200. Nonetheless, the tireless bluesman still played more shows and logged more miles than almost anyone else in the business. After a show in Israel around this time, B.B. and his band spent twenty-six hours in an airplane, traveling via Alaska to Detroit for the next performance. "Went straight from the airport to the gig," recalled James "Boogaloo" Bolden, the trumpeter. "Went straight to the club. Played three shows that night. Everybody was beat. We finished about four o'clock in the morning." As B.B.'s musicians collapsed around him, he signed autographs through the dawn.

B.B. had battled weight gain since middle age. In the early 1990s, he tipped the scale at three hundred pounds, far too heavy for a man of five ten. He was not controlling his diabetes. In 1992, one of B.B.'s musicians confided in Tommy Peters, "I don't know how long B.B.'s gonna make it." Peters, owner of B.B. King's Blues Club, caught up with B.B. on his bus after a Memphis show. "He was in terrible shape," Peters recalled. "His ankles were swollen. I told him, 'B.B., I want to come meet with you in the morning.'"

Peters had reached out to the Pritikin Longevity Center, a chain of weight-loss clinics favored by celebrities. The next day, Peters arrived at B.B.'s Peabody Hotel suite with an armload of Pritikin pamphlets. He laid the paperwork out on B.B.'s bed and made his case for B.B. to enroll at the clinic. B.B. didn't say much, Peters recalled: "But I could tell that he was taking it all in. He knew that if he didn't do something, he wasn't gonna be around much longer." Not long after, Sid Seidenberg telephoned Peters for more information. Seidenberg and B.B. traveled together to a Pritikin clinic in Miami. B.B. embraced the Pritikin regimen, trimming most meat and fat from his diet.

After that act of intervention, Tommy Peters was B.B.'s friend for life: B.B. never forgot an act of kindness. The next time they saw each other, at the MCA studios in Los Angeles, B.B. strode up to Peters and embraced him, proclaiming, "Son, I think you've given me at least fifteen more years of life." B.B. had shed sixty pounds. He confided more quietly, "Man, you've made it work again." Among other benefits, the Pritikin diet restored B.B.'s virility.

B.B. was in Los Angeles working on an ambitious new project.

The rise of the compact disc in the 1980s had redefined the long-playing album, nearly doubling its potential length. The medium spawned sprawling compilation albums and lavish box sets. In 1991, Polydor Records packed seventy-one James Brown songs onto four discs of *Star Time*, a set so compelling that it triggered a reappraisal of Brown's career. B.B. and his MCA label responded in the fall of 1992 with *King of the Blues*, four discs boasting seventy-seven songs that spanned six decades, starting with the 1949 Bullet Records single "Miss Martha King" and ending with five tracks from the U2 era. The collection was solid, well annotated, and well received but incomplete. The first disc covered the years 1949 to 1966: B.B.'s most important decade, the 1950s, thus occupied less than one disc. Andy McKaie, who produced the compilation, battled with multiple companies for access to the old Bihari recordings, which no longer belonged to the Biharis. Jules Bihari, dying of cancer, had sold the Modern Records catalog in 1984 to Nashville investors for a mere $375,000. The recordings changed hands again before fetching $1.8 million in 1990 from a consortium that included Virgin Records in the Americas and Ace Records, a specialty imprint, in Britain and Europe. McKaie gained permission to use just eight songs, including the chart-toppers "3 O'Clock Blues," "Please Love Me," and "You Upset Me Baby." He made the best of what he had, but by the third and fourth discs, *King of the Blues* wore thin. Music critics offered unequivocal praise for the package, unaware that much of B.B.'s best work was missing. By 1992, most of B.B.'s Modern Records catalog was long forgotten.

Along with box sets, the 1990s brought a bumper crop of all-star duets. For B.B.'s next studio album, *Blues Summit*, producers proposed to pair him with more than a dozen stars of his genre. Andy McKaie, the box-set producer, presented the *Summit* idea to B.B. at his Las Vegas home. "We started throwing names back and forth to each other," McKaie recalled. "We got virtually everybody we wanted." Recorded in Nashville and Berkeley, California, in early 1993, *Blues Summit* teamed B.B. with seemingly every living blues master who could still hold a microphone, wisely favoring artistry over marketability. Older fans delighted in hearing him sing "There's Something on Your Mind" with Etta James and "You're the Boss" with Ruth Brown. Nearly all of B.B.'s guests were African Americans, a choice that spoke volumes about where the great bluesman had come from and where his heart still dwelt. B.B.'s ribald repartee with his female collaborators brought the recordings to life. "He flirted with every one of them," McKaie recalled. The album's only real flaw lay in B.B.'s voice, which sounded ragged and hoarse on some cuts. Then again, B.B. was pushing seventy.

IN THE SPRING of 1994, B.B. traveled to China, a destination that had eluded him for decades. Commerce, rather than diplomacy, bridged its borders. Art Levitt, head of the Hard Rock Cafe chain, invited B.B. to perform at the May 14 opening of one of its rock 'n' roll kitsch restaurants in Beijing. Sid Seidenberg organized a far-flung Far East tour. B.B. returned to Australian cities he had conquered with U2. He played several dates in Japan and performed at Hard Rock venues in Taiwan and Singapore.

"My father wanted to break into China as a market," recalled Larry Seidenberg, Sid's son, who joined in the trip. But B.B. arrived to find that most of China already knew him. He loaded up on gadgets in Hong Kong, and he handed out guitar picks atop the Great Wall.

"I'm just happy to be here, and that the government let us play," B.B. said gamely. "Hopefully, the Chinese government officials will get out and boogie a little, too." China proved as repressive as the Soviet Union: government agents screened B.B.'s songs in advance after carefully translating the lyrics, struggling to find exact Mandarin equivalents for such blues idioms as "rock me, baby." At the Hard Rock, B.B. played a two-hour set to a handpicked audience of three hundred Beijing VIPs beneath a ceiling painted, Sistine Chapel style, with images of the Beatles, Rolling Stones, Elvis, and Chairman Mao. B.B. could not stir party officials to dance alongside the younger Chinese civilians and expatriates in the packed crowd. Outside the club, droves of actual B.B. King fans clustered at the door, unable to gain entry. Among them was China's biggest rock star, Cui Jian, who waited for an hour before leaving in a huff. "I think they are kissing the government's butt," he fumed. B.B. learned of the snub and anguished at the thought of heavy-handed guards turning away fans, but he said nothing. The rock star's protests made headlines, and not the kind B.B. or Seidenberg had wanted.

B.B. HAD NOT YET PENNED A MEMOIR. Charles Sawyer's biography now lay fifteen years in the past. In 1995, Avon Books announced plans to publish B.B.'s story in his own words. The cowriter was David Ritz, a white New Yorker who had emerged as the more or less official biographer of African American rhythm and blues. Ritz had cowritten memoirs with Ray Charles, Smokey Robinson, and Etta James. His posthumous Marvin Gaye biography, *Divided Soul*, was a classic. Ritz first glimpsed B.B. in 1957 at a Dallas club, where the teenaged Ritz was the only white patron. He first met B.B. ten years later in Buffalo, the introduction courtesy of his friend Charles Keil, author of *Urban Blues*. Ritz's literary collaboration with B.B. commenced after a chance meeting in 1993 at a Pritikin center, where Ritz watched B.B. and Etta James pick glumly at meals of boiled potato and fish. (Ritz was there as the soul diva's biographer.) The publisher promised a story spanning "the creativity, turbulence and excitement of a half century of musical evolution." Ritz commenced months of interviews, crisscrossing the country with B.B. on his tour bus.

B.B. spent the autumn of 1995 celebrating his seventieth birthday. At a September gig in Nashville, the Gibson guitar company presented him with the latest iteration of Lucille. The next month in Memphis,

B.B. jammed with Willie Nelson, Bobby Bland, Isaac Hayes, and Buddy Guy in an all-star tribute. A hometown paper put B.B.'s picture on its front page. When B.B. saw it, he gazed at the paper for a long time. Then he put it down and turned to Stafford Davis, his security aide. "Back when I first came here," B.B. said, "you knew that if they put your picture on the front page of the paper, it's to invite people to a lynching."

In December, Bill and Hillary Clinton presented Kennedy Center Honors to B.B. and four other icons of the arts, including playwright Neil Simon and actor Sidney Poitier, at a black-tie dinner in Washington. A-list celebrities queued up to meet the great bluesman. But the ceremony left B.B. feeling out of place, pinching the same nerve of unworthiness he had felt at Yale and the Fillmore. A chat with his fellow honorees calmed his nerves.

"We all came up similar," B.B. marveled to a reporter. "I was sitting next to Neil Simon, and he was telling me how we all started with nothing, how we all wanted to make it, how we all worked hard to make it. Some day, maybe I'll feel like I made it."

President Clinton introduced himself to B.B., telling the bluesman, "I saw you play once." B.B. thanked the president, wondering if he was being serious. Clinton continued, "I saw you at the Robeson Auditorium in Little Rock. I saw you and Bobby Bland there together." B.B. would visit the White House seven times during the Clinton years, collecting awards, delivering historic performances, and jamming with the nation's saxophonist in chief.

In the summer of 1996, politicians and press gathered at a new Memphis Welcome Center to unveil twin bronze statues of the city's two great musical sons, B.B. King and Elvis Presley. B.B.'s statue depicted him from about twenty years earlier, tall and trim in a rumpled suit, wincing with expressive effort as he squeezed a plaintive note from Lucille. Elvis looked positively youthful, wiry and taut as a high-school athlete, fringed Native American jumpsuit unlaced to midchest, acoustic guitar hanging casually at his side. B.B.'s statue was new. Elvis was merely refurbished: carved by a different sculptor, his statue had sat on Beale Street since 1980, ravaged by weather and fans, who couldn't resist breaking off strands of fringe from his Western shirt. The unveiling seemed to mark a moment of parity between B.B. and Elvis and between the city's Black and white musical traditions.

B.B. worked with Seidenberg to build the B.B. King brand. He hawked Smoky Bacon Cheeseburgers for Wendy's, beer for Budweiser, and a new line of blue M&M's, odd choices for a diabetic. (His pitches for Northwest Airlines and the Greyhound bus company rang more true.) In the summer of 1996, B.B. performed at the Olympics in Atlanta and played for U.S. troops in Bosnia. A second B.B. King's Blues Club had opened in Los Angeles. "B.B. is a conglomerate operation," Sid Seidenberg crowed. "We have fifteen employees, payroll, taxes, licensing of various products, posters, T-shirts, neckties."

Up to that point, the B.B. King story had been told in dribs and drabs. Keil had laid out a few bare facts in the 1960s with *Urban Blues*. Charles Sawyer's *Arrival of B.B. King*, in 1980, was light on formal biography, leaving space for a lengthy travelogue and in-depth analyses of B.B.'s musical style and Delta heritage. Much remained to be said. B.B. spent many months on the road with David Ritz, who patiently transcribed his life narrative from hundreds of hours of tape and then retold it in polished prose. B.B. lacked either the skills or confidence to review the manuscript on paper, so Ritz recited the entire book to him on B.B.'s tour bus as it rolled through the Midwest. He reached the last page as they pulled in to Des Moines. When Ritz finished, B.B. turned to his collaborator and said, "Beautiful. Thank you." B.B. did not ask him to change a word. Sid Seidenberg asked only that Ritz delete B.B.'s self-description as "dirty old man," though B.B.'s own stories seemed to bear it out.

The B.B. King of *Blues All Around Me*, released in the fall of 1996, taught by example. He offered scores of anecdotes, descriptive details, and stray facts that added up to a rich portrait of a complex man. Yet, in order to draw any conclusions about what made that man tick, the reader was forced into the role of armchair therapist: B.B. steadfastly refused to explore his own essential traits. B.B. revealed that he stuttered as a child, an affliction that might bespeak ancient trauma or suppressed rage, themes he then neglected to explore. "I have pleasant acquaintances with thousands of people the world over," B.B. wrote. "But few, if any, really know me. And that includes my own family. It's not that they don't want to; it's because I keep my feelings to myself." That was perhaps the most telling admission in *Blues All Around Me*.

"No one can tell the whole truth about himself," author W. Somerset Maugham wrote in his own autobiography, *The Summing Up*. B.B. tried, and David Ritz tried harder, laboring for months to draw the bluesman out. *Blues All Around Me* was the most B.B. King would ever say about himself. The rest of the story lay where it always had, etched within the grooves of his records.

B.B. dedicated the book to his children, whom he listed by name. For most of two decades, B.B. had told interviewers he was a father of eight. Five new children, all grown, staked paternity claims during the years of U2-inspired revival. Two more arrived in the early 1990s, bringing the total to fifteen. B.B. finally acknowledged that not all of them were biologically his, telling reporters the late-arriving children were "adopted." A few, including sons Willie and Leonard, had lived and worked with B.B. for years. Others he treated more like glorified VIPs, comping them tickets and receiving them as backstage guests when he visited their towns.

"He was born at a time when Black men didn't have money and didn't own land," recalled Stafford Davis, B.B.'s long-serving aide. "Children were a type of wealth," a currency that B.B. never forgot.

Yet, by labeling some of his children as adopted, B.B. sowed discord in his sprawling family. The eight original children clashed with their new siblings, each contingent wary of the other. "Every time my dad got more famous, I found out about a new sister," lamented Shirley King, the longest-tenured (if not quite the oldest) of B.B.'s children. "Now, three of us was born in 1949. Three was born in 1967. And I find that amazing, because my father couldn't have kids by his first wife, he couldn't have kids by his second wife, and all of a sudden he's a baby machine."

Fifteen children meant endless permutations of sibling rivalry. B.B.'s offspring squabbled in posh hotel lobbies and battled over the right to visit their father backstage, everyone desperate for access, recognition, and cash.

"They are not just draining his bank account. They are draining him physically and emotionally," recalled Lora Walker. "There are fistfights in hotel rooms. He is getting barred from hotels because of their behavior. They are embarrassing him in front of important people."

B.B. finally decided fifteen children were enough, even for him. Now, when a stranger approached him with a paternity claim, B.B. pressed for details: Who was the mother? Where and when had they met? He would check the facts against The Book, his tome of past paramours. Then he would politely reply, "No, I'm sorry, I'm not your father." He never took on another child.

In the summer of 1996, B.B. rented out half of a Days Inn in Greenville, Mississippi, to host a King family reunion, enough Kings to fill two buses, bringing his fifteen children together for the first time. B.B. led the entourage to Kilmichael to see the old Cartledge farm, Luther Henson's schoolhouse, and his mother's grave. B.B. wore a white cap that read, "#1 Grandpa." He reveled in family.

"He was showing the place that he had come from, trying to help the family understand who he was," Shirley King recalled. B.B. told his assembled children that he "wanted this family to be his legacy. He wanted this family to carry on and respect what he did": "He wanted us to be one."

He also wanted them to stop fighting. A few of B.B.'s children had arrived at the reunion with a list of other children they wanted him to disown. They challenged him to draw a line between the real children and the pretenders. At a sprawling family dinner, B.B. confronted them.

"Since there seems to be an issue with some of y'all over who is and who's not," he said, "I'd like to do a DNA test, if you all agree." The room fell to a hush. B.B. explained that he would not require any of his children to prove their parentage: he would provide for them in any case. But B.B. was not going to allow them to turn on each other. "So, if you want to do a DNA test," he said, "that's fine with me."

No one did. The insurrection was over.

B.B. could have admitted his infertility in his memoir. Instead, he perpetuated the fiction of fatherhood, blaming his ex-wives for failing to deliver children in marriage and lamenting what an inattentive parent he had been to his many scattered offspring born outside wedlock. Perhaps to paper over the dark secret, B.B. dwelt on sex to the point of obsession, from his prepubescent adventures with "Peaches" to his adolescent masturbation circles to his ceaseless quest to deflower farm girls to his autumnal fascination with pornography.

"After he gave up drinking," David Ritz recalled, "I think sex became a huge compulsion in his life."

B.B.'s tireless assistants now schlepped bag loads of pornographic videotapes from gig to gig in addition to their time-honored role as procurers of attractive women. Even as B.B. entered his seventies, he pursued sex in all guises with renewed vigor.

"He'd rent out a floor" in his luxury hotel "and have a woman in every room on that floor, and he'd just go from room to room at various points during the evening or during his stay and see who he was gonna see," recalled Myron Johnson, a latter-day valet.

B.B. loved dirty jokes. He had a few favorites, and close friends heard them over and over. One opened with a man coveting a convertible on a Cadillac lot. A salesman walks up and asks, "Why don't you get behind the wheel?" The customer climbs in. He caresses the steering wheel, and he moans, "Mmm, mmm, mmm," as if savoring a fine meal. The salesman asks if the customer is imagining driving down the road. "No sir," the customer replies, "I'm thinking about pussy." At the punch line, B.B. would laugh until tears streamed down his cheeks.

B.B.'s memoir did not name any of the women who inhabited his life after he and Sue divorced. That was B.B.'s way of honoring her. In the later years, "there were a lot of women, hundreds of women," recalled Lora Walker. "But one woman? No."

On the penultimate page of B.B.'s memoir, he drew a fascinating parallel. He recalled a trip through Louisiana with Big Red in the 1950s. The band walked into a diner, and all the white people walked out. The white owner recognized B.B., ran outside, and cried, "It's okay, folks. This is B.B. King, the singer." The white people filed back in. Whenever a new customer arrived, the owner pointed to B.B.'s table and said, "He's all right. He's B.B. King, the singer." Two decades later, the band was traveling through Europe by train. The train stopped in Holland. B.B.'s band walked into a café. Again, the dining room emptied. Again, the owner learned the identity of his famous patron, ran outside, and persuaded the white customers to return. "Now they're pointing and staring, and suddenly everything's cool," B.B. recalled. "Or is it?"

The juxtaposed stories showed how little had really changed. But here, again, B.B. simply laid out the facts and left the reader to react. Reviewers scoured the book for racial anger and, finding none, surmised that B.B. and his biographer had pulled their punches. Ritz, who had spent nearly two years with his subject, concluded that B.B.'s racial antipathy simply wasn't there: "He had no prejudice. For a guy who grew up in a period of American history where there was so much horror and vitriol and animus, I want to say that he came out almost unscarred. I was looking for scars. I didn't see any."

Or maybe Riley King's anger remained deep inside, concealed behind the expressive eyes and the ancient stutter, where perhaps it had always lived.

"If you hurt me," B.B. wrote, "chances are I won't tell you. I'll just move on. Moving on is my method of healing my hurt and, man, I've been moving on all my life."

CHAPTER 20

RIDING WITH THE KING

B.B. KING'S MEMOIR SOLD WELL, whetting the public's appetite for a new album. In late 1997, B.B. and Seidenberg delivered *Deuces Wild*, a second collection of collaborations that assembled some of the biggest names in pop. *Blues Summit* had dwelt in pure blues, and that was its strength. *Deuces Wild* ranged all over the map, sounding almost like tracks culled from a dozen different records. Predictably, some worked and some didn't. The opener, "If You Love Me," paired B.B. with Irish legend Van Morrison to fine effect. Then came a duet with Tracy Chapman, the young, African American singer-songwriter, on "The Thrill Is Gone." Chapman sounded great. B.B. sounded old. The third cut put B.B. with Eric Clapton, at last, on a splendid blues-pop reading of "Rock Me Baby." The rest of the tracks rose and fell on the strength of B.B.'s collaborators. Contributions from B.B.'s music-industry friends Bonnie Raitt, Dr. John, and Willie Nelson stirred the heart. Some other guests sounded outclassed. Nonetheless, *Deuces Wild* reached number 73 on the pop album chart, B.B.'s highest showing in twenty years, and number 1 on *Billboard*'s new blues album chart.

That fall, B.B. turned seventy-two. He explained to an interviewer what he wanted to give his fans, all of them: "a chance to know me almost as well as I know myself." As he approached his sixth decade as a working musician, B.B. soldiered on with the tenacity of a mountain climber, emboldened with every step to take another.

"I can tell you why he stayed on the road," said Sue King, his ex-wife. "Remember, when he started out, he wanted to make the blues acceptable. Okay, that was his goal. In the latter part of his career, every time he'd get to one level, there was an enticement from somewhere to go one more level. Every time, it was one more thing, one more level. I always think of it as a brass ring on the merry-go-round. He just couldn't stop."

Yet, by the late 1990s, a distinct theme of decline had crept into B.B.'s concerts. At a show in Dallas, B.B. "simply couldn't find the groove," the reviewer opined, "and sour notes tumbled out of Lucille with alarming regularity." Several months later, in St. Louis, B.B.'s voice "was all ragged edges without the barrel-chested bottom." B.B. settled into a chair after a mere handful of songs. He introduced and reintroduced his band. Sometimes he led the audience in interminable sing-alongs. "Fun is fun," one reviewer observed, "but with tickets priced at $34.50, I'd rather hear him than me."

B.B. now traveled in a leased VanHool bus from Belgium. This ride boasted a satellite dish, a kitchen, a full bathroom, six televisions, a horseshoe-shaped couch, a queen bed, and an engine that spat out status reports on computer printouts. This was his private chariot, capable of rolling twelve hundred miles on a single tank of gas.

The band, by contrast, still crisscrossed the nation in an old-fashioned motor coach, with seats that refused to recline. Out on the festival circuit, B.B.'s bandmates noticed that most of their peers traveled in modern buses equipped with bunk beds that afforded a good night's sleep. "Everybody else on the tour, Robert Cray, the Neville Brothers, they got tour buses with beds in them," drummer Tony Coleman recalled. The other bands generally boarded the bus after a show and rode to the next city, sleeping on the bus, then checked into a hotel and slept in comfortable beds until the next night's gig. Not B.B.: he liked to return from a gig to his cluttered hotel suite, typically into the arms of a waiting female companion. He and his band would strike out for the next town in the morning, which often dawned just an hour or two later. B.B. would sleep on his bus. The musicians would toss and turn in theirs.

"So the band would be bitching, 'God damn, I'm so sick of this fuckin' bus,'" Coleman recalled. But the musicians knew better than to complain, lest they lose their jobs. B.B. was not unfeeling toward their plight: he was unaware. "If he didn't see it, it didn't happen," recalled

Walter King, his nephew. Walter sometimes bought plane tickets with his own money to avert a marathon bus ride: "I wasn't gonna put my body through such trauma." Coleman tried another tack: on a festival tour in the late '90s, he accepted an invitation to travel on a different bus, with the festival crew, who slept in beds. Word of his insurrection reached Norman Matthews, who reported back to B.B., who summoned Coleman for a meeting.

"They tell me you ridin' with the crew," B.B. apprised Coleman. "You ridin' with the crew?"

"Yeah," Coleman replied.

"You think you better than those guys?" B.B. asked, referring to the other musicians.

"No," Coleman replied, "I just like to be more comfortable than those guys."

"You don't like the bus?"

"I most certainly do not."

B.B. instructed Coleman to rejoin his fellow musicians in the band bus. Coleman refused.

"Well, I tell you what, son," B.B. replied. "If you ride the crew bus again, you can stay with the crew. You don't have a job with me."

Not for the first time, Coleman resigned. Several months later, he and B.B. crossed paths again. B.B. told the drummer he had rented a new bus for the band, with beds. He asked, "You ready to come back to work now?" Coleman rejoined.

OFFSTAGE, B.B. CONTINUED to amass laurels. In December 1997, he presented a guitar to Pope John Paul II and performed holiday songs at the Vatican, a concert broadcast to a reported global audience of two billion. Later that winter, he appeared in the John Landis film *Blues Brothers 2000*, a forgettable sequel to the memorable original, from which B.B. had been excluded.

B.B. and Sid Seidenberg rushed out another record in the fall of 1998 to capitalize on the success of *Deuces Wild*. But *Blues on the Bayou* marked a conscious retreat from the commercialism of its predecessor.

Recorded on vintage equipment at a Louisiana studio with B.B.'s road band, *Bayou* sounded like an idealized version of B.B.'s live act from that era. Producers trucked in Cajun food, and musicians retreated to a fishing pond on breaks. "B.B. would do a lot of stuff off the top of his head when we recorded that album," recalled bassist Michael Doster. "The vibes were really good." The record kicked off with an instrumental, just like a B.B. King show. The performances were straightforward, with crisp horn parts penned by Walter King. The disc sounded, in fact, almost like a classic B.B. King recording of two or three decades earlier—except for Lucille. A new imprecision had blunted her attack. B.B. could no longer hit all of her notes cleanly. B.B. sputtered at the end of some solo runs and left the occasional string buzzing when it ought to be silent. He almost sounded inebriated.

"I think some of the problem was management of [B.B.'s] diabetes," Walter King recalled. "You can be like a drunk one minute, and you can be hyperactive the next. You can be extremely weak, where you can't use your fingers. The reason I know these things is because I'm a diabetic."

B.B. still played the guitar with his heart and his ears as much as with his hands. On *Bayou*, he alternately charged, strutted, and ambled through a set of B.B. originals, old and new. "I'll Survive," from the 1960 LP *King of the Blues*, took on new poignancy as an autumnal anthem. "Blues Man," a new song, was one of the sweetest things he ever recorded. "I'm a blues man," B.B. crooned, "but I'm a good man." The record earned B.B. his ninth Grammy.

Rolling Stone closed out 1998 with one of the longest features yet written on the blues king. The writer, Gerri Hirshey, reported that B.B.'s diabetes was getting worse. He had lost weight. He looked thinner, grayer, older, and wearier. "His pockets rattle with Ziploc bags of prescribed medications," *Rolling Stone* reported. He now claimed to be completely off alcohol and meat, although he also elicited titters onstage by boasting that his drink was spiked with Southern Comfort. He subsisted mostly on small, stabilizing snacks: hard-boiled eggs, butter beans, and the occasional sandwich from loyal aide Norman Matthews, washed down with Diet Cokes. By decade's end, B.B. performed entire concerts from his chair.

David Ritz had once attempted to tally the gigs B.B. had performed. Ritz gave up: such statistics were not kept in any official way. Gerri Hirshey gauged the number at "maybe 15,000." What Hirshey did not say, because it was unprovable, was that B.B. King had now probably played more concerts than anyone else in popular music. He had visited eighty-eight countries, surely another record. More than gambling or even sex, B.B. King was addicted to the road.

B.B. closed out the 1990s with customary dignity. In the autumn of 1999, he presented a copy of Lucille to President Clinton at a White House event touted as the "Concert of the Century." The show featured Eric Clapton, Al Green, country megastar Garth Brooks, and "Proud Mary" author John Fogerty. B.B. played "The Thrill Is Gone" with Clapton. When the song was over, B.B. patted the fifty-something Clapton on the shoulder and said, "You get better all the time, young man."

In October, B.B. released a new record titled *Let the Good Times Roll: The Music of Louis Jordan.* Jordan was King of the Juke Box, the great saxophonist and bandleader, a towering figure in the decades before and during B.B.'s own ascent. Stewart Levine took full advantage of the CD format, picking eighteen songs and arranging them much like Jordan's succinct and spirited originals. Several songs clocked in under three minutes. The stellar band featured saxophonists Hank Crawford and "Fathead" Newman from the old Ray Charles Orchestra, Dr. John on piano, and iconic rock 'n' roll drummer Earl Palmer. B.B. sang more than he played, and Lucille wasn't particularly missed: this was not an album of guitar blues. The performances sounded effortless. They were not. The sessions commenced while B.B. recovered from surgery to treat burst blood vessels in his eyes. He could barely see. "I had to sit in the studio with a pencil and point to every word as he was singing 'em," Levine recalled. "B.B. couldn't really read the lyrics." He probably knew most of the words by heart. But he faltered on the latter verses of "Is You Is, or Is You Ain't (My Baby)." In frustration, Levine leaned down to Dr. John at his piano and asked, "Do you want a piece of this?" The good doctor joined in, and the song became a jaunty duet.

With *Let the Good Times Roll*, B.B. had recorded three consecutive albums that could be termed artistic successes. He won his tenth

Grammy for the duet with Dr. John, in the category of best pop collaboration.

The Louis Jordan album was the last B.B. would record with Stewart Levine. But the two men remained dear friends. One night in Holland, in the summer of 2000, B.B. told Levine that Sue, his second wife, had been the love of his life. Later, back in L.A., B.B. telephoned Levine one night and said he wanted to go on a double date. B.B.'s date was Sue. He still saw her whenever he was in town, two or three times a year. Levine was a prominent producer and a great talker, and his wife was English. Levine recalled, B.B. "wanted us to come along because he wanted her," Sue, "to know that he knew people who were cultured." They went to The Mint, the historic L.A. nightclub. Both men did their best to impress Sue.

"She was a beautiful woman, you know," Levine recalled. "And she was so intelligent. And he was so happy."

BY THE CLOSE of the 1990s, B.B.'s health was tenuous. Sid Seidenberg's was worse. B.B.'s tireless manager had a bad heart and a bad hip, scheduled for surgical replacement in March 1999. Seidenberg quietly laid plans to sell his business to Floyd Lieberman, his fellow accountant and longtime deputy. Born in 1942, Lieberman had gone to work for Seidenberg in 1964, while still in college. He kept the books for thirty-five years, always in Seidenberg's shadow. Lieberman was nearly two decades younger than Seidenberg or B.B., with a compact frame, parted hair, and a full goatee. He shared Seidenberg's financial savvy and knew the inner workings of his business. By the start of 1999, Lieberman was already filling in for his ailing boss, serving as the de facto manager of Sidney A. Seidenberg, Inc.

Early that year, the two men met at a New Jersey diner to discuss terms for a handover. Seidenberg arrived with his wife, Edie. That struck Lieberman as odd: they were there to talk business. Once seated, Seidenberg announced his selling price for his share of the businesses he co-owned with B.B.: $5 million.

"Sid," Lieberman shot back, "are you out of your mind?" Lieberman was a salaried employee. He had never earned more than $175,000 a year. Seidenberg knew his deputy could never come up with $5 million. But Lieberman was ready with a counteroffer. In Seidenberg's absence, the deputy had persuaded B.B. to sign a new management contract. In effect, Lieberman had already supplanted his boss. Lieberman revealed the contract to Seidenberg. "You're lucky if you get $500,000 from me," he crowed. Edie Seidenberg began to cry. The Seidenbergs excused themselves from the table and went outside. Sid returned alone.

"Listen," Lieberman offered peaceably. "Where am I gonna get five million? You know what you paid me over the years. I'll give you one million." Seidenberg agreed.

In May 1999, Seidenberg suffered a heart attack. Surgeons performed triple bypass surgery. He spent time in rehab and then returned to his home in New Jersey. He was alive, but his days managing B.B. King were over. In January 2000, Seidenberg announced his replacement.

Seidenberg's tenure ended, and Lieberman's began, on a triumphal note. In January 2000, the managers blocked off an unprecedented eight weeks in B.B.'s schedule to record an album with Eric Clapton.

The notion of B.B. and Clapton recording together had floated around since their first fateful meeting in 1967. Whenever the blues travelers found themselves in the same place, Clapton recalled, "we'd try to get together and play," always promising each other they would make a record together. But years turned to decades, and the record never materialized. Finally, around 1998, Clapton had an epiphany. "I thought, I love this man, and I don't know how many opportunities we're going to have." Clapton would make it happen. He tendered an invitation. B.B. gleefully accepted. Clapton's last three records had gone platinum. His 1992 single "Tears in Heaven," cowritten with onetime B.B. collaborator Will Jennings, had reached number 2 on the pop singles chart. Clapton was hot.

The cover of the resulting album, *Riding with the King*, pictured Clapton at the wheel of a convertible and a serene B.B. stretched across the backseat. And that was more or less how the sessions played out.

Clapton took the lead, selecting a mix of new songs and B.B. King classics from the Modern Records vaults. "We'd try a contemporary song and then, when it was getting difficult, just as a moment of light relief, we'd do something from B.B.'s past," Clapton recalled. The sessions for *Riding with the King* alternated deftly between new and old.

Clapton would put on an old B.B. King record for the studio band to hear. "And then Eric would start playing," recalled Joe Sample, B.B.'s longtime collaborator, who took part. "Then, next thing you know, I had joined in, then [bassist] Nathan East joined in . . . then suddenly the whole band was playing, and Eric would say 'Turn on the tape!'" to begin recording. "They actually pulled the vocal mics right in front of them as they were sitting there playing the guitars. Never seen that in ages."

The album's titular opener was a lovely song penned in the 1980s by John Hiatt, the Americana singer-songwriter, reinvented here as a triumphant anthem. From there, the two guitarists glided effortlessly back to "Ten Long Years," an RPM single from 1955. Aside from the shimmering production, the song sounded as if it could have been recorded in the Eisenhower era, down to the vintage guitar salvos from Clapton, B.B., and various studio axe-men.

On *Riding with the King*, Clapton effectively reintroduced blues listeners to B.B.'s greatest body of work, the incendiary singles he had cut with the Bihari brothers. Clapton treasured the lost classics "Help the Poor," "Days of Old," and "When My Heart Beats like a Hammer," songs that few contemporary fans or critics had ever heard.

"Eric is a musicologist," recalled Nathan East, the bassist on *Riding with the King*. "He's one of the most serious musicologists I know. The mission was to try to come up with things that weren't so obvious."

Even "3 O'Clock Blues," B.B.'s first number 1 hit from 1952, was a revelation. Clapton took the first verse, and he sang it with earnest fervor. B.B. and Clapton traded gentlemanly solos across an eight-minute jam. The friendly rivalry inspired some of the sharpest solos and fiercest vocals B.B. would deliver in his autumn years. Juxtaposed with such magnificence, the "contemporary" numbers sounded oddly pedestrian and out of place. But Hiatt's wonderful "Riding with the

King" and its attendant video drove sales, which ultimately topped four million. Released in the summer of 2000, *Riding with the King* collected a Grammy and reached number 3 on the *Billboard* album chart, making it B.B.'s first and only top-ten pop album.

Once again, B.B. entered a new decade on a wave of commercial and artistic revival. *Riding with the King* was a success for Clapton and "a very, very big success" for B.B., Floyd Lieberman recalled. B.B. had earned a platinum-record award just once before, for his million-selling 1973 collection *The Best of B.B. King.* Lieberman secured a fifty-fifty split for B.B. and Clapton on royalties for *Riding with the King,* over the objections of Clapton's managers, who thought "Eric was doing a favor for B.B." and deserved a larger share, Lieberman recalled. B.B. also reaped songwriter royalties as the composer of four songs.

Sid Seidenberg had set himself up as part owner of B.B.'s various businesses, including Kingsid Ventures for licensing his name on T-shirts and restaurant menus and Sounds of Lucille for music publishing. Lieberman preserved that lucrative arrangement, and he claimed Seidenberg's 20 percent cut of B.B.'s earnings: 15 percent as his manager, 5 percent as his accountant. He negotiated a better deal for B.B. with his booking agents, trimming their commission from 10 percent to 7.5 percent. He raised B.B.'s asking price to appear in television and magazine ads to $500,000: Seidenberg had generally settled for $25,000 or less.

"And the money started coming in," Lieberman recalled. "Big time."

IN LATE 2000, just in time for the holidays, MCA Records released a compilation of thirty-four B.B. King songs titled *Anthology.* The collection was fine, so far as it went, which was back to 1962, when B.B. started at ABC-Paramount. True fans could seek out the latest releases from Ace Records. The British imprint produced a series of splendid B.B. King discs starting in the 1980s, focusing on his epic Modern Records sides. Then came *The Vintage Years,* a four-disc box set released by Ace in 2002. With 106 songs and a seventy-four-page book, even this was not a definitive B.B. King collection: it ended where MCA's *Anthology* began. But anyone who purchased both sets could finally hear B.B.'s five-decade career in its entirety. The Ace set spanned an era that yielded more than one hundred singles on the RPM and Kent labels, thirty-eight of which charted as rhythm-and-blues hits. As a document of artistry, *The Vintage Years* was probably the most important summation of B.B.'s recorded career to date and certainly the greatest compilation. Yet, in the United States, the British compilation passed almost unnoticed.

IN HINDSIGHT, B.B.'s jubilant autumnal jams with Clapton on *Riding with the King* seem well timed. In the new millennium, the years finally caught up with the King.

B.B. had been steadily narrowing his repertoire, paring down his solos, and talking more between songs. At some imperceptible moment, those concessions came to define his shows. A B.B. King concert of this era was less *Live at the Regal* and more *Prairie Home Companion*: a lot of talk, cornball humor, and sing-alongs, interspersed with the occasional song or song fragment. The concerts' dwindling quality, coupled with B.B.'s frequent onstage declamations of his many infirmities, naturally prompted interviewers to ask why he continued to tour. B.B. would reply that his life was the road, that he didn't know what else to do, that touring was the only way to ensure his fans would hear his songs. And B.B. was still padding his cumulative fortune, now well into seven figures. (The exact figure probably lay between $5 million and $10 million.)

Commerce, rather than artistry, now seemed to steer the B.B. King enterprise. He released a forgettable holiday album in the winter of 2001, *A Christmas Celebration of Hope* (a collection that, however ephemeral, snagged two more Grammys for B.B.). He presided over a pocket kingdom of five blues clubs. He appeared in ads for diabetes products—and also for the King Supreme, a feast of cholesterol and sodium from Burger King. A reporter from the *Wall Street Journal* asked B.B.'s new manager to explain why a vegetarian diabetic would tout the King Supreme. "We don't swear that we eat this product," Floyd Lieberman replied archly. "You think Bill Cosby walks around eating

Jell-O all the time?" When Burger King executives read Lieberman's comments, they pulled the ads.

When it really counted, B.B. could still bring the magic. He delivered a devastating "Sweet Sixteen" at Radio City Music Hall in February 2003, part of a marathon "Salute to the Blues" that gathered nearly every ambulatory blues legend onto a single stage. A month later, the *New York Times* declared B.B. "the last of the great bluesmen" in a sprawling profile by journalist Bernard Weinraub, who tapped the great blues writer Peter Guralnick to explain why B.B. mattered. "Almost single-handedly," Guralnick offered, "B.B. King introduced the blues to white America." Later that year, as if on cue, *Rolling Stone* named B.B. the third-greatest guitarist of all time, behind Jimi Hendrix and Duane Allman, both long dead. Ergo, B.B. King was the greatest living guitarist.

B.B.'s towering legend cut an ever-sharper contrast to the sad reality of a B.B. King show. In the winter of 2003–4, B.B. toured Florida with a flu so severe that he could barely talk, let alone sing. A critic termed a Jacksonville show "a night of single notes." A Toronto reviewer described the swelling entourage that now escorted the frail bluesman from gig to gig. "Although the bus was parked no more than three metres from the hall's back door," the newsman wrote, "King was bundled against the elements—thick overcoat, scarf, newsboy cap. As a towel was laid out at the foot of the bus door against the snow on the unplowed lot, a handler knocked to the ground the icicles that hung over the building's entrance. From there, surrounded by doting male helpers, King slowly shuffled through featureless hallways, all neutral colours and industrial carpeting, to find his way to the side of the stage. Once there, in darkness, he sipped from a plastic cup of water as assistants stripped him of his winter clothing." A month later, in Montana, B.B. told an interviewer he couldn't recall where he had been two weeks earlier.

Offstage, B.B.'s life was a parade of accolades. In the spring of 2004, Sweden's King Carl XVI Gustaf presented him with the Polar Music Prize, the Nobel of music. In February 2005, B.B. visited the Mississippi Capitol in Jackson for a long and tearful ceremony to mark a statewide B.B. King Day. The penniless sharecropper was now his state's most famous living resident, cast at the center of a campaign to market Mississippi and its blues heritage. (Seven years later, Mississippi would begin stamping Lucille on license plates.) "I've met kings and presidents," B.B. told the assembled lawmakers. "I've had a lot of honors. But none means quite so much to me as this, because I'm home now." A few months after that, in Memphis, B.B. attended a ceremony to rename a stretch of U.S. 61 as "B.B. King Highway."

ON A TOUR STOP OUTSIDE Chicago in March 2005, Martha Lee Davison came to see B.B. on his bus. B.B.'s ex-wife was seventy-five. She had raised seven children with her second husband, Rufus Davison, a distant relation of B.B. (The genetic link was Pomp Davidson, B.B.'s long-dead grandfather, whose name B.B. sometimes used to check into hotels incognito.) However acrimonious the couple's parting, B.B. and Martha remained friends. A cherished Davison family photo, taken on a previous visit, shows Martha sitting on B.B.'s lap, a few decades older than the shy teen in their staid wedding portrait, flashing a radiant smile.

Inside the bus, Martha dropped a bombshell. She told B.B. he was the father of her oldest son, Danny, born after the divorce. She said she had hidden Danny's parentage for half a century, but now she wanted him to know the truth. Twenty or thirty years earlier, B.B. might have accepted her claim without question. Now, B.B. told Martha the family should seek a DNA test: that would give them peace of mind. For reasons of their own, they never did.

Martha Lee Davison would die three years later, at seventy-eight. After her death, surviving children thickened the plot of paternity surrounding the marriage. They said Martha had given birth to twins during her years with Riley, but the babies had died in infancy. Was the family revealing a tragic secret, or had Martha planted the story to help her former husband sustain his fatherhood narrative?

B.B. had remained fond of Martha, but Sue was the love of his life. Around this time, B.B. invited his second ex-wife to attend his annual Mississippi Homecoming. One night in Indianola, B.B. planted Sue in the front row and serenaded her from the stage with an intensely personal performance of "The Thrill Is Gone," the song he had recorded for her. "There was no mistaking what he was doing," recalled Allan Hammons, B.B.'s friend. "He looked straight into her eyes."

The great bluesman could conceal the creeping symptoms of diabetic fog, could still power through a song in a high-stakes setting. He could not, however, hide his decline in a ninety-minute show. B.B. would play about 160 dates in 2005, perhaps the smallest total of any year in his career, with a five-week winter layoff for cataract surgery, time B.B. passed watching Roy Rogers movies in his Las Vegas home. He adopted a rough schedule of three weeks on, three weeks off, allowing more time to stretch out at home and catch up on *The Young and the Restless*, a soap opera to which he was so addicted that he stockpiled episodes on three recorders. When he traveled in the post-9/11 world, the bluesman favored his tour bus over airports and airplanes, despite the toll long road trips exacted on his bad back.

The greatest living guitarist followed a stage-show formula that one Minneapolis reviewer termed "50 percent comic, 25 percent singer and 25 percent guitarist." Even that calculation presumed B.B. followed a script, rather than repeatedly and unpredictably straying from it. In January 2006, he halted a show in Boston and spent several minutes talking to a female fan in the front row who had distracted him. Such interludes unsettled more than they amused, and they were becoming frequent.

B.B.'s MANAGEMENT and label celebrated his eightieth birthday, September 16, 2005, with an album titled *80* and credited to B.B. King & Friends. B.B. now recorded for Geffen Records. MCA had purchased the namesake imprint of producer David Geffen in 1990. But the Geffen label performed so well that it ultimately devoured its parent, and MCA ceased to exist.

Considering B.B.'s diminished powers, his new record was as good as could be expected, with the likes of Van Morrison, Eric Clapton, Elton John, and Sheryl Crow pitching in on vocal and instrumental chores. B.B. sounded ten years younger than the croaking crooner of prior releases. The opening collaboration with Irish soul shouter Morrison, on the prewar blues song "Early in the Morning," ranked among the finest latter-day performances in either man's catalog. Morrison himself, a noted curmudgeon, proved less than cordial, pacing the floor, grumbling, and walking in circles like a ruminating poet during idle moments in his session. Upon the Irishman's departure, B.B. turned to his producers and asked, "When I become a big rock star, can I act like that?" The album hit number 45 on the pop album chart, B.B.'s best showing since the Clapton collaboration. B.B. reaped another Grammy.

B.B.'s landmark birthday passed amid a flurry of commemoration. A new coffee-table book, *The B.B. King Treasures*, retold B.B.'s life story in condensed form, largely through his own words, alongside a trove of images and artifacts culled from across his career: The overall effect was something like a museum bound into a book.

WHEN B.B. DEPARTED for a two-legged European tour in the spring of 2006, he told his fans it would be his last. "B.B. was getting older," Floyd Lieberman recalled. So was his entourage. "And I was afraid, because there were a lot of incidents." A year or two earlier in Italy, Norman Matthews had appeared at Lieberman's hotel room with an unstaunchable nosebleed. Matthews had spent a week in a hospital as Italian doctors struggled to control his blood pressure.

B.B. touched down in England in March and performed in Sheffield and Manchester, Birmingham and Bournemouth. At Wembley Arena in London, "he looked terrible," a reviewer wrote. "After 12 minutes of inconsequential noodling from his band, Riley 'Blues Boy' King was helped onto stage by a platoon of minders. Obese and barely able to waddle, the king of the blues betrayed every last one of his 80 years, before he slumped into a chair that would not have been out of place at a school assembly." Then B.B. leaned in to the microphone and growled, "I know exactly what you're thinking. You're looking at ol' B.B. and you're thinking, 'Ol' B.B. can't cut it any more, he can't even stand.' And you know what? You're right. I'm diabetic, I got a bad back, my knees have gone and I can't remember a thing." He proceeded into a set that was more stories than songs.

The tour resumed in July with dates in Spain, Italy, and France. At the Montreux Jazz Festival in Switzerland, B.B. jammed with singer Gladys Knight, guitarists John McLaughlin and Stanley Clarke, and pianists Joe Sample and George Duke. "Maybe I should quit every night," he joked. Back home, B.B. teased crowds with hints that he was finished touring altogether, seeding speculation in the press. It wasn't true: B.B. seemed to be leveraging the threat of retirement as another rhetorical ploy to coax a reaction from the crowd, a pursuit that now occupied the better part of his shows. B.B. routinely interrupted songs after a single verse, lacking the attention span to complete them. His nightly monologue included the prediction "the papers are gonna kill me tomorrow" for talking too much during shows, a prophecy he then proceeded to fulfill. Offstage, B.B. increasingly relied on a wheelchair. Manager Floyd Lieberman pared back his schedule to just over one hundred performances a year.

"These days," one reviewer sighed, "attending a B.B. King concert is a little like visiting Mount Rushmore. You go to bear witness to its majesty. You don't expect it to move around much."

The Rushmore analogy was apt: by 2006, B.B. King was very nearly the last living icon of his musical era. Sarah Vaughan had died in 1990, Miles Davis in 1991, Ella Fitzgerald in 1996, Frank Sinatra in 1998, John Lee Hooker in 2001, Ray Charles in 2004. B.B. had wept at Brother Ray's funeral. James Brown would pass by year's end. Over the years, B.B. and Brown had traded friendly barbs about who, in fact, was the Hardest Working Man in Show Business.

"I've lost so many [friends], but I'm happy to be here," B.B. told an interviewer. "There is so much that I haven't done. At my age now, I feel like time is very short."

On May 3, 2006, Sid Seidenberg died at a hospice in Dover, New Jersey, at age eighty-one. Seidenberg had been the first to envision B.B. King as the Louis Armstrong of his era, a cultural icon whose achievements transcended his genre. B.B. never lacked the talent, the drive, or the desire to reach the top. But Seidenberg, alone among B.B.'s many artistic and commercial collaborators, divined the correct path. B.B. and Floyd Lieberman attended the funeral in New Jersey. B.B. embraced

Sid's family, but the service was tense. Edie Seidenberg, Sid's widow, forbade Lieberman to speak. Lines had been drawn.

Had Sid lived just a few months longer, he would have seen his vision's ultimate fulfillment. In December 2006, B.B. traveled to the White House to receive the Presidential Medal of Freedom, his nation's highest civilian honor. Duke Ellington had reaped the great medal in 1969, Count Basie in 1985, Ella Fitzgerald in 1992, Aretha Franklin in 2005. No blues artist—and no rock 'n' roller, Black or white—had yet donned the medal. Even Louis Armstrong didn't have one.

"He came up the hard way," said President George W. Bush, introducing B.B. "He's still touring, and he's still recording, and he's still singing, and he's still playing the blues better than anybody else. In other words: The thrill is not gone," he concluded, to peals of laughter from B.B. and the crowd.

The next month, B.B. spent two nights in a Texas hospital with influenza. He emerged seemingly unscathed. But people now greeted each B.B. King show as if it might be the last. When he took the stage at Eric Clapton's 2007 Crossroads Guitar Festival, on July 28 in Chicago, Clapton himself stood in the wings, snapping pictures with his camera as his eyes misted over. With Clapton watching, B.B. played a brief set that sounded like the old B.B. King. Between songs, he raised his red plastic cup and led the audience in a toast that invited thoughts of mortality. "May I live forever, but may you live forever and a day, cuz I'd hate to be here when you pass away," B.B. said. "And when they lay me out to rest . . . may the last voices I hear be yours," he continued, now turning to the teary-eyed Clapton, "sayin', 'While we was alive, we was friends.'"

B.B. had owned the crowd from the moment he took the stage at Clapton's festival. Such moments were few. In August 2007 at Madison Square Garden, according to a *New York Times* account, B.B. "pantomimed. He rucked up his shoulders so they nearly touched his ears, like a kid confronted with a perfect birthday present; he covered his face with one hand, opening a peek hole between two fingers; crossed his arms over his chest in ecstasy; made bug eyes in mock surprise;

squinted at his sidemen in mock suspicion." Reviewers simply laid out the facts: anything harsher, as a Cincinnati reviewer put it, "would come off as elder abuse."

B.B. paid his band to follow his every move: "to do what I do," as he once explained to nephew Walter King. They would have followed him off a cliff, and in the new millennium, that was where he often led them. At such times, performing behind him was purgatory.

"He can play whatever he wants, and the band will follow. So it never felt like he had restraints," Walter recalled. "And when I get up there, I'm gonna follow him whether I agree with him or not."

B.B. now traveled with medications to treat both diabetes and the creeping symptoms of dementia. When he took his pills, "he did great," recalled Dr. Darin Brimhall, B.B.'s personal physician from 2004 on. But "he lived on the road, so he didn't take his medications, didn't take them regularly, and he ate anything he wanted." His lapses were "a little bit of stubbornness and a little bit of denial," Brimhall recalled. Norman Matthews, "the one guy in the band who had no fear of B.B.," would chase B.B. around concert halls and hotel lobbies, bellowing, "You've gotta take your meds." Many of B.B.'s bad nights followed days when he refused.

IN THE SUMMER OF 2008, B.B. summoned Tommy Peters to Atlanta, where he was performing. On board the B.B. King bus, B.B. sought the accountant's help. B.B. trusted Peters, who had cared enough about B.B.'s well-being to send him to a weight-loss clinic. He asked Peters to read a stack of contracts between B.B. and Floyd Lieberman. Peters spent a week on the bus, poring over legal documents. "I read everything," he recalled, "and told him he was getting screwed."

In the months to follow, members of B.B.'s inner circle waged a quiet campaign to remove Floyd Lieberman: LaVerne Toney in Las Vegas; Tommy Peters in Memphis; Tina France, Sid Seidenberg's long-time aide, in New York; and a passel of lawyers. Most of them stood to gain if Lieberman went down.

* * *

GIVEN B.B.'S FRAILTY, no one could have expected what came next. In August 2008, Geffen released a new B.B. King album, and it was good.

B.B. was a benevolent despot, and that was fine while he was at the top of his game. He had impeccable instincts for reading an audience and channeling its collective mood with his songs. In later years, though, the affable dictator was losing focus, hence the interminable sing-alongs and painful blather. He now did his best work under the direction of another, ideally someone with a clear vision and a strong will. For his next LP, the label teamed B.B. with T Bone Burnett, a former Dylan sideman from Texas with piercing blue eyes, dirty-blond hair, and an ear for Americana. Burnett had produced convincingly retro soundtracks for the films *O Brother, Where Art Thou?* and *Cold Mountain* and wonderfully intimate records with British punker Elvis Costello and East L.A. rockers Los Lobos.

Burnett anchored the fragile bluesman to a sympathetic band, including the inimitable pianist Dr. John. Like Clapton before him, Burnett chose material that returned B.B. to his roots. "We started with T-Bone Walker and Lonnie Johnson," he recalled, revisiting songs and artists B.B. had loved since he first cranked up Aunt Mima's Victrola. The producer sought to invoke the sound and feel of B.B.'s recordings with Maxwell Davis and Modern Records in the 1950s: "I viewed them as by far the best examples of B.B. King records."

There was no need for guest artists. B.B. owned this set, singing and playing with an easy confidence on songs he had known for fifty years.

"The week or ten days we worked together on that record, he was strong and alert," Burnett recalled. "He was just killing it every day."

The resulting album, *One Kind Favor*, emerged in the summer of 2008. Its prevailing theme was weariness, established on the very first track. "See That My Grave Is Kept Clean" paid tribute to B.B.'s beloved Blind Lemon Jefferson. "Two white horses in a line, gonna take me to my burial ground," B.B. sang, his sepulchral baritone rising up out of a funeral-dance rhythm. Things only got darker from there. B.B. proceeded into a pair of mournful T-Bone Walker tunes, "I Get So

Weary" and "Get These Blues Off Me," and thence to Howlin' Wolf's "How Many More Years," Walker's "Waiting for Your Call," Lonnie Johnson's "My Love Is Down," and the Mississippi Sheiks' "The World Gone Wrong." B.B. and his band wallowed in heartbreak, despair, and disaster, finally sinking into the inky depths of Bessie Smith's "Backwater Blues," a hypnotic dirge that churned on for nearly eight minutes. The album concluded with a wistful Lonnie Johnson blues that harked back to B.B.'s defining song. "Tomorrow night," B.B. asked, "will all the thrill be gone?"

One Kind Favor would be B.B. King's final studio album, a fitting swansong. "I think there was a sense that it might be the last record he made," Burnett recalled. "I think he was playing for life or death."

A month later, to complement the aural tribute, B.B.'s supporters unveiled a brick-and-mortar monument to the great bluesman.

The $15 million B.B. King Museum and Delta Interpretive Center rose up in downtown Indianola around Mississippi's last standing red-brick cotton gin. Two architectural firms that bid on the project had independently, uncannily selected the same site, within whose boarded-up walls African American workers had once separated cotton fibers from seeds. The building resonated with Delta history. But when museum organizer Allan Hammons took B.B. to see it before construction, accompanied by manager Floyd Lieberman, their rental car pulled up to a "very bedraggled piece of real estate," Hammons recalled, a place choked with weeds, rusted vehicles, and construction flotsam. "This is the site?" Lieberman growled. A tense silence ensued. But then B.B. spoke, eyes welling with tears. "You know," he marveled, "I used to work in this building." Young Riley King had separated cotton at the old gin during his years on the Johnson Barrett plantation. Suddenly, the choice looked providential.

Curators combed through B.B.'s Las Vegas home like a forensic team to fill the exhibit space, affixing sticky notes to the items they wanted. (Some of his collections they mostly ignored, like the assortment of clocks that chimed at odd times, the stacks of discarded laptops, and the army of bobble-head dolls.) The only artifact B.B. denied them was a Gibson Les Paul, autographed to B.B. by Les Paul himself. "I believe I'd like to keep this one a little longer," B.B. explained.*

The B.B. King Museum and Interpretive Center opened on September 13, 2008, a hot and gusty Saturday. Encompassing twenty thousand square feet of Smithsonian-caliber dioramas, touch-screen films, and framed artifacts, the museum seemed an outsized landmark for sleepy Indianola, like an opera house in Mayberry. Then again, B.B. himself loomed larger than life. Organizers hoped to draw forty thousand visitors a year, four times the Indianola population. Within the dimly lit labyrinth, patrons could wend their way past a boat rescued from the Great Flood of 1927; sandstone footing from one of Riley King's boyhood shacks; B.B.'s stage outfits, in progressively larger dimensions; and B.B.'s home recording studio, transported from Las Vegas and reassembled piece by piece. After touring the museum, Delta tourists could stop by Club Ebony, the legendary chitlin' circuit roadhouse, which B.B. now owned.

When B.B. arrived at the finished museum in his wheelchair, he crossed his arms and patted his heart, as he sometimes did when receiving great honors. "Oh please," he gasped, "tell me this isn't just all about me." Later, B.B. sat on the stage of a small theater built to project images of the bluesman's life and loves. He grew misty at the thought of the one image that had eluded the curators: Nora Ella King, his mother. "I would pay $100,000, or whatever it would take, for a picture of her," he said, dabbing his eyes. "I don't even have a good picture of her in my mind."

Reporters politely wrote around B.B.'s conspicuous absence from the actual ribbon cutting, held in late morning on September 13, three days shy of his eighty-third birthday. "I was in dream heaven," he later joked. Floyd Lieberman wondered if B.B. had turned off his alarm.

Lieberman noticed a change in his client. B.B. had always signed contracts without reading them. Now, he took them and kept them, answering Lieberman's inquiries with, "My lawyer is looking at it." A

---

* B.B. intended to donate the guitar to the museum upon his death, Allan Hammons recounted to the author. But executors evidently lost track of his wish in the probate battles that followed. The guitar never arrived.

short time after the ribbon cutting, Floyd and his wife, Arlene, attended an event for the new museum. B.B. always greeted Arlene with a peck on the check. This time, he kissed her full on the mouth. Ashen, Arlene returned to Floyd's side and said, "Something is wrong."

All the hoopla over the museum and *One Kind Favor* album overshadowed another 2008 announcement: the rebranding of the blues station on the XM satellite radio network as "B.B. King's Bluesville."

Satellite radio offered listeners a clear signal from coast to coast, dozens of stations, and no commercials, for a monthly fee. XM Radio boasted nearly ten million listeners. Bill Wax, creator of the blues station, had turned up at the B.B. King Blues Club on Times Square in 2005 for an anniversary party. He introduced himself to Floyd Lieberman, who escorted Wax backstage, found B.B., and said, "This is the guy that does the blues radio show that you listen to all the time." B.B. rose to greet Wax. "Young man," he said, "I have wanted to meet you for a while now." B.B., a consummate technophile, was an early adopter of satellite radio. He marveled at this deejay, Wax, who played songs B.B. hadn't heard outside of his own tour bus in fifty years. "I was listening last week when you played Bukka White," he said.

Wax named B.B. honorary mayor of Bluesville. The satellite network paid $200,000 for the right to use his name. B.B. embraced the title with pride. B.B. visited Wax at his Washington, DC, studios whenever he passed through town, recording marathon interviews. In time, Wax suggested B.B. host his own show. B.B. agreed. Wax recorded the shows in B.B.'s Las Vegas home during his ever-longer breaks from the road. Wax would arrive at B.B.'s door at noon, when the great bluesman awakened. LaVerne Toney would meet him. Once B.B.'s secretary and housekeeper, LaVerne now oversaw his entire Las Vegas operation. Norman Matthews, who lived nearby, would bring breakfast and sit at B.B.'s side during the sessions. Wax was surprised at how little coaching B.B. required. Whatever his memory lapses on the road, B.B. remained a walking, talking encyclopedia of twentieth-century rhythm and blues. *You and Me with B.B. King* premiered on February 20, 2009.

"I think he realized that Father Time was catching up," Wax recalled, "and this was his last chance to tell the history the way he wanted it told."

Once again, B.B. was closing out a decade on a high note. In 2008 alone, he had christened a namesake museum, released a career-capping album, and reinvented himself as a satellite-radio deejay. All of those deals had been brokered by Floyd Lieberman. Comparing his own performance with his mentor's, Lieberman boasted, "I made more money for B.B. in ten years than Sid did in thirty-four years."

But B.B.'s relationship with Floyd Lieberman never approached the brotherly bond between B.B. and Sid Seidenberg. "B.B. always felt like Sid was his partner," recalled Tommy Peters, owner of the B.B. blues clubs. "He didn't have a problem sharing fifty-fifty with someone who was his partner."

In late 2008, LaVerne Toney summoned Las Vegas attorney Arthur Williams Jr. to B.B.'s home. She asked him to read B.B.'s will, which had been drawn up with Lieberman's help. Williams read the document. Then he turned to B.B. and said, "Mr. King, I will not let you walk out of here without changing that will."

In the lawyer's estimation, Lieberman "had everything in that will going to him or his family," rather than to B.B. or his family. Williams reviewed other contracts B.B. had signed and found that Lieberman had made himself part owner of a vast array of B.B.'s assets. The attorney asked B.B. how Lieberman had persuaded him to sign the forms. B.B. explained that Lieberman would present the documents to B.B. on the road, when he was distracted. B.B. didn't read them.

"B.B. wasn't a well-educated guy," Williams recalled. "So there's a lot of things that he didn't understand. And people like Lieberman took advantage of his lack of education to line his own pockets."

A week later, on December 18, 2008, Williams dispatched a letter to Lieberman. It instructed, "Your services will no longer be required." Williams sent copies to all of B.B.'s business associates.

Lieberman pushed back. He did indeed own between 25 and 50 percent of B.B.'s businesses. That had been B.B.'s arrangement with Sid Seidenberg. Lieberman had simply carried it forward. Lieberman also claimed a 20 percent cut of B.B.'s earnings: 15 percent as his manager and another 5 percent as his accountant, just like Sid.

A protracted court battle looked inevitable. Attorneys counseled B.B. to buy out his manager. B.B. agreed. Negotiations stretched into 2009. Lieberman walked away with roughly $3 million. "They were buying the stock out of a company that owned 50 percent of B.B. King," Lieberman recalled. "Everything was aboveboard. And I won."

Yet, by the close of 2009 and perhaps for the first time in his life, B.B. King was the sole owner of his own career.

CHAPTER 21

A GOLDEN CHAIN

IN AN INTERVIEW FOR THE JULY 2010 issue of *Ebony* magazine, a reporter asked B.B., "Is it true you have 15 children?" B.B. replied, "I've never had one." Then, he laughed.

Ever so gradually over two prior decades, B.B. had leavened his interviews with hints that not all of his children were truly his. He scattered other clues, like his reworked lyrics to the old country blues "I'm Gonna Move to the Outskirts of Town" at a Florida show in 2000: "We got nineteen children / And none of them, none of them, look like me."

B.B.'s comments to *Ebony* sounded like an eleventh-hour confession disguised as a joke. When the topic of paternity arose in another interview, B.B. spoke more plainly: "During all the time this was happening, there was no DNA [testing]. So I wouldn't swear that they all was mine biologically."

On the road in Jackson, Mississippi, not long after the *Ebony* piece, B.B. visited with two of his favorite people: Charles Evers, brother of the slain Medgar and organizer of many Mississippi Homecomings; and Sue, his ex-wife. They were talking on B.B.'s tour bus when Evers turned to the former couple and asked, "Why didn't you two have any children?" B.B. hesitated. His eyes turned sad, and he explained, "She had a couple of miscarriages, and it didn't work out." Then he turned to Sue, who later recalled, "I could see in B.'s eyes that he wanted me to lie." She nodded, affirming his story. "I did for the sake of him," she recalled. "He could have easily gotten out of this. Why he didn't, I don't know. And he paid dearly for it."

B.B. had given millions of dollars to his children across six decades. He telephoned them on their birthdays. He handed out fistfuls of cash when he saw them at gigs. At Christmastime, he parceled out $2,000 to each child, $1,500 to each grandchild. At one family reunion, he handed out checks for $10,000. In his golden years, though, B.B.'s attitude seemed to harden. He tailored his estate so that most of his wealth would pass not to his children but to his grandchildren and great-grandchildren, and only to finance their education. Dropping out of school in tenth grade was perhaps B.B.'s deepest regret, the one decision he would take back if he could live his life over. He would not permit his heirs to repeat the mistake. His will left no more than $5,000 in unfettered cash to any one child.

After Floyd Lieberman's exit, B.B. attempted an awkward power-sharing arrangement among the three people who ran his empire: LaVerne Toney; Tina France, former aide to Sid Seidenberg; and a succession of road managers. He called the troika his management team. "He was trying to safeguard himself against what had happened with Floyd," recalled Stafford Davis, his security aide. LaVerne became B.B.'s personal manager, running his household, paying his bills, and placating his family. France handled bookings, publicity, and merchandising. Sherman Darby remained road manager. When Darby died in 2009, his job passed briefly to Willie King, one of B.B.'s children, and then to Norman Matthews.

B.B. had resented Floyd Lieberman for curtailing his international travel. With Lieberman gone, B.B. went back overseas, touring Europe in 2009, Europe and South America in 2010. The tours required "pretty extensive medical clearance" forms from Dr. Brimhall. Brimhall worried not about B.B.'s diabetes or cognitive decline but about advancing arthritis in his legs: "The concern was, Would he fall? Would he be able to get around?" Brimhall recalled. In the spring of 2011, B.B. traveled from Australia to New Zealand to Hawaii, then played in Germany and flew home to perform on the West Lawn of the U.S. Capitol. After his annual Mississippi Homecoming in June, B.B. returned to Britain and played to sixty thousand rain-soaked fans at the Glastonbury Festival. A few days later, on June 28, he returned to Royal Albert Hall. That concert, recorded for release the next spring on CD and DVD, would serve as the final document of his recording career.

On bad days, the great bluesman could no longer get through a song, let alone a full performance. With his weakening vision, he struggled simply to see his audience. He seemed to know his limitations, and on *Live at the Royal Albert Hall*, B.B. peppered his rambling monologues with bitter quips. A few minutes in, he told the crowd he was going to bring out some special guests. But "I'm gonna let you get tired of me first," he said. B.B. then joked that one of his guests, blues guitarist Susan Tedeschi, was "a beautiful lady, but her husband is with her," drawing nervous laughter. He forgot the name of his record producer. He launched the band into "See That My Grave Is Kept Clean," then lost interest and allowed the song to collapse. "They don't know what I'm talking about, either," he said, to no one in particular. B.B. brought out the guests, Tedeschi and her guitarist husband, Derek Trucks. He flirted with Tedeschi, each gesture a bit more unsettling than the last. "I tried to marry his wife before he did," he said, gesturing to the couple, both now visibly stricken. He insisted that Tedeschi sit closer. As Trucks played a solo, B.B. loudly interrupted it with, "If I played like that, maybe I could get her, too." He accused his drummer of staring at Tedeschi. Five thousand British blues fans were left squirming in their seats.

B.B. HAD WEPT with joy upon the 2008 election of Barack Obama as president. "He did it," B.B. gasped over the phone to Lora Walker, his longtime friend. Four years later, in February 2012, the Obamas invited B.B. to perform in the East Room of the White House at an all-star tribute to the blues. Fellow bluesman Buddy Guy goaded the president and B.B. into singing verses of Obama's hometown anthem, "Sweet Home Chicago." That sentiment was touching, but the B.B. King who performed for the president that night was "difficult to watch," one writer recalled. B.B. sang his trademark song, "The Thrill Is Gone," in a listless moan. He "appeared to be lost beneath two layers of fog. He missed his cues and darted off on jags of confused banter," the reporter wrote. "Why was he even up there? Because he was a giant, of course. But more so because he was a man who couldn't let himself stop."

The B.B. King band was nearing its final incarnation. James "Boogaloo" Bolden remained as bandleader, a post he would hold till the end. Drummer Calep Emphrey had retired in 2008, leaving Tony Coleman in his stead. Cole Man departed in early 2013, weary of marking time as his boss blathered onstage. He had seen B.B. soil himself on a long flight from New Zealand to Hawaii in the spring of 2011, compelling his handlers to wrap him in an airplane blanket for a torturous journey through customs. He had watched a flu-afflicted B.B. vomit into a wastebasket during a 2012 performance in Lebanon, a misfortune captured on jumbotron screens. The final straw came when someone posted a YouTube video that showed Coleman drumming with one hand and texting with the other.

"I couldn't do it anymore," Coleman recalled. "You had people goin', 'B.B., shut the fuck up and sing!' You had half the audience upset because they paid $150, $200 a ticket, and you had the other half sitting there asking, 'Why is that poor man up there?'"

B.B. was up there for his musicians.

"He felt like he was responsible for everybody making a living," Coleman recalled. "And he loved everybody. We were on retainer. We got paid half salary whether we worked or not. And when we worked, we had bonuses coming from money that wasn't even accounted for. He was great to us," Coleman said, his voice breaking. "He was great."

B.B. had made LaVerne Toney promise she would never compel him to retire. When he reminded her of the pledge, LaVerne would reply, "Unless you go onstage without your pants on," bringing a smile to his face.

Amid a stream of caustic reviews in 2013, LaVerne received a letter from a promoter who didn't want to pay B.B.'s fee after a particularly weak performance. She showed it to Dr. Brimhall. They sat down with B.B. for a sort of intervention, asking him whether "it might be time to call it quits." Brimhall thought so. "You know," he told his patient, "it's not wrong to be done with dignity. Go out on top of the world, like you are right now." B.B. did not agree. "He was madder 'n hell," Brimhall recalled. "It wasn't a pleasant night."

No one had been able to work a crowd like B.B. King. Yet, by 2014, B.B. no longer seemed to know when he had a crowd to work. Onstage in packed concert halls, he sat cocooned within a bubble of sentience, dimly aware of the anxious musicians behind him and the lovely women in the front rows, oblivious to all else. The centerpiece of his meandering sets was no longer "The Thrill Is Gone," or even "Every Day I Have the Blues," but a marathon sing-along of the ancient country standard "You Are My Sunshine." As his memory and his senses failed him, B.B. found solace in playing the first song he had ever learned.

In April, at the Peabody Opera House in St. Louis, B.B. rambled and the band vamped for forty-five minutes before the group performed "anything resembling a song," a reviewer wrote. After a fifteen-minute sing-along of "You Are My Sunshine," the music stopped "and the show ground to an intensely uncomfortable halt." The reviewer asked why no one among B.B.'s sidemen or "surfeit of handlers" bothered to step in and help the addled bluesman. Instead, they "seemed more than content to stand respectfully by and watch him (metaphorically) die."

Walter King hated watching his uncle struggle. He felt sure that B.B.'s aides could restore order and decorum to his shows with "a bit more concerned support." Bandleader Boogaloo Bolden tried his best, but the responsibility ultimately lay with B.B.'s road manager.

Norman Matthews, B.B.'s closest friend, died in Las Vegas on May 11, aged eighty-five. The road manager's job passed to Myron Johnson, B.B.'s former valet. Johnson was fiercely loyal, but he lacked the gravitas of his predecessors: he could not speak bluntly to the boss. After the St. Louis debacle, B.B.'s management issued a statement of apology, dismissing the episode as "a bad night."

B.B. now had mostly bad nights. A reviewer in San Antonio constructed a timeline to document a terrible performance in May 2014:

9:21 p.m.—The B.B. King Blues Band started the show.
9:42 p.m.—B.B. took the stage, talked to the band, strapped in.
9:45 p.m.—B.B. talked, joked, and mugged for photos with fans, who crowded the stage despite pleas from ushers to retake their seats. Fans began to heckle. B.B. responded with, "Me no speak Spanish."

10:05 p.m.—B.B. played his first song.

10:34 p.m.—B.B. sang "You Are My Sunshine," forgetting the words.

10:42 p.m.—"You Are My Sunshine" dragged on, despite protestations from the crowd. "Try another chorus of it," B.B. commanded. "It's your song. I'm playing it for you."

10:44 p.m.—"You Are My Sunshine" finally ended, at the insistence of bandleader Boogaloo Bolden.

10:54 p.m.—B.B. announced, "Well, that's about it for us today." He remained in his chair for another ten minutes.

11:04 p.m.—B.B. rambled on to the thinning crowd. He finally said, "I buried my only friend yesterday," as three men arrived to help him to his feet and lead him from the hall.

B.B. was adrift and alone. He had outlived not only his music-industry peers but also dearer, lesser-known friends, men such as Bebop Edwards and Cato Walker. His best friend, Norman Matthews, had been something like a soul mate, a near-constant companion since the two entered manhood. Matthews had never actually retired: he'd died on the job. Sixty-five years earlier, B.B.'s father, Albert King, had instructed Matthews, "Take care of my son." Matthews did.

"We're friends," Matthews once said of B.B. "It never rain too hard or too much snow to get anything that he need, because he is the one that take care of me."

B.B. had no spouse and no full siblings, no one who had known him like Norman Matthews. When Matthews passed out of B.B.'s life, "it was as if the very last vestige of his past was gone," recalled Lora Walker, who had known B.B. nearly as long. "There was nobody left but me, and I didn't matter, because I was a girl. And I knew the stories. But Mr. Norman was the stories."

B.B. returned to the Delta in late May 2014 for the thirty-fourth Mississippi Homecoming, which organizers mercifully announced would be the last. He continued to play concert after concert: Michigan, Illinois, and Texas in June; Canada, New England, Pennsylvania, and Washington, DC, in July; Colorado, California, and Arizona in August. The shows were surreal. Many reviews now closed with politely worded entreaties for B.B. to pack it in.

"This isn't the B.B. King of 1969, or even of 1999," a reviewer wrote in Syracuse, New York, in July. "This is an 88-year-old legend who will draw a crowd even to watch him mumble."

On October 3, 2014, a chilly Friday, B.B. played the House of Blues in Chicago. Wind whipped the patrons arriving at the Dearborn Street club. Inside, B.B.'s wary musicians sensed trouble. After the customary instrumental opener, the bluesman failed to emerge from his dressing room. His daughter Shirley King, who lived in Chicago, was watching the show from her VIP seat. She eventually spotted B.B. in the wings, "and it looked like he was trying to get off the stage," she recalled. "I had never seen him act like that." At last, he walked onstage, or was walked onstage: it seemed to Shirley that B.B. was not moving of his own volition. Helpers lowered him into his chair. B.B. laboriously strapped on Lucille. The band launched into "Rock Me Baby." B.B. lifted his pick and attempted to play, brushing his hand weakly across the strings. The sound that rustled from the speakers reminded his nephew Walter King of playing cards flapping against bicycle spokes. B.B. limped through a halting set. Finally, B.B. stopped playing, "put his hands on his knees, and just stared out at the audience," Shirley recalled. He lifted the guitar strap back over his head and placed Lucille carefully back on her stand. He sat and stared at his guitar.

Boogaloo Bolden, B.B.'s bandleader, walked over and offered his boss a towel. He gestured to the stage hands to pull the curtain.

"Show's over," Boogaloo told B.B. "You're finished."

"Okay," B.B. said vaguely. He waved to the crowd, settled into a wheelchair, and rolled offstage for the last time.

Some minutes later, Boogaloo found B.B. in his dressing room, lying on a sofa. "How're you feeling?" he asked.

"I don't feel too good," B.B. replied. "Boogaloo," he continued, seeming to regain his focus. "You been with me a long time, and you never, ever heard me say this: I'm done. This is it. I'm done."

B.B. spent the night in a Chicago hospital. Then Myron Johnson helped him onto his tour bus, and B.B. returned to Las Vegas for the last time. When he arrived home, B.B. greeted LaVerne Toney with an enigmatic grin. "Ms. Toney," he said, "they're gonna give you hell." The remark struck her as strange. Then she realized B.B. was telling her to prepare for battle with his children.

B.B. slept for days on his California king bed, clad in gold pajamas and tucked beneath a gold comforter. Once in a while he would awaken, turn to Myron Johnson, and ask, "When's the next date?" or "When are we going back to work?" Johnson would gently remind him, "We're not going back on the road anymore. We're done." A small entourage attended the tired bluesman: Johnson, LaVerne Toney, sundry caregivers, and household staff. Barbara Matthews, Norman's widow, took his place at B.B.'s side, cooking meals and providing care.

Shirley, B.B.'s eldest daughter, talked her way into the house shortly before Christmas. "He seemed miserable," she recalled. "He couldn't sit up, he was unshaven, and his pajamas were dirty. He looked so frail and tired that it almost made me cry on the spot. I was able to give him a quick kiss on the cheek, but then I was escorted out." A week or so later, she visited again. She asked her father if he would accompany her to Palm Springs for a show, an odd request, given his condition. "Baby," he replied, "your daddy is tired, and I don't know if that's going to happen." Then Shirley asked if she could have a few of his jackets. B.B. had a vast collection of stage jackets, each more gaudily adorned than the last. He said yes. She gathered them up and attempted to leave, only to be stopped at the door by one of B.B.'s minders, who took them back, a skirmish in the escalating conflict.

"You know, there were only so many guitars, and there was only so much jewelry, and there were only so many stage coats," recalled Brent Bryson, an attorney who represented LaVerne Toney at the time. "Things would disappear."

B.B.'s children had enjoyed unfettered entrée to their father. He returned their calls and honored their pleas for cash. After the abortive concert in Chicago, it all stopped. "We no longer had access to him,"

Riley King Jr. told an interviewer. "We'd call, and his secretary would take our messages, and we'd never hear back from him."

LaVerne Toney held power of attorney for her boss, leaving her in command of his care and his funds. Theirs was a complex relationship. B.B. seemed to trust LaVerne above everyone else in his entourage. After four decades in B.B.'s employ, LaVerne wielded nearly all the powers of a spouse. Detractors sensed something sinister in her sway over her boss. LaVerne knew as much about B.B.'s sex life as Norman Matthews or Bebop Edwards ever had. She'd read The Book. Her only real rival within the King household was Patty King, one of his children, who happened to be staying in B.B.'s home as his health failed. This was the same Patty King whom B.B. had visited in prison two decades earlier. "I would cook his meals," Patty recalled. "He loved blueberry pie and pecan pie and pig's feet, macaroni and cheese." LaVerne and Patty feuded constantly over B.B.'s care. A standoff seemed inevitable.

Tony Coleman telephoned LaVerne in January 2015. He was flying to Las Vegas for the funeral of Melvin Jackson, B.B.'s former saxophonist. He wanted to see B.B. He had tried to reach his old boss directly, to no avail.

"He has a different number now," LaVerne told him, according to Coleman. "I don't want anybody calling him."

"Can you get him on the phone and let me say hello to him?"

"Well, I'll try," LaVerne replied. "But you know, he doesn't want to be bothered. He's just resting."

Coleman said he and LaVerne talked three more times, before, during, and after the January 10 funeral. "Well, I'll try," LaVerne kept saying. "But he doesn't want to be bothered."

LaVerne remembered differently: Coleman asked to see B.B. "maybe one time," she recalled, and B.B. told her he wasn't up to receiving visitors.

After the service, Coleman attended a Willie Nelson show at the House of Blues. Nelson asked Coleman how his old friend was doing: he hadn't talked to B.B., either. At the concert, Coleman received a call from a mutual friend. "I'm at B.B.'s house right now with Patty King," she said. The caller said that B.B. knew some of his old bandmates were in town and that he kept asking, "Where's my band? I want to see my band."

Coleman drove to B.B.'s house with fellow musician Stanley Abernathy. Patty left instructions at the guardhouse to let them in. When the two men entered the house, Patty motioned them upstairs: "He wants to see y'all." B.B.'s old sidemen walked into his bedroom. Coleman saw the emaciated frame of his former boss, clad in pajamas that looked several sizes too big. B.B.'s massive bed threatened to swallow him whole.

"He looked like a skeleton, almost," Coleman recalled. "I walked in. Stanley was behind me. He was lying there, he had the television on, he was watching a western movie." Guitars lay scattered around the room, a tableau that suggested the instruments had gathered to pay their respects.

"Hey, Tony Cole Man," B.B. said weakly. "Come on over here. Give an old man a hug." They embraced. Coleman sat on one side of B.B.'s bed, Abernathy on the other. "I wanted to go to Melvin's funeral," B.B. said, "but I just didn't feel up to it. But it's okay, because I'll be with him soon anyway."

"Man," Coleman protested, "you ain't goin' nowhere."

B.B.'s focus drifted. He rambled apologetically that the banks were closed, lamenting that he had no cash on him. He mistook his visitors for his children.

"We don't want any money, man," Coleman replied. "We're here to see you."

The spark of coherence seemed to come and go from B.B.'s eyes, Coleman recalled, like the luminosity of a lightbulb at the touch of a dimmer switch. B.B. pointed to the television screen: "That guy's getting ready to get shot. Watch this. BAM. See, I told you." He smiled.

Patty joined them in the bedroom. She pointed to a tray of untouched food: chicken, mashed potatoes, greens. "Why don't you try to make him eat something?" she asked. But the food was cold and congealed.

Coleman returned alone the next day. B.B. told the drummer he couldn't wait to go back out on tour. "His mind was going back and forth," Coleman recalled. "He still had it in his brain that he was going to work again, because that was all the man knew."

Patty pulled Coleman aside. She began to cry. "LaVerne's not taking care of my dad," she said. "We have to cut garbage bags and put them between the mattress and the sheet so he doesn't soak the mattress when he relieves himself." Patty said B.B.'s handlers had cut off his access to cash. "I can't even afford a toilet seat that's higher, so he doesn't have to squat down so low," she said. The drummer produced his own wallet, peeled off $200 in bills and handed them to Patty. "Thank you so much," she said. "LaVerne won't give me anything to help my dad."

Months passed. Word spread of B.B.'s ebbing health. A get-well letter from President Obama arrived in April. "Through the greatest joys and deepest sorrows," he wrote, "your music has been there, putting into notes the experiences that define us and reminding us of what it means to be alive."

On April 30, 2015, Patty summoned police to the house. She wanted B.B. hospitalized: he wasn't eating, and his urine looked oddly discolored. She accused LaVerne Toney of denying him proper care. Police called paramedics, who took B.B. to the hospital. Doctors determined he might have suffered a minor heart attack. They released him into home hospice care: B.B. was dying.

A probate battle loomed. Patty King took her accusations to the celebrity news site *TMZ* and shared a photograph of B.B. looking more dead than alive. *TMZ* reported that Patty and her boyfriend had filed a police report several months earlier, claiming that LaVerne had relieved B.B. of several Rolex watches, millions in cash, and a ring worth $250,000.

Another child, Karen King Williams, stepped forward on May 5 with fresh allegations. Karen said B.B.'s handlers had fleeced $453,000 from his bank accounts in a single month. She said LaVerne had barred B.B.'s family and friends from his deathbed, including A-list celebrities Eric Clapton, Willie Nelson, and Carlos Santana. She alleged that LaVerne wouldn't take him to a dentist to treat his abscessed teeth, claiming he was "broke."

B.B. had between $9 million and $10 million in the bank. LaVerne was struggling to maintain his care while protecting his fortune from his children, who, in her view, were trying to take it. She did her best to admit visitors to B.B.'s bedside, she recalled, and an exalted guest like Clapton or Santana "would never have been barred." But she would not allow any visitors on days when B.B. did not feel up to receiving them. The children's real complaint, LaVerne said, was that B.B. did not want to see them.

The children continued to campaign against LaVerne, joined now by old bandmates who felt jilted. Surreptitious photographs snapped by visitors showed B.B. "just in awful shape," recalled Tommy Peters, one of many who saw them. "He's urinating on himself in bed. Dirty mattress. He needed dental care. His teeth were rotting away." Peters sent Patty King money to buy B.B. a new mattress and fresh pajamas.

The fight moved to court. Karen Williams filed a petition seeking appointment as B.B.'s legal guardian, challenging LaVerne's power of attorney. "The family has been unable to account for what is reported to be in excess of $1 million," Karen said in a filing.

On May 7, a judge rejected Karen's claim. Separate investigations by the police and a social services agency found no abuse or neglect. LaVerne remained silent, but her attorneys hailed her courtroom victory. They denied the neglect claims and portrayed the action as a desperate cash grab by B.B.'s children, who could no longer tap their father directly for handouts. Three children held a press conference outside the Las Vegas courthouse. "We lost the battle," Karen Williams said, "but we haven't lost the war."

Eleven of B.B.'s fifteen children remained alive. News reports referred to them as "biological and adoptive." In fact, B.B. hadn't formally adopted anyone, though he had signed at least one birth certificate. Darin Brimhall and LaVerne Toney gently inquired about collecting samples of his DNA, evidence that might prove once and for all that he was not a father. B.B. refused.

A few more visitors were allowed in. One was Walter King. He and B.B. sat and watched westerns on television. They chatted about family. After a while, B.B. smiled at his nephew and said, "Son, you know how much I like my sleep. I'll see you later." They hugged. Walter said, "Love you, B." B.B. replied, "Love you." Walter departed, the last of the King's Men to see him alive.

Sue, B.B.'s beloved ex-wife, telephoned LaVerne and said she wanted to see him. "She said she would ask him," Sue recalled. She said no reply ever came.

A week passed. B.B. remained in round-the-clock hospice care. LaVerne and Myron Johnson traded twelve-hour shifts. B.B. didn't say much, but he had not missed the Shakespearean drama unfolding around him. "People want what they want," he said weakly to Johnson one day. "And they won't stop until they get it." Those were the last consequential words to pass B.B.'s lips.

B.B. and Johnson spent May 13 watching old cowboy films and episodes of *Perry Mason*. Johnson fed B.B. his dinner. He touched his employer on the shoulder and said, "Mr. B., I'm heading home to get some rest." As Johnson rose to leave, B.B. stopped him, reached over to take his hand, squeezed it gently, and pulled it to his lips. He looked Johnson in the eyes and kissed his hand.

Myron Johnson departed into the warm Las Vegas evening. B.B. slept through that night and most of the next day.

Twenty years earlier, B.B. had said in his memoir that he dreamed of dying while holding either Lucille or a woman, but he'd settle for passing in his sleep. And that was how he went, around 6:00 p.m. on May 14, 2015, with Myron Johnson back at his side, holding his hand. B.B. was eighty-nine.

Obituary writers around the globe labored to estimate B.B.'s inestimable contributions. Even now, fifty years after B.B. King's credentials as an American musical icon had been debated and affirmed, many writers hedged their bets. The *New York Times* placed him at "the apex of American blues" but no higher. *Rolling Stone* hailed him as the blues genre's "unrivaled ambassador" and a "larger-than-life" talent. *The Guardian*, in Britain, hit closer to the mark, noting that B.B. "represented the blues as Louis Armstrong once represented jazz, a single performer who could nevertheless stand, and speak, for the whole genre." Stewart Levine, B.B.'s beloved producer, put it more succinctly:

"His legacy is that he introduced America to its own music. And that's about as big a legacy as you could have."

No obituary writer seemed quite prepared to embrace that legacy. B.B. had almost singlehandedly written a new vocabulary of solo guitar, a lexicon that moved to the center of popular music and dominated it for a generation. While his final tally of gigs is unknowable, B.B. had probably performed more than seventeen thousand concerts in ninety countries. By the time of his death, B.B.'s technique of playing a guitar like a human voice was so ubiquitous, so universal, that the notion of this sound originating with a single man sounded absurd.

Rolling Stone compiled a list of ten legendary pop acts that "wouldn't exist without B.B. King": Jimi Hendrix, Stevie Ray Vaughan, Carlos Santana, Johnny Winter, and Robert Cray, along with the Butterfield Blues Band, Duane Allman's Allman Brothers, Eric Clapton's Cream, Peter Green's Fleetwood Mac, and Billy Gibbons's ZZ Top.

President Barack Obama observed, "B.B. may be gone, but that thrill will be with us forever. And there's going to be one killer blues session in heaven tonight."

ALMOST NO ONE had ever uttered an unkind word about B.B. King. Yet, within days of his death, his friends and loved ones were saying many unkind things about each other.

B.B.'s children gathered in Las Vegas on May 21, a week after his death, for a private viewing that they secured from a probate judge over LaVerne Toney's objections. The probate battle threatened to eclipse B.B.'s funeral in the press. "We're going to fight with every breath in our body," Patty King told reporters after the viewing.

The next two days belonged to B.B.'s family. His children planned a full slate of tributes in Las Vegas, even as B.B.'s handlers organized a largely duplicative schedule of events in Memphis and Indianola. The factions that had fought over B.B.'s custody and care now battled over his remains.

On a gray Friday afternoon, more than one thousand people turned out for a public viewing at a Las Vegas mortuary. Rita Washington, one of the children, greeted them at the chapel doors, handing out little postcards filled with family photos of her father. By the 3 p.m. start, a journalist reported, "the line of more than three hundred mourners snaked around the corner. They leaned on canes, sat in wheelchairs, and carried blue balloons as they waited to be led in for a viewing in small groups up to the casket." Some mourners broadcast B.B.'s songs from the tiny speakers of their smartphones. At the front of the queue sat Larry Montano, a retired sound technician of sixty-one from Palmdale, California, dressed in black and carrying a bouquet of blue roses. "I'm glad I came," he said, wiping his eyes. "But I don't want to remember him this way. I want to remember him when I saw him play, the night I shook his hand."

Inside the chapel, B.B. lay on a bed of white satin in an open casket, its lid emblazoned with an image of Lucille. Two guitars sat like sentries on either side, flanked by floral displays. Guards allotted the mourners ten seconds each of silent communion before motioning them on.

On Saturday, several hundred mourners gathered at a different Las Vegas mortuary for a memorial service. Carlos Santana paid his respects. Drummer Tony Coleman delivered a stirring eulogy.

"He fired me five times," Coleman said, pausing for a round of laughter. "But he hired me six times."

B.B.'s progeny dominated the room: nearly one hundred children, grandchildren, and great-grandchildren, by one estimate. At moments, their tributes sounded like rehearsals for probate court.

"My grandfather was king," said Landra Williams, daughter of Karen Williams, "not just king of the blues or Riley King but king of our family. In moments we shared with him, he cultivated a different, special relationship with each one of us."

Five children—Patty and Willie King, Barbara King Winfree, Karen Williams, and Rita Washington—now termed themselves a family board, aligned against LaVerne Toney. Some of the others remained neutral, perhaps waiting to see which side would prevail.

To all appearances, B.B. had died a natural death. Dr. Brimhall ascribed his passing to vascular dementia, a series of small strokes triggered by reduced blood flow to the brain, a consequence of chronic diabetes.

Nonetheless, on Monday, May 25, B.B.'s daughters Karen Williams and Patty King accused his caretakers of poisoning him. Patty said in an affidavit that she had seen Myron Johnson place two drops of an unknown liquid on his tongue every evening for months. "I believe my father was murdered," she claimed. The coroner ordered further investigation. Brent Bryson, LaVerne's attorney, dismissed the allegations as "defamatory and libelous" and lamented that a protracted probate battle was precisely what B.B. hadn't wanted. That much was certainly true.

On May 27, beneath a slate-gray sky, Memphis bade farewell to B.B. with a procession along Beale Street, which had grown into a thriving entertainment district on the strength of his name. A Dixieland band marched ahead of a black hearse that carried B.B.'s casket, playing "The Thrill Is Gone" and "When the Saints Go Marching In." Among the marchers was Herman Green, B.B.'s sideman from the 1950s, celebrating his eighty-fifth birthday. At the front of the procession walked Rodd Bland, son of Bobby and godson to B.B., carrying one of the bluesman's beloved Lucilles and wiping tears from his eyes. The elder Bland had died in 2013. Some of B.B.'s children pressed in against the hearse, clinging to its windows as if they feared it might drive off without them.

The caravan rolled south down Route 61 toward the Delta and its final destination, Indianola, flanked by enough police to protect a president. Sue rode in one of the trailing cars, joined by the mayor of Indianola and the director of the B.B. King Museum. All along the 135-mile route, Mississippians lined the road to record the procession on camera phones. Northbound motorists stopped their cars, climbed out, and stood in traffic lanes to watch. Parents clambered atop sport utility vehicles. Truckers parked their rigs. Fire trucks waited at every overpass, firefighters standing with hats in hands, American flags flapping from their ladders, tears gleaming in their eyes. Trailer parks emptied, their populations huddled along the highway with offerings of cut flowers laid out in the gravel. Hundreds of employees from a Dollar General shipping hub emptied the warehouse and gathered at the roadside to pay respects. Some mourners knelt and prayed as B.B. passed. Spectators pressed in so close and so hard that the procession slowed to thirty miles per hour. All of Mississippi, it seemed, had gathered to bury its King.

At dawn on a cloudy Friday, May 29, mourners lined up outside the B.B. King Museum. At 10 a.m., they filed into the restored red-brick cotton gin to view B.B. in his bronze coffin, his body clad in a purple satin shirt and floral tuxedo. Two Mississippi patrolmen stood guard, heads downcast, flanked by a pair of black Gibson guitars. B.B.'s records blared from outdoor speakers. One mourner, wearing a lace-trimmed top hat and calling herself the "Dance Queen of New Orleans," swayed emphatically to the beat. A local politician handed out fliers announcing that she and B.B. had been friends.

"B.B.'s been in my life, in my father's life, in my mother's life," said McClinton Samuels, a retired prison officer from New Orleans. Another mourner said she had flown in from Tokyo.

On Saturday morning, workers laid straw atop the mud around the empty grave that awaited B.B.'s casket on the museum grounds. Five hundred mourners crowded into the Bell Grove Missionary Baptist Church. Four burly state troopers blocked the doors, and the service began.

Myron Johnson recalled sitting with his boss at the Golden Spoon frozen-yogurt shop near his Las Vegas home: "just the two of us, him unrecognized, sitting on the patio, eating our favorite flavors, enjoying the summer breezes, telling jokes, sharing stories, and, yes, watching women." Johnson spoke bitterly of the probate feud that had framed B.B.'s final days. He mused that perhaps B.B. had "finally found in death what he never could in life: peace."

Phil Bryant, Mississippi's governor, gave a stirring tribute, a powerful white politician paying homage to a poor, Black sharecropper who had attained a station far above his own. "This man walked with presidents, . . . met popes, traveled the world as our ambassador to the blues of Mississippi. He lived his life just as he would want, and just as we would have wanted him to," Bryant said. "This humble, quiet man changed the world, but the world never changed him."

Presidents Obama and Clinton sent messages. Soul man Otis Clay belted out the gospel standard "When the Gates Swing Open," joined by Willie Rogers of the Soul Stirrers. Clay announced, "This is the last thing I'll do for B.B. King." Eight months later, Clay was dead as well.

In B.B.'s final years, he had grown obsessed with the Blind Lemon Jefferson song "See That My Grave Is Kept Clean." B.B. told his friend Allan Hammons to listen closely to the lyrics. Jefferson's song was literally funereal, dictating a set of instructions for burial. He sang of "two white horses in a line" and of a grave dug "with a silver spade" and a "church bell's tone" and a coffin laid down "with a golden chain."

It was a tall order. Asphalt lay beneath the soil where B.B. would be put to rest, so a silver spade would not suffice to dig a grave. Organizers found a pair of white horses to lead the procession and a backhoe to break through the asphalt. They improvised the golden chain.

Storm clouds threatened, so organizers shortened the route to the grave. Recorded church bells pealed through the outdoor speakers as B.B.'s brief final journey began. The first storm rolled in, spooking the horses and briefly halting the march. "It moved through quickly," one observer recalled, "bringing white sheets of lightning. The air turned cold. Wind rustled in the pecans and magnolias. Rain fell and thunder cracked." Another storm approached, so the procession resumed. "The honor guard led the way, followed by two white horses in a line, followed by the black horse carrying King's guitars," the observer recounted. "The thunder intensified as the hearse cut in front of the horses. The pallbearers got out and carried King's casket to the grave."

The elderly pallbearers struggled across the lawn, which rain had softened into spongy muck. The pallbearers faltered, and the casket tottered. Phil Bryant, the governor, leapt forward and grabbed a handle, steadying the others. Just as the bearers reached the shelter of the blue tent that covered the gravesite, the clouds burst anew.

The minister intoned, "Earth to earth, ashes to ashes, dust to dust," as B.B. King was lowered into his grave. The green casket straps had been painted a brilliant gold.

EPILOGUE

NOT TWO WEEKS HAD PASSED since B.B. King's funeral when the fight for his estate resumed. Attorneys for LaVerne Toney filed documents in early June 2015 asking a probate commissioner to approve her as executor. Dr. Brimhall testified that the mysterious droplets B.B.'s daughters had seen Myron Johnson place on his tongue were atropine, a drug to ease swallowing.

On June 25, a Las Vegas judge ruled against the children, leaving LaVerne in sole charge of B.B.'s estate. "He worked his entire life to provide for his family," the judge told the assembled family, shedding all pretense of dispassion. "The thing he left for you is his amazing body of work. Somebody has got to make sure that his legacy is protected."

In July, the Clark County coroner announced that an autopsy had found no foul play. B.B. had died a natural death.

The children attacked B.B.'s trust, filed in September 2014, alleging that lawyers had drawn up the document when B.B. was all but blind and afflicted with late-stage Alzheimer's disease. LaVerne insisted it was valid. The children fought on to remove LaVerne as representative of the estate, focusing on the allegation that she had improperly moved roughly $1 million out of B.B.'s personal bank accounts shortly after his death.

B.B. had left a scattered fortune. LaVerne had crisscrossed the nation on a sort of fiscal scavenger hunt, tracking down safe-deposit boxes B.B. had stuffed with loot in Las Vegas, Memphis, Indianola, and Chicago. B.B. wanted hard cash on hand in case he ever "got in trouble" on the road, she recalled, a measure of his lingering insecurity over the white-run worlds of finance and law. B.B. had also placed $1 million in a joint bank account with LaVerne, "in case anything ever came up" and she "couldn't get ahold of him," she recalled. Upon B.B.'s death, that account passed into LaVerne's name, and the children cried foul.

As the probate battle deepened, journalists began to question B.B.'s eleven remaining children on their paternity claims. LaVerne and her attorney produced a birth certificate purportedly proving that one of them, Karen Williams, was not, in fact, B.B.'s child. Reporters dug up Charlie Sawyer's biography and found the passage where Sawyer recounted B.B.'s failed fertility test, back in the early years of his marriage to Sue. Sawyer had politely written around the paradox. The fiction began to unravel.

Since B.B.'s death, three more claims of kinship had surfaced. Some children now spoke out against the others.

The children turned their attention to claiming shares of an estate they hoped might be worth $30 million. In fact, B.B. had died with less than $10 million in the bank, and the figure was shrinking with each month's legal bills.

The children alleged they had been shortchanged in B.B.'s will, dated 2007 and providing them $3,000 to $5,000 apiece. LaVerne claimed to be receiving nothing in the will apart from nominal compensation for her toils. B.B. had tied up most of his fortune in a trust to fund the education of his grandchildren, structuring the document so the money could be put to no other use. In the words of Luther Henson, his childhood teacher, B.B. wanted to guarantee his heirs "the one thing, if you get it, white people can't take it away from you."

The children finally ousted LaVerne Toney in 2016 over the $1 million she had allegedly removed from B.B.'s bank accounts. At age sixty-seven, LaVerne was "tired of all the bullshit, all the greediness," said Brent Bryson, her attorney. She walked away with a generous settlement.

The children claimed their full inheritance: about $3 million, from an estate diminished by litigation. Split among the heirs, the payments worked out to less than $300,000 per child.

By then, the probate feud had faded from the headlines, giving way to gentle reminders of the great bluesman's legacy.

In February 2016, public television aired the American premiere of *B.B. King: The Life of Riley*, a career-spanning documentary from

British director Jon Brewer: even now, fifty years after the British blues explosion, the Brits seemed more devoted than the Americans to scholarly study of American blues. Brewer interviewed surviving bandmates and celebrity friends from Bono to Clapton. Among all the written tributes to B.B. issued upon his death, one of the most poignant had come from Clapton, who noted most of "this music is almost a thing of the past now."

By 2015, the guitar sound B.B. had spawned was all but gone from the pop-music airwaves, along with guitars themselves. B.B. had inspired successive generations of guitar heroes. A 2009 documentary titled *It Might Get Loud* celebrated three of them, Jimmy Page of Led Zeppelin, U2's The Edge, and Jack White of White Stripes. The film marked the end of an era.

Synthesizers and software now ruled the radio: an endless parade of songs by rappers featuring other rappers, pop divas featuring other pop divas, pop divas featuring rappers, and so on, all suffused with electronically altered voices and an insistent, throbbing beat. The *Billboard* pop charts of 2010 and 2015 were strikingly diverse by comparison to the lists of twenty or forty years earlier, populated largely by non-white, non-male artists. But bands of boys were gone, and sadly, the guitars had gone with them.

Electric guitar sales in North America slid from around one and a half million a year to just over one million between the late 2000s and the late 2010s. "Maybe the guitar is over," Eric Clapton mused at a 2017 press conference. In May 2018, Gibson, B.B.'s brand, filed for bankruptcy. The B.B. King Blues Club in New York's Times Square hosted its final concert that spring.

But then, at year's end, Gibson rebounded with a limited-edition Lucille, offered in alpine white in a new collaboration with the B.B. King Family Trust, the education fund B.B. had left for his grandchildren. (Guitar sales would soar anew in 2020 amid the COVID-19 pandemic, which inspired many to embrace the instrument for musical therapy in quarantine.)

In September 2019, B.B.'s children auctioned off hundreds of his prized possessions, throwing open his inner sanctum of treasures, collections, and bric-a-brac. Bidders could rummage among B.B.'s effects online like nosy guests rifling through drawers at a cocktail party. The auction book revealed at every page a new facet of the bluesman's life: a framed photograph of Louis Jordan, signed by the artist with the words "How 'bout that?"; a hardbound Random House dictionary and thesaurus set, worn from heavy use as B.B. labored at self-improvement; stacks of quarter-inch tape filled with songs B.B. had recorded to play on the road; a framed portrait of Colonel Tom Parker, signed "my friend, B.B. King, the only one"; a letter from younger guitar legend Carlos Santana, signed "your student, fan and child"; a Three Stooges Christmas tie; dozens of loafers, in sizes eleven and twelve; ceremonial keys to dozens of cities; a pin from the city council of Grand Prairie, Texas; a silver belt buckle bearing the Great Seal of the state of Idaho; a get-well note from the Clintons; a photo taken with Jimmy Carter (sometime in his final decade, B.B. had managed to meet another president); the honorary doctorate from Yale; one black-vinyl volume of The Book, B.B.'s treasured compendium of paramours; a spiral notebook containing B.B.'s handwritten lyrics to Blind Lemon Jefferson's "See That My Grave Is Kept Clean," rendered in rounded capital letters; dozens of kaleidoscopic stage jackets; a platinum record for *Riding with the King*. By the auction's end, someone had paid $280,000 for a single guitar, a copy of Lucille presented to B.B. for his eightieth birthday.

On September 16, 2019, Google marked what would have been B.B.'s ninety-fourth birthday with an animated Google Doodle that celebrated his life. The digital age offered no greater honor.

In the spring of 2020, an African American man named George Floyd died on a Minneapolis street, facedown on the pavement, a white police officer's knee on his neck. His death launched a national dialogue about lingering symbols of white power. In Mississippi, the white, Republican governor signed a bill in June to retire and replace the state flag. Several southern states still flew banners decorated with winking symbols of the Confederacy. Mississippi incorporated the entire Confederate flag into its own, a gesture somewhat akin to some German province celebrating its identity with a swastika. That summer, another emblem of slavery in Mississippi came down.

In the fall, conflict erupted anew over B.B.'s estate. Wendell Pierce, an African American actor known for his work on the groundbreaking HBO series *The Wire*, announced on Twitter that he would portray B.B. in an inspirational docudrama about the bluesman's friendship with Michael Zanetis, the Los Angeles club owner and musician. That news brought a rebuke from managers of the estate, who said they were preparing the official B.B. King biopic, possibly starring *Saturday Night Live* veteran Kenan Thompson. The estate demanded a confusing clarification from Pierce. Zanetis fumed that his project was being suppressed. With much of Hollywood on lockdown in a darkening winter amid a surging pandemic, both projects remained on hold. But soon enough, some kind of normalcy would return, and then perhaps the films would move forward, to school a new generation of fans on a time when guitar heroes ruled the musical kingdom, and all of them bowed to one King.

LYRICS REFERENCED

"Every Day I Have the Blues," written by Peter Chatman, recorded by B.B. King and released in 1955 by RPM Records. Arc Music, Fort Knox Music Inc., Trio Music Co.

"How Blue Can You Get," written by Jane Feather, recorded by B.B. King and released in 1964 by ABC-Paramount Records. Modern Age Music Company.

"The Thrill Is Gone," written by Roy Hawkins and Rick Darnell, recorded by B.B. King and released in 1969 by BluesWay Records. Universal Music Careers.

"High Water Everywhere," written by Charley Patton, released in 1929 by Paramount Records. EMI Longitude Music.

"Prove It on Me Blues," written by Gertrude "Ma" Rainey, released in 1928 by Paramount Records. Spikedriver Music.

"It's Tight like That," written by Thomas Dorsey and Hudson Whittaker, recorded by Clara Smith and released in 1929 by Columbia Records. Chappell-Morris Ltd.

"B.D. Woman's Blues," written by Bessie Jackson (Lucille Bogan), recorded in 1935 and released in 1978 by Magpie Records. Spikedriver Music.

"Shave 'Em Dry," authorship unknown, recorded around 1933 by Lucille Bogan for Decca Records and released in 1968 by CBS Records.

"Devil Got My Woman," written by Skip James, released in 1931 by Paramount Records. Blind Basement Music.

"District Attorney Blues," written by Bukka White, released in 1940 by Okeh Records. Bukka White Music.

"Caldonia," written by Fleecie Moore, recorded by Louis Jordan and released in 1945 by Decca Records. Cherio Corporation.

"Somebody Done Changed the Lock on My Door," written by William Weldon, recorded by Louis Jordan and released in 1945 by Decca Records. Universal Music Corporation.

"She's Dynamite," written by Hudson Whittaker (Tampa Red), recorded by B.B. King and released in 1951 by RPM Records. Universal Music Careers.

"3 O'Clock Blues," written by Lowell Fulson (but credited to B.B. King), recorded by B.B. King and released in 1951 by RPM Records. Universal Music Careers.

"Beautician Blues," written by Roy Brown (but credited to B.B. King), recorded by B.B. King and released in 1964 by Kent Records. Universal Music Careers.

"You Know I Love You," written by B.B. King, released in 1952 by RPM Records. Universal Music Careers.

"Woke Up This Morning," written by B.B. King, released in 1953 by RPM Records. Universal Music Careers.

"You Upset Me Baby," written by B.B. King, released in 1954 by RPM Records. Universal Music Careers.

"Ten Long Years," written by B.B. King, released in 1955 by RPM Records. Universal Music Careers.

"Bim Bam," written by Don F. Harris and Dewey Terry Jr., recorded by B.B. King and released in 1956 by RPM Records. Sony/ATV Songs LLC.

"Sweet Thing," written by B.B. King, released in 1959 by Crown Records. Universal Music Careers.

"You Done Lost Your Good Thing Now," written by B.B. King, released in 1960 by Crown Records. Universal Music Careers.

"Sweet Sixteen," written by Ahmet Ertegun, recorded by B.B. King and released in 1960 by Kent Records. Universal Music Careers.

"Help the Poor," written by Charles Singleton, recorded by B.B. King and released in 1964 by ABC-Paramount Records. Unichappell Music Inc., Warsing Music.

"Aberdeen Mississippi Blues," written by Bukka White, released in 1940 by Okeh Records. Bukka White Music.

"Buzz Me," written by Dave Dexter Jr. and Fleecie Moore, recorded by B.B. King and released in 1967 by BluesWay Records. Cherio Corporation.

"The Jungle," written by B.B. King, released in 1967 by Kent Records. Universal Music Careers.

"All Over Again," written by Carl B. Adams, recorded by B.B. King and released by ABC-Paramount in 1965. Adams-Gipson Music.

"Lucille," written by B.B. King, released in 1968 by BluesWay Records. Songs of Universal Inc., Universal Music Careers.

"Why I Sing the Blues," written by B.B. King and Dave Clark, released in 1969 by BluesWay Records. Songs of Universal Inc., Universal Music Careers.

"Chains and Things," written by B.B. King and Dave Clark, released in 1970 by BluesWay Records. Songs of Universal Inc., Universal Music Careers.

"Blues Man," written by B.B. King, released in 1998 by MCA Records. Songs of B.B. King Inc., Universal Music Careers.

"See That My Grave Is Kept Clean," written by Blind Lemon Jefferson, recorded by B.B. King and released by Geffen Records in 2008. Tradition Music Co.

"Tomorrow Night," written by Sam Coslow and Will Grosz, recorded by B.B. King and released by Geffen Records in 2008. Bourne Co., Wilhelm Grosz Music Co.

DISCOGRAPHY

WHERE TO START A B.B. KING COLLECTION? A cursory search of the more than fifty proper albums B.B. cut in his lifetime, live and studio, reveals no *Purple Rain*, no *What's Going On*, no one landmark release that towers over the others. B.B.'s first, and greatest, decade as a recording artist was nearly over when the LP format took hold. Several of his early albums are little more than patchy singles collections. None of his studio albums ranks as an unqualified classic. His best live albums certainly do—but is *Live at the Regal* really better than the explosive *Blues Is King* or the impassioned *Live in Cook County Jail*? The volume and variety of B.B. King compilations defy comprehension. In this discography, I've tried to identify and briefly appraise each of B.B.'s live and studio albums and a few of the best compilations. I've erred on the side of inclusiveness with B.B.'s historic Modern Records releases, which blur the line between original work and compilation. I've added asterisks for recordings I consider essential. If you want to start somewhere, try one of the Ace collections, which revisit those breathless, deathless early years.

> *Singin' the Blues*, Crown Records, CLP-5020, spring 1957. B.B. King's first LP collected twelve of his biggest hits, including "3 O'Clock Blues" and "You Upset Me Baby."
>
> *The Blues*, Crown Records, CLP-5063, June 1958. A second singles collection, inevitably weaker than the first but still strong.
>
> *Compositions of Count Basie and Others*, Crown Records, CLP-5111/CST-143, 1959. Billed as "guest vocalist," B.B. plays no guitar. A forgotten curio.
>
> *B.B. King Wails*, Crown Records, CLP-5115/CST-147, June 1959. The first B.B. King LP to feature a collection of (mostly) new songs.
>
> *B.B. King Sings Spirituals*, Crown Records, CLP-5119/CST-152, late 1959. B.B.'s gospel album. Lucille sits silent.
>
> *The Great B.B. King*, Crown Records, CLP-5143, early 1960. A scattershot singles collection assembled around B.B.'s hit "Sweet Sixteen."

Compositions of Duke Ellington and Others, Crown Records, CLP-5153/CST-183, 1960. Another guest vocal date. Even after a decade of brilliant guitar work, B.B. was regarded primarily as a singer.

King of the Blues, Crown Records, CLP-5167/CST-195, 1960 or 1961. A strong set of new songs, featuring B.B. at his virile peak.

A Salute to Tommy Dorsey, Crown Records, CLP-5176/CST-201, 1960 or 1961. B.B.'s final guest-vocal appearance.

*My Kind of Blues, Crown Records, CLP-5188, 1960 or 1961. A mythic record among aficionados, reportedly recorded in a single day. B.B. called it his favorite album.

More B.B. King, Crown Records, CLP-5230, late 1961. The strongest of several Crown releases rushed out amid B.B.'s departure to a major label.

Twist with B.B. King, Crown Records, CLP-5248, 1961 or 1962. Shameless bandwagon jumping.

Easy Listening Blues, Crown Records, CLP-5286/CST-286, 1962. All-instrumental outing sounds like a good band whose vocalist has gone missing.

Mr. Blues, ABC-Paramount Records, ABC-456/ABCS-456, summer 1963. B.B.'s major-label debut ranks as one of the least bluesy collections released under his name.

Blues in My Heart, Crown Records, CLP-5309/CST-309, 1963. Strong if samey set of Crown leftovers. "Down Hearted" would evolve into the B.B. King signature "How Blue Can You Get."

*B.B. King, Crown Records, CLP-5359/CST-359, late 1963. A cannon blast of blues from the Bihari vaults, worthy of its name. One of B.B.'s finest Crown LPs.

Rock Me Baby, Kent Records, KLP-5012/KST-512, summer 1964. A single-disc greatest-hits collection from B.B.'s Modern Records years.

Let Me Love You, Kent Records, KLP-513/KST-513, late 1964. Another grab bag of old Modern Records songs, still better than B.B.'s ABC-Paramount studio recordings of that era.

*Live at the Regal, ABC-Paramount Records, ABC-509/ABCS-509, early 1965. A classic of live recorded blues, key to B.B.'s crossover ascent.

Live! B.B. King On Stage, Kent Records, KST-515/KLP-5015, spring 1965. A rehash of old singles, stitched together with fake crowd noises to sound live.

Confessin' the Blues, ABC-Paramount Records, ABC-528/ABCS-528, January 1966. More big-band schmaltz, an ignoble retreat from the spellbinding *Regal* set.

Blues Is King, BluesWay Records, BLS-6001/BL-6001, early 1967. An incendiary live set, chronicling the breakup of B.B.'s second marriage. Every bit the equal of *Regal*.

The Jungle, Kent Records, KST-521/KLP-5021, summer 1967. Another potent collection of scraps from the Modern Records vaults, perfectly timed to exploit B.B.'s new fame.

Blues on Top of Blues, BluesWay Records, BLS-6011/BL-6011, February 1968. Mercifully, the last album for a while to feature B.B. with a big band.

Lucille, BluesWay Records, BLS-6016, spring 1968. Ace producer Bob Thiele shrinks B.B.'s band and updates his sound. The epic title song helped seed the B.B. King legend.

From the Beginning, Kent Records, KST-533, December 1968. Terrific two-disc Modern Records compilation arrived just as legions of white youths with guitars were discovering the bluesman.

His Best—The Electric B.B. King, BluesWay Records, BLS-6022, February 1969. Pointless, if pleasant, collection of singles and leftovers.

Live & Well, BluesWay Records, BLS-6031, May 1969. The first B.B. King record in years to sound contemporary, thanks to new producer Bill Szymczyk. "Why I Sing the Blues" was the standout.

Completely Well, BluesWay Records, BLS-6037, late 1969. B.B.'s finest studio LP of the late '60s, featuring "The Thrill Is Gone" and inspired guitar work.

Indianola Mississippi Seeds, ABC Records, ABCS-713, late 1970. B.B. jams with Carole King, Leon Russell, and Joe Walsh on an all-star session. Strong but uneven.

Live in Cook County Jail, ABC Records, ABCS-723, early 1971. Another powerful live set, the last truly great B.B. King LP.

Live in Japan, ABC Records, GW-131~2, 1971. B.B.'s first double album, released only in Japan, featured several strong cuts alongside pointless filler.

B.B. King in London, ABC Records, ABCX-730, late 1971. A failed experiment, featuring some of Britain's finest musicians.

L.A. Midnight, ABC Records, ABCX-743, February 1972. B.B.'s first really aimless recording in half a decade. Guest guitarist Joe Walsh is drowned out by a tuba.

Guess Who, ABC Records, ABCX-759, fall 1972. Solid LP from an era that saw B.B. stray ever further into the realms of rock, soul, and funk.

Back in the Alley, BluesWay Records, BLS-6050, February 1973. Single-disc collection harvests the best cuts from B.B.'s years as a lost soul on the ABC-Paramount roster.

The Best of B.B. King, ABC Records, ABCX-767, February 1973. Picks up where *Back in the Alley* left off, collecting the best of B.B.'s work since his pop breakthrough.

To Know You Is to Love You, ABC Records, ABCX-794, summer 1973. Inconsequential Philly-soul outing delivered B.B. two minor hits.

Friends, ABC Records, ABCD-825, fall 1974. More forgettable Philly soul. An artistic dead end.

B.B. King & Bobby Bland: Together for the First Time . . . Live, ABC/Dunhill Records, DSY-50190/2, late 1974. A great idea gone wrong: old friends B.B. and Bland bicker and blunder through an unrehearsed live session.

Lucille Talks Back, ABC Records, ABCD-898, autumn 1975. Pleasant, forgettable outing clocks in under thirty minutes.

Bobby Bland & B.B. King: Together Again . . . Live, ABC Impulse!, ASD-9317, summer 1976. Second meeting with Bland repeats the errors of the first.

King Size, ABC Records, AB-977, early 1977. Finally, a collection of more or less straight blues from a mature B.B. King. His best studio outing since the "Thrill Is Gone" era.

Midnight Believer, ABC Records, AA-1061, spring 1978. The strongest B.B. King album in years, energized by B.B.'s new collaboration with producer Stewart Levine and the jazz-funk Crusaders.

Take It Home, MCA Records, MCA-3151, summer 1979. Another winning collaboration with the Crusaders and Levine.

B.B. King "Now Appearing" at Ole Miss, MCA Records, MCA2-8016, spring 1980. Limp live set, "sweetened" with studio trickery.

There Must Be a Better World Somewhere, MCA Records, MCA-5162, early 1981. Spirited session featuring songwriters Dr. John and Doc Pomus, evoking a lost era of Woodstock and weed.

Love Me Tender, MCA Records, MCA-5307, spring 1982. Abysmal foray into country-western music.

Blues 'n' Jazz, MCA Records, MCA-5413, spring 1983. A welcome return to B.B.'s R&B roots. B.B. contributed a brace of new songs, his first outpouring of original material in years.

The Unexpected . . . Instrumental . . . B.B. King . . . Just Guitar, Kent Records, KLP-2002, 1984. All-instrumental compilation, issued two decades after B.B.'s departure from Modern Records.

Six Silver Strings, MCA Records, MCA-5616, summer 1985. Slick, mid-'80s mess.

*The Best of B.B. King, Volumes One and Two, Ace Records, 1986 and 1987, CH-198 and -199. Vital collections from British Ace imprint.

King of the Blues 1989, MCA Records, MCA-42183, fall 1988. Released amid B.B.'s U2-inspired revival, this synthesized atrocity might mark the low ebb of his recording career.

Live at San Quentin, MCA Records, MCA-6455, summer 1990. Good autumnal live set from B.B. and his touring band.

Live at the Apollo, GRP Records, GRD-9637, spring 1991. B.B. fronts the Philip Morris "Superband," yielding a brisk big-band set that sounds about thirty years out of date.

There Is Always One More Time, MCA Records, MCAD-10295, fall 1991. Second teaming with songwriters Dr. John and Doc Pomus yields another warm, heartfelt set.

*King of the Blues, MCA Records, MCAD4-10677, fall 1992. Four-disc box set spans six decades, but licensing issues precluded proper appraisal of B.B.'s vital Modern Records years.

Blues Summit, MCA Records, MCAD-10710, summer 1993. All-star duet session pairs B.B. with virtually every living icon of rhythm and blues, from John Lee Hooker to Etta James, to fine effect.

Heart to Heart, GRP Records, GRD-9767, spring 1994. B.B. shares top billing with the white pop-jazz singer Diane Schuur, yielding a misguided menu of cocktail jazz.

Deuces Wild, MCA Records, MCD-11711, fall 1997. Second duets outing spans the pop spectrum, pairing B.B. with Eric Clapton, Van Morrison, Willie Nelson, and the Rolling Stones. Interesting but uneven.

Blues on the Bayou, MCA Records, MCAD-11879, fall 1998. Recorded on vintage equipment with B.B.'s road band. A strong autumnal release.

Let the Good Times Roll: The Music of Louis Jordan, MCA Records, 088-112-042-2, fall 1999. Stirring tribute to Louis Jordan, one of B.B.'s idols and prime influences.

The RPM Hits, 1951–1957, Ace Records, CDCHD-712, 1999; *The Best of the Kent Singles, 1958–1971*, Ace Records, CDCHD-760, 2000. Powerful collections from the British Ace label.

Making Love Is Good for You, MCA Records, MCAD-12241, spring 2000. Explicit sequel to *Blues on the Bayou* falls somewhat short of its predecessor.

Riding with the King, Reprise Records, 9-47612-2, summer 2000. Long-awaited collaboration with Eric Clapton delivered B.B. the biggest hit of his LP career. Clapton wisely focuses on the old stuff.

Anthology, MCA Records, 088-112-410-2, winter 2000. A fine collection, so far as it went—back to 1962, after B.B.'s golden era.

A Christmas Celebration of Hope, MCA Records, 088-112-756-2, winter 2001. Forgettable holiday fare.

The Vintage Years, Ace Records, ABOXCD-8, 2002. Perhaps the most important B.B. King compilation ever released, 106 songs and a seventy-four-page book that fully document the blues master in his prime.

Reflections, MCA Records, B0000532-02, spring 2003. Collection of big-band standards is a good idea brought to term about twenty years too late.

80, Geffen Records, B0005263-02, fall 2005. Third duets collection, pleasant but pointless.

Live, Geffen Records, B0009770-02, February 2008. Part musical performance, part Vegas cocktail monologue, *Live* documents the blues giant in decline.

One Kind Favor, Geffen Records, B0011791-02, summer 2008. B.B.'s last studio album is a fitting swansong, produced by Americana master T Bone Burnett.

Live at the Royal Albert Hall 2011, Shout! Factory, 826663-12946, 2012. Final document of B.B.'s recording career displays B.B. in full dementia, barely able to complete a sentence or a song.

THE KING'S COURT

DOZENS OF EXTRAORDINARY MUSICIANS populated the many B.B. King bands and orchestras that crisscrossed the world between B.B.'s first paid blues gigs in 1949 and his retirement in 2014. These were not ensembles of fixed membership, like the Beatles. Some of B.B.'s most memorable lineups endured for only a year or two. B.B.'s relentless touring schedule drove countless musicians away. B.B. regularly purged his ranks, driven by a tireless quest to remain at the top of his game. To fill empty seats on the bandstand, B.B. poached the talented crews of his R&B peers James Brown, Bobby Bland, Albert King, and Otis Clay. Later on, as B.B. entered his autumn years and his ambitions dimmed, he settled on a more or less permanent lineup. His most faithful sidemen, including drummer Calep Emphrey Jr., trumpeter James "Boogaloo" Bolden, and B.B.'s nephew, saxophonist Walter Riley King, remained with him for decades.

Rather than attempt to list every musician who played with B.B. or to catalog every iteration of his band, the following dramatis personae provides snapshots of the B.B. King ensemble at intervals across his six-decade career, drawing from newspaper accounts, liner notes, and photo captions. Thus, the entry marked "June 1956: *Pittsburgh Courier* profile" lists B.B.'s sidemen as reported by that African American newspaper in a 1956 account. The entry "March 1973: Wausau, Wis.," lists his musicians in a 1973 Wisconsin performance covered by the local paper. Letters stand for instruments: *g* for guitar, *k* for keyboards, *t* for trumpet, *s* for saxophone, *tb* for trombone, *b* for bass, *d* for drums.

Here, then, are the King's Men:

1949–50: early B.B. King bands. Robert Lockwood Jr. g, Johnny "Ace" Alexander or Ford Nelson k, Richard Sanders s, Herman Green s, Earl Forest or Solomon Hardy d.

1952–53: performing and recording personnel. Connie Mack Booker k, Floyd Jones t, Bill Harvey s, Evelyn Young s, George Coleman s, Fred Ford s, James Walker b, Ted Curry d, Charles Crosby d.

1955: Big Red crew. Millard Lee k, Kenny Sands t, Calvin Owens t, Evelyn Young s, Floyd Newman s, Lawrence Burdine s, Richard Lillie s, Earl Forest d, James Walker b, Ted Curry d.

June 1956: *Pittsburgh Courier* **profile.** Millard Lee k, Kenny Sands t, Lawrence Burdine s, Johnny Board s, James Merritt b, Ted Curry d.

1958: performing and recording personnel. Millard Lee k, Kenny Sands t, Henry Boozier t, Johnny Board s, Lawrence Burdine s, Louis Hubert s, Marshall York b, Ted Curry d.

November 1964: *Live at the Regal* **band.** Duke Jethro k, Kenny Sands t, Johnny Board s, Bobby Forte s, Leo Lauchie b, Sonny Freeman d.

November 1966: *Blues Is King* **band.** Duke Jethro k/b, Kenny Sands t, Bobby Forte s, Sonny Freeman d.

September 1970: *Live in Cook County Jail* **band.** Ron Levy k, John Browning t, Louis Hubert s, Booker Walker s, Wilbert Freeman b, Sonny Freeman d.

March 1973: Wausau, Wis. Milton Hopkins g, Ron Levy k, Eddie Rowe t, Cato Walker s, Bobby Forte s, Louis Hubert s, Joe Burton tb, Wilbert Freeman b, Sonny Freeman d.

April 1975: Burlington, Vt. Milton Hopkins g, Ron Levy k, James Toney k, Eddie Rowe t/b, Bobby Forte s, Cato Walker s, Joseph Burton tb, Jabo Starks d. (Bass duties probably shared.)

1978: *Arrival of B.B. King* **era.** Milton Hopkins g, James Toney k, Eddie Rowe t, Walter King s, Cato Walker s, Joe Turner b, Calep Emphrey Jr. d.

November 1985: Des Moines, Ia. Leon Warren g, Eugene Carrier k, James Bolden t, Walter King s, Edgar Synigal s, Michael Doster b, Calep Emphrey Jr. d.

May 1990: Scranton, Pa. Leon Warren g, James Toney k, James Bolden t, Melvin Jackson s, Walter King s, Michael Doster b, Calep Emphrey Jr. d.

1995–96: *Blues All Around Me* **era.** Leon Warren g, James Toney k, James Bolden t, Melvin Jackson s, Walter King s, Michael Doster b, Tony Coleman d, Calep Emphrey Jr. d.

Late 1999: *Makin' Love Is Good for You* **band.** Leon Warren g, James Toney k, James Bolden t, Stanley Abernathy t, Melvin Jackson s, Walter King s, Michael Doster b, Calep Emphrey Jr. d.

October 2006: *B.B. King Live* **band.** Charlie Dennis g, James Toney k, James Bolden t, Stanley Abernathy t, Melvin Jackson s, Walter King s, Reggie Richards b, Calep Emphrey Jr. d.

June 2011: *Live at the Royal Albert Hall* **band**. Charlie Dennis g, Ernest Vantrease k, James Bolden t, Stanley Abernathy t, Melvin Jackson s, Reggie Richards b, Tony Coleman d.

Sources: Ace Records, liner notes; King and Ritz, *Blues All Around Me*; and archives of the *Pittsburgh Courier, Scranton Times-Tribune, Des Moines Register, Arizona Republic, Burlington Free Press,* and *Wausau (WI) Daily Herald.*

ACKNOWLEDGMENTS

WHERE POSSIBLE, I HAVE RELIED on B.B. King himself and those who were closest to him to narrate his life. B.B. died in 2015, but he left a rich memoir and hundreds of interviews. Divorced since the mid-'60s, B.B. had no steady romantic partner, raised no children, and left no siblings. No one person could tell all or even most of his story. Many in his inner circle are long dead. Some, including B.B.'s enigmatic mother, Nora Ella King, left no trace. Others, including his father, Albert King, and his best friend, Norman Matthews, live on through archival interviews.

In reconstructing B.B.'s life, I spoke to dozens of surviving friends and relatives, bandmates and producers. Top billing must go to Sue King Evans, B.B.'s ex-wife and the love of his life; Lora Walker, his lifelong friend; Walter Riley King, his nephew; Allan Hammons, his longtime friend and organizer of his museum; and Charles Sawyer and David Ritz, his biographers. Each of those kind souls spoke to me more times than I can count. A few other sources, tapped many times over many months, deserve deep thanks, including bandmates Tony Coleman and Ron Levy; Bill Ferris, B.B.'s friend and tireless academic patron of the blues; security aide Stafford Davis; longtime friend Tommy Peters; producer Stewart Levine; Floyd Lieberman, who succeeded Sid Seidenberg as B.B.'s manager; and Larry Seidenberg, son of the late Sid.

Here, I hope, is a complete list of the other interviews I conducted in person and by phone, Skype, and email between 2018 and 2020. I beg forgiveness from the sources I may have forgotten.

In researching B.B.'s childhood, I spoke to many of the people listed above. I also interviewed Delcia Davis, widow of B.B.'s cousin Birkett Davis; Faye King, B.B.'s stepsister; Dr. Darin Brimhall, his physician; Jessie Mae Hemphill, his childhood classmate; and Hugh and Mary Jane Gibson, nephew and niece of Edwayne Henderson. Jocleta Cartledge, daughter-in-law of Flake Cartledge, spent half a day driving me and my daughter around the old Cartledge and Henderson farms in her pickup. Martha McKey and Fannie Henson Draine, daughters of schoolmaster Luther Henson, spoke to me within the one-room schoolhouse where their father once taught. Jerry Fair, of the storied Fair clan, shared his encyclopedic genealogical memories. Robert Terrell guided me through the exhibits at the B.B. King Museum. I reaped invaluable help from Wendy Hubbard, superintendent of schools in Montgomery County, Mississippi; Judy Moulder at the Mississippi Department of Health; Rachel Elizabeth Scott at the University of Memphis library; Robert Cruthirds and Gina Cordell at the Memphis Public Library; Ronald Lee at the Tennessee State Library; Wayne Everett Goins at Kansas State University; and John Dalton at the Equal Justice Initiative.

On B.B.'s young adulthood, his journey to Memphis in the late 1940s, his ascent to fame, and his tenure with Modern Records in the 1950s, I spoke to many of the sources listed above, as well as to Shirley Ann King, B.B.'s daughter; Dorothy Darr, wife of Charles Lloyd; Floyd Newman and Alfordson "Ford" Nelson, his surviving bandmates; Preston Lauterbach, author of the extraordinary *Chitlin' Circuit and the Road to Rock 'n' Roll*; Judy Peiser at the Center for Southern Folklore; Christine Cooper Spindel, an early WDIA employee; Natolyn Williams Herron, daughter of Nat D. Williams; Barbara Matthews, widow of Norman; Willis Edwards III, son of Willis "Bebop" Edwards Jr.; and Michael Bihari, son of Joseph Bihari. John Broven, an expert archivist of King's recordings, patiently explained the music business over many phone calls and emails. Neil Scaplehorn at Ace Records provided vital notes on the old RPM and Crown recordings. David Hardin at the National Personnel Records Center helped me interpret enigmatic Selective Service records. Garrick Feldman of the *Arkansas Leader* provided guidance on the real Lucille. Further thanks to Mike Stephenson and Tony Watson of *Blues & Rhythm*, Paul Kelly at *Rock's Backpages*, and Cilla Huggins of *Juke Blues*.

On B.B.'s fallow years, revival, and crossover ascent in the 1960s, I spoke to many of the sources above and to keyboardist Duke Jethro, producer Bill Szymczyk, bassist Jerry Jemmott, British blues pioneer John Mayall, photographer Glen Craig, and *Live at the Regal* producer Johnny Pate; Elvin Bishop, cofounder of the Butterfield Blues Band; Jerry Miller and Peter Lewis of Moby Grape; Russ Koberna of Kicks Inc.; blues revivalists Dick Spottswood, Dick Waterman, and E. D. Denson; Charles Keil, author of *Urban Blues*; journalist and *Rock Folk* author Michael Lydon; Darrell Spann, son of Pervis; and Harriet Seidenberg Turkanis, daughter of Sid. I had a brief and fruitful email exchange with Al Kooper.

On B.B. in the 1970s, 1980s, and 1990s, I spoke to the sources named above and to LaVerne Toney, B.B.'s top Las Vegas aide across five decades; Jim Abbott, longtime editor of the *Indianola Enterprise-Tocsin*; sidemen Joe Burton, Michael Doster, Russell Jackson, James Bolden, Charles Boles, and Wilbert Freeman; aides-de-camp Joe McClendon and Tina France; radio producer Gary Bird; filmmaker Michael Zanetis; and record producers Ed Michel, Steve Barri, and

Andy McKaie. I reaped timely help from *Soul Power* director Jeffrey Kusama-Hinte; Jesse Turner Jr., son of the late Jesse Turner Sr.; and State Department retiree Philippe du Chateau. Filmmaker John Landis told me the story of *The Blues Brothers*. Clarence Richard English, retired warden, took me back to 1970 at Cook County Jail. Myron Johnson, B.B.'s last road manager, recounted his final hours with the boss. Thanks to Mike Gianakos for plumbing the archives of *High Times* and to Noel Clay and Rasheeda Clements for answering my diplomatic inquiries.

On the final fifteen years of B.B. King's life, I spoke to many of the above and to his daughter Patricia King, attorneys E. Brent Bryson and Arthur Williams Jr., producers T Bone Burnett and Bill Wax, and bassist Nathan East.

I am indebted to researchers and archivists at several estimable libraries, including Greg Johnson at the University of Mississippi, Aaron Smithers at the University of North Carolina, Brenda Nelson-Strauss and William R. Vanden Dries at Indiana University, Daria Wingreen-Mason at the Smithsonian, Todd Harvey at the American Folklife Center, Rachel Scott at the University of Memphis, Jennifer Rose at the Sunflower County Library, and everyone in the Performing Arts Reading Room at the Library of Congress. Brett Bonner of *Living Blues* provided timely guidance and Airbnb tips. Malika Polk-Lee at the B.B. King Museum granted me entrée to their precious collection of archival interviews.

My friends Paul Dickson, Craig Singer, and especially Michael Dolan, music buffs all, provided invaluable advice in shaping this book. I owe deep thanks to Deborah Grosvenor, the consummate literary agent, who taught me most of what I know about the narrative arc; George Gibson at Grove Atlantic, whose superb edits posed all the right questions; and Sophie, my wife, my favorite editor and my favorite reader.

NOTES

Introduction

2 "empty of everything": Ron Levy, *Tales of a Road Dog: The Lowdown along the Blues Highway* (Pennsauken, NJ: BookBaby, 2013), Kindle edition, 87. This passage also draws from an author interview with Clarence Richard English on October 20, 2020, and from the *Chicago Tribune* of September 11, 1970, and February 21, 1971, the *Chicago Daily Defender* of September 17, 1970, and the *Chicago Sun-Times* of May 15, 2015.

2 "final and scary": James Maycock, "Pop: And That Is Why I Choose to Sing the Blues," *The Independent* (London), September 11, 1998.

4 "made me sad and glad": B.B. King with David Ritz, *Blues All around Me* (New York: Avon Books, 1996), 258 (also referred to in the notes as King's memoir).

1. Sharecropper

5 Albert probably entered: Kenneth Miller, "B.B. King's Father Succumbs," *Los Angeles Sentinel*, January 12, 1984.

5 Events tore Albert's family: Charles Sawyer, *The Arrival of B.B. King* (New York: Doubleday, 1980), 33–34.

5 Elnora's parents: The elder Davidson's nickname has been variously rendered as "Pop" or "Pomp."

6 When Albert called: Charles Sawyer, author interview, June 21, 2019.

6 a white farmer named Jim O'Reilly: Oddly, census records do not show that surname or anything like it in Itta Bena or environs. Perhaps O'Reilly was himself a tenant.

6 "When Mama went": King with Ritz, *Blues*, 7. The term "birth certificate" is used loosely. Though King believed the document existed, no record seems to have been filed with the state. In those times, records of sharecropper births and deaths often perished with the landlords who kept them.

7 When the Great: "Itta Bena Is Working Well," *Greenwood Commonwealth*, April 25, 1927.

7 Albert could not read: This passage draws from author interviews with Walter King and Charles Sawyer.

7 "My mother told me": This passage draws from a 2006 interview with King by Jim Dollarhide and Charles Sawyer in Mississippi for the B.B. King Museum and Delta Interpretive Center and from King's memoir.

7 "growing more and more": King with Ritz, *Blues*, 7.

8 Albert's drinking: In an interview on November 16, 2005, for the National Visionary Leadership Project, King told Camille Cosby, "My dad used to drink a bit—a bit too much, as far as my mother was concerned."

8 By the spring of 1930: King's memoir does not mention Herd. In his account, Nora Ella left Albert to rejoin her family in Kilmichael, fifty miles away.

8 "When a woman decides": Charles Sawyer, author interview, June 7, 2019.

8 Two-thirds of Mississippians: "Great Depression," undated article at the *Mississippi Encyclopedia* website, https://mississippiencyclopedia.org/entries/great-depression/.

8 "I didn't know": King with Ritz, *Blues*, 10–11.

8 Riley might have taken: In a June 1980 interview by John Jones for the Mississippi state archives in Jackson, King said the first school he recalled was "up near Berclair."

9 Bukka White was born: Potential birthdates for Bukka abound, but the 1910 census lists him as a boy of five.

9 "a little, one-store town": F. Jack Hurley and David Evans, "Bukka White," in *Tom Ashley, Sam McGee, Bukka White: Tennessee Traditional Singers*, ed. Thomas G. Burton (Knoxville: University of Tennessee Press, 1981), 190.

10 "looking like a million": King with Ritz, *Blues*, 25.

10 "old folk": King with Ritz, 27–28.

10 One distant relative: In a 2006 interview with organizers of the B.B. King Museum, a surviving member of the Fair family recalled Riley living with her sister and Riley's uncle, presumably William Pulley and his wife, Lucille Fair Pulley, in Berclair around 1931.

10 "We climb": King with Ritz, *Blues*, 5–6.

10 In 1931 or 1932: The date must be after 1930, because that year's census found none of King's people living in Kilmichael. Riley and his mother were in Itta Bena, living with Herd. Riley's grandmother Elnora was a hundred miles away in Chickasaw County.

11 "When Albert and Nora": Lessie Fair, interview by Jim Dollarhide and Charles Sawyer, Mississippi, 2006, for the B.B. King Museum and Delta Interpretive Center.

11 "She has a radiant face": King with Ritz, *Blues*, 3–4, 5–6, 16.

12 "I'm sorry, Mama": King with Ritz, *Blues*, 19–20.

13 "talked with his shotgun": King with Ritz, *Blues*, 8–9.

13 Riley remembered: Allan Hammons, author interview, September 24, 2018. Pomp Davidson, death certificate, Mississippi State Board of Health.

13 "But the blues hollerers": King with Ritz, *Blues*, 8–9.

14 Around the start of 1935: The family could not have left Chickasaw before then, because several members reported having lived there in 1935 on the 1940 census. But they could not have left much later, because Riley's mother died in Kilmichael before the year was out.

14 "we got out": King with Ritz, *Blues*, 7.

14 "All of them moved": Lessie Fair, Dollarhide and Sawyer interview.

14 Most of the actual farming: Sawyer, *Arrival*, 45.

16 "Good morning to you": Ted Hemphill, interview by Jim Dollarhide and Charles Sawyer, Mississippi, 2006, for the B.B. King Museum and Delta Interpretive Center.

16 "We had about five": Jessie Hemphill, author interview, April 1, 2018.

17 "Everything we ate": Fannie Henson Draine, author interview, April 1, 2018.

17 "snuff your little life": Jessie Hemphill, interview by Jim Dollarhide and Charles Sawyer, Mississippi, 2006, for the B.B. King Museum and Delta Interpretive Center.

17 "It's the one thing": Lora Walker, author interview, March 27, 2018.

17 Mississippi in 1930: Peter Irons, "Jim Crow's Schools," *American Educator*, Summer 2004.

18 "Y'all hear about": King with Ritz, *Blues*, 11–13.

18 "He was an A-1 student": This passage draws from Dollarhide and Sawyer's interviews with Ted and Jessie Hemphill and author interviews with Lora Walker. King's recollections come from his memoir.

18 "I would always make it": *B.B. King: The Life of Riley*, dir. Jon Brewer, Emperor Media, 2012.

19 "part séance": Sawyer, *Arrival*, 39.

19 "Archie Fair is the nearest": King with Ritz, *Blues*, 16.

19 "While they're not looking": King with Ritz, 16–18.

20 They were the I: The identities of the chords are a matter of some dispute. Biographer Charles Sawyer says that Fair taught King E, A, and B. Other sources suggest that Fair might have taught his young parishioner G, C, and D or perhaps C, F, and G. In terms of the musical relationship between the root (I) chord and its relatives, IV and V, it amounts to the same thing.

20 Folklorist Alan Lomax: Alan Lomax, *The Land Where the Blues Began* (New York: Dell, 1993), 347–48.

20 Riley appeared one day: Mary Jane Gibson, author interview, March 30, 2018.

21 "When I tightened": King with Ritz, *Blues*, 41.

21 "most modern": King with Ritz, 20–22.

21 reminded Riley of the field: King with Ritz, 22.

22 "to base his style": Francis Davis, *The History of the Blues* (New York: Hyperion, 1995), 145.

22 Riley couldn't hear: In interviews, King consistently recalled Johnson and Blind Lemon Jefferson as his greatest musical influences in childhood.

22 "He seed Riley": Lessie Fair, Dollarhide and Sawyer interview.

22 "I was afraid": King with Ritz, *Blues*, 28–31. Nora Ella was probably twenty-six or twenty-seven when she died, a year later.

23 She was twenty-six: This assumes a 1908 birthdate.

2. On the Run

25 "Staying in the cabin": King with Ritz, *Blues*, 33.

25 "could be a little mean": King with Ritz, 8.

25 "Everybody cared about me": Gerri Hirshey, "On the Bus with B.B. King," *Rolling Stone*, December 24, 1998.

26 "He would play with me": Wayne Cartledge, interview by Jim Dollarhide and Charles Sawyer, Mississippi, 2006, for the B.B. King Museum and Delta Interpretive Center. Wayne recalled meeting Riley when he was about three years old, in 1935.

26 "would go and drag": Lessie Fair, Dollarhide and Sawyer interview.

27 "Sometimes a bird": King with Ritz, *Blues*, 34–35.

27 Luther Holbert: Equal Justice Initiative, *Lynching in America: Confronting the Legacy of Racial Terror*, 3d ed. (2017), https://lynchinginamerica.eji.org/report/.

28 "I remember hearing": King, Cosby interview.

28 wired for electricity: In her interview with Dollarhide and Sawyer, Lessie Fair noted that "there wasn't even any electric across the river," alluding to the farmland where she and Riley lived. Her statement suggests that Kilmichael itself, north of the Big Black River, had power.

28 "Cowboy music": King with Ritz, *Blues*, 40.

28 "And for the longest time": Lora Walker, author interview, August 27, 2018. Sue King Evans and others also recalled the injury in author interviews.

29 "The guys had been tellin' me": Fred Schruers, "Mississippi Homecoming," *Rolling Stone*, November 30, 1989.

29 "Your food's in the safe": King with Ritz, *Blues*, 38.

30 Aunt Mima would end: This passage draws from the 1940 census and from Sawyer's *Arrival*.
30 Elnora died: Her age at death derives from the 1900 census, which put her birthdate in the latter half of 1885. All farm records were reported by Sawyer in *Arrival*.
31 "Big Jack": Jessie Hemphill, author interview.
31 he borrowed a furnish: Charles Sawyer transcribed Henderson's financial records in his biography, *Arrival*.
31 "I knew it was": David Ritz, *The God Groove* (New York: Howard Books, 2019), 120.
32 "I could see God's hand": Ritz, 120.
33 "tried to sound like": King with Ritz, *Blues*, 42.
33 "Once in a great while": King with Ritz, 43.
33 "Get your books": Jessie Hemphill, author interview. King remembered differently, writing in his memoir that his father came to get him at his home. King with Ritz, 46.
34 "rivers of whiskey": Sawyer, *Arrival*, 206.
34 "After [Elnora] passed": Lessie Fair, Dollarhide and Sawyer interview.
34 "You all right, Jack?": This passage draws from King's memoir, from an author interview of Jessie Hemphill, and from an interview of B.B. King conducted in Chattanooga, Tennessee, in June 1989 by an interviewer identified only as Tidwell.
34 "With Daddy there was": King with Ritz, *Blues*, 47.
35 The first meeting: King's thoughts and words in this passage draw from his memoir.
35 "I was never taught": *On the Road with B.B. King: An Interactive Autobiography*, CD-ROM, MCA Records, 1996.
36 attending private school: Jim Roberts, "From Itta Bena to Fame: B.B. King," *Tri-State Defender*, March 29, 1952.
36 "Professor Seal would talk": King with Ritz, *Blues*, 52.
36 "Someone cheers": King with Ritz, 51.
37 Mississippi would document: King biographer Charles Sawyer searched the *Advertiser* archives. Lynching statistics derive from the Equal Justice Initiative report *Lynching in America*. According to EJI staff attorney John Dalton, the agency has no record of a lynching at the time and place King recalled.
37 barely a year: In his memoir, King recalled that he had lived in Lexington three years earlier, in 1938. Yet, given the established date of his grandmother's death, that doesn't seem possible.
37 "The pressures of Lexington": King with Ritz, *Blues*, 53.
37 "Excuse me, ma'am": King with Ritz, *Blues*, 53–55.
38 "He was sitting": Jessie Hemphill, author interview.
38 "Who is that?": Lessie Fair recounted the conversation between John Fair and Riley King to Jim Dollarhide. Ted Hemphill provided Dollarhide the "log mule" quote.
39 "raised cotton and corn": Wayne Cartledge, Dollarhide and Sawyer interview.
39 "looked like a combination": This passage draws from Sawyer's *Arrival* and King's memoir.
40 "B.B. was my babysitter": Wayne Cartledge, Dollarhide and Sawyer interview.
40 "It's a little hard": Allan Hammons, author interview, September 24, 2018.
41 "I was in love": King with Ritz, *Blues*, 41.
41 "new life": King with Ritz, 41.
41 "had a battery-operated": Wayne Cartledge, Dollarhide and Sawyer interview.
41 One of the Hemphill boys: Jessie Hemphill, author interview.
42 "God has given everybody": Fannie Henson Draine, author interview.

42 After the 1942 harvest: This account, from biographer Sawyer, fits the facts bet-
ter than the one in King's memoir. King recalls returning from Lexington to
Kilmichael, discovering his kin have departed and immediately following them to
Indianola.

3. Indianola Mississippi Seeds

43 "it'll suck the soles": King with Ritz, *Blues*, 57.
44 "you could start walking": King with Ritz, 58.
44 "unheard of": Sawyer, *Arrival*, 50–51.
45 "He wore khaki pants": King with Ritz, *Blues*, 58–59.
45 "We used to say": Willie McClinton, interview by Jim Dollarhide and Charles Sawyer,
Mississippi, 2006, for the B.B. King Museum and Delta Interpretive Center; Delcia
Davis, interview by Jim Dollarhide and Charles Sawyer, Mississippi, 2006, for the
B.B. King Museum and Delta Interpretive Center.
45 Bay Lake School: Jim Abbott, "B.B. King: 'Indianola Is My Hometown,'" *Indianola
(MS) Enterprise-Tocsin*, June 23, 1977.
45 "like a woman": King with Ritz, *Blues*, 60.
46 The boys quarreled: Delcia Davis, Dollarhide and Sawyer interview.
46 "She was a dark-skinned": King with Ritz, *Blues*, 61. Riley's age is inferred from the
date of his arrival in Indianola. Angel's age is an educated guess.
46 "Finally, after the benediction": King with Ritz, *Blues*, 61–62. As with several other
signal events in King's childhood, his courtship of the doomed Angel resists docu-
mentation as historical fact. King spoke of her at length in his memoir and mentioned
her in a few stray interviews, but he never gave her full name or affixed a date, or
even a year, to her untimely death. A search of the *Indianola (MS) Sunflower Tocsin*,
which routinely covered the city's African American community, found no account
of a family wiped out in a traffic accident during King's time there as a single man.
47 prisoners of war: "Prisoners to Help Pick Cotton," *Indianola (MS) Enterprise*, September 30, 1943.
47 "the war got close": This passage draws from Andrew E. Kersten, "African Americans
and World War II," *OAH Magazine of History* 16, no. 3 (Spring 2002); Henry Louis
Gates Jr., "What Was Black America's Double War?," *PBS.org*, July 25, 2013, https://
www.pbs.org/wnet/african-americans-many-rivers-to-cross/history/what-was-black
-americas-double-war/; and King's memoir.
48 "quite a number": "Indianola Colored People Support 3rd War Loan," *Indianola (MS)
Enterprise*, October 14, 1943.
49 "came out of Mississippi": Peter Guralnick, *Feel like Going Home* (New York: Outer-
bridge and Dienstfrey, 1971), 46.
49 "The blues": Charles Evers, interview by Jim Dollarhide and Charles Sawyer, Mississippi, 2006, for the B.B. King Museum and Delta Interpretive Center.
50 "If they found out": King with Ritz, *Blues*, 64.
50 "we would sing": William R. Ferris, "Interview: B.B. King," *Southern Cultures*, Winter
2006.
50 "Why not us?": King with Ritz, *Blues*, 64–65.
51 a guitarist named Charlie Christian: King recalled in his memoir watching Christian
on a Mutoscope film. More likely, he heard the guitarist on disc. No known footage
exists of Charlie Christian in performance, said Wayne Everett Goins, a Christian
biographer, in an author interview by email on January 28, 2020.

51 ignoring the color line: Goodman had hired at least two other African-American musicians before Christian, including vibraphonist Lionel Hampton.

51 "a miracle man": King with Ritz, *Blues*, 67.

51 "women in tight dresses": King with Ritz, 68. King recalled seeing Parker play with McShann, but Parker may have left his band by the time King saw it.

52 "I'd climb up": King with Ritz, *Blues*, 73.

53 "Working the fields": Delcia Davis, Dollarhide and Sawyer interview.

53 "How come you ain't": Delcia Davis, Dollarhide and Sawyer interview.

53 "Maybe we could take off": This passage draws from an interview with King by William Barlow in Washington, DC, in February 1980, and from King's memoir.

54 The same tradition: William Barlow, *Voice Over: The Making of Black Radio* (Philadelphia: Temple University Press, 1998).

55 "a light-skinned beauty": King with Ritz, *Blues*, 82.

55 "Her smile warmed me": King with Ritz, 85–86.

57 "Once the fighting": Bryan D. Booker, *African Americans in the United States Army* (Jefferson, NC: McFarland, 2008), 49.

57 "Just me": This passage draws from author interviews with Charles Sawyer and Jerry Fair and from King's memoir. King's recollection of his military odyssey, while plausible, cannot be squared with the sparse military records that survive on draftee 22-72-25-243. A cryptic page from the 1944 Indianola draft registry lists twenty-nine African American men. Fourteen were rejected after their preinduction physicals for various reasons. Nine were inducted. The fate of the others, including King, was not recorded.

57 "How y'all doing?": This scene draws from King's memoir; from B.B. King with Dick Waterman, *The B.B. King Treasures* (New York: Bulfinch, 2005); and from Cosby's King interview.

58 "they ran me ragged": King with Ritz, *Blues*, 90.

59 "went to Camp Shelby": Delcia Davis, Dollarhide and Sawyer interview.

59 Venereal disease proliferated: G. St. J. Perrott, "Selective Service Rejection Statistics and Some of Their Implications," U.S. Public Health Service, April 1946.

59 "the most painful thing": Darin Brimhall, author interview, October 4, 2019.

59 the third assault: King recounted all three incidents to Lora Walker many years later in explanation for his infertility, sparing her the details of the VD treatment. He told the gonorrhea story to his second wife, Sue King Evans. Both women recalled the conversations in author interviews.

60 "About every weekend": Delcia Davis, author interview, December 26, 2018; Delcia Davis, Dollarhide and Sawyer interview.

61 "Why you do that?": Willie McClinton, Dollarhide and Sawyer interview.

61 "It's later in the afternoon": King with Ritz, *Blues*, 75.

61 "blues meant money": Ritz, *God Groove*, 121–22.

62 "After I got off": Tom Wheeler, "B.B. King: 'Playing the Guitar Is Like Telling the Truth,'" *Guitar Player*, September 1980.

62 "Everyone on the place": Missy Morgan, "They Remember Riley King of Indianola," *Indianola (MS) Enterprise-Tocsin*, June 5, 1980.

62 "He'd play that guitar": Delcia Davis, interviews by the author and Dollarhide and Sawyer.

62 "You can't sing": David Matthews, interview by Jim Dollarhide and Charles Sawyer, Mississippi, 2006, for the B.B. King Museum and Delta Interpretive Center.

62 "We were stuck": King with Ritz, *Blues*, 93.

63 "Hey, you could steal": B.B. King, interview by William R. Ferris, January 2, 2000, printed in *Reflections on American Music: The Twentieth Century and the New Millennium*, ed. James R. Heintze and Michael Saffle (Hillsdale, NY: Pendragon, 2000), 243–57.

63 "separated women": Preston Lauterbach, *The Chitlin' Circuit and the Road to Rock 'n' Roll* (New York: Norton, 2011), 123.

64 "His sound cut me": King with Ritz, *Blues*, 78.

64 "I had to keep working": King with Ritz, 80.

65 "You'll never do any": Sawyer, *Arrival*, 54.

65 "I didn't know": *On the Road* CD-ROM.

4. The Blues

67 "Their song was": George Pinckard, *Notes on the West Indies* (London: Longman, Hurst, Rees, and Orme, 1806), 1:231.

67 "merry repast": Frederick Law Olmsted, *Journeys and Explorations in the Cotton Kingdom of America* (London: William Clowes and Sons, 1861), 1:214.

68 "Our ears were beset": Charles Peabody, "Notes on Negro Music," *Journal of American Folklore*, July–September 1903, 148–152.

68 "the 'man' who left her": John W. Work, *American Negro Songs and Spirituals* (New York: Crown, 1940), 32.

69 "a lean, loose-jointed Negro": Davis, *History*, 25–26.

71 "almost as if": Ted Gioia, *Delta Blues* (New York: Norton, 2008), 36.

71 "One of the phonograph companies": Gioia, 38.

72 "a short and stubby woman": Davis, *History*, 74.

72 "unique in pre-Stonewall": Jonathan Ned Katz, "Ma Rainey's 'Prove It on Me Blues,' 1928," *OutHistory*, n.d., http://outhistory.org/exhibits/show/rainey/rainey2.

72 Francis Davis calls her: Davis, *History*, 76.

72 "all the femaleness": Mezz Mezzrow and Bernard Wolfe, *Really the Blues* (New York: Random House, 1946).

72 the nation's highest-paid Black performer: Gioia, *Delta Blues*, 40–41.

73 the standard first pressing: Gioia, 133.

73 "tore off the top": King with Ritz, *Blues*, 24.

74 "He darn sure could": Victoria Spivey, "Blind Lemon and I Had a Ball," *Record Research*, May 1966.

75 "The influence of the Delta": Gioia, *Delta Blues*, 1–2.

75 "among the most important": Robert Palmer, *Deep Blues* (New York: Viking, 1981), 57.

75 "a small, intense, fretful man": Samuel Charters, *The Blues Makers* (New York: Da Capo, 1991), 38.

76 "All the strutting": Gioia, *Delta Blues*, 51.

77 "I could make [the guitar] say": Gioia, 80.

77 tall and gangly: Charters, *Blues Makers*, 57.

78 Aunt Mima played: Tom Wheeler and Jas Obrecht, "B.B. King," in *The B.B. King Reader: 6 Decades of Commentary*, ed. Richard Kostelanetz (Milwaukee: Hal Leonard, 2005), 180.

79 "in Delta labor camps": Palmer, *Deep Blues*, 112–13.

80 "never recorded anything": Palmer, 127.

80 "slender, small-boned": Palmer, 111.

81 borrowed melodies and lyrical schemes: Davis, *History*, 128.

81 "the last *great* performer": Davis, 130.

82 "Because his music": King with Ritz, *Blues*, 78.

82 "the epitome of taste": King with Ritz, 125.

5. Memphis

83 "The Mississippi Delta begins": Jon Nordheimer, "Memphis: A City That Wants Never to Change," *New York Times*, January 26, 1973.

84 Beale Street: Lexis Withers, "Beale Street (1841–)," *BlackPast*, July 12, 2018, http://www .blackpast.org/aah/beale-street-1841.

85 "by word-of-Negro-mouth": Lauterbach, *Chitlin' Circuit*, 273–74.

85 Riley knew he had: William R. Ferris, *Give My Poor Heart Ease* (Chapel Hill: University of North Carolina Press, 2009), 199.

85 "I'd never seen anything": King with Ritz, *Blues*, 98.

86 "The sounds got me": King with Ritz, 99.

87 Spottswood Avenue: White told biographers he lived on Spottswood in 1946; Booker and Emma White are listed at 2605 Spottswood in the 1948 Memphis directory.

87 "Mr. Johnson is surely": King with Ritz, *Blues*, 100–101.

87 Bukka was a contemporary: This passage draws from several sources, particularly Hurley and Evans, "Bukka White."

88 "After that visit": William R. Ferris, "B.B. King at Parchman Penitentiary," *Living Blues*, Summer 1981.

88 "with a head full": This passage draws from Charters's *Blues Makers* and Burton's *Tennessee*.

88 The morning after: Margaret McKee and Fred Chisenhall, *Beale Black & Blue* (Baton Rouge: LSU Press, 1993), 128. Bukka's quote comes from King's memoir.

89 "His blues was the book": King's words and thoughts draw from his memoir.

89 The cousins often played: Sawyer, *Arrival*, 56.

89 T-Bone Walker first recorded: Allan Kozinn, Pete Welding, Dan Forte, and Gene Santoro, *The Guitar* (New York: Quarto Marketing, 1984), 74.

90 "B.B. used to come": Peter Guralnick, *Lost Highway* (Boston: David R. Godine, 1979), 60. Other details from Natolyn Williams Herron, author interview, September 28, 2018.

90 "Once in a great while": King with Ritz, *Blues*, 76.

91 Albert and Bukka: Hurley and Evans, "Bukka White," 191.

91 "missed her something fierce": This passage draws from King's memoir and from the *On the Road* CD-ROM.

91 Their departure drove: Delcia Davis, Dollarhide and Sawyer interview.

91 "I don't think": James Fair, interview by Jim Dollarhide and Charles Sawyer, Mississippi, 2006, for the B.B. King Museum and Delta Interpretive Center.

92 "Riley, where you been?": King with Ritz, *Blues*, 103.

93 "thick, heavy tone": Guralnick, *Going Home*, 67.

93 "high Indian cheekbones": Guralnick, 63–65.

94 guitar was an afterthought: Gioia, *Delta Blues*, 217.

94 "Poor recording": "Record Reviews," *Billboard*, July 10, 1948. The quip actually critiqued the single's A-side, "I Feel like Going Home." The reviewer dismissed "I Can't Be Satisfied" with the notation, "Same complaint as flip."

94 "I'd already been": King with Ritz, *Blues*, 107.

94 "For some reason": Hirshey, "On the Bus."

95 "I'll send for you": King with Ritz, *Blues*, 109. Most prior biographical sources have King making his second trip to Memphis in 1948. But he cannot have arrived before October 25 of that year, when the radio station WDIA began featuring African American talent. The date is probably closer to Saturday, March 26, 1949, the first appearance of the name "Bee Bee King" in the *Commercial Appeal* radio listings. In liner notes to *B.B. King—The Vintage Years*, Ace Records, ABOXCD 8, 2002, archivist Colin Escott notes that King joined the Musicians Union on March 31, further evidence of a March arrival.

95 Beale Street West: KWEM Radio, "History," n.d., http://www.kwemradio.com /History.html.

96 "I felt like I knew him": Paul Trynka, "B.B. King: Bright Lights Big City," *Mojo*, May 1998.

96 He found the harpist: This scene draws from accounts in King's memoir, Ferris's *Give My Poor Heart Ease*, and *Soul* magazine of April 6, 1970. These and other sources put Sonny Boy Williamson at KWEM in 1949; oddly, neither his name nor Wolf's appears in KWEM radio listings of that era. In some accounts, King said Sonny Boy was alone. The timing of King's visit to the station, on a Wednesday, comes from a 1988 interview with *Living Blues* magazine. Of all possible Wednesdays, the most likely date is May 23, 1946, three days before King's own name first appeared in radio listings.

98 The club on South Sixteenth Street: Rachel Silva, "Walks through History: Downtown West Memphis," April 11, 2015, Arkansas Historic Preservation Program.

98 "The joint was just": This scene draws from accounts in King's memoir and Stanley Booth's *Rythm Oil* (New York: Pantheon, 1992).

6. The Blues Boy

100 "What do you think": Christine Cooper Spindel, "Let's Put Him on the Air," *Oxford American*, Winter 2013; Spindel, *The Beginnings of Black Radio: My Years at WDIA Memphis* (Urbana, IL: Prairie Island, 2019), 1–5.

101 "the first four Negroes": Barlow, *Voice Over*, 52–55.

102 "For the first three": Christine Cooper Spindel, author interviews, October 3 and 4, 2018.

103 "a black man": This scene draws from King's memoir and Chester Higgins, "B.B. King Sings Blues with a Bounce," *Tan*, November 1969.

103 A less evocative retelling: Christine Cooper Spindel, author interviews.

103 "a short Jewish man": This passage draws from Louis Cantor's *Wheelin' on Beale* (New York: Pharos Books, 1992) and King's memoir.

104 "You're all right": This passage draws from King's memoir, author interviews with Christine Cooper Spindel, and Arnold Shaw's *The Rockin' '50s* (New York: E. P. Dutton, 1974).

105 "He just straightened up": Spindel, author interviews.

105 "Let's put him": Spindel, "Air."

106 "Man, it was horrible": Rufus Thomas, interview by David Less and Robert Palmer, Memphis, October 1976, Mississippi Valley Collection, University of Memphis.

106 "I'm going to rename you": This scene draws from author interviews with Christine Cooper Spindel and Cantor's *Wheelin' on Beale*.

106 "He was on every": This passage draws from King's memoir and author interviews with Christine Cooper Spindel.

106 This much is certain: This timeline draws from the daily "Radio Time Table" feature in the *Commercial Appeal.*

107 "That was ridiculous": King with Ritz, *Blues,* 115–16.

108 "I didn't tell Martha": This passage draws from King's memoir and author interviews with Lora Walker and Shirley Ann King.

109 Riley didn't have a band: King might have recruited one or two sidemen by this time, but he had no fixed ensemble.

109 "Who's that?": Colin Escott, "B.B. King: A Golden Anniversary (2000)," in Kostelanetz, *Reader,* 6.

110 "A low-down, heavy beat": "Record Reviews," *Billboard,* July 30, 1949.

110 "stood no taller": Lauterbach, *Chitlin' Circuit,* 181–82.

110 Accounts differ: An early feature on King, in the African American *Tri-State Defender* of March 29, 1952, supports Henry's version of events.

111 "a casual, heavyset fellow": Lauterbach, *Chitlin' Circuit,* 184–85.

111 "patron saint of Memphis": King with Ritz, *Blues,* 133.

111 "as far out as": Lauterbach, *Chitlin' Circuit,* 184–87, 199.

111 He played solo: In a 1998 interview, King told *Mojo* he "played alone for about two or three months" following his hire at WDIA. Trynka, "B.B. King."

112 "He and I had": The first quote is from King's memoir, the second from Escott, "B.B. King," 4.

112 "We were traveling": Brian Baumgartner, "Whoopin' and Hollerin' with Earl Forest," *Juke Blues,* Summer 2004.

113 Together they formed: Palmer, *Deep Blues,* 178.

113 "I went out there": This passage draws from three Lockwood interviews, the first broadcast in 1971 on radio station WRUW-FM in Cleveland, the second with Scott Dirks in 1995 for the Chicago Blues Archive, and the third with Jim Dollarhide and Charles Sawyer in Mississippi in 2006 for the B.B. King Museum and Delta Interpretive Center. King's quote comes from Trynka, "B.B. King." Conflicting facts in Lockwood's many interviews cast some uncertainty on the exact dates and tenure of their association.

115 "I could only visualize": King with Ritz, *Blues,* 118.

115 that thought gave way: King shared those thoughts in his memoir on page 118. Just how he recovered—and how long he was sick—is harder to say. King seems to have told his hepatitis story only once, in the memoir, and he did not give a timeline. His name appears regularly in radio listings of that era, which suggests his professional hiatus was brief.

115 "Take care of my son": This passage draws from a 2006 interview with Norman Matthews by Jim Dollarhide and Charles Sawyer for the B.B. King Museum and Delta Interpretive Center and from the program for Matthews's 2014 funeral. As for Matthews's employer, the city endured a procession of short-tenured mayors in the 1940s, but the timing favors Pleasants, who served from 1947 to 1949.

116 "It was a pattern": Shirley King, *Love Is King* (Albany, NY: BearManor Media, 2017), 14–15.

116 WDIA was a "daytimer": The reason is complicated science involving solar radiation. The same nocturnal phenomenon had allowed King to hear country stations in Nashville, three hundred miles away.

117 "It was rough": This passage and the section on gambling draw from King's memoir and from an author interview by email with Preston Lauterbach on September 24, 2020.

117 "Before Memphis": This passage draws from King's memoir, Wheeler's "B.B. King," Cantor's *Wheelin' on Beale*, and an author interview with Natolyn Williams Herron.

117 "had the most feeling": Shaw, *Rockin' '50s*, 96–98.

118 "isn't really a nightclub": King with Ritz, *Blues*, 129–30. More than a decade would pass before Lucille was named in print, which suggests the backstory of King's guitar was told only within his inner circle in the early years.

119 Twist remembered the date: Sideman Ford Nelson, on the other hand, distinctly recalled in author interviews that King had named his guitar by the time Nelson joined his ensemble in 1950.

119 "A large crowd": This undated and otherwise unidentified recording was supplied and authenticated by Allan Hammons from the archives of the B.B. King Museum. An Arkansas woman surfaced in 2015, claiming to be kin of the fabled Lucille. By her account, Lucille Banks was in Twist that night with her husband, who started the fight when he saw her dancing with another man. The real Lucille, if that was she, died in 2004, aged ninety-two. Garrick Feldman, "Lucille: Mystery Woman Solved," *Arkansas Leader*, September 4, 2015.

7. Lucille

120 "I wanted to sustain": King with Ritz, *Blues*, 127.

121 "That cry": King with Ritz, 127.

122 "I swivel my wrist": Ed Vulliamy, "B.B. King at 87: The Last of the Great Bluesmen," *The Guardian* (UK), October 6, 2012.

122 "I play lazy": B.B. King, interview by Sid McCore, December 29, 1979, Westwood One Radio, Archives of African American Music and Culture, Indiana University.

122 "I liked seeing": King with Ritz, *Blues*, 130.

123 "Both sounds": King with Ritz, 128.

123 "He just didn't think": Ford Nelson, author interview, October 31, 2018.

124 "Martha's disgusted": Stanley Booth, "Remembering the Man and Legend, B.B. King," *VanityFair.com*, May 15, 2015, https://www.vanityfair.com/culture/2015/05/remembering-legend-b-b-king.

124 "Y'all are a mess": This scene draws from King's memoir and Peter Guralnick's *Sam Phillips: The Man Who Invented Rock 'n' Roll* (New York: Little, Brown, 2015).

125 "We would go out": This passage draws from an interview with Ford Nelson by Jim Dollarhide and Charles Sawyer, Mississippi, 2006, for the B.B. King Museum and Delta Interpretive Center; Cantor, *Wheelin' on Beale*, 98–99; and author interviews with Ford Nelson and Lora Walker.

125 "By the way he spoke": This scene draws from King's memoir; from an article published September 8, 2008, in the *Memphis Commercial Appeal*; and from an interview with King on June 10, 2004, in Chicago for the American Academy of Achievement.

126 "Be careful": This scene draws from King's memoir, from the *On the Road* CD-ROM, and from an interview with Herman Green published in *Living Blues* in April 2009. Green recalled that a house fire had claimed the first Lucille, but King said the instrument was stolen from a car trunk in Harlem.

127 Edward and Esther Bihari: This passage draws from John Broven's *Record Makers and Breakers* (Urbana: University of Illinois Press, 2009), from Cantor's *Wheelin' on Beale*, and from a 1995 interview with Joseph Bihari by Steven L. Isoardi for the Oral History Program at UCLA.

127 "He was more a buddy": King with Ritz, *Blues*, 140–41.

128 Tuff Green's combo: Production credits are sketchy for these early singles, but King consistently recalled being backed by this ensemble on his first Modern Records recordings.

129 "Let's put it this way": Wheeler, "B.B. King."

129 "too conventional": Guralnick, *Sam Phillips*, 87–89; Broven, *Record Makers*, 151.

130 when Saul arrived: This passage draws from Guralnick's *Sam Phillips* and Broven's *Record Makers*.

130 "High-pitched warbler": "Rhythm & Blues Records," *Billboard*, September 23, 1950.

131 "He taught me": "Interview: B.B. King," *Living Blues*, May–June 1988.

131 "In those days": Harold Steinblatt, "Blues Is King," *Guitar World*, July 1991.

131 "tore the house down": Guralnick, *Sam Phillips*, 103–4.

132 "Y'all got a good group": Bill Greensmith, "We Got a Song Called 'Rocket 88,'" *Blues Unlimited*, July–September 1979.

132 "All I could picture": Guralnick, *Sam Phillips*, 105.

133 harbored high hopes: Guralnick, 112; "Record Reviews," *Billboard*, June 30, 1951.

134 "You know, I've watched": A. C. "Moohah" Williams, "What's Happening in the Big 'M,'" *Tri-State Defender*, November 24, 1951.

135 The "colored" YMCA: King's address comes from Lauterbach, *Chitlin' Circuit*. The YMCA address is from a 1953 city directory.

135 "an insomniac's lament": Gioia, *Delta Blues*, 330.

135 "nothing was happening": Joseph Bihari, Isoardi interview.

136 "When I got back": Joseph Bihari, interview by Jim Dollarhide and Charles Sawyer, Memphis, 2006, for the B.B. King Museum and Delta Interpretive Center.

8. On the Road

137 "No. 1 Blues Singer": "Stars Galore on Blues Show," display ad, *Atlanta Daily World*, January 6, 1952.

137 reached number 1: King's song actually rose and fell on two distinct *Billboard* charts, one tracking jukebox plays, the other sales. This narrative reports the song's highest showing on either chart. In January 1952, "Weepin' & Cryin'" vied with "3 O'clock Blues" atop *Billboard*'s jukebox chart. On the retail sales chart, King's song competed with Earl Bostic's "Flamingo."

137 "For the first time": Hal Webman, "Rhythm and Blues Notes," *Billboard*, February 9, 1952.

138 "God-fearing uncle": Jim Roberts, "From Itta Bena to Fame: B. B. King," *Tri-State Defender*, March 29, 1952.

138 Henry arranged: Sawyer, *Arrival*, 67.

138 B.B. took leave: Cantor, *Wheelin' on Beale*, 84, 92.

139 He curbed an impulse: King with Ritz, *Blues*, 148.

139 "At one point": Isabel Wilkerson, *The Warmth of Other Suns* (New York: Random House, 2010), 11–12.

140 "Goddamn": This scene draws from King's memoir and from "Tiny Bradshaw, Tab Smith Co-Headliners at Howard," *Washington Afro-American*, March 4, 1952.

140 One night during the stand: King with Ritz, *Blues*, 149–50.

141 "the nation's newest": "81 Theatre Presents Blues Sensation On Stage Wednesday," *Atlanta Daily World*, April 12, 1952.

142 "He had a big-throated": King with Ritz, *Blues*, 124.

142 "I bought some jewelry": King with Ritz, *Blues*, 157.

142 B.B. bought a new home: This passage draws from King's memoir and from author interviews with Walter and Faye King, B.B.'s nephew and stepsister.

143 "For all this work": King with Ritz, *Blues*, 152.

143 "I'm wondering if I'm working": King with Ritz, 158–59.

144 B.B. appealed for help: This passage draws from Delcia Davis interviews by the author and Dollarhide and Sawyer.

144 "Maybe it would have": King with Ritz, *Blues*, 151–52.

145 late summer of 1952: An ad in the August 8, 1952, edition of the *Arkansas State Press* may be the first to tout the King-Harvey ensemble.

145 "the George Washington": King with Ritz, *Blues*, 138.

145 B.B. and Harvey raided: This passage draws from an author interview via email with Dorothy Darr, the wife of Charles Lloyd, on April 1, 2019, and from Blake Alexander Wilkerson's paper "Manassas in the 1950s: Cultivating a Jazz Tradition," published in 2012 by the Rhodes Institute for Regional Studies.

146 B.B. now hired: Lora Walker, author interview, March 27, 2018.

146 an unannounced visit: Cantor, *Wheelin'*, 84.

146 "It was hard for us": King with Ritz, *Blues*, 158.

147 The pair were in town: Surviving clippings and programs show the tour passing through Houston around November 6. They do not document Diz and Bird's participation.

147 "and that made me feel": King with Ritz, *Blues*, 161–62.

147 "battle of guitars": Bob Rolontz, "Rhythm & Blues Notes," *Billboard*, November 15, 1952.

147 Costumery helped: Stafford Davis, author interview, March 6, 2020.

148 When the appointed day: This scene draws from Isoardi's Joseph Bihari interview and Colin Escott's "Notes on Selected Recordings," published in Kostelanetz, *B.B. King Reader*. Bihari contends these guitars were the original Lucilles, implying that King bestowed a name on his guitar three years after the legendary fire in Twist (unless we ascribe a later date to the fire).

148 "a laboratory of early": Preston Lauterbach, "Sympathy for the Devil," *Oxford American*, Winter 2014.

148 "didn't know a record": Charles Farley: *Soul of the Man: Bobby "Blue" Bland* (Oxford: University Press of Mississippi, 2011), 71.

148 "Let Evelyn book you": King with Ritz, *Blues*, 163.

149 "Robert was a nice guy": This passage draws from Lauterbach's *Chitlin' Circuit*, from *B.B. King Reader*, and from an October 15, 1973, interview with Robert Henry by Margaret McKee and Fred Chisenhall, authors of *Beale Black & Blue*.

150 They were known to sleep: Sebastian Danchin, *Blues Boy: The Life and Music of B.B. King* (Oxford: University Press of Mississippi, 1998), 49.

150 "If you give me $5,000": "Interview: B.B. King." King's account leaves unclear whether the Biharis upped Robey's $5,000 offer to $7,000 or paid him an additional $7,000, or $12,000 in all. In any event, King would wait several more years to buy a house.

150 "Socko Tour": "B.B. King, Famed Blues Artist, on 'Socko' Tour," *Chicago Defender*, May 9, 1953.

150 "blues shouting tornado": "B.B. King, Bill Harvey at Magnolia, Saturday Night," *Atlanta Daily World*, May 22, 1953.

150 Willis "Bebop" Edwards: This passage draws from feature articles in the *Mobile Press Register* of October 13, 1985, and November 2, 1990, and from author interviews with Willis Edwards III and Lora Walker.

152 a well-traveled boogie: This passage draws from Colin Escott's liner notes to *B.B. King—The Vintage Years*.

152 When a record company: This passage draws from author interviews with John Broven.

152 A top-ten B.B. King single: John Broven, author interviews, September 14 and 17, 2020.

153 "We worked with artists": Arnold Shaw, *Honkers and Shouters* (New York: Macmillan, 1978), 203. This passage also draws from Lauterbach's *Chitlin' Circuit* and author interviews with Floyd Lieberman, John Broven, and others.

153 "I'd never met 'Taub'": Escott, "B.B. King," 15–16.

153 The Black press: Dan Kochakian, "Blues Boys Kingdom Records," *Blues & Rhythm*, June 2015; "B.B. King Blues Ork Set for West Coast," *Chicago Defender*, January 30, 1954.

154 "We took our little review": This passage draws from King's memoir and from Farley's *Soul of the Man*.

155 B.B. debuted at the Apollo: This passage draws from *Variety* of June 2, 1954, the *Chicago Defender* of July 3, 1954, and a 2006 interview with Floyd Newman by Jim Dollarhide and Charles Sawyer for the B.B. King Museum and Delta Interpretive Center.

155 "indulged in pleasures": King with Ritz, *Blues*, 152–53. Ever the gentleman, King did not name the woman.

156 "He lived his whole life": Shirley Ann King, author interview, November 7, 2019.

156 "He looked like Nat Cole": These quotes come from King's memoir and from Escott's "B.B. King."

158 "Still sold over a million": Leroy Bonner, "King of the One-Nighters," *Blues Unlimited*, November–December 1977. An exhaustive search of *Variety* archives failed to unearth the rebuke alleged in Bonner's piece.

158 a thousand gigs: The total presumes King performed almost nightly from mid-1949, yielding an annual tally of at least 250 shows.

158 Evelyn Johnson told the press: "5th Anniversary in Music Trade Observed by King," *Billboard*, December 4, 1954.

158 "partying every night": This passage draws from King's memoir and from Cilla Huggins, "The Calvin Owens Story," *Juke Blues*, Summer 1995.

158 Around the close of 1954: The exact date of their parting is unclear. No news account after 1954 seems to document a King-Harvey performance. At least two print ads from early 1955 announce forthcoming concerts featuring both artists, but it is possible they were printed in arrears after the two had split.

158 Another reason was money: This passage draws from the series of Calvin Owens interviews for *Juke Blues* magazine, King's memoir, and John Broven's liner notes to *B.B. King—The Vintage Years* (Broven and Colin Escott each contributed essays).

159 "farewell dance": "Louis Jordan, B.B. King Set Box Office Record," *New York Age*, January 15, 1955; "Guest Talent at B.B. King Farewell Dance," *Los Angeles Sentinel*, December 23, 1954.

9. Big Red

160 "Well, Boss": All quotes in this passage come from author interviews with Lora Walker.

161 "Evelyn was fierce": This passage draws from King's memoir, Sawyer's *Arrival*, the Calvin Owens interviews in *Juke Blues* magazine, author interviews with Lora Walker, and Escott, "B.B. King," 11. Evelyn Young apparently lived with Bonita Cole for years after their departure from King's band; she subsequently married a man.

161 bisexual or gay: Huggins, "Calvin Owens."

161 B.B.'s first big band: This is the ensemble that lined up in front of Big Red for a famous photograph, which King described as "the first B.B. bus" and "the first B.B. band." Musicians came and went in the months before and after.

161 "old enough to be": This passage draws from an interview with Calvin Owens in *Living Blues* magazine of July–August 1998 and from King's memoir.

162 "You must learn": Floyd Newman, author interview, March 28, 2018.

162 "drinking days": King with Ritz, *Blues*, 125.

162 "would just as soon smoke": Charlie Frick, "High-Flying King of the Blues," *High Times*, November 1978.

162 "going to the bank": "Indianola Mentioned on Letterman," *Indianola (MS) Enterprise-Tocsin*, December 24, 1987.

163 "places so hot": Booth, *Rythm Oil*, 101.

163 "We were playing": Floyd Newman, author interview.

164 "really lived off the bus": Escott, "B.B. King," 11–12.

164 "When you rode with B.B.": Lora Walker, author interview, March 27, 2018.

164 "We need gas": This passage draws from Sawyer's *Arrival* and from an author interview with Floyd Newman.

164 bodies hanging from trees: Stafford Davis, author interview, March 6, 2020. Official sources document only a comparative handful of lynchings after 1949, the year King took to the road. But it is also widely accepted that many lynchings went undocumented.

165 "Somebody has to be": David Brown, "Citizen's Council Members Speak Out on Organization's Aims," *Delta Democrat-Times*, September 9, 1954.

165 "boy that done the talkin'": Federal Bureau of Investigation, "Prosecutive Report of Investigation" (on the death of Emmett Till), February 9, 2006; Richard Pérez-Peña, "Woman Linked to 1955 Emmett Till Murder Tells Historian Her Claims Were False," *New York Times*, January 27, 2017.

166 "What are you doing": King with Ritz, *Blues*, 177–78. King does not ascribe a date to the episode, but its placement in his memoir suggests the middle 1950s.

166 "You n——s are going": Lora Walker, author interview, March 27, 2018.

167 "shooting at anyone": King with Ritz, *Blues*, 177.

167 "taking care of": John Broven, liner notes to *B.B. King—The Vintage Years*, Ace Records, ABOXCD 8, 2002.

167 After a show in Austin: This incident, retold in King's memoir, seems to have drawn no news coverage, so we can only guess at the date.

168 "That's what you're getting": Marc Olden, "Interview with B.B. King," *Escapade*, June 1971. Apart from this example, no one involved in these backroom showdowns ever seemed to call police, perhaps on account of shady dealings on all sides.

168 "We had about 3,500 people": Farley: *Soul of the Man*, 140.

168 Big Red broke down: This scene draws from King's memoir and from Olden's "Interview."

169 "driving his Oldsmobile": Sawyer, *Arrival*, 135.

170 That Christmas night: This account is culled from Lauterbach's *Chitlin' Circuit*, from Sawyer's *Arrival*, and especially from Lauterbach's "Sympathy for the Devil" article, the most convincing among many accounts of Johnny Ace's death.

170 a star-studded funeral: "Famous Blues Singer of 'My Song' and 'The Clock' Buried," *Alabama Tribune*, January 7, 1955.

171 *Billboard* noted the trend: "1955: The Year R.&B. Took Over Pop Field," *Billboard*, November 12, 1955.

171 the occasional squib: The longest of these might have been a five-paragraph item that was published December 29, 1953, in the *St. Petersburg Times*, on a page devoted to "negro news."

171 "guitar magician": "B.B. King Opens at Savoy Thursday Night," *Los Angeles Sentinel*, December 8, 1955.

171 A subsequent feature: Conchita Nakatani, "R-B Star B.B. King's Group Lives in Style," *Pittsburgh Courier*, June 23, 1956.

172 star trumpeter Calvin Owens: Owens consistently recalled exiting King's band a year later, in 1957, but his absence from this 1956 photo spread suggests an earlier departure.

173 "Blues Battle": "Lil' Richard–B.B. King in Contest Here Friday Nite," *Arkansas State Press*, July 20, 1956.

173 "lighthearted and funny": King with Ritz, *Blues*, 182.

174 An item in the *Cash Box*: "*The Cash Box* Rhythm 'n Blues Ramblings," *Cash Box*, January 21, 1956.

174 B.B. was in love: This passage draws from interviews with Sue King Evans by the author on October 31, 2018, and by Jim Dollarhide and Charles Sawyer in Mississippi in 2006 for the B.B. King Museum and Delta Interpretive Center, and from King's memoir.

175 B.B. extended his contract: Kochakian, "Blues Boys."

176 "with the proper feeling": "Name B.B. King 'King of Blues,'" *New York Age*, September 1, 1956.

176 Blues Boys Kingdom: "B.B. King Heads Disc Setup Now," *Daily Defender*, December 3, 1956.

176 a twenty-acre farm: This passage draws from an author interview with Walter King and from B.B. King's memoir.

177 "there comes a time": Taylor Branch, *Parting the Waters: America in the King Years, 1954–63* (New York: Simon and Schuster, 1988), 139–40.

178 A grand jury: "Racial Bombing, Boycott Cases Dropped in Court," *Montgomery Advertiser*, November 27, 1957.

178 "If I could find": Guralnick, *Going Home*, 172.

179 "When I'd go over there": Charles Shaar Murray, "B.B. King: Uneasy Lies the Head That Wears the Crown," *Q*, February 1993.

179 "I saw all of them": King with Ritz, *Blues*, 141–42.

180 Goodwill Revue: This scene draws from coverage in the *Pittsburgh Courier* of December 22, 1956, from King's memoir, from Cantor's *Wheelin' on Beale*, and from Guralnick's *Last Train to Memphis* (New York: Little, Brown, 1994).

180 "How come cullud girls": Nat D. Williams, "Down on Beale," *Pittsburgh Courier*, December 22, 1956.

180 "just more white people": "*American Roots Music*: Oral Histories: B.B. King," *PBS.org*, 2001, https://www.pbs.org/americanrootsmusic/pbs_arm_oralh_bbking.html.

181 "Can't knock the money": Bonner, "One-Nighters."

182 "plunking his father's": Cy Schneider, liner notes to *Singin' the Blues*, Crown Records, CLP-5020, 1957.

182 scratchy on the first play: John Broven, "Crown LPs . . . and B.B. King," *Blues & Rhythm*, June 2003.

182 "undervalued and undersold": King with Ritz, *Blues*, 201.

182 "Sue surprised B.B.": Sue King Evans, author interviews.

183 October 14, 1957: This scene draws from coverage in the *Austin American-Statesman* and *Dallas Morning News* of October 15, 1957, from the *Mississippi Enterprise* of January 9, 1960, from court documents, and from King's memoir.

10. Fallow

185 "We couldn't work": Escott, "B.B. King," 14.

185 B.B.'s betrothed: Sue King Evans, author interview, September 2, 2020; Sue King Evans, Dollarhide and Sawyer interview.

186 B.B.'s contract: This passage draws from Broven's liner notes to *B.B. King—The Vintage Years* and *Record Makers*, from Escott's "B.B. King," and from King's memoir.

187 He timed the ceremony: This scene draws from author interviews with Sue King Evans and from David Maraniss's *Once in a Great City* (New York: Simon and Schuster, 2015), 12.

188 "B., your musicians love you": This passage draws from author interviews with Sue King Evans and from King's memoir.

188 B.B. and Sue had fun: This passage draws from author interviews with Sue King Evans and from King's memoir.

189 "screams of awe": "B.B. King Seeks Old Blues Sound," *Los Angeles Sentinel*, November 19, 1959.

189 "blood will run": Gertrude Samuels, "Little Rock Revisited—Tokenism Plus," *New York Times*, June 2, 1963.

189 "mob rule": U.S. National Park Service, "Little Rock High School Crisis Timeline," last updated July 27, 2020, https://www.nps.gov/chsc/learn/historyculture/timeline.htm.

190 "Something wrong, officer?": This scene draws from King's memoir and from Sue King Evans interviews by the author and Dollarhide and Sawyer.

192 archivist Colin Escott: Escott, "Notes," in Kostelanetz, *B.B. King Reader*, 297–98. Williams's single issued under a different title, "Hello Baby."

193 "Motherfucking, blues-singing B.B. King": This scene draws from King's memoir, which does not assign a date to the meeting. Its placement here assumes King caught Davis during his celebrated residency at Birdland in the summer and fall of 1959. King recalled that Davis performed with his classic sextet of that era.

193 "Move on, for what?": Miles Davis with Quincy Troupe, *Miles: The Autobiography* (New York: Simon and Schuster, 1989), 238–39.

193 "What you're doing": B.B. King, McCore interview.

194 a fertility test: This passage draws from author interviews with Sue King Evans.

194 Sue contented herself: Sue King Evans, author interview, October 31, 2018.

195 The decision to credit: Escott, "Notes," 286.

195 V. S. "Sonny" Freeman: This passage draws from Levy's *Road Dog* and author interviews with Wilbert Freeman, Sonny's brother.

195 B.B.'s bookings dropped apace: Broven, liner notes to *B.B. King—The Vintage Years*.

196 "The big companies": King with Ritz, *Blues*, 202.

196 "Jules was my man": Escott, "B.B. King," 15.

196 archivists later theorized: Ace Records, *My Kind of Blues* release page, n.d., https://acerecords.co.uk/my-kind-of-blues-the-crown-series-vol-1-mp3.

197 "Wanted just drums": King with Ritz, *Blues*, 202.

197 "I don't think anybody": B.B. King, speech at the National Press Club, Washington, DC, January 23, 1996.

197 "I could see": King with Ritz, *Blues*, 202.

198 "just about to get together": Willie Dixon with Don Snowden, *I Am the Blues* (London: Quartet Books, 1989), 207.

198 "You need a good company": King with Ritz, *Blues*, 208.

198 "had never sold less": Leah Davis, "B.B. King: The Thrill Ain't Gone," *Soul*, April 6, 1970.

199 "I'd like to stay": Joseph Bihari, Isoardi interview.

11. Regal

201 last bluesman standing: King voiced those feelings in interviews of that era and in his memoir. The date of his ABC signing comes from Broven's liner notes to *B.B. King—The Vintage Years*.

201 notwithstanding his nickname: Steve Barri, author interview, June 26, 2019.

201 parallel paths in the blues: In some early interviews, King named James as a primary influence on his own guitar style. But given that James began recording after King, it seems more likely King was simply a fan.

202 One night in 1961: This scene draws from the *Austin American-Statesman* of October 5, 1971, and from Vinny Cecolini's interview with Johnny Winter in *Jam Magazine* of March 2013. The date is approximate: Winter recalled being seventeen, an age he attained in February 1961.

203 "I played bills": King with Ritz, *Blues*, 210–11.

203 "never said a word": Joseph Bihari, interview with John Broven, Los Angeles, March 2, 2000.

205 "It hurts me": "Why I'll Always Sing the Blues," *Ebony*, April 1, 1962.

205 "a thump and a bump": King and Ritz, *Blues*, 217–18. The exact date of this crash and other details defy accurate reportage. The incident evidently drew no news coverage. Charles Sawyer put it "around 1961" in *Arrival*, while King's memoir placed it a year or two later.

206 "He never liked": Sue King Evans, author interview, February 14, 2019.

206 "real-life pain": King with Ritz, *Blues*, 212.

208 "a group of renegades": Elsie Carper, "Bombs Scare Grounds Race Group," *Washington Post*, May 16, 1961.

208 No state posed: Juan Williams, *Eyes on the Prize: America's Civil Rights Years, 1954–1965* (New York: Viking Penguin, 1987), 208.

209 "our greatest crisis": "Ole Miss Will Not Mix, Says Barnett," *Greenwood (MS) Commonwealth*, September 14, 1962.

209 "We didn't hang": Norman Matthews, Dollarhide and Sawyer interview.

209 the Gaston Motel: Diane McWhorter, *Carry Me Home: Birmingham, Alabama, the Climactic Battle of the Civil Rights Revolution* (New York: Simon and Schuster, 2001), 421–22, 427–30.

210 "We were two doors apart": King said this to Lora Walker, who recalled it in an author interview on September 15, 2020.

210 "just a blues singer": Lora Walker, author interview, September 15, 2020.

210 "Medgar Evers showed me": King with Ritz, *Blues*, 233.

211 "because this man": Lora Walker, author interview, September 15, 2020. King said those words to Walker after Evers's death.

211 earned fifty-four cents: J. Williams, *Eyes*, 197.

212 "about entirely new approaches": David Henderson, *'Scuse Me While I Kiss the Sky* (New York: Bantam, 1981), 76.

213 B.B. felt invisible: B.B. King, interview with John Broven, March 2, 2000.

213 Pate conferred with B.B.: Paul Gambaccini, "B.B. King Live at the Regal," *For One Night Only*, BBC Radio 4, London, December 27, 2011.

213 Its auditorium held: Ray Martinez and Bryan Krefft, "Regal Theater," *Cinema Treasures*, n.d., http://cinematreasures.org/theaters/992.
214 "probably the best": Gambaccini, "B.B. King Live."
214 "Oh, by the way": Duke Jethro, author interview, February 20, 2019.
214 probably played four sets: "Exciting Record Stars in New Regal Stage Hit," *Chicago Defender*, November 14, 1964.
215 "the audience just went wild": Gambaccini, "B.B. King Live."
215 "every night was different": Duke Jethro, author interview, February 20, 2019.
216 "eardrums fell out": James Joiner, "Fleetwood Mac Legend Mick Fleetwood: The 5 Best Drummers Ever," *Esquire.com*, November 5, 2014, https://www.esquire.com/entertainment/music/a30547/mick-fleetwood-best-drummers/.
217 "yellin' and screaming": Gambaccini, "B.B. King Live."

12. Revival

218 the BBC broadcast sides: Jas Obrecht, "Transatlantic Blues: How Britain's Blues Boom Saved American Rock and Roll," *Jas Obrecht Music Archive* (blog), July 19, 2010, http://jasobrecht.com/transatlantic-blues-how-british-musicians-helped-save-american-blues-and-rock/.
218 "the last American bluesman": Obrecht.
219 "Blues Boy" King: Bill Wyman, *Bill Wyman's Blues Odyssey: A Journey to Music's Heart and Soul* (London: DK Adult, 2001), 369.
220 "We didn't know any blues": *My Generation*, dir. David Batty, XIX Entertainment, 2017.
222 "With an amplified": Keith Richards with James Fox, *Life* (New York: Little, Brown, 2010), 108.
223 turned all the way up: Bob Brunning, *Blues: The British Connection* (London: Helter Skelter, 2003), 45.
223 "At first I played": Bruce Cook, *Listen to the Blues* (New York: Scribner, 1973), 178–79; Eric Clapton, *Clapton: The Autobiography* (New York: Crown Archetype, 2007), 325.
223 Clapton came late: This passage draws from author interviews with John Broven and Stefan Wirz's American Folk Blues Festival discography, https://www.wirz.de/music/afbf.htm.
224 "That set became": Dave Van Ronk with Elijah Wald, *The Mayor of MacDougal Street: A Memoir* (Boston: Da Capo, 2005), 46.
225 Dylan had also heard: This passage draws from Elijah Wald's *Dylan Goes Electric!* (New York: Dey Street Books, 2015), John Milward's *Crossroads: How the Blues Shaped Rock 'n' Roll (and Rock Saved the Blues)* (Boston: Northeastern University Press, 2013), and Bob Dylan's *Chronicles: Volume One* (New York: Simon and Schuster, 2004), among other sources.
226 Dick Spottswood: Dick Spottswood, author interview, March 13, 2019. This is Spottswood's version of the story. Some other versions credit Hoskins, alone, with locating Hurt.
227 "The number of people": Dick Waterman, author interview, June 27, 2020.
227 a record buff named John Fahey: E. D. Denson, author interview, March 19, 2019.
228 "moving tribute": Hurley and Evans, "Bukka White," 196–97.
228 "Now, isn't that nice": Gioia, *Delta Blues*, 364.
229 "He sat and played": Dick Waterman, author interview.
230 "B.B. who?": Sawyer, *Arrival*, 94–95.

230 "The Black blues culture": Elvin Bishop, author interview, March 18, 2019.

230 "I don't want any": Wald, *Dylan*, 197.

230 "Us white cats": Wald, *Dylan*, 222–23. Among many accounts of the Grossman-Lomax skirmish, this one taps the largest number of eyewitnesses and is thus favored here.

231 "with the gyrations": David Dann, "Michael Bloomfield at Newport," Mike Bloomfield: An American Guitarist, May 11, 2014, http://www.mikebloomfieldamericanmusic.com /newport.htm.

231 "electrified one half": Wald, *Dylan*, 202. As stated, Dylan had recorded with an electric guitar before this public debut.

231 "in the blink of an eye": Milward, *Crossroads*, 72–73.

13. Fillmore

233 "The critics went": King with Ritz, *Blues*, 221.

233 "Baby, you talk about": Phyl Garland, "Live and Electrifying," *Pittsburgh Courier*, February 27, 1965.

233 "where it really started": Eric Clapton, statement issued upon King's death, May 15, 2015.

233 "DNA": Gambaccini, "B.B. King Live."

233 500 greatest albums: "500 Greatest Albums of All Time," *Rolling Stone*, November 2003.

233 "Duke, they treat it": Duke Jethro, author interview, February 20, 2019.

234 surely the nadir: That opinion is the author's own. At the time, the Biharis' ruse worked, and music critics praised the "live" release.

234 "For a blues singer": "B.B. Says Deejays 'Ashamed' to Play Blues, Many Teens Are Rude," *Baltimore Afro-American*, February 27, 1965.

234 "clubs where you could": Duke Jethro, author interview, February 20, 2019.

235 "When people leave": "Rep. Winstead Feels 'Mystery at Last Solved,'" *Jackson (MS) Clarion-Ledger*, August 6, 1964.

235 "their mental I.Q.": J. Williams, *Eyes*, 258.

236 "white people should thank": Bentley Boyd, "History Has Treated Malcolm X Gingerly, When at All," *Newport News (VA) Daily Press*, May 27, 2007.

236 Employees managed to save it: Broven, liner notes to *B.B. King—The Vintage Years*.

236 B.B. spent $15,000: Major Robinson, "On the Line," *Pittsburgh Courier*, October 23, 1965.

236 arguably the apex: A rock-music fan would be hard-pressed to name a better year. In *Rolling Stone*'s 2003 list of the five hundred greatest albums, it ranked *Pet Sounds* second (behind *Sgt. Pepper's Lonely Hearts Club Band*), *Revolver* third, and *Blonde on Blonde* ninth.

237 The far greater sin: King's quotes in this account come from his memoir. Sideman Duke Jethro recalled the second guitarist but not his name or precise role.

237 The Biharis alerted ABC: John Broven, author interviews.

237 The IRS had haunted B.B.: This passage draws from King's memoir and author interviews with Sue King Evans.

238 "a matter of money": Duke Jethro, author interview, April 4, 2019. Burdine seems to have come and gone from King's employ more than once before his final departure: he did not perform at the famed Regal gig in late 1964, but a *Pittsburgh Courier* clipping from the following April lists him as a sideman.

238 "I knew he was going": King's side in this conflict comes from his memoir, Sue's from author interviews.

239 "to babysit the women": This passage draws from author interviews with Ron Levy and from supplementary material to his *Road Dog* memoir.

240 "He told me": Sue King Evans, author interview, February 7, 2019.

240   "I hope she changes": Mark Bricklin, "B.B. King Sings Blues as Wife Seeks Divorce," *Philadelphia Tribune*, July 26, 1966.

240   "It's tough": *B.B. King: The Life of Riley.*

240   B.B.'s family was growing: Author interviews with Lora Walker, Shirley Ann King, and Walter Riley King.

241   Charles Keil: Charles Keil, author interview, March 12, 2019.

241   "We were looking for": E. D. Denson, author interview.

242   "They didn't like B.B. King": Dick Spottswood, author interview.

242   "I doubt that more": Charles Keil, *Urban Blues* (Chicago: University of Chicago Press, 1966), 79.

242   "Whenever there isn't": Charles Keil, author interview; Keil, *Urban Blues*, 102–4.

243   "B.B. King is the only": Keil, *Urban Blues*, 102.

243   "I am primarily concerned": Keil, *Urban Blues*, 1.

243   Feather's full attention: Feather seems to have written King's name only once in his column before he reviewed *Urban Blues* in the *Los Angeles Times* on August 7, 1966, and then only in a quote from the saxophonist Charles Lloyd. Feather's *Urban Blues* review refers to the veteran bluesman as "a singer named B.B. King." The *Post* reviewed *Urban Blues* on August 11, the *New York Times* on August 14.

244   never striking a second: Kostelanetz, *B.B. King Reader*, 305.

244   B.B. surprised him: Sawyer, author interview, June 21, 2019.

244   "No matter how old": Phyl Garland, *The Sound of Soul: The Story of Black Music* (Chicago: Henry Regnery, 1969), 103.

245   "He was pulling": Elvin Bishop, author interview.

246   producers apparently permitted: Russ Koberna, author interview, April 9, 2019.

246   B.B. signed a new contract: "Long Contract Is Signed," *Arizona Daily Star*, November 29, 1966.

246   Lou Zito: Sawyer's *Arrival* asserts that King hired Zito immediately after firing Evelyn Johnson, who had been his de facto manager. Another biographer, Sebastian Danchin, writes on page 72 of *Blues Boy* that King employed "a succession of managers of varying ability." In any case, Zito's name does not appear alongside King's in clippings or production credits before 1966.

246   "At that time": Polly Walker, interview by Jim Dollarhide and Charles Sawyer, Memphis, 2006, for the B.B. King Museum and Delta Interpretive Center. Additional information from author interviews with Lora Walker.

246   "a large, wood-paneled room": This passage draws from Booth's *Rythm Oil* and from an author interview with Lora Walker.

247   plotted a sequel: This passage draws from author interviews with Duke Jethro, from an undated "Blues Is King" blog post by Otis Grand and David Mac on their *Blues Junction* website, http://bluesjunctionproductions.com/the_blues_is_king_bb_king_-_re-visited, and from a "Blues Is King" page at the Blues Foundation website, https://blues.org/blues_hof_inductee/blues-king-b-b-king/.

248   "was playing what he felt": Duke Jethro, author interview, April 4, 2019.

248   B.B. claimed not: while discussing his guitar in a 1980 interview for *Guitar Player* magazine, for example, King said, "To tell you the truth, I'm not even sure which pickup does what."

249   "complete fiascos": Sawyer, *Arrival*, 87. No independent record of either gig seems to survive, and Duke Jethro, Lora Walker, and Sue King did not recall B.B. performing for whites before the Sunset Strip dates.

249 "an indescribably soulful": This passage draws from reviews published February 15, 1967, in *Variety* and the *Los Angeles Times*.

249 "He bears down": Stanley Dance, "B.B. King: The King of the Blues," *Jazz*, February 1967.

250 "longhaired kids in tie-dyed outfits": This scene draws from King's memoir, from his 2004 American Academy of Achievement interview, and from the *On the Road* CD-ROM, as well as from Dollarhide and Sawyer's interview with Norman Matthews and other sources.

251 "Inside, a most remarkable assemblage": Sarah Hill, *San Francisco and the Long 60s* (New York: Bloomsbury Academic, 2016), 47.

251 "There wasn't a real": Peter Lewis, author interview, April 2, 2018.

14. Mythology

253 "The light was hitting": Carlos Santana, *The Universal Tone* (New York: Little, Brown, 2014), 170–71.

253 "I played that night": This passage draws from King's memoir and from a column penned by Bill Graham, published as "Blues Becoming Popular with Young Set," *Emporia (KS) Gazette*, February 22, 1968.

254 "The kids were tripping": Peter Lewis, author interview.

254 "I guess for most": Duke Jethro, author interview, April 4, 2019.

254 "They call him B.B. King": Ralph J. Gleason, "B.B.—the King of the Blues," *San Francisco Chronicle*, March 1, 1967.

255 "Tho most white Americans": Pat Dickelman, "B.B. Still the King," *Chicago Tribune*, May 7, 1967.

255 "the boy from Beale": Bill E. Burk, "B.B. King of the Blues, *Memphis Press-Scimitar*, May 26, 1967.

255 "Ladies and gentlemen": King with Ritz, *Blues*, 190. The date is an educated guess: King played a lengthy stand at the 20 Grand that summer. King recalled "a good number of whites" in the audience, which suggests the gig could not have come much earlier in his career.

256 The Biharis unearthed it: Kostelanetz, *B.B. King Reader*, 304.

256 "I noticed in the last year": James R. Bourne, "The Anatomy of B.B. King," *Down Beat*, July 27, 1967.

256 "I can remember": Duke Jethro, author interview, February 20, 2019.

256 the afterhours jam: This scene draws from author interviews with Elvin Bishop on March 18, 2019, and January 31, 2021, from David McGee's *B.B. King: There Is Always One More Time* (San Francisco: Backbeat Books, 2005), from Lillian Roxon's *Rock Encyclopedia* (New York: Grosset and Dunlap, 1969), and from *Melody Maker*'s interview with Eric Clapton in May 1968.

257 "Because of Jimi": King with Ritz, *Blues*, 241.

259 "That feeling on the guitar": "B.B. King," *Rolling Stone*, February 24, 1968.

260 "He calls his guitar": Ralph J. Gleason, "The Rhythm Section," *Honolulu Star-Bulletin*, December 31, 1967.

260 B.B. introduced her: The very first mention of Lucille in print was probably in the August 1, 1967, edition of the *Chicago Daily Defender*, in Lee Ivory's "Among the Stars" column.

262 "We stand amidst": Kevin Boyle, "After the Rainbow Sign: Jerome Cavanagh and 1960s Detroit," lecture, Walter P. Reuther Library, Detroit, November 30, 1999.

262 "I had a process": Michael Lydon, *Rock Folk: Portraits from the Rock 'n' Roll Pantheon* (New York: Dial, 1971), 64–66.

263 finally performed overseas: Danchin, *Blues Boy*, 82.

263 "They would stop you": Charles Boles, author interview, January 23, 2020.

263 "I have never had": Pauline Rivelli, "B.B. King," *Jazz & Pop*, July 1968.

264 "It was all about": King with Ritz, *Blues*, 235.

264 This was probably Pervis Spann: Most prior accounts have Seidenberg supplanting Zito as King's manager. But Seidenberg told biographer Sebastian Danchin (*Blues Boy*) that King briefly retained a Chicago man to replace the departing Zito. Seidenberg didn't name him, but it seems likely the man was Spann, who later claimed to have managed King profitably in this era. Spann's son, Darrell, confirmed their collaboration in an author interview on December 8, 2019.

264 "How are we doin'?": This scene draws from King's memoir, Sawyer's *Arrival*, and Danchin's *Blues Boy*. The timing, confirmed by Seidenberg aide Floyd Lieberman in an author interview, fits the announcement of King's new contract with ABC a month later, in June 1968. A *Billboard* listing in August seems to be the last mention of Zito as King's manager, and it might well have appeared after his departure.

264 Sidney Alexander Seidenberg: Larry Seidenberg, author interview, July 24, 2019. Other facts supplied by Harriet Seidenberg Turkanis via email correspondence.

265 "I felt like I'd known": King with Ritz, *Blues*, 236.

265 "I knew what a manager is": Danchin, *Blues Boy*, 74.

265 "He didn't smoke": Larry Seidenberg, author interview, July 25, 2019.

265 "For every million": Sawyer, *Arrival*, 108.

266 "Had he not been": David Ritz, author interview, August 14, 2019.

266 "Do you know Louis": King with Ritz, *Blues*, 237–38.

267 $750 to $1,000 a night: Roberta Skopp, "Sid Seidenberg: Management with Style," *Record World*, January 4, 1975.

267 Money poured in: This passage draws from King's memoir and from author interviews with Larry Seidenberg.

267 "like Ahab": Sawyer, *Arrival*, 89. Sawyer puts the bus theft in 1965. King, in his memoir, places it in 1966. But researchers at the B.B. King Museum found proof King renewed the vehicle's registration in 1967. Allan Hammons, author interview via email, February 1, 2021.

268 He called a meeting: This passage draws from King's memoir and from coverage in *Cash Box* of June 22, 1968, and *Montage* of February 1970.

268 "I want you to play": Marc Perrusquia, "Precious Lord! Saxophone Linked to MLK's Last Request to Be on Permanent Display at National Civil Rights Museum," *Memphis Commercial Appeal*, August 31, 2017.

268 "I felt I was doing": King with Ritz, *Blues*, 233–34.

269 "When B.B. comes downstairs": This scene draws from the "Blues Boy" chapter in Booth's *Rythm Oil*, pages 89–105.

270 "Albert King bears watching": Duke Jethro, author interview, February 20, 2019.

271 When B.B. performed: This passage draws from two Booth books, *Rythm Oil* and *Dance with the Devil* (New York: Random House, 1984).

271 *For Love of Ivy*: In fairness to former manager Zito, the *Ivy* deal was brokered before King decamped to Seidenberg.

272 had failed to publish: The closest the *Times* had come to a full article about King was its review of Charlie Keil's *Urban Blues*.

272 "field workers in collarless shirts": Michael Lydon, "B.B. King Sings the Blues Evra Day, Evra Day," *New York Times*, October 27, 1968.

272 "From that instant": Lydon.

273 The band departed Port Allen: This scene draws from Lydon's "B.B. King," from an author interview with Michael Lydon on December 7, 2019, and from accounts published in the September 24, 1968, *Baton Rouge State Times Advocate* and the September 28, 1968, *Philadelphia Tribune*.

273 "We're Wallaces": Lydon, "B.B. King."

273 Police arrived: "Negro Pair Treated at Local Hospital," *Baton Rouge State Times Advocate*, September 24, 1968. Additional details from Lydon, "B.B. King."

273 B.B., freshening up: Given that the band was refused service at the restaurant, one must assume King was allowed to use the bathroom at the neighboring service station.

274 "Wanted something to eat": Lydon, "B.B. King."

274 "Maybe soon": Lydon.

274 "When a lady says": Sawyer, *Arrival*, 77–78. This passage also draws from Bob Lardine, "Long Road to Top for B.B.," *Baltimore Sun*, May 26, 1970, and from author interviews with Shirley Ann King and Sue King Evans.

15. Live and Well

275 "All of a sudden": B.B. King, interview by Phyl Garland, March 1969, Archives of African American Music and Culture, Indiana University, Bloomington, IN.

275 "King has had the kind": Ralph Gleason, "King Has Divine Right to Crown," *Indianapolis News*, January 22, 1969.

276 "the Stones were breaking": Bill Szymczyk, author interview, May 7, 2019.

277 "I'd watch his foot": Jerry Jemmott, author interview, April 25, 2019.

277 that was what B.B. wanted: Jemmott.

278 "the most important blues recording": James Powell, "The B.B. King Experience," *Down Beat*, August 7, 1969.

278 Hendrix had journeyed to England: Ed Vulliamy, "When Jimi Hendrix came to London, he changed the sound of music for ever," *The Guardian* (UK), October 25, 2014.

278 "And as we walked": Alan Govenar, *Meeting the Blues* (Dallas: Taylor, 1988), 97.

278 "This is the moment": "B.B. Was in Tears at the End," *Blues & Rhythm*, August 2015. The passage is attributed to Ray Connolly of the *Evening Standard*.

279 "It's not so much instruments": Jerry Jemmott, author interview.

280 "set up the sound": This scene draws from author interviews with Bill Szymczyk and Jerry Jemmott, from King's memoir, and from the *On the Road* CD-ROM.

281 In the hours after: An alternate version of this story credits Herb Lovelle, the drummer and bandleader, with suggesting strings on "The Thrill Is Gone." Jerry Jemmott recalled that Lovelle, rather than Szymczyk, made most of the artistic decisions on the album.

281 "Are you the thrill?": Sue King Evans, author interview, August 17, 2019.

282 "history's first": Robert Christgau, "The Rolling Stones," Robert Christgau: Dean of American Rock Critics, n.d., https://www.robertchristgau.com/xg/music/stones-76 .php.

282 had even made a pilgrimage: Bill McGraw, "He Treated Stones Right in '64," *Detroit Free Press*, February 1, 2006.

283 "no sooner had the shutter clicked": John Greenwald, "BB," *Rolling Stone*, October 29, 1970.

283 "told me how they": King with Ritz, *Blues*, 260.

283 a stash of heroin: Booth, *Dance*, 126–27.

284 "The kids stood up": Rick Setlowe, "The Rolling Stones Gather No Moss but Much Moolah in Forum Freak-Outs," *Variety*, November 10, 1969.

284 The Stones held court: This scene draws from Booth's *Dance* and author interviews with Ron Levy.

285 "It's good that he still": Booth, *Dance*, 267–68.

285 "It's one of the great ironies": Roxon, *Rock Encyclopedia*, 273.

286 "being played on Top 40": Ralph J. Gleason, "Homage to the King of Blues," *San Francisco Examiner*, January 25, 1970.

286 the 500 greatest pop songs: "The Rolling Stone 500 Greatest Songs of All Time," *Rolling Stone*, special issue, December 2004, archived on Julian White's RockList website, http://www.rocklistmusic.co.uk/rstone.html.

286 "We didn't have to eat": Norman Matthews, Dollarhide and Sawyer interview.

286 "Hell, yes": *B.B. King: On the Road*, dir. Jon Brewer, Cardinal Releasing, 2018.

286 "We stood out there": Joe Burton, author interview, June 7, 2019.

286 "The King is in": Leonard Feather, "B.B. King Reigns at Nero's," *Los Angeles Times*, April 14, 1970.

286 "It was 3 a.m.": King with Ritz, *Blues*, 267.

287 Hampton Reese: This passage draws from Levy's *Road Dog* and Sawyer's *Arrival*.

287 "His thing was books": King with Ritz, *Blues*, 219.

288 "He taught himself": David Ritz, author interview, August 14, 2019.

288 "He was too proud": Sue King Evans, author interview, August 17, 2019.

288 "was, essentially, the same": John S. Wilson, "B.B. King Enlists Friends, Enchants Carnegie Audience," *New York Times*, May 4, 1970.

288 a $2 million federal lawsuit: The start of this litigation was covered in the *Baltimore Afro-American* of May 2, 1970, the end recounted in author interviews with Floyd Lieberman, Sidney Seidenberg's top aide. Lieberman could not recall whether the settlement included a cash payment for past royalties.

289 changed Carson's mind: Greenwald, "BB."

289 "Come on in": King with Ritz, *Blues*, 252–54.

290 B.B. hadn't actually set foot: Jim Abbott, author interview, July 21, 2019.

291 "it's the first time": *On the Road* CD-ROM. This passage also draws from an author interview with Clarence Richard English.

291 a dwindling audience: Sid Seidenberg claimed seventy million people had watched King perform on *Sullivan*. But a ratings analysis published November 5, 1970, in the *Hackensack Record* suggests *Sullivan* reached roughly eight million homes.

291 B.B. took the stage: This scene draws from King's memoir, Sawyer's *Arrival*, and author interviews with Ron Levy.

16. Back in the Alley

293 "do it like B.B. King": Jann Wenner, "The *Rolling Stone* Interview: John Lennon, Part One: The Working Class Hero," *Rolling Stone*, January 21, 1971.

293 "one of the greatest records": This passage draws from coverage in *Escapade* magazine of June 1971 and from an undated press release issued in the summer of 1971 by Sidney A. Seidenberg, Inc.

293 B.B. rented a luxury apartment: The date is estimated from the first mention of the apartment in print, in *Escapade*, June 1971.

293 "waddled around": George Goodman, "B.B. King, an Overnight Hit . . . after 21 Years of the Blues," *Look*, June 29, 1971.

294 "Oh, Slim": Levy, *Road Dog*, 64–65.

294 "He didn't want anybody": Ron Levy, author interview, June 3, 2019.

294 "treated as the international celebrities": Levy, *Road Dog*, 66.

296 Michel's handwritten notes: Ed Michel, author interview via email, May 19, 2019.

296 "They were behind": Johnny Black, "The Making of *B.B. King in London*," *Blues*, August 2015. King's quote was recounted by Jerry Shirley.

296 the tapes remained in a file: Ed Michel, author interview.

297 stay out of my way: Mark Camarigg, "All the King's Men," *Living Blues*, April 2009.

297 "I want to apologize": Sally Wright, "Glad Notes Greet 'Brother B,'" *Memphis Commercial Appeal*, August 28, 1971.

298 "This is MY man": Levy, *Road Dog*, 90–91.

298 "I could've killed": Joe Burton, author interview.

298 "He loved that farm": This passage draws from author interviews with Charles Sawyer and Sue King Evans.

299 "If you want to reform": Clarence Page, "B.B. King: 17 Jails in Only 18 Months," *Chicago Tribune*, March 8, 1972.

299 B.B. slipped: This passage draws from author interviews with Eddie Rowe (August 20, 2020) and Joe Burton.

299 "We buckled up": Levy, *Road Dog*, 76–77.

300 "Miz Ann": Joe Burton, author interview.

300 "He would bet thousands": Sue King Evans, author interview, September 18, 2020.

300 "He used to invite us": Joe Burton, author interview.

301 "B.B. King has": Lester Bangs, "The Best of B.B. King," *Rolling Stone*, March 29, 1973.

302 "I wasn't the kind of guy": Schruers, "Mississippi Homecoming."

302 "I'll come every year": Charles Evers, Dollarhide and Sawyer interview.

302 "It seemed like everybody": Joe Burton, author interview.

303 "Post would welcome": G. Edward Clark, March 15, 1973, Central Foreign Policy File, 1973–1979, National Archives, College Park, MD.

303 "Although Jefferson Airplane": William Pierce Rogers, July 27, 1973, Central Foreign Policy File.

304 "B.B. King's appearances": Oliver S. Crosby, November 28, 1973, Central Foreign Policy File.

304 "preferred raising his voice": Crosby.

304 "And I gotta say": Ron Levy, author interview, June 3, 2019.

305 "I liked hearing that": Bobby Bland, interview by David Ritz, Memphis, approximately December 2012. This was Bland's final interview.

305 "helpless, naïve, childish": Keil, *Urban Blues*, 114.

306 "B.B. was always ready": Steve Barri, author interviews.

306 "Both bands were massed": Vernon Gibbs, "Soul, Man: New York Johnny Meets L.A. Jane for a Medium Massage," *Crawdaddy*, November 1974.

306 "Whenever they would": Steve Barri, author interview.

306 "There was some weird shit": Ron Levy, author interview, June 3, 2019.

306 B.B. took great care: This passage draws from Sawyer's *Arrival* and author interviews with King's sidemen.

307 "I loved it better": King and Ritz, *Blues*, 263. Bland's comment is from Farley, *Soul of the Man*, 171.

307 "I was reading about": Stewart Levine, author interview, July 14, 2019.

307 The prospect of African American stars: This passage draws from author interviews with Stewart Levine, from *Q* magazine of June 2000, and from the *New York Times* of September 25, 1974, and July 2, 2009.

308 "a non-stop": This passage draws from author interviews with Levy and from his *Road Dog*.

309 "I'm running out of steam": Stewart Levine, author interview, July 13, 2019.

309 "The heavier the competition": Levy, *Road Dog*, 78–80.

17. Moscow on the Mississippi

310 "personal business transactions": Victoria Lucas Associates, "B.B. King Forms New Corporation," press release, February 5, 1975.

310 B.B. had dominated: King with Ritz, *Blues*, 270.

310 "If he doesn't want": Skopp, "Sid Seidenberg."

311 "The first time": Stewart Levine, author interview, July 13, 2019.

311 "I could do better": Joe Burton, author interview.

311 "When Sid was there": Burton.

312 "Sonny was a blues drummer": Eddie Rowe, author interview.

312 "the old camaraderie": Levy, *Road Dog*, 118.

312 a $200,000 ranch house: This passage draws from Sawyer's *Arrival*, King's memoir, and a 2006 interview with LaVerne Toney by Jim Dollarhide and Charles Sawyer in Las Vegas for the B.B. King Museum and Delta Interpretive Center.

313 "He asked me plenty": LaVerne Toney, author interview, October 24, 2020.

313 "He used to have": Stewart Levine, author interview, July 13, 2019.

314 "Whatever you see": LaVerne Toney, Dollarhide and Sawyer interview.

314 "It is probably": Sawyer, *Arrival*, 26–28.

314 "down to the cards": David Ritz, author interview, August 14, 2019.

314 a grisly medical procedure: This scene draws from King's memoir and from author interviews with Lora Walker, who supplied an approximate date.

315 "In recent years": Cliff Radel, "Cole, Spinners Wow Jazz Crowd," *Cincinnati Enquirer*, July 26, 1976.

315 "with Bland and King": Joel Selvin, "Yamashta's 'Go' Hangs Together," *San Francisco Examiner*, August 1, 1976.

316 "Things were getting": King with Ritz, *Blues*, 270.

317 "Bill, I'm not a speaker": This scene draws from author interviews with Bill Ferris and from Robert Palmer, "B.B. King: From Beale," *New York Times*, May 25, 1977.

317 "I'm just wondering": Jim Abbott, author interview, July 21, 2019.

318 "has a big place": Abbott, "B.B. King."

318 "He was despondent": Stewart Levine, author interview, July 13, 2019.

318 "And then this morning": Lydon, *Rock Folk*, 49–50.

318 "B. had a bad cold": Ron Levy, author interview, July 18, 2019.

319 "Little by little": King with Ritz, *Blues*, 270–71.

319 "To make another blues record": Stewart Levine, author interview, July 13, 2019; B.B. King, McCore interview.

320 When sessions commenced: This scene draws from author interviews with Stewart Levine and from McGee's *B.B. King*.

320 "general mismanagement": This passage draws from coverage in the *Tallahassee Democrat* of July 23, 1977, and the Gladys Knight memoir *Between Each Line of Pain and Glory* (New York: Hyperion, 1997).

320 Levine telephoned Seidenberg: This scene draws from McGee's *B.B. King*, King's memoir, and author interviews with Stewart Levine.

322 Critic Robert Christgau: Robert Christgau, "B.B. King: *Midnight Believer*," n.d., Robert Christgau: Dean of American Rock Critics, https://www.robertchristgau.com/get_chap.php?k=K&bk=70.

322 "You ever heard of": Walter King, author interview, July 29, 2019; Camarigg, "King's Men."

323 Another new face: This passage draws from author interviews with Walter King, Lora Walker, Stafford Davis, and Charles Sawyer.

323 "Norman held the record": Stafford Davis, author interview, January 10, 2020.

323 "Black Devil": Camarigg, "King's Men."

323 Matthews would sit: This passage draws from Linton Robinson's article "B.B. King—Seattle—1977," n.d., posted to his website at http://linrobinson.com/GIGS/bbking.pdf; George Lange's article "Norman and the King," posted to his blog *Lange Studio*, May 19, 2014, https://www.langestudio.com/blog-stream/norman-and-the-king; and author interviews with Michael Doster.

324 "Both of 'em was terrible": Joe McClendon, author interview, March 22, 2020.

324 The writer was Charles Sawyer: Charles Sawyer, author interviews.

325 "Hit at 11": Sawyer, *Arrival*, 4–9.

327 "Out of every dollar": Sawyer, 18.

327 "something like a million dollars": This passage draws from author interviews with Floyd Lieberman and from Dollarhide and Sawyer's interview with LaVerne Toney.

327 B.B. rolled out of Detroit: Sawyer, *Arrival*, 12–24; Charles Sawyer, author interview, June 13, 2019.

328 "become the single most popular": Pete Welding, "B.B. King: The Mississippi Giant, Part I," *Down Beat*, October 5, 1978.

328 "Either kiss my ass": Eddie Rowe, author interview.

328 B.B. populated his new ensemble: author interviews with Russell Jackson on September 16, 2019, and Tony Coleman on July 8, 2020.

329 "a little dictator": Russell Jackson, author interview.

329   A group from the Soviet: King with Ritz, *Blues*, 272.

330 B.B. and Seidenberg bought: Larry Seidenberg, author interview, September 14, 2019.

330 "I feel like I did": Jim Gallagher, "In Soviet Union, Reds Come Alive to B.B. King's Blues," *Chicago Tribune*, March 19, 1979.

330 untold hardships: This passage draws from a June 20, 2019, author interview with State Department retiree Philippe du Chateau and coverage in the *Minneapolis Star Tribune* of November 9, 1980.

330 "Every airport we passed": King with Ritz, *Blues*, 272.

330 "They had people sitting": Russell Jackson, author interview; Jane Cohen, "B.B. King and Sid Seidenberg Celebrate 25 Years," *Performance*, February 14, 1992.

331 "the impulsive Georgians": Andrea Lee Fallows, "The Blues Abroad," *New Yorker*, June 25, 1979.

331 "When we finally made it": This passage draws from King's memoir, from UPI coverage of his Moscow concert, and from author interviews with Joe McClendon.

331 "King teases his audiences": Fallows, "Blues Abroad."

18. Homecoming

333 "I'd be honored": Andy Slater, "King Puts Country in His Blues," *Atlanta Constitution*, March 12, 1982.

333 "You don't see our names": Trevor Carolan, "King of the Blues," *West Coast Music*, March 1981.

334 "were out of work": This passage draws from an author interview with John Landis on September 23, 2020, and from a Landis interview by Jeremy Kagan on June 11, 2013, for the Directors Guild of America.

334 "You never know": LaVerne Toney, author interview, October 24, 2020.

334 Patty Elizabeth King: This passage draws from coverage in the *Tampa Times* of July 30, 1979, *Jet* of August 16, 1979, and *People* of March 22, 1993.

335 B.B. refused to lip sync: John Swenson, "B.B. King: Thirty Years on the Road," *Rolling Stone*, February 21, 1980.

335 Proceeds aided victims: William R. Ferris, author interview, November 5, 2019. The tally of live releases includes King's three classic live sets and *Live in Japan* but not his collaborations with Bobby Bland.

336 "B.B. didn't like it": Russell Jackson, author interview.

336 B.B. King Day: This scene draws from coverage in the *Indianola (MS) Enterprise-Tocsin* on June 5 and June 12, 1980.

336 "four legendary performers": "B.B. King; Big Mama Thornton; Muddy Waters; Big Joe Turner; Lloyd Glenn," *Variety*, September 12, 1980.

336 his agent reached a deal: Charles Sawyer, author interview, June 13, 2019.

338 "the world that B.B. came from": This passage draws from McGee's *B.B. King* and from an author interview with Stewart Levine on July 13, 2019.

339 B.B. played 320 gigs: This passage draws from a Sidney A. Seidenberg press release of April 8, 1983, and from coverage in *Guitar Player* of March 1983.

340 "is such a gentleman": This scene draws from author interviews with Jim Abbott and from Robert Palmer, "At Mississippi Homecoming, B.B. King Unites Neighbors," *New York Times*, June 11, 1983.

341 "No, I don't think": Bill Nichols, "B.B. Bound to the Town That Birthed Him," *Jackson (MS) Clarion-Ledger*, June 26, 1983.

341 the country's first blues archive: This scene draws from *Living Blues* magazine of March–April 1986 and the *Philadelphia Inquirer* of September 3, 1983.

342 To thank B.B. for his gift: This passage draws from King's memoir; author interviews with Floyd Lieberman, William Ferris, Walter King, LaVerne Toney, and David Ritz; and property records.

342 B.B. evidently missed: David W. Johnson, "'Fixin' to Die Blues': The Last Months of Bukka White," *Southern Cultures*, Fall 2010.

342 Two deaths: This passage draws from the *New York Times* of May 1, 1983, and Robert Gordon's Muddy Waters biography *Can't Be Satisfied* (New York: Little, Brown, 2002).

342 The following winter: This scene draws from an author interview with Faye King and from coverage in the *Indianola (MS) Enterprise-Tocsin* and *Los Angeles Sentinel* of January 12, 1984, and the *Vancouver Province* of January 20, 1984.

343 "pretty down": This scene draws from author interviews with Michael Zanetis on December 21, 2020, and January 28, 2021, the latter via email.

344 "fucking around with drugs": Roger Wood, "True Blues Texas Trumpet," *Living Blues*, July–August 1998.

344 "I read once where": Tom Harrison, "Even a King Can Get the Blues," *Vancouver Province*, January 20, 1984.

344 "And the crowd picked up": Bill Milkowski, "B.B. King / Miles Davis," *Down Beat*, July 1986.

345 "Move over": Joe McClendon, author interview, March 23, 2020.

346 "Why wasn't I": John Landis, author interview, September 22, 2020.

346 "very '80s": Landis.

347 A well-traveled anecdote: Gary Graff, "Stars: B.B. King," *Billboard*, October 1, 2005. A search of this and other Vaughan sources does not yield a date for the encounter.

347 "To tell you the truth": Michael Doster, author interview by email, September 17, 2019.

348 a hoarse rasp: Walter King, author interview, July 29, 2019. B.B.'s concert schedule does not show the bluesman sitting idle for a full six weeks that winter. It does, however, show a near-total hiatus from early December 1985 to late January 1986.

349 "We're going to Ireland": This passage draws from King's memoir and U2's collective memoir, *U2 by U2* (New York: HarperCollins, 2006), and from author interviews with Tony Coleman, Joe McClendon, and Walter King.

19. Lovetown

350 the sophomore class: Hindsight suggests the music industry might have welcomed King into the Hall a year earlier, in 1986, with its inaugural class. King wasn't a rock 'n' roller, but the soul icons James Brown, Ray Charles, and Sam Cooke all made the first cut.

350 named his band after B.B.: "Remembering B.B.," *Rolling Stone*, June 18, 2015.

350 B.B. hosted a delegation: "They Enjoyed Trip to Visit B.B. in Vegas," *Indianola (MS) Enterprise-Tocsin*, August 13, 1987.

351 "that rare kind": John J. O'Connor, "TV: From Cinemax, B.B. King and 'Blues,'" *New York Times*, November 12, 1987.

352 "B.B. felt that urban contemporary": Gary Bird, author interview, October 23, 2020.

352 Bono had titled the song: This scene draws from the memoir *U2 by U2*, *B.B. King: The Life of Riley*, the film *U2: Rattle & Hum*, and King's memoir.

353 paid immediate dividends: This passage draws from coverage in the *Indianola (MS) Enterprise-Tocsin* of June 9, 1988, the *Chicago Sun-Times* of June 13, 1988, and *The Age* (Melbourne, Australia) of January 25, 1989.

353 "gave B.B. a new crowd": James Bolden, author interview, September 29, 2019.

353 "They, just like any": Stafford Davis, author interview, January 10, 2020.

354 "the least distinguished collection": McGee, *B.B. King*, 247.

354 "I don't want to compare": Gene Santoro, "E Pluribus Blues Man," *Down Beat*, February 1992.

354 "blacks get hurt": Bob Herbert, "Impossible, Ridiculous, Repugnant," *New York Times*, October 6, 2005; "Gravely Ill, Atwater Offers Apology," *New York Times*, January 13, 1991.

354 "I don't let nobody": Schruers, "Mississippi Homecoming."

355 "He was just the nearest": Carol Clerk, "B.B. King: When the Blues Comes to Town," *Melody Maker*, January 27, 1990.

355 Atwater wielded his influence: Tommy Peters, author interview, April 29, 2020.

355 "naked cruelty": "Gravely Ill."

355 "They would literally bet": "He's the Happiest Bluesman I Know," *The Guardian* (UK), March 17, 2006.

355 a surprise birthday party: Clerk, "B.B. King"; Joe McClendon, author interview, March 23, 2020.

356 "I remember how proud": Sue King Evans, author interview, November 7, 2019.

356 "I look for someone": Wheeler, "B.B. King."

356 "I think he thought": Stewart Levine, author interview, August 16, 2019.

356 "We're a family": Michael Doster, author interview, March 25, 2018.

357 "He was an enabler": Tony Coleman, author interview, July 8, 2020.

358 B.B.'s health: Walter King, author interviews.

358 dangerously low on energy: This passage draws from coverage in the *Anniston (AL) Star* of June 30, 1990, and author interviews with Walter King and Michael Doster.

358 former Beatles: Walter King interview, September 26, 2019. Walter remembered this episode clearly, but other sources close to King did not.

358 "In all of my forty-one years": Vincente Rodriguez, "B.B. Bounces Back," *Dallas Morning News*, June 10, 1990.

359 B.B. wept: Mary Campbell, "B.B. and Lucille Back on the Road Again," *Anniston (AL) Star*, June 30, 1990.

359 "I'll bet you thought": Bill Kohlhaase, "Coach House Show Proves B.B. Is Still King of Blues," *Los Angeles Times*, September 4, 1990.

359 "We do not negotiate": This passage draws from author interviews with Walter King and Michael Doster.

360 Sid Seidenberg finally prevailed: This passage draws from author interviews with Willis Edwards III, Lora Walker, and Stafford Davis. When Bebop died, in February 2001, King dispatched Norman Matthews and "Boogaloo" Bolden to Houston for the funeral. Mourners buried Bebop in his alligator shoes.

360 "We had gotten kicked": Walter King, author interview, July 11, 2020. The Truffaut reference comes from Hirshey, "On the Bus."

361 "They're gonna make": This scene draws from author interviews with Michael Zanetis and "B.B. King gets star on Walk of Fame," *The Dispatch* (Moline, Ill.), September 6, 1990.

361 "listen to a sixteen-piece": Stafford Davis, author interview, March 6, 2020.

362 "We'd be on these jazz festivals": Russell Jackson, author interview.

362 slackened the crazy pace: This passage draws from two press releases from Sidney A. Seidenberg, Inc., both issued on April 4, 1991.

362 "the original merchandiser": Tina France, author interview, December 5, 2019.

363 "It's only 11": This passage draws from coverage in the *Memphis Commercial Appeal* of April 24, 2019, and the *Austin American-Statesman* of August 21, 1982.

363 "Nobody wanted to invest": This passage draws from author interviews with Tommy Peters and coverage in the *Memphis Commercial Appeal* of May 4 and 5, 1991.

364 "Are you Polly Walker?": Lora Walker, author interview, September 15, 2020. Walker recalled the incident happening on the first Homecoming show after Darby joined King, which makes June 1991 the likely date. Further details from the *Indianola (MS) Enterprise-Tocsin* of May 30, 1991.

365 "It's almost like": Stewart Levine, author interview, August 16, 2019.

365 Sid Seidenberg's careful count: Sidney A. Seidenberg, Inc., press release, April 22, 1994.

365 "Went straight from the airport": James Bolden, author interview.

365 three hundred pounds: Tommy Peters, author interviews, April 27 and 29, 2020.

366 McKaie gained permission: Andy McKaie, author interview, August 18, 2019; John Broven, author interview, October 9, 2020.

366 offered unequivocal praise: In America, at least. In the United Kingdom, the Ace label had already begun a heroic effort to rekindle interest in King's greatest work.

367 "We started throwing": Andy McKaie, author interview.

367 B.B. traveled to China: This passage draws from author interviews with Tony Coleman and Larry Seidenberg and coverage in the *Seattle Times* of May 15, 1994, the *Hong Kong Standard* of May 16, 1994, the *Wall Street Journal* of July 29, 1994, and *Blues & Rhythm* magazine of March 1996. King and Seidenberg had aspired to visit China after the watershed 1979 Soviet Union tour, but the trip had fallen through. King hinted that the incoming Reagan administration was to blame.

368 "creativity, turbulence and excitement": Avon Books, press release, 1995.

369 "Back when I first": Stafford Davis, author interview, March 6, 2020.

369 "We all came up": Gary Pettus, "B.B. King," *Jackson (MS) Clarion-Ledger*, December 24, 1995.

369 "I saw you play": King with Waterman, *Treasures*, 138.

370 "B.B. is a conglomerate": Nazir Keshvani, "Partners in the Blues Business," *Straits Times* (Singapore), May 17, 1994.

370 B.B. spent many months: David Ritz, author interview.

370 "I have pleasant acquaintances": King with Ritz, *Blues*, 2.

371 "No one can tell": Paul Theroux, "The Trouble with Autobiography," *Smithsonian Magazine*, January 2011.

371 "He was born": Stafford Davis, author interview, March 6, 2020.

371 "Every time my dad": Scott Johnson, "B.B. King's Estate War," *Hollywood Reporter*, May 26, 2016; Shirley Ann King, author interview, October 18, 2020. This passage also draws from *Living Blues* of May–June 1988, *Ebony* of February 1, 1992, and the *Allentown (PA) Morning Call* of April 30, 1993, among other clippings.

371 "They are not just": This passage, including King's words, draws from author interviews with Lora Walker.

372 a King family reunion: This passage draws from author interviews with Shirley Ann King and Lora Walker and from Rita King, *On the Road with My Dad the King of the Blues Mr. B.B. King* (Rita King, 2014), Kindle edition, 174.

373 "After he gave up": David Ritz, author interview.

373 "He'd rent out a floor": "B.B. King," prod. James Greenberg, *Unsung*, TV One, season 13, episode 6, aired June 24, 2018.

373 B.B. loved dirty: Multiple sources shared this joke with the author.

373 "there were a lot": Lora Walker, author interview, November 5, 2019.

373 "It's okay, folks": King with Ritz, *Blues*, 295–96.

374 "He had no prejudice": David Ritz, author interview.

374 "If you hurt me": King with Ritz, *Blues*, 2.

20. Riding with the King

375 "a chance to know me": McGee, *B.B. King*, 300.

375 "I can tell you why": Sue King Evans, author interview, August 17, 2019.

376 a distinct theme of decline: This passage draws from concert reviews in the *Dallas Morning News* of February 24, 1997, the *St. Louis Post-Dispatch* of August 31, 1997, and the *Roanoke Times* of November 7, 1998.

376 a leased VanHool bus: This passage draws from author interviews with Tony Coleman and Walter Riley King. Specs on King's tour bus come from Hirshey, "On the Bus," and Cohen, "Celebrate."

378 "B.B. would do": Michael Doster, author interview, September 17, 2019.

378 "I think some of the problem": Walter King, author interview, September 26, 2019.

378 "His pockets rattle": Hirshey, "On the Bus." Credit for the assertion that King was addicted to the road must go to David Ritz, in an author interview.

379 B.B. closed out the 1990s: This passage draws from coverage in the *New York Times* of August 17, 1999, and the *Washington Post* of October 25, 1999.

379 "I had to sit": Stewart Levine, author interview, August 16, 2019.

380 "wanted us to come along": Stewart Levine, author interview, August 16, 2019.

380 B.B.'s tireless manager: Larry Seidenberg, author interview, August 19, 2019.

381 "are you out of your mind?": Floyd Lieberman, author interview, October 17, 2020.

381 Seidenberg's tenure ended: Seidenberg's exit and the Clapton collaboration were announced in press releases issued January 10, 2000, by Sidney A. Seidenberg, Inc.

381 "we'd try to get together": Eric Clapton, online chat, America Online, July 24, 2000, archived at Eric Clapton's website, http://www.eric-clapton.co.uk/interviewsandarticles/aoltranscript.htm.

382 Clapton took the lead: This passage draws from a June 28, 2020, author interview with Nathan East, Clapton's AOL chat of July 24, 2000, and a July 8, 2000, interview with Joe Sample by Tony Edser for the fan magazine *Where's Eric*.

383 ultimately topped four million: Bernard Weinraub, "Spinning Blues into Gold, the Rough Way," *New York Times*, March 2, 2003.

383 "a very, very big success": Floyd Lieberman, author interview, October 17, 2020.

384 The Ace set spanned: John Broven, "Behind the B.B. King Box," *Blues & Rhythm*, March 2001.

384 "We don't swear": Rachel Zimmerman, "B.B. King's Mixed Messages Give Some Fans the Blues," *Wall Street Journal*, February 5, 2002; Floyd Lieberman, author interviews.

385 "the last of the great bluesmen": Weinraub, "Spinning."

385 the third-greatest guitarist: David Fricke, "The 100 Greatest Guitarists of All Time," *Rolling Stone*, September 18, 2003.

385 an ever-sharper contrast: This passage draws from coverage in the *Florida Times-Union* of December 29, 2003, the *Toronto Globe and Mail* of January 24, 2004, and the *Great Falls (MN) Tribune* of February 11, 2004.

386 "I've met kings": King with Waterman, *Treasures*, 10.

386 On a tour stop: Diane Williams, *The Life and Legacy of B.B. King, a Mississippi Blues Icon* (Mount Pleasant, SC: History Press, 2019), 73–74.

387 "There was no mistaking": Allan Hammons, author interview, December 9, 2019.

387 hide his decline: This passage draws from *Rolling Stone* of September 8, 2005, and author interviews with Lora Walker and Stafford Davis. *Rolling Stone* reported King had taken a layoff of three full months, but a search of concert dates reveals no gap of nearly that length.

387 a stage-show formula: This passage draws from coverage in the *Minneapolis Star Tribune* of March 24, 2005, and the *Boston Globe* of January 31, 2006.

388 "When I become": This passage draws from a 2019 interview with a participant in the *Reflections* project who spoke on condition of anonymity.

388 "B.B. was getting older": Floyd Lieberman, author interview, October 17, 2020.

388 "he looked terrible": John Aizlewood, "BB Is Still the King: An Evening of Chewing the Fat as Blues Living Legend Lightens Up," *London Evening Standard*, April 5, 2006. This passage also draws from the *Washington Times* of July 5, 2006, and the *St. Petersburg Times* of April 27, 2006.

389 "These days": Don McLeese, "When B.B. King Plays, the Decades Melt Away," *Des Moines Register*, February 13, 2006.

389 "I've lost so many": Marti Parham, "B.B. King: Combats Health Scare to Thrill Fans Another Day," *Jet*, May 7, 2007.

389 the funeral in New Jersey: Floyd Lieberman and Larry Seidenberg, author interviews.

390 "He came up the hard way": "President's Remarks at Medal of Freedom Ceremony," *Washington Post*, December 15, 2006.

390 But people now greeted: This passage draws from coverage from UPI on January 28, 2007, and the *Chicago Tribune* of July 30, 2007.

390 Such moments were few: This passage draws from coverage in the *New York Times* of August 9, 2007, and the *Cincinnati Enquirer* of November 26, 2007.

391 "to do what I do": This passage draws from author interviews with Walter King and Dr. Darin Brimhall.

391 "I read everything": Tommy Peters, author interview, April 29, 2020.

392 "We started with T-Bone Walker": T Bone Burnett, author interview, November 18, 2019.

393 "very bedraggled piece": Allan Hammons, author interview, March 9, 2020.

394 The B.B. King Museum: This passage draws from coverage in the *Jackson (MS) Clarion Ledger* of September 14, 2008, *Rolling Stone* of September 15, 2008, the *Washington Post* of October 12, 2008, *Living Blues* magazine of April 2009, *McClatchy-Tribune Business News* of August 19, 2012, and author interviews with Allan Hammons, Robert Terrell, and Floyd Lieberman.

394 "My lawyer is looking": Floyd Lieberman, author interviews.

395 "This is the guy": Bill Wax, author interview, October 10, 2019.

396 "I made more money": Floyd Lieberman, author interview, September 10, 2019.

396 But B.B.'s relationship: This passage draws from author interviews with Floyd Lieberman, Arthur Williams Jr. (on September 19 and 24, 2019), and Tommy Peters.

21. A Golden Chain

398 "Is it true you have 15 children?": This passage draws from coverage in *Ebony* magazine of February 1, 1992, and July 2010, the *St. Petersburg Times* of April 8, 2000, and the *Arizona Republic* of November 15, 2009.

398 On the road in Jackson: Sue King Evans, author interviews.

398 B.B. had given millions: Floyd Lieberman, author interview, October 9, 2019.

399 "He was trying to safeguard": Stafford Davis, author interview, March 6, 2020.

399 "pretty extensive medical": Darin Brimhall, author interview, October 18, 2020.

400 "He did it": Lora Walker, author interview, March 27, 2018.

400 the Obamas invited B.B.: This scene draws from coverage in *Rolling Stone* of March 15, 2012, and the *Washington Post* of May 15, 2015.

401 "I couldn't do it anymore": Tony Coleman, author interview, September 12, 2019.

401 "Unless you go": Darin Brimhall and LaVerne Toney, author interviews.

402 "anything resembling a song": Daniel Durchholz, "B.B. King at the Peabody: How Things Just Got Weird," *St. Louis Post-Dispatch*, April 7, 2014.

402 "a bit more concerned support": Walter King, author interview, September 26, 2019.

402 "a bad night": Kevin C. Johnson, "B.B. King Apologizes for Poor St. Louis Perfor-
     mance," *St. Louis Post-Dispatch*, April 15, 2014.

402 A reviewer in San Antonio: Hector Saldaña, "B.B. King: The Thrill Is Gone," *San
     Antonio Express-News*, May 23, 2014. Saldaña's timeline is paraphrased.

403 "We're friends": Norman Matthews, Dollarhide and Sawyer interview.

403 "There was nobody left": Lora Walker, author interview, March 27, 2018.

404 "This isn't the B.B. King": Chris Baker, "B.B. King Struggles through Jazz Fest, and
     We All Love Him for It," *Syracuse Post-Standard*, July 13, 2014.

404 B.B. played the House of Blues: This scene draws from Shirley King's *Love Is King*
     memoir, from Brewer's *On the Road* documentary, and from an author interview with
     Walter King.

405 "Ms. Toney": LaVerne Toney, author interview, October 24, 2020.

405 "When's the next date?": LaVerne Toney and Myron Johnson, author interview,
     October 24, 2020. (Toney and Johnson were interviewed together.)

405 "He seemed miserable": S. King, *Love*, 142–44.

405 "You know, there were": Brent Bryson, author interview, July 21, 2020.

405 "We no longer had access": PennyLynn Webb, "The Thrill Remembered," *Palestine
     Herald*, August 10, 2015.

406 "I would cook his meals": Patty King, author interview, May 8, 2020.

406 "He has a different number": Tony Coleman and LaVerne Toney, author interviews.

408 "Through the greatest joys": "Barack Obama Signed Get-Well Letter to B.B. King
     Going for $17,500," *TMZ*, March 23, 2020.

408 Patty summoned police: This passage draws from coverage in *TMZ* on May 1 and
     May 5, 2015, and *The Daily Beast* of May 6, 2015, and from an author interview with
     LaVerne Toney.

409 "just in awful shape": Tommy Peters, author interview, May 12, 2020.

409 "The family has been unable": Ken Ritter, "Fight over B.B. King Goes to Court,"
     Charleston (WV) Daily Mail, May 8, 2015.

409 "We lost the battle": "Vegas Judge: No Evidence Bluesman B.B. King Is Being Abused,"
     Manila Bulletin (Philippines), May 8, 2015.

409 "biological and adoptive": Webb, "Thrill Remembered"; Darin Brimhall, author
     interview, October 4, 2019.

409 One was Walter King: Walter King, author interview, September 26, 2019.

410 "She said she would ask him": Sue King Evans, author interview, September 17, 2019.

410 "People want what": This scene draws from author interviews with Myron Johnson and
     LaVerne Toney, from Johnson's eulogy at King's funeral, and from Shirley King's *Love*.

410 Obituary writers: This passage draws from coverage in *Rolling Stone*, *The Guard-
     ian* (UK), and the *New York Times* of May 15, 2015, and from the *Unsung* television
     broadcast.

411 "wouldn't exist without B.B. King": Richard Gehr, "10 Legendary Acts That Wouldn't
     Exist without B.B. King," *Rolling Stone*, May 15, 2015.

411 "B.B. may be gone": White House, "Statement by the President on the Passing of
     B.B. King," press release, May 15, 2019.

411 "We're going to fight": Ken Ritter, "B.B. King Viewing Draws More than 1,000 in
     Las Vegas," *Arlington Heights (IL) Daily Herald*, May 24, 2015.

411 On a gray Friday afternoon: This scene draws from coverage in the *Las Vegas Review-
     Journal* of May 22, 2015, the *Los Angeles Times* and *Las Vegas Sun* of May 23, 2015, and
     the *Arlington Heights (IL) Daily Herald* of May 24, 2015.

412 "He fired me": Steven Moore, "Friends, Family, Fans Gather to Honor B.B. King," *Las Vegas Review-Journal*, May 23, 2015.

413 "I believe my father": "Lawyer Says Allegations B.B. King Was Poisoned 'Ridiculous,'" *Inland Valley (CA) Daily Bulletin*, May 25, 2015.

413 Memphis bade farewell: This scene draws from two YouTube videos of the King funeral procession: Kim Lloyd, "BB King's Funeral Procession down Beale St, Memphis," May 30, 2015, https://www.youtube.com/watch?v=I3qKntEq9po; Leigh M. Johnson, "B.B. King's Last Ride on Beale Street, Memphis," May 28, 2015, https://www.youtube .com/watch?v=R1sn3SsU1AM.

414 outside the B.B. King Museum: Richard Fausset, "Mississippi Offers Its Embrace as a Blues Giant Returns Home," *New York Times*, May 30, 2015.

414 workers laid straw: Thomas Lake, "'Always a Rotten Apple': B.B. King, Poison and the Daughters of an Infertile Legend," *The Guardian* (UK), May 31, 2015.

414 "just the two of us": Videotape of B.B. King funeral service, Indianola, Mississippi, May 30, 2015, archived at the Mississippi Public Broadcasting website, http://www .mpbonline.org/bbking/.

415 B.B. told his friend: This scene draws from author interviews with Allan Hammons and Lake's "Always a Rotten Apple."

Epilogue

416 "He worked his entire life": This passage draws from coverage in the *Lakeland (FL) Ledger* of June 9, 2015, the World Entertainment News Network of June 25, 2015, the *Dubuque (IA) Telegraph Herald* of June 27, 2015, and *CNN.com* of July 14 and 15, 2015.

416 "got in trouble": LaVerne Toney, author interview.

417 The children finally ousted LaVerne Toney: Brent Bryson, Shirley Ann King, and LaVerne Toney, author interviews.

418 "this music is almost": "Remembering B.B."

418 "Maybe the guitar is over": Geoff Edgers, "Why My Guitar Gently Weeps," *Washington Post*, June 22, 2017; Alex Williams, "Guitars Are Back, Baby!," *New York Times*, September 8, 2020; Roy Trakin, "Lockdown Blues," *Variety*, January 20, 2021.

420 conflict erupted anew: This passage draws from coverage in *Variety* and *TMZ* on October 25, 2020.

INDEX